EARLY CHRISTIAN FAMILIES IN CONTEXT

D1536865

RELIGION, MARRIAGE, AND FAMILY

Series Editors

Don S. Browning
David Clairmont

Early Christian Families in Context

An Interdisciplinary Dialogue

Edited by

David L. Balch and Carolyn Osiek

WILLIAM B. EERDMANS PUBLISHING COMPANY
GRAND RAPIDS, MICHIGAN / CAMBRIDGE, U.K.

Wm. B. Eerdmans Publishing Co.
255 Jefferson Ave. S.E., Grand Rapids, Michigan 49503 /
P.O. Box 163, Cambridge CB3 9PU U.K.

Printed in the United States of America

08 07 06 05 04 03   7 6 5 4 3 2 1

Library of Congress Cataloging-in-Publication Data

Early Christian families in context: an interdisciplinary dialogue /
    edited by David L. Balch and Carolyn Osiek.
        p.   cm.
    Includes bibliographical references.
    ISBN 0-8028-3986-X (pbk.: alk. paper)
    1. Family — Religious aspects — Christianity — History — Congresses.
    2. Rome — Social life and customs — Congresses. 3. Family —
    Rome — Congresses.   I. Balch, David L.   II. Osiek, Carolyn.

    BR195.F35E27   2003
    261.8′3585′093 — dc21

                                                    2003043428

www.eerdmans.com

Contents

Series Foreword

The Religion, Marriage, and Family series evolves out of a research project located at the University of Chicago and financed by a generous grant from the Division of Religion of the Lilly Endowment, Inc. The first phase of the project lasted from 1991 to 1997 and produced eleven books on religion and family. In late 1997, the Lilly Endowment gave the project an additional major grant that supports a second phase of research and publication. The books in the Eerdmans Religion, Marriage, and Family series come directly or indirectly from the initiatives of this second phase.

In some cases, the books will evolve directly out of the University of Chicago project. In other cases, they will be books written in response to that project or in some way stimulated by it. In all cases, they will be books probing the depth of resources in Judaism and Christianity for understanding, renewing, and in some respects redefining current expressions of marriage and family. The series will investigate issues of parenthood and children, work and family, responsible fatherhood, and equality in the family; the responsibility of the major professions in promoting and protecting sound marriages and families; the biblical, theological, philosophical, and legal grounds of Western family systems; selected classics of these traditions; and the respective roles of church, market, and state in supporting marriages, families, parents, and children.

The Religion, Marriage, and Family series intends to go beyond the sentimentality, political manipulation, and ungrounded assertions that characterize so much of the contemporary debate over marriage and family. It plans to develop an intelligent and accessible new literature for colleges and seminaries, churches and other religious institutions, questing individuals and families. Marriage and family issues are not just preoccupations of the United States; they have become worldwide concerns as modernization, globalization, changing values, emerging poverty, and changing gender roles disrupt traditional families and challenge the very idea of marriage throughout the world. It has been predicted that the emerging marriage and family crisis will be the central issue of the twenty-first century. The Religion, Marriage, and Family series hopes to contribute to more balanced and well-informed public debate on this issue, both in the United States and around the globe.

Early Christian Families has continuity with the biblical research of the Religion, Culture, and Family Project. It flows directly from the breakthrough scholarship of Carolyn Osiek and David Balch in *Families in the New Testament World: Households and House Churches* (1997). There they used the best insights from biblical, historical, and textual research, social and cultural anthropology, and the fields of classical Greek and Roman scholarship to throw new light on families both in and around early Christianity.

Early Christian Families carries this interdisciplinary project forward. It also shows with convincing power that to understand the uniqueness of families in early Christianity, one must also understand families in the Greek, Roman, and Hebrew social worlds. Hence, one needs to understand the contexts of early Christianity.

The richness of these contexts unfolds with illuminating complexity in *Early Christian Families.* Biblical scholars and theologians join forces with the world's leading classicists, archeologists, and historians to give us amazing new perspectives on intimate life in both the ancient world in general and early Christian families in particular.

This book will help contemporary debates, both within and outside religious communities, to move past the clichés that have dominated references to what is Christian and non-Christian with regard to families, marriage, and sexuality. Finally, the book has enormous implications for theological education, and a concluding section of articles by leading theological educators draws out those implications. *Early Christian Families* will make new contributions to theology, philosophy, and the human sciences as they struggle to understand the origins of contemporary families.

Don S. Browning and David Clairmont
series editors

Contributors

DAVID BALCH
Brite Divinity School
Texas Christian University

SUZANNE DIXON
Classics and Ancient History
University of Queensland

J. ALBERT HARRILL
Department of Religious Studies
Indiana University

ROSS S. KRAEMER
Department of Religious Studies
Brown University

CHRISTIAN LAES
Catholic University of Louvain

PETER LAMPE
University of Heidelberg

AMY-JILL LEVINE
Vanderbilt Divinity School
Vanderbilt University

MARGARET MACDONALD
St. Francis Xavier University

DALE MARTIN
Department of Religious Studies
Yale University

ERIC M. MEYERS
Department of Religion
Duke University

MARGARET M. MITCHELL
University of Chicago

CAROLYN OSIEK
Brite Divinity School
Texas Christian University

BERYL RAWSON
History (Arts)
Australian National University

RICHARD SALLER
Provost
University of Chicago

TIMOTHY SEDGWICK
Virginia Theological Seminary

MONIKA TRÜMPER
Archaeological Institute
University of Heidelberg

ANDREW WALLACE-HADRILL
The British School at Rome
and the University of Reading

Introduction

Interest in the early Christian family is a natural outgrowth of the dialogue between two presently thriving fields of scholarly inquiry: the study of social history and social structures in biblical and church historical disciplines, and study of the Roman family among ancient historians and classicists. The bibliography of works on the ancient Roman family written within the last three decades is enormous and ongoing. Studies of certain aspects of the family in biblical scholarship have always been of interest, e.g., the household codes and the Synoptic sayings about family, but attempts at full portrayals of the early Christian family are very recent.

One of the first of those attempts was *Families in the New Testament World: Households and House Churches,* by Carolyn Osiek and David Balch (Westminster John Knox, 1997), part of the University of Chicago project on religion, culture, and family directed by Don Browning and funded by the Lilly Foundation. Out of the collaboration between the two authors and their respective interests and contacts among ancient historians came the proposal to hold an interdisciplinary conference that would bring together scholars of the New Testament, early Christianity, early Judaism, and the Roman family to engage in presentations and dialogue that would be mutually beneficial, and to bridge the artificial disciplinary gap between scholars of ancient Judaism and Christianity, some with strong background and interest in archaeology and ancient history, on the one hand, and those of classical Greece and Rome on the other.

The conference was held at Brite Divinity School, Texas Christian University, Fort Worth, Texas, November 30–December 3, 2000, once again funded by the Lilly Foundation through Don Browning. Seven ancient historians, seven scholars of ancient Judaism and Christian origins, and one archaeologist presented papers and engaged in the dialogue. Most of the chapters in this volume began as papers presented and discussed there. Peter Lampe was invited but could not attend for personal reasons, and later sent his paper. Three other scholars, two New Testament scholars and the third a professor of Christian ethics, were asked to reflect with us on the implications of all this material for contemporary theological education.

Andrew Wallace-Hadrill moves "away from the standard image of the Roman *domus* as a 'single-family unit' and toward thinking of it as a 'big house' inhabited by a 'houseful' rather than a household; not only a parent-children-slaves unit, but a cluster linked by relationships that could vary from relationship and dependency to commercial tenancy." He also questions the "rigid distinction between the *domus* and the *insula*." Roman housing was rather "mixed in nature, between grand houses and blocks of flats and little shop units on the one hand, and buildings that formed focuses of local communal life on the other — baths, clubs, and corporations," various complexes, many of which often formed a neighborhood *(vicus)*. Further, he questions "the conventional wisdom that the rich and poor lived apart in imperial Rome, the rich in large airy houses on the hills, the poor crowded in unsanitary apartment blocks in the valleys."

Monika Trümper examines the houses of Delos as representative of Eastern types of housing in the Hellenistic period, and shows that courtyard and peristyle houses were common whereas the atrium or atrium-peristyle house, so well known in Italy, is totally absent. She speculates that the formal functions of the Roman atrium, such as the *salutatio,* were perhaps not as important for Romans living outside Italy, so that they did not carry their housing styles with them as they moved east. Thus Christian house churches would be found in a variety of different courtyard or peristyle housing units.

Eric Meyers takes us to domestic Palestinian architecture with special focus on Galilee, where he has excavated extensively. Here the courtyard house dominates, except in certain urban areas where Greco-Roman influence may sometimes be seen in the presence of peristyle-courtyard designs. With regard to the social construction of secluded females, he finds little architectural evidence that the confinement of women in the house was even possible.

Moving to the social and material environment of early Christian meals, Peter Lampe uses a constructivist approach to the sociology of knowledge to portray early Christians attempting to live the "equality" strictures of Galatians 3:28. He argues that they lived simultaneously in two mental constructs that became social when they shared experiences: the outside world in which everything proceeded as usual, and the inside world of the community in which they sincerely attempted to carry out this vision.

David Balch takes up the fascinating topic of wall paintings as found in Pompeiian houses, assuming them to be of the same kind that would be found in Roman houses elsewhere, and asks what influence they would have had on Christians who assembled under them. The frequent portrayals of mythological scenes of torture and violence could have provided ready-made pictures for the preaching of the gospel.

In the next section several authors look at the social presence of women in family life. Suzanne Dixon observes that scholars' focus on the idealization of illicit love by Roman elegists has overshadowed the evidence for happy marriages. The stereotype of the chaste and shy wife given in an arranged marriage, from whom a husband must depart in order to find sexual fulfillment, does not do justice to the evidence for the active sexuality of married women and the sexually fulfilling conjugal partnerships that existed in ancient Rome. This evidence must be kept in mind when assessing, for example, the background of the household codes.

Ross S. Kraemer examines the evidence for the lives of Berenice and Babatha, two Jewish women of Roman Palestine from very different social locations. Kraemer finds, perhaps unexpectedly, that in neither case does their identity as Jews have much to do with their lives and destinies. Rather they are very much part of the Greco-Roman context of their world.

Margaret Y. MacDonald looks at Celsus's claim that women and children were recruited for the Christian movement and encouraged to defy patriarchal authority, and that women in the household context were important agents in the spreading of the message. She finds some claims to their importance exaggerated, but many right on target. Not only as wives in mixed marriages, but as patrons, heads of households, mothers, and teachers, women were influential figures in evangelization. Celsus *was* right.

Richard Saller examines the interrelationship between labor and gender in the Roman household, or the economic aspects of women's contribution to the life of the family. Through use of literary texts and demographics, he concludes that female slaves of childbearing age were highly valued for their reproductive potential but not for their labor, whereas male labor was much more widely used and valued.

While recognizing that the categories of women, slaves, and children necessarily overlap, the next section is devoted to slaves and slavery in the world of the first Christians. Dale Martin shows through the examination of many inscriptions that, though slaves did not legally marry or have families, nevertheless they did both, and used the language of marriage and family in their funerary monuments even though the law nominally denied this to them. Slaves interacted with the free in many complex ways, including marital and parental relationships. These complexities must be kept in mind when assessing the role of slaves in early Christianity.

J. Albert Harrill highlights the conflicting stereotypes of the untrustworthy slave and the faithful slave, and shows how both are used in narratives involving slaves in early Christian texts. Even in the martyr narratives, where the overthrow of traditional Greco-Roman family values is at its most prominent, stereotypes of slave characters persist.

Carolyn Osiek looks at the thin evidence preserved for the lives of female slaves in Greco-Roman antiquity and asks how female slaves fared in early Christian communities. The common double standard that did not assign wrongdoing to the sexual exploitation of slaves, and the strange silence of Christian texts about these practices, raises questions about how the obedience of slaves was understood by slaves and owners.

Beryl Rawson, who has been studying Roman children for some time, gives us a survey of commemorative patterns of children in a society in which infant and child mortality was very high. Such personal commemorations and noting of relationships of deceased children declined noticeably in the Christian era. It is not known whether this was already an independent trend at the time or whether Christian influence is at work. Perhaps, she suggests, children were seen as part of a wider family, the church.

Christian Laes introduces a little-known phenomenon of Roman family practice: the language of *delicia* applied to children, child slaves, pets, and sometimes — but not always — child objects of erotic pleasure. The terminology is used not only in literary sources but in commemorative inscriptions as well. It declines sharply in the Christian period, while not disappearing altogether, perhaps because of a new evaluation of children.

Finally, three scholars offer their reflections on the implications of all of this for theological education. Amy-Jill Levine argues an uncommon thesis in the current intellectual climate: the more divinity students know about the cultural social, and material settings of early Christianity, the better homileticians, counselors, theologians, ethicists, and ministers they will be and the less likely it is that they will spew anti-Judaism or anti-Catholicism from their pulpits. Timothy Sedgwick offers the reflections of a moral theologian on the interplay between the shaping of ancient and contemporary Christian moral identity. New Testament scholar Margaret M. Mitchell looks intensively at the language of the Pastoral Epistles and compares it to that of funerary commemorations to show the longing for permanence that is expressed and which contemporary society finds it so difficult to grasp.

In concluding remarks (not included in this volume), Andrew Wallace-Hadrill reflected on his surprise at the lack of ideological gaps where he had expected to find them. Rather, there was a general harmony and consensus about method and presuppositions. All agree, for instance, that literary texts are not sufficient in themselves from which to draw conclusions. Epigraphic evidence and material culture must also be integrated into any analysis, not only of public but also of domestic social life. Images must from now on be part of any understanding of ancient culture.

Another area of agreement is on the diversity of cultural experiences in the ancient Mediterranean world. No longer can one be satisfied with simplistic generalizations and cultural stereotypes of "the Romans," "the Jews," or "the Christians." Each group had some distinctive characteristics but developed within a much broader cultural matrix that even contained some inherent contradictions. The early Christian family developed within a diversity of contexts, no one of which was "normative."

Yet a third area of broad agreement cited by Wallace-Hadrill was the consonances and differences of *our* attitudes and *their* attitudes. We have moved beyond the point of thinking that slavery was good for anyone who dealt with or experienced it, and have faced the reality that women did not have a distinctive voice that can now be recovered. Even the narrative of Perpetua has come under suspicion as an authentic woman's voice. The traditional approach to ancient history as solely military and political (called "maps and chaps" by Suzanne Dixon) has given way to interest in social life, perhaps largely because of the gender balance making its way into the scholarly population, of which this conference was illustrative. Instead of feeling that we must remain in a scholarly neutral position about all issues in ancient studies, we can also acknowledge that our interest in ancient issues is raised because of contemporary problems, e.g., an interest in ancient slavery because of the current problem of human trafficking that is taking place around the world, including Europe and North America.

This leads to another problem: How are we to judge the evidence of ancient practices that clash with the moral values of our own society, especially those issues raised directly in what we in various ways take to be "authoritative texts"? Such issues would include slavery and other divisions based on social status.

Both Wallace-Hadrill and Amy-Jill Levine in their concluding remarks raised a multitude of questions regrettably absent in the discussion, for the most part simply for lack of time. These questions included the whole social complex surrounding meals, with the exception of the connections created by David Balch, and the entire area of contraception, abortion, infanticide, and population control. Levine noted that citations from the Gospels were surprisingly absent, as well as analysis of the discrepancies between the Gospel information about children and what we know about childhood from other sources. The mention of Joanna in Luke 8:3 raises the question of relations between slave men and free women. Model female figures like Esther, who does not manumit her slave, and Sarah, who beats hers, raise questions about acceptable social conduct in the household. An analysis of expected treatment of slaves in the Mishnah would also be enlightening.

During the writing of *Families in the New Testament World,* the authors kept before us the idea that the early Christian or Jewish family was a Greco-Roman family "with a twist." Describing that twist, that set of characteristics that define the difference, was a major part of the endeavor of that book. This collection of papers certainly does not represent any kind of arrival point, but rather another step along the way. The participants are grateful to Don Browning; the Religion, Family, and Culture Project of the University of Chicago; and the Lilly Foundation for making this step possible. We are also grateful to Laurie Brink for her many hours of careful editing of manuscripts toward preparation of this volume. The interaction between biblical scholars, Christian historians, and ancient historians of Greco-Roman culture is no longer a luxury but a necessity if we are to construct a true picture of the early Christian family.

Finally, we are grateful to two doctoral students for their energy, time, acumen, and good humor employed in assisting us to edit this volume: Laurie Brink and Aliou Niang, the latter of whom provided the indices.

Abbreviations

AB	Anchor Bible
ABD	*Anchor Bible Dictionary,* ed. David Noel Freedman (Garden City, N.J.: Doubleday, 1992)
ACW	Ancient Christian Writers
AE	*L'Année épigraphique*
AGJU	Arbeiten zur Geschichte des antiken Judentums und des Urchristentums
AHB	*Ancient History Bulletin*
AJAH	*American Journal of Ancient History*
AJP	*American Journal of Philology*
AnBib	Analecta biblica
ANF	The Ante-Nicene Fathers
ANRW	*Aufstieg und Niedergang der römischen Welt*
ANTF	Arbeiten zur neutestamentlichen Textforschung
ARID	*Analecta Romana Instituti Danici*
BAGD	*A Greek-English Lexicon of the New Testament and Other Early Christian Literature,* ed. Walter Bauer, William F. Arndt, Wilbur Gingrich, and F. W. Danker, 3rd ed. (Chicago: University of Chicago Press, 2000)
BARev	*Biblical Archaeology Review*
BASOR	*Bulletin of the American Schools of Oriental Research*
BCH	*Bulletin de correspondance hellénique*
BETL	Bibliotheca ephemeridum theologicarum lovaniensium
BGU	Aegyptische Urkunden aus den Königlichen Staatlichen Museen zu Berlin, Griechische Urkunden. 15 vols. Berlin, 1895-1983.
BJRL	*Bulletin of the John Rylands University Library of Manchester*
BJS	Brown Judaic Studies
BTB	*Biblical Theology Bulletin*
BZNW	Beihefte zur *ZNW*
CCSL	Corpus Christianorum, Series Latina
CIG	*Corpus Inscriptionum Graecarum*
CIJ	*Corpus Inscriptionum Judaicarum*
CIL	*Corpus Inscriptionum Latinarum*
CLE	*Carmina Latina Epigraphica,* ed. F. Bücheler and E. Lommatzsch
Collezioni	*Le Collezioni del Museo Nazionale di Napoli: I Mosaici, Le Pitture, Gli Oggetti*

	di Uso Quotidiano, Gli Argenti, Le Terrecotte Invetriate, I Vetri, I Cristalli, Gli Avori, ed. Stefano De Caro (Milan: Di Luca Edizioni d'Arte, 1986)
CP	*Classical Philology*
CSEL	Corpus Scriptorum Ecclesiasticorum Latinorum
DAI	Deutsches Archaeologisches Institut Rom
De Caro	Stefano De Caro and Luciano Pedicini, *The National Archaeological Museum in Naples* (Naples: Electa, 1996)
DJD	Discoveries in the Judaean Desert (New York and Oxford: Oxford University Press)
EE	*Ephemeris Epigraphica*
FC	Fathers of the Church
FIRA	*Fontes Iuris Romani Anteiustiniani,* ed. S. Riccobono, 2nd ed. (Florence, 1968)
GR	*Greece and Rome*
HDR	Harvard Dissertations in Religion
HTR	*Harvard Theological Review*
HTRHDR	Harvard Theological Review, Harvard Dissertations in Religion
HTS	Harvard Theological Studies
HUT	Hermeneutische Untersuchungen zur Theologie
ICUR	*Inscriptiones Christianae Urbis Romae* (Rome, 1922-)
IEJ	*Israel Exploration Journal*
IG	*Inscriptiones Graecae*
IGSK	*Inschriften griechischer Städte aus Kleinasien*
ILCV	*Inscriptiones Latinae Christianae Veteres*
inv.	inventory number of a painting or a sculpture in the National Archaeological Museum, Naples
JAOS	*Journal of the American Oriental Society*
JBL	*Journal of Biblical Literature*
JDS	Judean Desert Studies
JECS	*Journal of Early Christian Studies*
JFSR	*Journal of Feminist Studies in Religion*
JHS	*Journal of Hellenic Studies*
JQR	*Jewish Quarterly Review*
JRA	*Journal of Roman Archaeology*
JRS	*Journal of Roman Studies*
JSNT	*Journal for the Study of the New Testament*
JSNTSup	Journal for the Study of the New Testament — Supplement Series
JSOT	*Journal for the Study of the Old Testament*
JSOTSup	Journal for the Study of the Old Testament — Supplement Series
JTS	*Journal of Theological Studies*
LCL	Loeb Classical Library
LIMC	*Lexicon Iconographicum Mythologiae Classicae* (Zürich: Artemis, 1981-97), 8 vols., each with two parts (text and plates), plus *Indices* (1999)
LSJ	Liddell-Scott-Jones, *Greek-English Lexicon,* 9th ed. (New York: Oxford University Press, 1996)
LTUR	*Lexicon Topographicum Urbis Romae,* ed. E. M. Steinby, 6 vols. (Rome: Quasar, 1993-99)

LXX	Septuagint
MAAR	*Memoirs of the American Academy in Rome*
MT	Masoretic Text
NEAEHL	*New Encyclopedia of Archaeological Excavations in the Holy Land*, ed. E. Stern et al., 4 vols. (New York: Simon and Schuster, 1993)
NovT	*Novum Testamentum*
NRSV	New Revised Standard Version
NTA	*New Testament Apocrypha*, ed. Wilhelm Schneemelcher, trans. R. McL. Wilson, rev. ed. (Louisville: Westminster John Knox, 1992)
NTS	*New Testament Studies*
PBSR	*Papers of the British School at Rome*
P. Fay.	Fayum Towns and Their Papyri, ed. B. P. Grenfell, A. S. Hunt and D. G. Hogarth (London: Offices of the Egypt Exploration Fund, 1900)
Pompei	*Pompei: Pitture e Mosaici*, Enciclopedia Italiana, 11 vols. (Rome: Arti Grafiche Pizzi, S.p.A., 1990-2003)
P.Oxy.	Oxyrhynchus Papyri
RAC	*Reallexikon für Antike und Christentum*
REA	*Revue des études anciennes*
RHE	*Revue d'histoire ecclésiastique*
RIDA	*Revue internationale des droits de l'antiquité*
RM	*Mitteilungen des Deutschen Archäologischen Instituts, Römische Abteilungen* = Römische Mitteilungen
RS	*Repertorium der christlich-antiken Sarkophage I: Rom und Ostia* (Wiesbaden, 1967)
SBL	Society of Biblical Literature
SC	Sources chrétiennes
SEG	*Supplementum Epigraphicum Graecum*
SHA	Scriptores Historiae Augustae
SJLA	Studies in Judaism in Late Antiquity
Smyrna	*Die Inschriften von Smyrna* (vol. 23, pt. 1 of *Inschriften griechischer Städte aus Kleinasien*)
TAM	*Tituli Asiae Minoris*
TAPA	*Transactions of the American Philological Association*
ThLL	*Thesaurus Linguae Latinae*
VC	*Vigiliae christianae*
Vg	Vulgate
VTSup	Vetus Testamentum, Supplements
WUNT	Wissenschaftliche Untersuchungen zum Neuen Testament
Zahn	Wilhelm Zahn, *Die schönsten Ornamente und merkwürdigsten Gemälde aus Pompeji, Herculaneum und Stabiae nebst einigen Grundrissen und Ansichten nach den am Ort und Stelle gemachten Originalzeichnungen* (Berlin: Georg Reimer, vol. 1 [1828, 1829], vol. 2 [1842, 1844], vol. 3 [1852, 1859])
ZNW	*Zeitschrift für die neutestamentliche Wissenschaft*
ZPE	*Zeitschrift für Papyrologie und Epigraphik*
ZRP	*Zeitschrift für Romanische Philologie*

I. Archaeology of *Domus* and *Insulae*

Domus and *Insulae* in Rome: Families and Housefuls

Andrew Wallace-Hadrill

While Saint Paul awaited trial in Neronian Rome, so legend has it, he lodged in a house in the Southern Campus Martius. That house was later turned into a church, S. Paolo alla Regola, by a pattern supposedly widespread in Rome,[1] like the houses where lived Pudens, the host of Saint Peter, and his daughters Pudentiana and Praxedes,[2] or Saint Clement, by tradition third bishop of Rome,[3] or the martyr brothers John and Paul.[4] The name Regola, which is also the name of the Rione, preserves, slightly distorted, the ancient Roman name for this district, Arenula, referring to the sandiness of the banks of the frequently flooding Tiber at this point. The road may have been called the Via Arenula in antiquity, though the twentieth century was to give this name to the new road which cut southward from the future Largo Argentina across the Ponte Garibaldi to Trastevere.

I start with Saint Paul in order to raise the question: Have we any chance of

1. On "house churches" and their origins in houses, see J. M. Peterson, "House Churches in Rome," *VC* 23 (1969): 264-72; L. Michael White, *The Social Origins of Christian Architecture,* vol. 1, *Building God's House in the Roman World: Architectural Adaptation among Pagans, Jews, and Christians,* HTS 42 (Valley Forge, Pa.: Trinity Press International, 1996); vol. 2, *Texts and Monuments for the Christian Domus Ecclesiae in Its Environment,* HTS 42 (Valley Forge, Pa.: Trinity Press International, 1997) On the legend of St. Paul and the Regola district, see W. A. Meeks, *The First Urban Christians: The Social World of the Apostle Paul* (New Haven/London, 1983), p. 9; U. M. Fasola, *Peter and Paul in Rome: Traces on Stone* (Rome, 1980).
2. *LTUR,* 4:166-68, s.v. "S. Pudentiana, titulus."
3. White, *Social Origins,* 2:219-28.
4. White, *Social Origins,* 2:209-18.

In this paper I return to themes already discussed in two papers: "Case e abitanti a Roma," in *Roma Imperiale: Una metropoli antica,* ed. Elio Lo Cascio (Rome: Carocci, 2000), pp. 173-220, and "Emperors and Houses in Rome," in *Childhood, Class, and Kin in the Roman World,* ed. S. Dixon (London and New York: Routledge, 2001), pp. 128-43. They are part of an ongoing project on domestic structures in imperial Rome.

reconstructing the sort of domestic setting which the traveler to imperial Rome might have encountered? Can archaeology restore to us the domestic fabric of the imperial city, and can we move from the archaeological traces to a picture of the sort of social and familial unit around which the buildings were constructed? Twelve years ago, when Beryl Rawson invited me to discuss what light the domestic structures of Pompeii could cast on the Roman family, I came face-to-face with the extraordinary difficulty of reading family structures from archaeological remains.[5]

I experimented, for instance, with the population statistics on various projections of the total town size to see if I could read back what the implicit size per average household was, hoping to establish whether the nuclear family made any sense as a hypothesis. I came to the conclusion that unless one posited a significantly higher density per household than the historical European norm, say of seven to eight persons per house, it would be hard to arrive at a sufficiently high population to meet our expectations. I found myself gradually moving away from the standard image of the Roman *domus* as a "single-family unit" and toward thinking of it as a "big house" inhabited by a "houseful" rather than a household; not only a parent-children-slaves unit, but a cluster linked by relationships that could vary from relationship and dependency to commercial tenancy. I also found myself questioning the conventionally rigid distinction between the *domus* and the *insula,* seeing in the former the single compact social unity of republican tradition, and in the latter the commercial block of flats that characterized the new imperial society.[6]

The difficulties I faced then are as nothing to those that face me today when I look at the capital itself. Let me return to S. Paolo alla Regola to illustrate both the enormous possibilities and the inherent difficulties. Though Saint Paul's supposed lodgings were converted into a church where no remains have been reported, the building immediately next door has produced one of the most spectacular examples of continuity in Roman housing, and of the possibility of reconstructing the urban fabric of antiquity. This area, already badly run down by the beginning of the twentieth century and regarded as a city center slum, was marked out for demolition and complete modernization, which the city administration of the postwar period took over in seamless continuity from fascism. Mercifully, incompetence delayed the demolition, so that by the late 1970s, when a major change of heart set in, a large portion of

5. Andrew Wallace-Hadrill, "Houses and Households: Sampling Pompeii and Herculaneum," in *Marriage, Divorce, and Children in Ancient Rome,* ed. Beryl Rawson (Canberra: Oxford University Press and Humanities Research Centre, 1991), pp. 191-227.

6. Andrew Wallace-Hadrill, *Houses and Society in Pompeii and Herculaneum* (Princeton: Princeton University Press, 1994).

the visible medieval fabric still stood. Lorenzo Quilici, in one of the most fiendishly difficult examples of standing structures archaeology, conducted a minute survey of the building, removing tons of late antique and early medieval rubble from the cellars, deliberately deposited in the process attested throughout the area which raised the streets and lowest inhabited levels by some seven meters.[7]

What Quilici found he described elegantly as a staggering example of structures inhabited continuously for two millennia, and constantly modified, adapted, and rebuilt over the course of time. For antiquity alone he was able to identify four major phases: the earliest, visible only at the lowest levels, cellars dated by the brick facing of the concrete to the late first century C.E.; above a major remodeling clearly dated by brick stamps to the Severan period, with several traces of mosaic flooring characteristic of that period; then signs of change of use, including the treading vats of a *fullonica* constructed against the Severan plasterwork; and finally in the fourth century another major remodeling, including the abandonment and infilling of the lower levels.

We see this story reproduced with many variants in example after example.[8] Effectively it is impossible to construct a building in the heart of Rome without encountering remains, and very frequently domestic remains, at a level a few meters beneath the modern streets. What is different about Rome now is that such remains are no longer simply bulldozed away; and the monthly publication of a color magazine, *Forma Urbis*, puts new discoveries in the public domain with remarkable speed and vividness. So, in recent months works in converting a cinema just behind the Fontana di Trevi have revealed remains of two *insulae* of the early empire.[9] It is evident that these had already been seen in 1946 when the concrete foundations of the cinema sliced through them. But willing collaboration between the developer and the Soprintendenza has shown a complex story of the *insulae* being redeveloped gradually until a traumatic destruction in the mid–fifth century. After that, levels are raised and reoccupation occurs, and the site is modified throughout the early Middle Ages. A closely comparable story has emerged from the excavation originally intended for a new car park beneath the Palazzo Spada, which ex-

---

7. L. Quilici, "Roma. Via di S. Paolo alla Regola. Scavo e recupero di edifici antichi e medioevali," *Notizie degli Scavi ser. VIII* 40-41 (1986-87): 175ff.

8. For an overview, see F. Guidobaldi, "Le *domus* tardoantiche di Roma come 'sensori' delle trasformazioni culturali e sociali," in *The Transformations of Urbs Roma in Late Antiquity*, Journal of Roman Archaeology Supplement Series 33, ed. W. V. Harris (Portsmouth, R.I.: Journal of Roman Archaeology, 1999), pp. 53-68.

9. Antonio Insalaco, "Vicus Caprarius: l'area archeologica," *Forma Urbis* VIII, 2 (February 2003): 4-19.

posed the extensive remains of second century C.E. mosaics from upper floors of an *insula* which collapsed in the lower levels and were abandoned in the fifth century.[10]

A particularly important aspect of Quilici's work was that he looked more broadly at the street network of the S. Paolo houses area, in order to establish to what extent the medieval housing simply followed the Roman street pattern.[11] Here he was assisted by a brilliant location by Emilio Rodrìguez-Almeida of a fragment of the *Forma urbis*. Notably, the endless discussions generated by the fragments of the Severan marble plan of Rome have focused on public monuments to the neglect of private houses.[12] This is largely because they are much easier to identify and locate. Because so many fragments are a few inches across, they contain nondescript patches of streets with little shops and houses that could be almost anywhere in the city.[13] The fragment or group of fragments concerned had two distinctive features: a partial street name, ..BLARIUS, and a long and gently curving feature in the shape of an ice hockey stick. This curve, Rodriguez-Almeida recognized, must be dictated by a bend in the Tiber, and it fitted perfectly with the line of the Vicolo Delle Zoccollette, the street named after the little slippered orphan girls whose orphanage had dominated the area in the Counter-Reformation period.[14]

Once the curve clicked into place, so did the rest of the street grid, and it was evident that with a few exceptions the medieval street pattern followed precisely that of antiquity. Even the exceptions are interesting. Where, for instance, in the Via Monserrato the street bulges outward in contradiction of the presumed straight Roman street plan below, at the site of the Venerable English College, whose documented presence on site goes back to 1362, it has been possible to demonstrate that the road was rerouted around the church of Saint Thomas of Canterbury, in the crypt of which the old Roman road can still be traced, and the traces of an old medieval tower in early prints suggest that this stronghold of the Savelli family deliberately privatized public space.

10. M. C. Rinaldoni and A. S. Scarponi, "Edifici antichi nei sotterranei di Palazzo Spada," *Forma Urbis* IV, 3 (March 1999): 4-13.

11. L. Quilici, "Il Campo Marzio occidentale," *Città e Architettura nella Roma Imperiale, ARID* 10 (1983): 59-85.

12. On the marble plan, see G. Carettoni et al., *La pianta marmorea di Roma antica: forma urbis Romae* (Rome, 1960); E. Rodrìguez-Almeida, *Forma Urbis Marmorea: aggiornamento generale 1980* (Rome: Quasar, 1981).

13. On these, note G. Lugli, "Il valore topografico e giuridico dell'*insula* in Roma antica," *Rendiconti della Pontificia Accademia Romana di archeologia* 18 (1941-42): 191-208; L. Pedroni, "Per una lettura verticale della Forma Urbis Marmorea," *Ostraka* 1 (1992): 223-30.

14. E. Rodrìguez-Almeida, "Forma Urbis marmorea, nuove integrazioni," *Bulletino della Commissione archeologica Communale in Roma* 82 (1970-71): 105ff.

Domus and *Insulae*

The implication of this example, when put together with the numerous other fragments of information we have, leads to what is in my view an exciting conclusion. Wherever we can test the matter, by detecting ancient levels below the medieval city, the medieval road pattern is basically faithful to the antique road pattern. There are some quite significant deflections, as at the English College, but you have to wait for the Renaissance before the creation of new processional routes like the Via Giulia,[15] the "trident" splayed from the Piazza del Popolo,[16] or the Via Sistina and the rest of Sixtus V's processional system with its obelisks.[17] This gives us a real chance to work back to much of the street plan of the imperial city, assisted by the fragments of the *Forma urbis,* and careful recording of the hundreds of fragments of ancient housing that have been forgotten as quickly as they emerge.

But how can we move from the macrocosm of the street network to the microcosm of the household? Here we are simultaneously vastly assisted and frustrated by the fourth-century listings of the buildings of Rome that go under the name of *Regionaries.* At first sight these lists are enormously promising for our purposes. Not only do they list, region by region through the fourteen Augustan *Regiones* of Rome, the public buildings, temples, baths, forums, porticoes, etc. (and this has always been a key document for locating public buildings), but they provide detailed statistics of the housing stock, enumerating the *domus* and *insulae* for each region, as well as *balnea, lacus,* and *pistrina.*[18] If we have reliable statistics for the density of the housing stock by region, and can wed it to an understanding of the street plan and numerous examples of actual structures, surely we can work back to a pretty good idea of how the housing stock fits into the topography of the city.

Alas, the statistics of the *Regionaries* are subject to long and agonizing dispute.[19] Let us pass over the minor variations between the two different versions,

15. See Luigi Salerno, Luigi Spezzaferro, and Manfredo Tafuri, *Via Giulia: una utopia urbanistica del 500* (Rome: Aristide Stadeerini, 1973).

16. See G. Curcio, *L'Angelo e la città. La città nel settecento* (Rome: Fratelli Palombi, 1987).

17. H. Gamrath, *Roma Sancta renovata: studi sull'urbanistica di Roma nella seconda metà del sec. XVI con particolare riferimento al pontificato di Sisto V (1585-1590)* (Rome: L'Erma di Bretschneider, 1987).

18. Arvast Nordh, *Libellus de regionibus urbis Romae* (Lund: C. W. K. Gleerup, 1949).

19. Gustav Hermansen, "The Population of Imperial Rome," *Historia* 27 (1978): 129-68; J. Arce, "El inventario de Roma: Curiosum y Notitia," in *The Transformations of Urbs Roma in Late Antiquity,* pp. 15-22; F. Coarelli, "La consistenza della città nel periodo imperiale: pomperium, vici, insulae," in *La Rome impériale: démographie et logistique. Actes de la table ronde*

and the failure of the figures for individual regions to add up to the totals given, so that the total number of *insulae* fluctuates from 44,000 to 46,000. Even if one takes the lowest figures, the land available within the Aurelian walls (a maximum of 1,783 hectares) can in no way accommodate this sort of density of *insulae*, or not at least if what we understand by *insula* is the sort of massive block of rental apartments of brick and concrete construction with which Ostia has made us familiar.[20]

On Guilhembet's calculations (and they are far from easy, because of the uncertainties over the precise boundaries of each region, and over what proportion of each was occupied by public buildings and imperial *horti* and the like, which left no room for private houses), the average figure for each *insula* is only some 224 square meters of ground-floor space, and that average reduces to some 75 square meters in the densest areas. We may note with interest that the housing becomes densest in the center of the city, around the Palatine and Capitoline and Forum, just where we would expect the highest concentration of public buildings. Does that show that the statistics are incredible, or that our assumptions about what the center of Rome was like, derived from our experience of the area as an archaeological park, are simply anachronistic?

One response is indeed to dismiss these statistics as a figment of the *mirabilia* literature which inflates the amazing size of Rome without real basis.[21] I have to say, I have much sympathy with the opposite position, articulated most eloquently by Filippo Coarelli, which sees in the *Regionaries* a reflection of hard information deriving from the office of the *praefectus urbi*.[22] We know that ever since Caesar's dictatorship, the *insula* was the basic unit of population census within the capital. As Suetonius explains (*Divus Julius* 41), this was the first time citizens were listed neighborhood by neighborhood, *vicus* by *vicus*, and through the owners of property, *domini insularum*. That is a vital system of knowledge for the imperial control of the city, when you are checking who is entitled to receive free grain or to enjoy the frequent other benefits that mark the privilege of the imperial capital, in an effort to ensure the ground support for imperial power. Augustus's reorganization of the city in *Regiones* and *vici*, with officially constituted boards of local officers, *vicomagistri* and

---

(*Rome, 25 mars, 1994*), Collection de L' École Française de Rome 230 (Rome: École Française de Rome, 1997), pp. 89-109.

20. J.-P. Guilhembet, "La densité des *domus* et des *insulae* dans les XIV régions de Rome: selon les *Régionnaires* représentations cartographiques," *Mélanges d' archéologie et d' histoire de l' École française de Rome* 108 (1996): 7-26.

21. So Arce, pp. 15-22.

22. Coarelli, "La consistenza della città nel periodo imperiale."

ministri, reveals the sophistication of Caesar's innovation, which gives the capillary control of the city real effect.[23]

Coarelli argues convincingly that the office of the *praefectus urbi* must have maintained these statistics, and regularly surveyed the properties and their inhabitants. He also believes, and this too I accept, that the marble *Forma urbis* was the public display of the city prefect's major instrument of knowledge and control, a precise mapping of the properties. Only one *domus* is actually named on the Severan plan, the *domus Cilonis,* the house of the very city prefect, Fabius Cilo, who had the plan inscribed. But we know that this version had predecessors going back probably to Augustus. Attached to the original survey maps will have been detailed lists of property owners, and the returns they gave about the citizens and noncitizens resident in their property. We are left to imagine the insight we could gain into the social and domestic structures of metropolitan Rome if only we had access to the prefect's office!

We at least have an oblique glance at this material through the *Regionaries.* Are the *domus* and *insulae* enumerated consistent with the units depicted on the marble plan, and with those we now excavate? All hangs on the definition of an *insula.* Coarelli argues, again surely rightly, that it must refer not to the urban unit of the "island" surrounded by roads, the original sense, nor to the architectural unit of a block of single construction, but to the unit of property which the prefect's men were busy surveying for their census.[24]

Here we can go back to an old exercise by Lugli, who took a number of areas with private housing from the marble plan and tried to split them into units.[25] The exercise is of course rather arbitrary, since the plan does not mark property boundaries; even so, it showed that it could be done within an average of circa 300 square meters per unit. Moreover, and this seems to me a helpful and significant observation, if one takes the known property boundaries of the *catasto* of the center of Rome in the seventeenth century, the average unit size is very comparable at 232 square meters. Here too the English College offers precious evidence, for its detailed records and plans of the numerous properties it owned and rented out illustrate the sort of patchwork of relatively small prop-

---

23. A. Fraschetti, *Roma e il Principe* (Rome and Bari: Laterza, 1990), pp. 204-73, is fundamental; also P. Zanker, *The Powers of Images in the Age of Augustus,* trans. Alan Shapiro (Ann Arbor: University of Michigan Press, 1988), pp. 129-35; R. Laurence, "The Urban *Vicus:* The Spatial Organization of Power in the Roman City," in *Papers of the Fourth Conference of Italian Archaeology,* vol. 1, ed. E. Herring, R. Whitehouse, and J. Wilkins (London: Accordia Research Centre, 1991), p. xxx.

24. Supported by E. Lo Cascio, "Le procedure di recensus della tarda repubblica al tardoantico e il calcolo della popolazione di Roma," in *La Rome impériale,* pp. 3-76.

25. G. Lugli, "Il valore topografico e giuridico dell'*insula* in Roma antica," pp. 191-208.

erties a big landowner could control: that too is a possible model to bear in mind for antiquity.[26]

We are talking about no more than a set of hypotheses, the plausibility of which must be tested on the ground. The suggestion is that imperial Roman housing consists not of a few vast apartment blocks, but of a patchwork of properties of very varied shape and size, some quite small, and with a surprisingly low average of around 250 square meters. Looked at from the point of view of numbers of inhabitants, we also arrive at a relatively low average per unit: the million inhabitants commonly attributed to Rome would fill some 46,000 units of domestic property at an average of twenty-two persons per unit. If we imagine a four- or five-floor property with one apartment per floor, that would give four or five inhabitants per 250-square-meter apartment, a generosity of space that would make the modern Roman green with envy. However it is in my view cautious to imagine a far greater variety, from large five-story blocks crowded with much higher numbers to smaller, more ramshackle properties with two or three floors each, not that far different from what we see at Herculaneum.

The Termini Quarter

I wish to move from these rather broad considerations to a case study, brought to public attention by an exhibition held in 1997 in the Museo delle Terme under the title *Antiche Stanze*.[27] It was an exhibition of an excavation that had been systematically suppressed and forgotten. In the late 1940s, after the war, when the Piazza dei Cinquecento was being dug up to install the new Metro station in front of Termini, an extensive area of ancient housing emerged. Part of it, a bath suite, had already been seen in the 1870s when the earlier station was constructed, and impressive sculptures underlined its importance; the bath duly appears, though incorrectly oriented, on Lanciani's plan. But now not only the bath but the whole block of housing around it became visible, with mosaic floors and frescoed walls of considerable quality. The structures were demolished as swiftly as they came out, and only the private notebooks and photographs of an archaeologist on site preserved the record.

What is particularly useful about the reconstruction of the plan that Rita Paris and her colleagues were able to produce is that we see not one rich house

26. See A. Majanlahti, "Mapping Rome: Urban Change in the Neighbourhood of Santa Caterina della Rota," *PBSR* 56 (2001): 393-95.

27. *Antiche Stanze: Un quartiere di Roma imperiale nella zona di Termini. Museo Nazionale Romano Terme Diocleziano*, Rome, December 1996–June 1997 (Milan and Rome: Mondadori, 1996). Parenthetical page references in the following text are to this work.

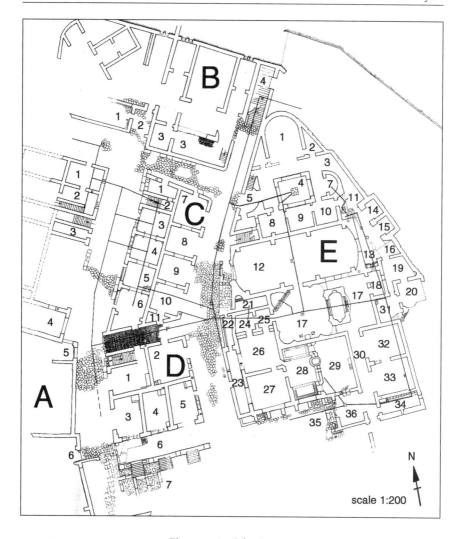

Figure 1. Antiche Stanze

in isolation, as so often, but something of the neighborhood around it. The rich house with mosaic floors occupies the triangular nose of a shiplike block (E1-11) (see detailed discussion, pp. 71-116). Its anatomy is not at all distant from that of a Pompeiian *domus,* though with significant variations: the entrance leads into a central court with a fountain (E4); on one side is a major reception room with an apsidal end to suit the curved seating pattern characteristic of the "sigma" of the high empire (E1). Opposite is a suite of smaller reception rooms/

bedrooms (E8-10). The services are tucked out of sight round the back (E14-20). Two staircases lead to upper floors; one is internal to the house (E5), the other external. The authors of the catalogue suggest that the external stair was for maintenance purposes only, for roof access, but this interpretation owes much to the conviction that one could not possibly have rental apartments above so smart a house (p. 71). Why not? The stair is broad, and could even have led directly to a third story.

The modern conviction that a rich *domus* was fundamentally different from an *insula* with its rental apartments evaporates on consideration of the rest of the block. The house was built simultaneously with the bath block against which it abuts, with a majority of brick stamps throughout dated to the reign of Hadrian, though modifications were made in the Antonine and Severan periods (p. 61). The magnificent hall (basilica, E12) leads to a sequence of curvilinear *frigidarium* (E17), two *tepidaria* (E26, 27) and *calidarium* (E28), with a supporting suite of changing rooms (E32, 33) and latrine (E34) (pp. 117-69). What is obvious is that this is not a private bath suite for the use of the household, but a public facility. One has to recall again and again that the great imperial baths did not supply the entire needs of the capital, but competed with the hundreds of private establishments which made profit by charging for use. The *Regionaries* give the enormous (and maybe inflated) number of 856 for these. Such a *balneum* was a valuable asset for income, as will have been the fullery immediately beside it (E21) (pp. 170-71).

But we need to look over the road too, at the double row of shops, split into two units, C and D, by a little lane, that form fourteen or so distinct units of operation (but surely not of ownership). Here too are evident traces of stairs to upper apartments, and just as in Pompeii, they may be internal to the shops (C5, D3, 4, 5) or for external access (C2, D1) (pp. 178-83). This dense block of shops and flats must have been a valuable source of rental income; that they were originally constructed in association with the *domus* is implied by the common drainage system. But while we may guess that shops, like bath, fullery, and even flats above the main residence, brought profits to the original proprietors of the *domus*, there would be nothing to prevent them and their successors from splitting the property into a series of separate lots, and indeed it is clear the property was split up in late antiquity (pp. 172-76). There is even a good chance that the original speculators were members of the imperial family, given the presence of stamped *fistulae* bearing the names of Marcus Aurelius and his daughter Vibia Aurelia Sabina, and a statue of Faustina, though all these are subsequent to the initial construction (pp. 61-62). Equally, even if all remained under a single owner, the urban prefect would surely have recorded the blocks as several units, though each had the same proprietor.

Rather harder to interpret is the northeastern building at the end of the little lane that runs between the grand house and the block of shops (B) (pp. 184-89). This part was already excavated during the initial construction of Rome's station in the 1860s. The plan shows one large, dominant room, which exceeds any room in the principal *domus* of block E; and an early photograph of John Henry Parker shows that it was two stories in height. Interpreted as the luxurious ground-floor flat of a block of apartments, it does not look like a normal domestic structure (p. 187). Its size suggests an assembly place like the shrine or college of the Augustales at Herculaneum, or the various collegial buildings of Ostia, and I offer the suggestion that it is the *schola* or meeting hall of some guild or association.[28]

In offering that suggestion, I invite you to think about Rome not so much as an undifferentiated sea of distinct units of housing, be they *domus* or *insulae*, flowing around the great public monuments, but as a series of cellular neighborhoods. The word *vicus* was taken over by Augustus in his project to impose formal neighborhood organization on the city, formalizing and bringing under control less official urban groupings represented by the *collegia* and associations of late republican Rome. The Augustan *vici* are in fact quite substantial: the 320 or so *vici* of the fourth-century *Regionaries* would contain an average 150 *insulae*, occupying an area of from one to ten hectares. The group of *insulae* of the Termini quarter would only be a fraction, perhaps no more than a tenth, of an entire *vicus*. But what is striking is the cellular composition of the housing stock wherever we glimpse it. It is essentially mixed in nature, between grand houses and blocks of flats and little shop units on the one hand, and buildings that formed focuses of local communal life on the other — baths, clubs, and corporations. Such clusters can reproduce and multiply like cells until one reaches the level of formal neighborhood organization imposed by the state. The absence of traces of internal sanitation and cooking facilities makes it likely that public baths, and nearby cookshops and bars, formed a key focus of communal life.[29]

This perception of the fabric of the ancient city as profoundly mixed,

---

28. On Ostia, see Gustav Hermansen, *Ostia: Aspects of Roman City Life* (Edmonton, Alberta: University of Alberta Press, 1982), pp. 56-89. Several collegial *scholae* are epigraphically attested: *LTUR*, 4:245-54; also *LTUR*, 1:259, for the *cella vinaria* and associated *collegium* in Trastevere.

29. On the Augustan *vici*, see A. Fraschetti, *Roma e il Principe* (Rome: Laterza, 1990), pp. 204-73; *Lexicon Topographicum Urbis Romae*, ed. M. Steinby, vol. 5 (1999), pp. 151-201. On *vici* at Pompeii, see R. Laurence, *Roman Pompeii: Space and Society* (New York and London: Routledge, 1994), pp. 38-50; W. van Andringa, "Autels de carrefour, organisation vicinale et rapports de voisinage à Pompéi," *Rivista di Studi Pompeiani* 11 (2001): 47-86.

which I first commented on for Pompeii, and am no less struck by in Rome, makes me unhappy with the conventional wisdom that the rich and poor lived apart in imperial Rome, the rich in large airy houses on the hills, the poor crowded in unsanitary apartment blocks in the valleys. That seems a retrojection of modern conditions, and the statistics Werner Eck assembles to substantiate the point seem to me to put too much weight on what can be inferred from lead pipes that bear the names of senators and equestrians.[30] *Fistulae*, in a word, may tell us more about the identity of the speculators who constructed property, or indeed of *domini insularum*, the rentier class, than of actual inhabitants. It is the same consideration that for me makes the *Lexicon Topographicum* such a limited guide to the housing of Rome.[31] Despite 195 pages dedicated to 433 *domus*, what we have is essentially a list of houses mentioned in literary sources bulked out by names from lead pipes. Of these, a mere dozen have secure physical traces. But over 100 cases exist of secure physical traces of domestic structures, whether of *domus* or *insulae*. It is from these, in my view, that we must start.

Within the *Insula*

In a final group of examples, I want to look at the internal organization of the Roman *insula*, and the implications for how it might be inhabited. While considerable attention has been given to this issue at Ostia, important evidence comes from Rome, and is oddly neglected. The *insula* at the foot of the Capitoline beneath the steps leading to S. Maria in Aracoeli is one of the extraordinary by-products of Mussolini's *sventramenti* of the 1930s. What Muñoz tore down was the small baroque church of S. Rita, which had swallowed up an early medieval church of S. Biagio in Campitello, and a set of apartments around it that seem to have been almost continuously inhabited for two millennia. There was no scientific publication of the excavation, though the underlying imperial *insula* was opened to tourist visits, and was presented in the Museo della Civiltà Romana in a fine model by Gismondi. Remarkably, and unlike the situation at Ostia, the structures survive in detail for the first four floors of the building, and ample traces remain of the fourth floor.[32]

---

30. W. Eck, "*Cum dignitate otium:* Senatorial *Domus* in Imperial Rome," *Scripta Classica Israelica* 16 (1997): 162-90.

31. See my review in the *Times Literary Supplement*, May 11, 2001, pp. 3f.

32. A. Muñoz, *Campidoglio* (Rome, 1930). J. Packer, "La Casa di via Giulio Romano," *Bulletino della Commissione archeologica Communale in Roma* 81 (1968-69): 127ff.; P. Chini, "L'insula dell'Aracoeli," *Forma Urbis* ann. IV, 6 (June 1999): 5-13.

We may note at once that the ground-floor plan bears little relation to that of the floors above — an observation which is significant when we consider that both the marble plan and most excavation give us the ground plan only. The bottom floor consists of the familiar row of shops, and would show up in hundreds of fragments of the marble plan as a series of rectangular units in a row. Above the shops is a mezzanine level, an arrangement that remained classic for Renaissance and baroque Rome too. The upper rooms were accessible by internal wooden staircases, and represented, as at Pompeii and elsewhere, the living quarters associated with the shop. The internal arrangements of the next floor up are less clear: a series of large interconnected rooms suggests a very large comfortable apartment, but the continuous habitation and possibility that structures have been significantly modified make this less than certain.

Most legible and striking is the fourth floor, which is subdivided by internal corridors into a series of suites of three rooms. There has been considerable disagreement over their function, and Amanda Claridge, for instance, inclines to an identification as slave quarters.[33] This seems to me to underestimate considerably the size and potential of each of these units. The end room is lit by two windows — externally the windows form groups of three, of which the third lights the corridor itself. This is surely the main living room, while the rooms behind serve as bedrooms and utility rooms. In present dank and dingy conditions it takes a leap of the imagination, but with painted plaster on the walls, and in all likelihood simple white mosaic flooring, such an apartment would rank with the forty-square-meter apartments in which many families live now in Rome. In any case, we must recall that such repetitive units of habitation were not constructed with particular family units or social groupings in mind, but as flexible space for renting in a changing market.

From the *insula* Aracoeli we may move to one final example that has an only too obvious connection to the house origins of Christian churches, SS. Giovanni e Paolo on the Caelian.[34] This is a theme about which we have learned much recently, thanks above all to the work of Federico Guidobaldi, whose article on houses as sensors of social transformations is a model of what can be done.[35] The early imperial *insula* that forms the core of the structure of the basilica (the brick stamps of the core are of 123 C.E., but this is substantially modi-

33. A. Claridge, *Rome*, Oxford Archaeological Guides (Oxford: Oxford University Press, 1998), pp. 232-34.

34. Antonio Maria Colini, "Storia e topografia del Celio nell'antichita," *Atti Pontifica Accademia romana di archeologia*, ser. III, 7 (1944): 164-70; R. Krautheimer, *Corpus Basilicarum Christianarum Romae* 1.4, 267-303; White, *Social Origins*, 2:209-18, for recent overview.

35. Guidobaldi, pp. 53-68.

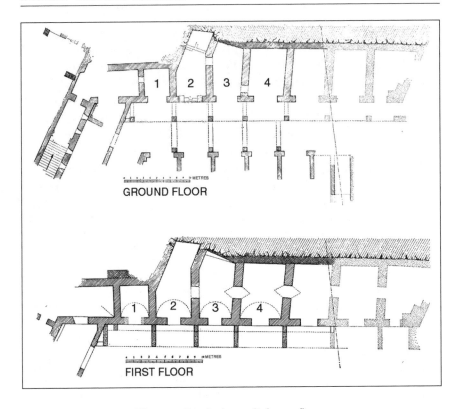

GROUND FLOOR

FIRST FLOOR

Figure 2. *Insula* Aracoeli, lower floors

fied and extended over the following century) is particularly visible in the flank that gives on the Clivus Scauri. Here we can see the familiar shop entrances, blocked in, and above them the brick-relieving arches that span groups of two or three tall rectangular windows, of proportions very similar to the *insula* Aracoeli. It seems to me reasonable to conjecture that groupings of three windows point to the same sort of arrangement of corridor and apartment.

But the blockings of these windows are not only medieval. Much of the brickwork is of the imperial period, and it seems that the *insula* undergoes a major transformation in the second half of the third century. Guidobaldi points out that after the end of a peak of construction in the early third century, building of *insulae* in Rome ceases completely. There are many instances of previous *insulae* being converted into large dwellings, including the *domus* Gaudentii, excavated by Carlo Pavolini under the military hospital, not far uphill from this site. Traces of conversion are also visible on the ground floor in-

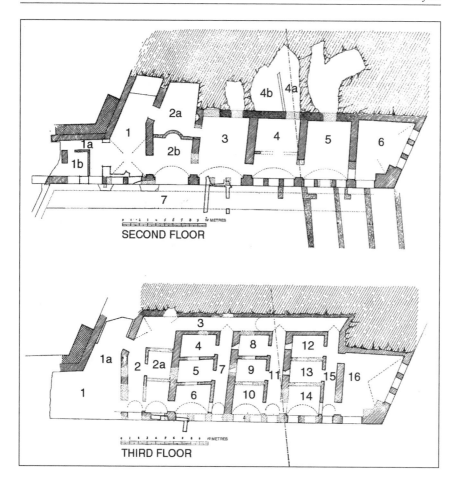

Figure 3. *Insula* Aracoeli, upper floors

side SS. Giovanni e Paolo. In the earlier phase we meet some large decorated rooms, including the courtyard area decorated with a large *nymphaeum*, with a scene of a marine Venus. Extensive redecoration takes place in the late third century, and the shops seem to be abandoned, replaced by decorated rooms like the "room of the Ephebes." By the fourth century the house becomes a house church, and the *confessio* beneath the stairs depicts the martyrdom of John and Paul.

What is so difficult to read is the sort of transformation that may be implied in the remodeling of *insulae*. Guidobaldi points to the shortage of building land — imperial Rome has reached its limits. It is hard to suppress the suspicion that the answer is also demographic, though Lo Cascio and others continue to argue vigorously for the populousness of late imperial Rome on the basis of figures for distribution of bread, wine, and pork.[36] If larger households are being established at the expense of the dense habitation made possible by little apartments, it would imply an easing of pressure on space.

But perhaps we should think too of changing social relations between the occupants of these buildings. Multiple apartments imply essentially commercial relationships; yet I have suggested that we should not overlook the possibility of a strong sense of community among such neighbors. Just as the corporation lists of Ostia name people together, and the columbaria bury them together, *insulae* may conveniently house them together.[37] What I would like to know is how these bonds develop in late antiquity, at a time when membership of trade corporations is being transformed from an option to a hereditary obligation. If we understood this better, we might understand the context within which Christian communities formed around martyr shrines in houses.

When we emerge into the early Middle Ages, we find new types of neighborhood solidarity: the family clan, a dense cluster around the big house of the leading family, is seen physically in the Rome of towers, the strongholds of the families who ran neighborhoods in sharp competition with one another.[38] It is this sense of neighborhood, rather than any sense of modern nuclear family, with which I think we need to come to grips. To do that, we need to take much more seriously the abundant evidence for the domestic fabric of the city that already exists.

36. E. Lo Cascio, "La popolazione," in *Roma Imperiale. Una metropoli antica* (Rome: Carocci editore, 2000), pp. 17-69, esp. 59f.

37. See J. R. Patterson, "Living and Dying in the City of Rome: Houses and Tombs," in *Ancient Rome: The Archaeology of the Eternal City*, ed. J. Coulson and H. Dodge (Oxford: Oxford University School of Archaeology, 2000), pp. 259-89.

38. J. Heers, *Family Clans in the Middle Ages: A Study of Political and Social Structures in Urban Areas* (Amsterdam: North-Holland Publisher, 1977).

Material and Social Environment of Greco-Roman Households in the East: The Case of Hellenistic Delos

Monika Trümper

Early Christian families lived and worshiped in the midst of Greco-Roman culture. It is known, primarily from literary references, that an important part of their lives took place in houses: early Christian communities met for prayer in the private houses of their members. During his journeys Paul preached, taught, and stayed in private homes. These houses, usually called "house churches," played a key role in the spread of Christianity, in the evangelization and religious education. However, there was nothing distinctively Christian about the physical setting of the early ἐκκλησίαι, since house churches were not adapted to or altered for specific religious functions. Thus they cannot be distinguished from contemporaneous domestic buildings. Even if a particular house was known to have been inhabited by Christians, this did not necessarily imply its use as a house church.[1]

Consequently, to understand the cultural and physical environment of early Christians, one can only take a look at the remains of contemporaneous domestic architecture in general, that is, Greco-Roman houses. Since Christianity developed in the western as well as the eastern part of the Roman Empire — Paul stayed in Rome and Italy but performed most of his missionary work in

1. Carolyn Osiek and David L. Balch, *Families in the New Testament World: Houses and House Churches* (Louisville: Westminster John Knox, 1997), pp. 5, 32-35, 206-14; L. Michael White, *The Social Origins of Christian Architecture*, HTS 42, vol. 1 (Baltimore: Johns Hopkins University Press, 1990), pp. 11-25; vol. 2 (Cambridge: President and Fellows of Harvard College, 1997), pp. 1-32.

I would like to thank Carolyn Osiek and David Balch for inviting me to the conference that gave rise to this volume and for including this essay here and for their improvements to my English text. I would also like to thank the other participants at the conference for comments and discussion, above all Andrew Wallace-Hadrill, to whose inspiring publications my own work owes much. Finally, I would like to note that only relevant literature published before 2002 is included here.

the East — both western and eastern domestic architecture have to be taken into account. For the western part the well-preserved Campanian cities Pompeii and Herculaneum, where life ceased just at the beginning of Christianity, offer the most complete view of domestic architecture. Their wide spectrum of house types has been the subject of many detailed studies and has already been discussed with regard to early Christian life.[2] There is no eastern equivalent for the Vesuvian cities. In the East, only very few urban houses of the first two centuries C.E. are well enough preserved and were both fully excavated and sufficiently published to allow the study of design and decoration as well as the classification of clear types. Moreover, this part of the Roman Empire comprises so many different countries and cultures that numerous local modifications in the layout and organization of houses are to be expected. Thus a satisfactory overview of eastern domestic architecture and the identification of universally valid house types can hardly be provided.[3]

For a high number of fully excavated and well-preserved houses, still the best eastern comparison for the Vesuvian cities is the settlement on the Cycladic island of Delos. In the French excavation since 1873, more than one hundred houses have been uncovered, with walls partly still preserved up to a height of from five to six meters. When leaving their houses the inhabitants carried most of their possessions with them, so almost no artifacts are left for interpretation. Nevertheless, large parts of the decoration, including wall paintings and different pavement types, are preserved and make it possible to gain a general impression of the setting. However, from a chronological point of view, Delian domestic architecture does not quite fit, since its heyday ended in the middle of the first century B.C.E. After a short period of independence (314-166 B.C.E.), the small polis-state Delos was declared a free port by the Roman conquerors in 166. It soon developed into a booming cosmopolitan trade center with merchants coming from all over the Mediterranean world. Although Delos was sacked twice, in 88 by the troops of Mithridates and in 69 by the pirates under Athenodoros, its desertion during the first century B.C.E. is predominantly due to the rivalry of increasingly successful Roman ports like Puteoli and Ostia. Life in Delos did not come to an abrupt halt, as is evidenced by remains of Roman *thermae* and several Christian basilicas, but it continued only on a much smaller scale.[4]

2. Osiek and Balch, *Families in the New Testament World.*

3. It is beyond the scope of this essay to give a detailed bibliography for houses in the eastern part of the Roman Empire. For the poor situation of research in Asia Minor, see Ulrike Wulf, *Die hellenistischen und römischen Wohnhäuser von Pergamon*, Die Stadtgrabung Teil 3. Altertümer von Pergamon XV,3 (Berlin and New York: Walter de Gruyter, 1999), p. 189.

4. Philippe Bruneau and Jean Ducat, *Guide de Délos* (Paris: Éditions E. de Boccard, 1983), pp. 20-30.

Despite its early date, the study of Hellenistic Delos can be instructive for the reconstruction of early Christian housing. As house types of Pompeii, dating largely before the first century c.e., can exemplify living arrangements in most Italian cities of the Roman Empire, the evidence of Hellenistic Delos might throw some light on the domestic architecture of those parts of the Roman Empire predominantly influenced by Greek-Hellenistic culture. To study Delian houses gives at least an insight into Hellenistic cosmopolitan life at the dawn of Christianity. Therefore in this essay, based mainly on the Delian houses, the following topics will be discussed:

1. The spectrum of house types in Delos.
2. The use and social significance of Delian houses: Do these houses reveal anything about the organization of their households and the social status of their inhabitants?
3. A comparison with other house types: How do Delian houses fit into western and eastern domestic architecture especially of the Pauline setting? Can they really be considered representative for Christian living conditions? Is it feasible that Paul during his journeys in the East encountered such houses, and did he meet different conditions when staying in Rome and Italy?

A satisfactory answer to these questions would require an extensive study of many different cities, which, partly for the above-mentioned reasons, is beyond the scope of this essay. Therefore comparison with eastern domestic architecture will be limited to few examples, with a representative number of excavated and published houses. Likewise, it is impossible to pay due attention to all the rich research literature on the Vesuvian cities. Instead the comparison will be restricted to a few remarks concerning, above all, the conspicuous differences between eastern and western houses.[5]

House Types in Delos

Constructing typologies serves first of all to sort and to categorize the archaeological evidence. Moreover, this is usually practiced in the more or less firm belief that different house types correspond to different social levels and that domestic architecture might thus reflect the social structure of the city or culture under examination. It is beyond the scope of this discussion to explain the

---

5. For an extensive survey of domestic architecture in the early Christian period, see Osiek and Balch, pp. 5-35.

methodology of defining "types." Potential criteria for the identification include shape, size, structure, number, and function of elements. The last, however, seems highly problematic, because the use and consequently the name of a room can rarely be determined. Only its importance, its rank within a house, can be estimated based upon characteristics like position, form, size, architectural elements (e.g., doors, windows, niches, columns), and above all, decoration with paintings and pavements. All wall plaster in Delos belongs to the masonry style (an equivalent of the first Pompeiian style). This style allowed differentiation in the use of colors and motifs, the extent of relief molding, and the number of frieze bands, but offered no place for figurative pictures except on the small friezes. A hierarchy of pavement types was based on different materials, the complexity of the composition and motifs. Among the vast majority of simple pavements with geometric patterns made of marble chips or large tesserae, only a few tesselated mosaics included figured *emblemata* made with tiny polychrome tesserae. Overall the perceivable figured decoration, being completed by statues and figurines of marble and terra-cotta, seems to have been rather limited. This also holds true for the scenes depicted, because in all three decoration types Aphrodisiac-Dionysiac themes predominate.[6]

Among the ninety-one completely excavated houses on Delos, one dominant standard type can be determined which has the shape of an elongated, rarely strictly regular rectangle with a central courtyard and rooms opening to the front and rear.[7] (Plate 1, houses I, III, IV, VI, VII; plate 4.) The front row, next to the street, comprises a vestibule and service rooms, often a latrine and a multifunctional room with a paved floor for activities with water,[8] whereas the back row consists of a characteristic group of rooms: a large room, *oecus maior*, with one or two annex rooms. These rooms probably constituted the main living area, and are generally larger and better decorated than the front rooms. The courtyard often occupies the whole width of the house, but is sometimes reduced by small rooms or simple shelters. Most of these houses are oriented toward the north and are equipped regularly with a well, a reservoir, or a cistern for water supply, a toilet, and drainage for rain and wastewater. Judging from

6. For the figured decoration, see Martin Kreeb, *Untersuchungen zur figürlichen Ausstattung delischer Privathäuser* (Chicago: Ares Publishers, 1988), with further bibliography.

7. The standard publication is still Joseph Chamonard, *Le Quartier du théâtre. Étude sur l'habitation délienne à l'époque hellénistique*. Exploration archéologique de Délos VIII (Paris: Éditions E. de Boccard, 1922/24); for a recent study on all excavated houses, see Monika Trümper, *Wohnen in Delos. Eine baugeschichtliche Untersuchung zum Wandel der Wohnkultur in hellenistischer Zeit*, Internationale Archäologie 46 (Rahden in Westfalia: Verlag Marie Leidorf GmbH, 1998), with further bibliography.

8. Kitchens can rarely be clearly identified.

the twenty-three still-preserved examples, their sizes range from 65 square meters to 200 square meters. Another sixteen houses are thought to follow this original design, even though they were modified in later phases.

Because of its frequent occurrence (43 percent), this type has been called "normal house type." Its elongated shape renders the normal house very suitable for grouping in rows. Indeed, there is no example of a freestanding normal house. Often two houses are combined to form a single block, but *insulae*[9] with up to six houses also occur. The double house blocks can be supplemented by an additional row of shops. Two dates have been suggested for the invention of this house type — the third century B.C.E. as the period of "independence," and the time of the free port after 166 B.C.E. — but to date, neither can be established with any certainty. In terms of relative chronology, normal houses are the earliest types, but they continued to be used until the last phases of occupation in all quarters.[10]

To classify the remaining houses is much more difficult. Neither size nor shape can be counted as convincing criteria. Instead, it seems more suitable to classify those houses that clearly present a higher standard of living than the normal house according to specific elements and their structure. Based upon these criteria, two further "types" can be determined which show strong similarities with the normal houses. Fourteen houses present a kind of enlarged normal house type with an additional row of rooms on one side of the courtyard (plate 1, house II; plate 4). These rooms are often richly decorated *(oeci minores, exedrae)* and, because of this, are usually taken as apt for representational purposes such as the reception of guests. The size of enlarged normal houses ranges from 120 square meters to 360 square meters.[11]

The highest living standard is provided by houses not only larger than the before-mentioned but also with a different shape: they are considerably wider, though rarely exactly quadrangular and even not always rectangular and regular in shape. The wider form allowed three or four rows of rooms to be grouped around the courtyard which normally comprises a peristyle (plate 2, houses B, C; plate 3, Maison des comédiens. Maison des tritons; plate 4). Elements of the normal house like the characteristic group of *oecus maior* with annexes are combined with a large variety of richly decorated rooms *(oeci minores, exedrae)*, which preferably open directly onto the courtyard — on as many sides as possible. Strictly isolated functional areas cannot be detected, although poorly decorated minor rooms and service areas clearly tend to concentrate ei-

---

9. The term is used in the modern sense defining a city block; Osiek and Balch, pp. 228-29.
10. Trümper, pp. 107-9.
11. Trümper, pp. 109-10.

ther in poorly lit, invisible corners of the house or in the front row next to the entrance, connected to the courtyard with as few doors as possible. Thus, not only the back part of the house but all visible sides of the peristyle courtyard could be reserved for the rich, prestigious rooms. An orientation of the main rooms to the north is realized wherever possible.[12]

These houses are usually classified as "peristyle houses." However, one has to take into account that this group is very heterogeneous in shape and size. Also, the peristyle, the characteristic element, is not limited to this particular group of houses. Some of the enlarged normal houses and even simple normal houses include peristyles, though always as later additions to the original plan (plate 1, house II). We keep in mind the limitations of this definition when we, for practical purposes, call this type peristyle houses here. What really distinguishes the peristyle house from the other two types is the availability and number of different lavishly decorated rooms for the reception of guests. Clear figures can hardly be provided: fifteen houses can be found that are larger than enlarged normal houses, that is, 360 square meters to 850 square meters. Two of those fifteen have no peristyle, which clearly shows that large houses are not automatically luxurious; two of the twelve houses with peristyles incorporated in the original design have fewer than 360 square meters surface. The date of introduction of peristyles in Delian domestic architecture has been intensely disputed, but up to now no peristyle can be dated before 166 B.C.E. with certainty. According to the relative chronology, peristyle houses are later than the first normal houses, some being dated by stratigraphy as late as the end of the second century B.C.E.[13]

In addition to these three types, the normal house, the enlarged normal house, and the peristyle house, there is a large variety of simple living units which cannot be classified into types or categories. The larger ones often have elements of the normal houses, that is, the basic equipment with courtyard, water supply, latrine, and sometimes even lavishly decorated rooms, but they do lack the characteristic structure and the specific group with *oecus maior* and annex rooms. The smaller ones, consisting mostly of only one or two rooms, are often combined with shops or workshops, the most simple lodging being the *pergula*, the mezzanine floor, in a *taberna* (plate 1, complex V; plate 2, houses A, D; plate 4).

Furthermore, apartments in upper stories have to be mentioned, not as a separate type — in fact, nothing is known about their size, structure, and elements — but only as a potential place for lodging (plates 1-4: UF = upper-floor

---

12. Trümper, pp. 81-90, 110-14.

13. Trümper, pp. 120-26.

entrance). According to the inventories of the temple of Apollo, rooms or apartments in upper stories could be let separately from the ground floor. The separate use of upper stories is confirmed archaeologically by the evidence of staircases that either had their own, separate entrance from the street, but within the confines of the building, or else were completely external, that is, constructed against the facades of houses. Findings show that most of the upper stories were decorated much more lavishly than their ground floor equivalents. Therefore their rank must have been equal if not superior to the ground floor, even if they did not have their own water supply.[14]

To summarize, there is a wide range of living units, from mezzanine floors within shops to extensive complexes with peristyle courtyards. Most of the houses share similar principles concerning the organization of space, regardless of their size and level. The basic design features a central courtyard and standard equipment with water supply, a toilet, drainage for wastewater, living and service rooms. The latter are concentrated in the front part of the house, in areas off the courtyard and in unlit corners. More richly decorated rooms tend to open directly onto the courtyard, being situated at the back part of the house opposite the entrance and, if space allows, on the sides of the court. Thus, in most Delian houses visitors had to traverse the whole house in order to reach the most representative rooms. But this structure was established within the confines of only one courtyard because houses were not extended horizontally, that is, grouped around several courtyards, but vertically, constituting usually no more than one additional story. Even if separate upper stories are attested by epigraphic and archaeological sources, multistoried apartment blocks seem to be missing.[15] Upper story rooms are generally much more lavishly decorated than their ground level equivalents, and must have been used accordingly if upper floor and ground floor were inhabited by one owner. Only one standard type, the normal house, could be clearly identified, whereas the other ones like the enlarged normal house and peristyle houses form less distinct groups. These three "types" can roughly be correlated to house sizes, measured on the ground floor level: the surface of normal houses and simpler house types up to 200 square meters (54 of 91 completely excavated Delian houses = 59 percent), that of enlarged normal houses and larger houses up to 360 square meters (22 of 91 = 24 percent), and that of large peristyle houses up to 850 square meters (15 of 91 = 17 percent).

14. Trümper, pp. 90-106.

15. With the exception of houses built against hills like the Maison de l'Hermès and some of the "Magasins" on the western coast, which might have functioned as large *synoikiai;* Bruneau and Ducat, pp. 215-19, 257-58.

Within single quarters or *insulae,* rather consistently houses of different sizes, including nonresidential space like shops or workshops, are mixed indiscriminately. There is no differentiation into "rich" and "poor," into noble or lower-class quarters. Even within *insulae* with the most lavish and distinguished houses, living units of different kinds are densely interwoven: in the Ilot de la maison des masques (plate 2), a medium peristyle house (house C) and two small courtyard houses (houses A, D), completely irregular in shape, are grouped like satellites around a lavish peristyle house in the center (house B). The rooms of the latter have been arranged in such a favorable manner around the peristyle courtyard that unattractive, unlighted corner rooms do not exist. The resulting shape is completely irregular, which, not being perceptible from the inside, has no negative effect on the big house but more so on the two small ones.

In the horizontal dimension, each living unit in the Delian *insulae* was clearly separated from the neighboring unit. Vertically, however, units were closely connected by sight and by the use of common space (plates 1-4, fig. 2): inhabitants of upper apartments could observe activities taking place in the ground floor courtyard, and most likely also had to intrude physically into this courtyard in order to get water. Unfortunately, information about private or official regulations as regards access to limited resources is lacking.

The Use and Social Significance of Delian Houses

If domestic architecture really mirrors the structure of a society, its standard social patterns and relations might be reflected in the layout of the houses. The structure of Greek society features clear distinctions between citizen and noncitizen, free man and slave, man and woman. The most important contrasts in Greek houses are often regarded as that between male and female space and that between patronal and servile space. Moreover, clear distinctions seem to have been drawn between household members and outsiders, usually guests or visitors. This polarization is often directly linked to a concept of "private" and "public" space, houses being divided into zones clearly marked for the use of either the family or visitors. The presence and extension of "public" space in a house is usually taken as an indicator of its social meaning and the social status of its owner. The concrete layout of the "public" spaces may allow deductions about the character and importance of social life in a house.[16]

16. From the rich literature concerning these questions, only very few representative works can be cited here: first has to be mentioned Andrew Wallace-Hadrill, *Houses and Society in Pompeii and Herculaneum* (Princeton: Princeton University Press, 1994), comprising several relevant

Trying to combine the structure of society and domestic architecture in Delos is quite a disappointing task. Specific patterns of social relationship within the houses cannot be convincingly reconstructed from the physical organization of space. Nor can house types be correlated with different social functions and levels, because despite excellent archaeological records, sufficiently detailed information on Delian society is lacking. According to the epigraphic sources, independent Delos was a normal Greek polis-state with the usual political institutions and a traditional social structure with clear differentiation between citizens, noncitizens, and slaves and a strong position of the family.[17] It is tempting to interpret the normal house type as the ideal townhouse for one single family in analogy to the many houses of classical cities like Olynthus and Priene. The traditional inward-looking courtyard house seems indeed very suited to the needs of a traditional Greek family. But even apart from the eminent chronological problems, a homogeneous picture of domestic architecture doesn't take into account the large variety of house types as described in the contemporaneous inscriptions. And the normal house type is certainly still widely used after 166 B.C.E. in a completely different sociohistorical context.

For the period of the free port, the archaeological record is decidedly better, but knowledge about the social structure is much more scanty: after 166 Delos became an Athenian cleruchy, but how long this political system really functioned and performed is still disputed. In the last quarter of the second century B.C.E., it might have been replaced by a multinational assembly that reflected the social structure of the free port, a cosmopolitan population probably being its most remarkable trait. Athenians, Romans, and Italians were the most important ethnic groups; Orientals figured prominently among the remaining foreigners. But any details about their respective numbers and about the social structure and organization of society remain the subject of much controversy. Although families of some importance and the formation of local polis elites of an old type are still attested epigraphically, it is far from certain that the family was the only dominant focus of the social structure in the milieu of the trade port. In addition, voluntary associations composed according to ethnicity or profession played an increasingly important role.[18] Against this

---

earlier articles not enumerated separately here; for recent research on Roman and Greek houses, see Jens-Arne Dickmann, *Domus frequentata. Anspruchsvolles Wohnen im pompejanischen Stadthaus,* Studien zur antiken Stadt 4 (Munich: Verlag Dr. Friedrich Pfeil, 1999); Lisa Nevett, *House and Society in the Ancient Greek World* (Cambridge: Cambridge University Press, 1999).

17. Claude Vial, "Délos indépendante," *Bulletin de Correspondance Hellénique,* suppl. X (1984).

18. For the period of Athenian dominance, see Pierre Roussel, *Délos, colonie athénienne* (Paris: Éditions E. de Boccard, 1916; 2nd ed., 1987).

background any attempt to identify the social level of owners of house types is condemned to fail. One can only suppose that modest houses have been constructed and inhabited by less well-off people while the large, lavish peristyle houses were in the possession of rich owners. But whether the latter were only some "nouveau riche" Trimalchios or really belonged to a politically influential aristocratic elite is open to speculation. This naturally has consequences for the reconstruction of social life within the houses, because it can consequently not be determined who used and frequented them.

Thus the archaeological evidence can be interpreted only with reference to the knowledge of Greek society in general. And within these boundaries, clear statements can be made about the relationship between household organization and social structures.[19]

If women (and children) were still largely present in Delos after 166 B.C.E., it remains unclear where they lived and worked. It is impossible to discriminate from the archaeological findings areas of specialized functions, let alone for exclusive use by women. In some classical houses the upper stories might have been reserved for women, as these are the most obvious areas for locating a *gynaikonitis* or the private quarters. This, however, was not the case in Delos, where upper stories were often inhabited separately, with the consequence that all needs of the inhabitants had to be met on one single story, ground floor or upper floor. In addition to that, even if upper-story rooms belonged to the ground floor apartment, the lavish decoration of the upper rooms excludes a purely "private" use since the richest rooms of houses usually served "public, male" representational needs.

If slaves were present, which is to be questioned for smaller houses and households,[20] they certainly moved around in the whole house in order to serve their masters. But most likely they lived in service rooms and areas as suggested by a graffito of a desperate slave in a small service room of the Maison du lac.[21] The servants' rooms were also the place for low-status activities such as working with water and cooking.[22] Since these rooms were often located and grouped in separated areas, frequently being accessible only by a long corridor, social ranks were distinctly segregated within the house (plates 1-3).

Determining which rooms were apt and reserved for the reception of outsiders in Delian houses is possible only if one accepts the widespread assumption that rooms of highest rank, i.e., the most richly decorated and favorably

---

19. For the following, Trümper, pp. 52-63, 87-90, 125-51.

20. Nevett, p. 13.

21. Chamonard, p. 423.

22. Probably rather for occasions like the *symposion* than for everyday meals.

positioned, fulfilled representative functions. Such rooms can indeed be identified. Their only common feature seems to be visibility and easy accessibility from the courtyard to which nearly all of them open. The rooms themselves, however, show a broad spectrum of forms and sizes (plates 1-3). There are but very few traditional quadrangular *andrones* for a fixed number of couches which were certainly used for *symposia;* however, couches for *symposia* could have been set up in all the unspecific rectangular rooms as well. Nevertheless, it is to be questioned whether the increase in both number and variety of prestigious rooms in a single house merely hints at an extension of the one and dominant form of Greek social life, the *symposion,* or might not indicate an increasing differentiation of forms of social life. In a trade port, numerous situations requiring a representative setting can be imagined, above all, various meetings with business partners during the day, or the regular exchange with members of associations. In contrast to the detailed reports by Roman authors, sources which describe the extent and forms of social life of either Delos or the Greek-Hellenistic world in general are not available. Therefore all these theories are subject to speculation.

This also regards the question of accessibility and openness of houses: Could visitors enter the houses only when invited or also when uninvited, at any time of the day or only at certain fixed hours? Even if Delian house owners had only few possibilities to distinguish house facades, entrance doors were designed differently to describe the resident's status (fig. 1). Additionally, many houses of higher standard were equipped with two generally visibly differentiated entrances or even vestibules: a narrow, modestly decorated one for domestic use and a well-positioned, representative one for the owners and especially their guests (plate 3, Maison des tritons). Many vestibules did not offer a direct passage from the street to the center of the house, a second door between corridor and courtyard preventing uncontrolled access and view (plate 2, house B; plate 3, Maison des comédiens; fig. 1).[23] Apart from practical considerations, such as increased security or protection from wind, the double doors might have served other purposes as well. A doorkeeper-slave, who either stayed and maybe even slept in between doors or in a small separate room next to the vestibule, could have conceded or refused access for unexpected visitors or clients who probably had to wait in the corridor until the porter opened the second door. This act might have been performed with deliberate care to increase the effect of a lavishly decorated interior and to put the rather dark vestibule in sharp contrast to the illuminated courtyard. When both doors stood open, a passerby in many cases could see right through the house, a visual axis running

23. Trümper, pp. 30-40.

Figure 1. Delos, Maison des comédiens;
reconstruction of entrance and vestibule

from the entrance through the courtyard to the most important rooms in the
rear, thus displaying the status of the occupier. In summary, many signs confirm the efforts of Delian house owners to mark the transition between public
street and private house and to regulate the progression into their house, maybe
in accordance with specific rituals of social life.

Even small houses often display the described characteristics and include at
least one better-decorated room, often the *oecus maior*. Additionally, status

Figure 2. Delos, Maison des comédiens;
reconstruction of the peristyle courtyard

symbols like peristyles and vestibules with two doors are not restricted to particular types or sizes of houses but are found from the most opulent houses to
the smallest ones. In the latter, these status symbols could be realized only by
subsequent alterations and usually in reduced and economical versions. This
phenomenon is quite well known, especially for Pompeii, and has been convincingly interpreted: in imitating and citing status symbols, the goal was not
only to "import something of the lifestyle of the prosperous and successful into
a humble home," but to bring a "sense of belonging" to a society "in which ideology and culture are defined by the elite."[24] The large spread of luxury and status symbols is predominately due to an intensive interchange between the dif-

24. Wallace-Hadrill, *Houses and Society*, p. 173; Paul Zanker, *Pompeji. Stadtbild und
Wohngeschmack* (Mainz: Verlag Philipp von Zabern, 1995), pp. 200-210.

ferent social levels, the use of status symbols not being restricted to privileged groups and houses. This seems highly probable for Delos as well, even if it will never be known whether, especially in the very modest houses, all these status symbols necessarily imply a representational function, a representational context like the reception of guests.

But if invited, a Delian would have found his way in any house, because despite the cosmopolitan composition of the population, the domestic architecture is surprisingly uniform in all aspects. This also applies to the decoration, which could most easily have been adapted to different traditions and tastes. Only very few clues point toward the ethnic origin of the patrons. These include, above all, liturgical paintings in niches, on altars, and on outside walls of thirty-two houses which are connected with the Compitalia, festivals organized to honor the lares of the crossroads (plates 1-3: A = Altar, niches, liturgical paintings).[25] The Compitalia were primarily celebrated by freedmen and slaves of both Greek and Oriental origin who were attached to Roman families. Thus the presence of these paintings suggests that the house in question was at some time owned by either a Roman or an Italian, though it remains uncertain when and for how long. Apart from the paintings, these houses do not differ in any aspect from all the other houses. This is quite remarkable given that Romans in these times were accustomed in their own country to completely different house types with atria. The phenomenon of an architectural koine can only partly be explained by high fluctuation in the trade port and possibly rapid turnover of ownership. Rather, it seems to have been a conscious choice. The mixed population voted for a kind of common architectural language spoken and understood by everybody; thus everybody should have been able to judge what one nowadays fails to comprehend: the social significance, the rank of each house.

Delian Houses and Greco-Roman Domestic Architecture

The comparison of Delian houses with those of other Greek-Hellenistic and Roman cities should demonstrate whether the typical features of Delian domestic architecture were unique to its location or common and widespread.

The Delian normal house type — the elongated rectangular row-house type with central courtyard, a line of service rooms in the front, and the living rooms in the rear — has a long tradition and is already prevalent in classical towns with strictly orthogonal plans like Priene or Piraeus (fig. 3). Since the

25. Trümper, pp. 134-37.

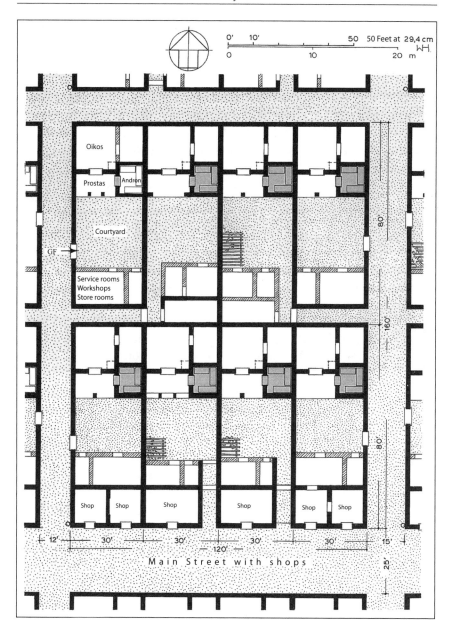

Figure 3. Priene, reconstruction of an insula with "Typenhäuser,"
fourth century B.C.E.

houses of these classical cities are taken to have been designed for a single traditional Greek family, one might conclude that this holds true for Delian normal houses as well. But the average classical house is not only larger than most of the normal houses, it also contains a special room for male representation, the *andron,* thus providing a higher living standard or at least a more differentiated use of the house.[26] The clearly gendered space of the *andron* has no counterpart; no specific female area, *gynaikonitis,* can be identified in classical houses, neither on the basis of architecture nor finds. Since literary sources emphasize the seclusion of women, especially from outsiders, a model of differentiation in time instead of space has been proposed: in general all rooms could have been used by all inhabitants; however, when male guests were visiting, women were kept secluded in separate parts of the house.[27]

A simple elongated row-house type is also found in the western part of the Roman Empire, most prominently in Pompeii. Row houses in Pompeii, datable to the late third or early second century B.C.E., show similarities with the Delian normal houses in shape and structure, with rooms opening off to the front and rear of an uncovered central space (fig. 4, types 1-3). Plot sizes of about 250-350 square meters (including gardens) are somewhat above the average of Delian normal houses but match those of classical "Typenhäuser."[28] Repertory and distribution of rooms differ considerably from Delian normal houses, the front line, e.g., containing *cubicula* instead of service rooms. Several Pompeiian row-house types include a *tablinum,* which is usually regarded as a status symbol conceived for representative upper-class rituals like the *salutatio* (fig. 4, types 1, 3, 4). Since the owners of Pompeiian row houses were identified as "peasant small-holders," a daily reception of clients in their *tablina* seems very unlikely. This phenomenon of a "basic house concept" for different house types might be compared to the Delian domestic architecture, its house types sharing similar principles in structure and characteristic elements, despite obvious differences in size and decoration.[29]

26. Wolfram Hoepfner and Ernst-Ludwig Schwandner, *Haus und Stadt im klassischen Griechenland. Wohnen in der klassischen Polis I,* 2nd ed. (Munich: Deutscher Kunstverlag, 1994): Priene, 207 square meters; Abdera, 207 square meters; Piraeus, 241 square meters; Miletus, 260 square meters; Olynthus, 294 square meters.

27. Nevett, pp. 36-39, 68-79.

28. Salvatore Ciro Nappo, "Urban Transformation at Pompeii in the Late Third and Early Second Century B.C.," in *Domestic Space in the Roman World: Pompeii and Beyond,* ed. Ray Laurence and Andrew Wallace-Hadrill, Journal of Roman Archaeology Supplement Series 22 (Portsmouth, R.I.: Journal of Roman Archaeology, 1997), pp. 92-120.

29. Striking similarities between the Pompeiian row houses and early atrium houses have been pointed out by Andrew Wallace-Hadrill, "Rethinking the Roman Atrium House," in *Domestic Space in the Roman World,* pp. 219-40, esp. 238-39.

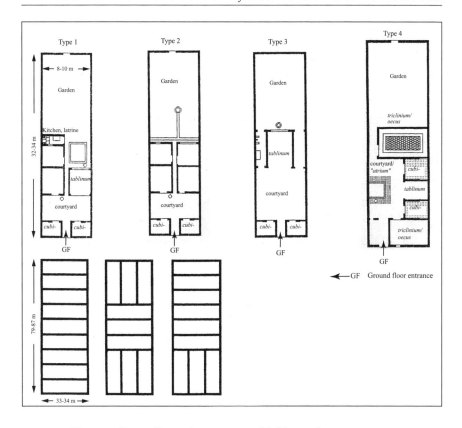

Figure 4. Pompeii, row-house types, third/second century B.C.E.

A whole spectrum of simple house types can be observed in different parts of the Mediterranean world, ranging from single-courtyard houses (with standard equipment, but lacking the characteristic form and layout of row-house types) to modest apartments with one or two rooms. A new study on Pergamenian houses gives an overview of all excavated houses in the city for the very first time.[30] Plans of all houses are available, but most are not fully published and therefore lack details about decoration and artifacts. The domestic architecture covers the period from the third century B.C.E. until the third century C.E., with many houses several times remodeled. Among the thirty-five houses are sixteen mainly Hellenistic single-courtyard houses with rooms mostly on two sides of the courtyard. The main rooms are preferably situated in the northern part and often preceded by a colonnade or anteroom,

30. Wulf, pp. 149-90.

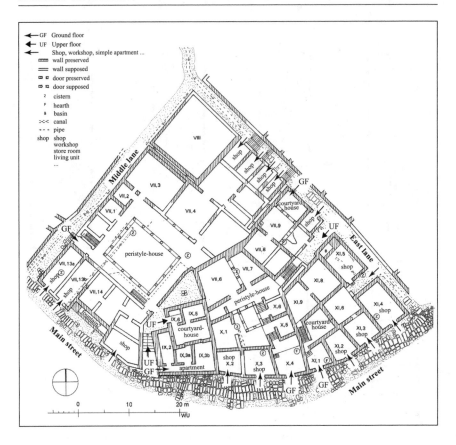

Figure 5. Pergamon, *insula* between Middle lane and East lane, first century C.E.

a feature unknown among Delian houses but quite usual for classical houses. The irregular shapes of these houses and the lack of both a common structure and particular elements like the characteristic group of three rooms in Delos are due to external factors, mainly the unfavorable topography of the steep slope in Pergamon. The modest houses have obviously been established on remaining terrain wherever possible. An excellent example is the completely irregular *insula* between Middle Lane and East Lane which, at the beginning of the first century C.E., contained a representative spectrum of simple house types (fig. 5): apart from two peristyle houses,[31] three courtyard

31. VII,1-4: 740 square meters; VII,6-7, upper-story rooms of X, 2-3, X, 1, 4-6: 370 square meters.

houses,[32] a simple apartment and probably fourteen shops/workshops/storerooms[33] which may have been used partly for living as well.[34] Even if the courtyard houses of Pergamon with ground floor areas of 135 square meters to 250 square meters are quite big, the living standard cannot be estimated because of the missing or unknown decoration; but the *andron,* the obliging element of classical houses, certainly is conspicuously absent.

An even wider spectrum of these rather modest house types can be studied in the Vesuvian cities, where they were built wherever possible, often in the direct neighborhood of large lavish houses. A good example is the Insula Arriana Polliana (fig. 6). Its overall shape is regular and fits into the orthogonal layout of Regio VI. However, the *insula* consists of a variety of units differing in size and shape: on the ground floor are three larger *domus* obviously without open courtyards, three shop-*tabernae* with *pergulae,* three residential *tabernae* with *pergulae,* and two bakeries with shops. Similar to Delos, the upper floor contains five separate apartments, ranging from simple ones with a surface of 50 square meters to most lavish ones of 170 square meters.[35]

The peristyle house has a long tradition in the East going back at least to the fourth century B.C.E. The late classical and early Hellenistic peristyle houses often represent a layout unknown in Delos with the organization of domestic space around two juxtaposed courtyards, which are clearly differentiated, one comprising a peristyle and lavish rooms, the other far more modestly equipped (fig. 7). They seem to correspond to Vitruvius's description of the Greek house with a richly decorated *andronitis* for the male public representation and the more modest *gynaikonitis* for the private family life. The development of such an elaborate, differentiated house type has been attributed to the increasing importance of social life, which required the provision of more space for the reception of visitors without the privacy of Greek family life being disturbed. Whereas according to Vitruvius each part had its own entrance from the street, the archaeological evidence presents three further forms of accessibility: both from a common entrance, the *gynaikonitis* only through the *andronitis,* and the *andronitis* through the *gynaikonitis.* These differences in accessibility might lead to the assumption that modes of differentiation between the parts varied

---

32. IX, 4-6, upper-story rooms of IX, 1-3: 150 square meters; XI, 1.6-9: 160 square meters; VII, 8-10: 135 square meters.

33. VII, 13.14; IX, 1-3; X, 2.3; XI, 2, 3, 4, 5; five shops on the East Lane.

34. Wulf, pp. 203-5.

35. Felix Pirson, *Mietwohnungen in Pompeji und Herkulaneum. Untersuchungen zur Architektur, zum Wohnen und zur Sozial- und Wirtschaftsgeschichte der Vesuvstädte,* Studien zur antiken Stadt 5 (Munich: Verlag Dr. Friedrich Pfeil, 1999), pp. 15-47, 176-86.

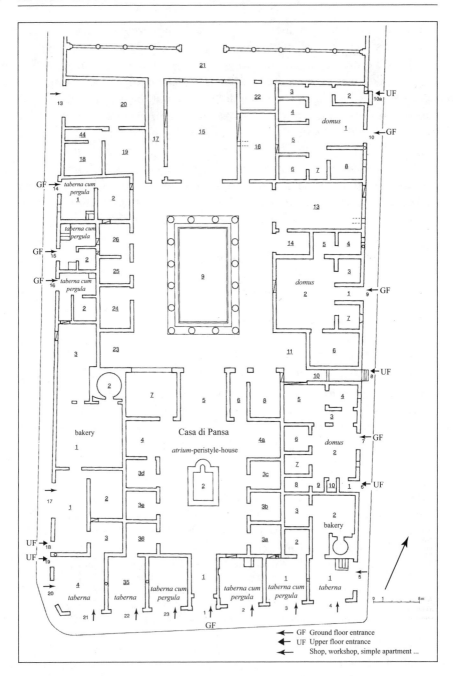

Figure 6. Pompeii, Insula Arriana Polliana; *atrium*-peristyle house
with different house types grouped around it, first century C.E.

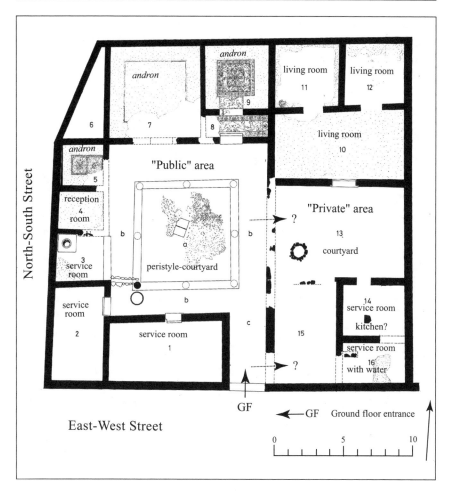

Figure 7. Eretria, Maison aux mosaïques, double-courtyard house,
fourth century B.C.E.

as well. Apart from a segregation of private and public space, there may have been different grades of public space.[36]

The multiplication of courtyards was not an overall common model, as proven by the existence of peristyle houses with one courtyard. All seventeen preserved examples of Pergamon fall into the latter category.[37] These peristyle

36. This cannot be discussed at full length here; for a recent overview of double-courtyard houses, see Nevett, pp. 107-26, 144-50.

37. Wulf, pp. 160-90. Some maybe had small courtyards in service areas, fig. 73; 3.4 (?); 74,5; 75,3.

houses show the same irregular shape as the Pergamenian courtyard houses, but, as in large Delian houses, there is an obvious attempt to establish a balanced relation between length and width, in order to have rooms opening to as many sides of the courtyard as possible (fig. 5). Despite their much larger ground floor area, ranging from 280 square meters to 2,400 square meters, the Pergamenian houses follow the same architectural principles as the Delian ones: they group a large variety of lavishly decorated rooms around the peristyle courtyard, and they shunt service rooms to separate areas near the entrance or in corners. A division of the houses into three distinct functional areas, public representational, private, and service areas, cannot be postulated as standard principle since only a few houses had upper stories which, according to finds, were richly decorated. Thus in most cases all needs concerning private living and public representation had to be met on the ground floor alone. In the two-storied houses the upper-floor rooms probably served both private and public use.

The absence of the double-courtyard house type from Pergamon and Delos is not due to the plot size. Some of the double-courtyard houses, with ground floor sizes of about 500-600 square meters, are considerably smaller than the Delian and especially the Pergamenian top-class examples. No attempt was made to separate zones of private living and public representation on a vertical scale, e.g., with private rooms in upper stories. Therefore, choice of the single-courtyard house type must have been deliberate. Even if this option for the single courtyard was mostly a phenomenon of the late Hellenistic period, it seemed equally attractive to the owners of Pergamenian peristyle houses and palaces of the third century B.C.E., and thus cannot be due to the specific history and social structure of Delos.[38] The difference between private living and public representation — if it ever existed — was obviously dissolved. Interpretation of the high number and often even predominance of luxurious rooms in one and the same house is highly problematic. Domestic activities could have been reduced or at least assigned lower priority, and thus were limited to a few unlit corner rooms. Alternatively, with a general increase of the living standard, parts of the domestic activities could have been executed in a more pleasant atmosphere. Finally, if part of the household, particularly women, still did not participate regularly in the more public aspects of social life, one could again imagine a model of differentiation in time rather than in space.

Most interesting is the observation that in both Pergamon and Delos the domestic architecture remained essentially Greek-Hellenistic, despite the Roman dominance and presence after 166 B.C.E. and especially 133 B.C.E. This

38. As Nevett, p. 166, proposed.

holds equally true for the major part of Ephesian houses, which kept their orig-inal "Hellenistic" design of rooms grouped around a central peristyle courtyard even in the prime of Roman power.[39]

The most typical trait of Roman houses is usually considered the atrium, a central covered space with an *impluvium,* surrounded by closed *(cubicula, triclinia)* and open *(tablinum, alae)* rooms, which are preferably arranged in a strictly symmetrical order. At least in the Campanian cities this architectural feature fulfilled until the end of the first century c.e. all social needs ranging from practical security to the correct performance of religious and social ritu-als. It was included in atrium houses and atrium-peristyle houses.[40] The addi-tion of a peristyle, which was usually surrounded by lavishly decorated rooms of different shapes and sizes *(oeci, exedrae, triclinia),* changed the symbolic function of the atrium and offered a much higher degree of differentiation of social practices: the atrium was reduced to the nucleus of less privileged activ-ity, the reception of clients, while the peristyle court was reserved for the privi-leged invited guests (fig. 6).[41]

Both atrium houses and atrium-peristyle houses are not only absent from Delos, Pergamon, and Ephesus,[42] but from most cities outside Italy. Conceiv-able remains point to a strong continuity of traditional house types like court-yard houses and peristyle houses in the East.[43] Why Romans living outside Italy chose to live in houses built in the Greek fashion is open to speculation. One might suppose that certain customs of Roman social life such as the *salutatio*

---

39. Peter Scherrer, ed., *Ephesos. Der Neue Führer* (Vienna: Österreichisches Archäologisches Institut, 1995), pp. 102-15; D. Parish, "The Architectural Design and Interior Décor of Apartment I in Insula 2 at Ephesus," in *Fifth International Colloquium on Ancient Mosaics, Bath 1987,* ed. Roger Ling, Journal of Roman Archaeology Supplement Series 9 (Portsmouth, R.I.: Journal of Roman Archaeology, 1995), pp. 143-58; Claudia Lang-Auinger, *Hanghaus 1 in Ephesos. Der Baubefund. Forschungen in Ephesos VIII/3* (Vienna: Verlag der Österreichischen Akademie der Wissenschaften, 1996), pp. 181-202, esp. 181, 199-202; Gilbert Wiplinger, "Die Wohneinheiten 1 und 2 im Hanghaus 2 von Ephesos," *Jahreshefte des Österreichischen Archäologischen Instituts in Wien* 66 (1997): 75-86; Hilke Thür, "Hanghaus 2, Wohneinheiten 4 und 6," *Jahreshefte des Österreichischen Archäologischen Instituts in Wien, Beiblatt* 67 (1998): 50-61.

40. Dickmann, *Domus frequentata,* pp. 49-126, 301-12.

41. Wallace-Hadrill, *Houses and Society,* pp. 3-61; Dickmann, *Domus frequentata,* pp. 127-255, 313-74.

42. The term "atrium" is often applied rather indiscriminately, e.g., to rooms that have four columns, or even an *impluvium,* but clearly lack the characteristic structure of Roman atrium houses. For the significantly different nature of "atria" in Ephesus and Pergamon: Lang-Auinger, pp. 199-202; Wolfgang Radt, "Pergamon. Vorbericht über die Kampagne 1992," *Archäologischer Anzeiger* (1993): 366-69.

43. Verification of this hypothesis has to await further research.

and the distinction between noninvited visitors and invited friends and guests were not important outside Italy, so that even Romans of high rank could have contented themselves with the eastern standard of peristyle houses. Likewise, these traditional social rituals might have been adapted to the space available, especially since Romans were eager to blend in with the local culture and taste.

A detailed discussion of controversial issues like the differentiation between Greek and Roman or the concepts of Hellenization versus Romanization is beyond the scope of this essay, but two points should nevertheless be emphasized at the end.

Despite the common organization of space around several nuclei, there is no correspondence between Greek multicourtyard houses and atrium-peristyle houses (figs. 6, 7). The Roman model exhibits a strict hierarchical organization with two public nuclei used for distinct public purposes. The Greek model, on the other hand — in the traditional interpretation — offered no differentiation of public spaces, but in compensation provided a private area for the exclusive use of household members.

The integration of peristyles in eastern, especially Delian, houses is certainly not due to Roman influence. Recent studies point out that the first peristyles added to Roman atrium houses at the end of the second century B.C.E. were purely "ambulatories" with at most one or two exedrae opening on to them. Only in a second phase, during the first century B.C.E., did the peristyle serve a comparable function to peristyle courtyards in Greek houses by becoming the focus of the most luxurious rooms of the house. In both cases the various lavish rooms around the peristyle were likely used according to similar needs: for the reception and entertainment of guests.[44]

To summarize: While traveling in the East, Paul would most likely have been exposed to all different Delian house types — small living units, simple courtyard houses, and lavish peristyle houses. As mentioned above, it cannot be determined in which houses or house types early Christians lived and assembled. But taking into consideration the spatial requirements of well-attended meetings, it is much more likely that Christians in the East gathered in larger peristyle houses rather than in modest courtyard houses. Just as in atrium-peristyle houses, they could have assembled in large rooms around the peristyle as well as in the courtyards themselves, which, at least in Delos, were paved and did not include gardens. Given the Delian background, it is likewise conceivable that Christians used upper rooms for their rituals.[45]

---

44. Jens-Arne Dickmann, "The Peristyle and the Transformation of Domestic Space in Hellenistic Pompei," in *Domestic Space in the Roman World,* pp. 121-36.

45. Osiek and Balch, pp. 30-35, 201-4.

If ἐκκλησίαι took place in such a peristyle house, it might have attracted neighbors of fairly different social statuses, given that in all cities mentioned here, living units ranging from simple shops to lavish houses were mixed indiscriminately within one single *insula*. With regard to Pompeii, Andrew Wallace-Hadrill has convincingly interpreted this jigsaw structure of the *insulae* as reflection of an equally complex social structure consisting of a *patronus* living in the central house with his dependents occupying the surrounding living units. In the case of Delos and Pergamon, a similar explanation is attractive but hypothetical.

Despite the continuity in the design of eastern domestic architecture from Hellenistic to Roman times, one crucial difference has to be emphasized at the end: Christians staying in eastern and western houses were exposed to significantly more figured art, especially wall paintings, than were the inhabitants of Delian houses. Themes and forms of representation might seem shocking and even offensive to present-day Christians, but were probably not considered outrageous or inappropriate by early Christians, who were familiar with and accustomed to Greco-Roman culture. Indeed, some pictures emphasizing pathos and suffering might even have been used by Paul to draw parallels to the gospel he preached, as David Balch has demonstrated in his contribution. In Delian houses Paul's sermons probably would have depended much more — if not solely — on words than on images.

The Problems of Gendered Space in Syro-Palestinian Domestic Architecture: The Case of Roman-Period Galilee

Eric M. Meyers

A consideration of domestic space in Roman-period Galilee with reference to gender issues and the family is particularly timely. Excavations in Galilee in the past two decades have been very productive, among the most important being Sepphoris, Capernaum, Jotapata, Bethsaida, and Qana, to mention only a few major new projects. Noteworthy even in this brief listing is the fact that among them only Sepphoris might be characterized as a large urban setting; the other sites are all considerably smaller, even Bethsaida not quite deserving of the designation of city.[1] In respect to gendered space, while the topic has been gaining ground for some time in the classical setting, only fairly recently has it gained any attention in the world of Syro-Palestinian archaeology.[2] As for how the structure of families might be related to private domiciles in Roman Palestine or archaeology, aside from a few isolated attempts,[3] there have been no systematic attempts to collect the data and interpret them in the light of new methods of analysis.

There are a number of reasons for this situation. First, there have been few archaeological publications that present the data in a usable form. Second, much of the evidence is slightly later, i.e., from the second to the fourth centu-

---

1. Rami Arav, letter to the editor, *BARev* 26, no. 5 (2000): 12, 14, 72, 74.

2. E. M. Meyers, "Roman-Period Houses from Galilee: Domestic Architecture and Gendered Spaces," *Albright/ASOR Centennial*, forthcoming.

3. S. Guijarro, "The Family in First-Century Galilee," in *Constructing Early Christian Families: Family as Social Reality and Metaphor*, ed. H. Moxnes (London and New York: Routledge, 1997), pp. 42-65; M. Peskowitz, "Family/ies in Antiquity: Evidence from Tannaitic Literature and Roman Galilean Architecture," in *The Jewish Family in Antiquity*, ed. S. J. D. Cohen (Atlanta: Scholars, 1993), pp. 9-38; C. M. Baker, "Rebuilding the House of Israel: Gendered Bodies and Domestic Politics in Roman Jewish Galilee c. 135-300 C.E." (Ph.D. diss., Duke University, 1997); this thesis has recently appeared as *Rebuilding the House of Israel: Architectures of Gender in Jewish Antiquity* (Stanford: Stanford University Press, 2002); Carolyn Osiek and David L. Balch, *Families in the New Testament World: Houses and House Churches* (Louisville: Westminster John Knox, 1997).

ries c.e. Third, it has not always been possible to identify the inhabitants of particular houses at certain sites: Were they Jews or non-Jews, Judeo-Christians or Christians? And in this connection some scholars have turned to the evidence of non-Jewish and non-Christian remains to discuss the household of the early Christians, especially in the West.[4] The use of ethnographic materials in relation to Roman-period Palestinian houses and households has been extremely helpful,[5] especially in demonstrating that the various spatial components of a particular domicile may not be associated with a single gender only; rather, the data show how certain functions such as weaving were movable, just as were particular items of furniture.

Before moving on to the more interpretive side of the archaeology of gender, it would be useful to summarize and describe briefly the kinds of houses that were used in Roman-period Palestine. The nomenclature used for the most part in this paper is Hirschfeld's. Most recently, however, Galor has questioned its appropriateness and called for a more inclusive nomenclature such as "condominium" or "apartment" to characterize the ancient Palestinian domicile.[6]

The Simple House

The most commonly found domicile in Roman-period Palestine is the single-room structure. The best preserved examples of this type of house are from the Hauran, south and east of Mount Hermon in the Golan.[7] These buildings may be situated with a courtyard either behind or in front of them and have been found in the vast majority of excavations; it is assumed that the majority of the population lived in such houses also. The general size of such domiciles varied from 20 to 200 square meters, though most were on the smaller side. The example from Khirbet Shema' represents the low end of that range, 40 square meters, including the upper story (fig. 1). An outer staircase there led directly to the second story, while a direct ground-level door opened into the main floor, which space served as a workshop or store. A street or alleyway ran alongside it. A baking oven and remains of other domestic (?) installations were found nearby to the west. The house is best presented in its last, Byzantine phase of use, fourth-

---

4. Osiek and Balch, pp. 5-35.

5. Y. Hirschfeld, *The Palestinian Dwelling in the Roman Byzantine Period* (Jerusalem: Franciscan Printing Press and Israel Exploration Society, 1995), pp. 217ff.

6. K. Galor, "The Roman-Byzantine Dwelling in the Galilee and the Golan: 'House' or 'Apartment'?" in *Miscellanea Mediterranea*, ed. R. R. Holloway (Providence: Brown University Press, 2000), pp. 118-19.

7. Hirschfeld, p. 24.

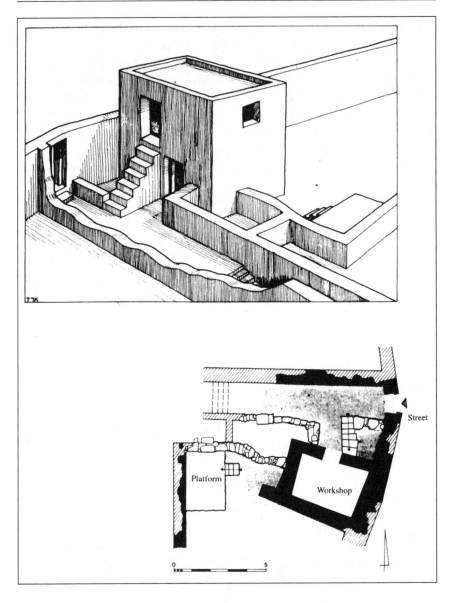

Figure 1. Plan and reconstruction of simple house
from Khirbet Shema', 4th-5th c. C.E.

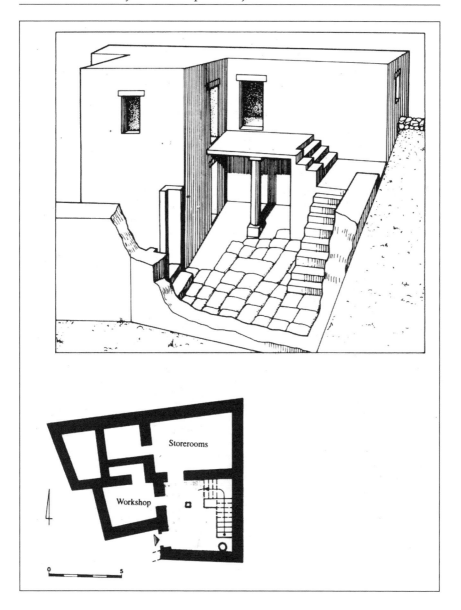

Figure 2. Plan and reconstruction of patrician house at Meiron, 2d-3d c. C.E.

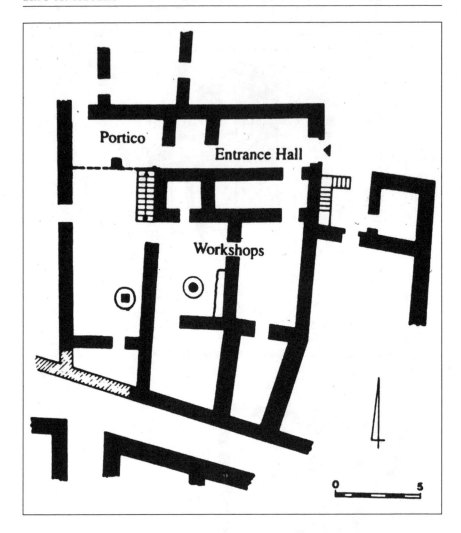

Figure 3. Plan of MI area in lower town

fifth centuries c.e., though it surely existed earlier. Its final use-phase is attested by the sherds and coins found on the tamped earth surface of the ground-level shop. Hirschfeld identifies this house as one of the smallest ever found in Palestine. Because of its size, the number of individuals residing in it was relatively few: six to eight individuals, parents, children, and some relatives. A *miqveh* for this southeast sector of town is located nearby and doubtless served a number of families and households in this sector.

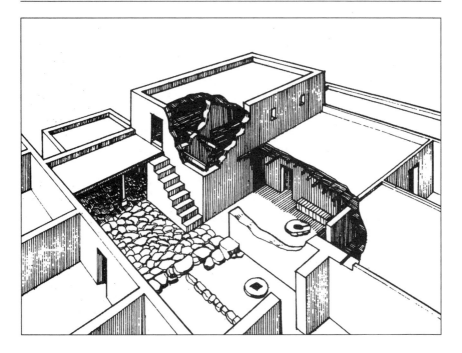

Figure 4. Reconstruction of MI complex showing courtyard,
work areas with sleeping quarters above

Another example of the small simple house type comes from nearby Meiron, and was called by the excavators the "Lintel House."[8] Its size is at least 80 square meters, but it is apparently only part of a larger complex, and is therefore incomplete. If it is to be related to the "Patrician House" that stands alongside it (fig. 2), even sharing the common space of a roof terrace, both are comparable in size to the largest houses of this type. Hirschfeld describes this type as a "two-wing" house, the two wings being perpendicular to one another, as is the case in the lower city of Meiron also.[9] Considering the relatively large size of these units, and keeping in mind that their full context was not uncovered, I conclude that the inhabitants enjoyed a good economic situation, and I would be hesitant to call them "peasants" as do Hirschfeld and Guijarro; well-to-do farmer or agriculturalist describes the situation better for me and eliminates the implication of low social status. Often the term "peasant" also carries the

8. E. M. Meyers, J. F. Strange, and C. L. Meyers, *Excavations at Ancient Meiron* (Cambridge, Mass.: ASOR, 1981), pp. 72-75.
9. Hirschfeld, pp. 31, 39.

connotation of being uneducated. Because of the nature of the finds in the Patrician House and their religious significance, such a connotation would be quite unjustified. Another example of the double-wing simple house type is found on the lower terrace at Meiron, which includes shops and workshops on the ground floor and a private *miqveh* that could serve the individuals in this unit, MI (figs. 3-4).[10] Its size, 180 square meters, puts it on the larger end of the type. The finds associated with this area and the elegantly carved doorposts strongly suggest that the occupants of this large house were well-to-do craftsmen or artisans, terms I would not equate with peasants.

There are many variations of the plan of the simple house; indeed, one of the best examples from the Golan, Kafr Nassej, has a broad building with a portico running in front of it.[11] I have only described several of the types I have excavated and hence refer the reader to Hirschfeld for further elaboration. It should be clear already from the variety of houses within the first category that it is very difficult to generalize about the organization of space and how it relates to the movement of individuals within that space except in relation to particular domiciles at particular sites. Moreover, it is also nearly impossible to identify individual spaces within these houses as task-specific. And yet, as I have already pointed out, certain spaces are very often interpreted in gender-specific ways that would place the female and her limited activities most often in closed internal space, or in space that is invisible to those without. The obverse would be true for males: they would conduct their activities mostly in public spaces outdoors.

The Complex House

Hirschfeld's second house type is an elaboration of the simple house, its construction accomplished through the addition of new wings or housing units built on three sides of the outer courtyard. Such an enlargement of property was undertaken due to the increase in numbers of the extended family, or it represented an expression of prosperity. It also offered a greater degree of privacy for individuals working in the courtyard, though it should be emphasized that it offered more direct access to the adjoining public areas also. These building types may be found in an urban apartment complex or rural farmhouse, which might consist of several dwellings around a central courtyard.[12] Often-

10. Meyers, Strange, and Meyers, pp. 33ff.
11. Hirschfeld, p. 24.
12. Hirschfeld, p. 44.

times the building history of a complex house is too complicated to determine: Was the house built at one time or were certain components added over time? This is very difficult to ascertain archaeologically because there are so many walls and so many repairs to them, as well as repeated buildup on the earthen floors within. The best examples of this type are found in the Hauran at Kafr Nassej and Umm el-Jimal, at Pella and Jerash of the Decapolis, at Ramat Hanadiv along the southern Carmel range, at 'En Yael near Jerusalem, or at Sebaste in Samaria.[13]

The Courtyard House

Another variant of the simple house, this type, like the simple house, continued the building traditions of the architecture of ancient Israel. Unlike the simple house that was more frequent in rural areas, the courtyard house was more common in urban contexts, though the example from Meiron's lower city had a courtyard, as did the Patrician House. This leads us to urge caution in defining categories too rigidly. Also, while in Roman-period Galilee there are only two cities, Sepphoris and Tiberias, Meiron is a "town," an intermediate stage between "village" and "city."[14] There is no reason why we might not find such a type in a prospering village as well, though it is less likely. Hirschfeld points out two variants of this type: a house with an inner courtyard without columns, an ancient local tradition, and a house with an inner courtyard with columns, an innovation taken from classical culture.[15] Such houses are also found in the Hellenistic period, as is the case in Marisa. The best examples of this type come from Jerusalem and date to the first century c.e., most notably the Great Mansion (600 square meters), the Burnt House (fig. 5), and the Herodian House of the Upper City (200 square meters).[16] The Triple Courtyard House at Capernaum, the courtyard houses at Korazin, and the large house on the western acropolis at Sepphoris (84.1) offer the best examples from Galilee. It is significant to note the presence of *miqva'ot* in the Jerusalem and Sepphoris contexts.

Examination of the contents of the Jerusalem houses leaves no doubt about their identification as Jewish homes, especially the presence of ritual baths and stone vessels. But the Jerusalem houses are all destroyed in 70 c.e.

13. Hirschfeld, pp. 44-56.
14. Ze'ev Safrai, *The Economy of Roman Palestine* (London and New York: Routledge, 1994).
15. Hirschfeld, p. 57.
16. Hirschfeld, pp. 57-61.

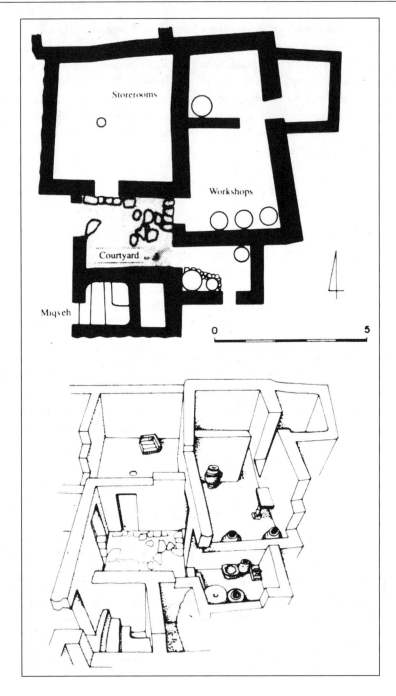

Figure 5. Plan of "Burnt House" at Jerusalem, 1st c. C.E., after Avigad

The Sepphoris example raises some very important issues about identifying the occupants of the building in the Roman period.[17] Parts of the house were originally built in the Hellenistic period and utilized in the early Roman period when the first stage of the house's construction was completed, circa 50 C.E. It was remodeled and expanded several times over the next centuries, but especially at the beginning of the fourth century C.E. when it assumed its present configuration, which was destroyed in the great earthquake of 363.

In an underground chamber near the south end of the building (84.1) in room I, a huge trash heap apparently closed up by renovations in the late third or beginning of the fourth century, a treasure trove of discarded objects, was found. They included a bronze miniature of Pan and Prometheus, and many third-century discus lamps that featured erotica on the central disc. However, among the pottery fragments of lamps was also one with a Torah shrine, clearly Jewish. And from the area that was Hellenistic in date and subsequently incorporated into the courtyard house in the Roman period came an ostracon with the earliest mention of a Jewish functionary at Sepphoris.[18] In addition, there are at least three *miqva'ot* in the building, though only two were in use at the same time. Among the faunal remains from this building and the entire western summit, there are no pig bones whatever to be found in the Roman period.[19] By the Byzantine era, when we find *terra sigillata* bowls stamped with crosses and even ostraca of a Christian character, and when the area is reconfigured architecturally after 363, the faunal remains produce 18 to 20 percent pig bones in all areas. The evidence, thus, in favor of seeing a Christian population move in during the Byzantine period is most convincing.

The location of this courtyard house with courtyard D and adjoining areas serving as the enclosed open space within the 200-meter structure is noteworthy. A narrow but elegantly paved roadway runs east to west along its northern end, and from it, one entered the third- to fourth-century structure by room Q. In the early Roman period access was from the north-south roadway into the entryway designated on the plan. The enlarged house not only provides ample space for extended family living, possibly as many as twenty-five taking into account a second story, but it also offers easy access to two neighborhood roadways or alleys as well as a high degree of privacy within the large house. Household chores were doubtless carried out in the open space (D) along with spinning and other crafts. Guijarro may be closer to the truth in pointing to

17. M. Chancey and E. M. Meyers, "How Jewish Was Sepphoris in Jesus' Time?" *BARev* 26, no. 4 (2000): 18-33, 61.

18. R. Nagy, E. M. Meyers, Z. Weiss, and C. L. Meyers, eds., *Sepphoris in Galilee: Crosscurrents of Culture* (Raleigh: North Carolina Museum of Art, 1996), p. 170.

19. Chancey and Meyers, pp. 25-26.

prominent landowners or clergy occupying such a household, and the presence of a large cache of ceramic incense shovels as well as many fragments of stone vessels dated to the early Roman period supports such an interpretation of this case.[20] To infer any more than this, however, namely, that some priestly families lived here and had considerable resources, would be going too far. We have no indication whatever that the occupants of this lovely mansion were tax collectors or leaders of the city. That they were very much at home with Hellenistic objets d'art, lamps, statues, etc., is obvious enough. The evidence of the *miqva'ot,* stone vessels, Jewish symbols on lamps, ostraca, the absence of pig bones, etc., clearly indicates that the household was Jewish and well-to-do in character.[21]

The Peristyle House

This type of house, a variant of the courtyard house, represents the clearest example of borrowing from the Greco-Roman architectural tradition.[22] The palaces at Herodian Jericho from the late Hellenistic and early Roman periods are built in the peristyle plan and also illustrate the influence of the Roman villa. Notable examples from the Hellenistic and Roman periods besides the House of Dionysos at Sepphoris include Tel Anafa, Samaria, Tel Judeidah and Khirbet el-Murag, Aphek and Jerusalem. The distribution of this type of house is very limited in Palestine, suggesting that such an overtly classical construction style had limited influence. However, I would not be surprised to find further examples of this type at Sepphoris, Beth Shean, or similar locations.

Let us briefly consider the significance of the House of Dionysos at Sepphoris in this context (fig. 6).[23] About 300 square meters of internal space commanding a unique position on the acropolis adjacent to the theater, the building was constructed in the first third of the third century c.e. and was destroyed in 363 by the great earthquake. By the time the building was completed, in the time of Rabbi Judah the Patriarch, Sepphoris was becoming a large multicultural city with Jews, Jewish Christians, and pagans occupying various

---

20. Guijarro, cited in L. V. Rutgers, "Incense Shovels at Sepphoris?" in *Galilee through the Centuries: Confluence of Cultures,* ed. E. M. Meyers (Winona Lake, Ind.: Eisenbrauns, 1999), pp. 177-98. See also my essay on this, *"The Ceramic Incense Shovels From Sepphoris: Another View,"* Festschrift for Ami Mazar, forthcoming.

21. E. M. Meyers, "The Pools of Sepphoris — Ritual Baths or Bathtubs?" *BARev* 26, no. 4 (2000): 46-49, 60.

22. Hirschfeld, pp. 85-97.

23. Nagy et al., pp. 111-15.

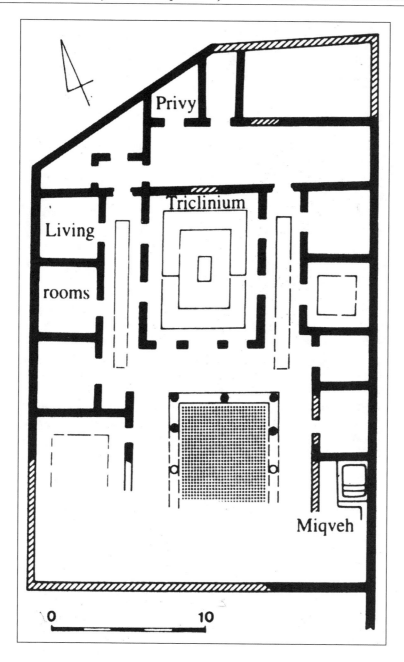

Figure 6. Plan of the Dionysus Mansion at Sepphoris, or Peristyle
House type. Note the *triclinium* at north end and privy in rear.
Side rooms were apparently used as guest rooms.

Figure 7. Central panel of Dionysus mosaic, which is the focus of the whole floor.
The scene depicts a symposium or drinking contest between Dionysus and
Herakles. Dionysus, god of wine and fertility, is shown leaning back with
drinking cup raised. Herakles is depicted under his name.

parts of the city. Rabbi Judah is also known to have been favorably disposed to
Greek as a language (*b. B. Qam.* 82b and 83a). Site selection for construction of
the Dionysos Mansion tells us nearly as much about the purpose and owners of
the building as do the wonderful mosaic panels on the floor of the triclinium or
banquet hall with their Greek labels (figs. 7-8). The single toilet and bath in the
northwest corner rooms reveal something about the high cost necessary to support such a facility. Several pools, a *miqveh*, and garden in the courtyard to the
south of the triclinium point to a lavish lifestyle, great wealth, or public sup-

Figure 8. A popular scene from Dionysus's mythology depicting his triumphal "procession" as he returned from his conquest of India

port. Because Sepphoris was administered internally by a *boulē* or municipal council, the mansion could be the place where it met, or where the patriarch welcomed guests, or where actors, performers, or distinguished visitors were hosted and housed. Meshorer believes the famous Caracalla coin that commemorates a treaty between Rome and the Sepphoris Council *(boulē)* supports the idea that the *boulē* was actually the Sanhedrin of the Jewish community, which at the time was at Sepphoris.[24] There is no reason why the leadership of the Jewish community should not feel right at home among these trappings of Hellenistic culture. Indeed, Rabbi Judah himself, redactor or editor of the Mishnah, according to rabbinic traditions and legends, is supposed to have been friendly with the Roman emperor Caracalla (Antoninus). The presence of a *miqveh* within such a context illustrates just how much at home the Jews were among these trappings of Hellenistic culture. Its presence on the eastern side of the courtyard suggests at the very least a period of Jewish usage, and the house could simply have served as the private domicile of one of Sepphoris's urban

24. Nagy et al., p. 198.

aristocracy. If it did serve as a meeting place for the municipal council, it would have included members of the different communities — by the fourth century also Christians — but most probably with a Jewish majority. In any event, it is quite clear that this elegant mansion was sited in a very special way; decorated in the most elaborate style with Greco-Roman mosaic art, with beautiful frescoes; and constructed in the classical architectural mode. Since it is located so close to what is surely an upscale Jewish quarter or neighborhood in the Roman period, it seems reasonable to conclude that its use was in the Jewish community. The lower city on the east, along the great *cardo*, no doubt housed many of the non-Jews and their buildings, though the presence of *miqva'ot* there suggests a large Jewish presence as well.[25] Thus far no inscriptional evidence has been found that would help us understand who planned the city's major expansion and classical character from circa 100 to 250 C.E. Whoever made such plans, at least in the Roman period, it was the Jewish community that first enjoyed the structures and ornaments of the city.

Gendered Space

Utilizing the above typology, let us now move on to the question of gendered space. A basic question underlying our inquiry about the house in Roman-period Jewish Galilee is whether or not the physical domiciles there reflect the construction of gender that one encounters in rabbinic texts. Insofar as houses were frequently modified over time, we should not think of domestic space in static terms. As the place in which the extended family lived, the house was ever changing to accommodate new individuals and realities. Yet if we were to inquire why the rabbis called the husband in a household *baal-ha-bayit,* "master of the house," we would begin to get a sense of the dominance of the male in the general ideological schema of the times. Also, domestic space, when considered apart from archaeology, has usually been considered part of the private as opposed to the public domain,[26] a designation that would identify most of the activities of the household as being female or in the domain of women. In order to dispel this still dominant public/private dichotomy with its specific connotations of gender and disposition to view work and status as something that re-

25. E. Netzer and Z. Weiss, "Architectural Development of Sepphoris during the Roman and Byzantine Periods," in *Archaeology and the Galilee: Texts and Contexts in the Graeco-Roman and Byzantine Periods,* ed. D. R. Edwards and C. Thomas McCollough (Atlanta: Scholars, 1997), pp. 117-30.

26. J. R. Wegner, *Chattel or Person? The Status of Women in the Mishnah* (Oxford: Oxford University Press, 1988), pp. 188-91.

sides outside the home,[27] let me begin by presenting the evidence from the town of ancient Meiron area I. According to Hirschfeld's nomenclature, the houses there are a development of the simple house and characteristic of the private domiciles in rural areas.[28]

What is so interesting at Meiron for gender considerations is the combination of work activities together with other activities of production and sustenance that may all be associated with this living and work complex. In the larger residence we find on the ground floor an eight-room configuration that empties onto a courtyard.[29] The nature of debris in this area suggests the existence of an upper story that doubtless functioned as sleeping quarters, very similar to the situation in the Old City of Jerusalem to this day. The size of the residence suggests a family or extended family of some means. Room E, which contained a stone workbench and an iron-handled bronze planer, was identified by the excavators as a cooperage, which produced wooden crates or barrels possibly for the Galilean trade in olives or olive oil. The adjacent room D was also identified as a work space, and room A was utilized as a passageway to the courtyard. Rooms F and C contained stone grinders necessary for the production of food. In addition, food grinders and bone and bronze needles were found in the courtyard, suggesting that food production and sewing took place there. The presence of a private *miqveh* off the courtyard should also be mentioned; it was apparently used by members of the family. In all, the building represents 180 square meters of space, including the 5 × 7 meter courtyard west of the house.

The implication of the Meiron residence for this presentation is quite clear: the interior of the house does not represent private space as distinct from work space. Rather, a variety of work was carried out there, consisting of food production, textile work, and carpentry. The public/private dichotomy simply cannot characterize this space where all manner of household, family, and everyday activities were carried on. Though inscriptional supports are lacking for husbands and wives working together, the organization of space suggests such a possibility as well as the involvement of family members in a variety of household tasks.[30] Indeed, at the Meiron residence it is difficult even to determine where one dwelling ends and another begins, let alone how all the rooms were meant to interconnect.[31] The house, whether in a village, town, or city, was

27. See Andrew Wallace-Hadrill, "The Social Structure of the Roman House," *PBSR* 56 (1988): 43-97.

28. Hirschfeld, pp. 30-31.

29. See Meyers, Strange, and Meyers, *Excavations at Ancient Meiron*, pp. 23-44.

30. Peskowitz, p. 32.

31. E. M. Meyers and C. L. Meyers, "Talmudic Village Life in the Galilean Highlands," *Bulletin of the Anglo-Israel Archaeological Society* (1982-83): 32-36.

rarely if ever isolated; rather it was a place of "dynamic arrangements, of access and exclusion, opening and closing, enclosing and disclosing, that shifted and varied with the time of day, the activity undertaken, the season of the year, relations between persons occupying or passing through, mechanisms of exchange and commerce, and so forth."[32] It is precisely this sense of fluidity that allows us to view domestic space and some of the material from those areas in the western acropolis at Sepphoris with new insight and vision. This examination of gendered space excludes the elaborate peristyle courtyard house or mansion with the Dionysos mosaic, which may have served as a meeting place for the *boulē,* as a guest house near the theater, or as a mansion for a wealthy aristocrat, as we have indicated above.

One of the few criticisms we may direct at Hirschfeld is that his otherwise commendable study of the house presupposes a narrative of privacy whether describing the courtyard as "a convenient barrier between the public and private domains" or characterizing the simple or complex house as offering "greater privacy."[33] But as we have already noted, it is very difficult to ascertain the true nature of relationships that obtained among the residents of any particular domicile. Courtyards in particular permit of multiple connections with neighbors and of multiple relationships among the people residing within the domicile. Hirschfeld states it this way: "Maintaining the privacy of the courtyard was apparently as important in the Roman-Byzantine period as it was in traditional Palestinian culture. In fact, the Jewish sources define the various types of courtyards according to the degree of privacy they provided."[34] But to restate our position, some courtyards "may serve as spaces for privacy while others are common space used by dwellings as an extension of household space, but hardly as a means of affording privacy."[35] In a topographic situation such as at Meiron, which is steeply sloped, several courtyards could be clearly observed from the upper slope, and even the lower rooftop of the lower house could serve as public space for the neighbors above.[36]

The Sepphoris house in unit IV is also known as area 84.1, and is briefly described in the Sepphoris catalogue (figs. 9-11).[37] As indicated above, this domicile is situated along the northern ridge of the westernmost residential area and is built alongside a very well preserved east-west roadway that connects the entire area with the area on the peak of the acropolis near the theater and

32. Baker, p. 65.
33. Hirschfeld, pp. 21-22.
34. Hirschfeld, p. 272.
35. Baker, p. 159.
36. Meyers, Strange, and Meyers, pp. 56-61.
37. Nagy et al., pp. 41-45.

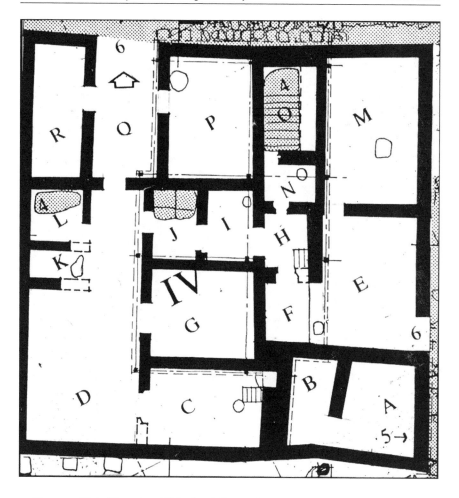

Figure 9. Unit IV or 84.1. This domicile on the western summit was occupied throughout the Roman period, ca. 30 B.C.E.–363 C.E. Rooms M and E and A and B were part of the earliest structure, though room C also existed in our earlier era and was occupied in Hellenistic times.

Dionysos Mansion. In the Roman period this house underwent numerous renovations, and parts may have taken shape originally in the Hellenistic period. Two *miqva'ot* have been identified in the structure. The earlier one, which dates from the early Roman period (end of the Second Temple period), is labeled L in the ground plan. It certainly continued in usage till circa 300, and may have been used into the fourth century as well. A much larger and more elaborate

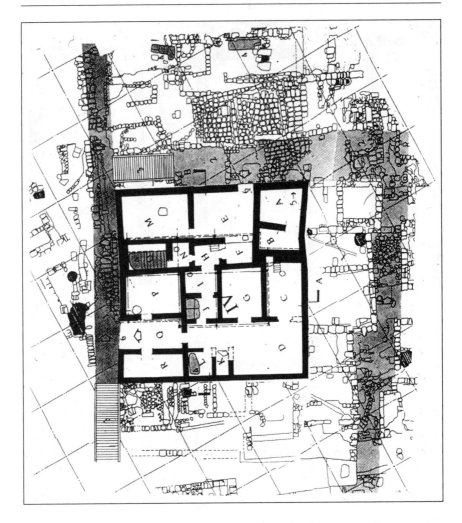

Figure 10. Unit IV or 84.1 in its larger setting. Note the east-west roadway running along the north face of the structure.

miqveh is identified as O on the plan, and by the fourth century has clearly been sealed over and the space put to other use. For several centuries the domicile had two ritual baths in simultaneous use, and both located near water cisterns.[38]

The main entrance to the house from circa 70 to 363 is labeled Q and provides immediate access to the east-west roadway. Room R, just to the west as one

38. Meyers, "The Pools of Sepphoris," pp. 46-49, 60.

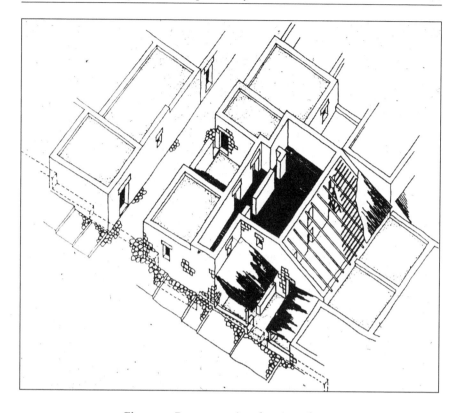

Figure 11. Reconstruction drawing of 84.1

enters facing south, doubtless provided easy storage for goods and supplies, and possible quarters for pack animals such as a donkey that might have carried the materials from the eastern market in the lower city, a fairly lengthy walk with heavy supplies. A small room K that might have served to collect water from the rooftops has a collection basin in its center. The main focal point of this section of the house, however, is the large unroofed courtyard D in the southwest corner. It is important to note that the courtyard is well situated with respect to the main northern entryway to the domicile (Q), and that the adjoining room to the east, room C, has a cistern and ample space for storage of work tools, and cool storage for food supplies; a similar case may be made for room G, which yielded a number of spindle whorls. Slightly to the north are rooms J and I; room J has a rather small stepped pool, either for washing vessels or purifying glass or metal ones; room I contains interlocking cisterns that were converted in the middle Roman period to underground storage. Also, abutting the east-west roadway is a very large storage room P, which had the greatest number of spindle whorls and items of personal adornment with extensive underground storage space for olives, olive oil, wine, etc. This lower section of the house most probably had a second story above units G, F, H, I, J, N, O, and P, no doubt residential private spaces such as we had at Meiron Insula I, hence the preservation of extensive items of personal use and adornment, spindle whorls, toggle pins, and hairpins.

Because so much of the area within the house was not sealed from above, save for the cisterns and underground chambers, it is difficult to do a definitive distribution chart of small finds and pottery types that might help us better understand room function and any association with gender. Before further consideration of these matters, let me point out a rather distinctive corpus of evidence in the Sepphoris house under consideration (84.1). First, there is the corpus of chalk or stone vessels that date to the early Roman period and most probably to the pre–70 C.E. era, similar to those found in Jerusalem and elsewhere in Galilee.[39] The vessels are clearly related to ritual purity and are found in virtually all early Roman loci from the western acropolis. In the context of 84.1, however, we may clearly relate these vessels to the two *miqva'ot* and possible smaller immersion pools for vessels already noted.

Of special note too are the fifty fragments and whole examples of round and rectangular incense shovels found in 84.1, more than have been found at any other Sepphoris excavation that has noted their presence.[40] All are of ceramic, which makes them a unique corpus since all other known examples are of bronze, though the Mishnah (*Kelim* 2.3, 7) mentions examples of ceramic. Many similar types are depicted in ancient Jewish art. Their chronological range spans the middle-late Roman period. They appear to be slightly later than the chalk vessels, but most others are used throughout the middle Roman period, at least up to circa 300, and probably to 363. Because of their similarity to the incense shovels in Jewish art, Rutgers has related the rectangular examples to the priestly *mahtah* used in the temple service;[41] the oval ones he has related to the *patera*, such as were found in the Bar Kokhba caves.[42]

---

39. See J. M. Cahill, "Chalk Vessel Assemblages of the Persian/Hellenistic and Early Roman Periods," in *Excavations at the City of David, 1978-1985*, Qedem 33 (Jerusalem: Hebrew University Institute of Archaeology, 1992); Y. Magen, "Jerusalem as the Center of Stone Vessel Industry during the Second Temple Period," in *Ancient Jerusalem Revealed* (Jerusalem: Israel Exploration Society, 1994); R. Deines, *Jüdische Steingefässe und pharisäische Frömmigheit: Ein archäologisch-historischer Beitrag zum Verständnis von Joh 2,6 und der jüdischen Reinheitshalacha zur Zeit Jesu* (Tübingen: J. C. B. Mohr, 1993).

40. Rutgers, p. 191, and Meyers, "Ceramic Incense Shovels."

41. Rutgers, pp. 178-83.

42. Y. Yadin, *Finds from the Bar Kochba Period in the Cave of Letters* (Jerusalem: Israel Exploration Society, 1963), pp. 46-63.

But there is something quite enigmatic about the incense shovels from Sepphoris: none appears ever to have been used. There is no trace of burning, no residue; yet there is no doubt that they are what they are: incense shovels. Rutgers concludes that since incense is associated with priestly function in the temple and matters of purity, they are indicative of priestly presence, a social reality we know well from rabbinic references.[43] But the suggestion that they were intended not to be used is something I am very uncomfortable with, so I would suggest alternatively that they possibly were used to hold sweet-smelling dried plants, a kind of potpourri, or were intended for burning scented oil, which would not leave a trace, or for containing a mixture of resin, spices, and herbs.[44] Such a hypothesis would allow therefore for the possible indication of priestly identity and at the very least the existence of an elite class at Sepphoris, which goes nicely with the evidence for what might be considered extreme concern with ritual purity, and a concomitant concern for keeping the air inside a very large house fresh with mild scent.

The array of artifacts from the rooms and spaces in and around the courtyard suggests a variety of domestic activities: grinders for food preparation, bone needles for sewing, toggle pins for clothing, loom weights, etc. The interior organization of space in 84.1 thus is analogous to the use and organization of space at Meiron in the lower town, area I. What is new at Sepphoris is that, similar to the priestly house in Jerusalem, accouterments associated with ritual

---

43. Rutgers, pp. 192-96, but cf. Meyers, "Ceramic Incense Shovels."

44. I have conferred with a number of paleobotanists and geologists who have suggested that a nonfunctional interpretation is highly unlikely. Annette Green, head of the Fragrance Foundation in New York City and author of numerous articles on the subject, informs me that the use of dry fumigants to provide scent to households was very common in antiquity and that the list of plants and spices used for such purposes is quite long. While not denying the priestly association that Rutgers had made, we may suggest that the use of fumigants in incense shovels was as much a reflection of social standing and class as it was of religious background, especially since both the vessel and the fumigants would have cost a not inconsiderable sum of money. Independently C. Meyers ("Fumes, Flames or Fluids? Reframing the Cup-and-Bowl Question," in *Boundaries of the Ancient Near Eastern World: A Tribute to Cyrus Gordon,* ed. M. Lubetski, C. Gottlieb, and S. Keller, JSOTSup 273 [Sheffield: JSOT, 1998], pp. 34-37) has dealt with the possible use of incense in Iron Age period cup-and-saucers from nearby Tel 'Ein Zippori. She concludes that the burning of incense or fumigants could well have occurred in domestic contexts as opposed to cultic, and that the use of imported resins "often mixed with herbs or spices from fumigation was somewhat more restricted for economic reasons. But even so, the notion that burning incense could mean only the burning of the costly fruit of trees or shrubs of South Arabia or West Africa must be rejected" (p. 36). This suggestion accords well with what we have proposed on the ceramic priestly shovels at Sepphoris. Where we do not find incense shovels that have been used with burnt material, it is quite possible that fumigants were burned on other type vessels, such as plates or even on cupped broken sherds.

purity, that is, *miqva'ot* and stone vessels, are found in abundance along with the later incense shovels, perhaps indicative of a priestly element in residence during and after the destruction of the temple in 70, no doubt an influential and wealthy group that could well have had an impact on the Sepphorean citizenry in adopting a pro-Roman stance in 68.[45] For the priests of the Second Temple, what mattered most was the status quo and preserving the temple service. Subsequently, when they disbursed to new centers after 70, such as to Sepphoris, they became part of the Galilean aristocracy.[46]

The inference drawn by Hirschfeld from the data presented above, that maintaining privacy was a major aspect of the courtyard house,[47] is one we must reject out of hand. Courtyard D in area 84.1 at Sepphoris was hardly a zone of privacy; rather, it could only have been the hub of a variety of activities that were carried out by the extended family that inhabited this house. Hirschfeld, however, does not take the privacy narrative to the extreme of declaring that one section of the house is for women and another for men, suggesting only that men were normally thought to be active in the courtyard closer to the roadway while the women concentrated their activities close to the inner courtyard.[48] Had Hirschfeld access to the Sepphoris material, the only other spaces that might qualify for such an interpretation would be rooms M and E in the older, northeast wing of the house. Since the roadway that runs just north of 84.1 is virtually intact to this day in its ancient configuration, it is plain that room M is contiguous with it. Similarly, the excavators have concluded that another ancient walkway or crossroad dividing *insulae* would have been located just east of rooms M and E where a modern walkway for tourists might be placed (no. 3), number 2 representing bedrock with occasional cut stones still in place from the early Roman road that was reused in the Byzantine period. In Hirschfeld's privacy scheme we would have to conclude that only women utilized courtyard D, a suggestion that cannot be supported by the data.

If one were to examine rabbinic literature systematically, a strong case for locating women in all sorts of diverse spatial contexts can be made, inside and outside the home; and men and women were also involved with fieldwork, production of goods, and moving about in towns, villages, and urban environments. If we may assume the presence of a significant priestly segment of society at Sepphoris, and especially in connection within domicile 84.1, then we must also be prepared to say that in an environment that took ritual purity

45. Meyers, *Galilee through the Centuries*, pp. 109-22.

46. L. Levine, *The Rabbinic Class of Roman Palestine in Late Antiquity* (Jerusalem: Yad Izhak Ben-Zvi, 1989), p. 171.

47. Hirschfeld, p. 272; Baker, p. 159.

48. Hirschfeld, p. 49; Baker, p. 161.

matters very seriously, women and men willy-nilly had to have had numerous contacts (not physical) during their daily activities. In the built environment of ancient Galilee it is virtually impossible to construct a scenario whereby men and women could have avoided each other either at home or outside the home. Even Meiron is mentioned in the list of priestly courses as the location of the clan of Yehoiariv.[49] And we have already observed the number and variety of work activities conducted in the MI complex; there the *miqveh,* however, was located off the courtyard, which would have facilitated its use by men and women in the compound.

There is no doubt that the urban environment of Sepphoris has contributed to the upscale nature of the households uncovered there, similar in fact to those uncovered in Jerusalem near the temple. Hence, while we can say that 84.1 is larger and more elaborate than the Meiron *insula,* and offers a greater possibility of privacy in respect to the availability of several *miqva'ot* in the household, we cannot infer from the data that the activities carried out at home were of lesser range or limited solely to women. I have not posited the size of the Sepphoris house because the eastern side is not as well preserved as the western side, the latter of which had an upper story. Assuming that the east was one story high, only since it is built on bedrock and is much higher upslope, 84.1 is nearly double the Meiron I household by the middle Roman period, or about 300 square meters, which probably accommodated more than twenty individuals by that time. The Jewish bride was transferred from the family of her father's home to that of the groom in Jewish practice; hence, along with elderly parents, aunts and uncles, and children, the number could soar quite quickly. While the full shape of 84.1 in the early Roman period is not known, because so many portions of the western sector go back to that era, it is possible that two households and/or homes were combined in the mid–second century to create a much larger unit of space, in which case each half of the larger unit might have been comparable in size to MI in the pre–70-135 c.e. era. In any case, the suggestion of Guijarro that the average size of the first-century family in Galilee was four, seems much too low, especially in view of the practice of sons bringing their wives home with them.[50] If I am correct in assuming that two houses and households might have existed side by side in late Second Temple times but were combined in the space occupied by 84.1 from circa 135 to 363, each half in the earlier setting would have had ample water storage space, at least one *miqveh* each, each unit with a courtyard, and each bordering on one or more

49. Avi-Yonah, *The Holy Land From the Persian to the Arab Conquest* (Grand Rapids: Baker Book House, 1977), p. 133.

50. Guijarro, pp. 60-61.

streets or alleyways which constituted important activity areas for residents. Such places were areas where various people, men and women, met and congregated, not to mention nearby water areas as well. What the implications were for the families when the two units were possibly combined into one is difficult to say. But these priestly families, as aristocratic as they might have been, and as committed as they were to high standards of ritual purity, were pretty much obliged to perform a considerable rate of work activity at home, whether it be food preparation or textiles. The nearby pedestrian traffic along the adjoining walk and roadways assured both men and women an easy outside access to markets, shops, fields, reservoirs, etc., all likely places for regular contact as at home.

Conclusion

A consideration of Syro-Palestinian domestic architecture with special attention to Galilee has demonstrated above all how the built structures of Roman-period Palestine reflect local building traditions, though for the peristyle house we have clear-cut evidence of the influence of Greco-Roman architectural and building traditions. On the courtyard house, except for the "town" of Meiron, we have observed that the overall urban context is key to understanding the full significance of the archaeological remains, especially evident in the examples from first-century Jerusalem. The general rarity of the villa or peristyle-courtyard type in Jewish nonurban settings reveals that domestic architecture may not be the best means of assessing the degree of Hellenization for the masses of Roman-period Jews.

On the other hand, a consideration of domestic space in Jewish Galilee has resulted in the view that Jewish households cannot be considered areas of confinement or concealment for women. Rabbinic sources treat women's public appearances at marketplaces or in the street with great concern, requiring modesty of dress and demeanor. In view of the archaeology of domestic space, however, it is difficult to feminize women's work at home, which has led to the creation of a myth of women denied access to the outside world and its mundane affairs in contrast to men who were devoted to Torah study and worldly occupations. Such was the way the rabbis reconstructed a Judaism that was devoid of a temple after 70 C.E. and that was presumably dominated by men in all walks of life. But the material world of Roman-period Palestine clearly shows that women participated far more fully in crafts, daily household labors and management, and hence had a much higher degree of recognition and responsibility than one might infer from literary sources alone.

The built environment also demonstrates how Roman-period Palestine was opening up to the emerging open-market economy, the main by-products of which were increasing urbanization and Hellenization. Ultimately such a changing environment led to a much higher degree of participation of women in the full range of social and professional activities. Only when the rabbinic literature is studied alongside the material and cultural world gleaned from archaeology will we be in a better position to appreciate the "true" role of women in ancient Jewish society.

II. Domestic Values: Equality, Suffering

The Language of Equality in Early Christian House Churches: A Constructivist Approach

Peter Lampe

What does modern brain research have to do with theology? Currently a lot of research focuses on the human brain, which poses challenges to the different sciences. Old questions of humanity are considered anew. How do we arrive at certain knowledge? Is this at all possible? What is "consciousness"? How should we understand "reality"?

As rifts have developed in the concept of "logical empiricism" since the 1970s, new approaches to the term "reality" have been attempted within the framework of interdisciplinary studies. One of these, a constructivist model stimulated by the sociology of knowledge, is presented here. This model describes under which conditions everyday realities — contexts of meaning that are valid for many subjects — originate.

The model will then be applied to a New Testament theme, the language of equality. Further early Christian examples as well as a more detailed theoretical discussion can soon be found elsewhere.[1]

The Model

The bulwark of logical empiricism, which once seemed so strong, has weakened since the 1970s. Patricia Smith Churchland words it more critically: "Logical empiricism, though still admired for its clarity and rigor, is now generally as-

1. See Peter Lampe, *Die Wirklichkeit als Bild. Das Neue Testament als Grunddokument abendländischer Kultur im Lichte konstruktivistischer Epistemologie und Wissenssoziologie* (Neukirchen: Neukirchener, forthcoming 2004); see also Peter Lampe, "Wissenssoziologische Annäherung an das Neue Testament," *NTS* 43 (1997): 347-66.

For Professor Emeritus Christoph Burchard. This essay was translated from the German by Margaret Birdsong Lampe.

sumed to have collapsed."[2] The dissolution of the logical-empiric bulwark resulted from its assumption that statements based on empirical sensory data
were unchanging foundations for the structures of knowledge, while the theoretical statements built upon these foundations were changeable and could be
replaced by better ones as they came along. Empirical sensory data statements
were thought to be independent from these theoretical statements.[3] However,
this was a fundamental mistake, as Mary Hesse, for example, demonstrated in
1970.[4] No language of observation is independent of theories; the theories inform perception. No term in an observational statement is so firm that it cannot be reclassified.

Since the collapse of logical empiricism in the last decades, the term "reality" has to be rethought. What is called reality rests neither solely outside in the
world, as the naive realists postulated, nor solely in the mind, as George Berkeley (1685-1753), for example, believed. The answer to the riddle lies somewhere
between the extreme poles of ontological idealism and naive realism. But
where?

There have been many attempts to answer this question, and I have chosen
for discussion what is in my opinion an important contribution: *constructivism*. Since the 1980s, it has been articulated in various ways by several disciplines. Building on the painful realization that perception and recognition cannot lead to a reflection or reproduction of the ontic reality, that even improved
recognition methods do not bring us closer to this reality, the basic
constructivist thesis states: the subject creates its own reality. *Reality is a construction of the brain.* Besides the traditional philosophical-epistemological reasons supporting this thesis, thanks to current brain research we now see that
there are also neurobiological reasons.[5]

If reality is a construction of the brain, this of course does not mean that
the constructionists consider deviating into solipsism, according to which the
world exists only in human ideas — in the sense of "Only I exist, and every-

2. Patricia Smith Churchland, *Neurophilosophy: Toward a Unified Science of the Mind-
Brain*, 3rd printing (Cambridge, Mass.: MIT, 1988), p. 271.

3. Logical empiricism was based on the logic of Gottlob Frege and Bertrand Russell. It tried
to represent science as a system of logical relations between observational foundations on the
one hand and theoretical superstructures on the other, between individual cases on the one
hand and general laws, set patterns, and regularities on the other. From a logical-empiricist perspective, all statements that are not logically defining statements require empirical sensory data
statements for their verification; for this purpose they need to be brought into the right logical
relation with these observational statements.

4. Hesse, "Is There an Independent Observation Language?" in *The Nature and Function of
Scientific Theories*, ed. R. Colodny (Pittsburgh: University of Pittsburgh Press, 1970), pp. 36-77.

5. For this, see the book cited in n. 1.

thing else is my imagination." No, an ontic reality, which is independent from us and our consciousness, does exist. Parts of it can even be *experienced,* but they are not *recognizable* and *knowable.* The ontic world is experienced insofar as it repeatedly puts up barriers against which our actions run. Such resistance is a decisive indication for the existence of an ontic reality. But this "world of objective obstacles, of ontic barriers, between which we act" remains "principally inaccessible and indescribable."[6]

The constructed reality is "objective" insofar as it represents an intersubjective, social reality. And with this we have reached the point where epistemological constructivism and sociology of knowledge start to overlap. For constructivism, all "knowledge that proves itself to be useful in intersubjective, over-individual, institutionalized contexts" is "objective."[7] The collective usefulness of knowledge is a sociological category. In other words, we have come to the constructivist-oriented sociology of knowledge. It affirms that the individual subject interprets the social- or culture-specific constructions as "outer" and "objective" realities.[8]

The Berlin sociologists Horst Stenger and Hans Geisslinger attempted to connect epistemological constructivism with the constructive theoretical perspective of the sociology of knowledge (Berger-Luckmann, for example). In an exciting empirical analysis, they examined how social, intersubjective reality comes to exist. Which processes of construction come into play? Under what conditions do groups form their realities?

In establishing their theoretical framework, the two authors started with the concept of meaning. For the constructivists, the meaning that phenomena have is a product of a constructive cognitive process. People, relationships, or physical objects are not meaningful *in themselves.* Rather the individual subject as well as a society, a culture, *construct* meaning. How do they do this? Two steps are carried out. One recognizes a phenomenon by attributing a meaning to it ("this is a table"). Meaning then unfolds in a second step as it becomes associated with other units of meaning ("table" — "a place to put something," "sit," "write," "eat," "community," etc.). When units of meaning are put together into a system, a so-called *context* of meaning emerges.

A subjective context exists in a subject's head. And this mental context be-

---

6. E. von Glasersfeld, "Konstruktion von Wirklichkeit und der Begriff der Objektivität," in *Einführung in den Konstruktivismus* (Munich: Oldenbourg, 1985), p. 19.

7. Cf. H. Stenger and H. Geisslinger, "Die Transformation sozialer Realität: Ein Beitrag zur empirischen Wissenssoziologie," *Kölner Zeitschrift für Soziologie und Sozialpsychologie* 43 (1991): 247-70, here 250.

8. Cf. Stenger and Geisslinger, p. 250.

comes a social context when the subject makes it known to and relevant for other subjects. In this way the mental context becomes intersubjective.

A characteristic of constructed contexts is that they are based on axiomatic theorems. The psychoanalytical context, for example, rests on the axiomatic assumption of the unconscious. A theological context rests on the assumption of a powerfully acting God who reveals God's self. When a context develops and unfolds, becoming more and more differentiated, then also the *categories* are made available that allow the content of the respective axiom to be *experienced*. In this way, within the context of psychoanalysis, the processes and structures of the unconscious become *observable*. Or in the theological context, God becomes someone who can be *experienced* — whether in the history of Israel, in the works of a Nazarene, or, as for the Corinthians, in spiritual-charismatic experiences such as glossolalia. Axioms and categories produce evidence in this way. The contexts confirm themselves.

Stenger and Geisslinger report about a two-week field experiment that took place at a retreat center in the upper Pfalz area. The everyday social reality of a group of teenagers was transformed during the course of this experiment so that by the end of it, they all were firmly convinced of two things. First, they believed their nightly dreams were affected by underground streams running under their bedrooms, and that this even occurred in a reciprocal manner: not only did the underground streams influence their dreams, but the level of their dream activity could also affect the level of the water in these streams. Secondly, they believed that locations occurring in their dreams could be put on a map and then found during a nighttime walk through the upper Pfalz area. During this walk at night through the Bavarian countryside, which actually took place, a buffalo was seen sleeping in a field, a mole's hill towered to two meters, and a door frame stood in the middle of the landscape without a house.

How do such experiences originate? They sound like fantasy only to those unlucky enough not to have participated in the new social reality of this group. There is no room here to relate the entertaining individual steps of the experiment or to report how a new construction of meaning, a newly constructed reality, was made plausible to the members of this group. Various sources of evidence make new contexts of meaning seem plausible. However, the discussion of these sources would burst the frame of this article. The categories important for us here are:

- "constructed reality" = "context" = "context of meaning,"
- "objective" = "intersubjective" or "transsubjective,"
- "objective, social context" = "social reality" versus
- "subjective, mental context."

Early Christian Equality as "Social Context"

In Galatians 3:28 Paul states that whatever the worldly differences among the Galatians may be, they are abolished. "There is neither Jew nor Greek, slave nor free, male nor female." The text differentiates between two social contexts, two constructs of reality, which stand both beside and in opposition to each other. On the one hand is the worldly, Hellenistic-Roman context in which Jews and Greeks are differentiated from each other, the not legally free from the free, the men from the women. On the other hand, the Christian community has changed the paradigm. In their new social context, these differentiations among people are no longer made. In the house churches and in the Christians' interactions with each other, such worldly differences are considered irrelevant, so that the one person stands equal to the other. This is what is meant by "you all are one" (εἷς). You are all together one and the same; nothing differentiates you. A paraphrase capturing the meaning would be: "You all are the same as each other." Contrary to popular assumption, the masculine εἷς cannot mean that they all are "one (church) body." The neuter of σῶμα (body) contraindicates this.

In Galatians 3:28 this new context first of all is a subjective, mental context in Paul's head. However, it also represents a social context, a new social reality in the early Christian congregations. How can this conclusion be made?

In 3:27-28 Paul refers to the early Christian understanding of baptism (in baptism and in the postbaptismal existence, worldly differences among the baptized become irrelevant; regardless of their worldly status, all who are baptized are assured of the same closeness to Christ). The apostle reminds the Galatians of this early Christian construction of reality. If this construct existed only in *Paul's* head, then he would first have to convince the Galatians of its validity; he would first have to push to objectivize (= intersubjectivize) it. However, he does not do this. Rather, he presupposes that a successful objectivization of the construct has already taken place. He takes the construct for granted and uses it as a building block in the argumentation in the letter to the Galatians — as a building block with an argumentative function that does not need to be proved itself.

Paul argues to the Galatians that observing the Torah, especially circumcision, does not give anyone an advantage over the uncircumcised Gentile Christians. Without differentiations, all Christians are "children of God through faith" (3:26). *"In Christō,"* the difference between Gentile and Jewish Christians is irrelevant. This means, however, that the differences between slaves and free people, between men and women, mentioned in 3:28 go beyond the frame of the chapter and indicate a traditional formula that is older than the letter to the Galatians. This conclusion is also supported by the fact that here there is an accumulation of words that are hardly used in other Pauline texts — and never in this combination again: the ἔνι (there is), which is found three times here, otherwise occurs only in 1 Corinthians 6:5 in Paul's writing, and ἄρσεν (male) and θῆλυ (female) appear only in Romans 1:26-27. This pre-Pauline traditional piece presents a formula with three parallelisms.

After all, we can assume that the irrelevance of worldly differences among Christians was not only a mental concept in Paul's head but also a transsubjective construct of reality in the heads of the congregational members. But that does not necessarily mean that these congregations always behaved accordingly. As we frequently can observe in ourselves, there are frictional losses between mental context and behavior. However, although such losses doubtlessly occurred, our early Christian sources also document behavior that does correspond to the construct of irrelevant worldly differences. In the first Christian generation, *women* did have notable influence in Christian congregational life, as numerous studies have shown. It was not before the end of the first century that a significant effort was made to cut back this influence.[9] Although the integration of *Jews and Gentiles* could create severe problems in the church (e.g., Gal. 2), often enough Gentile Christian congregations, such as in the capital city of Rome, did integrate Jewish and Gentile Christians without any problems and without giving one group priority over the other.[10] *Slaves* could be treated as *pares* in a brotherly or sisterly way, as Paul shows in the letter to Philemon. He places himself at the same level as the slave Onesimus, who had converted to Christianity (Philem. 6, 12, 16-18), and he expects Onesimus's master to waive his legal rights as master and to take Onesimus back as an equal and a brother in a loving way (16-17).

We can assume from all of this that the irrelevance of ethnic, legal, social-economic, and gender differences, thus the equality of all congregational members, was part of the constructed social reality of the first Christian generation — at least in the Pauline churches.

Does this mean that the old, Hellenistic Roman social context was totally discarded by the Christians? Not at all. Otherwise the baptized would have to emigrate from this world, which was not Paul's intention (1 Cor. 5:10).

When Christians walked the streets or markets of a Hellenistic city and mixed with pagan people and visited them in their homes, moving around in the social context of the Hellenistic Roman culture, they fully belonged to *this*

---

9. For further details, see, e.g., Peter Lampe and Ulrich Luz, "Nachpaulinisches Christentum und pagane Gesellschaft," in J. Becker et al., *Die Anfänge des Christentums: Alte Welt und Neue Hoffnung* (Stuttgart: Kohlhammer, 1987), pp. 185-216, here 189-93.

10. Cf., e.g., Peter Lampe, *Die stadtrömischen Christen in den ersten beiden Jahrhunderten,* 2nd ed. (Tübingen: Mohr-Siebeck, 1989), pp. 53-63.

context. They worked as slaves, lived their roles as men and women, and were influenced by their Jewish or pagan pasts. These differences were not abolished in the worldly, social context. To the contrary, considering the impending eschaton, in 1 Corinthians 7 Paul even encouraged the Christians to remain in their given roles in the worldly context and not to try to be freed if slaves or to end a marriage with a pagan partner. All were supposed to stay in the same worldly status they had when they were baptized (Gal. 3:27) and changed paradigms from the worldly to the Christian social context. Paul expected everyone to stay in his or her κλῆσις (vocation).

Paul further concretized this recommendation: within the worldly context in which Christians continued to live after baptism, they should not actively try to change their status, but should accept changes if these are imposed on them passively. If a master decided to free a slave, this should be accepted; if a pagan partner in a mixed marriage definitely wanted to separate, then this should be done (1 Cor. 7). Whatever worldly status the environment placed on Christians, the baptized should voluntarily accept these worldly roles in light of the quickly approaching eschaton.

What then changed with baptism? What is exciting is that after baptism, the Christians lived in *two* contexts. When they were living their everyday lives "outside" the house churches in the pagan world as slaves or women or masters, the equality maxim of the Christian context was merely a mental context.

Is such a coexistence of mental and social contexts possible? In fact, it is possible, and here it can be seen how well the theoretical instrument of a constructivist sociology of knowledge fits to the early Christian constellation illustrated by Galatians 3:28.

In social interactions an individual can have a social as well as one or more differing mental contexts of meaning in his or her head. For example, in a crowded sports stadium a spectator can be excited by a team and its talent and therefore integrate well into the social context of the athletic competition and its enthusiasm but at the same time have a second mental context working in his or her head — for example, a social-psychological context, which motivates this spectator also to observe the behavior of the crowd and to interpret it in social psychological categories. Since the participants in a situation are always free to have another mental context in their heads besides the social context of the situation, there are often amazing differences in the reality of these different participants in the same situation. Only in rare cases is a situation something transsubjectively unified and monolithic.

In relation to the early Christians, this means that outside in the "world," Christians moved within the social context of the Hellenistic Roman society as they continued to play their roles of slaves, free people, men and women. At the same time, however, they had a mental context in their heads, saying that such worldly differences were invalid before God and in the Christian congregation.

This *mental* context became *social* as soon as Christians met. Then they often interacted with each other as brothers and sisters by abstracting from the worldly differences of the old social context and not regarding each other any more κατὰ σάρκα ("according to the flesh," 2 Cor. 5:16).

It was possible that some Christians did not fully lose themselves in this new social context, but also had the context of the Hellenistic Roman society as a mental context of meaning in their heads at the same time. For example, a man who was successful and socially elevated in the world could feel embarrassed if he was too familiarly greeted by a Christian slave in the house church,[11] or if women like Prisca,[12] Junia,[13] or the patroness Phoebe (Rom. 16:1-2) took over leading functions in the congregations. A man also could be irritated by two simultaneous contexts in his head if during the worship service he felt fascinated by the erotic aura of a female Christian, although this did not fit with the new social context of Galatians 3:28 — "neither male nor female." It was not for nothing that Paul pushed for women chastely to cover their heads during worship services (1 Cor. 11:2-16).[14] According to Galatians 3:28, the old gender roles were supposed to lose their strength in the new social reality of the Christian congregation. This means also that the erotic "electricity" between the sexes was supposed to diminish — at least as much as possible (even though this was not possible for everybody; cf. 1 Cor. 7:29, 32, especially 7:37-40).

Such people with two simultaneous contexts in their heads caused the "frictional loss" mentioned above, which often can be diagnosed when a reality construct is transposed into behavior. This transposition frequently entails some "watering down" of the reality construct.

Other Christians, however, probably lost themselves and integrated more completely in the new social context. At least during the congregational meetings in the house church, they blocked out the context of meaning that the "world" and the Hellenistic Roman society provided.

The early Christians lived in two contexts and moved back and forth be-

11. Cf. 1 Tim. 6:2: Those slaves "who have believers as their masters must not be disrespectful to them because they are brethren, but must serve them all the more."

12. In Rom. 16:3; Acts 18:18, 26; 2 Tim. 4:19, she is mentioned before her husband. Together with him, she hosted several house churches.

13. According to Rom. 16:7, she either was an apostle herself or at least most highly respected by the apostles.

14. In order to justify his ruling, Paul gives reasons other than the danger of distracting men. However, his ruling of course also dampened eroticism, no matter whether Paul consciously intended this or not.

tween them. Whenever they shifted from one to the other, the mental context became social — and the social became mental. It depended on which people they interacted with: fellow Christians or pagans.

In my opinion, the constructivist instrument provides an adequate tool for describing the coexistence of the two realities that are hinted at in New Testament texts such as Galatians 3:28.

Not all early Christian groups could handle the tension between two such differing social contexts in their lives. If we jump one and a half generations to the 90s, the Asia Minor author of Revelation found that at his time the coexistence of the Roman Hellenistic and early Christian contexts was highly antagonistic, and he refused to integrate in the Hellenistic Roman context. This heightened antagonism arose in Asia Minor as the emperor Domitian's priesthood had started to propagate the imperial cult as obligatory for all. In Laodicea, for example, a temple to the emperor was erected by the officials in 83 C.E.; in Ephesus, a colossal statue of the emperor towered in the area of the Diana temple. The syncretistic association of the indigenous religions with the cult of the emperor had climbed to its apex in Asia Minor. The author of Revelation accordingly portrayed the Roman emperor as a hideous beast, which was assisted by a second monster, representing the imperial priesthood of the provinces.[15] The apocalyptic writer complained that the imperial priests "cause all, both small and great, both rich and poor, both free and slave, to be marked on the right hand or the forehead, so that no one can buy or sell unless he has the mark, that is, the name of the beast" (Rev. 13:16-17). This is comparable to Pliny's *Epistle* 10.96.10: Christians were discovered when they did not buy sacrificial meat at the market, when they neither took part in public festivals nor swore in the name of the emperor. Those who did not worship the divine emperor risked their lives (Rev. 13:15). Some believers had already been executed (2:13; 6:9-11). The writer of Revelation expected a large persecution of Christians in Asia Minor (which, however, never took place) and felt the present to be full of hardship (1:9; 2:9-10, 13; 7:14; 13:7-10; 16:6; 17:6; 18:24; 19:2, 20; 20:4), which he had "to suffer through" and "persevere with patience" (2:7, 11, 17, 26; 3:5, 11-12, 21; 21:7; cf. 1:9; 2:2-3, 19; 3:10; 12:11; 13:10; 14:12). "Do not fear what you are about to suffer. . . . Be faithful unto death" (2:10); "blessed are the dead who die in the Lord henceforth" (14:13). It was essential not to deny the name of Christ, not to give in to the imperial cult (3:8). For the writer of Revelation, the alternative between Christ and the emperor was absolutely exclusive.

Against this background, he compared the Roman Hellenistic context with the Christian one in an antithetical manner and caricatured the former as mimicking the latter:

---

15. Cf. in Rev. 13:1-10 the emperor and in 13:11-18; 16:13 the priesthood of the imperial cult.

- At the pinnacle of the Christian context stands God; at the pinnacle of the Roman Hellenistic context stands the Diabolos.
- As Christ receives his power from God, so does the emperor from Diabolos (13:2, 4).
- As the risen Christ carries his death marks (5:6), so is the emperor Domitian a revived Nero and carries Nero's healed death wound on his body (13:3, 12, 14).
- As God, Christ, and the Holy Spirit belong together, so the Diabolos, emperor, and pseudoprophetic beast (the priesthood of the imperial cult) form a satanic "trinity" (16:13; 20:10).
- The pseudoprophetic beast gives life like the Holy Spirit (13:15 together with 11:11) and disguises itself as a lamb like Christ but with horns (13:11).
- The Christian mark of baptism is reflected in the mark of the beast (7:3; 13:16).

For the writer of Revelation, the new Christian social context was a reality that was opposed to and in competition with the social context of meaning of the Hellenistic Roman environment. This also manifested itself morally. In the "world" murder (18:24) existed, rising prices and hunger scourged the provinces (6:5-6), while in Rome the pagans were feasting and partying (17:4; 18:12, 16), and "slaves and human souls" (18:13) fell under the wheels. In the Christian anticontext constructed by the apocalyptic writer, however, loving as brothers and sisters was valid, and *differences between "small" and "great" vanished* (1:9; 20:12; 19:5). Yes, affirmed the writer of Revelation, even Christ will *share* his throne with the Christians like a good brother (3:21; 20:6), in spite of all the hierarchical behavior in the world — and in the church. The writer of Revelation nonchalantly *ignored* the *hierarchical structures* that also had emerged in the Christian congregations by the end of the first century. Prophecy was the only church office he wanted to acknowledge in earthly Christian congregations (cf. 10:7; 11:18; 16:6; 19:10; 22:6, 16).

Radical apocalyptic antithetical statements and the refusal in any way to integrate into the old Hellenistic Roman context characterize this type of dealing with the coexistence of the two contexts. All evidence indicates that, like many other early Christian teachers, the author of Revelation chose to step out of a settled life in the Hellenistic Roman society and become a wandering prophet in Asia Minor.[16] He emigrated from the worldly context and conse-

---

16. See Peter Lampe, "Die Apokalyptiker — ihre Situation und ihr Handeln," in U. Luz, J. Kegler, P. Lampe, and P. Hoffmann, *Eschatologie und Friedenshandeln,* 2nd ed. (Stuttgart: Katholisches Bibelwerk, 1982), pp. 59-114, here 109-11.

quently also did not shy away from readiness for martyrdom. "Do not fear what you are about to suffer. . . . Be faithful unto death" (2:10).

His Christian context, that is, his Christian reality, was radicalized and therefore entirely exclusive in regard to the Hellenistic Roman context. He transsubjectively shared it with other prophetic radicals, but not with the majority of the Christians of his time.

The other and most often preferred way early Christians dealt with the tension between the two coexisting social contexts was by toning down the new Christian context of meaning a little instead of being radicalized by it. In other words, the new Christian context became partly accommodated to the Hellenistic Roman context. Thus, over time, hierarchical structures also developed in the church in spite of the doctrine of equality. And the influence of originally equal women in the early church was pushed back many places by the end of the first century.[17]

Galatians 3:28, this uncomfortable statement of the first generation, in the post-Pauline literature certainly did not enjoy great popularity. The letter to the Colossians, written by one of Paul's students, does refer to the passage: "There cannot be Greek and Jew . . . slave, free" (Col. 3:11). However, the "neither man nor woman" from Galatians 3 is missing already. And in Colossians 3:22–4:1 the Christian slaves are warned to be obedient to their masters — only a few verses after the programmatic sentence that there is "no more slave or free."

The principle of equality — not only before God but also in the life of the Christian congregations — often risks fading into an old traditional phrase. But often enough it described — and continues to describe — a social reality of the church, in other words, an intersubjectively shared social context, a construct of reality carried by a whole community. Whenever this happens, this constructed reality is much more than a mere subjective, mental context of some lonely dreamers.

17. See above, n. 9.

Paul's Portrait of Christ Crucified (Gal. 3:1) in Light of Paintings and Sculptures of Suffering and Death in Pompeiian and Roman Houses

David L. Balch

Paul baptized the household of Stephanas in Corinth, as he remembered while writing from Ephesus (1 Cor. 1:16; 16:15-16), where the church was meeting in the house of Aquila and Prisca (1 Cor. 16:19; see Rom. 16:3-5a). Carolyn Osiek and I investigated how Stephanas's household might have lived in their house, and what it meant to worship in the house of Prisca and Aquila.[1] While doing that earlier research, I found the work of Andrew Wallace-Hadrill on Pompeii and Herculaneum. His new insights informed our book, and the Lilly Endowment conference papers in this book, sponsored again thankfully by Don Browning, grew out of those research questions. Greco-Roman houses, unlike many modern ones, were filled with art, with paintings, mosaics, and sculptures. The question that generates this essay is: When Paul preached in such houses, or when there was a Eucharist or a baptism, might there have been art in the house that could help those gathered to understand the sermon or the eucharistic dinner conversation?[2]

Recent studies of Roman domestic art focus not only on Pompeii and Herculaneum, but also on the Roman West (Spain, Gaul, Germany, Britain, and Dacia) and the Greek East (especially Ephesus). Indigenous traditions influenced the paintings, but especially in the beginning, Italian centers were determinative.[3] Lavagne observes that the paintings were discussed by those who viewed them at symposia: "You musn't forget your classics even at dinner!" (Petronius, *Satyricon* 39.4, which Petronius meant ironically; trans. Bracht and

---

1. See Carolyn Osiek and David L. Balch, *Families in the New Testament World: Houses and House Churches* (Louisville: Westminster John Knox, 1997), p. 202 and passim.

2. For early Christian development of art despite their critique of pagan art, see Paul Corby Finney, *The Invisible God: The Earliest Christians on Art* (Oxford: Oxford University Press, 1994), chaps. 1–3.

3. Henri Lavagne, "Römische Wandmalerei: Bilanz jüngerer Forschungen und neue Sichtweisen," in *Römische Glaskunst und Wandmalerei*, ed. Michael J. Klein (Mainz: Philipp von Zabern, 1999), pp. 21-24, at 21.

Kinney). These recent studies show that styles and themes of this art typically originated in Rome and spread to the provinces in the East and the West. One would find datable styles and a limited number of themes in Rome and Pompeii, and in the first centuries B.C.E. and C.E., comparable styles and themes in other Greco-Roman cities.

The thesis of this paper is that Greco-Roman domestic, tragic art emphasizing pathos would have provided a meaningful cultural context for understanding Paul's gospel of Christ's passion. Although Dionysian themes are more prominent than scenes of suffering and death in Roman domestic art, tragic art portraying suffering was surprisingly significant in domestic contexts — where Christians lived and worshiped.[4] The gospel itself (e.g., 1 Cor. 15:3-8) and the rituals of baptism (Rom. 6:3-4) and the Eucharist (1 Cor. 11:23-26) all focus on the meaning of Christ's death. One of these meanings was that his death was an expiation at the cost of his blood (Rom. 3:25-26). Paul proclaimed that Christ's death was voluntary (Gal. 1:4; see 2:20 and 2 Cor. 5:14-15), and he coordinated the confession of Christ's saving death with an anthropology that emphasized believers suffering and dying with Christ (2 Cor. 1:5-6).[5] If we imagine Christians in Antioch, Ephesus, Corinth, or Rome reading manuscripts of the Greek Bible (LXX) in their houses, this essay asks what domestic pictures they would be seeing. I assume that the interpretation of the biblical texts would have been influenced consciously or unconsciously by the visual representations valued in Greco-Roman domestic culture.

Would Jews too have seen such visual representations? During Paul's lifetime, most Jews in Israel did not have figurative art in their homes, but there were exceptions. When Josephus was sent to Galilee in 66 C.E., just before the war with Rome, he informed the leaders of Tiberias that he "had been commissioned by the Jerusalem assembly to press for the demolition of the palace erected by Herod the tetrarch, which contained representations of animals (ζῴων μορφὰς) — such a style of architecture being forbidden by the laws" (*Vita* 64-65, trans. Thackeray in Loeb).[6]

---

4. I owe this precise wording to John R. Clarke (personal letter, April 2002). See his *The Houses of Roman Italy, 100 B.C.–A.D. 250: Ritual, Space, and Decoration* (Berkeley: University of California Press, 1991). Bettina Bergmann, "The Roman House as Memory Theater: The House of the Tragic Poet in Pompeii," *Art Bulletin* 76, no. 2 (1994): 225-56, at 249: "In the Roman world, tragic myth pervaded the very heart of family life, the *domus*." On the following Pauline references, see Sam K. Williams, *Jesus' Death as Saving Event: The Background and Origin of a Concept*, HTRHDR 2 (Missoula: Scholars, 1975), pp. 31, 47; he compares 2 Macc. 6:14 and 4 Macc. 6:29.

5. See Ernst Käsemann, "On Paul's Anthropology," in his *Pauline Perspectives*, trans. Margaret Kohl (Philadelphia: Fortress, 1971), pp. 1-31.

6. See Lee I. Levine, *Judaism and Hellenism in Antiquity: Conflict or Confluence?* (Peabody, Mass.: Hendrickson, 1998), pp. 56-58, on Josephus, *Antiquitates Judaicae* 15.267-79.

In the early third century c.e. at Beth-She'arim in lower Galilee, Rabbi Judah I was buried in catacombs that exhibit representational art.[7] But already in the first century c.e., Greco-Roman domestic culture in the form of a peristyle house with Romano-Campanian frescoes had invaded Jerusalem.[8] Animals were depicted in houses of the Herodian period in Sepphoris as well as on Mount Zion and in the Jewish Quarter of Jerusalem.[9] A late first century c.e. inscription, dated probably between 60 and 80, from a synagogue in Phrygia (Asia Minor), refers to an "edifice" (*oikos*, l. 1) constructed by Julia Severa.[10] The edifice was renovated probably by the early second century by the Jewish leaders Publius Tyrronios Clados, *archisynagogos* for life; Lucius the son of Lucius, *archisynagogos;* and Popilios Zoticos, archon. A portion of the inscription reads: "They have decorated the walls and the ceiling *(egrapsan tous toichous kai ten orophen)*, and they made the security of the gates and all the rest of the decoration *(panta kosmon)*" (ll. 7-8, 10).[11] The Jewish author of "Pseudo-Phocylides" (ll. 3-8), written perhaps in Syria, begins moral exhortations with the Ten Commandments, but the prohibition of images disappears![12] The Jewish Christian Gospel of Matthew (22:20), also written in Syria, allows the use of coins with human "images." In the first century c.e., some Jews in Antioch and Jerusalem began accepting the artistic depiction of animals in houses and palaces and of humans on coins; in the second century they represented animals and humans in their rabbis' burial caves. More obviously, when Paul converted Gentile households, they would have had frescoes on their domestic walls.

In Galatians 3:1 Paul exclaims, "You foolish Galatians! Who has bewitched you? It was before your eyes that Jesus Christ was publicly exhibited

7. Levine, *Judaism and Hellenism,* chap. 4, and Levine, "Beth-She'arim," in *Oxford Encyclopedia of Archaeology in the Near East,* ed. Eric M. Meyers (New York: Oxford University Press, 1997), 1:311.

8. L. A. Roussin, "Mosaics," in *Oxford Encyclopedia of Archaeology in the Near East,* 4:51. Nahman Avigad, "Jerusalem," in *NEAEHL,* 2:730-34, p. 734 for the House of Columns.

9. Silvia Rozenberg, "The Absence of Figurative Motifs in Herodian Wall Painting," in *I Temi Figurativi nella Pittura Parietale Antica (IV sec. a.C.–IV sec. d.C.),* ed. D. S. Corlàita (Bologna: University Press, 1997), pp. 283-85, 415-16, at 284.

10. See the text with discussion in L. Michael White, *The Social Origins of Christian Architecture,* vol. 2, *Texts and Monuments for the Christian Domus Ecclesiae in Its Environment,* HTS 42 (Valley Forge, Pa.: Trinity Press International, 1997), pp. 307-9 nn. 45-46.

11. Louis H. Feldman, *Studies in Hellenistic Judaism,* AGJU 30 (Leiden: Brill, 1996), p. 582, translates: "and they donated the (painted) murals for the walls and the ceiling, . . . and made all the rest of the ornamentation."

12. John M. G. Barclay, *Jews in the Mediterranean Diaspora: From Alexander to Trajan (323 BCE–117 CE)* (Edinburgh: T. & T. Clark, 1996), pp. 341-42.

(προεγράφη) as crucified!" (NRSV).[13] Paul portrayed Christ crucified by his preached words and deeds (see 2 Cor. 13:4; Gal. 6:17). Speakers sketching word pictures in houses that had beautiful frescoes on their walls was common. Lucian,[14] while speaking in such a house, says a beautiful house excites the speaker, that "something of beauty flows through the eyes into the soul," then into the words; and the painter of such word pictures has Euripides or Sophocles as a model (*De domo* [περὶ τοῦ οἴκου] 4, 6, 13, and 23, trans. Harmon in Loeb).

Lucian ("Essays in Portraiture" [Εἰκόνες] 4, trans. Harmon in Loeb) paints a verbal picture of the emperor Verus's mistress, Panathea of Smyrna, comparing her, for example, to Alcamenes' Athenian Aphrodite (the Venus Genetrix). He thinks "Homer . . . the best of all painters" (τὸν ἄριστον τῶν γραφέων Ὅμηρον; 8). Lucian compares Panthea with Aspasia, the consort of Pericles, who was painted (γραφεῖς) by Aeschines, the friend of Socrates, who painted (ἐγέγραπτο) on a small canvas, but Lucian says his figure is colossal (17). He compares her to Theano, Sappho, and Diotima (18), and Lycinus says, "paint (γράφου) more of them!" (19). Lucian's word picture is painting. Lucian summarizes, "I painted (ἐγραψάμην) her soul, not made of wood and wax and colors, but portrayed with inspirations from the Muses" (23).

Persons who lived in Greco-Roman houses outside Israel in the first century C.E. would typically have *seen* tragic stories on their walls. At the conclusion of his insightful fourth chapter on salvific death in Greek literature, Williams cites modern scholars who document the influence of Aeschylus and especially Euripides on literature four or five centuries later.[15] But we do not have to guess which stories Greeks and Romans, including Christian Gentiles, valued; in Pompeii we can still see which ones they chose to have painted on the walls of their houses. In the first and most of the second century, Christians did not build church buildings;[16] rather they lived and worshiped in the same

13. Compare Hans Dieter Betz, *Galatians,* Hermeneia (Philadelphia: Fortress, 1979), pp. 131-32, and contrast B. S. Davis, "The Meaning of προεγράφη in the Context of Galatians 3.1," *NTS* 45, no. 2 (1999): 194-212.

14. Christiane Reitz and Ulrike Egelhaaf, "Ekphrasis," *Der Neue Pauly,* ed. H. Cancik et al., 3 (1997): 942-50, 946 on Lucian and Vergil. See Ann Vasaly, *Representations: Images of the World in Ciceronian Oratory* (Berkeley: University of California Press, 1993), a reference for which I thank Beryl Rawson. Also Karl Lehmann-Hartleben, "The *Imagines* of the Elder Philostratus," *Art Bulletin* 23 (1941): 16-44, and Jas Elsner, *Art and the Roman Viewer* (Cambridge: Cambridge University Press, 1995), chap. 1, two references for which I thank John R. Clarke, whose *Art in the Lives of Ordinary Romans: Visual Representation and Non-Elite Viewers in Italy, 100 B.C.–A.D. 315* (Berkeley: University of California Press) will be published in 2003.

15. Williams, p. 159 nn. 41 and 42.

16. See White, pp. 210-11, on the oldest Christian church buildings.

houses in which they had lived before they were converted. What would Paul's word picture of Christ crucified have looked like, and would some Greco-Roman domestic paintings and sculptures have helped make his gospel comprehensible?

Iphigenia

Iphigenia at Aulis is Euripides' final extant tragedy and was presented in 405 B.C.E. Earlier (414-412) he had written *Iphigenia in Tauris*.[17] In Euripides' earlier play, Iphigenia rejects death, not being willing to become a sacrifice, but in his final tragedy she willingly gives herself for her country. Assembled to sail against Troy, the Greek fleet was becalmed at Aulis. The seer Calchas informed them that Artemis was angry (89-93), and that only by sacrificing Agamemnon's eldest daughter, Iphigenia, would the fleet be able to set sail and capture Troy. Through the play Agamemnon vacillates, but Iphigenia willingly sacrifices her body for Greece, bowing to the will of the gods. Her mother, Clytemnestra, asks Achilles: "will he [Agamemnon] drag her away by force if she is unwilling (οὐχ ἑκοῦσαν) to go?" (1365, trans. Morwood). Iphigenia, however, affirms, "I have made the decision to die" (1375) for "the overthrow of the Phrygians"; "and if the barbarians try to seize our women from happy Greece in the future, it lies with me to stop them" (1379-81).

> If Artemis has decided to take my body (ἐβουλήθη τὸ σῶμα) am I, a mere mortal, to oppose the goddess? . . . I give my body to Greece. Sacrifice me (θύετ') and sack Troy. . . . It is right that Greeks should rule barbarians, mother, and not barbarians Greeks. For they are slaves and we are free (τὸ μὲν γὰρ δοῦλον, οἵ δ' ἐλεύθεροι) (1395-1401). . . . Allow me to save Greece (σῶσαι) (1420), . . . the benefactor of Greece (1447), . . . for the sake of Greece (ὑπὲρ γῆς Ἑλλάδος) (1456). You brought me up to be a light for Greece. It causes me no regret that I die (θανοῦσα δ' οὐκ ἀναίνομαι) (1502-3).

At the conclusion of the present play a messenger goes to Clytemnestra to inform her of the final event (1532-1629). Many scholars doubt the genuineness of the ending and debate when it was added and by whom, but the visual tradition

17. Emanuel Löwy, "Der Schluss der Iphigenie in Aulis," *Jahreshefte des Österreichischen Archäologischen Instituts in Wien* 24 (1929): 1-41, at 34 n. 1. Quotations are from *Euripides, Iphigenia among the Taurians, Bacchae, Iphigenia at Aulis, Rhesus*, trans. James Morwood (Oxford: Oxford University Press, 1999); text ed. by F. Jouan in Budé (1993). The parenthetical numbers in the text refer to lines in the play.

with which I am concerned focuses on these lines, so I quote some of the messenger's words.

> And when King Agamemnon saw the girl coming into the grove to be slain, he groaned loudly, turned his head away from her and burst into tears, pulling his robe in front of his eyes. But she stood near to her father and said . . . "I gladly give my body for my fatherland (σῶμα τῆς ἐμῆς ὑπὲρ πάτρας) and for the whole land of Greece. Lead me to the altar of the goddess . . . and sacrifice me (ὕπερ θῦσαι δίδωμ' ἑκοῦσα). . . . Therefore let no Greek lay a hand on me. I shall offer my neck with a brave heart in silence." (1547-60)

> And the seer Calchas drew a sharp sword from its scabbard, . . . and put a garland round the girl's head. . . . The priest took the knife, uttered his prayer and looked at her throat to see where he should strike. As for myself, a great anguish began to lay hold on my heart. . . . But suddenly there was a wonder (θαῦμα) to behold. Everyone would have heard the thud of the blow clearly, but the girl had sunk into the ground, nobody knows where. (1566-83)

Artemis herself supplied a substitute, a mountain deer, whose blood she accepted. But Clytemnestra's child lives among the gods (1609, 1612, 1622). Artemis removed her to Tauris, where she was a priestess for the goddess.

After Euripides died, there was a competition to paint Iphigenia. Timanthes won over Colotes, and his picture is described by later authors: "The artist had depicted an expression of grief on the face of Calchas and of still greater grief on that of Ulysses, while he had given Menelaus an agony of sorrow beyond which his art could not go. Having exhausted his powers of emotional expression he was at a loss to portray the father's face as it deserved, and solved the problem by veiling his head and leaving his sorrow to the imagination of the spectator" (Quintilian, *Institutio oratoria* 2.13.13, trans. Butler in Loeb; see Cicero, *Orator ad M. Brutum* 22.74).

Löwy argues that Timanthes' painting is the source of the interpolated conclusion of the present play, since the two are so similar:[18] in the conclusion to the play and in the painting, Agamemnon is veiled.

Like the textual tradition, the visual tradition presents both an unwilling and a willing Iphigenia; in the first she is carried to the altar in the arms of two men, in the second she stands alone on her own feet.[19] In Aeschylus's play *Aga-*

---

18. Löwy, pp. 20, 33, 38-39.

19. Stefano De Caro, "Ifigenia in Aulide su una Brocca Fittile da Pompei," *Bollettino d'Arte* 23 (1984): 39-50, at 42, and Lilly Kahil and Pascale Lilant De Bellefonds, "Iphigeneia," in *LIMC* 5.1.717, 720, 726-27, fig. 40 and #64; also 5.2, p. 473, figs. 41-42.

memnon, "Iphigenia is sacrificed to Artemis; there is no mention of the story . . . that at the last minute the sacrifice was averted; and years later Klytemnestra will assume her daughter to have perished."[20] The postbiblical Jewish tradition of the sacrifice of Isaac on Mount Moriah exhibits the same ambiguity. Genesis 22, like Euripides' tragedy, has God substitute an animal for Isaac at the last minute; despite the biblical story, however, Jews developed a midrash that Isaac died — voluntarily sacrificing himself.[21] In the second century B.C.E. Jewish martyrs refused to understand themselves simply as victims of their Hellenizing persecutors. Rather they willingly gave themselves as martyrs "for the law" (2 Macc. 6:28; 7:9, 23, 37), and they revised the biblical story of Isaac accordingly.

Both Euripides' tragedy and the Jewish midrash are similar to Christian baptismal, eucharistic, and theological language: Jesus willingly gives his body and blood as a sacrifice for us. Williams has already observed the textual similarities between Euripides and Paul. But this story was also known through domestic frescoes in Roman cities during the decades that Paul preached Christ crucified. The Iphigenia in Tauris was painted in Pompeii on the walls of the House of the Lyre Player (I 4,5.25),[22] in the House of Pinarius Cerialis (III 4,4),[23] the House of L. Caecilius Iucundus (V 1,26),[24] and the House of the Tragic Poet (VI 8,3.5).[25]

The painting in the House of the Lyre Player is in an exedra (35), the central picture on the east wall. The Popidius family that owned this house was in the service of Nero. The similarity between Iphigenia's brother, Orestes, and Nero in the painting has led to the hypothesis of direct imperial influence either on the painter or on the maker of the cartoon that was used as a model.[26] Nero

20. Hugh Lloyd-Jones, "Artemis and Iphigenia," *JHS* 103 (1983): 87-102, at 88.

21. See Jon D. Levenson, "The Rewritten Aqedah of Jewish Tradition," in *The Death and Resurrection of the Beloved Son: The Transformation of Child Sacrifice in Judaism and Christianity* (New Haven: Yale University Press, 1993), pp. 173-99.

22. Casa del Citarista, the central picture in exedra (35), inv. 9111 (*Pompei*, 1:117-77, at 134). See Joanne Berry, ed., *Unpeeling Pompeii: Studies in Region I of Pompeii*, Soprintendenza Archeologica di Pompei (Milan: Electa, 1998), pp. 27-39. Note: in the text above, I translate many non-English terms, e.g., *casa* by "house," but in the footnotes I do not.

23. Casa di Pinarius Cerialis (*Pompei*, 3:435-77, at 435, 461).

24. Casa di L. Cecilio Giocondo, in the tablino (i), inv. 111439 (*Pompei*, 3:574-620, at 589, fig. 2).

25. Casa del Poeta Tragico, in peristyle (10), inv. 9112 (*Pompei*, 4:527-603, at 552-53). The paintings in the House of the Tragic Poet date to the reign of Nero, or less likely, to the reign of Vespasian (Bergmann, pp. 228 n. 15, 248 n. 48). On the varied, gendered meanings of Iphigenia for Roman viewers, see Bergmann, pp. 249-51, 54: she is the cause and cost of war, an exposed woman, and she died to save others; competition for women can rupture male bonds (Homer, *Iliad* 19.56-60, 86-94), and she is an allegory of the bride. The altar in this fresco means that her father, King Agamemnon, perpetrates impious family worship.

26. *Pompei*, 1:118.

sang of "Orestes the matricide" (Suetonius, *Nero* 21.4; 39.2; 46.1): both killed their mothers. The dimensions of the picture (2 × 3 meters) are exceptional in Campanian painting and may be modeled after the style developed for the House of Augustus on the Palatine.

Löwy sees no resistance in the Iphigenia of the House of the Tragic Poet, understanding her rather as a martyr already looking for her salvation to Artemis, whom the painter has pictured among the clouds with the animal that will be her substitute (see plate 5).[27] However, Kahil and De Bellefonds observe that this pose, Iphigenia carried by two men while raising her arms to heaven, is exactly that of earlier Etruscan urns belonging to the tradition in which she does not consent.[28]

In 1835 Zahn sketched a picture of Iphigenia at Aulis that he found in a room near the House of Modesto (see plate 6).[29] He described the painting: "The background of the painting is black. Iphigenia wears a green garment with a violet trim; she has brown hair and gold earrings. She appears to have a branch in her right hand. The priest Calchas wears a bright red, short skirt, the lower part of which has blue trim. A sorrowful Achilles sits to Iphigenia's left, veiled by a red garment. The lance point of Achilles and the sacrificial knife of the priest are steel blue." Löwy corrects Zahn's identification: the veiled figure is not Achilles but rather Agamemnon.[30] And the authors of *Pompei* reverse the right and left sides of the painting; that is, Agamemnon is on the viewer's right and Calchas on the left.[31] Perhaps the printers reversed Zahn's drawing. M. de Vos found the picture in the National Archaeological Museum in Naples, which enabled the authors of *Pompei* to print it correctly.

Iphigenia stands on her own feet, not carried by anyone, while the priest Calchas cuts a lock of her hair with the sacrificial knife against the background to the viewer's right of Artemis's temple. When Paul preached Christ crucified, who willingly died for us, some of his auditors may well have been familiar with this visual representation; both he and they could even have been viewing it while Paul preached. In this respect the cultural/religious gap between Paul and his Greco-Roman auditors was not wide. The voluntary, sacrificial deaths of Iphigenia, Isaac, and Christ are strikingly similar.

27. Löwy, pp. 32, 41.

28. Kahil and De Bellefonds, p. 726.

29. Zahn II.61. *Pompei*, 4:342-44, places the Casa di Modesto at VI 5,13, some distance from the room (VI 5,2) where this painting has traditionally been located.

30. Löwy, p. 6.

31. *Pompei*, 4:290-93, figs. 5 and 6, the room located in Pompeii at VI 5,2 (nameless); however, the authors are not certain that this picture was found in this room, nor are they sure to what house the room belonged.

Figure 1. House of the emperor Titus, Rome: sculpture of the priest, Laocoon,
with snakes coiled around him and his two sons, sculpted by Hagesander,
Polydorus and Athanodorus of Rhodes. Now in the Belvedere Court
of the Vatican Museum, Rome.

Laocoon

In 1506, in the presence of Michelangelo himself, the sculpture *Laocoon* was discovered. The ancient sculptors' tragic presentation of human suffering, the
classic *exemplum doloris,* became the most celebrated statue of the Renaissance
(see fig. 1).[32] Giuliano da Sangallo at once recognized the statue as the one

32. Bernard Andreae, *Laocoon und die Gründung Roms,* Kulturgeschichte der Antiken Welt
39 (Mainz: Philipp von Zabern, 1988), pp. 13, 23. With its emphasis on the human body, a new

praised by Pliny,[33] who judged it preferable to all other paintings and sculptures:

> because [when there are two or more sculptors] no individual monopolizes the credit nor again can several of them be named on equal terms. This is the case with the Laocoon in the palace of Emperor Titus, a work superior to any painting and any bronze. Laocoon, his children and the wonderful clasping coils of the snakes were carved from a single block *(ex uno lapide)* in accordance with an agreed plan *(de consilii sententia)* by those eminent craftsmen Hagesander, Polydorus and Athanodorus, all of Rhodes. (*Naturalis historia* 36.37-38, trans. Erichholz in Loeb)

This great sculpture, now in the Belvedere Court in the Vatican Museum, dominates the modern understanding of the story. Scholars debate its date, who the sculptors were that created it, and whether it is an original or a copy. *Laocoon* was also painted in the House of Menander (I 10,4)[34] and in the House of the Laocoon (VI 14,28.33)[35] in Pompeii. I will summarize discussions of the sculpture without pretending to decide issues that have been debated for five centuries, then focus on the domestic paintings.

Vergil (*Aeneid* 2.40-56, 199-231) tells the story. The Greeks attacking Troy under Agamemnon apparently gave up the fight and sailed away, leaving a wooden horse as an offering. The priest of Apollo, Laocoon, did not want to recognize that the gods had decided on the fall of Troy and its rebirth in a newly founded Rome. He warned the Trojans against the wooden horse; therefore, the gods made the priest himself an offering. Athena sent her snakes over the ocean, who attacked the priest and his two sons. Versions differ about whom they killed — all three, the father and one son, or both sons — but the Trojans interpreted their deaths as punishment of the priest. They tore a hole in their city wall and hauled the horse into Troy. The prophet Cassandra, daughter of the king of Troy, Priam, also fought against bringing the wooden horse into the city, saying it was full of warriors. But as fated, no one believed her prophecy. Odysseus[36] and his

---

interest over against the Middle Ages, the *Laocoon* sculpture fascinated Renaissance culture. Paul too focused on the body (e.g., Gal. 6:17; 2 Cor. 4:10).

33. Andreae, *Gründung Roms*, pp. 33-34.

34. Casa del Menandro (I 10,4), the picture in ala (4), the central fresco on the south wall, with two related pictures on the east and north walls (*Pompei*, 2:240-397, at 285, fig. 68). See Berry, pp. 22-25, and John R. Clarke, *The Houses of Roman Italy, 100 B.C.-A.D. 250* (Berkeley: University of California Press, 1991), esp. pp. 14-16, 170-94.

35. Casa di Laocoonte (*Pompei*, 5:341-62, at 352-53, fig. 16, inv. 111210). A picture of Polyphemus and Aeneas is in the next room, the *tablinum*, inv. 111211.

36. One may read Homer's stories of Odysseus for an example of growing wise by endur-

Greeks inside the horse were then able to burn the city, but the Trojan Aeneas, following the will of the gods, fled the burning city and founded a new Troy in Italy — Rome.

The story was promoted by Julius Caesar, Augustus Caesar, and Vergil, but not only by the political and literary elite in Rome. The National Archaeological Museum in Naples exhibits a statuette of Aeneas, Anchises, and Ascanius from Pompeii.[37] De Caro writes that it may derive from a traditional pictorial pattern: Aeneas carries his father, who holds a reliquary containing the Penates, and with his right hand he leads his son. It may have been a trinket, or perhaps an element in a *lararium* in the house of a Pompeiian who cherished traditions of the Julio-Claudian period. Zanker observes that "images such as that of Aeneas were well nigh ubiquitous in Roman cities during the Early Empire."[38] It was so well known even in small towns that it could be caricatured for comic effect with an expectation that the joke would be understood. Zanker prints an image of these same three characters, Aeneas carrying his father and leading his son, painted on a villa wall at Gragnano near Pompeii (see plate 7).[39] The caricature pictures three long bodies of monkeys who have short legs and the heads of dogs; both Aeneas and his son are pictured with long penises.[40]

Andreae argues that the three sculptors of the marble statue named by Pliny worked in the time of Tiberius Caesar. They copied an earlier bronze original by Phyromachus, whose original sculpture had been commissioned by the Attalid king of Pergamon in Asia Minor, Eumenes II (197-159 B.C.E.).[41] Simon argues rather for a date under Nero or Vespasian.[42] A third scholar, Kunze, insists against Andreae that the marble group in the Vatican is the original of the sculpture to which Pliny refers, and he dates it to 30-20 B.C.E., earlier than

---

ing suffering without being overwhelmed (Horace, *Epistle* 1.2.18-22), a reference for which I thank A. Wallace-Hadrill.

37. De Caro 271. F. Canciani, "Aineias," in *LIMC* 1.2.303, #96, exhibits a similar figure from Rome.

38. Paul Zanker, "Augustan Political Symbolism in the Private Sphere," in *Image and Mystery in the Roman World: Papers Given in Memory of Jocelyn Toynbee* (Gloucester, 1988), p. 1.

39. Paul Zanker, "Immagini come Vincolo: Il Simbolismo Politico Augusteo nella Sfera Privata," in *Roma: Romolo, Remo e la fondazione della città. Roma, Museo Nazionale Romano* (Milan: Electa, 2000), pp. 84-91, fig. on p. 85, inv. 9089, first century C.E.

40. See Otto J. Brendel, "Der Affen-Aeneas," *RM* 60-61 (1953-54): 153-59, with Taf. 61. Brendel (p. 153) notes other caricatures in Pompeii, e.g., of pygmies in Nile landscapes.

41. Andreae, *Gründung Roms*, and *Laocoon und die Kunst von Pergamon: die Hybris der Giganten* (Frankfurt: Fischer Taschenbuch, 1992).

42. Erika Simon, "Laokoon und die Geschichte der Antiken Kunst," *Archäologischer Anzeiger* (1984): 643-72 with Abb. 1-21, and "Laokoon," *LIMC* 6.1, 196-201, and 6.2, 94-95.

Andreae.[43] The two Pompeiian paintings (late third and fourth style), on the other hand, were generated by Vergil's text published in 19 B.C.E. The one in the House of Menander follows Vergil (*Aeneid* 2.220) in placing the snake above the head of the Laocoon, and the painter in the House of Laocoon reflects Vergil's description of the older son (2.202, 213-15). But the marble group does not assume Vergil, since it is only loosely connected with the flight of Aeneas from Troy.

Salvatore Settis examines inscriptions concerning Hagesander and his father's sculptural workshop and concludes that they were active in Rhodes in 50-40 B.C.E.[44] He concludes that the *Laocoon* must have been sculpted not in Rhodes but in a shop in Italy between 40 and 20 B.C.E.,[45] a judgment concerning the date that he shares with R. R. R. Smith. As Smith has observed, these baroque figures are a "disturbing" presence in the calm, sovereign world of Augustan art.[46] Settis contrasts another sculptural school, that of Pasiteles and Stephanus, with the baroque sculpture *Laocoon*. Stephanus created an athlete in neoclassical style, a sculpture dated 40-30 B.C.E., that is, contemporary with Settis's dating of *Laocoon*.[47] He also contrasts the contemporary portraits of Caesar and Pompey, political rivals in the 50s B.C.E. The portrait of Pompey imitates Alexander the Great, emphasizing pathos, while that of Caesar emphasizes control. There was a conflict of styles in the mid–first century; one emphasized and the other de-emphasized pathos.[48] The *Laocoon* sculpture is "neo-Pergamonic"; the athlete of Stephanus is "neo-Attic." The marble *Laocoon* presupposes the art of Pergamon, specifically the Pergamon Altar and the battle between Athena and the giant Alcyoneus.[49] There was a similar contrast in the rhetoric of the period. Demetrius, *On Style* 36, distinguishes four styles: simple, grand, elegant, and powerful. These may all be combined, except that the grand and the simple styles exclude each other. Settis describes the *Laocoon* as grand, the athlete of Stephanus as simple. The portrait of Pompey is powerful and elegant; the portrait of Caesar is simple and powerful.[50] Against prevailing categories, however, Settis asserts that Augustan style included all these elements, including the Pergamene.[51]

---

43. Christian Kunze, "Zur Datierung des Laokoon und der Skyllagruppe aus Sperlonga," in *Jahrbuch des Deutschen Archäologischen Instituts* 111 (1996): 183-84, 221.

44. Salvatore Settis, *Laocoonte: Fama e stile* (Rome: Donzelli, 1999), pp. 29-41.

45. Settis, p. 50.

46. Settis, p. 56, citing R. R. R. Smith in *JRS* 79 (1989): 215.

47. Settis, pp. 56-60.

48. Settis, p. 61.

49. Settis, pp. 62, 72, as argued by Andreae.

50. Settis, p. 63. See Andrew Wallace-Hadrill in *JRS* 79 (1989): 157-64.

51. Settis, p. 62.

The domestic paintings are interpreted by Schefold,[52] Maiuri,[53] the *Enciclopedia Italiana*,[54] and Settis. Schefold observes that of all the Greek sagas, the Trojan War became the most important for the Romans: the Trojan Aeneas became the father of Rome. For second-style painting, scenes of Troy, that is, of conflict, were characteristic, as Vitruvius noted (7.5.3). These disappeared in the third and fourth styles, for which youth and love become dominant values, a change Schefold regarded as a decline *(Verarmung)*.[55] These scenes return in the late fourth, the Vespasianic style. In the House of the Criptoporticus (I 6,2) there is a series of eighty-three scenes, seventy-five of which are from the *Iliad*. The final one is the flight of Aeneas with his father and son from Troy.[56] The choice of visual representations and their order corresponds with that of the Iliad Tablets.[57] This correspondence assumes a tradition of such pictures in schoolbooks, although the painter in the House of the Cryptoporticus used a picture book from the time of Alexander that recalls the Alexander mosaic in the House of the Faun (VI 12,2). The Cryptoporticus series emphasizes Cassandra's warning against the wooden horse, probably balanced on the left end of the series by a Laocoon where there is room for three to five more pictures.[58] The Hellenistic poet pseudo-Lycophron (*Alexandra* 1226-82), Vergil (*Aeneid* 2.246-47), and Horace (*Ode* 3.3) all have Cassandra prophesy not only the fall of Troy, but also the future greatness of Aeneas's descendants, as long as they do not degenerate into the ancient impiety of Troy.[59] Romans loved visual representations of the prophet Cassandra, for example, in the House of the Five Skeletons (VI 10,2) and in Nero's Golden House, flanked by Hector and

---

52. Karl Schefold, "Die Troiasage in Pompeji," *Nederlands Kunsthistorisch Jaarboek* 5 (1954): 211-24.

53. Amedeo Maiuri, *La Casa del Menandro e il suo Tesoro di Argenteria*, 2 vols. (Rome: La Libreria dello Stato, 1933), 1:39-52, and vol. 2, pls. IV, V. The three paintings are still in situ. See Roger Ling, "The Insula of the Menander at Pompeii: Interim Report," *Antiquaries Journal* 63 (1983): 34-57, pls. V-XII and figs. 1-12.

54. *Pompei*, 2:276-85.

55. Schefold, "Troiasage," p. 219.

56. See *Pompei*, 1:193-277 and 280-329, the second-style paintings at 201-22, figs. 13-46, including fig. 46 of Aeneas's flight from Troy; the fourth-style reliefs of the *Iliad*, bks. 22-24, at pp. 296-305, figs. 20-43. See Richard Brilliant, *Visual Narratives: Storytelling in Etruscan and Roman Art* (Ithaca, N.Y.: Cornell University Press, 1984), pp. 61-65. Compare the series of perhaps one hundred panels discussed by Filippo Coarelli, "The Odyssey Frescos of the Via Graziosa: A Proposed Context," *PBSR* 66 (1998): 21-37.

57. Schefold, "Troiasage," p. 212. See Brilliant, pp. 54-60.

58. Schefold, "Troiasage," pp. 212, 215, 220-22.

59. Schefold, "Troiasage," pp. 220, 222. Other domestic pictures of Cassandra warning against the wooden horse: *Collezioni* 136-37, #90, inv. 8999; also 152-53, #208, inv. 9010.

Andromache.[60] She prophesied the theft of the Palladium, which had guaranteed the city's security, which Romans believed was later deposited in the temple of the Vestal Virgins in Rome. The corresponding male prophet is Laocoon, whose destiny was tied to Aeneas's, because Laocoon's death shocked Aeneas into realizing that Apollo willed the destruction of Troy.

It is no accident that the marble *Laocoon* group was created about 40 B.C.E., Schefold writes, when thoughts of the disintegration of Rome disturbed so many, and it is even more important that Nero gave this statue an important place in his Golden House. Nero composed a poem on the destruction of Troy that he performed in 64 C.E. while watching Rome and his own Domus Transitoria on the Palatine burn. The destruction of Troy/Rome was probably to be followed by a new golden age, presided over by the Lord of the Domus Aurea.[61]

I will briefly describe the three paintings in the House of Menander,[62] which are not simply illustrations, but three examples of perilous rebellion.[63] They are from the same cycle concerning the fall of Troy, have the same style and structure (quite small), and were certainly painted by the same artist.[64] They are very close to Vergil (*Aeneid* 2.201ff., 238ff., 246ff.), and probably reproduce manuscript illustrations of the epic poem.[65] The three paintings in ala (4) as well as those in the atrium and the *tablinum* are in the grand style, while others in the house are simpler; the three in ala (4) represent the beginning of the fourth style.[66]

Cassandra is the subject of the central picture (on the east wall; 62.5 × 62.5 cm.; see plate 8). On the right the wooden horse is on a cart to purify its feet. A person with a double flute announces the triumph of Troy, but Cassandra points out the fatal error. With one hand she pushes the horse, with the other she tries to tear open its stomach to reveal the deception. A portion of the city

---

60. Schefold, "Troiasage," p. 221. For one viewer's response, see Philostratus, *Imagines* 1.10: Cassandra.

61. Schefold, "Troiasage," pp. 222-23, citing A. von Salis, *Antike und Renaissance* (Zürich: Eugen Rentsch, 1947), p. 137.

62. See Maiuri, 1:39-52; also *Pompei*, 2:240-42, 276-85.

63. Schefold, "Troiasage," p. 222.

64. *Pompei*, 2:281.

65. *Pompei*, 2:277, 281, 284, citing Simon, p. 649, who calls these Pompeiian paintings the earliest illustrations of Vergil. Ling (personal e-mail) is less confident about illustrated texts of Vergil before 79 C.E.

66. *Pompei*, 2:240. Also Ling, "Interim Report," pp. 49, 52, who dates them between 50 and 62 C.E., the years during which the apostle Paul was active. But in *The Insula of the Menander at Pompeii: The Structures*, vol. 1 (Oxford: Clarendon, 1997), p. 56, Ling is inclined to date the atrium and ala paintings after 62 C.E.

wall above has been breached to admit the wooden horse. Above is also the temple of Athena, enclosed by an ample porch and approached by a frontal stairway; priests are inside the temple.

The *Death of the Laocoon* (on the south wall; 64 × 67.5 cm.; see plates 9 and 10) is the painting that has deteriorated the most. It has two planes. In the center is Laocoon as a priest with his head encircled by a white wreath and with a snake wrapped around his right, raised arm looking him in the face. One knee is bent and rests on the altar. Immediately to his left, the bull destined for sacrifice has already been wounded by the sacrificial ax and is bleeding; he forcefully runs away from the two snakes. Below, the sacred bronze table has been overturned; there is a metal vase, and there are two other objects, perhaps cymbals. At the bottom of the picture are the two sons of Laocoon, also victims of the wrath of Athena, one already dead, lying on the ground with his adolescent face turned up. The other son, nude, has his knee on the ground and, like his father, is being attacked by a snake while trying to flee. Above there are two distinct groups of spectators or servants of the cult with the Phrygian cap, four above the bull and three on Laocoon's left behind a podium. One of the three raises his hand in terror. Further above are the wall of the city and the figures of an old man and a woman. The old man, perhaps Priam, has a Phrygian cap and a bandaged chin; he raises his right hand in terror at the sight of this monstrous prodigy. This painting is quite similar to one of the same subject in the House of the Laocoon.

The *Night of Troy* (on the north wall; 63.5 × 70 cm.; see plate 11) has two episodes in one painting: the violent capture of Cassandra and the first dramatic encounter of Menelaus with the adulterous Helen. On the viewer's right, Aias or Odysseus aggressively seizes Cassandra as she holds the Palladium with her left hand (Vergil, *Aeneid* 2.402ff.). On the viewer's left, Menelaus in armor seizes Helen's hair, who is nude and defends herself with her hands. Priam, between Cassandra and Helen, seems to be the center of the painting.[67] There is some dissonance between the original myth and this melodramatic, Roman, anecdotal elaboration.

Settis notes that the marble sculpture of the Laocoon made such an impact after 1506 that it obscured every other representation of the story.[68] Before contrasting the different versions, Settis adds a relief from Gandahra, emphasizes Petronius's story (*Satyricon* 89) of Laocoon in front of the wooden horse, recalls the illustration of a Vatican manuscript of Vergil that is similar to the Pompeiian paintings, and adds two fragments of a relief in terra-cotta from

---

67. *Pompei*, 2:227.
68. Settis, p. 66.

Tarsus.[69] Two terra-cotta fragments from Tarsus are in the Louvre and probably belong to a Laocoon group. Since this paper concerns Paul, it is intriguing that there are fragments of the Laocoon group from his birthplace. Settis's additional illustrations generally represent Cassandra and Laocoon in the context of the fall of Troy, as does the painting in the House of Menander. Here the female and male prophets are iconographic synonyms. When the story of Laocoon is presented, methodologically one could substitute Cassandra before an altar. An iconographic formula they have in common is a bent knee pointing to an altar. In the House of Menander, the artist used this formula both for Laocoon and for Cassandra before the Palladium, a pathos formula, in which one takes refuge before an altar.[70] Often the other leg is tense, and the person raises an impotent hand to heaven.

Therefore, the marble *Laocoon* of Athanodorus, Hagesander, and Polydorus is an exception. Their Laocoon takes refuge on the altar and nearly collapses in the extreme tension of his defense. His right knee is bent but does not point to the altar; rather he is virtually seated. In his passion, terror, and death, that right knee, although marble, seems to move with the twisted body. The three sculptors have created a variation of the story that differs from other presentations, especially in that it is only loosely related to the fall of Troy. The father grieves impotently, seeing his two sons threatened. The clients for such a sculpture of vibrant, nervous passion, of such explosive tension, in the last half of the first century B.C.E., would have been Pompey and Mark Anthony.[71] Augustan classicism rendered such passion marginal, except, of course, that the emperor Tiberius (may have) owned such sculptures at Sperlonga, Nero stole some for his Golden House (see below), and Titus had exactly this neo-Pergamene work in his house. For the subject of this article, the later history of the *Laocoon* group is more important even than the debate about its origin. Its later history is or may have been entwined with another group, the *Dying Galatians*.

The *Dying Galatians*

I include the *Dying Galatians* in this paper on domestic pictures for two reasons. First, the visual representation of defeated enemies is common in Roman iconography. In Pompeii the *Triumph of Dionysus* is painted on the triclinium

---

69. Settis, pp. 67, 70, with pls. 31, 36-37, 40-41, 45.
70. Settis, p. 68.
71. Settis, p. 75.

wall (16) of the House of Marcus Lucretius (IX 3,5.24).[72] An enemy prisoner, his hands tied behind his back, sits on the shield that had been taken from him. These are elements of Hellenistic victory iconography represented in Roman imperial art, for example, in the *Sebasteion* at Aphrodisias, which celebrates the Caesars as conquerors of the provinces, typically represented as women. In Pompeii the scene is painted on a dining room wall.

Second, Nero stole sculptures of the dying Galatians for his Domus Aurea (an unusual *domus,* but for the purposes of this paper, still a "house"),[73] as Pliny reports (*Naturalis historia* 34.84).[74] This is confirmed by Dio Chrysostom (*Orationes* 31.148) and Pausanias (10.7.1). Then Vespasian placed these statues in the Temple of Peace in his new forum, "an edifice erected to commemorate his victory over the Jews, the 'barbarians' assimilated from the Roman point of view to the Galatians."[75] Schefold and others (see nn. 61 and 73) think the marble *Laocoon* was also among the statues in Nero's Domus Aurea. The Jew Paul, who became a Christian, was martyred in this artistic/political context. But I return to the origin of the *Dying Galatians.*

Attalos I became the ruler of Pergamon after fighting the Syrian Seleucids and the invading Gauls/Galatians. To commemorate his victories, shortly after 223 B.C.E. he erected monuments in the sanctuary of Athena on the Acropolis, that included *Gaul Killing Himself and His Wife* (see fig. 2). The statue can be viewed from several directions.[76] Seen from the left, the Gaul glares at his enemy and seems to be drawing his wife close to him. From the front, however, his face is covered, vividly revealing his wound and that his powerful sword thrust is suicidal. He seems about to topple over his wife. Schalles says this reveals clas-

---

72. Casa di Marcus Lucretius, *in triclinio* (16) (*Pompei,* 9:141-313, at 261-63, figs. 178-79). On the *Sebasteion* at Aphrodisias see n. 93 below.

73. See Eric M. Moormann, "'Vivere come un uomo': L'Uso dello Spazio nella Domus Aurea," in *Horti Romani: Atti del Convegno Internazionale, Roma, 4-6 maggio 1995,* ed. Maddalena Cima and Eugenio La Rocca (Rome: "L'Erma" di Bretschneider, 1998), pp. 345-61. Moormann agrees (p. 357) with Coarelli's hypothesis that Nero placed both the *Dying Galatians* and the *Galatian Killing Himself and His Wife* in the Octagonal Room of the Golden House.

74. Cited by Filippo Coarelli, *Da Pergamo a Roma: I Galati nella città degli Attalidi* (Rome: Quasar, 1995), p. 15.

75. Coarelli, *Da Pergamo,* p. 16. See J. Packer, "Forum Traiani," in *LTUR,* 2:348-56 with fig. 116. The Galatian sculptures were created at the same time as the Maccabean revolt, and two centuries later they symbolically represent the defeat of the Jews. The sculpture *Galatian Killing Himself and His Wife* would have influenced Roman readers' understanding of Josephus's narration of the suicides at Masada (*Jewish War* 7.320-406). Did this sculpture also influence Josephus, who knew Vespasian's Temple of Peace (7.158-62), as he narrated the suicides?

76. See H.-J. Schalles, "Pergamon: Sculpture," in *Dictionary of Art,* ed. Jane Turner (New York: Grove Press, 1996), 24:413-16, at 413.

Figure 2. Sanctuary of Athena on the acropolis in Pergamon,
stolen by Nero for his Domus Aurea, then placed by Vespasian in
the Temple of Peace in his new forum: large sculpture of a Gaul
killing himself and his wife. Now in Palazzo Altemps, Rome.

sical views of the Galatians, their apparent courage, strength, and boldness, but
also their naïveté and stupidity, ultimately their lack of stamina. Greeks perceived an antithesis between their own cultured moderation and such barbarians, who since the fifth century had submitted to Greek genius and power.

After the final victory over the Gauls (168-165 B.C.E.), Eumenes II built the
biggest relief cycle known from antiquity, the Great Altar in Pergamon, now re-

constructed in the Berlin Museum. The Great Frieze depicts a gigantomachia, in which the gods, with the help of the mortal Hercules, suppress a revolt by giants, descendants of the earth mother Ge, preserving order and reason in the world. The Great Frieze then compares the gods and the giants with the Pergamenes and the Gauls: the Pergamene kings claimed descent from Hercules. In the east frieze, the first one to confront the viewer, Athena downs the giant Alcyoneus, whom Andreae has shown is a model for the Laocoon, who in pride also did not submit to Athena at Troy. Andreae insists that both sculptures exhibit not only suffering, fear, and tragedy, but also blindness against the will of the gods.[77]

The priest Laocoon died because he opposed the goddess Athena, who willed the destruction of Troy. Nero sang of the destruction of Troy while Rome burned (Suetonius, *Nero* 12.3; 21.1, 3; 38.2-3; Tacitus, *Annales* 15.39). Later he built the Domus Aurea, in which he placed the *Dying Galatians* and, according to some modern art historians, also the marble *Laocoon*. In this same time and place, Christians practiced a "pernicious superstition" according to Tacitus: "[The Christians] were covered with wild beasts' skins and torn to death by dogs; or they were fastened on crosses, and, when daylight failed were burned to serve as lamps by night. Nero had offered his Gardens for the spectacle and gave an exhibition in his Circus" (Tacitus, *Annales* 15.44, trans. Jackson in Loeb; see Suetonius, *Nero* 16.2).

Christians confessed a Lord other than Caesar or the Roman state,[78] which put them in conflict with the core value of Roman society.[79] Romans thought that Laocoon, the Galatians, and the Christians deserved to die, but this raises the question whether viewers had ambivalent reactions, for example, satisfaction that the priest Laocoon, who opposed the will of the gods, was punished, but perhaps also pity? Tacitus answers this question in relation to the Christians: "Hence, in spite of a guilt, which had earned the most exemplary punish-

77. Andreae, *Gründung Roms*, p. 210, which agrees with Schefold (see n. 63) and R. R. R. Smith, *Gnomon* 63 (1991): 356-57. See B. Knittlmayer and W.-D. Heilmeyer, eds., *Staatliche Museen zu Berlin: Die Antikensammlung. Altes Museum — Pergamonmuseum* (Mainz: Philipp von Zabern, 1998), pp. 232-75, esp. p. 244.

78. On conflicts between the earliest Christians and Rome, see Gerd Theissen, *The Gospels in Context: Social and Political History in the Synoptic Tradition*, trans. Linda M. Maloney (Minneapolis: Fortress, 1991), chaps. 3 (on Mark 13) and 5 (on Q, e.g., the temptation story in Matt. 4:1-11, with v. 9: "All these [kingdoms of the world] I will give you, if you will fall down and worship me").

79. See G. B. Conte, "Virgil's Aeneid," in his *The Rhetoric of Imitation: Genre and Poetic Memory in Virgil and Other Latin Poets*, trans. C. Segal (Ithaca, N.Y.: Cornell University Press, 1986), p. 144, who refers to "the supremacy of the state as an embodiment of the public good, with the acceptance of divine will as providential guidance."

ment, there arose a sentiment of pity, due to the impression that they were being sacrificed not for the welfare of the state but to the ferocity of a single man" (*Annales* 15.44).

The Crucifix on the Palatine

Some have suggested that the first visual representation of Christ dying on a cross that was actually drawn on a wall may be a graffito found on the Palatine Hill and now exhibited in the Palatine Museum (see fig. 3).[80] It sketches a man on a cross, who has the head of an ass. To the left is the sketch of a man who raises his left hand toward the figure on the cross, and a graffito under the two figures reads, "Alexamenos adores god" (ΑΛΕΞΑΜΕΝΟΣ ΣΕΒΕΤΕ[81] ΘΕΟΝ). Tertullian confirms (*Ad nationes* 1.114.1) that Christians were accused of worshiping a divinity with the head of an ass. There is a second graffito above and to the right of the crucified figure, a "Y," which has been interpreted as a moan; however, the Y is not part of the original graffito.[82] Tomei dates the image to the first half of the third century C.E.

Maser objects to the traditional interpretation: the graffito is supposed to show the Christian Alexamenos honoring the cultic image of the cross in the third century, but honoring such images began only in the fourth or fifth century.[83] Maser may or may not be right; some archaeologists have indeed wanted to attract tourists. He does make one incorrect assumption, that Christians must themselves have been honoring physical images before such a caricature could have been drawn. First, Lucian "wrote" oral word pictures of Panathea, when presumably no artist had painted her on a wall or sculpted her in marble. Second, caricature was popular in Pompeii, for example, of Augustus's ideology. In that case the caricaturist also painted animals, monkeys with the heads of dogs. The Pompeiian caricaturist was imitating physical images and paintings on walls, but Lucian was not. It would have been possible for a Roman soldier to caricature Christian word pictures of Christ crucified, as Paul said he

80. See Maria Antonietta Tomei, *Museo Palatino*, English ed. (Rome: Electa, 1997), pp. 104-5, #78: "the original interpretation . . . appears to be the most convincing: the author of the drawing makes fun of a Christian."

81. Instead of ΣΕΒΕΤΑΙ.

82. Heikki Solin and Marja Itkonen-Kaila, *Graffiti del Palatino,* Acta Instituti Romani Finlandiae 3 (Helsinki: Helsingfors, 1966), p. 211.

83. Peter Maser, "Das sogenannte Spottkruzifix vom Palatin: Ein 'frühchristliches' Denkmal im Widerstreit der Meinungen," *Das Altertum* 18 (1972): 248-54, with Abb. 1-2, here 250.

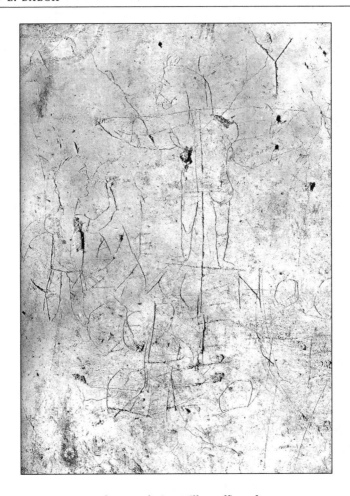

Figure 3. Barracks on Palatine Hill: graffito of man on cross
who has the head of an ass. To the lower left another man
raises his hand toward the figure on the cross. An inscription
under the two reads, "Alexamenos adores god."
Now in the Palatine Museum, Rome.

was "writing" (Gal. 3:1), without the soldier having seen them honoring physical images in their worship. It remains a possibility that this graffito caricatures the worship of Christ dying on a cross.[84]

84. See Robin Margaret Jensen, *Understanding Early Christian Art* (New York: Routledge, 2000), p. 131 with n. 2; 134 with n. 11, citing Thomas F. Mathews, *The Clash of Gods: A Reinterpretation of Early Christian Art* (Princeton: Princeton University Press, 1993), pp. 48-50 with fig. 33.

Conclusion: Comparisons and Contrasts

The thesis of this paper is that contemporary, domestic tragic art emphasizing pathos would have provided a meaningful cultural context, whether consciously or unconsciously assimilated, for understanding Paul's gospel of Christ's suffering and his saving death. When Paul portrayed Christ crucified in the earliest churches in Greco-Roman houses, his audience might well have been aware of and could even have been observing a painting on the wall of Iphigenia at Aulis. Both Iphigenia and Christ voluntarily gave their bodies as a sacrifice — for Greece (Euripides) or the ungodly (Paul). The powerful representation of Iphigenia, however, could also have led to misunderstanding: she died so that "Phrygians" and not Greeks would be slaves, whereas those (Galatians!) baptized in the early Pauline churches denied the value of such ethnic distinctions (Gal. 3:28).

The priest of Athena, Laocoon, died rebelling against her will; he opposed the destruction of Troy, which she had decreed. In the House of Menander the prophet Cassandra is an iconographic synonym of Laocoon: she too opposed the will of the gods and suffered the consequences (see Euripides, *Trojan Women*). Romans would most easily have understood the crucifixion of Christ and his disciples as legitimate punishments (Suetonius, *Nero* 16.2; Tacitus, *Annales* 15.44). For Christians, however, Jesus died not opposing but submitting to the will of God (e.g., Rom. 4:25; 8:32; compare Mark 14:36). Vergil and Nero, on the one hand, and Paul, on the other, had fundamentally different understandings of the meaning of human suffering and death as they relate to God(s), providence, and the Roman state.

The Pergamene king Eumenes II sponsored the sculpting of some of the most moving statues created in the Greco-Roman world, the *Dying Galatians*, in order to celebrate his victory[85] over those barbarians after decades of war. Julius Caesar had these statues copied for his gardens on the Esquiline Hill, Nero stole them for his Domus Aurea, and Vespasian placed them in the Temple of Peace in his new forum to celebrate his burning of Jerusalem. They symbolize the victory of the Olympian gods over the giants, of the Athenians over the Persians, of the Pergamene kings over the Gauls, of Vespasian over the Jews, and Schefold adds, of Stoic order over Eastern Isiac mysticism.[86] In crises Jews

---

85. Andreae, *Gründung Roms,* pp. 171, 214, emphasizes that Eumenes' goal was the Galatians' "annihilation."

86. Karl Schefold, *Der religiöse Gehalt der antiken Kunst und die Offenbarung,* Kulturgeschichte der Antiken Welt 78 (Mainz: Philipp von Zabern, 1998), pp. 334-37; note his discussion (p. 432) of sculptures of Marsyas and the gospel. See Philostratus the Younger, *Imagines* 2: Marsyas.

like Jesus and Paul and those in Jerusalem who rebelled against the Seleucids in 165 B.C.E. or against Rome in 66 C.E. fit into this Greco-Roman order as martyrs who were defeated, committed suicide, or were crucified. This social and religious experience may have been mocked by a soldier on the Palatine Hill, if the graffito of Alexamenos worshiping his god caricatures Christ on a cross.

One problem with the reconstruction in this paper, however, is that "the earliest known [Christian] representations of Jesus' crucifixion date to the early fifth century, and are extremely rare until the seventh."[87] The lack of early Christian visual representations of Jesus' death corresponds to scholars' observation about Paul's theology in the century after he died: "the authority of Paul is, to be sure, acknowledged in a formal way but Paul's fundamental view of justification is hardly to be found."[88] Jensen argues that the problem is not as severe as it seems; for example, in those early centuries visual representations such as that of the lamb of God and the sacrifice of Isaac carried similar symbolic value. Observations in this paper (see nn. 46, 55, 71) raise the following question in relation to the lack of early Christian visual representations of Jesus' death in catacomb and sarcophagus art: If neo-Attic art displaced neo-Pergamene art in the culture generally, to what extent did early Christian art reflect Greco-Roman culture by abandoning the baroque Pauline images?

On the other hand, Jensen refers to visual representations of the cross, the staurogram, in early Christian papyri, the oldest Christian artifacts. Christian scribes developed a unique system of abbreviating approximately a dozen words, sacred names *(nomina sacra)* and others, including the noun *(stauros)* and verb *(stauroō)* for "cross/crucify." Three of the most important of these papyri are P[46] (the Pauline Epistles without the Pastorals but including Hebrews), P[66] (the Gospel of John 1–21), and P[75] (the Gospels of Luke 3–24 and John 1–15). Some scholars date these three papyri in the late second century, while others place them in the early third,[89] that is, earlier than or contemporary with the

---

87. Jensen, chap. 5, here p. 131. Compare Graydon F. Snyder, *Ante Pacem: Archaeological Evidence of Church Life before Constantine* (Macon, Ga.: Mercer University Press, 1985), pp. 165-66. In a companion article "The Suffering of Isis/Io and Paul's Portrait of Christ Crucified (Gal 3:1): Frescoes in Pompeian and Roman Houses and in the temple of Isis in Pompeii," *Journal of Religion* 83/1 (Jan. 2003): 24-55, I discuss an analogy; frescoes of Io/Isis, the earliest of which is in the House of Livia on the Palatine (ca. 30-20 B.C.E.), exhibit her suffering, which several later copies of this painting suppress.

88. Georg Strecker, *Theology of the New Testament*, trans. M. E. Boring (Louisville: Westminster John Knox, 2000), p. 18. This is nuanced in William S. Babcock, ed., *Paul and the Legacies of Paul* (Dallas: Southern Methodist University Press, 1990).

89. Kurt Aland, *Studien zur Überlieferung des Neuen Testaments und Seines Textes*, ANTF 2 (Berlin: De Gruyter, 1967), pp. 91-92, 102, dates P[46] and P[66] "around 200" and P[75] to "the beginning of the third century."

graffito on the Palatine discussed above. P[46] abbreviates the verb "to crucify" eight times and the noun "cross" twelve times by omitting the diphthong "au" from *st(au)ros/st(au)roō*.[90] But in P[66] the abbreviation becomes an aesthetic image. Eleven or twelve times in the fragmentary text of John 19 (vv. 6 [perhaps three times], 15 [perhaps twice], 16, 18, 19, 20, 25, 31, and perhaps 41), not only is "au" omitted, but the letters tau (τ) and rho (ρ), thrown together in the abbreviation, are combined to form a staurogram, e.g., in verse 19, Pilate had the title σ⳨ου put on the cross. Curiously, once in P[66] the verb is neither abbreviated nor represented, but simply written *estaurōsan* (John 19:23). Thus in one of the earliest Christian artifacts we have, text and art are combined to emphasize "Christus crucifixus."[91] Similarly in P[75] the staurogram occurs twice (Luke 14:27; 24:7) and the abbreviation once (Luke 23:26). Also in the third century, P[45] has the abbreviation twice (Mark 8:34; Luke 14:27); P[80] (consisting of only one verse, John 3:34) has two staurograms, not in the text but concluding the verso and recto sides of the papyrus; and P[91] has one staurogram (Acts 2:36). In conclusion, there are four early papyri with the staurogram (P[66], P[75], P[80], and P[91]) and two that abbreviate "cross/crucify" (P[45] and P[46]). The staurogram constitutes a Christian artistic emphasis on the cross within the earliest textual tradition. It is not surprising, then, that a Christian apologist, Minucius Felix, *Octavius* 29.6 (closely related to Tertullian's *Apology,* written in 197 C.E.), responded to critics that "crosses are not objects that we worship."[92]

Finally, the art we have seen reinforces ethnic divisions. Pergamene art dramatizes the differences between Athenians and Persians, Pergamene victors and Galatian losers. Augustus's architecture in the Roman Forum, both the Temple of Apollo and his victory arch, portrayed his battles not as civil war but as conflicts of Romans against Eastern barbarians.[93] With its sources in the East, earliest Jewish Christian baptism rejected this ideology: despite their gathering in Greco-Roman houses that architecturally reinforced status, they confessed that God's call and not ethnic identity determines human worth (Gal. 3:28). Then as

90. Aland, p. 175.

91. Matthew Black, "The Chi-Rho Sign — Christogram and/or Staurogram?" in *Apostolic History and the Gospel: Biblical and Historical Essays Presented to F. F. Bruce on His Sixtieth Birthday* (Grand Rapids: Eerdmans, 1970), pp. 319-27, at 327.

92. G. W. Clarke, *The Octavius of Marcus Minucius Felix,* ACW 39 (New York: Newman, 1974), p. 106, cited by Jensen, p. 141. She also (p. 138) quotes Tertullian, *Adversus Marcionem* 3.22, who recommends tracing the symbol of the cross on the forehead "in all the ordinary actions of daily life."

93. See Paola Guidobaldi, *The Roman Forum,* Soprintendenza Archeologica di Roma (Milan: Electa, 1998), p. 37, and R. R. R. Smith, "The Imperial Reliefs from the Sebasteion at Aphrodisias," *JRS* 77 (1987): 88-138, at 98: "it is always victory over barbarians of various kinds: Britons, Armenians, and the like."

now, feminists have legitimate cause to reject the value that women like Iphigenia should sacrifice themselves for men.[94] Neither ethnic nor gender roles are to determine status in the Christian assembly. Christ did not die for Greece, or Rome, or North America, or for straight men, but according to Paul's polemical thesis, for the "ungodly" (Rom. 1:18 with 4:5), in that cultural context, for Laocoon, Cassandra, and the Galatians — for whom Paul portrayed Christ crucified (Gal. 3:1). Paul's polemical gospel was disturbing because he embodied, proclaimed, and challenged key Roman ideological values.[95]

94. See Osiek and Balch, chap. 5, for some ways that the Pauline churches modified gender roles.

95. Another key difference is that those who painted Iphigenia, Laocoon, and Cassandra, and who sculpted Laocoon and the dying Galatians, sacrificed animals to their deities, but Christians replaced actual sacrifices with sacrificial language, a major change in the history of religion. See Gerd Theissen, *The Religion of the Earliest Churches: Creating a Symbolic World*, trans. John Bowden (Minneapolis: Fortress, 1999), chap. 7, and Richard L. Rubenstein, "Atonement and Sacrifice in Contemporary Jewish Liturgy," in *After Auschwitz: Radical Theology and Contemporary Judaism* (Indianapolis: Bobbs-Merrill, 1966), pp. 92-111, a chapter not included in the 2nd ed. (1992).

III. Women

Sex and the Married Woman in Ancient Rome

Suzanne Dixon

Classical scholarship has radically changed its focus in the last thirty years, to encompass the majority traditionally excluded from earlier narratives of war and elite politics. Slaves, women, children, the free lower classes, and the family have largely superseded battles and consulships within the "territory of the historian." Emotions and sexualities are now acceptable, even commonplace topics of publication. Studies of Roman marriage and family relations in the late republic and early empire are based no longer solely on jurists' opinions from edited legal compilations but on sophisticated source readings, which locate texts historically and distinguish between laws and social ideals. The long-standing conviction that pagan approaches to marriage and family differed radically from those of Christians has also been progressively modified by recent scholarship, while a growth area of historical scholarship, on constructions of sex and the body, has yielded new and productive discussions of pagan/Christian difference.

Classical scholars of the current generation have published extensively on women, sex, sexualities, and marriage.[1] Married sex, however, remains a ne-

1. Initially, scholarship on the sexualities of the ancient Mediterranean concentrated disproportionately on classical Greece, so leading books and articles by D. Halperin, E. Keuhls, J. Winkler (not to mention Foucault himself) were significant in formulating the principles of new scholarship, but overall of indirect relevance to Rome. An important landmark study by A. Richlin, *The Garden of Priapus: Sexuality and Aggression in Roman Humor* (New Haven: Yale University Press, 1983), has been reissued with a new introduction. Both Richlin and J. P. Hallett pioneered studies of Roman sexualities in the 1970s and 1980s based primarily on imaginative literature. Works which focus on visual material include C. Johns, *Sex or Symbol? Erotic Images of Greece and Rome* (Austin: University of Texas Press and British Museum, 1982; reprint, 1991); N. Kampen, ed., *Sexuality in Ancient Art* (Cambridge: Cambridge University Press, 1996); J. Clarke, *Looking at Lovemaking: Constructions of Sexuality in Roman Art, 100 B.C.–A.D. 250* (Berkeley, Los Angeles, and London: University of California Press, 1998). Archaeological and iconographic methodology is explored in A. Koloski-Ostrow and C. L. Lyons, eds., *Naked Truths: Women, Sexuality, and Gender in Classical Art and Archaeology* (London and New York:

glected area. The sexualized married woman is discussed, if at all, only as an adulteress, but the husband's perspective has been touched on: some scholars of Roman history and literature have promoted the idea that Roman men looked to prostitutes, slaves, and mistresses for sexual satisfaction rather than to the wives assigned them through marriages arranged by family committees with a view to political and financial alliance — and, of course, children.[2] These scholars point to the idealization of illicit love by Roman elegists as confirmation of a dominant cultural attitude, but in this chapter I shall examine the proposition that their view rests ultimately on an unexamined, inherited construction of Romans as "other" and the assumption that arranged marriages must necessarily be unromantic and asexual.

Without falling into the opposite fallacy of a cozy human-nature belief that Romans were just like "us," I venture to suggest that Roman expectations of marriage and specifically of sexual satisfaction, even passion, within marriage were not necessarily as "different" as others have suggested. Exploration of such intimate questions, problematic even for social scientists in our own age of information overload, raises significant methodological issues for ancient histori-

---

Routledge, 1997). See also A. Rousselle, *Porneia: On Desire and the Body in Antiquity* (Oxford: Blackwell, 1988; French original, Paris: Presses universitaires, 1983); D. Konstan and M. Nussbaum, eds., *Sexuality in Greek and Roman Society* (Providence: Brown University Press, 1990); A. Richlin, ed., *Pornography and Representation in Greece and Rome* (New York: Oxford University Press, 1992), and J. P. Hallett and M. B. Skinner, eds., *Roman Sexualities* (Princeton: Princeton University Press, 1997). Foucault has naturally had a great impact but has not always been viewed favorably, to say the least: in her highly critical 1991 review of classical writings on sexuality, "Zeus and Metis: Foucault, Feminism, Classics," *Helios* 18, no. 2: 160-80, Amy Richlin argued that Foucauldian studies have compounded the exclusion/dismissal of female subjectivities. Cf. L. Dean-Jones, "The Politics of Pleasure: Female Sexual Appetite in the Hippocratic Corpus," in *Documenting Gender: Women and Men in Non-Literary Classical Texts,* ed. D. Konstan, *Helios* 19, nos. 1-2 (1992): 72-91; E. Greene, "Sappho, Foucault and Women's Erotics," *Arethusa* 29, no. 1 (1996): 1-14; and (for opposing views) the contributions by Halperin (chap. 1) and Cohen and Saller (chap. 2) in *Foucault and the Writing of History,* ed. J. Goldstein (Oxford: Blackwell, 1994). M. Skinner's overview, "Zeus and Leda: The Sexuality Wars in Contemporary Classical Scholarship," *Thamyris* 3, no. 1 (1996): 103-23, is very helpful. For a guide to scholarly approaches and bibliography on Roman marriage, see S. Treggiari, *Roman Marriage* (Oxford: Oxford University Press, 1991), and B. Rawson, ed., *Marriage, Divorce, and Children in Ancient Rome* (Oxford: Oxford University Press, 1991).

2. E.g., J. P. Hallett, "The Role of Women in Roman Elegy: Counter-Cultural Feminism," *Arethusa* 6, no. 1 (1973): 103-24; Hallett, *Fathers and Daughters in Roman Society: Women and the Elite Family* (Princeton: Princeton University Press, 1984), pp. 219-43; R. O. M. Lyne, *The Latin Love Poets from Catullus to Horace* (Oxford: Clarendon, 1980), e.g., pp. 8-13, 17; K. Bradley, "Ideals of Marriage in Suetonius's *Caesares,*" *Rivista storica dell'antichità* 15 (1985): 77-95, esp. 86-91; E. D'Ambra, "The Calculus of Venus: Nude Portraits of Roman Matrons," in *Sexuality in Ancient Art,* pp. 219-32.

ans. I have dealt elsewhere with the political, material, and sentimental aspects of elite Roman marriage.[3] My aim here is not to prove the unprovable — that all Romans had loving and sexually fulfilled marriages — but to provide a sampler of suitable sources and some ideas about how we might interpret and combine them. I shall highlight evidence for expectations of sexual interest, excitement, and even obsession within Roman marriage in the literary, male-centered sources of the late republic and early empire (approximately 201 B.C.E.–second century C.E.). I shall also suggest ways in which we might try to retrieve a female perspective from traces of folklore.[4]

As a first step in this ambitious project, let us review ideas about "Romans" which hover behind so many scholarly and popular arguments. Popular ideas about the ancient Romans continue the mix of irreconcilable stereotypes which gained currency in the novels of the nineteenth and films of the twentieth century. The self-controlled disciplinarians of schoolbooks reappeared in these media, but lost their proverbial dignity (along with their togas) at dinner parties, which invariably degenerated into orgies. Serious students of Roman social institutions have not been immune to the screen, print, and digital images which continue the tradition today. Constructions of Roman women are similarly contradictory: the received view is that respectable Roman matrons generally exercised a social and economic independence which contrasted dramatically with the situation of their Greek contemporaries. Indeed, the "emancipation" of Roman women has been a popular and academic commonplace which has served a range of moral and symbolic purposes. But from time to time another image is invoked: the Roman woman as victim of an archetypal patriarchal system. Both surface in readings of Roman marriage as a loveless institution defined by duty rather than feelings.

Christian discourse on Roman marriage, women, and family relations has a venerable history of its own. Diatribes against such practices as infant exposure were important weapons in the battle for souls in late antiquity.[5] Nor did

---

3. E.g., S. Dixon, "The Marriage Alliance in the Roman Elite," *Journal of Family History* 10 (1985): 353-78; Dixon, "The Sentimental Ideal of the Roman Family," in *Marriage, Divorce, and Children in Ancient Rome*, pp. 99-113; Dixon, *The Roman Family* (Baltimore: Johns Hopkins University Press, 1992), pp. 61-97.

4. Classical scholars use the term "literary" to include prose history, letters, and speeches from antiquity, as well as poetry and other forms classed as literary by modern historians. "Nonliterary sources" include legal (i.e., juristic) writings, papyri, inscriptions, and graffiti. On the possibility of retrieving female voices from "between the spaces" of male-centered texts, see B. Gold, "'But Ariadne Was Never There in the First Place': Finding the Female in Roman Poetry," in *Feminist Theory and the Classics*, ed. M. S. Rabinowitz and A. Richlin (New York and London: Routledge, 1993), pp. 75-101.

5. See especially M. Corbier, "Child Exposure and Abandonment," in *Childhood, Class, and Kin in the Roman World*, ed. S. Dixon (London: Routledge, 2001), pp. 52-73.

the classical revival exonerate Rome. Long after the eighteenth-century publication of Gibbon's interpretation of the military and political collapse of the Roman Empire, scholarship ran with his presumption of moral decline and his juxtaposition of pagan and Christian values — something so self-evident as to require no substantiation. This clear-cut pagan-Christian dichotomy, which provided a convenient tool for historical explanation, has been severely eroded by later twentieth-century scholarship ever since Beryl Rawson's considered challenge in 1966 to oft-repeated but quite unfounded statements about the popularity of concubinage and the lack of "family life" in parts of the Roman Empire.[6] Recent works have authoritatively debunked the entrenched belief that Constantine instituted radical changes to laws governing marriage and parenthood in the fourth century because, as the first Christian emperor of "Rome," he wished to promote a more humane approach to children and regarded marriage as a sacrament and divorce as a sin.[7] Scholars are now fine-tuning the more gradual and subtle impact of Christianity on marital and kin ideologies within the European tradition.[8]

Deciding which sources to use and how to weight them is crucial to any inquiry into Roman expectations of marriage. The notion that Roman marriages were loveless unions designed solely to produce children stems from a disproportionate reliance on love poetry and on certain didactic and moralizing genres. Such sources are important, not least because of their impact on our cultural heritage: Latin love poetry influenced courtly love conventions and later European poetry, and its themes linger on in pop music, while Seneca's pronouncements on marriage and married women in the first century of the Christian era inform the prescriptions of Saint Augustine and Saint Jerome, whose voices echo still. Nor am I one of those historians who dismiss out of hand the possibility of mining poetry for historical purposes. We can certainly employ both elegiac poetry and didactic essays for historical reconstruction of ancient ideologies, provided we identify the purpose and context of each work and discriminate between prescription, fantasy, and practice. This process is surely vital for historians of any social phenomenon. I provide specific exam-

6. B. M. Rawson, "Family Life among the Lower Classes at Rome in the First Two Centuries of the Empire," *CP* 61 (1966): 71-83.

7. See especially J. Evans Grubbs, *Law and Family in Late Antiquity: The Emperor Constantine's Marriage Legislation* (Oxford: Clarendon, 1995).

8. On marriage, see H. S. Nielsen, "The Value of Epithets in Pagan and Christian Epitaphs from Rome," and on attitudes to children and their "right to life," see M. Corbier, "Child Exposure and Abandonment," both chapters in *Childhood, Class, and Kin in the Roman World*. On the legal position of women under Christianity, see A. Arjava, *Women and Law in Late Antiquity* (Oxford: Clarendon, 1996).

ples of how we might apply these critical principles to a study of Roman attitudes to sex and marriage.

Along with the choice of sources, we have to determine how to weigh conflicting views which might emerge from them. We need to monitor our own prejudices and eschew glib generalization. I have already suggested that scholarly insistence on the unemotional character of Roman marital relations may reflect contemporary Western revulsion at the idea of arranged marriages. The very notion poses a challenge to dominant modern ideologies of romantic individualism, which construct marriage as the consequence of "falling in love" and put the bridal couple at the center of negotiations. But it is a great logical leap from the mode of arrangement to the expectations and content of a marriage. Overgeneralization from any single aspect of ideology or practice is risky: marriages in the modern West do not always conform to their ideal formulation.

Moreover, the fact that a society emphasizes one aspect of marriage (such as production of children) need not preclude other emphases (on sexual pleasure, for example). Romantic Western ideologies of marriage, after all, do not discount social compatibility or economic security in marriage, nor did Romans undervalue marital happiness. And, if we're collating evidence of attitudes, we must acknowledge that both cultures have produced a mass of antimarriage jokes and proverbs, which defy simple reading.

Cultural consistency may be a fiction, a pitfall of academic inquiry, which seeks always to impose meaning. It is tempting for a social historian, confronted with apparently conflicting views, to shape selected testimony into a more coherent perspective. It is understandable that historians of classical antiquity, faced with a mass of fragmentary and haphazardly preserved materials, pick and choose, both to sustain a thesis and to suit their own specialist training (in epigraphy, iconography, or historiography, for example). Consulting and assessing diverse sources makes the historian's task more difficult but may well reveal a more believable range of Roman beliefs (or postures) than the comfortable schoolroom stereotypes. Tombstone inscriptions reflecting mainstream ideologies of marriage and married love, commissioned and presumably authored by widows and widowers alike, provide one counter to the antimarriage commonplaces of Latin literature. To be sure, epitaphs are shaped and limited by the conventions of a genre which — then as now — elevated marital fidelity and harmony but was unlikely to refer to sex. They are a salutary reminder that the tone and even the content of an ideological statement might vary with the medium. We are, after all, used to politicians and editors who alternate between representing the youth of today as the hope of the nation and portraying them as the embodiment of cultural decline. Genre skewing and exclusions must be taken into account in reading ancient sources, too.

The selection, combination, and reading of sources is thus the methodological kernel of this chapter. The topic puts female subjectivity at the center, thereby raising a central concern of women's history: whether and how we can retrieve a female voice, let alone lived female experience, from sources composed overwhelmingly by and for elite Roman citizen males. Different strategies have been proposed for tackling this core problem: reading against the text and reading between the spaces of Roman poetry are possibilities advocated by literary scholars in the wake of French feminists.[9] These techniques have been little used by historians of ancient Rome but might yield new findings from much-worked texts. I shall show how Juvenal's notorious sixth satire and the strictures of Seneca and Plutarch reveal the authors' familiarity with the phenomenon of lovesick husbands. Perhaps we can go even further and extract traces of a female perspective on conjugal sex from male-oriented and male-authored Roman sources, which incidentally pass on women's proverbial sayings, folkloric practices, and religious rituals.

Spellbound: Ritual and Magic

Male authors and state inscriptions make few references to rituals connected with the female life cycle and predominantly managed by women. Some ceremonies were closed to men; others were not secret but, being all-female, were on the margins of masculine consciousness (like mother-daughter relations). Odd pieces of information about them surface if they impinge on masculine narratives, but otherwise we have to read between the lines.[10] Experts on religion have worked hard at piecing together such scattered and sometimes enigmatic material, from which Gagé, for example, has theorized that Roman matrons constituted an extrafamilial group which performed diverse religious

---

9. The principles and their relationship to French feminism are elaborated in several chapters of *Feminist Theory and the Classics*, as well as Gold's chapter, cited in n. 4 above.

10. References to the all-female rites of the "Good Goddess" *(Bona Dea)* or "Great Mother" *(Magna Mater,* Cybele) are typical: the official transfer of the "Great Mother" to Rome from the East in 204 B.C.E. at a time of national catastrophe is solemnly recounted by Livy 29.14; the rites of the Good Goddess were disrupted in December 60 B.C.E. by the presence of a man in drag, allegedly Publius Clodius Pulcher, the lover of Caesar's wife Pompeia — the resultant trial and gossip are retailed in Cicero's *Letters to Atticus* 1.12-16. Contrast Juvenal's extravagant version (*Satire* 6.314-34) of what went on at the solemn all-female rites with Plutarch's equally speculative (but serious) account — *Life of Cicero* 9.

functions and acted as a formal body which managed the ritual transitions of young girls to womanhood and marriage.[11]

Certain female religious rites — particularly some linked with Juno, Venus, and Virile Fortune *(Fortuna virilis)* — were concerned with marital happiness, fertility, and the beauty and sexual desirability of married women. The goddess Juno was invoked by women for marriage and weddings (as Juno Pronuba), for childbirth (as Juno Lucina), and for reconciling couples who had fallen out (as Juno Viriplaca = Husband-Pleaser/Placator).[12] At the July Nonae Caprotinae young Latin girls held mock battles and women (presumably married women) exchanged abuse and feasted on sacrificed goat *(capro)* under a wild fig apparently in connection with fertility rites involving Juno and Faunus.[13] The ceremony shared elements with the February Lupercalia in Rome, when naked youths, Luperci, ran around the city boundaries and struck with thongs of goat-hide women who wished to become pregnant.[14] Antiquarians, ancient and modern, have speculated on the intriguing elements of these festivals, but for our purposes it is enough to know that they existed and associated animal lasciviousness with approved female fertility.[15]

The Lupercalia and Nonae Caprotinae were typical examples of rites performed in the classical period and containing archaic elements little understood by Romans of the late republic and early imperial eras (as the bishop Gelasius pointed out, section 16 of his attack on the Lupercalia). In his *Fasti*, a poetic explication of the religious calendar, which unfortunately was never completed, Ovid attempted to make sense of the imperfectly understood April rituals of Venus and Virile Fortune and their interconnection — probably confusing the picture irrevocably for posterity. He describes how married women took special potions of poppy, milk, and honey and bathed in warm springs wearing only a myrtle garland in the course of annual rites designed to make them sexually attractive to their husbands.[16]

---

11. J. Gagé, *Matronalia. Essai sur les dévotions et les organisations cultuelles des Femmes dans l'ancienne Rome* (Brussels: Latomus, 1963), pp. 7-8.

12. See G. Wissowa, *Religion und Kultus der Römer* (Munich: Beck, 1912/1971), pp. 181-90, for the various festivals and rites of Juno; Valerius Maximus 2.1.6 for the procedure of Viriplaca.

13. *CIL* 4.1555; Plutarch, *Romulus* 29; Varro, *On the Latin Language (De lingua Latina)* 6.18. And see Wissowa, p. 184.

14. Ovid associates the rites with the woodland god Faunus at *Fasti* 2.267-302 and gives a historical etiology, involving wolves and the goddess Juno Lucina, for the whipping at lines 424-52. Plutarch gives more detail in his *Life* of Julius Caesar, 61.

15. See especially Ovid, *Fasti* 2.266-474, and cf. Macrobius 1.11.36-38, J. G. Frazer, LCL (Cambridge: Harvard University Press, 1931), pp. 389-94. Cf. M. Beard, J. North, and S. Price, *Religions of Rome*, vol. 2 (Cambridge: Cambridge University Press, 1998), pp. 119-24.

16. Ovid, *Fasti* 4.1-164, is an elaborate etiology. Only lines 133-56 detail the rituals. See also

Married women's concern with their beauty, their sexual allure, and their fertility was thus legitimated and encoded in Roman culture. It is possible that, as in many modern societies, these topics were a significant element of female social and conversational exchanges and are, like the wisdom of ancient mid-wives, largely lost to the historical record. The recurrent references to enticing the husband and pleasing him sexually to avoid his straying seem to reflect standard advice and, like expectations of mutual sexual gratification, are embedded in wedding rituals.

Surviving wedding songs tend to be literary versions rather than raw originals. They stand in contrast to the more somber but detailed celebrations of wives and marriages found in funeral orations epitaphs, and popular exemplary tales of heroically loyal wives, preserved orally within families and regions, which made little reference to sexuality and reproduction apart from praise of the wife's chastity and maternity.[17] A poem of Catullus (no. 61) illustrates the point. It is thought to have been commissioned for the wedding of his friend Manlius Torquatus. Problems of interpretation inevitably present themselves. As so often, Catullus adapted an existing Greek tradition, in this case that of the *epithalamium*. Alternate verses are allocated to the boys' and girls' choirs that accompany the couple in a procession which may not always represent the reality of Roman ceremonial, but Catullus explicitly includes a literary version of the obscene and mocking "Fescennine" songs (*fescennina iocatio*, Catullus 61.120), which we know *were* part of Roman wedding ritual. The singers' reminder to the groom that he must now put aside certain bachelor pleasures forms part of the poetic version:

> Anointed groom, you're supposed to be having trouble
> giving up boys, but you must give them up. . . .
> We know you've only tried acceptable pleasures.
> But the same things are not permissible to a married man.   (61.134-41)

The bride is cautioned in her turn:

E. Stehle, "Venus, Cybele and the Sabine Women: The Roman Construction of Female Sexuality," *Helios* 16, no. 2 (1989): 143-64, for an analysis of ritual rather different from mine.

17. Wives are praised in tombstones for being content with one husband (i.e., not remarrying once widowed) or, more explicitly, with one bed — see R. Lattimore, *Themes in Greek and Latin Epitaphs* (Urbana: University of Illinois Press, 1942), p. 296. Women are also praised, in stock bereavement letters *(consolationes), laudationes* (funeral eulogies), and their derivatives, for welcoming motherhood (in contrast to the probably imaginary selfish society women who avoid pregnancy for the sake of their figures, e.g., Seneca, *Ad Helviam* 16.3) — e.g., Pliny, *Epistle* 8.5, on Macrinus's unnamed wife. On the preservation of stories in regions and families of heroic wives, see my 1991 chapter, "Sentimental Ideal."

Bride, you, too, make sure you do not deny
what your husband asks,
lest he go elsewhere to look for it.   (61.144-46)[18]

The combination of admiration for the beauty and desirability of bride
and groom, the overlapping references to sex and the reproductive aim of marriage in this *epithalamium* may constitute a refined literary reflection of the
raunchier, more down-to-earth traditions of knowing sexual advice from the
older generation. What better reminder do we have of the force of genre and
the flexibility of the poetic viewpoint than this passage from Catullus 61? The
poet who elsewhere pilloried amorous and political rivals and idealized, illicit
love, toys in this wedding song with notions of married sex not just as a reproductive duty but as fun and passion which should lead to children:

. . . Play — however you like your pleasure
— and give him children soon.
Such a venerable name should not be without children.   (61.204-6)

Earlier in the song the modest bride has been lured from her home by the
assurance that the husband is ready to foreswear adultery and to seek out the
sexual delights of his new wife.[19] The song, which maintains the fiction of the
stages of the wedding ceremony, delivers her to the groom's house, where he lies
ready for her on the marriage bed, burning with a deep flame of desire as great
as hers (ll. 165-72). The singers end with the couple in the bridal chamber:

Close the door, bridesmaids.
We've had our fun.
Now, you fine pair, have a good life
and go to it, make the most of your thrusting youth,
consummating your conjugal duty over and over again.[20]

Catullus skillfully rolls reproduction, bawdy sex, and conjugal propriety,
even duty, into a satisfying climax. Behind the literary conceits and ritualistic

---

18. Catullus's wording is echoed by Martial in a much later (satiric) caution to a wife,
couched in deliberately subversive and grossly explicit terms; Martial 12.96.7-8.

19. Catullus 61.97-106, where Catullus follows the reference to the husband's eagerness for
her nubile nipples with a sensuous image of his insinuating himself in her embrace, like a vine
entwining a tree.

20. Catullus 61.221-28. On the rituals of the Roman wedding and their relation to the virtues of wives and the hope of fertility, see also G. Williams, "Some Aspects of Roman Marriage
Ceremonies and Ideals," *JRS* 48 (1958): 16-29, and Treggiari, *Roman Marriage*.

compliments, we can discern certain recurrent elements of the dominant culture and its assumptions about married love, sex, and passion.

Jealousy and infidelity also play their part in conventional advice to the wife. In his *Conjugal Precepts,* a work purportedly presented as a wedding present to a young couple in Roman Greece in the early second century C.E., Plutarch addressed himself specifically to the bride, urging her to suppress her own sexual jealousy if the husband sought gratification elsewhere and to avoid the *common wifely practice* of resorting to spells and potions to enhance her desirability. He does not deny the efficacy of such measures, but claims they reduce the husband to a state of chronic stupor.[21]

Governing elites in the ancient world displayed a certain ambivalence toward magic. The Roman state legislated against many magical practices, but augury and other forms of omen reading were enshrined in official tradition. Pliny the Elder poured scorn on the claims of sorcerers, but, like Cato the Elder before him, passed on traditional cures and prayers replete with magical elements.[22] Apotropaic phalli were visible and ubiquitous — on house fronts, street corners, public baths, and adorning bodies in the form of amulets and other jewelry.[23] In Roman literature sorcery is associated with marginals, and witches are typically represented as older, lower-class women, but superstitious belief in magic is in fact attested in prominent senatorial men and members of the imperial family.[24] Papyrological spell manuals, curse tablets, and other ma-

---

21. Plutarch, *Conjugal Precepts (Praecepta coniugalia)* 5 (= *Moralia* 139a). See also n. 26 below.

22. Legislation (the *lex Cornelia*) — *Digest* 10.2.4.1. Pliny the Elder denounced magic in his *Natural History* book 30 (e.g., 1-15 on *magi*), but cites cures which hinge on auspicious timing and the magical power of letters, 28.5.-9. Consider, too, his comments on the accuracy and understanding of ravens in divination, 10.32-3; cf. Cato the Elder, *On Agriculture* 160, for a traditional cure aided by incantation and sympathetic magic.

23. See Johns, pp. 15-35, for illustrations and discussion; on public displays and meanings of phalli, see B. Kellum, "The Phallus as Signifier: The Forum of Augustus and Rituals of Masculinity," and J. Clarke, "Hypersexual Black Men in Augustan Baths: Ideal Somatypes and Apotropaic Magic," both in *Sexuality in Ancient Art,* pp. 170-83 and 184-98, respectively.

24. The witches of Horace, *Epode* 5, and Ovid, *Fasti* 2.571-82, are fairly typical. According to the section of Octavian/Augustus's biography dedicated by Suetonius to his "religious" leanings, the first Roman emperor not only set great store by astrology and dreams but displayed a range of superstitious practices (Suetonius, *Divus Augustus* 90-92, with relevant additions in the following sections). His grandson Germanicus was a strong believer in magic. In his account of Germanicus's final illness, Tacitus (*Annales* 2.69, 74; 3.7, 12-14) seems to endorse the fear of magic and the culpability of the female poisoner. Poison and magic were frequently linked — see following discussion and n. 26 below. On approaches to literary references to magic, see C. R. Phillips, "Seek and Go Hide: Literary Source Problems and Greco-Roman Magic," *Helios* 21, no. 2 (1994): 107-14.

terial remains attest the widespread use of magic and the range of purposes for which it was used.[25] Love charms could be and were employed by both sexes, but the presumption of authors like Plutarch, that married women routinely resorted to potions and spells to secure their husbands' sexual fidelity and for the related purpose of ensuring their fertility, gains some support from material remains.[26] This association of fertility, wifely sex appeal, and husbandly fidelity and the overlap among religion, magic, and cyclic rituals are evident, for example, in the Lupercalia and wedding celebrations examined above.[27]

25. Examples of actual spells are given by J. G. Gager, ed., *Curse Tablets and Binding Spells from the Ancient World* (Oxford: Oxford University Press, 1992), and G. Luck, *Arcana Mundi: Magic and the Occult in the Greek and Roman Worlds* (Baltimore: Johns Hopkins University Press, 1985).

26. Love magic was illegal (penalties are listed by the jurist Paul, *Opinions* 5.23, 14-19), but such spells are well represented in the collections cited in the preceding note. Potions were regarded, perhaps justifiably, with particular suspicion, and legal penalties were most severe for potions which proved fatal (not their intended aim). C. Faraone ("Sex and Power: Male-Targetting Aphrodisiacs in the Greek Magical Tradition," *Documenting Gender*, ed. D. Konstan, *Helios* 19, nos. 1-2 [1992]: 92-103) suggests (pp. 98-99) that married women's potions might have been sedatives designed to make the husband less threatening and more tractable — compare Roman wives' prayers to Juno Viriplaca (husband-placator). Examples cited by biographers and historians also suggest that legal penalties failed to deter wives (and others) from employing love magic. The instances are worth recording only because their consequences were extraordinary. Thus love potions feature in Suetonius's *Life of Caligula* 50 and *Lives of the Poets* 43 because they are rumored to have (unintentionally) caused insanity or death. Tacitus, *Annales* 4.22, recounts a sensational scandal of 24 c.e., in the course of which the noble Numantina was tried and acquitted of driving her ex-husband by magical incantations and potions to murder his new wife. Apuleius, a second century c.e. literary celebrity who did dabble in magic, had to answer charges that he had used charms to ensnare the wealthy widow Pudentilla (*Apology* 9ff. and passim). And see Gagé, p. 15, on possible connections (or confusions) between Venus and poison (*venenum*).

27. Modern preoccupation with fertility control has led to interesting work on contraceptive/abortive practices in the ancient world (Dixon, *The Roman Family*, pp. 119-23; T. Parkin, *Demography and Roman Society* [Baltimore: Johns Hopkins University Press, 1992], pp. 99, 115, 119-20), but has tended to obscure the much stronger interest in ensuring fertility in the ancient world (cf. the remarks of K. Hopkins, "Contraception in the Roman Empire," in *Comparative Studies in Society and History* 8 [London: Cambridge University Press, 1965/66], pp. 124-51), which pervades medical and folkloric "women's medicine" — Rousselle, esp. pp. 24-26, on women's care of their own health. On the nurses, midwives, and *sagai*, healers with magical associations, see E. Nardi, *Procurato aborto nel mondo greco romano* (Milan: Giuffrè, 1971), pp. 239-40. Cf. H. Parker, "Women Doctors in Greece, Rome and the Byzantine Empire," in *Women Healers and Physicians: Climbing a Long Hill*, ed. L. Furst (Lexington: University of Kentucky Press, 1997), pp. 131-50. Pliny the Elder cites in his *Natural History* (20.226; 28.81) famous examples of female doctors and midwives, some of whom wrote manuals.

Sex-Bound: Besotted Husbands

The figure of the husband enslaved by passion for his wife is as much a literary cliché as the enslaved lover in thrall to his *domina,* or "mistress."[28] He appears in discrete genres, usually as a warning to husbands to avoid this dreaded fate. Juvenal's long sixth satire is designed to show the impossibility of happy marriage and the extreme improbability of female virtue. It contains the following passage:

> The bed in which a wife lies is always ringing with quarrels and complaints — there's little chance of sleep in it. The time she hassles her husband, the time she's worse than a tigress deprived of her cub, is when *she,* aware of her own secret misdeeds, invents grievances, either pouring her venom on your boy-favourites or making up a girlfriend and calling up the abundant tears she always keeps on stand-by, just waiting for her orders to gush forth. And you take it as proof of her love, poor worm, you pride yourself on it and kiss away her tears! (Juvenal 6.268-77)

Jealousy, tears, and reproaches lead to caresses and, by implication of the setting, to full consummation, much as they do in the conventional sequences of love poetry. The marriage-bed location adds piquancy and confirms the presumption of sexual passion and mutual physical jealousy between spouses.[29] *This* marriage bed is not merely for dutiful procreation. This wife resembles the turbulent object of love poetry, this wife is a "mistress," *domina,* of the manipulated husband. For what it is worth, Juvenal is representing besotted husbands as a sadly recognizable phenomenon.[30]

More dignified genres carried similar warnings. Philosophers also cautioned husbands against the dangers of infatuation with their wives and urged

28. Love as slavery for the normally dominant partner is one of the stock clichés of erotic poetry, Greek and Latin, lamenting the cruelty, fickleness, and mercenary character of the boy or girl who thus subjugates the social superior. Latin poets used the term *domina* — elsewhere a standard word for the respectable *materfamilias* who headed a household and supervised its slaves. The term, and the role-reversal concepts, were adopted in later courtly and Renaissance love conventions.

29. I discuss below the basis for suggesting a context is sexual. Compare Johns, pp. 121-22, on her decision to analyze the rather domestic Gallo-Roman second century c.e. terra-cotta of an embracing couple in bed with a dog at their feet and bedclothes covering most of their bodies: "The fact that the pair are in bed, and that they are exchanging caresses, seems to justify the inclusion of the piece in the class of erotic representations." It is even more difficult to pin down what makes a literary work "erotic." Sex is usually implied, not described, in so-called erotic poetry — see further chapter 3 of my book, *Reading Roman Women* (London: Duckworth, 2001).

30. Seneca *On Marriage,* gives numerous, allegedly historical examples, 81-83.

them to make (conjugal) love in a rational frame of mind.[31] Another caution is contained in Lucretius's long poem, *On the Nature of Things (De rerum natura)*, an Epicurean view of the universe. Explaining and theorizing on love, sex, and reproduction, Lucretius elaborates on the philosophical commonplace that sex ought to be undertaken sensibly, with a view to legitimate procreation: "There is no need for *wives* to wriggle seductively, for the woman prevents conception and repels the semen if in the throes of her pleasure she pulls her crotch away from her husband's loins and pants heavily with the full force of her lungs. . . . That is why prostitutes make a habit of squirming around, so that they do not fall pregnant and swell up — as well as ensuring that the sex-act should be more fun for the men. This seems quite inappropriate behaviour for our wives!" (4.1268-71, 1274-77). This passage is commonly invoked to reinforce the view that Roman men expected few fireworks in the marital bed. But we need to read on. Elsewhere in book 4, dedicated to sex and generation as embodied in the goddess Venus, Lucretius recommends adventurous positions to facilitate conception and repeats the commonly held view that women needed to have sexual pleasure in order to conceive.[32]

The younger Seneca (ca. 4 B.C.E.–65 C.E.) also warned husbands about the danger of excessive sexual enjoyment in marriage. His caution is linked to the stock theme of whether the philosopher — assumed, in spite of theoretical and actual admission of female philosophers to many of the schools, to be male — should marry. The standard answer was that, ideally, he should not, for marriage — and sex — was a distraction from higher concerns. Marriage *could* be justified philosophically for its general social advantages, as could marital sex, if it were directed at respectable reproduction. Saint Jerome preserved excerpts from a treatise by Seneca the Younger on this theme.[33] Seneca also saw fit to warn the philosophically inclined husband against the dangers of excessive sexual attachment to one's wife:

> The beginnings of married love are honourable, but its excesses make it perverse. After all, it makes no difference how a disease is actually caught. For this reason, Sextius has written in his *Opinions*: "The man who makes love

31. The philosophers' sayings on marital sex collected by Treggiari in *Roman Marriage*, app. 3, pp. 511-13, are mostly about adultery.

32. Lucretius 4.1263-67. The association between sexual pleasure and conception goes back to the Hippocratic corpus and was continued by Roman practitioners such as the second century C.E. Soranus — Dean-Jones, p. 90 n. 57.

33. *On Marriage* esp. 45-59. See Jerome/Hieronymus (*Adversus Iovinianum* 1). Many readers will be familiar with the Christian theological tradition of such views and their recent authoritative reiteration.

too ardently to his own wife is an adulterer." And indeed it is a disgraceful thing to feel any love for another man's wife, but also to feel too much for your own. The wise man ought to love his wife reasonably, not passionately. He controls the onset of erotic excitement and is not rushed headlong into sex: there is nothing more disgusting than making love to your wife as if she were your mistress. (Seneca, *On Marriage* [*De matrimonio*] 84-85)

It is moot whether Seneca took his own advice, for his attachment to his wife was well known, but for our purposes the notable point of the warning to husbands is that it was seen as necessary and, indeed, became a cliché.[34]

Plutarch voiced a similar sentiment to bride and groom on the dangers of being overwhelmed by sexual passion early in the marriage. Such feelings, he reminded them, are more transient than long-term affection.[35] One is reminded of the typical jokes made at modern weddings about honeymooners. We need to read such warnings in context and allow for generic emphases — on marital discord (Juvenal), on ensuring conception (Lucretius), on philosophical restraint (Seneca). Far from being confined to the ancient world of arranged marriages, the idea that enduring love is built on something more solid than instant attraction is a recurrent form of popular wisdom that is typically offered by one generation and ignored by another. Today such advice reverberates in such popular culture forms as tabloid women's magazines and daytime television talk shows (also pitched at a female audience). So in cultures in which individuals are free to choose their own spouses, the older generation still points to the danger of being swept away by ephemeral passion into unwise life choices. The same sentiment seems to underpin Lucretius's philosophical recommendation of the "better" love, based on character and withstanding the test of time, which he contrasts with the thunderbolt effect of sudden passion;[36] Seneca's juxtaposition of solid love with the delusion of erotic passion (an adaptation of another commonplace of the love poets);[37] and Plutarch's advice to the young married cou-

---

34. In the preceding passage, 81-83, Seneca elaborates on the delusional/demented nature of physical passion. That is the context of his "historic" examples (cited above) of husbands who were ludicrously attached to their wives; see Tacitus, *Annales* 15.63, for Seneca's love for his wife.

35. Plutarch, *Conjugal Precepts* 139.9. It is characteristic that the modern equivalent appeals to pop science: overwhelming romantic infatuation is now put down to biochemical responses (pheromones). In the ancient world, you could blame Aphrodite or Venus.

36. Lucretius 4.1278-83. Treggiari, *Roman Marriage*, rightly points out that this is not explicitly confined to married love, but the context makes that the obvious application for the reader, since it follows the description of proper married sex — see the quote below.

37. Although they rail against it, the love poets tend to dwell on the delusional type of love. Catullus is unusual in attempting to describe a different kind of feeling for Lesbia — character-

ple, that excessive passion burns out while love based on deeper foundations of companionship and mutual respect is longer-lasting and more reliable. Like the warning to the bride from Catullus's choristers to comply with all her husband's sexual demands, the advice seems to reflect Roman folk wisdom, this time directed more at men than at women. Old husbands' tales, perhaps.

Genre Crossing: Erotic Motifs Go Conjugal

Latin poets built on themes and meters inherited from Greek lyric poets to construct a new form, Latin love elegy, with its own special conventions and rules. The stock characteristics of the beloved are much the same, but they are embedded in a narrative around the one named love object ("Lesbia," "Cynthia," "Corinna").[38] Roman elegy was by definition about illicit love: it romanticized the hopeless, tempestuous passions of those who had no wish or means to marry. As we have seen, some modern scholars have used this theme to support the notion that passionate love was distinct from Roman marital experience. It is therefore striking that ancient authors writing to or about their wives sometimes appropriated certain conventions of erotic poetry, such as the presumption of sexual, physical obsession with the beloved and the need for her (even his) presence.[39] Cicero, in prose, and Ovid, in verse, both wrote impassioned appeals to their wives from exile, posited on the husbands' emotional (and even political) dependence on their wives. The extreme nature of their situation intensified their history of shared hardship and love.

The question naturally arises whether we should class this kind of thing as sexual. The distinction between passionate attachment and explicitly sexual references is sometimes blurred by the use of common language and motifs familiar from the elegiac poets, such as the recurrent image of the beloved, and love as a wasting disease or enslavement. Consider Cicero's references in 58 B.C.E. to his wife "always moving before my eyes day and night,"[40] or Ovid,

---

istically, in a nostalgic reproach: "I loved you then not only as the crowd loves a mistress but as a father loves his children and sons-in-law" (Catullus 72.3-4).

38. Catullus is credited with beginning this convention, but his poetry was not seen by ancient authors as part of the genre of love poetry.

39. On this general application of elegiac conventions to married love, see A. M. Guillemin, *Pline et la vie littéraire de son temps* (Paris: Belles Lettres, 1929), pp. 140-41. Cf. Dixon, *Roman Family*, pp. 83-90 (focusing on romantic rather than erotic feelings).

40. Cicero, *Letters to His Friends (Epistulae ad familiares)* 14.2.3. Cf. 14.3.5. Pliny, in the letter quoted below (7.5), also used this motif of the absent beloved's image appearing before him and keeping him from sleep.

writing more than seventy years later from an even bleaker exile, of his wife's image appearing before him in his illness.[41] In a poem to his wife urging her to leave Rome and join him in his native Naples, Statius (*Silvae* 3.5) reviewed the course of their unequal love. She had been married before, but for him love was a new experience, a sudden, overwhelming blow from Venus. She had "transfixed his heart" and subjected him, a willing victim.

Women also wrote of love, even married love, but our surviving examples of their poetry give us less help than we might have hoped for in our search for female subjectivity. We do have some trace of a female voice in surviving poetry. Martial refers (10.35, 38) to a Sulpicia who wrote chaste verses, apparently about her husband, in the late first century C.E., but they have not survived. Poems by another, earlier female poet of the same name have, however, been preserved.[42] Her verses celebrate her love for "Cerinthus" in quite passionate terms: "I burn more than the other girls. The fact that I burn, Cerinthus, is no trial, if the same flame burns in your breast for me" (3.11 [4.5], 5-6) and "Won over by my prayers, Venus has brought him here and delivered him to my embrace" (3.13 [4.7], 3-4). As far as we know, this Sulpicia was unmarried. Poem 3.12 [4.6] seems to imply that marriage was expected to follow this love. Her claim (3.13 [4.7], 1-2) that her love was not shameful but should be published abroad has led to speculation that "Cerinthus" was a pseudonym for her fiancé,[43] but, although we can identify this Sulpicia as a historic figure, we have no way of knowing if her poetry revolved around a living person or a poetic fiction.[44]

At the end of the first century C.E., Pliny the Younger, then in his forties or fifties, and writing to his newish teenaged (third) wife Calpurnia, adopted the stock elegiac motif of the excluded lover — in this case it was the wife's bedroom, not the mistress's home, from which the author was excluded by circum-

---

41. Ovid, *Laments (Tristia)* 3.3.15-20, on the hallucinations he sees in his weakened state, and 21-28 on elaborations of the theme of love and separation. Ovid was fifty years old when he was exiled ca. 8 C.E. He died at Tomis, on the Black Sea, ten years later.

42. In published versions of Tibullus, bk. 3 [4], but editors differ on whether to attribute only 3.13-18 [4.7-12] to her.

43. See Treggiari, pp. 121-22, 302-3.

44. Sulpicia was granddaughter of a famous jurist and niece of a patron of literature. Typically, her poetry was attributed to Tibullus until quite recently. See J. Hallett, "Martial's Sulpicia and Propertius," in *Woman's Power, Man's Game: Essays in Classical Antiquity in Honor of Joy K. King*, ed. Cynthia M. DeForest (Chicago: Bolchazy-Carducci, 1993), pp. 322-53; originally published in *Classical World* 86, no. 2 (1992): 199-24; M. Skoie, "Sublime Poetry or Feminine Fiddling: Gender and Reception: Sulpicia through the Eyes of Two Nineteenth Century Scholars," in *Aspects of Women in Antiquity*, ed. Larsson Lovén and A. Strömberg (Jonsered, Sweden: Paul Åstrom, 1998), pp. 169-82.

stances which are not detailed: "I am seized by unbelievable longing for you. The reason is above all my love, but secondarily the fact that we are not used to being apart. That is why I spend the greater part of the night haunted by your image; that is why from time to time my feet lead me (the right expression!) of their own accord to your room at the times I was accustomed to come and see you; that is why, in short, I retreat, morbid and disconsolate, like an excluded lover from an unwelcoming doorway" (Pliny, *Epistle 7.5*).

Such extravagant protestations — like the elegiac originals — might often have been hollow conventions. It is difficult to say. Again we need to consider which examples are to be classed as specifically sexual. Oddly enough, this question is not posed of elegiac poets — whose works form the basis of generalizations about the sex lives of elite Roman males. Yet these poets make few explicit references to sex with the beloved or even to the body of the beloved.[45] It is the background and the association which make such references "sexual." The lover in Roman elegy is meant to be enslaved by his "mistress," and their love — especially his love — is a recurrent theme. Sex is not conveniently separated and the poet-lover's longing for the mistress's physical presence is accepted as part of an erotic narrative. To modern critics, though, Juvenal's satiric marriage bed full of tears and jealousy, followed by reconciliation, is less sexual than comparable scenes in elegy, and the yearning or excluded husband (versus the yearning or excluded elegiac lover) is interpreted sentimentally. The judgment on what makes a particular love poem "sexual" is ultimately subjective.[46] The scholarly inclination to class literature as erotic only if it celebrates illicit relationships is arbitrary and may reflect modern expectations.

An Inconclusive Conclusion

What can we extract, then, from this sampler of sources? At the least, that it was unremarkable — if regrettable — for Roman husbands to display passionate love for their wives. So strong indeed was the cultural presumption that Roman men did expect sexual pleasure in marriage, particularly in the early years, that

45. Sex is implied, as in many of our media, by symbolic references to "bed" or "the night." On the vagueness of Roman bodily references to the beloved, especially the female beloved, see Richlin, *The Garden of Priapus*, pp. 44-55, esp. 47.

46. Once more it is worth citing Johns, pp. 121-22, this time on her decision to exclude "'low-key' erotic images" of clothed, standing couples kissing or embracing from her discussion of erotic art "although they may be said to contain a potential erotic force." The decision is even more difficult with literature. See below on the characterization of poetry and letters by spouses employing erotic motifs.

husbands were conventionally cautioned against sexual infatuation with their wives. Wedding songs constructed the bride as beautiful and sexually desirable, as modestly eager for sexual pleasure. Letters from husbands (however artificial) construct the wife as the object of longing and love, an appropriate focus for the extravagant, erotic language of love poetry.

To be sure, the authorial emphasis is on the masculine perspective. It assumes female desire, but incidentally. Female subjectivity remains elusive. We are driven to seek it not only in the meager remains of female-authored texts within dominant genres (particularly the epitaph and love poetry), but in the "spaces" of the male-centered texts and what they reveal, almost in passing, of female culture — magic, religious rituals, rites of passage, and proverbial intergenerational advice.

Certainly Roman women as a group were not accorded the sexual freedom of their male equivalents, and were expected to comply with their husbands' sexual whims. As with fertility, the ultimate responsibility for sexual failure tended to be laid at their door, and transgressive wives were gossiped about more intensively than errant husbands. But wives were not without weapons — religion, charms, popular advice, and respectability among them. The relative social and economic freedom of Roman women also gave them access to a lifestyle of shared interests with their partners which is even reflected in erotic literary conceits as well as tombstones and laudatory stories about wifely loyalty, chastity, and industry. Source criticism reveals predictable genre differences in content and perspective, but there is little evidence overall of an entrenched distinction in Roman culture of ideas current in modern societies: of a wife/ whore distinction, of motherhood or respectability making a woman less sexual or less attractive than a slave or mistress.

Married sex was not extensively discussed in Roman sources, but it is not discussed at all by those who now write about sex and marriage (separately) in the ancient world. That is understandable. In concentrating on the privileged literary forms, it is evidently easy to miss (or dismiss) references to conjugal sex and sexual attachment in favor of the more glamorous treatments of adulterous and cross-class passion. Ultimately we can only speculate about the relationship between expectations and reality, for men and women, in marriages of the past. But we should view with skepticism any overconfident claims of what lived experience *must* have been. Consider the following statement by an expert in Latin love poetry: "By tradition, upper class marriage was at best an institution in which a man and woman could enjoy friendship, mutual respect and affection, and be partners in the maintenance of the *domus* and the propagation of the family. In no case was it likely to be, nor was it traditionally expected to be, an institution of love in all love's aspects, combining reciprocated passion and affection, and the rest."[47] Perhaps not. We can hardly know people's feelings on such matters even in our own social circles. We need to be skeptical of concluding practice from public posturings — and that applies equally to protestations of passionate love and jokes about lovesick or spellbound husbands. But if we can cast aside our preconceptions, we should at least consider the possibility that scholarly faith in the authenticity of tempestuous (but perfectly metric) illicit love narratives and the associated, a priori insistence on the loveless, passionless nature of arranged Roman marriages and the sober sexlessness of Roman matrons might have more to do with highly selective source readings based on outdated and baseless cultural prejudices than with what the ancients might have said.

47. Lyne, p. 17.

Typical and Atypical Jewish Family Dynamics: The Cases of Babatha and Berenice

Ross S. Kraemer

Given the largely incontrovertible beginnings of Christianity as a movement within Judaism,[1] a paper on typical and atypical Jewish families and family dynamics in the first two centuries of the common era might seem entirely appropriate for a conference on early Christian families. The earliest of such families, after all, would have been comprised almost entirely of Jews. Yet I want to propose at the outset that the study of Jewish families in the early centuries of the Roman Empire may not be all that crucial for the study of early Christian families. Although they do not take this position explicitly in their recent book, our colleagues and hosts for this conference, Carolyn Osiek and David Balch, may share this assessment, since their work locates early Christian families almost entirely within the context of the larger Greco-Roman world.[2] Most of this pa-

1. Burton Mack (*The Lost Gospel: The Book of Q and Christian Origins* [San Francisco: Harper Collins, 1993]) and a few others have recently argued for a reconstruction of the origins of the Jesus movement in an ethnically and religiously mixed association of persons living in the Galilee, only some of whom would have been "Jewish," but this reconstruction has many problematic components to it that are, however, beyond the scope of this paper.

2. Carolyn Osiek and David L. Balch, *Families in the New Testament World: Houses and House Churches* (Louisville: Westminster John Knox, 1997). Most of the material they consider for context comes from non-Jewish sources.

This paper expands my treatments of Babatha, Berenice, and issues in the study of Jewish women in the Greco-Roman period published elsewhere, especially "Jewish Mothers and Daughters in the Greco-Roman World," in *The Jewish Family in Antiquity,* ed. Shaye J. D. Cohen, BJS 289 (Atlanta: Scholars, 1993), pp. 89-112; "Jewish Women and Women's Judaism(s) at the Beginning of Christianity," in *Women and Christian Origins,* ed. Ross Shepard Kraemer and Mary Rose D'Angelo (New York and Oxford: Oxford University Press, 1999), pp. 50-79; "Berenice," in *Women in Scripture,* gen. ed. Carol Meyers (Boston: Houghton-Mifflin, 2000), pp. 59-61. Many of the literary sources for Berenice and some on the Babatha papyri are now included in my book *Women's Religions in the Greco-Roman World: A Sourcebook* (New York and Oxford: Oxford University Press, 2003).

per will consider what we know of the families of two Jewish women who lived within about a century of Jesus and his earliest followers, and how that comports with other evidence we have for Jewish families in the Greco-Roman Mediterranean generally. I will suggest that this evidence is generally, if not entirely, consistent with the overall evidence for non-Jewish families in the same period, an observation already to be found in recent scholarship on Jewish families in antiquity.[3] One possible conclusion is that the demographics and dynamics of Jewish families may not shed any more light on early Christian families than does the study of Roman-period families broadly, for at least two reasons. First, as Shaye Cohen writes in the introduction to *The Jewish Family in Antiquity:* "The striking conclusion that emerges [from the four papers in the central section] is that the Jewish family in antiquity seems not to have been distinctive by the power of its Jewishness; rather, its structure, ideals, and dynamics seem to have been virtually identical with those of its ambient culture(s)."[4] Second, while it may be true that the earliest families we might retrospectively identify as "Christian" were comprised largely if not entirely of Jews, this ceases quickly to be the case.

The Available Evidence: A Brief Overview

Since the context of this paper is a discussion of early Christian families, I have limited my chronological parameters mostly to the first and second centuries C.E. The evidence comes from a variety of sources. Public and personal documents preserved on papyri, including a handful of marriage and divorce documents, found both in Egypt and in the region of the Dead Sea provide some details of demographics, although the best information for such things as age at first and subsequent marriages; numbers of marriages; numbers, sex, and names of children; age at death; and so forth is available principally from burial inscriptions and to a lesser extent from donative and other inscriptions found mostly in the diaspora, and dated mostly to the third and fourth centuries C.E. Our most significant historical source is, of course, Josephus, particularly his narratives of the Herodian family in his *Antiquities of the Jews* and the *Jewish War,* but also a few telling remarks about his own family arrangements in the *Life.*[5] The works of Philo of Alexandria provide, regrettably, little insight into

---

3. See especially Cohen, *The Jewish Family in Antiquity.*

4. Cohen, p. 2; one of those four papers was my own contribution, "Jewish Mothers and Daughters."

5. *Life* 414-15. See Kraemer, "Women's Judaism(s)," pp. 57-58.

the actual family arrangements and dynamics of Jews in Alexandria and Egypt in the first centuries B.C.E./C.E. Various literary works known or thought to be dated roughly to this period offer tantalizing representations of family demographics and dynamics, whose correspondence to social reality and practice is difficult to determine: here we might include Pseudo-Philo's *Biblical Antiquities*, 4 Maccabees, the *Sentences of Pseudo-Phocylides*, and of course, early Christian Gospels, particularly the Synoptics. Works like Tobit and Susanna offer fascinating portraits of ancient family dynamics, but the difficulties of dating these, and identifying their probable social context, make it prudent to omit them from the present discussion.[6]

Some may wonder why I have not included anything from the corpus of rabbinic literature in this category. The use of rabbinic sources in general as evidence for Jews and Jewish life in the first and second centuries C.E. is notoriously problematic. Most rabbinic sources are significantly later than the period under consideration, and it is extremely difficult to determine how much of rabbinic materials reflect actual Jewish practices, either of rabbis and their immediate circles, or of Jewish communities more broadly in the Roman period.[7] For the purposes of this paper, then, I have found it wiser to omit these materials from consideration.

In this paper I will focus primarily on what we know of the families of two

---

6. For some discussion, see Kraemer, "Jewish Mothers and Daughters in the Greco-Roman World." In that article I also analyzed the representation of family dynamics in the work usually known as *Joseph and Aseneth* (my own preferred title is now just *Aseneth*), but I would no longer do so, having come to the conclusion that *Aseneth* is most likely a relatively late production (third-fourth centuries C.E.) that may or may not be Jewish: Ross Shepard Kraemer, *When Aseneth Met Joseph: A Late Antique Tale of the Biblical Patriarch and His Egyptian Wife, Revisited* (New York and Oxford: Oxford University Press, 1998).

7. Not everyone, of course, shares my reluctance on this point: the best attempt to use rabbinic materials to investigate some of these questions is the work of Tal Ilan, in three volumes: *Jewish Women in Greco-Roman Palestine: An Inquiry into Image and Status*, Texte und Studien zum Antike Judentum 44 (Tübingen: J. C. B. Mohr [Paul Siebeck], 1995); *Mine and Yours Are Hers: Retrieving Women's History from a Literature* (Leiden: Brill, 1997); and most recently, *Integrating Women into Second Temple History*, Texte und Studien zum Antike Judentum 76 (Tübingen: Mohr Siebeck, 1999). For some methodological difficulties in Ilan's approach, see my review of *Jewish Women in Greco-Roman Palestine* in JAOS 118, no. 4 (1998): 570-73, and the review by Lieve Teugels of *Integrating Women* in the *Journal for the Study of Judaism* 31, no. 3 (2000): 322-25. For a different approach, see Miriam B. Peskowitz, *Spinning Fantasies: Rabbis, Gender, and History* (Los Angeles: University of California Press, 1997); see also Cynthia Baker, "Rebuilding the House of Israel: Gendered Bodies and Domestic Politics in Roman Jewish Galilee c. 135-300 C.E." (Ph.D. diss., Duke University, 1997); see also the review by Shira L. Lander, of Ilan, *Jewish Women*, and of Peskowitz, *Spinning Fantasies*, in *CCAR Journal: A Reform Jewish Quarterly* (summer 2000): 61-68.

Jewish women in this period: a member of the elite Herodian royal family, Berenice, a great-granddaughter of Herod the Great, who was born within a few years of the death of Jesus, and a somewhat more ordinary woman named Babatha (or perhaps Babta),[8] who was born about seventy-five years later, and whose affairs were somehow implicated in the Bar Kokhba revolt of the early 130s (see below). I do so at least partly because we know relatively more about both women than we do about virtually any other individual Jewish women in antiquity, and because, taken together, their lives appear to exemplify both typical and atypical Jewish families of this period and locale.

The Lives of Berenice and Babatha

Berenice

Berenice was born around 28 c.e., one of the five children of Agrippa I and Cypros, according to Josephus.[9] A great-granddaughter of Herod the Great, she ultimately became the lover of a Roman general named Titus, who is perhaps far better known in Jewish history for his role in the destruction of the Second Temple, and his building of an arch commemorating his triumph over the Jewish revolt that still stands in Rome today. According to the reports of several later Roman historians, Titus and Berenice apparently wanted to marry, but for the son of a Roman emperor (Vespasian) who ultimately became emperor himself, marriage to a Herodian Jewish princess was out of the question.[10]

Berenice's complicated, fascinating life, including her complex family relationships, may be glimpsed through a relatively wide range of ancient sources. Josephus, while silent on her relationship with Titus, provides the most details; Suetonius, Tacitus, Dio, and several other ancient historians treat her affair with

8. Her name is usually spelled Babatha; in *P. Yadin* 16, it is spelled Babtha.

9. See *Antiquities* 18 §132, for the names and numbers of the children. The date of Berenice's birth is derived from Josephus's statement that Berenice was sixteen (and already married to her second husband, Herod) when her father, Agrippa I, died. Nikos Kokkinos, refuting D. Schwartz and others, argues that Agrippa died in mid-44 c.e.; app. 5, "Date of Agrippa I's Death," in Nikos Kokkinos, *The Herodian Dynasty: Origins, Role in Society, and Eclipse*, Journal for the Study of the Pseudepigrapha Supplement Series 30 (Sheffield: Sheffield Academic Press, 1998), pp. 378-80.

10. The references to Berenice are conveniently collected, with detailed notes in some cases, in Menahem Stern, *Greek and Latin Authors on Jews and Judaism*, 3 vols. (Jerusalem: Israel Academy of Sciences and Humanities, 1980), nos. 231 (Quintilian 4.1.19); 275 (Tacitus, *Histories* 2.2.1); 298 (Juvenal, *Satire* 6.156); 318 (Suetonius, *Divine Titus* 7); 433 (Cassius Dio 66.15); 532 (*Epitome of the Emperors* 10.4-7).

Titus. She makes a brief appearance in Acts 25:13–26:32, where she, her brother Agrippa, and a substantial retinue hear Paul's defense and collectively pronounce him blameless.[11] She was honored with a statue and accompanying inscription in Athens, where she is called "great" queen; a Latin inscription from Beirut also calls her "Queen."[12]

None of our sources describes her childhood directly, although as I will discuss later, we may deduce some things about it from what we know about her parents. It seems reasonable to suppose that she received some formal education and that she may have been fluent, if not literate, in several languages, Greek, Latin, and Aramaic.[13] At a relatively early age (between about thirteen and fifteen)[14] she was married to a man from an elite Alexandrian Jewish fam-

11. For my analysis of Luke's treatment of Berenice, see Kraemer, "Berenice."

12. *IG* 3:556 (*CIG* 361) and *AE* 1928:82; *Comptes rendues de l'Academie des Inscriptions* (1927), pp. 243-44. Interestingly, the *IG* inscription is not included in Jean-Baptiste Frey, *Corpus Inscriptionum Judaicarum*, 2 vols. (Vatican City: Pontificio Instituto di Archeologia Cristiana, 1935-52), nor in Baruch Lifshitz's prolegomenon to the revised edition of vol. 1 (New York: Ktav, 1965). The appropriate volumes for the two inscriptions have not yet appeared in the new Cambridge volumes of Jewish inscriptions edited by David Noy. They are treated by Grace H. Macurdy in her article "Julia Berenice," *AJP* 56 (1935): 246-53, and in her chapter, "Royal Women in Judaea," in *Vassal Queens and Some Contemporary Women in the Roman Empire,* Johns Hopkins University Studies in Archaeology 22 (Baltimore: Johns Hopkins University Press; London: Oxford University Press, Humphrey Milford, 1937; reprint, Chicago: Ares Press, 1993), pp. 63-91.

13. Berenice was almost certainly born in Rome, and spent the early years of her childhood in the imperial court, where she might well have learned Latin as well as Greek. She lived subsequently in Tiberias (where probably she would have spoken Greek, and perhaps learned Aramaic, although not necessarily), in Syria, in Alexandria, and then in Palestine. Her extensive sojourns in Rome and other foreign kingdoms certainly suggest that she could have been fluent in Latin, and perhaps learned other indigenous languages as well.

14. The actual date of the marriage is unknown, and therefore, Berenice's age at the time. Various dates, from 41 C.E. (David Braund, "Bernice," in *ABD*, 1:677) to 43 or 44 C.E. (A. Fuks, "Marcus Julius Alexander," *Zion* 13-14 [1948-49]: 15-17 [Hebrew], cited in Louis Feldman, Josephus, *Antiquities* 19 §277, LCL [Cambridge, Mass., 1965], 9:343 n. g; Mary Smallwood, *The Jews under Roman Rule, from Pompey to Diocletian: A Study in Political Relations,* SJLA 20 [Leiden: Brill, 1976; reprint, 1981], p. 385 n. 106) have been proposed. Kokkinos surmises that Agrippa I arranged the marriages of his daughters in late 41 C.E., at a major birthday celebration when he was himself fifty-two: presumably the marriage of Berenice and Marcus would have required some time for appropriate preparations, and would thus have taken place quite late in 41, or sometime in 42 (Kokkinos, p. 294). If Kokkinos is right that Agrippa died in mid-44 when Berenice was already married to Herod, that marriage cannot have taken place any later than late 43/early 44. Thus 41 is a reasonable guess, but 42 would work also for the marriage to Marcus. The discussion in Emil Schürer, *The History of the Jews in the Age of Jesus Christ,* a new English version revised and edited by G. Vermes, F. Millar, and M. Goodman, 3 vols. (Edinburgh: T. & T. Clark, 1986), 1:572 n. 59, raises the possibility that Marcus and Berenice were be-

ily, Marcus Julius Alexander, the son of Alexander, alabarch of Egypt, making her the niece by marriage of Philo of Alexandria and the sister-in-law of Tiberius Julius Alexander (who ultimately became procurator of Judea, prefect of Egypt, and an adviser to Vespasian and Titus during the Jewish revolt).[15] After Marcus died, her father Agrippa I then married her to his brother, Herod of Chalcis, with whom she had two sons.[16] In 50 C.E., at approximately age twenty-two, she was a widow for the second time.

After Herod's death Berenice did not immediately remarry. Rather she appears to have ruled as queen with her brother, Agrippa II.[17] The narrative from Acts is set during this period. According to Josephus, Berenice's relationship with her brother was rumored to be an incestuous one, though his report is not substantiated in several other writers, and may reflect his own hostility toward Berenice for her support of one of his opponents.[18] To thwart the rumor, so

---

trothed only and the marriage to Marcus never took place, although Josephus says quite plainly that Marcus married (γαμεῖ) Berenice.

15. For discussion of Tiberius Julius Alexander, see, inter alia, Stern's notes to Tacitus, *Histories* 1.11.1, with bibliographic references in *Greek and Latin Authors,* pp. 7-8. One might wonder how his presence in Jerusalem during the war would have affected Berenice, who would appear to have been involved with Titus by now.

16. See *Antiquities* 19 §277 for the marriage; for the two sons, Berenicianus and Hyrcanus, see *Antiquities* 20 §104.

17. Macurdy offers evidence that Berenice's title of queen derives from her joint rulership with Agrippa: "Royal Women in Judaea," pp. 84-91; also her almost identical article, "Julia Berenice." Tal Ilan asserts without discussion that it derives from her marriage to Herod, king of Chalcis ("Josephus and Nicolaus on Women," in *Geschichte — Tradition — Reflexion. Festschrift für Martin Hengel zum 70 Geburtstag,* vol. 1, *Judentum,* ed. Hubert Cancik, Hermann Lichtenberger, and Peter Schäfer [Tübingen: J. C. B. Mohr (Paul Siebeck), 1996], pp. 221-62, here 229), but as Macurdy's discussion indicates, the question is quite complex. In addition to the inscriptions, her designation as queen occurs in several Roman writers.

18. See Macurdy, "Julia Berenice," pp. 250-51, and "Royal Women in Judaea," pp. 88-89. Macurdy doubts that the allegation of incest was true and suggests that Josephus's hostile portrait of Agrippa and Berenice, including this allegation, stems from Josephus's anger at Agrippa for his patronage, and Berenice for her support, of Josephus's opponent, Justus of Tiberias (*Vita* 343, 356). Feldman notes that "Juvenal vi. 156-160 likewise alludes to this report when he speaks of the famous diamond that the 'barbarian' Agrippa gave to his 'unchaste sister'" (LCL, 9:467 n. 6), but see the more complex discussion of this passage in Stern, 2:100, including the question of whether these terms apply to Agrippa and Berenice or to Ptolemy and Cleopatra. The Latin is actually *incestae.* Ilan argues that Josephus is here (and elsewhere in his account of Berenice) following a priestly author concerned with Berenice's apparent violations of Jewish ancestral laws: Ilan, "Josephus and Nicolaus," p. 233, with references to the work of Schwartz in numerous notes. Ilan argues that, in fact, much of Josephus's material on women comes from his sources: she is scathingly critical of Grace Macurdy for an uncritical acceptance of the material in Josephus, but does not seem to tackle the question of why Josephus uses this material as he does.

Josephus relates, Berenice persuaded one Polemo, king of Cilicia, to marry her (and to agree to be circumcised for the occasion, since he wasn't Jewish).[19] Josephus claims that Polemo agreed principally because of Berenice's wealth and that the marriage failed quickly, when Berenice, motivated by ἀκολασία (inappropriate sexual desire),[20] deserted (or perhaps divorced)[21] Polemo. In the writings of Josephus, Berenice last appears in Jerusalem during the war when, barefoot and penitent, she implores the Roman procurator Gessius Florus to desist from his slaughter of Jews in Jerusalem.[22]

The remainder of Berenice's life is known from sources other than Josephus. When, precisely, she and Titus met does not appear to be known.[23] Roman historians concur, though, that Titus was deeply in love with her. After the war Berenice and her brother Agrippa went to Rome with Titus. One Roman historian, Dio Cassius, says Berenice acted in all respects as though she were Titus's wife, creating enough tension between Titus and the Roman aristocracy that she was forced to leave Rome.[24] When Titus was proclaimed emperor in 79 C.E., after the death of Vespasian, she returned to Rome, apparently hoping, finally, to become his legitimate wife, but sufficient pressure was brought to bear on Titus that he dismissed her for good.[25] Two years later, on September 13, 81, Titus died, just shy of his forty-second birthday.[26]

Blaming Josephus's sources conveniently defers questions about their accuracy and rehabilitates Josephus. For a similar assessment of the function of Ilan's source criticism, and a detailed critique, see the lengthy review by Lieve Teugels of Ilan's most recent book, *Integrating Women into Second Temple History*, in the *Journal for the Study of Judaism* 31, no. 3 (2000): 322-25.

19. *Antiquities* 20 §145-46. On the question of which Polemo Berenice married, see N. Kokkinos, app. 6, "Identity of Polemo, Husband of Berenice II," pp. 381-82, in his *Herodian Dynasty*. Kokkinos identifies him as [Caius] Julius Polemo II of Pontus and Cilicia, and dates the marriage to the early sixties (when she would have been in her early to mid-thirties).

20. The term is difficult to translate precisely: Feldman's choice is "licentiousness." It is the opposite of σωφροσύνη, which, applied to women, primarily signified sexual chastity.

21. καταλείπω.

22. *War* 2 §310-14. According to Josephus, Berenice was in Jerusalem at the time to fulfill a Nazarite vow: whether related to the war or other causes, is unclear from the text.

23. Titus accompanied Vespasian to Jerusalem in 67 C.E.; left and then returned, ultimately taking control of the Roman troops in Jerusalem, and destroying the city and the temple in August of 70. He had divorced his second wife ca. 64. If they met around 67, Berenice would have been about thirty-nine; Titus, who was born on September 30, 39, would have been about twenty-eight.

24. Dio Cassius, *Historia Romana* 66.15.3-5, preserved in Xiphilinus. Text, translation, and commentary in Stern, no. 433 (2:378-39).

25. Suetonius, *Divus Titus* 7.1. Text, translation, and commentary in Stern, no. 318 (2:126-28).

26. Perhaps at the instigation of his brother, Domitian: Suetonius, *Domitian* 2.3; Cassius

Babatha

In the late 1950s Israeli archaeologists excavating a cave associated with Simeon bar Kokhba, leader of the second Jewish revolt against Rome (ca. 132-35 C.E.), found a set of papyrus documents rolled up in a leather bag. These turned out to contain the personal papers of a Jewish[27] woman named Babatha, who was probably born around the year 100, and who may have died in the revolt.[28] (Several skeletons, both male and female, were found in the cave, along with various personal items, such as mirrors, sandals, bowls, etc., and it is not impossible that Babatha herself is among those dead.) Her archive includes marriage contracts, loan documents, guardianship papers, land registrations, and more. Written in Greek, Aramaic, and the regional language of Nabatean, transacted in diverse legal jurisdictions and involving Jews, Roman citizens (who may or may not have been Jews), and Nabateans, these papyri throw into sharp relief the diverse cultural and legal environments in which Babatha and those around her lived their lives. They offer us the most detailed portrait yet of an actual Jewish woman from Greco-Roman antiquity.[29]

We know less of the outlines of Babatha's life than we do of Berenice's, though we know some of the specifics in surprising detail. Babatha was born to a couple named Simeon and Miriam, between about 90 and 105 C.E., in an area known as the Roman province of Arabia, just south of the Dead Sea.[30] Whether

---

Dio 66.26; see also Philostratus, *Life of Apollonius of Tyana* 6.32, where Apollonius predicts to Titus that he will meet a death from the sea: Philostratus explains this as a reference to Domitian poisoning Titus with an extract of sea hare.

27. Kokkinos addresses the question of whether Babatha herself was actually Jewish "by faith" — his suggestion is that she might have been what he calls an "Idumaean Jewess." Part of the discussion centers on the fact that in *P. Yadin* 16, a registration of land document, she swears an oath on the τύχη of the emperor that she has registered her property in good faith; part on the fact that she has what Kokkinos calls "an unavoidable link with Idumaea." Kokkinos, p. 294 n. 106; he cites here Glen Bowersock, "The Babatha Papyri, Masada and Rome," *JRA* 4 (1991): 336-44; Martin Goodman, "Babatha's Story," *JRS* 81 (1991): 169-75; and B. Isaac, "The Babatha Archive: A Review Article," *IEJ* 42 (1992): 62-75.

28. Naphtali Lewis, ed., *The Documents from the Bar Kochba Period in the Cave of Letters: Greek Papyri*, JDS 2 (Jerusalem: Israel Exploration Society, Hebrew University, Shrine of the Book, 1989), esp. pp. 3-5; also Yigal Yadin, *"Bar Kokhba": The Rediscovery of the Legendary Hero of the Second Jewish Revolt against Rome* (New York: Random House, 1971), for description of the find, with illustrations.

29. Although on the question of her "Jewishness," see above, n. 27.

30. This date is admittedly speculative. *P. Yadin* 12, dated to 124 C.E., records the appointment of two guardians for Babatha's son, Jesus. It appears that orphaned (i.e., fatherless) sons may have required guardians until they were twenty-one: anecdotal evidence may be found, inter alia, in Philostratus's *Life of Apollonius of Tyana*, bk. 1.13. Lewis (p. 88) hypothesizes that the

she had siblings is unknown. Her parents were financially comfortable, owning land, houses, and orchards in their village. One of the earliest documents in her archive records a deed of gift from her father, Simeon, to her mother, Miriam, transferring all his property in the village of Ma'oza, including houses, court-yards, gardens, and so forth.[31] (Babatha's second husband, Judah, makes a similar gift to his own daughter, Shelamzion, at the time of her marriage.)[32] Some of this property is subsequently enumerated in a registration document filed by Babatha in December 127. The absence of a similar deed of gift from Miriam, while still living, to Babatha may suggest that Babatha inherited the property when her mother died. We know nothing of the specifics of her childhood, except that she was not taught to read and write.[33]

Her first marriage was to a man named Jesus (in Greek; Joshua in Aramaic), with whom she had a son, also named Jesus. Whether she had other children is unknown: the existing papyri make no mention of them. Her husband Jesus died while their son was still legally a minor. The boy remained in Babatha's care, but two guardians, both men, were appointed to administer Jesus' estate and provide for the son.[34]

Sometime around 125 (the precise date is unclear),[35] Babatha married

---

elder Jesus must have died not long before the appointment of the guardians, perhaps in the same year (124) or the year before. In some of the latest papyri, dated to 130-31, the son, Jesus, is still under the legal care of his guardians: therefore he should have been no older than twenty in 131, which would have made him no older than his early teens in 124. If this were Babatha's first marriage, and Jesus her first child, we might imagine her to have been no older than about twenty when he was born, so depending on his age, she could have been anywhere from her early twenties to her late thirties or more in 124.

31. *P. Yadin* 7. Kokkinos points out that Eleazar was originally from Idumea, and had moved to Ma'oza.

32. *P. Yadin* 19.

33. In *P. Yadin* 15, a document regarding the guardianship of her son, Eleazar signs for Babatha "because she does not know letters" (ll. 34-35: Ἐλεάζαρος Ἐλεαζάρου ἔγραψα ὑπὲρ αὐτῆς ἐρωτηθεὶς διὰ τὸ αὐτῆς μὴ εἰδέναι γράμματα).

34. *P. Yadin* 12, dated to 124.

35. Lewis proposes (p. 58) that the marriage must antedate the earliest papyri which have Judah functioning as Babatha's guardian, namely, *P. Yadin* 14 and 15, dated to October 11 or 12, 125, based on the practice of husbands acting as their wives' guardians. Lewis concedes, though, that Babatha is not explicitly named as Judah's wife until *P. Yadin* 17, dated to February 128. After Judah died, Babatha acquires at least three different guardians: *P. Yadin* 22, 25, and 27; in *P. Yadin* 26, written on the same day as 25 (July 131), she has no guardian. Unless one wants to argue that Babatha was married, in short succession, to all these men, it seems clear that unmarried women utilized the services of guardians to whom they were not married. Despite Lewis's assumption that Judah became Babatha's guardian because he was her husband, it seems at least quite possible that the marriage followed the guardianship, which is what the papyri seem

again. Her new husband was a man named Judah, who already had a living wife, named Miriam, and a daughter, Shelamzion. Babatha's papyri thus provide the only known documentation of a polygynous Jewish marriage in this period.

Several years later Judah died.[36] His death appears to have thrown his extended family into protracted legal disputes, leaving Babatha and Miriam to wrangle over the effects of the estate and giving Babatha's affairs a distinctly modern resonance. One papyrus in particular, dated to July 9, 131, records a dispute between Babatha and Miriam over the household property of their late husband, Judah.[37] Babatha summons Miriam to appear before the governor, to explain why Miriam seized everything in the house. Miriam replies that she had previously warned Babatha to stay away from the house, and that Babatha had no claims against Judah's estate. Another papyrus testifies to her disputes with her late husband's relatives over the ownership and disposition of date orchards: Babatha sells a date crop from an orchard which she claimed after Judah's estate failed to repay her dowry and deposit.[38]

Not long after, the Bar Kokhba revolt broke out (around 132). En-Gedi, where Babatha lived, was a stronghold of the revolt. Documents and artifacts pertaining to the revolt, including those of Bar Kokhba himself, were found in the same cave as Babatha's papyri. Some scholars have speculated that Babatha, like others caught in the revolt, may have fled to the caves in the Judean desert for refuge, and there met their deaths. Babatha appears to have had a more specific connection to the revolt: her cowife, Miriam, was apparently a member of the same family as the author of a letter to Bar Kokhba: one Jonathan, son of Be'ayan.[39] But if Babatha is not among the cave's dead, it seems likely that she was never able to return to retrieve the personal archive left there, perhaps for safekeeping.

---

themselves to say. Hence the date of the marriage cannot be later than 128, and might or might not have been earlier. In *P. Yadin* 7, Babatha's father makes over all his property in Ma'oza, present and future, to Babatha's mother. It also specifies that should their daughter, Babatha, be widowed, she gets permanent use of a house until she remarries. In *P. Yadin* 16, the land registration, Babatha identifies herself as daughter of Simeon, not wife of Judah, and indicates that she and Judah live in separate domiciles. This datum may be read in at least two ways: If Babatha and Judah are married, they may maintain separate residences due to the polygamous nature of the marriage. Alternatively, since the father's deed of gift provided a house for Babatha if widowed, so long as she did not remarry, Babatha and Judah may have resided separately because, contrary to Lewis, they were not yet married.

36. Between April 128 and June 130. (See the discussion in Lewis, p. 88.)

37. *P. Yadin* 26.

38. *P. Yadin* 22 (130 C.E.)

39. Y. Yadin, "Expedition D — the Cave of the Letters," *IEJ* 12 (1962): 241-44.

Interestingly, there is even some possibility of a historical connection between Babatha and Berenice. Babatha's stepdaughter, Shelamzion, was engaged in a dispute with two of her cousins, the minor, "orphaned" sons of her father's brother, over property that her father (Babatha's second husband) had deeded to her.[40] Babatha herself was also involved in the dispute. One of the guardians representing the boys was a woman named Julia Crispina.[41] Crispina's father's name was Berenicianus, known to be the name of one of Berenice's sons by her marriage to Herod.[42] Tal Ilan has suggested that Julia Crispina was in fact the granddaughter of Berenice, an identification that is chronologically feasible and supported (though perhaps not conclusively) by additional evidence.[43] Other scholars, though, have been more skeptical of the connection.

Comparative Demographics and Family Dynamics

The lives of Berenice and Babatha both conform to much of what we already know about family demographics and dynamics in the first and second centuries C.E., and allow us to situate the discussion of Jewish families within the larger context of the Greco-Roman Mediterranean. I will begin with some observations about demographics.

Though customs seem to have varied widely, most women in the Greco-Roman Mediterranean, including Jewish women, appear to have married, or otherwise entered into active sexual and reproductive lives, at a fairly early age, anywhere from twelve to twenty.[44] The first marriages of free women were typi-

---

40. In *P. Yadin* 20, the guardians renounce their prior claim against Shelamzion, but continue to litigate with Babatha in *P. Yadin* 25.

41. *P. Yadin* 20, 25.

42. Josephus, *Antiquities* 20 §104.

43. See Tal Ilan, "Julia Crispina, Daughter of Berenicianus, a Herodian Princess in the Babatha Archive: A Case Study in Historical Identification," *JQR* 82, no. 3-4 (1992): 361-81. The identification is dismissed rather cavalierly by Jonas Greenfield, "'Because He/She Did Not Know Letters': Remarks on a First Millennium C.E. Legal Expression," *Journal of the Ancient Near Eastern Society* 22 (1993): 39-43. A more reasoned discussion of the probability and problems may be found in Kokkinos, pp. 293-94.

44. Enslaved women or women otherwise unable to contract licit marriage would still generally have become "sexually active." There is now an extensive secondary bibliography on these topics: for an excellent recent overview, with considerable references, see Anne Hanson, "The Roman Family," and Bruce W. Frier, "Roman Demography," both in *Life, Death, and Entertainment in the Roman Empire,* ed. D. S. Potter and D. J. Mattingly (Ann Arbor: University of Michigan Press, 1999), pp. 19-66 (Hanson), pp. 85-109 (Frier). Frier notes that in Egyptian census returns, "free women began to marry at age twelve, but by their fifteenth birthday only about 12

cally to older men: a difference of ten or fifteen years seems common. Women who did not themselves die early (frequently from childbirth, illness, accidents, and sometimes starvation) could routinely expect to be widowed, and to enter into additional marriage(s). First marriages were regularly a matter of family arrangements, often negotiated between the couple's fathers, or between the bride's father and her future husband. Subsequent marriage arrangements might often involve more active participation by the woman herself, particularly when her own father was no longer alive.

Although the question is complicated, recent research has suggested that in the absence of other factors such as illness, diet, infertility, and so forth, women who were sexually active could expect to continue to become pregnant, give birth, and nurse children in a pattern of what Bruce Frier calls "natural" fertility. Drawing partly on the evidence from Egyptian census data, Frier suggests that women could expect to become pregnant every two to three years throughout their childbearing years.[45] The average life expectancy at birth appears to have been in the low twenties. Children who survived to age ten, then, appear to have had an average life expectancy of another thirty-five years; mortality rates that Frier notes are considerably higher than those in early modern Europe.[46] In their study, Osiek and Balch also cite the work of Thomas Wiedemann, who estimates that given ancient mortality rates for infants and children, only about 40 percent of the population could expect to live past age twenty. To end up with two adult children themselves of an age to reproduce, a woman would have had to give birth at least five times: three of those five children would die before reaching adulthood.[47]

Interestingly, these demographic patterns are illustrated reasonably well by the few bits of personal history provided by the first-century Jewish historian Josephus, toward the end of his apologetic autobiography. In 67 C.E., after he either surrendered to the Romans or was taken captive by them at the end of the siege of Jodefat (Jotapata), Vespasian had him marry another captive, a young

---

percent of women were married. The bulk of female marriage took place between ages fifteen and twenty" (p. 91). He also notes that by age fifty, only 40 percent of surviving women were still married. A less detailed, more general survey of these issues may also be found in the introductory chapters of Osiek and Balch, *Families in the New Testament World;* their detailed discussion of domestic architecture is particularly nice.

45. Frier, p. 98.

46. Frier, p. 89; discussion of the general issue of mortality may be found on pp. 87-90.

47. Thomas Wiedemann, *Adults and Children in the Roman Empire* (London: Routledge, 1989), p. 15, cited in Osiek and Balch, p. 67. Richard Saller suggested to me that the work of Bruce Frier and Roger S. Bagnall, *The Demography of Roman Egypt* (Cambridge and New York: Cambridge University Press, 1994), is more reliable.

woman who was παρθένος and from Caesarea; whether she was Jewish is unclear. He would have been about thirty years old at the time, and does not appear to have been married previously. Since she is called παρθένος, it seems reasonable to assume that this first wife would have been relatively young, and
considerably younger than Josephus himself. The marriage dissolved quickly
once Josephus was freed. He says only then that he married again, apparently in
Alexandria: whether we are to infer that his wife was herself Alexandrian is,
here too, unclear.[48] This second wife was the mother of three children, of whom
two died. The sex of the two who died is not known (they are merely called
παῖδων), but the one who survived was a son named Hyrcanus. Josephus subsequently divorced her because she displeased him, whatever that means. This
marriage would appear to have lasted at least a few years, and perhaps as many
as ten, depending on the interval between pregnancies and how long each child
lived. After his divorce Josephus married a third time, at which point he would
have been at least in his mid-thirties, and probably closer to forty. By his third
wife he had two sons, Justus and Simonides, also called Agrippa.[49] All told, he
was married at least three times, and had at least five children, three of whom
survived.[50]

It may also be worth pointing out that these same demographic patterns
appear to describe the family of Jesus as well, at least as represented in the Synoptic traditions. These three portray Jesus as one of a large family of two or
more other brothers and two or more sisters (Mark 3:31-35; Matt. 12:46-50; Luke
8:19-21);[51] the names of his brothers are given in Mark 6:3//Matthew 13:55 as
James, Joses (Matthew: Joseph), Simon, and Judas, although his sisters go unnamed. The age difference between his mother, Mary, and her husband, Joseph,
is never explicitly stated, but one way to understand the lack of reference to Joseph in the Gospel narratives, apart from the stories of Jesus' birth and childhood, is as a consequence of his death before Jesus' public career, consistent
with the pattern identified above.[52]

To return to Berenice and Babatha, the experiences of both women regarding marriage, at least, turn out to be fairly typical. Berenice's first marriage, to

48. Josephus, *Life* 414-15.

49. Josephus, *Life* 427.

50. Feldman apparently took this as evidence that Josephus was difficult to live with, but in
fact, it seems demographically ordinary, although admittedly the first marriage was highly artificial, and Josephus does dismiss the second wife because she "displeased" him.

51. For further discussion of these passages, see my entries in *Women in Scripture*.

52. Another, of course, is theological, in which case Joseph's absence cannot be taken as an
indication of anything about his age, although we are still left with the image of a fairly typical
family: aging widow with numerous children, at least some of them "grown."

Marcus Julius Alexander, son of Alexander the alabarch of Egypt (and nephew of Philo of Alexandria), was arranged by her father, Agrippa I.[53] Though the exact date of this marriage is uncertain, Berenice must have been in her very early teens at the time, since she was already married for the second time at age sixteen, after Marcus's death left her a widow.[54] It is difficult, if not impossible, to determine how old Marcus was when they married, or whether he had been married before. He was the older brother of Tiberius Julius Alexander, who would seem to have been born after Tiberius became emperor in 14 C.E.[55] Since Tiberius Julius Alexander was procurator of Judea circa 46-48 C.E., prefect of Egypt, and a major adviser to Titus during the siege of Jerusalem, it seems reasonable to assume that he was born not long after the emperor Tiberius's ascension. If we draw on the general demographic patterns I noted earlier, it also seems reasonable to think that the brothers would have been at least two to three years apart, making Marcus born no later (or not much later) than 12 C.E.[56] This would have made him about sixteen years Berenice's senior, consistent with the age spread of many ancient marriages. There seems to be no information about Marcus's prior marital history, and it is quite possible that Berenice was his first (and only) wife. No children are known from this marriage.

Berenice's second marriage, also arranged by her father, was to her paternal uncle, Herod king of Chalcis. Kokkinos estimates that Herod would have been born circa 10 or 9 B.C.E.:[57] he would have thus been about thirty-eight years

---

53. Kokkinos, who claims there were strong ties between the two "families" based on reciprocal aid, implying that the marriage of their children is a further strengthening of those ties (p. 295), seems to have glossed over something important here. As I discuss below, when Agrippa was in dire financial straits, he sought a loan from Alexander, who refused him, but agreed to loan the money to Cypros, "marvelling (καταπεπλημένος)" at her devotion to her husband and her many virtues. Cypros promised to repay the loan herself. Kokkinos, however, obscures this crucial distinction and writes that "Alexander had saved Agrippa's life in the past by lending large sums of money to him." It is interesting that Feldman's marginal header in the Loeb edition reads "Agrippa obtains a loan from Alexander the alabarch" (9:103). Not inconceivably, the subsequent marriage between the two children is related to this loan. While a more feminist perspective might cast the marriage as a fairly typical use of women as a medium of exchange in relationships between powerful men, Alexander's hostility to Agrippa, and his willingness to loan the money to Cypros, instead suggest a more complex dynamic. It's not clear how Josephus knows any of this.

54. Josephus, *Antiquities* 19 §354.

55. Thus explaining his name. I am grateful to my colleague at the University of Pennsylvania, Robert A. Kraft, for discussions on Marcus and Tiberius.

56. Although a closer interval is certainly possible: Berenice and Agrippa II appear to have been only a year apart.

57. Kokkinos, p. 304; see also p. 272.

older than Berenice, and in his mid-fifties when they married. Herod's first wife was Mariamme, a granddaughter of Herod the Great (through her mother, Olympias): they are known to have had one son. Kokkinos points out that we do not know whether that marriage ended in Mariamme's death or in divorce, and suggests it is even possible that the marriage to Berenice was bigamous.[58] The marriage to Berenice lasted six years, until Herod died in 50 c.e., leaving Berenice twenty-two years old, again a widow, now with two children.

As I mentioned earlier, Josephus (or perhaps, as some scholars have suggested, a source on which he drew for these events)[59] claims that Berenice remained widowed for a considerable period of time after Herod's death, and was suspected of an incestuous relationship with Agrippa. Sometime in the early sixties c.e., when she would have been in her early to mid-thirties, Berenice was briefly married to a non-Jew, Polemo, king of Cilicia, who, so Josephus relates, agreed to be circumcised for the marriage. Josephus's language suggests that Berenice herself arranged the marriage, prevailing on Polemo in order to quash the rumors of incest. But it is hard to assess how the marriage was contracted. By suggesting, however tacitly, that Berenice both arranged the marriage herself and then abandoned her husband out of her own lack of sexual self-control, Josephus (or perhaps his source) manages to impugn Berenice's reputation even further than the allegation of incest, by suggesting that she acts in an inappropriately autonomous manner. By arranging the marriage and abandoning it (or perhaps actually initiating the divorce), Berenice usurps roles Josephus (and of course many others) perceives of as appropriately male: the active roles of fathers and husbands. Still, the questions are complex and depend in part on how much autonomy we might reasonably expect a woman of Berenice's stature and age to have exercised. Certainly her father was no longer alive to contract the third marriage, and she herself was considerably older. Although one might have expected Agrippa II to participate in the marriage of his sister, after the death of their father, we cannot really ascertain from Josephus what role Agrippa might have played either in the marriage to Polemo or in its dissolution. In any case, to the best of our knowledge this was the last of Berenice's formal marriages, though her most historically significant liaison, with the eventual Roman emperor Titus, was still to come.

Parenthetically, it's also interesting that Berenice and her siblings were all born when their father, Agrippa I, was in his late thirties or older. He was in his

58. Kokkinos, p. 308; he does note in the conclusion (p. 353) that at least one other Herodian, Herod the Great, was known to have engaged in polygamy (polygyny).

59. As I noted above, n. 18, Ilan argues that Josephus is here (and elsewhere in his account of Berenice) following a priestly author concerned with Berenice's apparent violations of Jewish ancestral laws: Ilan, "Josephus and Nicolaus," p. 233.

late thirties when his first son, Drusus (who died relatively young), was born, and almost forty when Agrippa II was born. He was about forty when Berenice, the oldest daughter, was born, forty-six when Drusilla was born, and about fifty when the youngest sister, Mariamme, was born. How old Cypros was at the time is not known.[60]

Babatha's marital history lacks the political weight of Berenice's, but is nonetheless telling. Her age at her first marriage, to Jesus son of Jesus, is uncertain. Jesus left Babatha a widow while their son, also called Jesus, was still relatively young. Sometime around 125 C.E. Babatha entered into a polygynous marriage with Judah. Their marriage contract, written in Aramaic, was among Babatha's papers, but its opening lines are poorly preserved and do not allow us to determine its precise date, nor whether Babatha's father was a party to the contract.[61] This marriage, too, ended with the husband's death.

Without considering the thorny problems of what legal systems and standards may have applied in either case, it is clear that both women entered into licit, publicly recognized marriages. Berenice's third marriage, to Polemo, ended with both parties still living, but whether it was terminated by a formal divorce, and if so, of what legal nature, raises complex questions that I cannot address here.[62]

---

60. Kokkinos (p. 276; see also his discussion, p. 160) speculates that she could not have been born before the marriage of her parents, Phasael I and Shelamzion, ca. 20 B.C.E., and she may have been born as late as the turn of the century. Since she is still bearing children around 38 C.E., it seems reasonable to imagine that a late date makes more sense, in which case she would have been something like ten years or more Agrippa's junior.

61. To the best of my knowledge, the second volume of the papyri still has not been published, although the volume is described as forthcoming in H. Cotton and A. Yardeni, DJD 27 (published in 1997). The marriage contract itself, however, was published in 1994: Yigal Yadin, Jonas C. Greenfield, and Ada Yardeni, "Babatha's Ketubbah," *IEJ* 44, nos. 1-2 (1994): 75-101; see also Mordechai A. Friedman, "Babatha's Ketubbah: Some Preliminary Observations," *IEJ* 46, nos. 1-2 (1996): 55-76. The only legible signatories to the contract are Judah, Babatha, and a witness named Toma.

62. Recent studies suggest that there is more evidence for Jewish women initiating divorce proceedings than previously known and/or recognized. Particularly important is *P. Se'elim* 13, from the region of En-Gedi in the Judean desert, probably a divorce bill given from a woman, Shelamzion, to her husband, Eleazar. Initial notice of the papyrus appeared in J. T. Milik, "Le travail d'édition des manuscrits du Désert de Juda," in *Volume du congrès Strasbourg 1956* = VTSup 4 (Leiden: Brill, 1956), p. 21. The papyrus was published by Ada Yardeni, *Nahal Se'elim Documents* (Jerusalem: Israel Exploration Society and Ben Gurion University in the Negev Press, 1995). Yardeni espoused the view taken by the late Jonas Greenfield that the papyrus is not a *get*, but rather the receipt for a *get* issued to a woman. Tal Ilan, however, argues that the more plausible interpretation is that Milik's initial assessment was correct ("Notes and Observations on a Newly Published Divorce Bill from the Judaean Desert," *HTR* 89, no. 2 [1996]: 195-202, with Aramaic text and English translation).

As for their childbearing, determining the number of children Jewish women are likely to have had is difficult to do on the basis of the available evidence, though much suggests that it would have been similar to that of non-Jewish women. As with non-Jewish women, many factors would have been relevant here, including economics, maternal health, knowledge of birth control techniques, and so forth. Jewish women's experience of infant and child mortality is similarly likely to have been consistent with that of non-Jewish women, with perhaps one exception. It has been suggested that Jews were less likely to practice abortion and/or to expose unwanted children, though the evidence is not unambiguous and Frier suggests that contraception and abortion were primarily used in nonmarital sex.[63] It is interesting to note that a number of Herodian marriages, where economic advantage may be presumed, produced at least five children who lived to adulthood.[64] Despite Wiedemann's claim that it would take five births to provide two adults old enough to reproduce themselves, this surely does not mean that every woman with five children surviving to adulthood had been pregnant something like twelve or thirteen times, but it does suggest that such families might well have experienced some failed pregnancies and prior childhood deaths![65]

Berenice is known to have had only two children, both boys, from her marriage to her maternal uncle Herod, while Babatha is known only to have had one child, Jesus, by her first husband, Jesus; no children are mentioned from the marriage with Judah, who himself seems to have had only the daughter, Shelamzion, by his wife Miriam (although this datum may be more due to the selective nature of the papyri than anything else). Berenice had no known children with Marcus, and neither her (short) marriage to Polemo nor her affair with Titus is known to have produced children, or at least children who survived long enough to warrant mention. Both their childbearing histories seem comprehensible from the facts of their marital histories alone. Berenice's marriage to Marcus may have been too brief (as little as a few months, and less than three years)[66] to produce children, or

---

63. Frier, pp. 98-99.

64. Herod the Great and Mariamme (daughter of Hyrcanus); Aristobulus and Berenice; Phasael and Shelamzio(n); Agrippa I and Cypros had five children, but one son, Drusus, died before adolescence (Josephus, *Antiquities* 18 §132).

65. Families with five living children are well attested from Asia Minor in the third and fourth centuries, largely due to the practice of erecting antemortem burial inscriptions listing the names of those who could be lawfully buried in a particular sarcophagus, tomb, etc. Numerous examples may be found in *Monumenta Asiae Minoris Antiqua*, 8 vols. (Manchester: Manchester University Press, for the American Society of Archaeological Research by Manchester; London: Longmans, Green, 1928-62).

66. The longest possible duration of the marriage would be from late 41 C.E. (if Kokkinos is

at least children who survived past a brief infancy. Her marriage to Polemo appears to have been similarly brief, and by then she would have been in her middle to late thirties, not necessarily past childbearing age but certainly at an age where fertility might have been a question.[67] Her age also seems likely to account for the lack of children conceived with Titus; by 75 c.e., when she goes to Rome and lives with Titus publicly, she would have been about forty-seven (Titus would have been about thirty-six).[68] In Babatha's case, too, the relatively brief duration of her marriage to Judah might account for the absence of children (assuming that the absence of their mention in any of the papyri is sufficient to conclude that there were none).

Aspects of Family Dynamics for Babatha and Berenice

Babatha's papyri enable us to describe a web of relationships that point to relatively small "nuclear" families enmeshed within wider networks of kinship. These "nuclear" families include that of Babatha and her parents, Miriam and Simeon; Babatha, her first husband, Jesus, and their son, Jesus; the "blended" family of Babatha, Judah, Miriam, and Shelamzion; the nuclear family of Shelamzion and her husband, Judah, known as Cimber; and the nuclear family of Jesus, brother of Judah (Khthousion), his unnamed wife, and their two sons. In these papyri we seem to be dealing with family structures where male kinship relations predominate (and probably also with patrilocal residence practices, whereby wives go to live either with their husbands' families or in a nuclear familial residence where the dominant kinship relations remain those of the husband and his male relatives). In these papyri Babatha appears deeply enmeshed in the affairs of the families of her two husbands and their male relatives. It is telling that the two family trees reconstructed by Lewis (the editor of the Greek papyri), following Yadin, contain the names of nineteen men and

---

right that this is when the betrothal would have taken place, if not the marriage itself) to sometime shortly before the death of Agrippa I in 44, at which point Berenice is now married to Herod of Chalcis. In this period, if we follow Frier, we might expect Berenice to have conceived once, with several possible outcomes: she might have miscarried or borne a child who died very young. Alternatively, she might still have been too young to bear children: some evidence suggests that the average age of menarche in the Roman period would have been relatively high (for references and brief discussion, see Kraemer, "Jewish Mothers and Daughters," pp. 104-5).

67. See Frier, p. 96, for discussion of the rapid decline in fertility after age thirty or so.

68. There are other possibilities, including her use of birth control (this would have been, after all, "nonmarital" sex), the possibility that she did have children who are not mentioned in the sources, who did not survive, and so forth.

only four women. Eleven wives remain nameless, identified on the chart only by a female symbol. Despite the fact that the papyri represent the personal archive of a woman,[69] they show us predominantly networks of fathers, sons, and brothers, but not mothers, daughters, and sisters.

As for relationships among men, the papyri show us glimpses of precisely the kinds of dynamics our general demographic survey envisions: boys whose fathers die while their sons are relatively young, leaving those sons to be raised by widowed mothers, dependent (the sons and perhaps the mothers!) financially on court-appointed guardians. This is the case not only for Babatha's son Jesus, but also for the sons of Judah's brother, also named Jesus.[70] In the papyri we see glimpses of the relationship between brothers in the apparently intertwined affairs of Judah and his brother, Jesus. These relationships exhibit signs of strain in the disputes over property following the death of the two brothers.

Babatha's own father appears to have died sometime after 120 C.E., when he made out a deed of gift to her mother, transferring various properties to her in the event of his death, but clearly before Babatha's marriage to Judah.[71] How old Babatha was at the time is obviously uncertain; she could have been as young as about fifteen, but also as old as thirty or so. Shelamzion, whose age we don't know, also loses her father relatively young, although after she marries Judah Cimber.[72]

The Yadin papyri say virtually nothing about mother-daughter relationships, two of which are nevertheless documented: Babatha and her own mother, Miriam, and Shelamzion and her mother (also named Miriam). The same demographic patterns that frequently left sons and daughters fatherless at

69. Usually taken to be Babatha, although I continue to think it possible that they represent a collection ultimately assembled by her stepdaughter, Shelamzion.

70. This may, by the way, have interesting implications for the resonance of strong father imagery in religious systems where the demographic reality is that many men lost their fathers while they were still young, and many men die before their own sons are grown, limiting the majority (?) of father-son relationships to those between men in their thirties and forties (or more) and young boys. Such vastly uneven relationships may afford little opportunity for ties between fathers and their grown sons. We might expect relationships between brothers to be strengthened in such situations and to offer a somewhat different way in which to explicate both the sibling language of early Christian communities and even the nature of the father-son language and imagery in works like the Gospel of John.

71. *P. Yadin* 7.

72. Judith Hallett has argued that at least in elite Roman circles of this period, father-daughter ties were extremely important, in *Fathers and Daughters in Roman Society: Women in the Elite Family* (Princeton: Princeton University Press, 1984). Judah's provisions for Shelamzion might point in the same direction, but they might also be a consequence of her being an only, or only surviving, child. See also Kraemer, "Jewish Mothers and Daughters."

an early age also meant that children who did not lose their mothers as a result of childbearing might well have had living mothers well into their own lives. Babatha's mother may have died prior to her marriage to Judah, but we do not know for certain.[73] Shelamzion's mother, Miriam, is clearly alive at the time of her daughter's marriage, and for some time thereafter. What the tenor of these relationships might have been like is a complex question. I have suggested, in an earlier article, that Jewish mothers, like their non-Jewish counterparts, might have had less attachment to their daughters than to their sons, and less investment in those relationships, for a variety of reasons that I won't rehearse here.[74] Nothing in these papyri provides definitive affirmation or disconfirmation of that argument, although, as we shall see, a few interesting observations emerge from a consideration of the more complex polygynous family dynamic.

Unquestionably, the most interesting family dynamic evidenced in these papyri is the polygynous household. Such families are generally assumed to be atypical,[75] but whether it was more common than we realize is currently impossible to say. The discovery of these papyri reminds us that we know little about the actual family practices of relatively ordinary people. How such a marriage might have worked is similarly hard to tell. If Babatha and Judah were married at the time of the land registration recorded in *P. Yadin* 16, we might conclude that Babatha lived in her own home in Ma'oza while Judah lived with his first wife, Miriam.[76] As I noted early, after Judah's death Miriam and Babatha wrangled both personally and in court over Judah's estate. *P. Yadin* 26, dated to July 9, 131, provides some details: Babatha summons Miriam to explain why Miriam seized everything in the house of their mutual husband, Judah. Miriam counters that she had previously warned Babatha to stay away from Judah's possessions, and that Babatha had no claims against Judah's estate. This may suggest they lived in separate houses, but the papyrus is hardly conclusive.

If the relationship between Babatha and her cowife was strained after the death of Judah, and perhaps before, Babatha's relationship with her stepdaughter, Shelamzion, may be more intriguing. In *P. Yadin* 17, dated to February 21, 128, Babatha loans Judah a sum of 300 denarii in silver coin, a sum identical to

73. Some of the properties that Simeon deeded to Miriam in *P. Yadin* 7 are subsequently listed in Babatha's declaration of land in *P. Yadin* 16. Yadin speculated that Babatha had inherited them from her mother, who would therefore now be dead.

74. Kraemer, "Jewish Mothers and Daughters."

75. Kokkinos points out that only Herod the Great engaged in polygynous marriage, but Lewis (p. 23 n. 6) adduces several other examples from the work of L. M. Epstein, *Marriage Laws in the Bible and the Talmud* (Cambridge, 1942).

76. The document actually says only that Babatha resides in her own home, while Judah resides in his; no mention is made of Miriam.

the cash portion of Shelamzion's dowry, as evidenced in Shelamzion's marriage contract, dated six weeks later, to April 5. The presence of Shelamzion's marriage contract among Babatha's papers could be taken as possible testimony to a close tie between Babatha and her stepdaughter, although I periodically wonder whether one couldn't account for the entire archive as the property of Shelamzion, who continues to have an interest in Babatha's affairs by virtue of the marriage to her father, Judah, especially if the estate is still under contest.[77] Given the fact that Shelamzion had family connections to the rebels, her presence in the cave seems more obvious than Babatha's, although admittedly our knowledge here is extremely limited.

Missing from the Yadin papyri is a sense of the wider ancient *familia* that included slaves and freedpersons. Conceivably this is due to the specific nature of these documents, since it seems odd that persons of significant financial resources would have had no slaves or servants (nor, for instance, have ever themselves been freedpersons).

Berenice was one of four children surviving to adulthood, enmeshed in a very large complex of family relationships. These include the relationships of her natal family, their spouses and children as well as complex Herodian ties to the imperial family. The Herodian household also had slaves and freedpersons.[78] According to Luke 8:3, one person who provided financial support to Jesus and his followers was a woman named Joanna, identified as the wife of Herod's ἐπίτροπος.

Josephus provides some fascinating details about Berenice's family, although his motives and sources are not above suspicion. Her father, Agrippa I, was raised in Rome in the imperial household,[79] where his mother, also named Berenice, had close ties to some imperial women. While in Rome he married his first cousin, Cypros.[80] Josephus claims that while his mother was alive, Agrippa reined in his natural tendency to extravagant spending, but that once she died he rapidly ran through his entire fortune[81] and returned destitute and suicidal to Judea.[82] At this point Cypros, whom Josephus portrays as a devoted wife,

---

77. I made this suggestion already in "Jewish Mothers and Daughters," p. 100 n. 23.

78. See, e.g., Josephus, *Antiquities* 18 §155, for Agrippa's freedman Marsyas; *Antiquities* 18 §156 for Protos, a freedman of Agrippa's mother, Berenice; Thaumastus, a slave whom Gaius gave to Agrippa (who appears to have freed him, appointed him ἐπίτροπος, but then "left" him to Agrippa II and Berenice, *Antiquities* 18 §194).

79. With Drusus, son of Tiberius; Josephus, *Antiquities* 18 §143.

80. See Kokkinos, p. 276.

81. Josephus, *Antiquities* 18 §145.

82. Kokkinos, pp. 272-79, dates Agrippa's return to the mid-thirties, well after the death of his mother, Berenice, which he thinks occurs shortly before the birth of her granddaughter, who

sought help from her sister-in-law Herodias, who was now married to her paternal uncle, Herod the tetrarch. In response, Herodias and Herod brought Agrippa (and his family) to the city of Tiberias (on the western shore of the Sea of Galilee) and gave him a job as ἀγορανόμος (commissioner of the markets) and a living allowance. When this arrangement, and others, proved untenable, Cypros again intervened on her husband's behalf, this time securing a loan from Alexander the alabarch, Philo's brother and Berenice's eventual father-in-law, after Alexander had refused to loan Agrippa money directly.[83] Cypros then returned to Judea with her children (presumably at least Agrippa II and Berenice),[84] while Agrippa returned to Italy. There he subsequently obtained additional loans and used the funds to cultivate relationships with the imperial family.[85]

Although we should be exceedingly nervous applying modern categories to ancient families, it is certainly tempting to see Berenice as the product of a somewhat dysfunctional family, including a father with designs on power who was unable to support his family and a mother who might easily be labeled, in modern terms, an enabler, repeatedly bailing out her husband when he proved unable to provide for his family. How, precisely, this dynamic affected their children is difficult, if not impossible, to assess, but it is worth noting that Berenice would have spent her childhood repeatedly uprooted, moving from Rome, where she was almost certainly born, to the relative backwater of Tiberias, to Syria, to Alexandria, and then to Judea. She subsequently went through at least four relationships with men (Marcus, Herod of Chalcis, Polemo of Cilicia, and Titus), and seems to have been deeply attached to her brother, Agrippa II, who was only about a year older than she.

Josephus portrays the relationship between Berenice and her much younger sister Drusilla as particularly fraught with tension. In a marriage arranged by their brother Agrippa II, after the death of their father, Drusilla was first

---

is then named for her. The arrangement seems not to have lasted long — according to Josephus, Herod taunted Agrippa for his dependence on his brother-in-law, so that Agrippa sought assistance from an old Roman friend, Flaccus, then governor of Syria. There, however, Agrippa became embroiled in an intrigue that destroyed his friendship with Flaccus.

83. As noted above (n. 14), there are interesting questions about the relationship between this loan and the subsequent betrothal of Berenice and Alexander's son, Marcus. In any case, Josephus claims that Alexander gave Cypros the money because of her love for her husband and all the rest of her virtues: *Antiquities* 18 §159.

84. Drusus, the oldest brother, might have been dead; the two younger daughters may not yet have been born.

85. Specifically, with the emperor Tiberius and with his son, Gaius, leading to his eventual political comeback, as it were.

married to Azizus, king of Emesa, who Josephus says agreed to be circumcised for the occasion.[86] Not long after, the Roman procurator of Judea, Felix, fell in love with Drusilla and persuaded her to leave her husband and marry him. Josephus blames Berenice directly for her sister's actions, claiming that out of jealousy over Drusilla's great beauty, Berenice treated her abusively, causing Drusilla to "transgress ancestral laws."[87] Macurdy thought, though, that Josephus himself was responsible for assigning blame to Berenice. Drusilla's true motives remain unknown.[88]

Comparative Family Dynamics — Extrapolating to Larger Jewish Communities?

Since, perhaps somewhat rashly, I titled this paper "Typical and Atypical Jewish Family Dynamics," I probably need to say something about the degree to which the elements of the family dynamics of each might be typical or atypical of Jewish families in this period. This, however, is complicated not only by the limited amount of evidence available for comparison, but by questions of deciding who counts as evidence for "Jewish" families. Interestingly, Kokkinos's recent book on the Herodian family questions how much the Herodians really count as "Jews" (of the family as a whole, he writes: "[They] only came to be Jewish by the accident of the forced conversions of the Idumaeans. Balancing on the edge of Judaism, some members tipped one way and some the other").[89] Regrettably, for all his detailed and fascinating discussions of Herodian history, Kokkinos seems still to subscribe to fairly traditional equations of Jewish = rabbinic. Babatha, too, he sees as possibly Idumean, and perhaps only Jewish by marriage to Judah (of her earlier marriage to Jesus he says nothing).

86. Josephus, *Antiquities* 20 §139. Agrippa had apparently previously contracted with Antiochus for a marriage with Drusilla, but Antiochus reneged, not wishing to adopt Jewish practices (μὴ βουληθεὶς τὰ Ἰουδαίων ἔθη μεταλαβεῖν).

87. Josephus, *Antiquities* 20 §143. Josephus does not specify precisely what was the transgression of ancestral laws; the options include instigating divorce, leaving the marriage without a proper divorce, and marrying a non-Jew who had not been circumcised and adopted Jewish practices.

88. Ilan comments that it's curious that Josephus claims that Agrippa's three daughters all left their husbands (Drusilla leaving Azizus to marry Felix, Berenice leaving Polemo, and Mariamme leaving her husband, Julius Archelaus, to marry Demetrius, alabarch of Alexandria; Josephus, *Antiquities* 20 §147). She suggests that it "bears the stamp of an attempt to malign the king's descendants" (*Jewish Women*, p. 145 n. 27). Given my discussion of the family dynamic in which they were raised, though, one might also argue that other factors lay behind their actions.

89. Kokkinos, p. 360.

Regardless of whether it is wise to extrapolate from the family dynamics of Berenice and Babatha to contemporaneous Jewish families, it is worth observing that both Josephus's descriptions of Berenice's family affairs and the Babatha papyri are revealing of the degree to which these families adhere to and are constructed around pervasive ancient notions of gendered hierarchy.[90] In the interests of time, let me give just two examples, one for each.

Whatever motives Josephus may have had for his portrait of Berenice, he appears most critical of her when her actions violate fundamental ancient cultural assumptions that women should be subordinate to appropriate male authority, when, for instance, she takes it upon herself to arrange (perhaps) and then to terminate her marriage to Polemo. Blaming her actions on excessive or inappropriate sexual desire might seem to modern readers like a stereotypical critique of women's sexuality, but it may also be understood as part of a general ethos in which both men and women were expected to exercise appropriate self-control, although women were thought to have much less ability to do so, and to require male assistance and guidance, as well as overt control on occasion. Conversely, he is more approving of her in other contexts, such as her abject supplication before Gessius Florus on behalf of the Jews during the siege of Jerusalem. Similarly, Josephus criticizes other Herodian women who act autonomously when they ought to acquiesce to appropriate male authority, and praises women, like Cypros, who demonstrate appropriate female virtues of marital fidelity and loyalty.[91]

Comparable notions of gender undergird the Babatha papyri as well. One significant issue here is the whole notion of guardianship — not only for Babatha, but also for her son and the sons of her deceased brother-in-law, Jesus. Children and grown women alike require male guardians to function for them in the legal universe in which only free adult males are competent actors. That children require guardians is also probably related to the notion that women require guardians, for one who herself requires a guardian should not be able to function as guardian.[92] Other aspects of the judicial system(s) may be viewed in

90. Here I have in mind models drawn, although not uncritically, from the work of Michel Foucault, particularly *The History of Sexuality,* trans. Robert Hurley, 3 vols. (New York: Vintage Books, 1978-86).

91. There are numerous other examples here: Josephus's critique of Herodias for her marriage to Herod but his relative praise for her subsequent devotion to him in times of adversity; see my entry for Herodias 1 in *Women in Scripture,* pp. 92-94; also perhaps Antonia in Josephus, *Antiquities* 18 §179-86.

92. Like everything else, this is actually somewhat more complicated. At least one woman, Julia Crispina, functions as a guardian for the minor children of Babatha's deceased brother-in-law, Jesus; and Babatha does not always utilize guardians in her papers.

a similar light: men are regularly present and active in legal proceedings, whereas women are generally absent or present by proxy. Men and women alike are known by their relationships to male relatives, whereas female lineage is regularly omitted and obscured. The marriage contract for Shelamzion and Judah Cimber is clearly a contractual relationship between two men, regardless of whether it can be considered specifically "Jewish" or not,[93] and an exchange between them: the bride *is* what is exchanged. She is thus constructed as property and object, not subject with agency. Judah the father gives his virgin daughter to Judah the husband. Judah the father gives to Judah the husband a sum of money, together with the bridal trousseau, which Judah the husband must return if he ever returns the bride, in effect. Judah the husband promises his wife's father that he will feed and clothe both Shelamzion and the children to come. Shelamzion, of course, promises nothing, since she is not an active party to the contract. However, the contract foresees potential action by Shelamzion or by those acting on her behalf: Judah the husband agrees that he will return the dowry on demand, in silver, and further agrees to penalties should he not do so immediately.[94]

93. See Hannah Cotton's arguments that the marriage (and divorce) documents from the Dead Sea area, including *P. Yadin* and *P. Se'elim*, suggest that the marriages of Jews, from a legal standpoint, are not distinctively Jewish at all (and that "Jewish" marriage, as opposed to the marriages of Jews, is a rabbinic invention: "there is nothing specifically Jewish about this marriage contract, apart from the clauses concerning the distinction between male and female children . . . it would be methodologically unsound to claim that, because the documents reflect halakhic rules familiar to us from tannaitic literature, these rules should be described as Jewish" [DJD, 27:274]).

94. The phrase "whenever she shall demand" (ὁπόταν . . . ἀπαιτήσει) seems to suggest that she could initiate termination of the marriage, something that troubles Lewis. The marriage contract of Salome Komais and Jesus son of Menahem, also found in the same cave but not part of Babatha's archive, offers another example of a similar clause; it, too, seems to assume Komais's right to instigate divorce by demanding back the dowry, though actually this contract is a little more ambiguous than that of Shelamzion — strictly speaking, it may refer to her right to determine the form of the return of the dowry. The document seems to say that Jesus pledges all his property, which he owns now, or may come to own, as security for the dowry, and that Komais could move against any of his property should she so choose. Subsequent publication of another Judean desert papyrus has provided even stronger support for women initiating divorce proceedings; above, n. 62. Furthermore, the actual practices evidenced in the papyri point to more complex social realities, where women do occasionally function as actors, but the general, and shared, underlying paradigm appears operative.

Salient Differences, If Any, between
Jewish Families and Non-Jewish Families

What can we say about the salient differences, if any, between Jewish families and non-Jewish families that are comparable in other respects? Two areas on which we might focus are the practice of polygyny (which was illegal under Roman law) and divorce practices. Both Jews and non-Jews allowed the termination of marriages prior to the death of one spouse. It has long been argued that Jewish women were unable to initiate divorce proceedings, a view taken by Josephus, although several of the Judean papyri, including Shelamzion's marriage contract, do strongly suggest alternative views and practices. While this vexed question of who triggers the termination is interesting, it doesn't alter the fundamental availability of divorce for all sorts of reasons.[95] Furthermore, given my suggestion that all our sources point to an underlying Foucauldian paradigm of gender and hierarchy, it makes sense that women, as "passive" partners in the marriage, would in general not be expected to take the "active" role of instigating/initiating divorce — something hardly confined to Jews.

Conclusions

Writing this paper has persuaded me that there is much interesting additional work to be done on Jewish families in the Roman period, but it has not changed my perception that much about those families is not distinctively Jewish. So I return here to my opening observation: ironically, the study of Jewish families, while fascinating in itself, is not as germane to the study of early Christian families as it might initially seem. Most Christians whose family dynamics can be reconstructed are unlikely to have been born Jews and/or to have drawn their ideas of family dynamics primarily from a Jewish context. Even if they did, the dynamics of Jewish families do not appear appreciably different from those of non-Jews (of similar class and status conditions) in the early imperial Roman period. Finally, although the context of the conference allowed insufficient time

---

95. The cases of several elite Herodian women demonstrate that elite women could in practice initiate the termination of unsatisfactory marriage. Scholars like Kokkinos may account for this seeming departure from "Jewish law" by casting the Herodians as marginally Jewish, but the recent arguments about *P. Se'elim* 13, concluding that it is in fact a divorce deed from a woman to a man, suggest, together with additional prior evidence, that Jewish women could, at least in certain communities, instigate divorce proceedings. For some discussion of the evidence that Roman women in general were also unable to instigate divorce directly, see Myles MacDonald, "Divorce Initiated by Women," *AJAH* 8 (1983): 54-80.

and space to develop this last argument, it seems to me highly plausible that the emergence of a distinctive "Jewish" family, at least in terms of certain practices such as marriage and divorce, may well be a rabbinic innovation that is itself a response to issues of Jewish identity and community maintenance and boundaries in the Roman period.[96]

96. Michael Satlow, *Jewish Marriage in Antiquity* (Princeton: Princeton University Press, 2001), appeared too late for use in this paper: he has a brief discussion of the marriages of Babatha and Salome Komais, pp. 97-100. Some of these issues are explored in Susan Marks, "Jewish Weddings in the Greco-Roman Period: A Reconsideration of Received Ritual" (Ph.D. diss., University of Pennsylvania, 2003).

Was Celsus Right? The Role of Women in the Expansion of Early Christianity

Margaret Y. MacDonald

In the opinion of the second-century pagan intellectual Celsus, the Christian family was at the very heart of the growth of a troublesome new movement. The subordinate members of households were especially prominent among the gullible crowds. As recorded by Origen, Celsus describes the early Christian missionary tactics as follows: "Their injunctions are like this. 'Let no one educated, no one wise, no one sensible draw near. For these abilities are thought by us to be evils. But as for anyone ignorant, anyone stupid, anyone uneducated, anyone who is a child, let him come boldly.' By the fact that they themselves admit that these people are worthy of their God, they show that they want and are able to convince only the foolish, dishonorable and stupid, and only slaves, women and little children."[1]

According to Celsus, Christians lead adherents to turn against the heads of households and those in legitimate positions of authority — they encourage insubordination within the family group:

> In private houses we see wool-workers, cobblers, laundry workers, and the most illiterate and bucolic yokels, who would not dare to say anything at all in front of their elders and more intelligent masters. But whenever they get hold of children in private and some stupid women with them, they let out some astounding statements as, for example, that they must not pay any attention to their father and schoolteachers, but must obey them; they say that these talk nonsense and have no understanding, and that in reality they neither know nor are able to do anything good, but are taken up with mere empty chatter. But they alone, they say, know the right way to live, and if the children would believe them, they would become happy and make their home happy as well. And if just as they are speaking they see one of the schoolteachers coming, or some intelligent person, or even the father him-

---

1. Origen, *Contra Celsum* 3.44 (see also 3.50), in *Origen, "Contra Celsum,"* trans. Henry Chadwick (Cambridge: Cambridge University Press, 1953).

self, the more cautious of them flee in all directions; but the more reckless urge the children on to rebel. They whisper to them that in the presence of their father and their schoolmasters they do not feel able to explain anything to the children. But, if they like, they should leave father and schoolmasters, and go along with the women and little children who are playfellows to the wooldresser's shop, or the cobbler's or the washerwoman's shop, that they may learn perfection. And by saying this they persuade them.[2]

In Celsus's account women and children are clearly depicted as targets for Christian missionaries, but they are also presented as active in the missionary enterprise themselves. Teachers are said to instruct the prospective members to go along with women and children to the various shops in order to attain perfection, seemingly to receive further instruction and initiation. While we should probably not press the text for logical consistency, there is an interesting movement from house to house or house to shop (which could presumably mean one section of the house to another) in this text. The initial contact is made in houses where gullible, illiterate, and subordinate members of the household are present, but the possibility of someone in authority overhearing is very real indeed. Bolder recruits (children mostly) are presented as being accompanied by women and children to the wooldresser's shop — or to the cobbler's or to the washerwoman's shop — apparently a place where there will be greater opportunities for instruction. All of this suggests an intriguing relationship here between secrecy, concealment, and the involvement of women and children that I will explore further below.

In analyzing Celsus's depiction of women's involvement in the evangelizing tactics of the early Christians, we are confronted immediately by one of the most difficult methodological issues facing historians who investigate the involvement of women in the expansion of the movement: the problem of drawing historical conclusions based on texts where women are represented in such a way as to further the agendas of male authors. From the target audience for missionary efforts, to the nature of the shops propounded as the locus of activities, to the secretive and insubordinate behavior of adherents, to the stress on the initiative of women and children, the attempt to denigrate early Christianity by appealing to the gender and status of its main proponents is unmistakable. In fact, women figured prominently in Celsus's polemical critique of early Christianity as he set out to attack the religion on the basis of its origins, major tenets, and social manifestations.[3] Celsus's approach was to be expected. New

---

2. Origen, *Contra Celsum* 3.55.

3. On Celsus and women, see Margaret Y. MacDonald, *Early Christian Women and Pagan Opinion: The Power of the Hysterical Woman* (Cambridge: Cambridge University Press, 1996), pp. 94-126.

and illegitimate religious groups in antiquity were typically attacked by high-lighting their attraction for women and their corrupting influence upon women.[4] Predictably, we see these themes repeated in the pagan criticism of Christianity, which predates or is contemporary with Celsus. Celsus's treatise has much in common with the reactions of such authors as Marcus Cornelius Fronto or Lucius Apuleius, but it also differs from these others in a significant way.[5] His account surpasses mere rumor, general impression, or stereotype. He clearly had a detailed knowledge of Christianity and had read such important texts as the Gospel of Matthew and probably various gnostic sources.[6] More-over, the picture Celsus painted of the importance of the house to the expansion of Christianity finds support in early Christian texts, which speak of groups meeting in houses (e.g., Rom. 16:5; 1 Cor. 16:19; Philem. 2) and of entire households joining the church (e.g., 1 Cor. 1:16; Acts 16:11-15). There is also significant evidence for the participation of women in early Christianity, and though it is not free of ambiguity, it has points in common with Celsus's presentation. I have previously argued that, when evaluated critically, pagan opinion about early Christianity can offer an alternate window into the lives of early Christian women to complement what can be deduced on the basis of Christian sources.[7] To stress the involvement of women and children in the expansion of Christianity clearly suited Celsus's rhetorical purposes, and his treatment certainly cannot be taken at face value, but there is enough corroborating Christian evidence that we may reasonably ask the question: Was Celsus right?

The impression of prominence, even of predominance, of women in early Christian circles that one finds in pagan critique of early Christianity has found a counterpart in modern scholarship on the Christianization of the empire. In his magisterial study *Pagans and Christians*, Robin Lane Fox has written that "Christian women [were] prominent in the churches' membership and recognized to be

---

4. See, for example, Juvenal, *Satire* 6. On women in Greco-Roman criticism of various Eastern religions, David L. Balch, *Let Wives Be Submissive: The Domestic Code in 1 Peter* (Chico, Calif.: Scholars, 1981), pp. 65-80.

5. See, for example, the anti-Christian oration by Marcus Cornelius Fronto recorded in Marcus Minucius Felix, *Octavius* 8-9; Apuleius, *Metamorphoses* 9.14 (note, however, that this text could refer to either a Jewish proselyte or a Christian woman).

6. R. Joseph Hoffmann, *Celsus on the True Doctrine* (Oxford: Oxford University Press, 1987), p. 36. See also Harold Remus, *Pagan-Christian Conflict over Miracle in the Second Century* (Cambridge, Mass.: Philadelphia Patristics Foundation, 1983), p. 270 n. 68; Pierre de Labriolle, *La réaction païenne: étude sur la polémique antichrétienne du 1er au VIe siècle* (Paris: L'Artisan du livre, 1948), pp. 124-27.

7. See MacDonald, *Early Christian Women and Pagan Opinion*. On early Christianity generally, see Robert L. Wilken, *The Christians as the Romans Saw Them* (New Haven and London: Yale University Press, 1984).

so by Christians and pagans," recalling the claims of Adolf von Harnack about women playing "a leading role in the spread of this religion."[8] Most recently, the involvement of women has been central to Rodney Stark's thesis about the rise of Christianity. In his chapter on women Stark makes claims about women out-numbering men in early Christian circles, about them enjoying higher status in church circles than in the Greco-Roman environment generally, and about their ability to affect church growth on account of marriages to pagans. It is this last aspect of Stark's work that is of most interest for this paper. Stark is clearly drawing on a particular sociological notion of conversion that focuses on the use of available social "networks" in contributing to the expansion of the group.[9] The network in question here is the extended household of antiquity.

Yet some interpreters (sometimes adopting a feminist perspective) have been reluctant to ascribe a major role to women in the Christianization of the empire and have warned against an uncritical reading of the evidence. They have argued that in the realm of ancient literature, including both early Christian texts and pagan critique of early Christianity, the depiction of women's influence may have much more to do with the intention of male authors than with the activities of real Christian women. Focusing particularly on the Christian literature of the later empire, Kate Cooper has spoken of a "topos of womanly influence" in Christian literature as an element of "cultural continuity with the earlier Empire." Concentrating on evidence from Jerome, Chrysostom, and Augustine, Cooper argues that texts which describe the influence of women on their male partners and have been understood to mean that married men were converted by their wives should not be taken at face value. Her thesis is that such discourse was part of a rhetorical strategy in power competitions between men, such as that between married, householder clergy and celibates over Christian leadership.[10] In a similar vein, Judith Lieu has raised critical

---

8. Robin Lane Fox, *Pagans and Christians* (New York: Knopf, 1987), p. 308. See Adolf von Harnack, *The Mission and Expansion of Christianity in the First Three Centuries,* trans. James Moffat (1908), Torchbook Edition, introduction by Jaroslav Pelikan (New York: Harper and Brothers, 1961), p. 368; cf. pp. 393-98; also Peter Brown, "Aspects of the Christianization of the Roman Aristocracy," *JRS* 51 (1961): 1-11. See discussion by Elizabeth A. Castelli, "Gender, Theory, and the Rise of Christianity: A Response to Rodney Stark," *JECS* 6, no. 2 (1998): 242.

9. See Rodney Stark, *The Rise of Christianity: A Sociologist Reconsiders History* (Princeton: Princeton University Press, 1996); also R. Stark and W. S. Bainbridge, "Networks of Faith: Interpersonal Bonds and Recruitment in Cults and Sects," *American Journal of Sociology* 85 (1980): 1376-95. For an evaluation of this theoretical perspective for understanding conversion among other theories, see Brock Kilbourne and James T. Richardson, "Paradigm Conflict, Types of Conversion, and Conversion Theories," *Sociological Analysis* 50 (1988): 1-21.

10. Kate Cooper, "Insinuations of Womanly Influence: An Aspect of the Christianization of the Roman Aristocracy," *JRS* 82 (1992): 150-64, here 155.

questions about earlier evidence concerning the involvement of women. Noting some parallels with Josephus, she has argued that a novelistic tendency may well shape the account of the conversion of Lydia (Acts 16:11-15) and of the noble women of Thessalonica in Acts (17:4, 12; cf. 17:33-34), and for similar reasons, the story of Thecla "tells us little about 'real' women's conversion to Christianity in the second century."[11] She concludes: "The gendering of conversion is a matter of rhetorical and not of statistical analysis. The move from rhetoric to social experience must remain hazardous."[12]

The disjunction between the bold claims of Stark and some ancient historians and the sobering cautions of other interpreters (to the point where one might become hesitant to make any claims about real women at all) has led me to examine the evidence once again. In investigations of the role of women in the expansion of Christianity, scholars have dealt with two types of evidence. They have made claims about the number of women attracted to early Christianity and about the greater attraction of women to early Christianity. It follows that women may have contributed to the expansion of early Christianity by the sheer force of their presence.[13] Secondly, they have focused on the specific activities of early Christian women (e.g., their role in evangelizing pagan partners) in contributing to the expansion of Christianity. This study is of the latter type. In this essay I will concentrate on literary texts which suggest that women — many of them unnamed in the texts and probably quite "ordinary"

11. Judith M. Lieu, "The 'Attraction of Women' in/to Early Judaism and Christianity: Gender and the Politics of Conversion," *JSNT* 72 (1998): 16-19.

12. Lieu, p. 20.

13. I consider the numerical estimates of the sex ratio of early Christianity to be of necessity so tangential as to be of questionable use. Archaeological remains and epigraphic evidence are a potential source of information here, but to date the findings are not conclusive. See, for example, the prosopographical and epigraphical evidence discussed by Michele Renée Salzman in "Aristocratic Women: Conductors of Christianity in the Fourth Century," *Helios* 16 (1989): 207-20. While her results offer reasons to be cautious about women playing a major role in Christian expansion, in the end her pool of cases is simply too small to be really conclusive. See also her similar discussion in "How the West Was Won: The Christianization of the Roman Aristocracy in the West in the Years after Constantine," in Carl Deroux, ed., *Studies in Latin Literature and Roman History, Collection Latomus* 217 (1992): 451-79. Similarly, as noted by Castelli, Rodney Stark probably puts too much weight upon limited evidence to come to conclusions opposite to that of Salzman in dealing with the evidence from a fourth-century house church in North African Cirta where a disproportionately large number of women's articles of clothing were listed in an inventory: *Gesta apud Zenophilum,* CSEL, 26:185-97, at 187.4-10; cited in Castelli, p. 242 n. 29. See Stark, p. 98; also Fox, p. 310. However, important archaeological evidence such as that discussed by Osiek and Balch has a great deal to teach about how the physical parameters of women's lives may have shaped their contributions to the expansion of Christianity.

according to the standards of their day — were actively doing things that contributed to the expansion of church groups.[14] Much of the discussion of the role of women in the Christianization of the empire has concentrated on the Roman aristocracy of the fourth century because of the significant body of evidence from this period. But in this essay I wish to focus on the earlier periods about which much less is known, but which are clearly critical for the expansion of early Christianity — the first and second centuries c.e.

Women in the Pauline Mission

If one is to study the role of women in the expansion of Christianity, an obvious place to begin is with the women who participated in Paul's mission. Clearly women such as Prisca and Phoebe had leadership roles in the Pauline circle, but can we say for sure that they contributed in direct ways to the group's expansion? Of course, the difficulty of answering this question is compounded by the fact that the manner of Christianization of the empire remains a subject of debate; even Paul's own modus operandi is far from certain, especially given the difficulty harmonizing Paul's letters with the depiction of Paul as a missioner in Acts. Despite these difficulties, however, many recent interpreters have confidently asserted the involvement of women in the missionary efforts of the Pauline circle. The fascinating references to women leaders in the Pauline churches have been analyzed by Elisabeth Schüssler Fiorenza and others, and it is impractical to repeat the results of their analysis here.[15] However, it is important to note that interpreters have usually not distinguished precisely between women's involvement in the expansion of early church groups and the other types of leadership they undertook among believers. This is no doubt due to the fact that the NT evidence by no means suggests a rigid demarcation between types of leadership. A woman leader of a house church such as Prisca (1 Cor. 16:19; Rom. 16:3-5) is also depicted as engaging in evangelizing efforts

14. On ordinary women, see Harold Remus, "Unknown and Yet Well-Known: The Multiform Formation of Early Christianity," in *A Multiform Heritage: Studies on Early Judaism and Christianity in Honor of Robert A. Kraft*, ed. Benjamin G. Wright (Atlanta: Scholars, 1999), pp. 79-93.

15. See Elisabeth Schüssler Fiorenza, *In Memory of Her: A Feminist Theological Reconstruction of Christian Origins* (London: SCM Press, 1983). On missionary activities of women in the Pauline churches, see, for example, pp. 167, 183. On the leadership of women in general in Pauline circles, see Ross S. Kraemer, *Her Share of the Blessings: Women's Religions among Pagans, Jews, and Christians in the Greco-Roman World* (New York and Oxford: Oxford University Press, 1992), pp. 136-38, 174-76, 65-86.

(Acts 18:24-26). But for the purposes of this paper, it is essential to try to distinguish as much as possible between local leadership and leadership efforts with an outward orientation — indications of activities that clearly win new members.

Among the strongest evidence we have that some of the women mentioned in Paul's letters understood themselves and were understood by others as fostering the spread of the gospel is the fact that they are named as partners — missionary partners — continuing the practices of the Jesus movement (cf. Mark 6:7; Luke 10:1 — though here not presented as male-female pairs). As has frequently been observed, these partnerships did not always involve a man and a woman (such as Prisca and Aquila [Rom. 16:3-4; 1 Cor. 16:19] or Andronicus and Junia [Rom. 16:7]), but sometimes involved teams of two women (such as Euodia and Syntyche [Phil. 4:2-3] or Tryphaena and Tryphosa [Rom. 16:12]). The nature of the arrangements between these pairs was not limited to "husband and wife"; in fact, it is by no means impossible that even those who understood themselves as such had given up sex for the sake of the gospel (cf. 1 Cor. 7:5, 36-38). The "sister-wife/woman" (1 Cor. 9:5) was not necessarily the conjugal mate of one's preconversion life.[16]

Because they are described as prominent among the apostles — clearly a designation of paramount significance for Paul's identity and in earliest Christianity — Andronicus and Junia are especially intriguing missionary partners (Rom. 16:7).[17] It must be admitted that the term "apostle" (ἀπόστολος) carries a broad range of meanings in Paul's letters and can refer simply to a messenger or emissary of the church (e.g., 2 Cor. 8:23). But Paul frequently uses the term to refer to itinerant preachers of the gospel (2 Cor. 11:4-6, 13; 12:11-12). If we place the description of this pair of "apostles" within its context of Romans 16, which often alludes to precarious activities undertaken for the sake of the gospel, there seems little reason to doubt that Paul referred to Andronicus and Junia (de-

---

16. The meaning of 1 Cor. 9:5, where Paul speaks of the right of an apostle to be accompanied by a "sister as wife," is debated. See Mary Rose D'Angelo, "Women Partners in the New Testament," *JFSR* 6 (1990): 73-74, 78-81; Fiorenza, *In Memory of Her*, pp. 172-73. Note especially that the term γυνή, usually translated "wife" in this text, can mean simply "woman."

17. It is possible that the Greek text should be taken to mean that Andronicus and Junia were prominent among the apostles in the sense that they were valued by apostles without being apostles themselves. The most straightforward reading, however, accepts that they are actually being called apostles. Note also that Junia has sometimes been understood to be a man. See discussion in Margaret Y. MacDonald, "Reading Real Women through the Undisputed Letters of Paul," in *Women and Christian Origins*, ed. Ross Shepard Kraemer and Mary Rose D'Angelo (Oxford and New York: Oxford University Press, 1999), pp. 209-10.

scribed as Paul's fellow prisoners) as apostles who partook in the missionary enterprise.

Of the male-female pairs, however, we possess the most information about Prisca and Aquila. They are both called Paul's coworkers (Rom. 16:3: συνεργός), a term Paul can use to single out males in leadership roles (e.g., Rom. 16:9; Phil. 2:25), including such important fellow workers in the spreading of the gospel as Timothy (Rom. 16:21; 1 Thess. 3:2) and Titus (2 Cor. 8:23). Euodia and Syntyche also belong to this group (Phil. 4:3). Paul even describes himself, along with Apollos, as God's fellow workers who plant what in the end only God can grow — the community (1 Cor. 3:9). Like Paul himself, the "fellow workers" seem to do things that are understood as expanding the church while at the same time nurturing existing communities. One of the most remarkable texts in all of the New Testament concerning the evangelizing role of a woman is Acts 18:24-26, where both Priscilla (in Paul's letters she is called Prisca) and Aquila are said to have taught Apollos in Ephesus, a learned Jew who had great knowledge of the Scriptures. Although Apollos already had some knowledge of the Christian message, Priscilla and Aquila are said to have taken Apollos aside and "explained the way of God more accurately" (Acts 18:24-26). Given the tendency of the author of Acts sometimes to downplay the leadership role of women, the presentation of Priscilla as an evangelizing teacher is especially striking.[18] The author of Acts probably meant for us to understand that Priscilla and Aquila took Apollos into their home, which also served as a house church, the basic cell of Christian organization. If one combines the evidence from Paul's letters with that from Acts, it seems that Prisca and Aquila had houses in three major cities in the ancient Mediterranean world: Corinth, Ephesus, and Rome (1 Cor. 16:8, 19; Rom. 16:3-5; Acts 18:2-3; 18:18–9:1). They were leaders of a house church in Ephesus and probably also in Rome.[19] Moreover, the reference to Paul staying and working with them in Corinth suggests that this may also have been the case here (Acts 18:2-3).[20]

18. See Clarice J. Martin, "The Acts of the Apostles," in *Searching the Scriptures: Volume 2, A Feminist Commentary,* ed. Elisabeth Schüssler Fiorenza (New York: Crossroad, 1994), pp. 785-86. On women in Luke-Acts, see also Mary Rose D'Angelo, "Women in Luke-Acts: A Redactional View," *JBL* 109, no. 3 (1990): 441-61.

19. It should be noted that for textual reasons and from evidence related to the manuscript tradition, Rom. 16 has sometimes been considered to have originated as a separate letter (maybe intended for Ephesus) that only later became inserted into the main body of Romans. In that case, Rom. 16:3-5 would refer to the church that meets in the house of Prisca and Aquila in Ephesus and not in Rome. For more detailed discussion of the texts concerning Prisca and Aquila, including the chronology of events related to their move from city to city, see MacDonald, "Reading Real Women," pp. 202-4, and "Rereading Paul: Early Interpreters of Paul on Women and Gender," in *Women and Christian Origins,* pp. 240-41.

20. Acts 18 presents Paul as arguing in the synagogue and persuading Jews and Greeks. But

While Prisca and Aquila's teaching of Apollos might offer evidence for the involvement of women in a type of evangelization, it does not provide evidence of women making initial contact with nonbelievers — Apollos was already familiar with the Christian message to a certain extent. Yet the evidence from Acts is suggestive especially when one considers Celsus's description of Christians leading the recruits back to their shops for further instruction. Moreover, Paul describes the efforts of Prisca and Aquila with language that recalls the perils of mission. He states that they have risked their necks on his behalf and on behalf of others; we may surmise that he is talking about the dangers of travel and perhaps also the risks of initial contacts with people whose family members objected to this association (cf. 1 Cor. 7:12-16). Such an association between danger and the life of missionary partners is also evident in the description of Andronicus and Junia (Rom. 16:7), and especially in the description of Euodia and Syntyche's contribution to Pauline Christianity (Phil. 4:2-3). While we cannot be absolutely certain of this, Paul's language implies that these women were involved in the evangelization of nonbelievers. They were apparently successful despite having experienced opposition from nonbelievers (though opposition from internal opponents cannot be ruled out entirely). They are described, with a verb that recalls the struggles of war or the violent contests of the games (συναθλέω), as coworkers who fought at Paul's side. The only other use of the term in the NT appears earlier in Philippians to refer to the struggle of the community against some external threat that Paul himself experienced (1:27-30; cf. 1 Thess. 2:2; Acts 16:19-40).[21]

The references to Prisca and Aquila sharing Paul's craft (Acts 18:3) and the evidence for their frequent displacement from city to city are in keeping with the growing scholarly consensus that geographical mobility for trade and business was central to the expansion of Pauline Christianity.[22] But the mission of Prisca and Aquila differed from that of Paul in important ways, perhaps indicating a certain independence. In addition to the fact that Paul chose to work without a partner (having renounced his right to be accompanied by "a sister-wife" [1 Cor. 9:5]), to the best of our knowledge he did not set up a church in his house. In the work of Prisca and Aquila, the leadership of the local community presumably played a larger role, but it is by no means clear that this more "settled" life actually was less successful in winning new members. In one of the few places where Paul tells us how new members might be won, he speaks of outsid-

---

this does not preclude the use of the house for church meetings and for such important rituals as baptisms (Acts 18:7-8; cf. 16:40).

21. See Francis X. Malinowski, "The Brave Women of Philippi," *BTB* 15 (1985): 62.

22. See, for example, Wayne Meeks, *The First Urban Christians: The Social World of the Apostle Paul* (New Haven: Yale University Press, 1983), pp. 16-17.

ers witnessing an early church meeting presumably in a house church (cf. 1 Cor. 14:23-25). But could the household base of the mission of Prisca and Aquila have meant that Prisca actually was a more influential missioner than her partner? The fact that Prisca's name appears before that of Aquila in Romans 16:3 and in Acts 18:18, 26 is usually taken as a sign that she was of higher status than her partner, but could it not also mean that she was more successful at winning new members? How the physical meeting of church groups in the house may have enhanced women's leadership and missionary efforts is a subject that requires further investigation.

With Euodia and Syntyche's leadership (Phil. 4:2-3; cf. Rom. 16:12) we have evidence of women clearly conducting their work for the sake of the gospel in the first instance without male counterparts. This type of independence is even more striking with respect to Phoebe (Rom. 16:1-2; Mary [16:6] and Persis [16:12] may also be women working for the sake of the gospel without specific partners), the woman who traveled to Rome perhaps bearing Paul's letter and/or for business purposes. Among the most tangential theories about her identity, but among the most suggestive for this essay, is that Phoebe was viewed by Paul as a central player in his plans for a Spanish mission (Rom. 15:23-24).[23] In calling Phoebe a "benefactor" (προστάτις) of many community members and of Paul himself, Paul implies that he has been dependent upon her sphere of influence to expand his mission in Cenchreae or elsewhere (the commendation Paul offers Phoebe, however, is also an indication of her dependence upon him). Perhaps Phoebe offered her house for meetings or acted as a host to traveling Christians; she may well have been of service to Paul by introducing Paul to others who became community benefactors.[24] The titles used to describe Phoebe offer evidence that the extension of her influence included the winning of new members. Like Apphia, the prominent member of the house church greeted in Paul's letter to Philemon, Phoebe is called a "sister" (ἀδελφή) — a term that could be used to refer to the female member of a missionary partnership (cf. 1 Cor. 9:5) and whose male equivalent was a frequent designation for Paul's collaborator Timothy (Philem. 1; 2 Cor. 1:1; 1 Thess. 3:2). The significance of the use of the term "deacon" (διάκονος) to describe Phoebe's role is not com-

23. Robert Jewett, "Paul, Phoebe and the Spanish Mission," in *The Social World of Formative Christianity and Judaism: Essays in Tribute to Howard Clark Kee,* ed. Jacob Neusner, Ernest S. Frerichs, Peter Borgen, and Richard Horsley (Philadelphia: Fortress, 1988), pp. 142-61.

24. On Phoebe, see Caroline F. Whelan, "Amica Pauli: The Role of Phoebe in the Early Church," *JSNT* 49 (1993): 67-85; Roman Garrison, "Phoebe, the Servant-Benefactor and Gospel Traditions," in *Text and Artifact in the Religions of Mediterranean Antiquity: Essays in Honour of Peter Richardson,* ed. Stephen G. Wilson and Michel Desjardins (Waterloo, Ontario: Wilfrid Laurier Press, 2000), pp. 63-73.

pletely clear.[25] But it is indisputably a term (often translated "minister," "servant," or "helper") that Paul uses to describe his own identity and the identity of coworkers who are involved in spreading the gospel (e.g., 1 Cor. 3:5; 2 Cor. 3:6; 11:23; cf. Rom. 11:13; 1 Cor. 16:15; 2 Cor. 5:18; 6:3; Col. 4:7).[26]

There is strong evidence suggesting that the women named as leaders in Paul's letters engaged in activities that contributed directly to the expansion of the movement. Such terms as "sister," "deacon," "coworker," or "apostle," which are used to describe these women, are not unambiguous. But when taken together and compared to their usage (or the use of masculine equivalents) to describe men, including Paul himself, we are left with a very strong impression of missionary activity. Describing the precise nature of this activity is much more difficult. The references to travel and crafts indicate opportunities to circulate the gospel on the road, in shops, and in the midst of trade. Allusions to the institution of patronage, the leadership of house churches, and sequestered teaching opportunities point to women using their households in various ways to foster the growth of the movement. Among the most fascinating information emerging from this survey is the ever present suggestion of danger. These women were clearly taking risks for the sake of the gospel.

Rhetorical attempts to control the lives of women and to use female identity as a means of articulating community norms and boundaries are present in Paul letters (e.g., 1 Cor. 11:2-11; 14:33b-36), and become even more pronounced in later periods. As we move beyond Paul's day, incidental references to "real" women become rarer and women's identities increasingly become constructs operating through such literary genres as apology, martyrology, and novelistic accounts. It is difficult to judge the impact of such texts on women's lives or to what extent they reflect the reality of the existence of women. Thus we are fortunate indeed that Paul revealed so much incidentally in the exchange of greetings and recommendations about real women. As if by accident we are informed that the roles of women coworkers were like those of men. With respect to missionary couples, for example, there is no indication of the female partner having a different or diminished role in relation to the male partner. Later patristic exegetes offered the women partners a much more restricted script.

---

25. The use of the term must be distinguished both from its usage to describe an office which formed part of the threefold organizational framework of bishop, presbyter, and deacon that emerged in some circles at the beginning of the second century and from the female office of "deaconess" that developed considerably later. Paul's use of the term is in fact quite flexible, being employed in the plural along with "overseers" to refer to local leaders of a community or perhaps even to believers in general in Phil. 1:1.

26. Fiorenza has argued vigorously for the missionary connotations of the term διάκονος and its cognates. See *In Memory of Her*, p. 171.

Clement of Alexandria interpreted 1 Corinthians 9:5 as a reference to spiritual marriage where the woman missionary partner acted as a helpmate who ministered in her own right only to other women. He stressed the fact that only women could enter the women's quarters in houses without scandal being aroused.[27] Clement's reading is shaped by the intention to present an appropriate male and female division of labor at the end of the second century c.e., but his presentation does raise interesting questions about the role of women in making initial contact with other women. Clement is writing at about the same time as Celsus, when suspicions about the illicit activities of Christians are clearly high. The secret penetration of the house emerges in the comments of both pagan and Christian as a Christian missionary strategy. Similarly, in the fourth century, the ministry to women in pagan households was described as a special duty of the deaconess because it would have been too dangerous to send a male official.[28] All of this should not be read uncritically back into Paul's day, when tension between the church and the world was much less pronounced and Christianity would most likely not have appeared to an outsider as a clearly distinct entity. The named women leaders we encounter in Paul's letters were probably continuing in the leadership roles they had as pagan and Jewish women in other groups and associations.[29] Yet even in the earliest period, there is evidence that women joining church groups was causing household tensions (1 Cor. 7:12-16; cf. 1 Pet. 3:1-6) and, as discussed above, that women were taking some types of risks for the sake of the gospel.

Widows, Teachers, and Prophets

The evidence concerning widows in early Christian literature indicates that networks of women contributed to the expansion of Christianity among women and children. Both Paul's letters and Acts bear testimony to the importance of the presence and influence of widows among the first generations of believers (e.g., 1 Cor. 7; Acts 6:1-2; 9:36-43). For example, in keeping with the tendency to stress the involvement of well-to-do women in the rise of Christianity, the author of Acts presents Tabitha of Joppa as a community patron who bestowed goods on widows who were less fortunate. Tabitha may have

---

27. Clement of Alexandria, *Stromateis* 3.6.53.3.

28. *Apostolic Constitutions* 3.15. See MacDonald, "Reading Real Women," p. 203.

29. Kraemer, *Her Share*, pp. 191-98; Bernadette J. Brooten, *Women Leaders in the Ancient Synagogue*, BJS 36 (Chico, Calif.: Scholars, 1982); Valerie Abrahamsen, "Women at Philippi: The Pagan and Christian Evidence," *JFSR* 3 (1987): 17-30.

been a widow herself, though one of independent means.[30] Perhaps as a reflection of the importance of widows to the expansion of church groups, the author presents the miraculous raising of Tabitha from the dead as the catalyst for a missionary thrust with news circulating by means of the witness of the saints and the widows (Acts 9:41-42).[31] But in the literature coming from about the beginning of the second century we find conclusive evidence of organized groups of women, some even exercising the "office of widow." The letters of Ignatius, *The Shepherd of Hermas,* and the Pastoral Epistles all come from approximately the same period and offer evidence of women living together in the same house and/or being members of the same house church. Calling for Polycarp to be the protector of widows (Ign. *Pol.* 4.1; cf. Pol. *Phil.* 6.1; *Herm. Sim.* 9.27.2-3), Ignatius also greets "the virgins called widows" (Ign. *Smyrn.* 13.1). In this greeting the group of women is distinguished from believing families made up of householders, wives, and children in a manner that suggests a diverse group of celibate women living together perhaps with some children.[32] One gets the same impression from the intriguing instruction found in *The Shepherd of Hermas:* "Grapte shall exhort the widows and orphans" (*Herm. Vis.* 2.4.3). We know virtually nothing about Grapte, but it seems likely that she was a well-to-do woman leader of a house where believing widows and children lived and worshiped together. That well-to-do women in early Christianity opened their homes to other women is also suggested by 1 Timothy 5:16. The practical support that early church groups could offer women and children in otherwise destitute circumstances was in all likelihood an important factor in winning new female members. If this was not the case, it is difficult to make sense of texts such as 1 Timothy 5:16, where their sustenance is clearly an issue of community concern if not at the center of a community dispute (cf. Acts 6:1).[33]

In 1 Timothy 5:3-16 the author of the Pastorals sets out to limit the burden of widows on the church, to define and to limit the "office of widows," and generally to control the behavior of widows. But unwittingly, the author may have offered us a window into the network of women that contributed to the expansion of Christianity. In critiquing the lives of widows, the author appeals to stereotypical opinions about the excessive and inappropriate religious inclinations

---

30. Bonnie Bowman Thurston, *The Widows: A Women's Ministry in the Early Church* (Minneapolis: Fortress, 1989), pp. 32-35.

31. On the importance of healings and exorcisms for the expansion of Christianity, see especially Ramsay MacMullen, *Christianizing the Roman Empire (A.D. 100-400)* (New Haven and London: Yale University Press, 1984).

32. MacDonald, *Early Christian Women,* pp. 225-26.

33. MacDonald, *Early Christian Women,* pp. 227-29.

of women. Among other things, they are said to be idlers, gossips, busybodies, and gadabouts, going from house to house, saying the things that should not be said (1 Tim. 5:13; cf. 2 Tim. 3:6). They are in all likelihood perpetuating an ascetic teaching that the author of the Pastorals cannot abide (cf. 1 Tim. 4:3). Yet, given the great interest in the reputation of the community in the works, and the author's admission that some widows have already contributed to the defamation of the community, it seems likely that the author is aiming to limit activities that were designed to draw new recruits into their ranks.[34]

The vision of roving women in the Pastorals has much in common with Celsus's depiction of the church as contributing to insubordinate behavior among women and children. Both bear the strong imprint of conventional views concerning the effect of illegitimate religion upon women. But the polemic does not mask the historical activities of women completely. When dealing with widows in particular, the evidence is solid enough to suggest that by the end of the first century the activities of groups of women would have been visible to outsiders and, as the story of Tabitha and the treatment of widows in 1 Timothy 5:3-16 suggest, a contributing factor in the expansion of Christianity. Widows as a group were visible enough in the wider world to be singled out by at least one pagan author. When Lucian of Samosata told the tale of the conversion to Christianity of the philosopher Peregrinus, he spoke of aged widows and orphan children waiting near the prison, at the very break of day, presumably to pray or to offer some type of service to those who were in prison.[35] But the strongest evidence for widows engaging in "evangelizing" activities comes from just outside the period I am mainly discussing, the early third century. The *Didascalia Apostolorum* displays many conventional views on the virtues and vices of women. The relationship between the teaching concerning widows and the specific activities of women is by no means always clear. But the instructions concerning how widows should relate to nonbelievers are precise and nuanced enough that we may be fairly confident that they are based on actual encounters between pagan and Christian. In the opinion of the author of the *Didascalia Apostolorum*, these encounters can often lead to problems. But interestingly, the author does not ban them altogether. Rather the writer allows the widows to answer preliminary questions "in refutation of idols and concerning the unity of God." More complicated questions concerning Christology and eschatology, however, need to be referred to male church leaders: "For when the Gentiles who

34. On the relationship between the treatment of women and communal relations with society at large in the Pastoral Epistles, see MacDonald, *Early Christian Women*, pp. 154-82.

35. Lucian, *The Passing of Peregrinus* 12-13. On the historical reliability of Lucian's satirical account and its use in the study of early Christianity, see MacDonald, *Early Christian Women*, pp. 73-82.

are being instructed hear the word of God not fittingly spoken, as it ought to be, unto edification of eternal life — and all the more in that it is spoken to them by a woman — how that our Lord clothed Himself in a body, and concerning the passion of Christ: they will mock and scoff, instead of applauding the word of doctrine; and she shall incur a heavy judgement for sin."[36]

The attempt to restrict the activities of widows severely once again is unmistakable. But the small amount of latitude given to widows to answer rudimentary questions might well represent an indirect acknowledgment of the power of widows to make initial contact with potential converts and to generate interest in Christianity (even if, in the author's view, such interest subsequently needs to be perfected by the appropriate male authorities).

The treatment of widows in the *Didascalia Apostolorum* is in keeping with a common attitude displayed in early Christian texts toward women teachers, prophets, and visionaries, many of whom were celibate. The texts bristle with often indirect acknowledgments of their power, and strong measures to control them (e.g., 1 Cor. 11:2-16; Rev. 2:19-23). This ambivalence is no doubt related to the ambivalent reaction these women received as ambassadors of the new faith. In Lucian of Samosata's account mentioned above, the presence of old women and children in early Christian circles clearly serves to strengthen an already negative picture. But in contrast, drawing special attention to the presence of women among church groups, Galen of Pergamum praised their "restraint in cohabitation" and defined their nature as a philosophical school.[37] In highlighting the involvement of both men *and* women, Galen's comments recall Philo's favorable description of a Jewish ascetic community, the Therapeutae society, and also have much in common with Justin's description of celibate men and women who proudly display their example before the whole of humanity.[38]

Judith Lieu has argued that Galen's description of Christian women and the involvement of women in Gnosticism and Montanism offers evidence that some women may have found Christianity intellectually attractive and may have been drawn to church groups for that reason.[39] At the end of the second

---

36. R. Hugh Connoly, ed., *Didascalia Apostolorum* (Oxford: Clarendon, 1929), pp. 132-33 (chap. 15).

37. The text here is based on an Arabic source translated and edited by Richard Walzer, *Galen on Jews and Christians* (London: Oxford University Press, 1949), p. 15. For a full discussion of the meaning of this text, including textual issues, see MacDonald, *Early Christian Women*, pp. 82-94.

38. Philo, *On the Contemplative Life* 12, 32-33, 68-69, 83-88 (cited in Ross S. Kraemer, ed., *Maenads, Martyrs, Matrons, and Monastics: A Sourcebook on Women's Religions in the Greco-Roman World* [Philadelphia: Fortress, 1988], pp. 27-28). See Justin, *First Apology* 15 (ANF, 1:167).

39. Lieu, p. 9.

century, Celsus's investigation of early Christianity turned up a number of women teacher-leaders, apparently as founders of groups. Though it suited his agenda to stress this female initiative, these women do figure prominently in gnostic and apocryphal sources: Helena, Marcellina, Salome, Mariamme, and Martha.[40] Celsus also speaks of the early Christian belief in a "power flowing from a certain virgin Prunicus," and calls some Christians "Sybillists" — the Sybil was a prophetess of obscure origin known from Jewish and pagan sources and also mentioned in *The Shepherd of Hermas*.[41] It seems likely Celsus had encountered early Christian groups — including gnostic groups — where women were prophets, visionaries, or teachers.

About the time Celsus composed his critique of early Christianity, two women, Priscilla and Maximilla, were greatly honored leaders in a revivalist movement known as the New Prophecy (or Montanism), and their oracles were written down and accorded high status.[42] Further evidence for the prophetic activities of women is found in *The Martyrdoms of Saints Perpetua and Felicitas*. This document presents Perpetua as a powerful visionary and, though it is by no means certain, has been understood as reflecting Montanist elements rooted in an early third-century, North African context.[43] Because a portion of this work claims to have been written by Perpetua herself, it has frequently been judged to be highly significant for the history of early Christian women. Recently, however, Ross S. Kraemer and Shira L. Lander have raised reservations about the historicity of the document, the claims of female authorship, and the extent to which it can be taken to reflect the experiences of real women.[44] Yet, despite these reservations, the document raises many interesting questions about the relationship between conversion, martyrdom, and the religious "displays" of women more generally. Although it enhances the martyrdom discourse to speak of the conversion of jailers[45] and the power of a prison "love feast" to lead witnesses to faith,[46] the prison/martyrdom arena was clearly a place where early Christian women might have made a public impression.

---

40. Origen, *Contra Celsum* 5.62. See discussion in Hoffmann, p. 42. Unfortunately much of Celsus's text concerning these women has been lost.

41. Origen, *Contra Celsum* 6.34; on the Sybil, *Herm. Vis.* 2.4.1.

42. Christine Trevett, *Montanism: Gender, Authority, and the New Prophecy* (Cambridge: Cambridge University Press, 1996), p. 154. See also Kraemer, *Her Share*, pp. 157-59.

43. See Ross S. Kraemer and Shira L. Lander, "Perpetua and Felicitas," in *The Early Christian World*, ed. Philip F. Esler, vol. 2 (London and New York: Routledge, 2000), pp. 1061-62.

44. Kraemer and Lander, pp. 1051-58.

45. *The Martyrdoms of Saints Perpetua and Felicitas* 16; cited in Kraemer, *Maenads*, p. 104. *Acts of the Christian Martyrs*, trans. H. Musurillo (Oxford: Clarendon, 1972), pp. 106-31.

46. *The Martyrdoms of Saints Perpetua and Felicitas* 17.

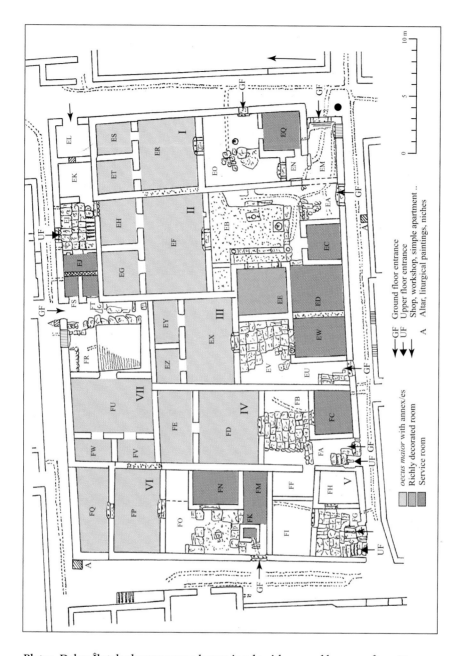

Plate 1. Delos, Îlot des bronzes; row-house *insula* with normal houses, after 166 B.C.E.

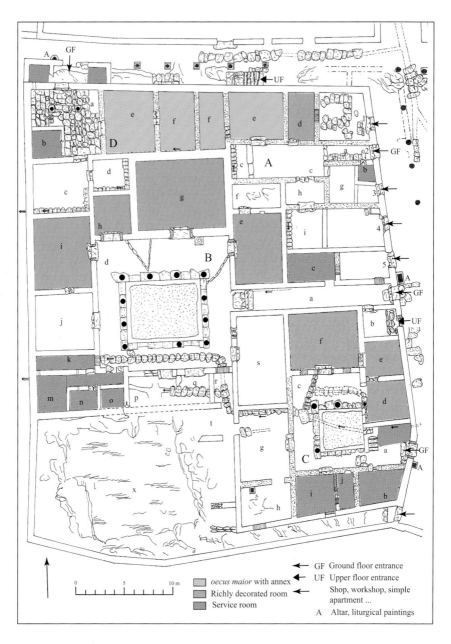

Plate 2. Delos, Îlot de la Maison des masques; *insula* with two peristyle houses, two simple courtyard houses, and shops, after 166 B.C.E.

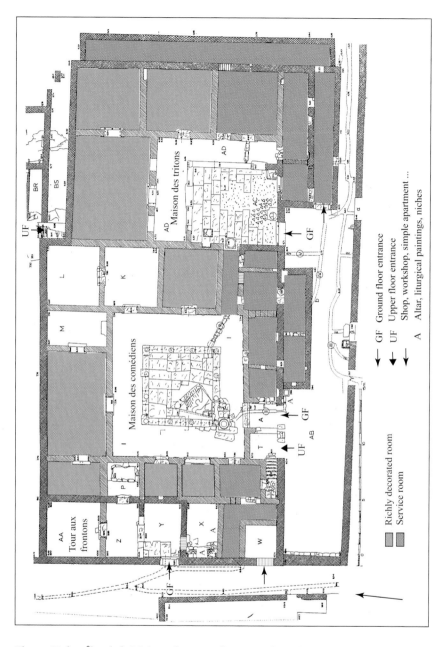

Plate 3. Delos, Îlot de la Maison des comédiens; *insula* with two peristyle houses and tower, last quarter of the second century B.C.E.

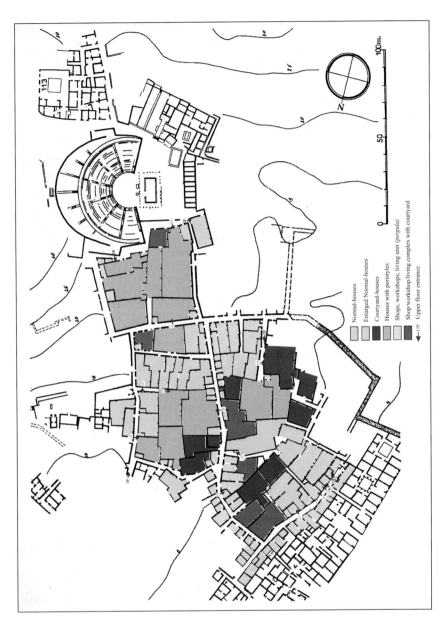

Plate 4. Delos, Quartier du théâter; house types, third (?)-first century B.C.E.

Plate 5. House of the Tragic Poet (VI 8,3.5), Pompeii: fresco of the sacrifice of an unwilling Iphigenia at Aulis carried by two men, Calchas the seer standing on the right, her father Agamemnon seated on the left with his robe drawn over his head, the goddess Artemis with a substitute deer above in heaven. Now in the National Archaeological Museum, Naples.

Plate 6. House of Modesto (?), Pompeii: fresco of the sacrifice of a willing, standing Iphigenia, the seer Calcas on the left cutting a lock of her hair, the sorrowing father Agamemnon seated on the right.

Plate 7. Villa near Pompeii: caricature of Aeneas carrying his father, Anchises holding the household deities, and leading his son, Ascanius; all three have bodies of monkeys, short legs and heads of dogs. Aeneas and his son are sketched with penises. Now in the National Archaeological Museum, Naples.

Plate 8. House of Menander (I 10,4), ala 4 Pompeii: fresco of Cassandra, a prophet warning against the wooden horse before Troy. Above are the city wall and the temple of Athena, in situ.

Plate 9. House of Menander (I 10,4), ala 4: fresco of the death of the priest Laocoon, with the sacrificial bull running away from the snakes. His two sons are below, one already dead, the other being attacked by a snake. Two groups of spectators are above.

Plate 10. House of Menander (I 10,4), ala 4: the entire south wall with the painting of Laocoon in its center. This is one wall of a side room opening onto the atrium that exhibits these three frescoes (plates 8, 9, and 11) of Homeric scenes.

Plate 11. House of Menander (I 10,4), ala 4: the Night of Troy with two episodes. Aias or Odysseus seizes Cassandra as she clings to the image of Athena, and Menelaus seizes the adulterous Helen by her hair. Priam, king of Troy and father of Cassandra, stands in the center observing his daughter captured.

Children

In early Christian literature the care of orphans was often paired with the care of widows as a duty of the church (e.g., James 1:27; *Herm. Man.* 8.10; *Barn.* 20.2; Ign. *Smyrn.* 6.2; cf. Jer. 7:6; Deut. 24:19-22). But the references to the widows and orphans most particularly in *The Shepherd of Hermas,* but probably also in Lucian's description of the imprisonment of Peregrinus, illustrate that the association of orphans with widows as a group in the early church was more than a stylized way of speaking about those in need. Here I would like to concentrate especially on the orphans and other children who appear in early Christian literature.

Given the very limited possibilities for birth control in ancient society and the fact that the house was a meeting place for church groups, it is reasonable to assume that children were very rarely absent when early Christians gathered. No children are singled out in conjunction with the male-female missionary partners of Paul's day, but it is difficult to know what to make of this. Clement of Alexandria would have us believe they were engaged in spiritual marriages. But even in light of such ascetic arrangements (the matter is disputed by scholars; cf. 1 Cor. 7:2-7), children must often have been part of the lives of individuals before they came into contact with the movement. What are the chances, for example, that Prisca and Aquila or Andronicus and Junia did not have children? The avoidance of sex and procreation goes back to the earliest period and is certainly an important aspect of early Christian history, but did it really limit the involvement of children to any significant degree? The exhortation to Grapte to instruct the widows and orphans reminds us that celibate women may have been as involved with caring for children as those who had male partners. As in the modern day, what constitutes "family" is clearly flexible.

The sources do in fact indicate the presence of children, and even their role in the expansion of the movement. Most obviously, the direct address to children in the household codes of Colossians and Ephesians (Col. 3:20; Eph. 6:1-2) indicates that the authors expect children to be present when the letters are read aloud in the midst of the assembly. Ephesians 6:1-4 includes fairly lengthy teaching on the relationship between Christian parents and their children, calling fathers to raise their children "in the discipline and instruction of the Lord." According to John M. G. Barclay, this phrase refers to a "specifically Christian way of raising children, and perhaps a specifically Christian body of instruction to be imparted to them."[47] This interest in the Christian socialization of chil-

---

47. John M. G. Barclay, "The Family as the Bearer of Religion," in *Constructing Early Christian Families: Family as Social Reality and Metaphor,* ed. Halvor Moxnes (London and New York: Routledge, 1997), p. 77.

dren is repeatedly found in the teaching of the Apostolic Fathers (1 Clem. 21.6, 8; Did. 4.9; Pol. Phil. 4.2). In Polycarp's letter to the Philippians, such socialization is presented as the special duty of wives. The Pastoral Epistles offer specific evidence of women being involved in the Christian socialization of children. Timothy's faith is said to have been kindled by the influence of his grandmother Lois and of his mother Eunice (2 Tim. 1:5).[48] Given modern expectations of mother-child relations, one might naturally suppose that this type of socialization took place primarily between mothers and young children. But Suzanne Dixon has brought evidence to light indicating that Roman mothers continued to exert considerable influence on their adolescent sons, even in such areas as education and career patterns.[49] That the grandmother Lois and mother Eunice are presented as sharing this agenda is also not particularly surprising, as a good deal of evidence points to a strong bond between married daughters and their mothers.[50]

We should also consider the circumstances of children who were part of families where only one parent was a member of the church. Paul mentions these for the first time in his argument concerning the preservation of mixed marriages in 1 Corinthians 7:12-16.[51] The manner in which Timothy is presented as the child of two generations of believing women suggests that he is being presented by the author of the Pastorals as the "fruit" of a family circumstance where faith was propounded by the women of the house. It is likely that many children simply accompanied their believing parent into the church without making a deliberate choice to join a new movement. But at the parent's side faith would have been absorbed, and it is conceivable that the children played an important role in the winning of other nonbelieving members of the household. Young children were left in the care of, and/or came into contact with, a variety of people in the ancient household, including slaves, nurses, and surrogate parents of various kinds.[52] If Celsus's views even somewhat accurately reflect church efforts to recruit children, there is good reason to suspect that such children would have contributed to the expansion of Christianity. Although it comes from a much later period, there is at least one delightful text that envisions the specific missionary activity of a child. In his correspondence

---

48. On the importance of Christian teaching being absorbed at the mother's side, see Jean Delumeau, La religion de ma mère: les femmes dans la transmission de la foi (Paris: Cerf, 1992).

49. On the relationship between the Roman mother and her adolescent son, see Suzanne Dixon, The Roman Mother (London and Sydney: Croom Helm, 1988), pp. 168-203.

50. Dixon, pp. 220-28.

51. For a full discussion of this complicated text, see MacDonald, Early Christian Women, pp. 189-95.

52. Dixon, pp. 159-61.

with Laeta, Jerome casts Laeta's daughter in the role of unrelenting child evangelist in relation to her pagan grandfather: "When she sees her grandfather, she must leap upon his breast, put her arms around his neck, and, whether he likes it or not, sing Alleluia in his ears."[53]

The Household and Conversion

While asceticism and marriages between pagans and Christians (see below) continued to challenge the boundaries of conventional family existence, it is fair to say that by the latter decades of the first century Christianity became grafted onto conventional patterns of family life in some church circles.[54] At times the household base of early Christianity was actually sanctified, with familial images merging with metaphorical descriptions of the relationship between the human and the divine (e.g., Eph. 5:22-33; 1 Tim. 3:15). Ephesians even names God as the Father from whom every family *(patria)* is named (3:14-15), suggesting "the sanctification of lineage as a divinely-ordained gift."[55] This reinforcement of conventional life is revealed most explicitly, however, in the household codes found repeatedly in the literature of the late New Testament and early patristic era (cf. Col. 3:18–4:1; Eph. 5:21–6:9; 1 Pet. 2:18–3:7; 1 Tim. 2:8-15; 5:1-2; 6:1-2; Titus 2:1-10; 3:1; *Did.* 4.9-11; *Barn.* 19.5-7; *1 Clem.* 21.6-9; Ign. *Pol.* 4.1–5.2; Pol. *Phil.* 4.2-3). Modern research on the origin and functions of the codes has revealed that the degree of explicit apologetic interest varies from one document to the next, but we should clearly look to the need for apology in seeking to understand why this type of hierarchical ethical exhortation emerged in church groups at this time.[56] Generally speaking, the tendency to include household-code teaching surfaces when Christianity emerges as a clearly identifiable group in ancient society and struggles to survive in an increasingly hostile environment. Moreover, the emergence of household codes occurs largely simultaneously with what Ramsay MacMullen has identified as a decline in references to explicit missionary activity starting at the turn of the

---

53. Letter 107, Jerome to Laeta, excerpt from Kraemer, *Maenads*, p. 130; see pp. 127-30.

54. Barclay, p. 77.

55. Barclay, p. 76.

56. See Balch, *Let Wives Be Submissive*. Balch draws parallels between the New Testament use of the code and the apologetic function of the topos of household management in other ancient texts. See pp. 54-55, 73-76. See also Margaret Y. MacDonald, *Colossians and Ephesians*, Sacra Pagina Series, ed. Daniel J. Harrington, S.J. (Collegeville, Minn.: Liturgical Press, 2000); E. Elizabeth Johnson, "Ephesians," in *The Women's Bible Commentary*, ed. Carol A. Newsom and Sharon H. Ringe (Louisville: Westminster John Knox, 1992), pp. 340-41.

second century. He argues that Christians of this period were essentially cautious when it came to large-scale public appearances and identifies the fairly sequestered settings of home and work as the circumstances where most conversions took place.[57]

What MacMullen describes as a move in the literature toward greater seclusion corresponds to what interpreters have identified as a shift with the household codes away from the fairly open possibilities for women's leadership in Paul's day toward increasing restriction within the household. Yet for the purposes of this essay it is important to remember that the restriction of women's leadership opportunities does not mean that women necessarily played less of a role in the growth of the movement in all cases. With all the limiting of women's authority inherent in the household codes, the codes nevertheless include at least one tacit acknowledgment of women's power. As the instructions concerning the relationship between believing wives and nonbelieving husbands in 1 Peter 3:1-6 illustrate, sometimes hierarchical teaching masks tacit acknowledgment of the ability of women to influence the household by perpetuating the growth of the movement. The ideal Christian wife could serve as a symbol of group identity (cf. Eph. 5:22-33) and the perfect, modest, and discreet mediator between the church and the nonbelieving world (1 Pet. 3:1-6).[58]

Although it is communicated through literary artistry rather than ethical exhortation, an apologetic agenda also underlies the Acts of the Apostles. In an effort to link the rise of Christianity with family institutions and modes of operation, the author of Acts highlights a pattern of early Christian expansion for which there is important corroborating evidence in Paul's letters (e.g., 1 Cor. 1:16): the conversion of the head of the household followed by the remainder of the household. Acts includes four stories of household conversions, beginning with the programmatic story of Cornelius (10:1–11:18; cf. 16:11-15; 16:25-34; 18:1-11). All speak of conversions using the same "οἶκος" formula, "and/with [all] his/her household," apparently recalling for the reader the mission of evangelizing households given to the seventy-two in Luke (Luke 10:5-7).[59] With a specific

---

57. MacMullen, *Christianizing the Roman Empire*, pp. 33-42. Note the similar observation made by Martin Goodman: "[I]t is a separate question how many Christians believed a proselytizing mission to be desirable after the eschatological fervour of the first generations. Against any view that such a mission was generally seen by Christians as applicable in later times is the treatment of the texts of Jesus' commission to the apostles (Matt. 28:19-20; Mark 16:15-16) in patristic writings of the second to fourth centuries." See Goodman, *Mission and Conversion: Proselytizing in the Religious History of the Roman Empire* (Oxford: Clarendon, 1994), p. 106.

58. MacDonald, *Early Christian Women*, pp. 240-43.

59. David Lertis Matson, *Household Conversion Narratives in Acts: Pattern and Interpretation*, JSNTSup 123 (Sheffield: Sheffield Academic Press, 1996), pp. 87-88.

focus on Acts 16, which includes the story of the conversion of Lydia and her household, Michael White has demonstrated the problems with establishing direct historical correlation between the narrative and the situation in first-century Philippi, noting the tendency for the narrative instead to revolve around the conventional. He argues that the author of Luke-Acts is interested in making a point about the shape of the Christian movement using an established model from the environment: "That model asserts the position of the extended household (including the *pater-* or *materfamilias,* children, slaves, friends, freedmen, and other clients) is the locus of the movement."[60]

In the story of the conversion of Lydia and her household (Acts 16:11-15), the interest of the author of Acts to highlight the conversion of households intersects with the desire to highlight the attraction of well-to-do women to Christianity. As a dealer in purple dyed garments with a house large enough to host several guests, Lydia obviously meets the grade. The setting for Lydia's conversion is Philippi, but in other cities Paul finds converts among leading women, including Thessalonica (17:1-9), Beroea (17:10-15), and Athens (17:16-34). An interesting corollary to this success among leading women is the failure at Pisidian Antioch, where "prominent" and "devout" women team up with leading men to oppose Paul (13:50).[61] The sympathy of powerful women seems to be one of the themes developed by the author of Acts in an effort to communicate the respectability and independence of early Christianity.[62] In addition to apologetic crafting, Judith Lieu has argued that Acts shares the novelistic tendency of second-century Greek and Jewish novels that appear to exaggerate the social influence of women.[63]

It is probably best not to look for direct correlation between the story of Lydia and the real circumstances of Paul's day. Rather, for the author of Acts Lydia represents the ideal woman convert, a facilitator of Christian growth to the ends of the earth (Acts 1:8) whose own house serves as a base for the movement (16:15, 40). Lydia herself may never have existed, but women like her almost certainly contributed to the rise of Christianity from Paul's day onward. Lydia has been compared to such "real" women as Phoebe (Rom. 16:1-2), discussed above, and Nympha (Col. 4:15), who is described as a woman leader of a house church in the context of the document which introduces the household code into Pauline Christianity. The inclusion of traditional household ethics in

60. See Michael White, "Visualizing the 'Real' World of Acts 16: Toward Construction of a Social Index," in *The Social World of the First Christians,* ed. L. Michael White and O. Larry Yarbrough (Philadelphia: Fortress, 1995), p. 259.

61. Matson, pp. 140-41.

62. Lieu, p. 16.

63. Lieu, p. 17.

works of the latter decades of the first century and early decades of the second century did not mean that influential women completely disappeared from early Christian texts. The works of Ignatius of Antioch, for example, contain both household-code teaching (Ign. *Pol.* 4.1–5.2) and references to prominent women such as Tavia (who is apparently at the head of a household or may lead a house church), the wife of Epitropus (who is greeted along with her house and children), and Alce (Ign. *Smyrn.* 13.2; Ign. *Pol.* 8.2-3). As male authors began to propound more restricted and conventional roles for women, they nevertheless continued to offer considerable latitude to well-to-do women. This may be in part because women such as Nympha or Tavia were very important to the success of the mission, but it was also no doubt because their exertions of influence as heads of households and patrons were within the boundaries of societal expectations for the prominent women of their day.[64]

Christian women who were married to pagans, however, posed a definite challenge to societal expectations concerning the prerogatives of the paterfamilias.[65] Rodney Stark argues that such marriages were nevertheless ultimately of great importance for the growth of early Christianity, noting that they were a mechanism by which "Christians managed to remain an *open network*, able to keep building bonds with outsiders, rather than becoming a closed community of believers."[66] Central to his thesis is the ruling by Callistus in the early third century that women could live in "just concubinage" with their mates.[67] This ruling apparently responded to the problem of upper-class women seeking to preserve their wealth, for legal marriages with Christians of lower rank would have meant the loss of inheritance. Thus, Stark asks, "If highborn Christian women found it so difficult to find grooms that the bishop of Rome permitted 'just concubinage,' how was he to condemn middle- and lower-class Christian women who wed pagans, especially if they did so within the church guidelines concerning the religious training of children?"[68] As Stark

---

64. For example, see Ramsay MacMullen, "Women in Public in the Roman Empire," *Historia* 29 (1980): 208-18; MacMullen, "Women's Power in the Principate," in his *Changes in the Roman Empire: Essays on the Ordinary* (Princeton: Princeton University Press, 1990), pp. 169-76.

65. For an illustration of how the religious activities of women could be viewed as an assault upon the head of the household, see Apuleius, *Metamorphoses* 9.14. See full discussion of this text in MacDonald, *Early Christian Women*, pp. 67-73.

66. Stark, p. 115.

67. Reported in Hippolytus, *Philosophumena (refutatio omnium haeresium)* 9, 12, 24, cited in Marie-Thérèse Raepsaet-Charlier, "Tertullien et la législation des mariages inégaux," *RIDA* 29 (1982): 262. Note that Michele Renée Salzman has pointed out that this was not a problem unique to the Christian community and Roman legislation was drawn up to respond to it (p. 213).

68. Stark, p. 112.

himself acknowledges, there are many voices, including that of Tertullian, strongly condemning the practice of Christian women entering into new marriages with pagan men, but he sees this as a further indication that such marriages were actually occurring in significant numbers.[69]

All of this evidence needs to be evaluated carefully. There is no question that marriages between pagans and Christians existed in the church from Paul's day, and that they virtually always involved a Christian woman. Despite the encouragement to let these marriages continue under some circumstances (for Paul it is the nonbelieving partner's willingness to remain in the union that is the determining factor [1 Cor. 7:12-16]), these marriages are clearly problematic. Most obviously, there is the problem of pollution (cf. 1 Thess. 4:4-5; 1 Cor. 6:15-20; cf. 2 Cor. 6:14). Though his apologetic genre should make us cautious about drawing conclusions about real persons and specific events, Justin Martyr describes the circumstances of the woman from Rome who eventually divorces her philandering husband in a manner that may offer insight into typical reactions of Christians to mixed marriages; he speaks of her revulsion at having to share his table and his bed.[70] Tertullian states categorically that believers contracting marriages with Gentiles are "guilty of fornication" and should be excommunicated, citing 1 Corinthians 5:11: "with persons of that kind there is to be no taking of food even."[71] Drawing upon the examples from pagan life where wealthy householders forbid their slaves to marry outside the household, Tertullian describes Christian women who seek marriage to pagan men as "conjoining to themselves the devil's slaves." In Tertullian's view it is the wealthiest Christian women who are subject to such temptations, those with a proclivity for the more capacious house (in our terms, the bigger house in the suburbs!).[72] Such forceful language may indicate that some women wish to enter into marriage with pagans, but it is equally possible that Tertullian is using such aspirations as a particularly good example of the moral weakness of women without there being necessarily many instances of women seeking out such arrangements at all.

In addition to the problem of pollution, the theory that exogamous marriage (particularly the contracting of new marriages between Christian women and pagan men) was central to the growth of early Christianity must be measured against evidence of mounting tension in the households of those engaged in mixed marriage (cf. 1 Cor. 7:15) that culminates in violence against Chris-

---

69. Stark, pp. 112-13.

70. See Justin, *2 Apology* 2.

71. Tertullian, *To His Wife* 2.3 (ANF 4).

72. Tertullian, *To His Wife* 2.8 (ANF 4). See discussion of this in Raepsaet-Charlier, pp. 254-63.

tians. Instructions concerning marriage between believing women and nonbelieving men in 1 Peter 3:1-6 include the call for silence and reserve, coupled with a clear attempt to bolster the confidence of these women with the instruction that they are to let nothing terrify them (v. 6).[73] Clement of Rome connects the suffering of believing women who were divorced by pagan husbands with the indignities suffered by women during martyrdom (1 Clem. 6.1-4; cf. Tertullian, Apology 3, ANF 3). While often more fantastic than historical, the Apocryphal Acts of the Apostles nevertheless include many accounts of women's attraction to Christian asceticism culminating in refusals to marry or go on living with pagan men, the result being blind rage and violence directed especially at apostles.[74] There are enough points of contact with other early Christian texts to suggest that, at least to some degree, these texts reflect the circumstances that real women faced.

Given all this tension, violence, and concern about the polluting influences of the pagan partner, we are left with the question of why these marriages were tolerated at all. Part of the reason may have been pragmatic. In order to survive, Christian women may sometimes have needed to keep their allegiances secret, and Christian exhortation may have justified a way of life from which there may well have been no safe escape. But the motives announced by the texts themselves fit to some degree with Stark's theory. For Paul and the author of 1 Peter the motivation to preserve the union is clear: such marriages bear the inherent potential of spreading the gospel. In 1 Peter 3:1-6 the woman is cast in the role of quiet evangelist in her own home. Justin presents the Roman woman as trying to persuade her unchaste husband initially, apparently heeding Paul's advice (2 Apology 2). If church texts present these marriages as potentially winning converts, we should perhaps be hesitant to discount them. But the problem is that there is so very little evidence of success in the convincing of husbands in this period. In fact, there is evidence in the distinctly opposite direction. In Justin's account, the woman ends up divorcing her husband despite numerous attempts to reform him. The Apocryphal Acts time and time again describe the husband's opposition to the wife's attraction to ascetic Christianity and rarely include the conversion of husbands.[75] But if women were not very often successful in converting their husbands, perhaps they contributed to the

73. MacDonald, Early Christian Women, pp. 195-204.

74. See, for example, Acts of Peter 34, E. Hennecke and W. Schneemelcher, eds., New Testament Apocrypha, vol. 2, English translation by Robert McL. Wilson (Philadelphia: Westminster, 1965), p. 317. Cf. Justin, 2 Apology 2.

75. See Ross S. Kraemer, "The Conversion of Women to Ascetic Forms of Christianity," Signs 6 (1980): 298-307. Kraemer offers the following examples: Andronicus in the Acts of John 63 and Misdaeus in the Acts of Thomas 170 (p. 300).

preservation of an "open network" (to use Stark's phrase) in other ways: by influencing children (1 Cor. 7:12-16; 2 Tim. 1:5) and perhaps also slaves (1 Tim. 6:1). Perhaps the preservation of the marriage was often not based on any real hope of the Christianization of the marriage per se, but on the hope of winning some members of the household and those with whom the wife might come into contact as she went about her daily affairs.

Thecla, the Missionary

I have saved discussion of the most dramatic image of a woman winning household members (though not members of her own household) for the end of this chapter. In the *Acts of (Paul and) Thecla,* Thecla is portrayed as a missionary teacher who dies only "after enlightening many with the word of God" (3.43).[76] But the evidence from this work is by no means easy to evaluate. Earlier theories about the prominent role assigned to a woman offering a window into the ascetic world of women have given way to great hesitation to view this account and other stories contained in Apocryphal Acts of the Apostles as historical in any way.[77] Because these works have so much in common with ancient novels, their value for describing the lives of real women is difficult to judge. In comparing the *Acts of (Paul and) Thecla* to ancient romances, Kate Cooper has argued that even the centrality of asceticism in the work should be evaluated critically and from a literary perspective:

> The Acts of Paul makes clear the usefulness of the heroine's continence as a narrative device to propel the conflict between the apostle and a symbolic representative of the ruling class of the cities he visits. . . . The challenge by the apostle to the householder is the urgent message of these narratives, and it is essentially a conflict *between men.* The challenge posed here by Christianity is not really about women, or even about sexual continence, but about authority and the social order. In this way, tales of continence use the narrative momentum of romance, and the enticement of the romantic heroine, to mask a contest for authority, encoded in the contest between two pretenders to the heroine's allegiance.[78]

---

76. For translation, see n. 80 below.

77. See Kate Cooper, *The Virgin and the Bride: Idealized Womanhood in Late Antiquity* (Cambridge, Mass., and London: Harvard University Press, 1996). See especially pp. 62-63, where she questions these earlier theories.

78. Cooper, *Virgin and the Bride,* pp. 54-55.

Cooper's important work calls into question naive historical readings of the *Acts of (Paul and) Thecla* and theories about women's storytelling or authorship underlying the text. While I would agree that authority and the social order are central to the true meaning of this work, I would not go so far as to say that the challenge posed by Christianity "is not really about women." It is important not to lose sight of the significant points of contact between the *Acts of (Paul and) Thecla* and other less novelistic texts. We know that ascetic communities of women existed, such as seem to be in view in this work, especially in the depiction of the household of the widow Tryphaena. We also know that the prerogatives of the pagan paterfamilias were threatened by women who were attracted to early Christianity, ascetic or otherwise. We know that marriages between pagan men and early Christian women existed, even if it is difficult to determine their frequency. Perhaps most importantly, the literature speaks of church groups dealing with awkward situations on account of the involvement of Christian women in such arrangements. When women were converted to Christianity under such circumstances, we can only assume that they took the initiative. This is not to suggest that Thecla ever existed or that the influence of a woman has not been exaggerated, greatly surpassing the bounds of the history. But I think that in this early Christian text, women's influence is exaggerated because women's influence was real and perceived as dangerous. Christianity's conflict with the social order and civic responsibility involved both the real and imagined activities of women. Cooper may be correct in identifying the two main conversation partners in the *Acts of (Paul and) Thecla* as men, but I would argue that this conversation makes sense in this early Christian text only because of a combination of women's initiative, social expectations concerning women's proper roles, and the special significance attached to the honorable behavior of women in defining group identity.[79]

At its most basic level, the battle about authority and social order in the *Acts of (Paul and) Thecla* is expressed in terms of a battle for houses in the city, with a special concern for the activity of women in these houses. The work has significant points in common with the other texts we have been considering. As it is presented in the *Acts of (Paul and) Thecla,* the church meets in houses (e.g., 3.2-7; cf. 3.41) and conversion is a household affair (e.g., 3.7, 23).[80] Onesiphorous, for example, is described as having left the things of this world to follow Paul with all of his house (3.23). Similar to 1 Timothy 5:13-15, which describes widows who perpetuate a network of false teaching from house to house, the

---

79. See MacDonald, *Early Christian Women,* pp. 240-43.

80. References are to the translation of the apocryphal *Acts of Paul and Thecla,* by W. Schneemelcher, in Hennecke and Schneemelcher, pp. 353-64.

text describes Thecla's frequent movement from house to house. But this time such movement is celebrated. The wealthy widow Tryphaena, whose own daughter has died (cf. 3.27-29), offers shelter to Thecla. Thecla is presented as resting in the house of Tryphaena for eight days, instructing her in the word of the Lord. The maidservants are said also to believe, and there is great joy in the house (3.39). A new family has been created whose bonds are not of flesh and blood, but of Christian commitment.[81] Even after Thecla sets out on the road again, Tryphaena continues to support her work, sending her gifts of clothing and gold for the poor (3.41). The households of women envisioned in 1 Timothy 5:16; Ignatius, *Letter to the Smyrnaeans* 13.1; and *Hermas, Vision* 2.4.3 come to mind, as do the hints in various texts that women spread the gospel to other women, children, and slaves, and supported those in need.

In the *Acts of (Paul and) Thecla*, Thecla takes on masculine characteristics (e.g., 3.25), and adopts a public and visible evangelical role of the type for which there is very little evidence for either Christian men or Christian women in this period. But if we understand the text as a symbolic depiction of what was at stake especially for women who joined the church and worked to secure its survival and expansion in various ways (and for men who were seen to be associated with such women), in my view we are much closer to history. The suspicions of shamelessness and sexual immorality that follow Thecla throughout the account are echoed throughout pagan critique of early Christianity. The fantastic depictions of the violence endured by Thecla find a corollary in the usually much more subtle depictions of household strife and violence found in other texts. Yet what is perhaps most interesting about the *Acts of (Paul and) Thecla,* and most useful as a means of clarifying the historical indications we find in other texts, is the importance attributed to household settings in the expansion and struggle for success of early Christianity.

Conclusion

In this paper I have drawn attention to the existence of divergent scholarly opinion concerning the involvement of women in the expansion of Christianity. With respect to the first two centuries c.e., I have found that the evidence justifies neither the bold claims of some scholars concerning the influence of women in the Christianization of the Roman Empire, nor the extreme skepticism of others. For the earliest period in particular we find incidental references to women who contributed to the expansion of the movement. But the evi-

---

81. For fuller discussion, see MacDonald, *Early Christian Women,* pp. 172-78.

dence also includes many texts where women are represented in order to further the agenda of male authors in various ways; the relationship between these texts and the lives of real women is much more difficult to determine. Yet the results of literary and rhetorical analysis of such texts can be incorporated within the process of historical reconstruction. Comparison of the relevant early Christian texts, consideration of the Greco-Roman setting, and careful attention to literary genre can work together to produce a reliable picture of the involvement of women in the expansion of early Christianity. This picture, however, is not uniform (i.e., mainly stemming from marriages between Christian women and pagan men), but multifaceted — involving women in such diverse roles as patrons, heads of households, mothers, teachers, and various kinds of ambassadors of the new faith. Nevertheless, the picture has a unifying element: household life. The attempt to identify the specific activities of women that contributed to the expansion of the gospel leads time and time again to the household: either women meeting together in a house, seeking to build believing homes, or struggling to preserve Christian allegiance in the home of a pagan householder.

To return, then, to the question with which we began: Was Celsus right? If we look beyond the polemic (though the polemic is part of the story!), largely, yes. Women did move in and out of houses and shops, taking risks and leading people — including children — to join the movement without permission from the "proper" authorities. They did so, it seems, while conducting their daily business. No doubt they sometimes remained largely invisible, but in other cases they met with real resistance both inside and outside of church groups. This combination of boldness, affront, and concealment is for me one of the most interesting and little understood features of the rise of early Christianity.

Women, Slaves, and the Economy
of the Roman Household

Richard Saller

The topic of labor and gender in the Roman household is both theoretically interesting and substantively important. The fact that the subject is understudied is due no doubt in part to the woeful inadequacy of information, but it is also part of a more general picture of long neglect of women as economic actors. Moses Finley's *Ancient Economy* has no listing in the index for "women"; although women receive scattered attention in the book, the reader would not guess that Roman women owned a substantial fraction of the capital and provided a large part of the labor in the Roman Empire. I pick Finley's book *exempli gratia*; the same point could be made about Rostovtzeff's *Social and Economic History of the Roman Empire* and other standard works.[1] What is more, in the field of women's studies of the Roman world, relatively little attention has been devoted to women's economic roles, to judge from the bibliographies of recent collections devoted to women of classical antiquity.[2]

The neglect has certainly not been complete, but I believe the reasons for the relative neglect are closely related to the reasons that give the topic its fundamental theoretical interest. In the social sciences and history there is a large gulf between cultural approaches to understanding human behavior and economic approaches based on assumptions of universal human rationality. Cultural historians of gender tend to shy away from economistic analyses, while the mainstream of economists (until recently) have analyzed households as the basic unit of consumption and the firm as the basic unit of production, without reference to gendered individuals. It is a special irony that Finley, the leading advocate of the idea of an embedded economy, was uninterested in the way eco-

---

1. M. I. Finley, *The Ancient Economy* (Berkeley and Los Angeles: University of California Press, 1973); M. I. Rostovtzeff, *Social and Economic History of the Roman Empire* (Oxford: Oxford University Press, 1957).

2. Richard Hawley and Barbara Levick, *Women in Antiquity: New Assessments* (London: Routledge, 1995); Tanja Scheer, "Forschungen über die Frau in der Antike. Ziele, Methoden, Perspektiven," *Gymnasium* 107 (2000): 143-72.

nomic behavior was embedded in a gendered construction of labor and property rights.

And yet across human societies labor is more or less universally patterned by gender. As Cathy Lynne Costin points out, "because the division of labor and gender identity are so deeply entwined, it is an interesting and important observation that can help us understand the nature and origins of gender as a structuring social principle, namely the incredible strength of the tendency to mark men and women as separate, as well as the dynamic that gender played in the organization of production in complex societies."[3] Costin cites the cross-cultural tabulation of Murdock and Provost to show that between societies there can be much variation in whether a particular craft is coded "male" or "female," but it is a rare society that codes crafts indiscriminately as "female" and "male."[4] Murdock and Provost were concerned mainly with preindustrial production, but the pattern of gender coding has not disappeared with industrialization. Claudia Goldin, a Harvard economist, in her influential work *Understanding the Gender Gap: An Economic History of American Women,* acknowledges that her research impressed on her the persistent influence of long-held norms and expectations on women's participation in the labor force, even in the fluid labor markets of the twentieth century. Labor may be broadly utilitarian, but it is channeled and organized in ways fundamentally marked by the cultural values of gender.[5]

The configurations of the gendering of labor have major implications for the individual experiences of women and men in a society, and also for economic production in aggregate. Ester Boserup underlined this basic point in her classic work, *Women's Role in Economic Development.* From one developing society to another, Boserup found large variations in women's participation in agricultural and urban production. For instance, the strong moral teaching in Arabic societies against public visibility of women has had a powerful, depressing effect on women's contribution to agricultural fieldwork and urban commerce. The lower participation of women, in turn, has limited the potential for economic growth. Boserup concluded that "under-utilization of female family labor" is not "exceptional" even in impoverished areas, and "the prejudice

---

3. Cathy Lynne Costin, "Exploring the Relationship between Gender and Craft in Complex Societies: Methodological and Theoretical Issues of Gender Attribution," in *Gender and Archaeology,* ed. R. P. Wright (Philadelphia: University of Pennsylvania Press, 1996), p. 123.

4. George P. Murdock and Caterina Provost, "Factors in the Division of Labor by Sex: A Cross-Cultural Analysis," *Ethnology* 12 (1973): 203-25.

5. Claudia Goldin, *Understanding the Gender Gap: An Economic History of American Women* (New York: Oxford University Press, 1990).

against women's work in the field is an important cause of . . . poverty" in some regions.[6]

The experiences and treatment of women vary across societies and are affected, inter alia, by their relation to production and property. The evidence from Rome illustrates how separate property rights within the family can give a woman the leverage to command deference from family members and the broader society.[7] Though the evidence for the Roman laboring classes is inadequate, comparative studies suggest that women's participation in economic production can also lead to higher esteem and better treatment of women, resulting in better nutrition and lower mortality rates for girls and adult women.[8]

Altogether, it is clear that women's role in economic production is an important subject, and not only because women constituted about half the population of the Roman Empire. Women's work in Rome has received some attention, especially from Susan Treggiari in the urban sphere and from Walter Scheidel in the rural sphere. In the 1970s Treggiari published an important series of papers comprehensively describing the occupations of women in the city of Rome. These articles are thorough in their deployment of epigraphic and juristic evidence and offer valuable general observations. Scheidel's articles collect the meager sources for rural labor by women and interpret them with the guidance of historical comparisons.[9]

I hope to add a little to the previous scholarship (1) by considering the limited evidence within the framework of Roman conceptions of household production and management and (2) by considering the interrelationships between urban and rural production. The typical wealthy Roman estate owner

6. Ester Boserup, *Women's Role in Economic Development* (London: Allen and Unwin, 1970), p. 72.

7. J. A. Crook, "Women in Roman Succession," in *The Family in Ancient Rome: New Perspectives*, ed. B. Rawson (Ithaca, N.Y.: Cornell University Press, 1986), pp. 58-82.

8. Boserup, pp. 48-51; Stefan Dercon and Pramila Krishnan, "In Sickness and in Health: Risk Sharing within Households in Rural Ethiopia," *Journal of Political Economy* 108 (2000): 688-727; Walter Scheidel, "The Most Silent Women of Greece and Rome: Rural Labor and Women's Life in the Ancient World (I)," *GR* 47 (1995): 204.

9. Susan Treggiari, "Domestic Staff at Rome in the Julio-Claudian Period, 27 B.C. to A.D. 68," *Histoire Sociale* 6 (1973): 241-55; Treggiari, "Jobs in the Household of Livia," *PBSR* 30 (1975): 48-77; Treggiari, "Jobs for Women," *AJAH* 1 (1976): 76-104; Treggiari, "Lower Class Women in the Roman Economy," *Florilegium* 1 (1979): 65-86; Scheidel, "The Most Silent Women of Greece and Rome (I)"; Scheidel, "The Most Silent Women of Greece and Rome: Rural Labor and Women's Life in the Ancient World (II)," *GR* 48 (1996): 1-10; Scheidel, "Reflections on the Differential Valuation of Slaves in Diocletian's Price Edict and in the United States," *Münstersche Beiträge zur antiken Handelsgeschicte* 15 (1996): 67-79; Scheidel, "Quantifying the Sources of Slaves in the Roman Empire," *JRS* 87 (1997): 159-69.

had both a townhouse staffed by a *familia urbana* (urban slave staff) and rural estates worked by a *familia rustica* (rural slave staff). In keeping accounts the Roman master (male or female) typically kept these two staffs conceptually separate. Paulus notes that some legal authorities distinguished the *familia urbana* from the *familia rustica* on the principle of residence; others made the distinction based on type of work; but Paulus thought the distinction was best made on the basis of where the slaves appeared in the accounts, drawing their *cibaria* or rations (*Digest* 32.99 pr).

In considering the dynamics between urban and rural, I will pay special attention to the female slave, the *ancilla*. The *ancilla* is a crucial figure for understanding the economic productivity of the Roman household and the reproduction of the slave labor force. Recent heated arguments about the supply of slave labor over the centuries of the empire have focused on the sex ratio in the slave population.[10] It is claimed that there was not enough work for *ancillae* to warrant a balanced sex ratio capable of full reproduction.[11] I believe it is possible to bring a little more evidence to bear on this problem, though it is unlikely to resolve the debate.

One issue I will not try to tackle is the subjective experiences of female laborers, in particular female slaves. I know of no source from which to provide an authentic voice for this group. Furthermore, the male authors of the extant texts are (shockingly) insensitive to the sensibilities of *ancillae*. Horace's notorious advice to stay out of trouble by using an *ancilla* as a sexual outlet shows no interest in the partner as a sentient human being (*Sermones* 1.2.117). Musonius Rufus, in his discussion of sexual indulgence (XII. *Peri aphrodisiōn*), argues that men should observe the same moral restraint in sexual activity as their wives — no double standard. Musonius acknowledges that some Roman males see nothing wrong with a master's sexual relations with his own slave woman, "since every master is held to have it in his power to use his slave as he wishes."[12] Musonius refutes this reasoning, not by appeal to respect for the *ancilla*'s inviolability, but by the analogy of how intolerable a *domina*'s relations with a male slave would be. This lack of interest in, and concern for, the slave's sensibilities makes it difficult to guess at her coping responses to what surely were degrading experiences. The rituals and routines of Roman house-

---

10. W. V. Harris, "Demography, Geography and the Sources of Roman Slaves," *JRS* 89 (1999): 62-75; Scheidel, "Quantifying the Sources of Slaves in the Roman Empire"; Keith Bradley, "On the Roman Slave Supply and Slavebreeding," in *Classical Slavery*, ed. M. I. Finley (London: Frank Cass & Co., 1987), pp. 42-64.

11. Harris, p. 69.

12. See the contribution of Carolyn Osiek in this volume.

holds symbolically reaffirmed the hierarchy of the *matrona's* honor and *ancilla's* lack of it.[13]

The basic unit of production and consumption in antiquity was the household or the *familia* (slave staff). The Romans, for all their intricate development of legal institutions, never developed the concept of the private corporation as an entity transcending the individual or a few partners. Relatedly, the Romans did not develop a notion of wage labor as an impersonal relationship with a faceless corporation. Working for someone else entailed a personal relationship with overtones of dependence, whether as a slave or debt bondsman or *filiusfamilias.* This much the economic historians of the previous generation, such as Finley, Ste. Croix, and Brunt, stressed. But these historians did not think through all the implications of having economic production embedded in the family and household.[14]

Domus or household in Roman society covered units of very different sizes and complexity: rural and urban, large slave *familiae* and small immediate families. The small, rural family without slaves was probably the most common type, but is the one we know least about. The large slave *familiae* were, by an order of magnitude, the biggest private productive units in the Roman Empire, and as such, raised issues of organization and management for Roman owners of the sort that interests microeconomists today. Here I want, first, to consider some of the basic values, principles, and assumptions that shaped the *familia* as a productive unit, and then to look at the evidence for women's labor in urban and rural households.

The starting point is very familiar and widespread in societies based on plow agriculture: that is, the gendered division of spheres between female domestic work and male fieldwork with the plow and draft animals. This ideology was grounded in an ideology of the natural strength of men and weakness of women. It is so familiar that I need not dwell on it.[15] The controversies over the implications and consequences of the ideology arise among historians on several counts. First, in some plow cultures the ideal of female domesticity has been undergirded by an ideology of honor and shame, which encourages women to be kept in the home away from the public (male) gaze. The extent to

---

13. Richard Saller, "Symbols of Gender and Status Hierarchies in the Roman Household," in *Women and Slaves in Greco-Roman Culture,* ed. S. Murnaghan and S. Joshel (London: Routledge, 1998), pp. 85-91.

14. For Greek households and the implications of the family life cycle, see Thomas W. Gallant, *Risk and Survival in Ancient Greece: Reconstructing the Rural Domestic Economy* (Stanford: Stanford University Press, 1991).

15. Sarah B. Pomeroy, "Women in Roman Egypt: A Preliminary Study Based on Papyri," in *ANRW* II.10.1 (1988): 712, citing Ulpian, *Digest* 50.4.3.3.

which Roman culture shared these Mediterranean values of honor and shame is a matter of debate, though no one would assert that the Roman ideals were as extreme as the Athenian or later Arab ideals. Second, there is the question of how the ideology affected female slaves. One might think it was irrelevant to slaves as honorless property, but there are reasons to think that the deepest Roman assumptions about the male/female opposition affected the condition of *ancillae* as well as free women, even though slaves were in principle without honor.[16] Third, it is argued that this ideological overlay must have dissolved in the face of the harsh realities of subsistence agriculture. Scheidel emphasizes the discrepancy between ideals and behavior in his conclusions, arguing on utilitarian grounds that slave and free women participated in agricultural labor.[17] This is an important issue, and although I would argue that Scheidel's skepticism is overstated, there is no point in pretending that the evidence is adequate to offer a definitive answer.

The female/male differentiation of productive roles gave the materfamilias of the household the role of *custos* or guardian.[18] The contents and significance of this role were most fully elaborated by Xenophon in his *Oeconomicus*, and were later quoted by Columella as fully applicable to Rome.[19] As *custos*, the materfamilias had the responsibility to guard and preserve the stores of the *domus*, to exercise *frugalitas* in their consumption, and to manage the slave staff of the household.[20] Though subordinate to the paterfamilias, the *matrona*'s custodial responsibilities were important, both in small subsistence households and in larger units with slaves. In the former, effective supervision of consumption could be the difference between survival and starvation, or at least between good health and malnutrition. In a larger slave household, supervision of a coerced labor force was one of the principal challenges of household production.

The female ideal of the domestic *custos* is related to another ideal, the well-ordered *domus*, which had both a moral and a functional dimension. The materfamilias was the guardian of the chastity of the *domus*, in which the slaves

16. Paul Erdkamp, "Agriculture, Underemployment, and the Cost of Rural Labor in the Roman World," *Classical Quarterly* 49 (1999): 556-72, sees gender ideology as irrelevant to female slaves.

17. Scheidel, "The Most Silent Women of Greece and Rome (II)"; Scheidel, "Reflections on the Differential Valuation of Slaves in Diocletian's Price Edict and in the United States"; Scheidel, "Quantifying the Sources of Slaves in the Roman Empire."

18. T. E. V. Pearce, "The Role of the Wife as Custos in Ancient Rome," *Eranos* 72 (1974): 16-33.

19. Sarah B. Pomeroy, *Xenophon, "Oeconomicus": A Social and Historical Commentary* (Oxford: Oxford University Press, 1994); Columella 12.pref.7.

20. Pearce, "The Role of the Wife as Custos in Ancient Rome."

were organized in clearly defined jobs.[21] Treggiari observed that "in the more elaborate households specialization was, if not economical in man-hours, effective in maintaining morale among the servants and prestige for the employer. It was considered the mark of a cheese-paring owner if one slave did two jobs (Cicero *Pis.* 67; Aelius Aristides *Rom. Or.* 71B)."[22] Given the dominance of the household in production and consumption, this ideal may have had significant economic ramifications and is worth further thought below.

The centrality of the *domus* and *familia* as units of production invites us to think about what constitutes "economic production." Notoriously, economists' statistics for gross domestic product have not conventionally included the value of "women's work" in the home.[23] The modern discipline of economics cannot take credit for this oversight: the Romans had a comparable conception that emerges from legal discussions. Here the law is a good guide to the basic practical assumptions of Roman estate owners. Propertied Romans wrote wills that included brief shorthand terms based on the daily functioning of their estates. Two concepts that shed light on the economic organization of their households and farms are *penus* and *instrumentum,* both of which could be bequeathed by a testator and hence required definition.

Penus was the household store of food and drink intended for consumption by the paterfamilias, his *uxor* and *liberi* (wife and children), and the slaves and draft animals kept around him for personal use (*Digest* 33.9.3 pr, Ulpian). The slaves around the master were distinguished from those working at the villa. In the curious phrase of the great republican jurist Q. Mucius Scaevola, this was a distinction between those slaves who worked and those "who did not work" (*qui opus non facerent, Digest* 33.9.3.6; also A. Gellius, *Noctes Atticae* 4.1.17). The dividing line between slaves who worked and those "who did not work" might be ambiguous in some cases. Jurists disagreed over the categorization of weavers (male and female) living in the urban *domus* (*Digest* 33.9.3.6). Despite the ambiguities, there was a deep feeling among Roman masters that one class of slaves earned their keep, most clearly by *opus rusticum* (rural work), and another class did not. When the regretful father in Terence's *Heauton timorumenos* decided to punish himself by getting rid of the amenities of life, he sold off his "*ancillas, servos,* except who earn their own keep by doing rural work *(opere rustico faciundo)*" (142-43). The quintessential slave "who does not work" was the *ancilla* attending the matron of the house —

21. Pearce, p. 29; Richard P. Saller, "Familia, Domus, and the Roman Concept of the Family," *Phoenix* 38 (1984): 336-55.

22. Treggiari, "Jobs for Women," p. 93.

23. See http://www.admin.uiuc.edu/NB/95.10/01womenstip.html for a calculation that inclusion of unpaid domestic work would increase the global GNP by one-third.

worse yet, an entourage of ten *ancillae* dressed in jewelry and fancy clothing, who can bring financial ruin on a man (449-54). Of course, to stereotype the *ancilla* as an attendant "who does not work" was to ignore the considerable labor required to feed and clothe a household (see below), but it was no more out of touch with reality than the recent stereotype of the housewife who contributes nothing to economic production. Both stereotypes embody a gendered valuation of labor.

Related to the distinction between slaves who do and don't work, but not wholly congruent with it, was the distinction between slaves who had an *artificium,* or skill, and those who had an *officium,* or a duty that required no training. Examples of the former are cooks and weavers; an example of the latter is a litter bearer (*Digest* 32.65.1, Marcian). In this distinction lies a rudimentary sense of the economists' concept of human capital — that is, the value of education and training workers. To the extent that males were more trained in an *artificium* than females, the gendered valuation of labor would have been grounded in the realities of production.

The second concept with economic implications is *instrumentum.* It was common for Roman testators to bequeath a farm *(fundus)* with the *instrumentum* needed to work it. Since farms were among the largest units of production, the *instrumentum* could be extensive and unwieldy, and its precise contents uncertain and changing at the margins. Consequently, compilers of the *Digest* devoted a substantial title to defining *instrumentum* (33.7). As with *penus,* the juristic interpretation of *instrumentum* must have coincided with the customary practices and understandings of Roman owners if it was to carry authority. Ulpian refers to Sabinus's definition of the *instrumentum* of a farm as "those things which are provided for the producing, gathering, and preserving of the fruits. Thus, for producing, the men who till the soil and those who direct them or are placed in charge of them, including stewards and overseers, also domesticated oxen and beasts kept for producing manure, and implements useful in farming, such as plows, mattocks, hoes, pruning hooks, forks, and similar items" (*Digest* 33.7.8 pr). Clearly, this is a down-to-earth, practical discussion, not some flight of juristic imagination. Practicality required consideration of the support staff for the field hands, who had to be fed, clothed, and housed. The support staff (about whom, more below) came under the heading of *instrumentum instrumenti* — inelegantly translated as "the equipment of the equipment" — and was assumed to be part of a bequest of the *instrumentum* (*Digest* 33.7.12.5, Ulpian).

As an alternative to a *fundus* with the *instrumentum,* a testator could bequeath a *fundus instructus.* This was a broader concept, including the *fundus* and its *instrumentum,* plus everything placed on the farm so that the paterfamilias may be better equipped.[24] Significant for our purposes, the *fundus instructus* included, along with working slaves, the *"contubernales, id est uxores"* of these slaves and their children (*Digest* 33.7.12.33, Ulpian). But it did not include those slaves who were just passing through and were not intended by the master to reside on the *fundus* (*Digest* 33.7.12.37, Ulpian).

Now I want to summarize the scattered evidence for women's labor in the various types of *domus* and *familia*, urban and rural, small and slave households. I will not repeat the comprehensive descriptions of Treggiari and Scheidel, but try to draw attention to the points that seem to me especially telling. The challenge is to figure out how to generalize from the scattered scraps of evidence.

Consideration of women's labor in the urban artisanal class must start from Treggiari's studies of the funerary inscriptions from Rome listing occupations.[25] In this category we should imagine families — free, freed, and slave — practicing a craft and/or selling goods and services. The activities ranged from the manufacture of clothing, jewelry, or perfume, to the sale of fruits and vegetables, to the provision of prepared food, wine, rooms, and sexual services.

Treggiari drew several important conclusions from the list of occupations. First, women are attested in many fewer occupations than men: 35 for women in comparison with 225 or so for men.[26] Furthermore, Treggiari noted the gendered distribution by occupation: "Women appear to be concentrated in 'service' jobs (catering, prostitution); dealing, particularly in foodstuffs; serving in shops; in certain crafts, particularly the production of cloth and clothes; 'fiddly' jobs such as working in gold-leaf or hair-dressing; certain luxury trades such as perfumery. This is a fair reflection of at least part of reality."[27] In short, women are found in what Ester Boserup dubbed the "bazaar and service sector," found in a number of areas of the developing world.[28]

Sandra Joshel's quantitative summary of participation by gender in the workforce of Rome reinforces Treggiari's point. A comparison of women's occupational distribution with men's in Joshel's table 3.1 highlights the rarity or absence of women in banking, building, transportation, and administration. The category of job in which women and men are most nearly balanced is

---

24. I mistakenly conflated *fundus instructus* with *instrumentum* in Saller, "Pater Familias, Mater Familias, and the Gendered Semantics of the Roman Household," *CP* 94 (1999): 182-97, without consequences for the argument there.

25. See also Jane F. Gardner, *Women in Roman Law and Society* (Bloomington: Indiana University Press, 1986), pp. 233-55.

26. Treggiari, "Lower Class Women," p. 78.

27. Treggiari, "Lower Class Women," p. 78.

28. Boserup, p. 91.

"skilled service," but a breakdown of the specific jobs in this category (barber, hairdresser, masseuse, entertainer) reveals gendered patterns here as well. The funerary inscriptions listing occupations are by no means a cross section of the workforce, but represent those workers who took enough pride in their jobs to identify with them on their tombstones.[29] The absence of women in some but not other occupational categories may not be a direct, unmediated reflection of their absence in those jobs, but is surely related to their lower participation in certain kinds of labor.

Here are the gender asymmetries in occupational participation, from Roman epitaphs (*CIL* VI), as tabulated by Joshel.[30]

Occupation	Men		Women	
Building	112	(100%)	0	
Manufacture	282	(85%)	49	(15%)
Sales	99	(92%)	9	(8%)
Banking	42	(100%)	0	
Professional	101	(84%)	19	(16%)
Skilled service	40	(53%)	35	(47%)
Domestic service	235	(73%)	86	(27%)
Transportation	55	(100%)	0	
Administration	296	(97%)	10	(3%)

Treggiari drew a second general conclusion from the inscriptions with regard to the independence of women with jobs: "The frequency with which a woman is paired with a man, usually a husband, in the same trade suggests that many of them worked alongside husbands."[31] In view of the (male) Roman ideal of subordination of wife to husband, this "working alongside" is likely to have been on unequal terms and may be part of the reason for the lower epigraphic visibility of women in occupations, as suggested by Natalie Kampen.[32] The division of labor within an artisan family often left women, boys, or girls with the responsibility of minding the shop.[33]

The relative rarity of women with an *artificium* in the epitaphs may be linked to the evidence for apprenticeship practices. It is a pity that we do not

29. Sandra R. Joshel, *Work, Identity, and Legal Status at Rome: A Study of the Occupational Inscriptions* (Norman: University of Oklahoma Press, 1992), p. 16.

30. Joshel, p. 69 (tab. 3.1).

31. Treggiari, "Lower Class Women," p. 76.

32. Natalie Kampen, *Image and Status: Roman Working Women in Ostia* (Berlin: Mann, 1981), p. 125.

33. Treggiari, "Lower Class Women," p. 73; Kampen, pp. 112-13; *Digest* 14.3.8.

have for Rome a set of apprenticeship contracts of the sort found in Roman Egypt. Most of the Egyptian contracts concern weaving and range in duration from one to five years.[34] The terms varied by occupation and within occupations. Apprentices in weaving generally received monthly rations of wheat and oil (or the equivalent in cash) in the first year or two, and then additional wages if they continued, presumably to compensate the value of their skills from training.[35] In the few dozen contracts most apprentices are free boys; some are slave boys and slave girls; and not one is a freeborn woman.[36] As Bradley notes, this pattern "implies that daughters in artisanal families, like their counterparts in upper-class society at Rome, may not normally have been trained for work other than that of a traditional, domestic sort, but were instead prepared only for marriage and child-bearing."[37] While acknowledging the usual caveats about generalizing from Roman Egypt to the whole empire, I find the fit between the gendered occupational distribution in Rome and the gendered pattern of apprenticeship contracts in Egypt very suggestive. And to judge from modern development economics, the gender bias against free women in the crafts may have had several interrelated consequences: less training of women, hence lower productivity and lower wages for women, hence less economic independence and possibly lower valuation of women in their families, and less growth in productivity for the economy as a whole.[38]

34. Keith Bradley, *Discovering the Roman Family* (Oxford: Oxford University Press, 1991), p. 107; Jane Rowlandson, *Women and Society in Greek and Roman Egypt: A Sourcebook* (Cambridge: Cambridge University Press, 1998), p. 268.

35. See A. C. Johnson, *Roman Egypt: Economic Survey of Ancient Rome,* vol. 2 (Baltimore: Johns Hopkins University Press, 1936), pp. 388-91, for a summary of contract terms.

36. Bradley, *Discovering the Roman Family,* p. 108.

37. Bradley, *Discovering the Roman Family,* p. 108. Peter Van Minnen, "Did Ancient Women Learn a Trade outside the Home? A Note on SB XVIII 13305," *ZPR* 123 (1998): 201-3, disputes Bradley's conclusion on two grounds. First, Van Minnen identifies three possible apprenticeship contracts involving freeborn girls. One of these is much later, another is of uncertain reading, and only one is clearly counter to Bradley's generalization. As a result, Bradley's summary should be slightly revised, but the conclusion about the absence of freeborn girls remains substantially the same. Second, Van Minnen argues that freeborn girls probably learned crafts in their own homes in order to avoid threats to their chastity, generating no contracts. Some girls no doubt learned skills at home, but if home training had been as valuable as apprenticeship outside the home, we would expect that freeborn sons would also have been trained in this way at no cost. The basic point stands, I think: to the extent that apprenticeship added valuable skills, freeborn women were for the most part cut off from that added labor value.

38. Urbanization in the Roman Empire is generally assumed by economic historians to be an index of economic growth, but Boserup points out that in some modern developing countries the migration of families from the countryside to the towns has led to increased productivity for males but less economic opportunity and lower productivity for the females. Boserup, p. 175.

The big urban *domus* could be a very large unit with scores or even hundreds of members. Of course, the basic distinction in these households was between the free owner's honorable family and the honorless slaves. Treggiari has described in detail one of the prominent characteristics of the large household, the fine differentiation of duties and titles that, along with the personal names, were the identities marking domestic slaves in columbaria.[39] Plautus's comedy *Mercator* revolves around the distinction among female slaves between those who did the menial household work and those who attended the *domina*. A dissipated young man returns from abroad to his parents' home with an attractive *ancilla,* the target of his passion. He attempts to disguise his personal attachment by claiming that the *ancilla* is meant to be a gift for his mother, but the girl's beauty raises doubts about the son's story. His father asserts that the mother should not have an attractive attendant *(pedisequa)* and needs only functional *ancillae* who will do the tedious chores of weaving, grinding grain, cutting wood, spinning, sweeping, cooking, and taking a beating (396-98). Wool spinning was of course the quintessential women's work, represented as honorable in the foundation legend of the republic (Livy 1.57.9). In the empire, jurists associate spinning with *ancillae* more often than any other type of labor (*Digest* 7.8.12.6; 24.1.31.1; 33.7.16.2).[40] Wool working was honorable enough to suit the matron and even the first empress. Other domestic duties of the *ancilla,* such as washing the latrine, were among the most sordid and degrading in the household (Plautus, *Curculio* 577; Cicero, *Tusculanae disputationes* 5.20.58).

By contrast to the hardworking women, attendants *(pedisequae)* were a luxury signaling status (Plautus, *Aulularia* 500); and as a representative of status, they could be the vehicle for dishonoring the mistress. Among the ways to inflict an insult *(iniuria)* on a matron, Ulpian mentions the seduction of the matron's attendant (*Digest* 47.10.1.2 with 47.10.15.16). Another aspect of the display in the largest Roman houses was the avoidance of female slaves in many of the serving jobs.[41] Since *ancillae* were presumably as capable of dining room service, the preference for young men, who could have been working in the fields, was a form of conspicuous consumption. This is a point of contrast between the Roman slave system and New World plantations, where males were rarely assigned to domestic service.[42]

In view of the broad Roman ideology of gender hierarchy, it is not surprising that women are also rarely attested in administrative and managerial jobs in

---

39. Treggiari, "Domestic Staff at Rome in the Julio-Claudian Period, 27 B.C. to A.D. 68."

40. Treggiari, "Jobs for Women," pp. 82-85.

41. Treggiari, "Jobs in the Household of Livia"; Treggiari, "Jobs for Women."

42. Robert W. Fogel, *Without Consent or Contract: The Rise and Fall of American Slavery* (New York: Norton, 1989), p. 46.

the household.[43] The limited evidence for the teaching of slaves suggests that education in literacy and arithmetic probably benefited males rather than females.[44]

Let me conclude this summary of women's labor in cities with a few general points. First, the level of urbanization of a society is a good rough guide to the level of economic development insofar as it reflects the proportion of the population that can be spared from food production to produce goods beyond subsistence. The best estimates for the level of urbanization of the Roman Empire fall in the range of 10 to 20 percent — that is, a small fraction of the populace, but an important one for the economy. Second, to judge from comparative evidence from twentieth-century urbanizing societies, it would not be surprising if the cities of the empire had an unbalanced sex ratio in favor of males. Premodern cities were population sinks with high mortality rates; they were not self-reproducing and depended on a flow of migrants from country to city; the migrants were often disproportionately male because single males had more employment opportunities.[45] Employment for women in Rome, slave or free, was mostly domestic service: some of these jobs (midwifery, hairdressing, weaving) involved skills that required training, but most of those mentioned in Plautus's stock description were unskilled, tedious jobs requiring only time and energy. If we consider the productivity of this labor, there is no reason to believe that urban women's labor realized noticeable improvements in productivity from the time of Plautus to the time of the great jurists four centuries later — a very long time span of near stagnation. As Treggiari noted, the highly differentiated occupational organization of the large households may have produced social status, but did not yield an efficient workforce maximizing measurable output. And if male slaves were underemployed, the female slaves in these households were probably even more so.[46]

The bulk of the population and economic production was in agriculture — probably over 80 percent of the people and two-thirds to three-quarters of

43. Treggiari, "Domestic Staff," p. 46; Treggiari, "Jobs for Women," p. 77; Kampen, pp. 121, 133; Joshel, p. 69 (tab. 3.1).

44. S. L. Mohler, "Slave Education in the Roman Empire," *TAPA* 71 (1940): 262-80.

45. Boserup, p. 86.

46. Though the well-ordered, minutely differentiated staff was in part grounded in a desire for social status, it may also have had an element of economic rationality. In the sprawling, involuntary labor force of a large *domus*, accountability for specific tasks must have presented a challenge to masters. One strategy to account for which slaves were doing their jobs, and which were not, was to divide tasks into small, discrete units for which one and only one slave was held responsible. However, unless the discrete tasks neatly coincided with full-time work, this strategy also entailed idle time for the slave.

production. Consequently, it is regrettable that we are so badly informed about women's labor in agriculture. Walter Scheidel was able to survey the ancient evidence for field labor and animal husbandry in only four and a half pages, and that included Greek as well as Roman texts. As I understand it, Scheidel's basic argument is that beneath the ideology of the outdoor male/domestic female division of labor lay the realities of survival, which required women to work in the fields. This seems to me valid, but does not go far enough. To say that in all societies people will do almost anything under the pressure of bare survival may be a truism, but that truism should not obscure the possibility of significantly different patterns of female labor in agriculture, even among poor, subsistence societies, as Boserup's data showed.

In considering rural women's labor, we might start from a broad distinction between the peasant family farm and the larger estate employing slaves or other nonfamily labor. In the nearly complete absence of evidence, Scheidel is likely to be right that in some regions, at some times, and in some circumstances women contributed labor to agricultural production, but without more evidence that claim will unavoidably remain vague. It is to be expected that there was regional variation across the empire in the division of family labor on the farm, but our ability to specify the variation is hampered by the scarcity of information and by the rhetorical coloring of the few fragments available. As Scheidel points out, Greek and Roman authors associated female field labor with marginal and barbarous peoples, such as Strabo's native Spaniards.[47] These texts may tell us more about Roman ideology than regional farming practices. More revealing about actual practices are the documents from Roman Egypt. Women are occasionally found in agricultural labor (as the olive carrier in P. Fay. 91),[48] but the documents generally suggest asymmetrical gender participation in agriculture. Rowlandson found that "it apparently remained extremely rare for women to undertake a tenancy of agricultural land: scarcely a handful of examples survive among the nearly 1,000 land leases of Roman or Byzantine date, although leasing of land by women to male tenants was not uncommon."[49] And from the state's point of view, "male landowners were required to cultivate, or at least to pay taxes on, unproductive public land. Women were officially exempt from this burden on the grounds of their weakness and unsuitability to agricultural tasks."[50] Rathbone, in his close study of

47. Scheidel, "Most Silent Women (II)," pp. 5-8; Christine Tina Saavedra, "Women on the Verge of the Roman Empire: The Socioeconomic Activities of Iberian Women" (Ph.D. diss., University of Chicago, 2000).

48. Rowlandson, p. 231.

49. Rowlandson, p. 220.

50. Rowlandson, p. 221.

the records from the Appianus estate, briefly noted that "there is no known case of the employment of women, either permanently or casually, for agricultural tasks on the Appianus estate."[51] This documentary evidence is indirect, but it does suggest both the expectation and the reality of much less female than male participation in the cultivation of the land in Roman Egypt.

We are somewhat better informed about labor on large estates, though here too the evidence is at best elliptical. Columella provides a description of the responsibilities of the *vilica*, the bailiff's wife, who by virtue of her partnership with the *vilicus* had important supervisory duties. According to his pseudohistorical account, in the good old days the *dominus* and *domina* were so heavily involved in the work of the *fundus* that little was left for the *vilicus* and *vilica* to do (12.pref.8). By contrast, in Columella's day the materfamilias was idle and self-indulgent, and shrugged off the household duties to the *vilica*. The qualities to be sought in a *vilica* included moderately good looks (to hold the attention of the *vilicus*), freedom from vices of character such as (female) superstition, a capacity to take care of the work indoors so that the *vilicus* could work outside. In the house the *vilica* was supposed to supervise the work and tend to the health of sick members of the *familia*. She had the major responsibility to inspect, store, and keep track of perishable and nonperishable items, according to Columella with reference to Xenophon's *Oeconomicus* (12.3.5). And the *vilica* was obliged to keep a stock of wool on hand, so that on cold or rainy days when women could not be expected to be outdoors doing *opus rusticum*, they could be kept busy making cloth (12.3.6).

Columella's comment about the *opus rusticum* of slave women raises the major question of how the majority of slave women were exploited on the farm. Some historians, citing this text, have argued that slave women were not subject to the ideology of honorable domesticity and hence were used in the fields, at least at harvest time.[52] Other historians have suggested that the outdoor male/indoor female dichotomy affected slave women as well as free, limiting the use of female slaves in agriculture and hence lowering productivity of the rural slave labor force as a whole.[53] As a point of comparison, it is useful to look at the U.S. South. There a higher proportion of slave women (69 percent) than men (58 percent) were field hands.[54] Plantation owners in assigning tasks

51. Dominic Rathbone, *Economic Rationalism and Rural Society in Third-Century A.D. Egypt: The Heroninus Archive and the Appianus Estate* (Cambridge: Cambridge University Press, 1991), p. 164.

52. Erdkamp, p. 571; Scheidel, "Most Silent Women (I)," p. 208.

53. P. A. Brunt, *Italian Manpower, 225 B.C.–A.D. 14* (Oxford: Oxford University Press, 1971); G. E. M. de Ste. Croix, *The Class Struggle in the Ancient Greek World* (London: Duckworth, 1981).

54. Fogel, pp. 45-46.

regarded women as three-quarters of a field hand, or less if they were pregnant.[55]

Roman estate owners appear to have thought of rural female slaves differently from their American counterparts, insofar as they considered slave women as adjuncts rather than a central element of the workforce in the fields.[56] Columella's reference to *opus rusticum* is vague and could encompass almost any outdoor task, including the tending of small animals, mentioned elsewhere;[57] the phrase need not imply regular work in the fields.[58] Comments of the jurists, especially their concepts of *fundus instructus* and *instrumentum instrumenti*, contain an assumption that many slave women did not participate in what was regarded as the central productive work of the farm, and so could not be categorized as part of the *instrumentum* itself. As part of the support staff (the *instrumentum instrumenti*), some *mulieres* baked bread, kept the villa, served in the kitchen as *focariae*, spun wool *(lanificae)*, and cooked the *pulmentaria* for the *familia rustica* (*Digest* 33.7.12.6). Ulpian also thought it a reasonable assumption that a testator would wish the *uxores* and *infantes* to go along with the *instrumentum* on the grounds, not that they worked, but that "it is not to be believed that he wished to inflict a harsh separation" on the slave families (*Digest* 33.7.12.7; so also *Sententiae Pauli* 3.6.35 for *uxores eorum qui operantur*, "wives of those who work"). Similarly, in the discussion of *fundus instructus*, slave women and children who could not be categorized as either directly productive workers or support staff were captured under the heading of *fundus instructus* because they were wives *(uxores)* and offspring of the male workforce (*Digest* 33.7.12.33). I do not imagine that these women were idle; rather, I picture them in the situation of the slave shepherds' wives described by Varro, cooking, keeping house, and helping their husbands with the flocks (*Res rusticae* 2.10.6). Though these texts are not detailed, I take them to mean that the slave wives' primary responsibility was domestic, though they did some farm work. The productive value of the domestic work should not be underestimated. As Boserup noted of low-technology societies, "it is not always realized how very time-consuming is this crude processing of basic foods," which in Africa and Latin America could take thirty hours per week or more.[59] By comparison, slave women of the U.S. South typically put in full days of work in

55. Deborah Gray White, *Ar'n't I a Woman?* (New York: Norton, 1985), p. 121; Larry Hudson, *To Have and to Hold: Slave Work and Family Life in Antebellum South Carolina* (Athens: University of Georgia Press, 1997), p. 4.

56. Cf. Scheidel, "Most Silent Women (I)," p. 212.

57. Scheidel, "Most Silent Women (II)," p. 4.

58. As suggested by Scheidel, "Most Silent Women (II)," p. 3.

59. Boserup, pp. 164-65.

the fields and then did the domestic work in their off-hours. A Southern planter would not have excluded slave women from the *instrumentum*, as defined by Roman jurists.[60] Overall, the juristic texts at least suggest — though they are hardly adequate to prove — that labor on Roman estates was not organized to exploit female slave labor to the fullest extent possible.

In addition to the wives and children of field hands, the juristic texts point to another group of women and children on country estates.[61] The wives and children of some urban male slaves serving in the townhouse resided at the villa. The jurists give the barest glimpse of this arrangement when they refer to the slave who, after the death of his master, traveled to the farm to join his family. Does he fall into the *familia urbana* of the testator or the *familia rustica*? (The answer is the former.) I imagine that for estate owners it was cheaper to house and maintain slave nonworkers in the country than in the city, where space was cramped and food was more costly. This is an illustration of the economic interrelationship of the *familia urbana* and *familia rustica*.

Overall, the scarce and fragmentary evidence suggests that the Romans' fundamental ideas about gendered division of labor affected the participation of women in every sector, from agricultural field work to crafts to domestic service to management and administration. A gendered division of labor makes Rome no different from nearly every other human society, but it is worth reflecting on the consequences of the particular configuration of gendered labor in Rome's slave society.

Roger Bagnall and Bruce Frier briefly comment in their masterful *Demography of Roman Egypt* that it is pointless to speculate on the relative valuation of slave women's economic production and biological reproduction.[62] In a sense they are right, to the extent that the question cannot be definitively answered. On the other hand, the question has such important implications for central issues of Roman history that it is worth saying certain things with appropriate cautions.

The valuation of women's work is in part a matter of cultural categories of value — i.e., what counts as "productive"? Two related distinctions in Roman thought resulted in a diminished appreciation of the work done by women. The first is the distinction between labor "productive" of things that could be sold for an income and services within the household that did not realize any in-

60. Brunt suggested that "one may doubt if either women or children were used as much on Roman as on American plantations," but he did not argue or develop the point. Brunt, p. 707.

61. Bradley, "Roman Slave Supply," p. 58.

62. R. S. Bagnall and B. W. Frier, *The Demography of Roman Egypt* (Cambridge: Cambridge University Press, 1994), p. 158 n. 83.

come. The former was associated in particular with rural field labor, the latter with domestic labor, especially attendants. The second distinction is between those slaves who work and those who do not work. What we know of the tasks done by slave women would place them largely in the category of unproductive nonworkers. So when a character in Plautus's *Truculentus* (533) is presented with the gift of two *ancillae*, the response is, "do I need more *ancillae* to feed?" Though the situation in this comedy was highly contrived, the sense that *ancillae* often do not produce enough to cover their keep fits with basic Roman assumptions devaluing women's work.

If the labor of *ancillae* was limited and undervalued, one would expect to find either that the prices for female slaves were correspondingly lower than for males or that the value represented in prices for female slaves was based on their reproductive capacities. We do not have really good price series for Roman slaves, but Diocletian's Price Edict does indicate a bureaucrat's perception of the relative values of female and male slaves. Scheidel has analyzed the price list and compared it with U.S. prices.

Maximum Prices for Ordinary Slaves in Diocletian's Edict

Age	Male	Female	(% of male price)
0-8	15,000	10,000	(67%)
8-16	20,000	20,000	(100%)
16-40	30,000	25,000	(83%)
40-60	25,000	20,000	(80%)
60+	15,000	10,000	(67%)

These are prices in denarii for ordinary, unskilled slaves. Scheidel demonstrates that the relative valuations by age and gender are not too different from relative valuations by gender and age for U.S. slaves, and hence are realistic.

The prices for women are somewhat lower than for men, but not drastically so. In the early and late years of life, the maximum price for females was two-thirds that of males. The price for slave boys and girls was equal in their midteens, as the girls were entering their childbearing years and just before boys were fully mature field hands. At their peak of productivity in their adult years, female slaves were valued at 83 percent of male slaves. The maximum price of female slaves after their childbearing years dropped sharply, more sharply than the price listed for male slaves, but the price did not drop to zero — a reflection of the tacit recognition that slaves "who do no work" really did have productive value. The prices of the edict may be interpreted to show that the women's work of *ancillae* was valued but not as highly as male labor, and that they were more highly valued for their reproductive capacity than in the

U.S. South.[63] Given the higher value attached to men's labor than women's, it is at first sight surprising to find twice as many female foundlings as males benefiting from the extant wet-nursing contracts.[64] Owners were willing to pay in the range of 150-250 drachmae over two years in the first and second centuries c.e. to have a foundling nursed. Despite the expectation of high levels of childhood mortality and the lower value of surviving female slaves, a rough calculation suggests that it made financial sense to take in and nourish female foundlings.[65]

Altogether, the disparate scraps of evidence suggest to me that Roman slave owners valued the reproductive capacity of female slaves, who in the early em-

---

63. K. R. Bradley, "The Age at Time of Sale of Female Slaves," *Arethusa* 11 (1978): 243-52; Andrew Dalby, "On Female Slaves in Roman Egypt," *Arethusa* 12 (1979): 255-59, with Bradley's reply; Scheidel, "Reflections," pp. 72-74 nn. 20, 24. Using the numbers in the wet-nursing contracts, one might start from the assumption that the value of a slave baby (outside Alexandria) in the first two centuries c.e. was about 200 drachmae (the cost of a wet nurse to feed a costless foundling). If a slave woman gave birth every three years, the value of her childbearing would have been around 60-70 drachmae a year. The value of domestic service was probably on the order of 150 drachmae a year, and other jobs were of higher value. These crude calculations seem to me to fit reasonably well with Scheidel's analysis of the differential prices by age in the Price Edict: after age forty the maximum price of female slaves went down only by 20 percent, suggesting greater value attached to production than to reproduction. For wet-nursing contracts, M. Manca Masciardi and O. Montevecchi, *I contratti di baliatico. Corpora Papyrorum Graecarum* 1 (Milan: Azzate; Varese: Tipolitografia Tibiletti, 1984), pp. 32-35; for slave prices, H.-J. Drexhage, *Preise, Pieten/Pachten, Kosten und Loehne im Roemischen Aegypten bis zum Regierungsantritt Diokletians* (St. Katharinen: Scripta Mercaturae Verlag, 1991), pp. 249-79; Johnson, pp. 279-81, *especially* P.Bour. 16 and P.Oxy. 95, and for wages, pp. 306-10, especially P.Oxy. 736 and *BGU* 894.

64. K. R. Bradley, "Wet-Nursing at Rome: A Study in Social Relations," in *The Family in Ancient Rome*, pp. 201-29; Rowlandson, p. 275. On second thought, the larger number of female foundlings must reflect the likelihood that more female newborns than males were exposed.

65. Though the prices for sale of slaves in Roman Egypt are scattered and do not amount to a meaningful series, it appears that prices for a young female slave (outside Alexandria) averaged about 1,200 drachmae. If so, to spend 204 drachmae (8.5 dr/mo × 24 mos, including the oil allowance) to nurse a foundling would make sense on the following calculation. The investment entailed a substantial risk (ca. 50 percent) that the child would not survive to productive or reproductive adulthood; that sum, invested in loans at interest, would have roughly doubled in value over the twelve to fourteen years of rearing; and the child would have required an additional investment of ca. 50 drachmae a year in maintenance after infancy. During the later years of childhood, enough return on the investment could have been realized in the form of household service to offset the cost of food (to judge by the apprenticeship contracts). The resulting total value of the investment — 204 dr × 2 (for risk) × 2 (for forgone interest) + 50 dr/yr (maintenance) × 5 years × 1.5 (forgone interest) = 1,191 dr — is comparable to the cost of an adult female slave. Of course, this calculation is extremely crude, but it does answer the argument of some historians that it would have made no financial sense to raise foundlings, especially females. See note 63 for references to prices for sale and wet-nursing.

pire must have produced the great majority of the next generation of slaves.[66] On the other hand, the physical labor of female slaves was depreciated by male cultural norms and social arrangements. Women appear not to have been trained for skilled work to the same extent as men, and they were not used as fully in agricultural work as men or as American female slaves. Comparative evidence suggests that these norms and attitudes toward women's labor may have had wide ramifications for the experiences and status of women, though those are difficult to illuminate with Roman evidence alone.

66. I am persuaded by Scheidel, "Quantifying the Sources of Slaves in the Roman Empire," against Harris, "Demography, Geography and the Sources of Roman Slaves," on the primacy of reproduction as a source of slaves over the centuries. Harris's argument that one in five freeborn infants was exposed and enslaved — that is, one per family on average — strikes me as wholly implausible.

IV. Slaves

Slave Families and Slaves in Families

Dale B. Martin

Scholars of the New Testament and early Christianity have long recognized the significance of slavery for the history of early Christian groups. Though no one any longer accepts the older notion that Christianity was a "slave religion" or a movement comprising a huge number of slaves, it is universally recognized among scholars that Christian groups included slaves and freedpersons, and that they sometimes played significant roles within the movement and its controversies. The case of Philemon and Onesimus alone is often invoked to illustrate the way social relations, including slavery, were rendered more complicated and sometimes controversial by the conversion of individuals and households to Christianity.

The household and family themselves have become increasingly significant subjects for scholars studying early Christianity, as is demonstrated by this very collection of essays. Scholars are now quite cognizant of the fact that early Christian groups were "house churches" and that at least many of them, the Pauline churches most noticeably, were socially constructed to reflect the structures and relations of the Greco-Roman household.[1] What may merit further attention, however, is the relation between slaves and families. Contrary to some modern assumptions, slaves in antiquity were sometimes able to maintain familial structures of their own — even though slaves could not legally marry and the children of slaves were legally the property of the parents' owners. And, perhaps more remarkably for modern readers, slaves sometimes played nonservile "roles" in the households of other persons. How do we think about the reality of ancient slavery and family when we realize that a slave could sometimes be treated as a spouse, a parent, a child, a brother or sister, or even a

---

1. But see the recent argument by Jorunn Oekland, which I find convincing, that Paul's rhetoric in 1 Corinthians represents an attempt to configure the meetings of the gathered ἐκκλησία as "sanctuary space" instead of "household space." See "Women in Their Place: Paul and the Corinthian Discourse of Gender and Sanctuary Space" (Ph.D. diss., University of Oslo, 2001).

"patron" or "client" of someone else (either another slave or a nonslave)? In order to provoke more consideration of the varieties of ancient slave and familial life, this article illustrates, by funerary inscriptions, the variety of social structures in which slaves maintained "families" themselves and played what we might call familial roles in the households of others.

The scope of the article is limited. I make no pretense of settling statistical questions — of suggesting, for instance, what percentage of slaves had what sorts of families. Nor does this article claim that even a great many slaves, much less a majority, maintained family structures of any sort, whether nuclear, partial, or extended families. I merely offer here a look at several funerary inscriptions that contain evidence of slave families and slaves in families in order to provide an impression of the familial lives of at least some slaves in antiquity.

Anecdotal Historiography

The historical evidence here offered is admittedly anecdotal. I recognize that historians are famously, and for the most part rightly, allergic to anecdotal historiography. When faced with a few inscriptions that portray a few slaves maintaining extended, sometimes rather large and complex family structures, we immediately want to ask, "So, how representative is this particular example for the overall historical reality of slavery and family?" I am sensitive to such concerns. But I also want to point out that the difference between thorough, respectable historiography and anecdotal historiography can be exaggerated, certainly when we are speaking of the social history of the ancient world and possibly of history of other periods as well. As is widely acknowledged, we have too little dependable data from the ancient world to allow us anything like reliable demographic accounts. Even if we use thousands of funerary inscriptions, for example, we must admit that such evidence is "anecdotal" when compared to modern historical demography. Moreover, it must be admitted that every study of ancient slavery attempts to paint a larger portrait of the reality of slavery by using pieces of evidence — the occasional mention of slaves in literature, images of slaves in fiction, scraps of information derived from chance finds of papyri and epigraphy — that could be suspected of limited relevance. So I would insist that ancient historiography, due to the nature of the sources, is always "anecdotal" to some extent. Though recognizing the possible perils of offering a handful of funerary inscriptions as evidence of ancient slave life, I do believe these data provide *some* accurate historical account of at least the lived experience of *some* ancient slaves. I am, that is, unabashedly offering here a version of anecdotal historiography.

Nuclear Families

First, we may note that when we have funerary inscriptions that appear to be intentionally set up to reflect family structures (what I have elsewhere called "familial inscriptions"),[2] we find different kinds of structures. In a study of 115 slave inscriptions from Asia Minor, I counted 74 that give some evidence of family structure, 11 of those (or 15 percent of 74) show evidence only of a couple, and 36 (49 percent of 74) provide some evidence of the nuclear family (that is, husband, wife, and at least one child, but excluding mention of other relations).[3] Thus 47 inscriptions provide evidence for slave couples or nuclear family structures, about 64 percent of the "familial" inscriptions, constituting a substantial majority. This should not surprise us since we can imagine that it would have been easier for slaves to maintain a nuclear or "couples only" family than an extended family of some size.

It has generally been assumed by scholars that slaves would more likely have coupled with other slaves from the same household.[4] This may have been the case with a couple named Amor and Roma. The two names constitute a palindrome. The most likely explanation for their names, according to an ingenious suggestion by Kent Rigsby, is that they were slaves of the same person who couldn't resist the wordplay. Perhaps they were even purchased and named at the same time. In any case, they apparently went on to marry and produce children of their own, having begun as slaves in the same household.[5]

Extended Families

We should not, though, exaggerate the predominance of nuclear family structures for slaves. The study mentioned above also counted 17 extended family inscriptions (23 percent of 74) as well as 10 inscriptions (13 percent of 74) in which

2. Dale B. Martin, "The Construction of the Ancient Family: Methodological Considerations," *JRS* 86 (1996): 40-60.

3. See Dale B. Martin, *Slavery as Salvation: The Metaphor of Slavery in Pauline Christianity* (New Haven: Yale University Press, 1990), p. 161, tab. C.

4. See Carolyn Osiek's essay in this volume; Keith R. Bradley, *Slaves and Masters in the Roman Empire: A Study of Social Control* (New York: Oxford University Press, 1987), p. 74.

5. The couple's names in the Greek inscription are Eros and Roma. Rigsby notes that though Eros is a not uncommon name for a man, Roma is very rare for a woman. He therefore suggests that these were Greek equivalents of their Latin names, Amor and Roma. See Kent J. Rigsby, "Graecolatina," *ZPE* 102 (1994): 192-93; see also *SEG* 44 (1994), #526. For an inscription in which we can be certain that the man and woman are both slaves of the same master, see *TAM* 3.762.

people apparently unrelated by the traditional ties of blood or marriage provide funerary inscriptions for themselves. If we add together these extended and communal inscriptions, we have 27 inscriptions (36 percent of 74) that may reflect familial or familial-like social structures that do not fit the couples-only or nuclear model. Thus, even for the slave inscriptions, admittedly representing only those kinds of slaves who *could* put up such inscriptions, the nonnuclear structures are in a relation vis-à-vis the nuclear structures by a proportion of 36 percent to 64 percent. That simple comparison, however, provides only a minimal impression of slave families. I will now point out several inscriptions that illustrate the remarkable variety of kinds of families apparently possible for slaves.

Some are basic extended family inscriptions. Indeed, a number of them look just like free or freed extended families of the time. Take, for example, the inscription of Syros III:

Σύρος γ', ὑκέτης κληρονόμων τῆς γενομένη[ς
Αὐρ(ηλίας) Περικλείας, θυ(γατρὸς) Αὐρ(ηλίου) Περικλέ[ο]υς Ἑρ(μαίου)
Κε[υ]α, ἐφέσει τῶν δεσ-
ποτῶν τὴν σωματοθήκην ἑαυ[τ]ῷ καὶ τῶ γυναικὶ αὐτοῦ
Παμφυλία καὶ τῇ θυγατρὶ αὐ[τοῦ Ἀ]γοράστῃ καὶ τῶ ἀνδρὶ τῆς θυγατρὸς Καλ[ο]κ[έρω?] καὶ τῶ προενόντι ἀνεψιῶ
αὐτοῦ Τροκονδα· [ἕτερος] δὲ ο[ὐ]δ[ε]ὶς ἄλλο . . .

Syros III, slave of the heirs of the former [i.e., deceased] Aurelia Perikleia, daughter of Aurelius Perikleos Hermaiou Keua, by permission of the masters, [provides] the sarcophagus for himself and his wife Pamphylia and his daughter Agoraste and the husband of his daughter Kalokeros and for his deceased cousin (?) Trakondas. No other corpse . . . etc.[6]

Here is a male slave of a woman's heirs, who are not named (which poses the question of why she is named and they are not); the slave provides for himself, his wife, daughter, son-in-law, and an ἀνεψιός (cousin?). He is the only one called a slave, but no one else bears a name that would indicate free or freed status, so they may all be slaves. We cannot be certain. In any case, this constitutes a fairly traditional extended family for the time: it is certainly extended since it includes the son-in-law and a cousin of some relation, but it is not particularly large; most extended families in funerary inscriptions from Asia Minor are not large.[7] (The inscriptions are almost never dated, and it is impossible in most

---

6. *TAM* 3.769. Translations of this and the inscriptions that follow are my own.
7. See Martin, "Construction," pp. 52-53.

cases to date them by any means, but most scholars assume the majority come from around the second to third centuries.)

Another common aspect of extended family inscriptions from this area is that even though they portray extended families, they often do not contain *complete* nuclear families. Take, for example, the epitaph of Georgos, which is dated by the editors to around 150 C.E.:

Γεωργὸς Μολεους, οἰκέτης Πλάτωνος leaf
Οβριμοτου, κατέστησεν τὴν σωματοθήκην τοῖς ἐξ αὐτοῦ τέκνοις
Ἀγοράστῳ καὶ Ἀρτέμει καὶ τῷ γενομένῳ αὐτοῦ
ἀδελφῷ Πολυ-
δεύκῃ καὶ ἑαυ-
τῷ ἐφέσει τῶν
δεσποτῶν

Georgos, slave of Platon Obrimotes, "established the sarcophagus for his children Agorastos and Artemeis and for his former [i.e., deceased] brother Polydeukes and for himself by permission of the masters," etc.[8] Here a slave man provides a sarcophagus for himself, his son and daughter, and his brother, but does not mention a wife.[9]

In these first two examples the provider of the tombstone explicitly calls himself a slave; we may conjecture that the others in the family are slaves, but we cannot be sure. One inscription, though, appears to represent a three-generational slave family.

Κατεσκεύασαν τὸν τύμβον Φειδίας,
Μάρων, Εὐδαίμων, δοῦλοι Ἀρχεπόλε-
ως, ἑαυτοῖς καὶ πατρὶ καὶ μητρὶ καὶ
γυναικὶ Φειδίου Ἐλπίδι καὶ γυναικὶ Μάρωνος Σωτηρία καὶ παιδίοις τῶν ἐκ
Φειδίου καὶ Μάρωνος τῶν προγεγρα-
μένων γυναικῶν· ἑτέρῳ δὲ μηδενὶ ἐξαίσται·

Pheidias, Maron, Eudaimon, slaves of Archepolis [m.] constructed the tomb for themselves and father and mother and for the wife of Pheidias, Elpis, and the wife of Maron, Soteria, and for the children of the aforerecorded wives of Pheidias and Maron, but for no other is it permitted [to be buried], etc.[10]

8. *SEG* 41 (1991) #1302; *Termessos* III 224/225 = *Termessos* IIIA 29 no. 27.
9. For the family tree of the master, see *TAM* 3.301.
10. *TAM* 2.1032.

Here we have three brothers, all slaves of the same man, along with their parents, who for some reason are not named but are probably slaves of the same man also. Provision is also made for two wives and the children of the wives. Since the children are not named, they may not yet exist; but then again, they may. We may therefore be witnessing a remarkable stability of three generations, all slaves, within one extended family.

Note that the brothers call the children (in rather awkward wording, at that) their wives' children rather than their own. One possible reason is that that was legally the case: offspring of a slave couple would be officially children of the woman but not the man. But male slaves in these inscriptions often *do* call their children just that: their own children. So it is also possible that the children are the wives' offspring by other fathers or previous husbands, though I think that is unlikely here.

We do have inscriptions, though, that indicate just such a situation. Take, for instance, this one, which portrays a slave family with "his and her" children.

Τὸν τύνβον κατεσκεύασε Γαμικός,
δ]οῦλος τῶν σὺν Μηνοδώρω, ἑαυτῶ
κὲ τέ]κνοις κὲ γυνεκὶ κὲ τέκνοι<ς> αὐτῆς τῆς Θευτί<σ>?-
κης?] κὲ νύνφες κὲ ἐγγόνοις·

Gamikos, slave of the associates of Menodoros, constructed the tomb for himself and children and for his wife Theutiske and her children and daughters-in-law (? νύνφες) and descendants ... etc.[11]

Gamikos is a slave of "those around Menodoros," probably heirs or clients.[12] We are not told whether his wife and other family members are also slaves, though I think they probably are. At any rate, he calls his own children his, and his wife's children hers, and all, including in-laws and other descendants (who may occur?), are included in the funerary arrangements.[13]

---

11. *TAM* 2.1019.

12. For other cases in the same area of someone being called a "slave of those around" someone, see *TAM* 2.1005 and 2.1018.

13. It is not completely clear to me why Theutiske's name comes in the inscription where it does, so far after her designation as γυνή, but I think it must in fact be her name rather than someone else's (for example, the name of her [female] owner). And the name surely is not supposed to be connected to νύνφες, which comes at a location in the inscription (after the conjunctive and just before the other "descendants") that indicates that these "daughters-in-law" or "young women" must here remain unnamed. The odd spelling of νύνφες is not an indication that it should be taken as genitive, but is due to the shift in spelling in which -αις becomes -ες, just as και in the inscription is written κε.

We may rightly imagine that such extended slave families were much more possible for slaves in better, more powerful positions. Imperial slaves, especially those in managerial positions on the large estates and other enterprises in Asia Minor in the Roman imperial period, were doubtless better able than most slaves to maintain an extended family. The "slave of Caesar" Telesphoros Julianos, for instance, erected this inscription in the late first or early second century:

Τελέσφορος Καίσαρος
δοῦλος Ἰουλιανὸς ἑαυτῷ
ζῶν καὶ Κλ. Ὀλυμπιάδι καὶ Οὐ-
αλερίοις φλαουιανῷ καὶ Σε-
κούνδῳ τοῖς τέκνοις αὐτῆς
ζῶσι, καὶ Ἀλβανίᾳ Βικτωρείνῃ
θ(ανούσῃ) καὶ ἀπελευθέροις καὶ δού-
λοις τοῖς προσήκουσιν αὐτῷ

Telesphoros Julianos, slave of Caesar, for himself while living and for Claudia Olympia, and for Valerius Flavianus and Valerius Secundus, her living sons, and for Albania Victorina, deceased, and for all the freedpersons and slaves who belong to him, etc.[14]

Managerial slaves who were not members of the imperial household would have been in similar situations. A slave πραγματευτής (business manager) left behind this provision for his family:

[Ἡ] σορὸς καὶ ἡ περὶ αὐ[τ]ὴν κάμαρα καὶ ὁ πα[ρα]κείμενος βω-
μὸς καὶ ἡ παρεστῶσα στήλη λευκόλιθος, δαδούχου Γ(αίου) Ἰου(λίου)
Θιλίππου συγκλητικοῦ, δούλου πραγμ[α]τευτοῦ καὶ γυν[αι]κὸς καὶ
τέκν[ων] καὶ ἐκγόν[ων καὶ Θ]ρεμμάτ[ων . . .

The coffin and the vault about it and the altar lying before it and the stele of white marble standing nearby (all are those of) the slave *pragmateutes* [manager] of the Dadouchos [torch-bearer, a local civic honor] Gaius Julius Philippus, of senatorial rank, and [the πραγματευτής'] wife and children and grandchildren and *thremmata. . . .*[15]

This slave manager is able to provide a burial complex that would house the remains of himself, his wife, his (unnamed) children and grandchildren,

---

14. *Smyrna* 23.225.
15. *BCH* 5 (1881), p. 346, #8.

and his "thremmata," which here is probably to be understood as equivalent to the Latin *verna* and refers to homebred slaves. The burial complex includes a coffin or sarcophagus *(soros)*, a vault *(kamara)* around it, a base or altar nearby *(bōmos)*, and a stele standing nearby. It must have been an impressive monument to this managerial slave's extended family.

Mixed Households

In spite of our assumption that slaves must have tended to couple within the same household, and thus that the members of their families must have generally been all members of the same household, we do have instances when that was not the case. We have families in which some members are free or freed while others are slaves and in which members do not all belong to the same household.

> Αὐρ(ήλιος) Δοῦλος Μαρκιανοῦ Λολίου, ἀπ(ελεύθερος), τὴν σωματοθήκην
> ἑαυτῶ καὶ Ἑλένη, τῇ γυ(ναικὶ) αὐτοῦ, καὶ Πρωτοπαίω, τῶ υἱῶ αὐτοῦ,
> οἰκέταις Αὐρ(ηλίας)
> Γῆς Ἑρ(μαίου) Ὁπλεους·

> Aurelios Doulos, freedman of Markianos Lolios, [provided] the sarcophagus for himself and Helene, his wife, and Protopaios, his son, slaves of Aurelia Ges, daughter of Hermaios Oples . . . etc.[16]

It is of course possible that the patron of this freedman and the mistress of his wife and son are members of the same family or household, but we certainly cannot assume that. The freedman is mentioned in another inscription from the same area, there designated as the father of a deceased woman named Aurelia Korkaina (*TAM* 3.838), who is being commemorated by her husband and is either free or freed. But there is no indication of any patron's family. The female owner of the man's wife and son, Aurelia Ges, is also named in another Termessus inscription (*TAM* 3.382), and the editors there provide something of a family tree for some of her other relatives. But there is no mention there of any name similar to Markianos Lolios. So we probably have here a family in which the father is a freedman from one household, and his wife and son are slaves of a different household. He (later?) also had a free or freed daughter who was commemorated by her own husband whose name is unknown (that inscription is fragmentary).[17]

---

16. *TAM* 3.421.
17. For discussion of mixed slave-free marriages in Asia Minor, see L. P. Marinovic, E. S.

We also encounter families in which the male provider is a slave while the other members of his family are free.

Τόνδε τὸν τύμβον Διονύσιος, οἰκονόμος τῆς πόλε-
ως, κατεσκεύασεν ἑαυτῷ καὶ Τύχῃ Ὑγείας Ὀλυμπηνῇ
καὶ Χαιρούσῃ καὶ Διονυσίῳ τέκνοις καὶ Ἀρτείμα καὶ Ἀγαθόπο-
δι καὶ Ναυκληρικῷ τοῖς Ὑγείας Ὀλυμ(πηνοῖς)· ἑτέρῳ δὲ οὐδενὶ . . .

Dionysios, οἰκονόμος of the city, constructed the tomb for himself and Tyche, [daughter?] of Hygeia, an Olympene, and for Chairouse and Dionysios [their? his? her?] children, and Artemas and Agathopous (m.) and Nauklerikos, Olympenes, of Hygeia, but for no other (etc.). . . .[18]

There are several uncertainties here. I have called Dionysios a slave, though he does not explicitly label himself as such, because οἰκονόμοι of cities in this time and area were often, though not always, public slaves.[19] Furthermore, though he mentions that his wife and others are "Olympenes," he doesn't refer to himself that way. Granted, the precise meaning of "Olympene" is itself not completely clear, but it may refer to a citizen of Olympus, which is where the tomb is located.[20] Since Dionysios does not refer to himself as an Olympene, though his wife and other family members are, that may be another clue that he is a public slave. Finally, it is unclear whether Hygeia is the mother or former owner of Tyche, and thus whether the three men named later are Tyche's brothers or fellow freedpersons or both. The editor takes Hygeia to be Tyche's mother, a conclusion with which I agree, because I would expect a more explicit designation of them as her freedpersons if that were the case. Though all this is based on some conjecture, I take it that we have here a public slave who provides a funerary inscription for himself, his wife, their daughter and son, and his three brothers-in-law, all of whom are free. Of course, this sort of situation would have been easier for a managerial, public slave to maintain than for slaves in lesser positions. But it demonstrates how families comprising mostly free persons could be headed by a slave patriarch.

We also find households in which the wife is a freedwoman while the husband remains a slave. We might be tempted to suppose that though male slaves

---

Golubcova, I. S. Sifman, and A. I. Pavlovskaja, *Die Sklaverei in den östlichen Provinzen des römischen Reiches im 1.-3. Jahrhundert* (Stuttgart: Franz Steiner, 1992), pp. 88-90.

18. *TAM* 2.1151.

19. See Martin, *Slavery as Salvation*, pp. 15-17, 174-76.

20. Though slaves in these inscriptions *almost* never refer to themselves as "Olympenes," in the immediately preceding inscription, *TAM* 2.1150, the donor, Trokondas, seems to call himself both a slave and Olympene.

may have been freed for any number of reasons, women were most often freed in order to serve as wives to their patrons.[21] That may be true, though we have few means to test the hypothesis — and no means at all for establishing anything remotely approaching statistical representation. Moreover, there is some counterevidence. When we have a male who is a slave of one household with a wife who is a freedwoman of a different household, it is not likely that his wife was freed only for marriage. Take this inscription from Termessus, for example:

Ἀρτέμων ὁ καὶ Ζωτικός, οἰκέτης Αὐρ(ηλίου) Ἀρτέμωνος
Ἀπολ(λωνίου) Ἀρ(τειμου) ε’ Ἀλικρεους, τὴν σωματοθήκην ἐφέσει τοῦ δεσ-
πότου ἑαυτῶ καὶ Αὐρ(ηλία) Κορκαινα Κορκαινου, τῆ γυ(ναικί), καὶ τῆ
προ-
εντεθαμμένη
Πασαγάθη, τῆ πρ<ο>γό-
νη·

Artemon, also called Zotikos, slave of Aurelios Artemon Apollonios [son of?] Arteimas V Alikreous, [provided] the sarcophagus, by permission of the master, for himself and for Aurelia Korkaina [freedwoman] of Korkainos, his wife, and his previously interred step-daughter [?] Pasagathe . . . etc.[22]

The man remains the slave of a man and provides burial for his wife, who is a freedwoman of a man other than her husband's owner, and for his stepdaughter (probably; the interpretation of προγόνη is not entirely certain). Why he doesn't call the girl the daughter of his wife, which is a common practice in such inscriptions, is unclear to me. Might the girl be his stepdaughter by a previous wife? Of course, it is possible that Korkaina was freed by her master Korkainos in order to be his wife and later was divorced, after which she married the slave Zotikos. But I think that less likely than the simpler hypothesis that she was freed for other reasons than marriage.[23]

21. The situation obviously existed; see Susan Treggiari, *Roman Marriage: Iusti Coniuges from the Time of Cicero to the Time of Ulpian* (Oxford: Clarendon, 1991), p. 120.

22. *TAM* 3.338. For the tomb of the father of the master, see *TAM* 3.263.

23. We *may* have other cases of free or freed wives with slave husbands, though the status of the husbands is uncertain. I refer to inscriptions in which a woman provides an inscription for herself, a husband, and sometimes others, and the husband's name is given as being "of" a name that appears clearly to be feminine. In *TAM* 2.952, for instance, Neike, who is either free or freed and calls herself an "Olympene," provides a lengthy inscription for a rather large extended family, including several people of no apparent blood or marriage relation. Her husband is called "Protanikos, also known as Drakon, of Lychiarchis," possibly meaning that he is a slave of a woman. Furthermore, Neike calls all the children mentioned "her" children rather than "their" children, which may further support the hypothesis that her husband is a slave.

More counterevidence to the idea that women were usually freed for marriage becomes apparent when we find freedwomen providing inscriptions for themselves and their husbands, and the husbands are not their patrons. Take this inscription, for example:

Ἀφροδεισία, ἀπελευθέρα
Ἀπολλωνίου, τὸν τύμβον ἑαυτῇ καὶ ἀνδρὶ Ἑρμαίῳ καὶ υἱῷ
Ζως<ί>μῳ καὶ γυναικὶ καὶ τέκνοις
καὶ Ἐφηβικῇ καὶ τέκνοις Ἀφροδεισία καὶ Ἐλπιδᾶ καὶ Ἀπφίῳ Ἀσκλη-
πιάδου, ἄλλῳ δὲ οὐδενὶ . . .

Aphrodeisia, freedwoman of Apollonios, [provides] the tomb for herself and her husband Hermaios and son Zosimos and [his] wife and children and Ephebike and [her?] children Aphrodeisia and Elpis and Apphion [son?] of Asklepiades, but for no other . . . etc.[24]

Or this one, in which a freedwoman of two male priests (brothers?) provides an inscription for herself and her dead husband:

Αὐρ(ηλία) Καρικὰ, ἀπε(λευθέρα) ἱ(ερέων) Αὐρ(ηλίων) Ἀπελλᾶ καὶ
Ἡλιοφόρου, τὴν σωματοθήκην ἑαυτῇ
καὶ τῷ προενειμένῳ αὐτῆς ἀνδρὶ Αὐρ(ηλίῳ) Ὠφελίμῳ μόνοις.

Aurelia Karika, freedwoman of the priests Aurelios Apellas and Aurelios Heliophoros, [provides] the sarcophagus for herself and her previously interred husband Aurelios Ophelimos alone, etc.[25]

Finally, when considering the reasons for freeing female slaves, we must reckon with the many cases in which women are freed by other women, who obviously would not be freeing them in order to marry them. There are many such cases, and they are relatively unremarkable, so I will not quote any explicitly (but for examples, see *TAM* 2.1003; 3.224; 3.259; 3.365; 3.747). In some the inscription is provided by a man (sometimes himself freed) for himself and his wife, who is a freedwoman of a woman. We may imagine that in some of those cases, perhaps, the man bought his wife out of slavery in order to marry her. So we could say that in those instances the women were freed, in a sense, for marriage. But that would be a rather different situation from when a woman is freed by her

24. *TAM* 2.941. See also *TAM* 3.430; 3.662.
25. *TAM* 3.539.

master so he can marry her. Women slaveholders must have had all sorts of reasons to manumit their slave women, though those reasons are not always clear.

Thus far in this section I have concentrated on those families in which one partner was slave while the other was free or freed. But we also find other kinds of mixed households. Sometimes one generation would be freed while another would remain slave. One freedwoman of a priest, for instance, provides burial for herself and her parents, who seem still to be slaves of the same priest:

Αὐρηλία Σωτηρίς, ἀπελευθέρα ἱ(ερέως) Αὐρ(ηλίου) Τι(βερίου) Οπλητος, τὴν σ[ω]μα[τ]οθή[κη]ν ἐαυτῇ . . .

Aurelia Soteris, freedwoman of the priest Aurelios Tiberios Oples, [provides] the sarcophagus for herself and for her father Bales and mother Soteira, slaves [of Oples?], etc.[26]

And sometimes even extended family members, though slaves, could be included in the funerary arrangements of free relations, as in this case:

Αὐρ(ήλιος) Εὐπρέπης Δορᾷ τὴν σωματοθήκην ἐαυτῷ καὶ τῇ προενειμένῃ ἀδελφῇ
καὶ τῷ ἀνεψιῷ αὐτοῦ Σοκλεῖ, οἰκέτῃ Νεικιανῆς Αρμαστης, ἀπὸ Λυκιαρχίας,
καὶ τῇ γυνεκὶ αὐτοῦ
τοῦ Σοκλέος Λαμ-
προτύχῃ καὶ τοῖς
ἐξ αὐτῶν τέκνοῖς
ἄλλῳ δ<ὲ> μηδενὶ

Aurelios Euprepes Dora [provides] the sarcophagus for himself and his previously interred sister and for his cousin Sokles, slave of Neikiane Armasta, from Lykiarchia (?), and for the wife of Sokles, Lamprotyche, and their offspring, but to no other, etc.[27]

Though I'm not certain that "cousin" is always the correct translation of ἀνεψιός, it is nonetheless clear that Sokles is not of the immediate family of the provider, and that he is a slave of a woman apparently unrelated to the other persons in the inscription.[28] A slave man and his immediate family are, therefore, included in the familial inscription of a free male relative.

26. TAM 3.772.
27. TAM 3.485.
28. The slave owner may be the woman mentioned in 3.277, who there provides for herself and her deceased daughter.

One last category of these "mixed households" is interesting for the light it sheds on the possible roles available to women in household structures. I refer to the fact that we sometimes encounter what we might call "female-dominant households." I provide a few examples.

Ἑλενούς, δούλη Αὐρ(ηλίας) Ἀρτεμεισίας
κατεσκεύασα τὸν τύμβον ἑαυτῇ καὶ
ἀνδρὶ καὶ τέκνοις καὶ ἐνγόνοις καὶ
γαμβρῷ Φιλοσεράπι καὶ δούλῃ μου Μελίννῃ
καὶ ἀνδρὶ αὐτῆς Ἁρποκρᾷ καὶ τέκνοις αὐτῶν. ἑτέρῳ δὲ μηδενὶ . . .

Helenous, slave of Aurelia Artemeisia, constructed the tomb for herself and husband and children and grandchildren and son-in-law [?] Philoserapis, and for my slave Melinne and her husband Harpokras and their children, but for no other . . . etc.[29]

Here a female slave of a female owner provides an extended family inscription — though if she actually has a husband, children, and grandchildren, why doesn't

---

29. *TAM* 2.967. It is unclear to me exactly what relation is referred to in these inscriptions by the term γαμβρός, though I think it most probable that it refers to a son-in-law, judging by a comparison of where the term occurs in other inscriptions of the area. The place of the term in *TAM* 2.1068 suggests that there it refers to sons-in-law (and maybe including daughters-in-law?) because it comes right after the term for "children," and later in the inscription the term "the brothers of his wife" occurs (thus suggesting that "brother-in-law" was not covered by γαμβρός earlier in the inscription). A similar case may be *TAM* 2.986, where a freedman lists his relations in this order: self, wife, daughter, γυναικάδελφος (wife's brother), γαμβρός, and grand-children (or descendants: ἐγγόνοι). Though we would expect the term for son-in-law to come after "daughter," γαμβρός nonetheless seems here to mean "son-in-law." I think it much less likely that it refers to the wife of the γυναικάδελφος, because it is masculine. Other inscriptions from the same area that seem to use the term to refer to a son-in-law: *TAM* 2.1096; 2.1148. On the other hand, the occurrence of the term in *TAM* 1109 is a bit more confusing. There a woman provides an inscription and includes herself, her husband, her children and grandchildren (the children and grandchildren are not named), and only then mentions a man named Grammation, whom she calls her γαμβρός. But then she lists Grammation's wife Auxityche. If Auxityche were the woman's daughter (thus making Grammation the donor's son-in-law), we would expect her relation to the donor to have been made explicit. Another possibility, though, is that Auxityche is a second or previous wife of Grammation, who at some point was also mar-ried to the donor's daughter (this seems to be what the editor is suggesting). In any case, I have here translated γαμβρός as son-in-law because a survey of the inscriptions tends to suggest that relation, though the meaning is not certain. The problem with *TAM* 2.967 is that if Philoserapis is Helenous's son-in-law, I would have expected her to mention the name of her daughter to whom he was married.

she name any of them, seeing that she explicitly names other persons who are to be included? In this case, as in some others, we may suspect that she includes the relations only in the hope that she may someday have them (Philoserapis may be some other "in-law" relation rather than a son-in-law; see n. 29). In any case, she either has or hopes to have an extended family. She also provides for her own slave woman and that woman's husband and children. Note the dominant position held by the women in the inscription: as the donor, as slave owners, and in Melinne's case as the first-named person of her own nuclear family.

We have a similar inscription from a freedwoman:

Π]ραξία, ἀπηλευθερωμέ-
νη] Ἀμαροῦτος Ὀβολέο<ς?> [Ὀλυν-
πηνῆς, κατεσκεύασα [τύν-
βο]ν ἑαυτῇ καὶ τέκνοις μου [καὶ
δ]ούλη Ἀγατητύχῃ καὶ παιδίοις [αὐ-
τ]ῶν καὶ οἷς [ἐ?ὰ]ν δόξῃ τοῖς
προδηλο[υ-
μένοις
τέκνοις
μου Ἡρα-
κλείτω καὶ
Εὐ?]αισθήτ[ω
<ἤ>δη?, οὓς καὶ
παρακαλῶ
συνχωρῆσαι
ἐνκηδευθῆ-
ναι καὶ Δά-
ω]νι· ἑτέρω
δὲ μηδε-
νὶ . . .

Praxia, freedwoman of Amarous Oboles, Olympene, constructed the tomb for myself and my children and slave Agatetyche and their [sic] children and for any that seem proper to my previously designated children Heracles and Euaisthetos, whom also I ask to allow a place for Daon also to be buried, but to no other, etc.[30]

The freedwoman does not explicitly mention a husband (though it is possible, but I think unlikely, that her patron or Daon is her husband). We have no

30. *TAM* 2.1103.

indication of what relation Daon is; he may be a lover or just an acquaintance. But again, the dominant position held by the females is notable.

Lastly for this category I will mention an inscription by an apparently free woman who is married to a man who is probably a slave, in which case it would be understandable that she takes the position of "head of the household":

Αὐρηλία Ροδοὺς Ἑρμαίου Διονυσιδώρου Ὀλυμπηνὴ κατεσκεύασα
τὸν τύμβον ἑαυτῇ καὶ τῷ ἀνδρί μου Δημητρίῳ καὶ τοῖς τέκνοις
ἡμῶν καὶ ἐγγόνοις καὶ τῇ γλυκυτάτη προϋποκειμένη
τροφίμῃ Ὀλυμπιάδι καὶ Ἑρμαίῳ Διονυσιδωρου, πατρί μου,
καὶ μητρί μου Χρυσογονία καὶ τῷ δευτέρῳ ἀνδρί
μου Μακαρίῳ, οἰκονόμῳ τοῦ Λυκίων ἔθνους· ἑτέρῳ δὲ
οὐδενὶ . . .
Ἐπέτρεψα
δὲ
κηδευθῆ-
ναι αὐτὸν
σύντρο-
φόν μου Εὐπρέπην
Ὀλυμπη-
νὸν
καὶ γυναῖκα
αὐτοῦ Αὐρηλίαν
Ὀλυμπηνήν.

Aurelia Rhodous, daughter of Hermaios Dionysidoros, Olympene, constructed the tomb for myself and my husband Demetrios and for our children and grandchildren and for the sweetest, previously interred τροφίμη Olympene [here a proper name] and Hermaios Dionysidoros, my father, and my mother Chrysogonia and for my second husband Makarios, οἰκονόμος [manager] of the ethnos of the Lycians, but to no other, etc. . . . I have permitted also to be buried in this my σύντροφος [foster brother?] Euprepes, Olympene, and his wife Aurelia, Olympene.[31]

By calling a man her σύντροφος, is Rhodous indicating that she was herself a θρεπτή, which usually refers to a person taken up or bought as a child and raised in someone else's household? Such persons were sometimes slaves or at least in a quasi-servile relation to the head of the household, even though they were often treated more like children. At any rate, Rhodous appears to be the

31. *TAM* 2.1163.

head of an impressive extended household. She provides burial space for herself, her first and second husbands, her father, her mother, her descendants, her fellow "foster child" (if that is how we should take σύντροφος) and his wife, and her "sweetest," deceased τροφίμη. Out of context, it is impossible to be certain about this last relation. It could refer to Rhodous's own mistress or "foster mother," or to a "foster daughter" of Rhodous herself. I take her second husband Makarios to be a public slave for a couple of reasons: first, his name occurs late in the inscription and with only one name, while others named in the inscription are given patronymics or are said to be "Olympenes," or both; second, οἰκονόμοι of this time and region seem usually to be slaves, in this case, I think, a public slave. Of course, as a public slave manager, Makarios would have held a bit higher (informal) status than an ordinary slave, and thus his marriage to a free or freed woman.

We have seen a few examples of the different kinds of family structures and types in which slaves lived or themselves maintained. But these familial inscriptions are also useful for illustrating the different roles slaves might play in families, by which I mean that the persons, though slaves, occupied also other familial roles in relationships to other people who were not slaves.

Slaves in "Familial" Roles

First, we may note that familial inscriptions allow us to illustrate not only possible sizes and types of families but also their internal structures. The inscriptions reflect the social spacing of persons within families; they plot people's places in the text of the inscription and sometimes even in the geography or stratigraphy of the burials themselves. For example, we would normally expect slaves to occupy the lowest status positions in households, so it is no surprise when we encounter funerary inscriptions in which slaves, and sometimes freedpeople or θρεπτοί, are allowed burial in the ὑποσόριον of the familial vault or burial structure, that is, in a vault or vessel below the main sarcophagus or vessel holding the remains of the rest of the family's members. Thus an οἰκονόμος named Zosimos, who is himself probably a slave, provides a tomb for himself and the ὑποσόρια for his θρεπτοί and θρεπταί, his own slaves whom he reared from a young age.[32]

But slaves could occupy roles in families other than mere slave or slave owner. A common one, most modern scholars imagine, was as spouses, in some cases wives in all but the legal sense, of men. We expect that it was common, for

32. *TAM* 2.437; see also 2.322; 2.438.

example, for Roman soldiers to purchase women as *contubernales* for themselves since soldiers were forbidden to marry. Such a situation may be reflected in this inscription:

Γαίῳ Ἰουλίῳ Φρόν-
τωνι οὐετρανῷ ἥ-
ρωϊ ἀνέστησε τὸν
Βωμὸν Γαμικὴ [ἡ]
θρεπτὴ αὐτοῦ [εὐ]-
χαριστίας καὶ φ[ιλ]-
ανδρίας ἐν[εκεν]

For Gaius Julius Fronton, veteran, hero. Gamike, his θρεπτή, erected the altar for the sake of thanksgiving and love of man.[33]

A more complicated, and confusing, situation confronts us in the inscription of Dionysios, the city οἰκονόμος, quoted above (*TAM* 2.1151). In spite of the interpretation problems I mentioned above, it appears that Dionysios is a public slave with a free or freed wife named Tyche, whose mother was Hygeia. Indeed, the editor of the inscription takes Hygeia to be the mother of Tyche and remarks that, since Dionysios is a slave, Tyche is not really his wife but his *paelex*, his lover or "mistress." (We are not told explicitly who the parents of the children are, though Dionysios is certainly the father and I suspect Tyche the mother.) Thus we apparently have here a situation in which a free woman is spouse to a slave man. The slave is in the role of father and patriarch in a family of otherwise free persons.

Slaves could also imitate the practice of their free neighbors of buying a wife for themselves.

Ἕσπερος Ἑσπέρου υἱός, Τιβερίου δὲ
Κλαυδίου Πωλίωνος Φαίτρου οἰκονόμος Σωτηρίδι τῇ ἑαυτοῦ συν-
βίῳ συνζησάσῃ αὐτῷ ἔτη ἑπτὰ καὶ
ἀπολιποίσῃ αὐτῷ τέκνα τρία μνή-
[μ]ης χάριν τελευτησάσῃ ἐτῶν εἴκοσι

Hesperos, son of Hesperos, οἰκονόμος of Tiberius Claudius Polion Phaitros, for Soteris, his own wife, who lived with him for seven years and left behind

---

33. S. Sahin, *Die Inschriften von Arykanda* (*IGSK* 48); probably first century c.e. See the brief discussion in *SEG* 44 (1994), #1147.

for him three children. For the sake of memory for the one who died at the age of 20.[34]

Hesperos does not say he is a slave, but the editors take him to be such, and because he is an οἰκονόμος, I think it likely he is. If he were freed, we would expect him to have a Roman name. Soteris was thirteen when she began to live with Hesperos, and she may have been bought for that purpose. An οἰκονόμος could easily have purchased just such a slave to be his spouse.

We can be more certain about the status of a man named Stephanos, who provides for burial for himself and a woman named Laina, whom he "reared":

Στεφάνου οἰκέτου. Ἐγὼ
κηδευ[θ]ήσομαι καὶ
Λαῖνα, ἣν ἀνεθρεψάμην.

[The sarcophagus] of Stephanos, slave. I permit also Laina, whom I reared [to be buried here], etc.[35]

Here it seems fairly certain that this slave man bought and reared a woman to be his spouse.

Another intriguing twist on the theme of servile spouses is provided by a few inscriptions that suggest that such relationships were experienced even by "same-sex couples." What are we to make, for example, of this inscription?

Ἀρτέμων [δίς], οἰ(κέτης) Ἑρμέου, τὴν σωματοθήκην τοῖς γονεῦσιν αὐτοῦ κ<ὲ> ἑαυτῶ κὲ
τῶ ἐκτρ[α]φέντι ὑπ' αὐτοῦ Ἐρωτικῶ·
ἄλλω δὲ οὐδενὶ . . .

Artemon II, slave of Hermes, [provides] the sarcophagus for his parents and for himself and for the one reared by him, Erotikos, but for no other, etc.[36]

Artemon, a male slave of a male owner, provides for himself and his parents and his θρεπτός, whom he calls "Erotikos." Eros as a slave name is rather common for the Roman imperial period. But Erotikos (or its feminine equivalent) is rare, though we can find a very few other instances. (I know of three masculine and one feminine.)[37] Is it too much to suppose that the name

34. SEG 28.1045; second century C.E.?

35. TAM 2.338.

36. TAM 3.357.

37. See P. M. Fraser and E. Matthews, A Lexicon of Greek Personal Names, vol. 3A (Oxford: Clarendon, 1997); vol. 2, ed. M. J. Osborne and S. G. Byrne (Oxford: Clarendon, 1994), s.v.

Erotikos, which presumably would have been given to the θρεπτός by Artemon at the time when he, probably, purchased the boy, indicates that Artemon obtained a child with the purpose of rearing him to be his lover?[38] We know, of course, that same-sex coupling was common in the ancient world, and we know that slave owners took their slaves to be appropriate objects for sexual attention.[39] And, as I have shown, sometimes those attachments went beyond mere sexual gratification to imitate marriage. We may in some inscriptions be seeing something like "same-sex marriages" between male owners and their male slaves.

To move to other familial roles besides that of spouse, we know that many slaves must have played the role of ersatz children in the homes of others. The case of the θρεπτοί in these inscriptions is not entirely clear. Were they foundlings raised in the home but not necessarily as slaves? Or were they slaves who were bought or found when infants and raised as slaves but in a special category within the household? We cannot be certain. I think that at least some of the many θρεπτοί found in familial inscriptions from Asia Minor must have been either slaves or persons raised in a quasi-servile state. Yet they clearly were treated much like children, as we can tell from the positions their names occupy on tombstones and the phrases used by their owners/parents about them. Many of them must have been slaves who played the role of a child (even if somewhat "second-class" children) in the family.[40] How did this combination of identities — slave as also son or daughter — affect their lives and experiences of slavery and family?

We even have some inscriptions in which people seem to have been the owners of their actual children. We have manumission inscriptions in which fathers manumit their own slave children.[41] Funerary inscriptions provide similar evidence:

d(is) m(anibus)·
Spenis · vixit · ann(is) ·
VI · m(ensibus) · VIIII · d(iebus) · XXIIX · domi-

---

38. A Latin inscription (*TAM* 4.147) portrays a man supplying an inscription for his *verna*, a man named Vitalis, who lived twenty-two years. The slave is called *amantissimus*, but the term was common enough that we should probably avoid reading erotic meaning into its use here.

39. For sexual relations between slaves and owners, see Hans Klees, *Sklavenleben im klassischen Griechenland* (Stuttgart: Franz Steiner, 1998), pp. 155-75, and the article by Carolyn Osiek in this volume.

40. Golubcova takes θρεπτοί to be house slaves in a special relation to the owners, but nonetheless slaves; see Marinovic et al., pp. 90-92.

41. See references and discussion in Klees, pp. 171-72, and 172 n. 105.

ni · et · parentes · Primitivus · et · Sotira · dolentes
   fecerunt.

θεοῖς · καταχθονίοις.
Σπῆνις · ἔζησεν · ἔτη
ς’ · μῆν(ας) · θ’ · ἡμ(έρας) · κη’ · οἱ κύρι-
οι · καὶ · γονεῖς · Πρειμιτεῖ-
βος · καὶ Σωτείρα · πονοῦν-
τες · ἐποίησαν.

To the chthonic deities. Spenis lived six years, nine months, and twenty-eight days. Primitivus and Sotira, masters and parents, suffering, provided [the tomb].[42]

Are Primitivus and Sotira using both "masters" and "parents" literally (perhaps they were really his owners and just came to think of him as their son, or really his parents who just describe themselves as his "lords")? Are they using both terms to refer to themselves? Or do we have two owners, named, supplying the inscription along with the unnamed parents? I think this possible but unlikely. In that case the parents would likely be named or not referred to at all, and it is even less likely that the masters would be mentioned as helping to pay for the inscription but not named. If he really is both their slave and their son, how did that work? Did they buy him and then adopt him? Were they themselves slaves and his natural parents? But if so, why would they call themselves his "masters"?[43]

We have a similar case in a Latin inscription from a location near Philippi. A sixteen-year-old keeper of a *taberna* calls himself a homebred slave. He calls his owner his "father" and also mentions his "mother."

Vitalis C. Lavi Fausti
ser., idem f., verna domo
natus, hic situs est, vixit

---

42. *IG* 10.2.1.666.

43. I am grateful to Beryl Rawson for calling to my attention (in private correspondence) a few Latin inscriptions from Rome in which the word *dominus* is used in the presence of more intimate familial ties. In *CIL* 6.21787 a father is *dominus;* in 6.36351 a mother *seems* to be a *domina* (the text is fragmentary); in 6.2233 a man is called both brother *(frater)* and *dominus;* and in 6.11511 a six-year-old son is *dominus.* Professor Rawson herself doubts that these are references to slave masters, but offers no alternative explanation. For other possible cases of combinations of slave and familial relations, see Marinovic et al., pp. 39, 58.

annos XVI, institor tabernas
Aprianas, a populo acceptus,
idem ab dibus
ereptus. Rogo
vos, viatores, si quid minus
dedi mesura ut patri meo adicere,
ignoscatis. Rogo per superos
et inferos, ut patrem et matre
commendatos abeatis.
Et vale.

Vitalis, slave of Gaius Lavus Faustus, likewise son, *verna* born in the house-hold, lies here; he lived 16 years, manager of the *taberna* of Apriana, approved by the people but snatched away by the gods. I ask you, travelers, if I gave you some lesser amount so that I might profit my father, forgive. I ask those above and below that you keep my father and mother commended. And fare-well![44]

Again, there are uncertainties of interpretation. Vitalis names his father, though not his mother. He may have been the offspring of a union between his owner-father and one of his father's household slaves; he was thus raised as a slave in the household of his free father. How do we imagine Vitalis experienced his slavery in such a case? How did persons experience their identities when their owners were also their parents?

Finally, we should turn our attention to the important Greco-Roman patron-client system. Of course, slaves were themselves in an unofficial client position in relation to their owners — running their businesses, attending them, performing many of the functions that clients provided for their patrons — certainly after manumission but also in many cases before. But we also have evidence of slaves in a position of "client" to people who were not their owners. An imperial slave οἰκονόμος, for instance, provided a votive inscription in Asia Minor that honored both himself and a free Roman who was not his owner but who apparently functioned at least on this occasion as something like his pa-tron:

Τὸν ναὸν σ[ὺν
τοῖς ἀγάλμ[α-
σιν κατεσ[κεύ-
ασεν Ε[ὐτ]ύχη-

---

44. Hermann Dessau, *Inscriptiones Latinae Selectae* 7479.

ς] Σεβ(αστῶν) οἰκονό-
‹ν›μος χωρίων
Κωνσι[δ]ιανῶ[ν
σὺν Φα]υστε[ί-
νω καὶ Νεικ[ε-
ρωτιαν[ῶ καὶ
Ἑρ[μ]ᾶ [τέκν]οις
αὐτο[ῦ, εὐ]πο-
ροῦντος Κ[λαυ-
δίου Οὐ[α]λερι[α-
νοῦ το[ῦ] κρατ[ίς-
του ἐπι[τ]ρό[που.

Eutyches, imperial manager of the estate of Considiana, with Faustinus and Neikerotianos and Hermas, his children, built the temple with the statues, with the most excellent procurator Claudius Valerianus making it possible.[45]

We do not know how involved Claudius Valerianus was in the life or business of the imperial slave οἰκονόμος. Anderson speculates that the equestrian procurator may have furnished the land on which the temple was built. In any case, at least in this inscription he occupies the role of the slave's patron.

Other inscriptions portray slaves as something like clients connected, at least by funerary arrangements, with the households of persons other than their owners. In the inscriptions from Olympus on the southern coast of Asia Minor, this is especially true for sacred slaves, that is, people who apparently were owned by a sanctuary or a god and who performed services for whatever social entity ran the sacred precinct. I have found several such cases, but will provide only one:

Αὐρ(ήλιος) Δίσκος Β' Ὀλυμπηνὸς κατεσκεύασεν
ἑαυτῶ καὶ γυνεκὶ Κρατείη Ζωσιμᾶτος
καὶ τ[έ]κνοις καὶ Ἐπικτοῦτι Νεικενέτης
τῆς καὶ Βερνείκης [sic] · συνχωρῶ δ' ἐγὼ ἡ Κρά-
τε[ι]α [ἐν]κηδευθῆναι Σένεκαν ἱερόδουλον
καὶ γυ[ναῖκα] αὐτοῦ Ῥόδαν καὶ υἱῶ τοῦ Σένε-
κος ['Ελ?]ένω καὶ γυναικὶ αὐτοῦ Δρακοντίδι
καὶ παιδίω τῆς Ῥόδας Λέοντι, ἑτέρω δὲ οὐδενὶ.

45. J. G. C. Anderson, "An Imperial Estate in Galatia," *JRS* 27 (1937): 18-21.

Aurelios Diskos II, Olympene, established [the tomb] for himself and wife Krateia [daughter] of Zosimas and children and Epiktous [slave?] of Neikenete, who is also [called] Berneike. I, Krateia, also allow to be entombed within: Seneka, sacred slave, and his wife Rhoda, and the son of Seneka, Helenos, and his wife Drakontis and the child of Rhoda, Leon, but no other, etc.[46]

If we take this familial inscription to represent a household, we have a rather large, complicated, extended family that includes a sacred slave with his wife, his son and daughter-in-law, and her son, and another man who seems to be a slave of a different household and whose owner is a woman. Both the sacred slave and the other man, Epiktous, occupy roles normally held by clients of the household. How are we to interpret this relationship? How did these slaves' relationship to Diskos, who was not their owner, affect their experiences of slavery itself? At any rate, we must assume that their identities and senses of themselves were not formed purely by their identities as slaves or by their relationship to their owners. Both their "family lives" and their slavery were complicated by multiple factors of identity formation — indeed, by multiple identities.[47]

Finally, we should note that just as slaves could be clients, so they could be patrons. They obviously were in a position of patronage vis-à-vis those people who were their own slaves or freedpersons, and we have seen funerary inscriptions portraying such relationships. But it is a bit more surprising when we find inscriptions suggesting that slaves could function as patrons for people who were not their own slaves or freedpersons:

Ἀβάσκαντος, δοῦλος πρα-
γματευτὴς Αὐρ(ηλίου) Μακεδόνος, τὸν
τύμβον κατεσκεύασα ἑαυτῶ καὶ τῆ γλυκυ-
τά]τη μου θυγατρὶ Θεοδώρα καὶ τέκνοις αὐτῆς
καὶ υἱῶ?] μου Ἀστερίω καὶ Ἑρμῆ Παπίου Ὀλυμπηνῶ καὶ
τῆ γυν]αικὶ αὐτοῦ Ἑρμιόνη καὶ τέκνοις αὐ-

Abaskontas, slave πραγματευτής [business manager] of Aurelios Makedon, constructed the tomb for himself and my sweetest daughter and her children

---

46. *TAM* 2.1000.

47. In *TAM* 2.1023 a female sacred slave joins with a freedman and his wife and another person to establish a burial place for themselves and their offspring. In *TAM* 2.1062 a sacred slave of the god Hephaistos provides an inscription for himself, his wife, his son, and the wife and offspring of his son. In a fragmentary inscription (*TAM* 2.1089) a sacred slave and his wife are allowed burial in the extended family tomb of an apparently otherwise unrelated man.

and my son [?] Asterios, and for Hermes [son] of Papios, Olympene, and his wife Hermione, and [his? their?] children.[48]

Note that Abaskontas does not mention a wife; he may not have had one or she may have died or left him in a "divorce" (since slaves did not legally marry, of course, they would have needed no legal divorce). His daughter seems to have children, but no husband is named for her either. The son is also apparently unmarried, at least at the time of the commemoration. What is fascinating is that another nuclear family, that of the apparently free man Hermes, is included in the funerary arrangements of someone who is a slave of someone else. Hermes occupies the position of a client to the slave. Of course, it was no doubt easier for a slave business manager, who thereby held higher than normal informal status than most slaves, to command both the financial and social strength to function as a patron for an otherwise unrelated free man. But this sort of relation was nonetheless possible.[49]

Conclusion

Though the evidence I have presented is admittedly sparse and anecdotal, it does allow us to form an impression of the variety of family structures and experiences that must have been possible for at least some slaves in Asia Minor in the early Roman Empire. And we have also seen that slaves, in spite of being slaves, could "serve" as husbands, wives, children, parents, lovers, siblings, patrons, and clients in relations with slave, freed, and free people.

What did it mean for these slaves to function as someone's ersatz family member? How did it affect their experiences of slavery *and* family? We cannot know the answers to such questions, of course, but we must allow our imaginations more room to think about how human beings in antiquity experienced both family and slavery. And that may complicate the way we imagine slavery, family, household, and their relation to one another in early Christianity.

48. *TAM* 2.1020.

49. We may have a similar situation in *TAM* 2.1044. See also *TAM* 3.663, where a male slave of a female owner provides a sarcophagus for himself, but then there occurs the name of another (free or freed?) male apparently also allowed burial. Perhaps the other man's name was added later or originally omitted by mistake? The second man, of course, could be the slave's brother, but they have no names in common, and there is no indication of relation. So the second man may have been included in the slave's sarcophagus as the slave's friend, lover, client, or any combination of those roles.

The Domestic Enemy: A Moral Polarity of Household Slaves in Early Christian Apologies and Martyrdoms

J. Albert Harrill

The presence of slaves in the ancient household made the Greco-Roman family an inherent place of danger. Slaves were considered necessary as the ultimate domestic *insiders* doing the master's will in faceless attendance and total subordination. This abstraction is, of course, the articulated viewpoint of ancient slaveholders; some modern interpreters might find the answer to whether ancient slaves agreed easy to intuit, but in fact that second issue is difficult to decide historically because of the limited nature of the primary source material.[1] Ancient slaveholding ideology regarded chattel slaves (to paraphrase Aristotle) nothing but mere "tools" breathing around the house, at work performing the labor necessary for the ancient home economics.[2] But these tools were dangerous to have around the house, being chattels with an agency needing permanent restraint by fundamental dishonor and violent domination to maintain their natal alienation and social death. Greco-Roman slaveholding ideology, therefore, constructed "the slave" as an oxymoron, the "insider-outsider" — a person-and-nonperson — of enforced and so dubious loyalty in an unequal power relation of chattel bondage.[3] This oxymoronic construction of "the

---

1. Ancient evidence originates from members in the slave-owning social orders of the aristocratic elite. For cases of possible exception (such as Terence and Epictetus), evaluation of the primary source material, and contrast to the kinds of primary evidence used to do the history of modern slavery, see J. Albert Harrill, *The Manumission of Slaves in Early Christianity*, HUT 32 (Tübingen: Mohr Siebeck, 1995), pp. 18-30.

2. Peter Garnsey, *Ideas of Slavery from Aristotle to Augustine*, The W. B. Stanford Memorial Lectures (Cambridge: Cambridge University Press, 1996), pp. 107-27; P. A. Brunt, "Aristotle and Slavery," in his *Studies in Greek History and Thought* (Oxford: Clarendon, 1993), pp. 343-88.

3. My definition of "slave" combines the hermeneutical principle of slave-as-chattel by the Roman historian M. I. Finley, *Ancient Slavery and Modern Ideology*, ed. Brent D. Shaw, 2nd ed. (Princeton: Markus Wiener, 1998), pp. 135-92; Finley, "Slavery," in *International Encyclopedia of the Social Sciences*, ed. David L. Shils (New York: Macmillan and the Free Press, 1968), 14:307-13, and the hermeneutical principle of slavery-as-social-death by the historical sociologist Orlando Patterson, *Slavery and Social Death: A Comparative Study* (Cambridge: Harvard University

slave" served classical culture as a rhetorical, historical, and literary topos of moral polarity.

This essay examines this moral polarity in apologetic and martyrdom literature of second- and third-century Christianity. My thesis is that both genres contain tales suspiciously similar to "pagan" anecdotes of slaves in wider classical culture. From one side came the "faithful slave" of familial loyalty; the flip side brought the "enemy slave" of domestic betrayal. Either way, by saying that only one kind of person in the household — the slave — could be the source of familial ruin, apology and martyrdom sought to contain the anxiety that danger could reside in other kinship family members, and so were able to offer a partial explanation for the problem of persecution. Slaves faithful to the last provided at least a thread of moral continuity.[4] As discourses, apology and martyrdom articulated the role of slaves in Christian families under persecution with topoi similar to those used by classical authors because these topoi were rhetorically advantageous, not because they necessarily record actual events.[5]

The slave-as-domestic-enemy expressed proverbial, gnomic wisdom circulating in the Greco-Roman milieu of ancient Christianity. Couched in ancient warfare imagery and Roman military culture, it warned that "You have as many enemies as you have slaves" (e.g., Seneca, *Epistle* 47.5). The proverb pictured every slave a potential instigator of family betrayal and sedition, an "obvious" situation because of the full integration of slaves into ancient family life. The flip

---

Press, 1982), pp. 13, 35-101. Harrill, *Manumission of Slaves*, pp. 13-17; Harrill, "Paul and Slavery," in *Paul in the Greco-Roman World: A Handbook*, ed. J. Paul Sampley (Harrisburg, Pa.: Trinity Press International, 2003).

4. Cf. G. Maslakov, "Valerius Maximus and Roman Historiography: A Study of the *Exempla* Tradition," *ANRW* 2.32.1 (1984), p. 451.

5. For martyrdom as a discourse (rather than a "thing"), see Daniel Boyarin, *Dying for God: Martyrdom and the Making of Christianity and Judaism*, Figurae: Reading Medieval Culture (Stanford: Stanford University Press, 1999), p. 94; Tessa Rajak, "Dying for the Law: The Martyr's Portrait in Jewish-Greek Literature," in *Portraits: Biographical Representation in the Greek and Latin Literature of the Roman Empire*, ed. M. J. Edwards and Simon Swain (Oxford: Clarendon, 1997), p. 40; Elizabeth A. Castelli, "Visions and Voyeurism: Holy Women and the Politics of Sight in Early Christianity," *Protocol of the Colloquy of the Center for Hermeneutical Studies*, n.s., 2 (1995): 12; Judith B. Perkins, *The Suffering Self: Pain and Narrative in the Early Christian Era* (London: Routledge, 1995), pp. 104-23. The literature on martyrdom is extensive but concentrated mostly on the criminal charges and possible relation to actual court proceedings. Older scholarship assumed these accounts to be contemporary or accurate trial records *(commentarii)*. The best survey is Timothy D. Barnes, "Pre-Decian *Acta Martyrum*," *JTS* 19 (1968): 509-31 (with Barnes, "Legislation against the Christians," *JRS* 58 [1968]: 32-50). See also Hippolyte Delehaye, *Les passions des martyrs et les genres littéraires*, 2nd ed., Subsidia hagiographica 13b (Brussels: Société des Bollandistes, 1966).

side of this proverbial wisdom celebrated its moral polarity — the "faithful slave" accepting the master's authority and point of view so fully as to endure torture and to give all, even life itself, to save the master's home. The moral polarity of the enemy slave and the faithful slave also reinforced Roman ideologies of gender construction: betrayal by one's own domestics questioned the legitimacy *(potestas)* of the householder's right to dominate others, both inside and outside the home. In short, it unmade the man (the *vir*).[6] Ancient Christian authors recognized this polarity as both moral and essential to classical historiographic tradition, and they exploited its reversibility, using one slave exemplum, its flip side, or both, whichever best suited the rhetorical goals of the moment.

The first section below examines the domestic enemy proverb and its origins in material culture by surveying the physical environment of the ancient house and the integration of slaves in Greco-Roman domestic work, religion, and family relations. The second section explores the use of the domestic enemy proverb in early Christian apology. The third section interprets the stories about slaves in martyrdom accounts as the moral exemplum of domestic fidelity. I shall explore slave moral polarity in apologies and martyrdoms in order to evaluate the degree to which Christian tales of slaves, especially in martyrdom, subverted Greco-Roman ideologies of the family. Against a standard consensus in early Christian studies, I shall argue that such slave tales did not entirely overthrow the hierarchy of the Roman family.

The Slave as Domestic Enemy: A Tale of Mastercide

In 61 C.E. Pedanius Secundus, the emperor's deputy at Rome *(praefectus urbi)*, was murdered at home by his own slave. The details on why are unclear: either the domestic expected to be freed at a previously agreed price or the slave and master were competitors for the affection of the same slave boy-toy. The particular motivation did not concern the Roman senate. After some debate and despite protests from the populace about the innocents, the senate ordered in accordance with ancient custom the immediate execution of *all* slaves "residing under the same roof" *(sub eodem tecto mansitaverat)*, in this case 400, no matter how loyal or high ranking, as an example to others of how Rome would re-

---

6. Richard Alston, "Arms and the Man: Soldiers, Masculinity and Power in Republican and Imperial Rome," in *When Men Were Men: Masculinity, Power, and Identity in Classical Antiquity,* ed. Lin Foxhall and John Salmon, Leicester-Nottingham Studies in Ancient Society 8 (London: Routledge, 1998), p. 215.

spond to mastercide.[7] Accepting such a high number as historical is difficult, given the archaeological evidence for resident domestic space in even the largest extant *domus* or *insula* uncovered at Rome. But as Andrew Wallace-Hadrill pointed out in the discussion that followed the oral presentation of this paper, the murdered master was *urban prefect*, the magistrate placed in charge of, among other things, public slaves (slaves owned by the state) employed in the Roman aqueducts, baths, and other public works throughout the city.[8] When public slaves in the entire city are included, 400 of them "residing under the same roof" of the prefect's "house" becomes more intelligible.

At the games, some emperors even made the execution of mastercides a public exhibition of performance art. With the construction of the Roman Colosseum (Amphitheatrum Flavium), what had once been a theater of mimes became an execution staged for real. A criminal would play that "guilty wretch who had plunged a sword" into his master's throat. The slave was hung (for real) "on no sham cross" and gave "his naked flesh to a Calcedonian boar." "His lacerated limb lived on, dripping gore, and his whole body no longer looked like a body." Thus he "met with the punishment he deserved" and suffered a double penalty of crucifixion and condemnation to the beasts.[9] The condemned was a commodity whose ritual execution was more remarkable as spectacle *(spectaculum)* than as punishment. The visual display celebrated in "real theater" was a powerful mechanism of social control.[10] The public execution of mastercides was spectacle that had to be swift and brutal because Romans imagined that such slaves, if not made examples of, would inspire slave rebellion, even open warfare, in the household, city, and state; the legacy of Spartacus died hard. Mastercides reinforced the proverb that the slave was *the* domestic enemy.

7. Tacitus, *Annals* 14.42-45; Richard P. Saller, "Slavery and the Roman Family," in *Classical Slavery,* ed. M. I. Finley, "Slavery and Abolition" special issue 8 (London: Frank Cass, 1987), pp. 65-66.

8. However, the exact scope of the urban prefect's jurisdiction at this period is unclear, especially since the other city magistrate, the urban praetor, presided over major civic events, such as the games, which would have employed numerous public slaves. The standard work on public slaves is Walter Eder, *Servitus Publica,* Forschungen zur antiken Sklaverei 13 (Wiesbaden: Franz Steiner, 1980).

9. Martial, *Spectacles* 7.8-10; Ramsay MacMullen, "Judicial Savagery in the Roman Empire," in his *Changes in the Roman Empire: Essays in the Ordinary* (Princeton: Princeton University Press, 1990), p. 205; see also Richard C. Beacham, *The Roman Theatre and Its Audience* (Cambridge: Harvard University Press, 1992), p. 136.

10. Cf. K. M. Coleman, "Fatal Charades: Roman Executions Staged as Mythological Enactments," *JRS* 80 (1990): 63; Andrew Feldherr, *Spectacle and Society in Livy's History* (Berkeley and Los Angeles: University of California Press, 1998), pp. 4-50.

The domestic enemy proverb originates in its material culture, the close physical environment of the Greco-Roman house. That ancient house, either *domus* or *insula,* arranged slaves pervasively, in every aspect of domestic responsibility, which gave rise to masters' fear of slave plots and sedition. In such integration, the material conditions of slaves varied greatly, depending on the slave's specific domestic function and the master's resources and general care to provide.[11]

Wealthy slave owners managed numerous domestics in a hierarchy of multifarious jobs, with slaves even owning other slaves (*servus vicarius;* evidence that some slaves themselves belonged to the slave-owning ranks).[12] The architecture of the Roman house kept slaves in their place; they were left to sleep in narrow cells *(cellae, cellulae)* that also doubled as storage rooms.[13] Slaves also slept in the hallways, on the roof, or wherever else space was available. (In contrast to the situation in the American South, in which slaves typically lived in separate "slave quarters" outside the master's manor, ancient slaves lived under the same roof as their owners.) Within the aristocratic house, slaves had jobs of extraordinary specialization. There were bath attendants, masseurs, hairdressers, barbers, announcers of the guests, waiters, tasters, choristers, child minders (παιδαγωγοῖ), secretaries, business managers *(procuratores),* physicians, and cooks.[14] As cooks and servers, slaves figured prominently at Roman banquets *(convivia),* surrounding the dining area. The elder Pliny refers to waiters standing as "legions" *(mancipiorum legiones)* who protect "our food and drink," but who also pilfer (*Natural History* 33.26). Seneca notes the "the crowd of standing slaves" at meals and condemns the customary practice of making them stand stationary "all night long," hungry, silent, and in trembling fear of punishment (*Epistle* 47.3). The character Trimalichio, in Petronius's *Satyricon,* gives each guest his own table, "so these filthy slaves won't make us so hot by crowding past us" (34).[15] Since early Christian worship centered around ritual meals (Eucharist and the agape), the teeming slave waiters at Roman *convivia* are note-

11. Keith Bradley, *Slavery and Society at Rome,* Key Themes in Ancient History (Cambridge: Cambridge University Press, 1994), p. 89.

12. Bradley, *Slavery and Society,* pp. 2-3.

13. Bradley, *Slavery and Society,* p. 84. See also Michele George, "*Servus* and *Domus:* The Slave in the Roman House," in *Domestic Space in the Roman World: Pompeii and Beyond,* ed. Ray Laurence and Andrew Wallace-Hadrill, Journal of Roman Archaeology Supplement Series 22 (Portsmouth, R.I.: Journal of Roman Archaeology, 1997), pp. 15-24.

14. Jérôme Carcopino, *Daily Life in Ancient Rome: The People and the City at the Height of the Empire* (New Haven: Yale University Press, 1968), pp. 70-71; Bradley, *Slavery and Society,* pp. 61-65; Andrew Garland, "Cicero's *Familia Urbana,*" *GR* 39 (1992): 163-72.

15. John H. D'Arms, "Slaves at Roman Convivia," in *Dining in a Classical Context,* ed. William J. Slater (Ann Arbor: University of Michigan Press, 1991), pp. 179-80.

worthy. Some scholars suggest a model for the early Christian house church that relies heavily on Roman atrium-style villas, such as those found at Pompeii and Herculaneum, which housed such lavish Roman *convivia*.[16] Tenement apartment buildings *(insulae)*, another probable setting for Christian congregations and their ritual meals, also had specialized and full integration of slaves into each activity of domestic life.

Tacitus makes a revealing observation about slave presence in every part of the Roman house, by contrasting the Roman situation with the German. "Their . . . slaves are not organized in our fashion: that is, by an exact definition of services throughout a household. Each freedman remains master of his own house and home: the master requires a certain quantity of grain or cattle or clothing from the slave, as if from a tenant farmer. The slave so far is subservient; but the rest — the services of the household — is discharged by the master's wife and children" (*Germania* 25.1-2). Tacitus deemed slave quarters absolutely separate from the owner's residence odd indeed.[17]

The religious life of Roman slaves, whether in houses or apartments, required participation in the daily ritual of the household cult, which centered around the family idols *(lares)* that represented the ancestral spirit *(genius)* of the estate owner *(paterfamilias)*.[18] During one pagan rite in January (the Compitalia), the family hung male and female dolls for each free member of the house *(domus)* but woolen balls for each slave. While the ritual integrated slaves as house members, the representation nonetheless also subordinated them as dehumanized, genderless balls. The interplay of gender and status distinctions also was part of religious festivals for the benefit of slaves, the Saturnalia in December and the slaves' holiday on August 13 *(servorum dies festus)*. Both celebrations "recognized the permeability of the boundary between master and slave status in the household, but only as the exception that confirmed that boundary."[19] Given the inclusive nature of Greco-Roman polytheism as an open religious system, domestic religious activity was most likely tolerant of diversity. Slaves did their own (often unnoticed) private worship alongside that of the master's culture, society, or position in religious associations *(collegia)* — with (again) the main exception of the household domestic

16. Carolyn Osiek and David L. Balch, *Families in the New Testament World: Houses and House Churches* (Louisville: Westminster John Knox, 1997).

17. Bradley, *Slavery and Society*, p. 84.

18. On *paterfamilias* meaning "estate owner," see Richard P. Saller, "Pater Familias, Mater Familias, and the Gendered Semantics of the Roman Household," *CP* 94 (1999): 182-97.

19. Richard P. Saller, "Symbols of Gender and Status Hierarchies in the Roman Household," in *Women and Slaves in Greco-Roman Culture: Differential Equations*, ed. Sandra R. Joshel and Sheila Murnaghan (London: Routledge, 1998), p. 90.

cult.[20] Slaves brought alien religious observance even into Christian homes, where (unlike pagan homes) it was not supposed to be, according to the theology of many patristic authors. Tertullian, for example, reports of a Christian householder who went on a journey and whose slaves took advantage of his absence to garland his front gate in celebration of their (formerly inconspicuous) regular pagan rites for the season, evidence for the open religious system of paganism being tenacious even in the (ideally closed) ancient Christian household.[21] Tertullian uses the episode to exhort the strict discipline required to police idolatry in the family, especially among the (often unnoticed) family slaves.

In contrast, Roman jurists, magistrates, and other aristocratic pagan thinkers expressed little need for policing such garden-variety slave *superstitio,* until it endangered "ancestral tradition" *(mos maiorum)* of the family cult and "piety" *(pietas),* "public prayer" *(vota publica),* and "divine providence" *(providentia)* of the Roman state.[22] The jurist Vivian considered a daft slave who "from time to time" joined "religious fanatics" and their "ecstatic utterances" a weirdo, to be sure, but nonetheless a chattel with "minor mental defects" only. Likewise, the loony slave who formerly had "indulged in Bacchanalian revels around shrines" and danced in Maenadic frenzy uttering Bacchic "responses" was no more a market liability for the master than chattel having a high fever once. Even persistence "in that bad habit" of cavorting around occult shrines and uttering glossolalia meant (for Vivian and jurists who respected his opinions) a slave gone a bit mental but not having the physical defect of disease, thus lowering market value. Vivian understood slave curiosity for strange rites to be irrational experimentation, harmless and puerile, and not legal-economic liability for the owner.[23]

However, masters' tolerance of infantile superstition had limits. Prime concern was *superstitio* that subverted family and state, which was believed to have

20. Jan Theo Bakker, *Living and Working with the Gods: Studies of Evidence for Private Religion and Its Material Environment in the City of Ostia (100-500 AD),* Dutch Monographs on Ancient History and Archaeology 12 (Amsterdam: J. C. Gieben, 1994), pp. 42-43, 194; the standard work on slave religion is Franz Bömer, *Untersuchungen über die Religion der Sklaven in Griechenland und Rom,* 3 pts., Abhandlungen der Akademie der Wissenschaften in Mainz, Geistes- und sozialwissenschaftliche Klasse, Forschungen zur antiken Sklaverei 14 and 14.3, revised by Peter Herz (Wiesbaden and Stuttgart: Franz Steiner, 1982², 1960, 1990).

21. Tertullian, *Idolatry* 15.7-8 (CCSL, 2:1116); Robin Lane Fox, *Pagans and Christians* (New York: Knopf, 1987), p. 296.

22. On pagan piety, see Robert L. Wilken, *The Christians as the Romans Saw Them* (New Haven: Yale University Press, 1984), pp. 48-67.

23. *Digest* 21.1.9-10; Ramsay MacMullen, *Enemies of the Roman Order: Treason, Unrest, and Alienation in the Empire* (Cambridge: Harvard University Press, 1996), p. 332 n. 26.

caused in part the bloodiest slave revolts in Roman history. The rebel leader of the First Sicilian Slave War (ca. 136-132 B.C.E.) was a slave named Eunus with deep devotion to the Anatolian mysteries of the Great Mother and the Syrian goddess (Atargatis/Astarte). Roman sources brand Eunus a religious fraud, a wizard who gained supporters by breathing fire sparks through a walnut.[24] Roman fears pointed also to the Thracian gladiator Spartacus and especially his prophetess wife, a Maenad initiated into mysteries of Dionysus.[25] Masters' anxiety over their slaves engaging in antifamily *superstitio* persisted long after the major slave wars of the late republic because slaves — while fundamental outsiders — continued to live, labor, worship, and die within negotiated domestic space.

To deal with this anxiety, some Greco-Roman moralists condemned cruelty to slaves. Posidonius, for example, blamed the arrogant abuse of a single master, Damophilus of Enna (among whose agricultural slaves revolt first broke out), for the First Sicilian Slave War, on the logic that the "public transcript" (we would say) of slaves proved that they would never rebel without cause: "the slaves were coming to be treated worse and worse, and were correspondingly more and more alienated from their owners" (*apud* Diodorus Siculus 34/2.26).[26] Additionally, the Stoic moralist Seneca condemned the condition of many households that gave rise to the domestic enemy proverb in the first place. He writes that

> wretched slaves aren't even allowed to move their lips in order to speak. Every sound is suppressed by the threat of a beating; and not even unintentional noises like coughing, sneezing or hiccups are exempted from chastisement. If the silence is disturbed by any sounds, it must be atoned for by a dire punishment. Throughout the night they stand there hungry and silent. That's how it comes about that those who aren't allowed to talk in the presence of their master will tell tales about him behind his back. But those slaves who are allowed to talk not just in their master's presence, but actually with the master, were ready to offer their neck on his behalf, and to turn aside onto their own

24. Keith Bradley, *Slavery and Rebellion in the Roman World, 140 B.C.–70 B.C.* (Bloomington: Indiana University Press, 1989), pp. 55-56. Note also the slandering of the Bacchanalia by the claim that a *Graecus ignobilis* first introduced the cult to Italy, and the repeated discrediting of Catiline and his conspiracy with the taint of servile association; Keith Bradley, "Slaves and the Conspiracy of Catiline," *CP* 73 (1978): 330; Harrill, *Manumission of Slaves*, p. 149 n. 91.

25. Bradley, *Slavery and Rebellion*, pp. 92-93; see Tacitus, *Annals* 15.46.

26. For an excellent critique of the reliance on the "public transcript" to explain the causes of slave resistance and revolt, see James C. Scott, *Domination and the Arts of Resistance: Hidden Transcripts* (New Haven: Yale University Press, 1990), pp. 70-107.

head danger that was threatening him: they talked when they served dinner, but kept quiet when they were being tortured. Thus there is the proverb [*proverbium*] which originates from the same arrogant attitude, that we have as many enemies as we have slaves. (*Epistle* 47.3-5)[27]

Seneca bemoans abuse of slaves by masters as unmanly behavior and a sign of fallen morality: the domestic enemy proverb is not old gnomic truth but recent bad coinage reflecting inferior mastery on the part of contemporary slave owners.[28] Yet the proverb persisted in Roman cultural understanding despite Seneca's condemnation. As late as the fifth century, an author like Macrobius had to repeat Seneca's reproof, with explicit reference to the proverb (and quoting Seneca nearly verbatim): "What do you suppose was the origin of that oft-quoted and arrogant proverb which says that in every slave we possess we have an enemy? They are not natural enemies, but we make them our enemies by the inordinate pride, insolence, and cruelty that we show toward them, when luxurious living makes us so prone to anger that to be crossed in anything leads to an outburst of violent rage. . . . That is why these slaves who may not speak before their master speak of him behind his back" (*Saturnalia* 1.11.13-15).[29]

Greco-Roman authors echo Seneca's concern without explicit mention of

27. Translation in Thomas Wiedemann, *Greek and Roman Slavery* (London: Routledge, 1981), p. 233. Ancient grammarians also commented on the proverb, and its moral polarity: *quot hostis tot servi* ("We have as many slaves as we have enemies," because war captives were enslaved); Sinnius Capito 17 (Gino Funaioli, ed., *Grammaticae romanae fragmenta collegit. Volumen prius,* Bibliotheca scriptorum Graecorum et Romanorum Teubneriana [Leipzig: Teubner, 1907], p. 463; Wallace M. Lindsay, ed., *Sexti Pompei Festi. De verborum significatu quae supersunt cum Pauli epitome,* Bibliotheca scriptorum Graecorum et Romanorum Teubneriana [1913; reprint, Hildesheim: Georg Olms, 1965], p. 314).

28. This belongs to Seneca's wider critique of proverbs generally, and his exhortation for moral progress beyond dependency on gnomic compilations learned in school exercises (*Epistle* 33.5-9); Abraham J. Malherbe, *Moral Exhortation: A Greco-Roman Sourcebook,* Library of Early Christianity (Philadelphia: Westminster, 1986), pp. 118-20.

29. Translation in Percival V. Davies, *Macrobius: "The Saturnalia"* (New York: Columbia University Press, 1969), p. 76. For the fifth-century date for Macrobius, see Alan Cameron, "The Date and Identity of Macrobius," *JRS* 56 (1966): 35-38. Cicero also employs the "enemy within" topos, in his speech against Catiline: "If my slaves feared me," Cicero declares, "as much as all your countrymen fear you, I would think that I should get out of my house" (*Catiline Orations* 1.17). The proverb endured well beyond antiquity; see the fourteenth-century Italian humanist Petrarch, *De remediis utriusque Fortunae* 1.33 (Conrad H. Rawski, *Petrarch's Remedies for Fortune Fair and Foul* [Bloomington: Indiana University Press, 1991], 1:101-3), and Iris Origo, "The Domestic Enemy: The Eastern Slaves in Tuscany in the Fourteenth and Fifteenth Centuries," *Speculum* 30 (1955): 321-66, on slaves in medieval Tuscany; Cissie Fairchilds, *Domestic Enemies: Servants and Their Masters in Old Regime France* (Baltimore: Johns Hopkins University Press, 1984), on servants in old-regime France.

the proverb. Juvenal, for example, assumes the criminality of slaves to be "obvious" and satirizes the difficulty of the aristocrat trying to keep secrets, precisely because of the hoard of oxymora (the insider-outsider) in his house:

> Do you suppose that a rich man has any secrets? . . . Let him shut the windows and close every chink with curtains; let him fasten the doors, remove the light, turn everyone out of the house, and permit no one to sleep near — yet the tavern-keeper close by will know before dawn what he was doing at the second rooster crow; he will hear also all the tales invented by the pastry-chef [*libarius*], by the chief cook [*archimagirus*] and the carvers [*carptores*]. For what defamation [*crimen*] will they hesitate to concoct against their master when a slander will avenge them for their whippings? . . . There are many reasons for right living; but chief of all is this, that you need pay no attention to the talk of your slaves. For the tongue is the worst part of a bad slave. (*Satires* 9.103-21)

This maxim recurs in Pseudo-Lucian: "For slaves know all that goes on [in the household], whether good or bad" (*The Ass* 5). As with Posidonius and Seneca, the call for humane treatment of slaves (analogous perhaps to animal rights activism today) was motivated by a concern to help the abuser — and especially the *dignitas* that arrogance degrades in the master.[30] This evidence does not prove some ancient social justice activist program (Stoic or otherwise) to abolish slavery as an institution or an ideology.

At no period in Roman history was concern for masters higher than during the civil wars that destroyed the late republic. Appian, in the imperial era, narrates episodes of domestic slave betrayal back then, even *before* torture was applied, stressing the shock of its regularity and abundance. But the "faithful slave," that rare hero, holds the narrative spotlight as a moral exemplum of slave loyalty (*fides servorum*) even to the death that protects the life of the master, a monumental spectacle testifying imitation.[31] Livy uses also this topos: "Men's fears were many and various; above all the rest stood out dread of their slaves. Everybody suspected that he had an enemy in his own household, whom it was not safe to trust" (3.16.3). In his panegyric on Trajan, Pliny the Younger praised

---

30. William S. Anderson, "Anger in Juvenal and Seneca," *University of California Publications in Classical Philology* 19, no. 3 (1964): 160-65.

31. Appian, *Civil War* 4.4.22-23; 4.4.26; 4.4.28-29; 4.6.39; 4.10.81; 4.12.94-95. On the "faithful slave" topos, see Holt Parker, "Loyal Slaves and Loyal Wives: The Crisis of the Outsider-within and Roman *Exemplum* Literature," in *Women and Slaves in Greco-Roman Culture*, pp. 152-73; Joseph Vogt, "The Faithful Slave," in his *Ancient Slavery and the Ideal of Man* (Cambridge: Harvard University Press, 1975), pp. 129-45.

the emperor as good in contrast to the bad Domitian: "For no longer are our slaves the emperor's particular friends. . . . You have freed us from the fear of an accuser within our own households" (*Panegyric* 42.3). Additional (and redundant) episodes appear in the handbook of illustrative examples, "Of the Fidelity of Slaves," in the *Memorable Doings and Sayings*, by Valerius Maximus (6.8.1-7). Classical historiography, then, set such moral exempla against a historical backdrop of the past to teach that the instability and disorder found in former periods confirm the clear and present danger of contemporary violence in the family to the state.[32] The greatest such danger to the family was slave autopsy, precisely a thesis of Greco-Roman historiography found in Christian apologies and martyrdoms.[33]

Vision and Authority: Slave Autopsy in Early Christian Apology

In his *Legatio,* addressed to the Roman emperors Marcus Aurelius and Commodus, Athenagoras defends Christian ritual practice as harmless by, among other things, appeal to the autopsy of household slaves owned by Christians.[34] To dismiss the charge that the Eucharist is cannibalism, Athenagoras argues that "Furthermore, we have slaves, some many, some few, and it is impossible to escape their observation. Yet not one of them has ever told such monstrous lies about us."[35] Few scholars have commented on this passage, except to note that it is "interesting" because other apologists like Tertullian (*Ad nationes* 1.7.15) and Justin Martyr (*2 Apology* 12.4) indicate the contrary (that household slaves have betrayed their Christian owners to Roman authorities at every opportunity). Reading the apologies as social description (even literal transcripts of actual trial hearings), many commentators attempt to solve the problem of patristic contradiction geographically, by conjecturing that the ex-

---

32. Maslakov, p. 451.

33. Influential on my analysis is the excellent work of spectacle and autopsy by Feldherr, p. 5 and passim.

34. On autopsy (eyewitness) as a method of validation in classical culture, see John Marincola, *Authority and Tradition in Ancient Historiography* (Cambridge: Cambridge University Press, 1997), pp. 63-86; John Buckler, "Plutarch and Autopsy," *ANRW* 2.33.6 (1992): 4788-4830; Llewelyn Morgan, "The Autopsy of C. Asinius Pollio," *JRS* 90 (2000): 51-69.

35. Athenagoras, *Legatio* 35.3 (SC 379.202 = William R. Schoedel, ed., *Athenagoras: "Legatio" and "De Resurrectione,"* Oxford Early Christian Texts [Oxford: Clarendon, 1972], pp. 82-83). For the charge of cannibalism and ritual murder (so-called Thyestean banquets), see Stephen Benko, *Pagan Rome and the Early Christians* (Bloomington: Indiana University Press, 1984), pp. 54-78; Wilken, p. 17.

perience of Justin in Rome and of Tertullian in Carthage was different from that of Athenagoras in Athens.[36]

What patristic scholars overlook is that these slave episodes are *apologetic* and show remarkable correspondence to stock moral exempla. Greco-Roman literary and rhetorical topoi (as opposed to actual events) were the sources of these Christian tales. Christian apologists copied "pagan" moral exempla of household slaves, exploiting their moral polarity, in order to neutralize the value of slave autopsy as a witness for the charge of religious crime in the family. Key to this interpretation is to read early Christian apology as *discourse* rather than *transcript*.[37]

In his apology, Athenagoras describes the vulnerability of the family to slave autopsy. He explains that it is "impossible to escape" the observation of "our domestic slaves" (*Legatio* 35.3). His argument depends on proverbs about slaves, gnomic wisdom ignored at one's peril.[38] No behavior at home escaped the slave's gaze. If unlawful atrocities did actually take place in the Christian household, slaves would have seen them and rushed by their very nature as domestic enemies to inform against the family. Yet because there was nothing unlawful for them to spy, slaves had nothing to tell, convincing "proof" (in Athenagoras's mind) why domestics have never informed against their Christian masters. Yet Athenagoras does not mention the alternative explanation for reticence to inform Roman authorities, the possibility of slave loyalty to the family even to the death. He presents a veritable argument from silence. Athenagoras's fallacy reveals the reversibility and moral polarity of the domestic enemy proverb. While authenticating slave autopsy, the proverb also seemingly discredits such witness as a lie.

Doing Athenagoras one better, Tertullian exploits this legal paradox in his

---

36. Leslie W. Barnard, trans., *St. Justin Martyr: The First and Second Apologies*, ACW 56 (New York: Paulist, 1997), p. 195 n. 64; Lawrence P. Jones, "A Case Study in 'Gnosticism': Religious Responses to Slavery in the Second Century CE" (Ph.D. diss., Columbia University, 1988), pp. 139-40.

37. My thesis builds upon Boyarin, p. 95, on martyrdom as a "discourse" rather than a "thing."

38. Athenagoras relies on proverbs in other places, such as *Legatio* 34.3 (Schoedel, pp. 81-83) on harlots. For Greco-Roman proverbs influencing the thinking of other early Christian authors, such as Irenaeus, see Robert M. Grant, *After the New Testament* (Philadelphia: Fortress, 1967), p. 168; for the rhetorical use of proverbs (and maxims) in classical culture, see George Kennedy, *The Art of Persuasion in Greece* (Princeton: Princeton University Press, 1963), pp. 5, 99, 101, 108, 270, 278, 289; Jan Fredrik Kindstrand, "The Greek Concept of Proverbs," *Eranos* 76 (1978): 71-85; Walter T. Wilson, *Love without Pretense: Romans 12.9-21 and Hellenistic-Jewish Wisdom Literature*, WUNT 46, 2nd ser. (Tübingen: Mohr Siebeck, 1991), pp. 9-39.

early apologetic work *Ad nationes.* Through diatribe with an imaginary pagan interlocutor, he explains:

> If they [sc., the Christians] themselves are not the betrayers, it follows that it must be strangers. Now how could strangers get intimate knowledge, since all mysteries [sc., mystery religions of Isis, Eleusis, Mithras, and the like] — even those lawful — keep away strangers, unless the unlawful mysteries are not so careful? Could it not be rather that strangers are capable of showering accusations to such a degree as to invent?
>
> But, you may say, the curiosity of household slaves [*domesticorum curiositas*] has obtained such knowledge though peepholes and crevices.
>
> So what of domestics betraying their secrets to you? Why shouldn't they, when they are all betrayers?
>
> Indeed they are, and isn't it more likely that such betrayal should occur when atrocities like these are in question, when a righteous indignation destroys the trust within the household? When it can no longer contain what horrifies the mind, and what the eye shutters at?
>
> If this were true, the wonder is that the one who, with such impatient justice, leapt forth to turn informant did not likewise eagerly desire to show proof, and that the one who heard, did not care to see for himself, since no doubt the reward is the same for the informant who offers proof and for the hearer who convinces himself of the credibility of the testimony.[39]

If Christian assemblies were as secret as reputed, Tertullian argues, then it is unlikely the atrocities alleged to them would be known publicly. Outsiders, then, are much more likely to know nothing about them, and so must have concocted them. To the apologist, the only other possible explanation for how outsiders got alleged "insider" information would have been the (always untrustworthy) rumor and gossip begun by household slaves owned by Christians.

---

39. Tertullian, *Ad nationes* 1.7.14-17 (CCSL, 1:19); E. Evans, "Tertullian Ad Nationes," *VC* 9 (1955): 38; André Schneider, "Notes critiques sur Tertullian, Ad Nationes I," *Museum Helveticum* 19 (1962): 181. Pliny and Tacitus served as literary sources for *Ad nationes,* informing Tertullian's mocking denunciation of torture to extract information; see A. R. Birley, "Persecutors and Martyrs in Tertullian's Africa," in *The Later Roman Empire Today: Papers Given in Honour of Professor John Mann,* ed. D. F. Clark, M. M. Roxan, and J. J. Wilkes (London: Institute of Archaeology, 1993), pp. 41-42. The passage recurs in Tertullian's *Apology* (on the literary relationship between *Ad nationes* and *Apology,* see Timothy D. Barnes, *Tertullian: A Historical and Literary Study,* 2nd ed. [Oxford: Clarendon, 1985], pp. 49, 104-6), but with domestics edited out and the diatribe redacted into a more focused apostrophe discrediting rumor generally, rather than slave autopsy per se (*Apology* 7.6-7 [CCSL, 1:99]). Perhaps, in the end, Tertullian did not find what he wrote previously in *Ad nationes* convincing. Interestingly for our study, Tertullian cites another classical proverb, about the fast flight of rumor's falsehood (*Apology* 7.8).

But, Tertullian asks rhetorically, what master ever took seriously the puerile tattle of slaves? The diction is striking: slaves are "impatient" *(impatientiae)* and "leap forth" *(prosilire)* to turn informant; they "eagerly desire" *(gestire)* to show proof. Such language points to the dramatic theme of the *servus currens,* a device of Greco-Roman comedy to provoke humor by stereotyping slaves as infantile adults whose puerile self-absorption and lack of control invariably confuse news they report.[40] In any case, the point of Tertullian's diatribe is clear — there is no proof that Christians actually commit the alleged atrocities. There is either outright concoction by pagan prosecutors or only the always suspect slave gossip leading to the rumor. Tertullian's diction is key. He indicates *curiositas* to be the source of rumor, an undignified vice of lower sorts in Greco-Roman cultural understanding.[41]

Tertullian follows a standard philosophical distinction. Plutarch, for example, condemned curiosity as a "disease" that "infects" with "slavish envy and desire," his target being the vulgar officiousness which earlier Greek comedy satirized, especially in Aristophanes. The moralist contrasts *good* interest in proper intellectual subjects, like natural science, and *bad* "curiosity" *(curiositas;* πολυπραγμοσύνη; better translated "officiousness" or "meddling") into things deemed attractive merely because they are hidden *(Moralia* 515B-523B, *De curiositate).* The theme recurs in *The Golden Ass,* by Apuleius, an older contemporary of Tertullian and a fellow African, with the asinine downfall of Lucius because of his *curiositas* for the occult. In this Greco-Roman context, the *curiosi* are spies, gossipmongers, and skulking informers, the Peeping Toms of the ancient world — and who listens to Peeping Toms?[42] Tertullian stereotypes slaves by the *curiositas* vice to encourage prejudice against domestics and blame for the persecution of Christians, testifying to his deep implication in ancient slaveholder ideology.

In a later work, the *Apology,* Tertullian changes his mind (but not his slave ideology) and accepts betrayal as (rather than blaming betrayal on) the unavoidable consequence of living Christian lives: "We are daily besieged, we are

---

40. For *servus currens,* see J. Albert Harrill, "The Dramatic Function of the Running Slave Rhoda: A Piece of Greco-Roman Comedy (Acts 12.13-16)," *NTS* 48 (2000): 151-53, and literature there cited.

41. P. G. Walsh, "The Rights and Wrongs of Curiosity (Plutarch to Augustine)," *GR* 35 (1988): 73-85; J. L. Penwill, "Slavish Pleasures and Profitless Curiosity: Fall and Redemption in Apuleius' *Metamorphoses,*" *Ramus* 4 (1975): 49-82; Joseph G. DeFilippo, "*Curiositas* and the Platonism of Apuleius' *Golden Ass,*" *AJP* 111 (1990): 471-92.

42. Walsh, pp. 74-81; William Fitzgerald, *Slavery and the Roman Literary Imagination,* Roman Literature and Its Context (Cambridge: Cambridge University Press, 2000), pp. 104-5; Carlin A. Barton, *The Sorrows of the Ancient Romans: The Gladiator and the Monster* (Princeton: Princeton University Press, 1993), pp. 88-89.

daily betrayed; oftentimes in the midst of our meetings and gatherings, we are surprised by assault."[43] Tertullian finds solace in the Greco-Roman proverb (from a play of Terence) that truth brings forth hate.[44] Tertullian explains: "Truth and hatred came into existence together. As soon as the former appeared, the latter began its enmity. It has as many foes as there are outsiders, particularly among Jews because of their jealousy, among soldiers because of their blackmailing, and even among the very slaves of our own household because of their corrupt nature."[45]

Letting the Greco-Roman slave proverb guide his theology, Tertullian then uses it as a hermeneutical key to read Scripture. He claims that "our domestics" have caused persecution "through whose agency the betrayal has been appointed,"[46] alluding to a gnomic saying of Jesus on the conditions of discipleship: "And one's foes will be members of one's own household" (Matt. 10:36).[47] Tertullian further laments over "that desperation and excessive malice with which the most abandoned slaves do not even hesitate to slay their masters. For it is written in my Gospel that 'Satan entered into Judas.'"[48] Tertullian uses the Judas story of betrayal as the hermeneutical key to neutralize the shock of household slave betrayal.

This finding helps solve our original problem, the patristic contradiction of Athenagoras (slaves never betray their Christian owners) and Tertullian and Justin (slaves routinely betray, even more so under torture). Justin in particular writes that the authorities "dragged to torture also our domestic slaves [οἰκέτας τῶν ἡμετέρων], either children or women, and by dreadful torments forced them to admit those incredible actions."[49] The answer lies in the moral polarity

43. Tertullian, *Apology* 7.4 (CCSL, 1:99).

44. Terence, *Andria* 68. The proverb is not identified as such by Tertullian.

45. Tertullian, *Apology* 7.3 (CCSL, 1:98-99). My translation disagrees with that in the FC — "because of human nature" (Rudolph Arbesmann, Emily Joseph Daly, and Edward A. Quain, trans., *Tertullian: Apologetical Works; and Minucius Felix: Octavius*, FC 10 [Washington, D.C.: Catholic University of America Press, 1950], p. 26) — which has the passage express the later, Augustinian doctine of "original sin." Tertullian's point is that betrayal is a vice of slaves by their very nature as domestic enemies (*"Tot hostes eius quot extrani . . . ex natura etiam ipsi domestici nostri"*), not a vice of "all" humans generally (including Tertullian).

46. Tertullian, *Scorpiace* 10.11 (CCSL, 2:1089).

47. Cf. Édouard Massaux, *The Influence of the Gospel of Saint Matthew on Christian Literature before Saint Irenaeus*, vol. 2, *The Later Christian Writings*, New Gospel Studies 5.2 (Macon, Ga.: Mercer University Press, 1992), pp. 48-49, although commenting on *Martyrdom of Polycarp* 6.1, not Tertullian. For Matt. 10:36, its relation to the Q Gospel, and its allusion to Mic. 7:6, see Christoph Heil, "Die Rezeption von Micha 7,6 LXX in Q und Lukas," *ZNW* 88 (1997): 218-22.

48. Tertullian, *Ad Marcionem* 5.6.7 (CCSL, 1:680).

49. Justin, *2 Apology* 12.4 (Edgar J. Goodspeed, ed., *Die ältesten Apologeten: Texte mit kurzen Einleitungen* [Göttingen: Vandenhoeck & Ruprecht, 1914], p. 87).

of the domestic enemy proverb cutting both ways. Athenagoras can claim that the *lack* of slave betrayal proves Christian innocence because "obviously" slaves would betray their masters at the slightest chance. Yet, with identical appeal to a hermeneutics of "plain sense," Justin and Tertullian can assert the same Christian innocence based on the *abundance* of slave betrayal. Rather than evidence of different geographic or historical circumstances, the patristic arguments are contradictory because of the rhetorical moral polarity inherent in ideological discourse that the slave is domestic enemy. The idealized test of this moral polarity was the spectacle of martyrdom.

Torture and Truth: The Slave Body as Spectacle in Early Christian Martyrdom

Early Christian martyrdom was quite literally spectacle *(spectaculum)*. As such, it participated in the wider cultural use of *spectaculum* in rhetorical and historiographic traditions. Spectacles were of two different kinds in Roman imperial society. One was superficial entertainment — the shows *(ludens)* of the circus and the arena — a hollow image pointing away from the location of real power. The visual corollary was a higher form of spectacle, the ocular display in national monument fashion of the "realities" of power *(imperium)* for public awe and emulation.[50]

In contrast to what Tertullian and Justin say, few martyrdom accounts show slaves turning in their masters. But slaves in martyrdoms nonetheless display both kinds of spectacle by virtue of the moral polarity that the idea of *slave* manifests. When the slave is the instigator of persecution by betraying the master under torture, the spectacle is reduced to an image empty of meaning and truth, opposed to the "realities" of divine power. The slave standing by the master and testifying innocence to the death is a monument of faith, a spectacle of real divine *imperium* for the other characters and the reader to emulate. Martyrdoms contain spectacles in this latter, meaningful sense, the goal being transcendence, of literature itself as secondhand reflection of reality, and very autopsy (or *deiknymena*) of God for the reader (or auditor).[51]

For example, the *Martyrdom of Polycarp* has the bishop flee into the countryside, changing farm hideouts to avoid capture, only to have one of his own

50. Feldherr, pp. 6-7, 13-14; David Potter, "Martyrdom as Spectacle," in *Theater and Society in the Classical World,* ed. Ruth Scodel (Ann Arbor: University of Michigan Press, 1993), pp. 53-88.

51. I apply to martyrdom the discussion in Feldherr, pp. 8, 100, and passim.

domestics under torture betray his whereabouts. By a Gospel theme seen previously in Tertullian, the author tries to neutralize the reader's shock with the hermeneutical key of the domestic enemy proverb. The narrator explains: "When they did not find him, they arrested two young slaves, and one of them confessed under torture. For it was indeed impossible for [Polycarp] to remain hidden, since those who betrayed him were of his own house, and the police captain who had been allotted the very name, being called Herod, hastening to bring him to the arena that he might fulfill his appointed lot to become a partaker of Christ, while they who betrayed him should undergo the same punishment as Judas."[52] The comparison with Judas may appear exaggeration, but it becomes intelligible in light of the absolute loyalty owed the master in Roman slaveholder ideology.[53] A central tenet of Roman mastery was the need to achieve, in a series of specific, concrete events, not just slave obedience to individual commands but also slave acceptance of the master's viewpoint so fully as to anticipate the master's wishes and to become an extension of the master's will. A personalized form of power, mastery was the extreme in a continuum of domination in the hierarchies of Roman personal relations, the distinctly Roman virtue known as *auctoritas*.[54]

The torture of Polycarp's domestic slave to obtain truth requires further contextualization. In their juridical examinations, the Greeks and Romans "marked the body of the slave as a privileged site for the production of truth

---

52. *Martyrdom of Polycarp* 6.1-2 (Herbert Musurillo, trans., *The Acts of the Christian Martyrs*, Oxford Early Christian Texts [Oxford: Clarendon, 1972], pp. 6-7); parallel in Eusebius, *Historia ecclesiastica* 4.15.11-12; hereafter *HE*. Hans von Campenhausen ("Bearbeitungen und Interpolationen des Polykarpmartyriums," in his *Aus der Frühzeit des Christentums: Studien zur Kirchengeschichte des ersten und zweiten Jahrhunderts* [Tübingen: Mohr Siebeck, 1963], pp. 261-63) argues the section about a magistrate named Herod and the allusion to Judas (*Mart. Pol.* 6.2–7.1a) to be an interpolation (in part, simply because Eusebius omits it), a hypothesis not persuasive to recent commentary; Gerd Buschmann, *Das Martyrium des Polycarp*, Kommentar zu den apostolischen Vätern (Göttingen: Vandenhoeck & Ruprecht, 1998), pp. 140-60; Buschmann, *Martyrium Polycarpi — Eine formkritische Studie: Ein Beitrag zur Frage nach der Entstehung der Gattung Märtyrerakte*, BZNW 70 (Berlin: Walter de Gruyter, 1994), pp. 48-53, 178-82; Boudewijn Dehandschutter, "The Martyrium Polycarpi: A Century of Research," *ANRW* 2.27.1 (1993): 493-97; Dehandschutter, *Martyrium Polycarpi: Een literair-kritische studie*, BETL 52 (Leuven: Leuven University Press, 1979), pp. 140-55, 225; Leslie W. Barnard, "In Defence of Pseudo-Pionius' Account of Saint Polycarp's Martyrdom," in *Kyriakon: Festschrift Johannes Quasten*, 2 vols. (Münster: Aschendorff, 1970), 1:193-97.

53. Judith M. Lieu, *Image and Reality: The Jews in the World of the Christians in the Second Century* (Edinburgh: T. & T. Clark, 1996), p. 88.

54. Kathleen McCarthy, *Slaves, Masters, and the Art of Authority in Plautine Comedy* (Princeton: Princeton University Press, 2000), pp. 22-23.

through torture."[55] The term in Greek for this process is *basanos* (touchstone), the flinty slate used to test the purity of silver or gold by the streak that it left on the stone when scraped against the metal. In the logic of ancient slaveholding ideology, "the tortured slave has no choice but to 'break' into a truth that she or he contains but does not possess. Defined by torture, the slave cannot witness freely: the slave must give witness when coerced."[56] This touchstone theory of torture and truth marked the slave body as a site of meaning to be excavated by flogging, burning, and racking.[57] The typical whip used for such purposes had metal pieces attached to its thongs and was meant to make deep, cutting wounds: the victim was either hung up, with feet weighted down, or stood with arms tied to a beam across the shoulders. Burning called for boiling pitch, hot metal plates, and flaming torches applied directly to the skin. Racking by the "little horse" *(eculeus)* or "lyre-strings" *(fidiculae)* meant tearing the body limb from limb. Slave owners weary of the effort could hire the services of professional torturers. An advertisement of one torture-and-execution business survives in an inscription from Puteoli, offering flogging and crucifixion as standard options for a flat, low rate.[58]

Questioning slaves by torture was both routine and required under criminal law of Rome (and Athens).[59] Because the slave was considered naturally criminous, the slave's truth could be obtained only through her or his body. Although the Roman jurists debated among themselves the merits of slave testimony given under torture — wouldn't the victim admit to anything to stop the pain? (Quintilian 5.4.1; *Digest* 48.18.1.23-24) — torture nonetheless was considered the best means to question a slave, since in ancient slaveholder ideology only the brutal violence of torture could force a slave to overcome servile inclination to lie.[60] The

---

55. Virginia Burrus, "Torture and Travail: Producing the Christian Martyr," in *A Feminist Companion to Early Gnostic and Patristic Thought,* ed. Amy-Jill Levine (Sheffield: Sheffield Academic Press, forthcoming), p. 2 (in typescript).

56. Burrus, p. 2.

57. Burrus, "Torture and Travail"; Kate Cooper, "The Voice of the Victim: Gender, Representation and Early Christian Martyrdom," *BJRL* 80, no. 3 (1998): 152-53; Page duBois, *Torture and Truth* (London: Routledge, 1991), pp. 35-38, 47-68.

58. Bradley, *Slavery and Society,* pp. 166-67.

59. Michael Gagarin, "The Torture of Slaves in Athenian Law," *CP* 91 (1996): 1-18; duBois, pp. 63-74; P. A. Brunt, "Evidence Given under Torture in the Principate," *Zeitschrift der Savigny-Stiftung für Rechtsgeschichte (romanistische Abteilung)* 97 (1980): 256-65; Olivia Robinson, "Slaves and the Criminal Law," *Zeitschrift der Savigny-Stiftung für Rechtsgeschichte (romanistische Abteilung)* 98 (1981): 213-54; Peter Garnsey, *Social Status and Legal Privilege in the Roman Empire* (Oxford: Clarendon, 1970), pp. 213-16.

60. Garnsey, *Social Status,* p. 215; duBois, pp. 36, 66-68; Alan Watson, "Roman Slave Law and Romanist Ideology," *Phoenix* 37 (1983): 58-59.

Martyrdom of Polycarp confirms the truth excavated from the slave body, for the tortured domestic correctly led the police chief to Polycarp's hideout.

The *Letter of the Churches of Vienne and Lyon* provides another test case for the moral polarity of slave character, and one of the most revealing.[61] The account, written by Christians who managed to escape the massacre in the amphitheater at Lyons (177 C.E.), possibly by Irenaeus himself,[62] appears in a fragment quoted by Eusebius (*Historia ecclesiastica* 5.1-3). The *Letter* reports:

> The arrests continued, and every day the finest [οἱ ἄξιοι] were taken to fill up the number of the martyrs. The result was that they collected all the most zealous Christians of the two communities and those on whom everything depended. Arrested too were some of our pagan slaves [ἐθνικοί τινες οἰκέται]. For the governor had publicly ordered a full-scale investigation of all Christians. Thus the slaves, ensnared by Satan and terrified of the tortures they saw the faithful suffering, at the soldiers' instigation falsely accused the Christians of Thyestean feasts and Oedipean intercourse, and many other things that it should be sinful for us even to think of or even speak about or even to believe that such things could ever happen among people.[63]

The spectacle terrorizes the pagan slaves into betrayal without torture for their "testimony." The author contrasts the pagan slaves' fake autopsy (vacuous spectacle) with the authentic autopsy of fidelity in the martyrs (meaningful spectacle). Because the touchstone of torture was never applied to the servile betrayers, their testimony is blind before the realities of God's power.[64]

61. For literary and historical background, see Frederick W. Weidmann, "The Martyrs of Lyons," in *Religions of Late Antiquity in Practice,* ed. Richard Valantasis, Princeton Readings in Religions (Princeton: Princeton University Press, 2000), pp. 398-412; see also the older but disappointing analysis in William H. C. Frend, *Martyrdom and Persecution in the Early Church: A Study of the Conflict from the Maccabees to Donatus* (Oxford: Basil Blackwell, 1965), pp. 1-21; Jean Colin, *L'Empire des Antonins et les martyrs gaulois de 177,* Antiquitas, ser. 1; Abhandlungen zur alten Geschichte 10 (Bonn: Rudolf Habelt, 1964).

62. Pierre Nautin, *Lettres et Écrivains chrétiens des IIᵉ et IIIᵉ siècles,* Patristica 2 (Paris: Cerf, 1961), pp. 54-61; for source and redaction issues, see Winrich A. Löhr, "Der Brief der Gemeinden von Lyon und Vienne (Eusebius, Ecclesiastical History V, 1-2 (4))," in *Oecumenica et Patristica: Festschrift für Wilhelm Schneemelcher zum 75. Geburtstag,* ed. Damaskinos Papandreou, Wolfgang A. Bienert, and Knut Schäferdiek (Stuttgart: W. Kohlhammer 1989), pp. 135-49.

63. *Letter of the Churches of Vienne and Lyon* 1.13-14 (Musurillo, pp. 64-67 = Eusebius, *HE* 5.1.13.14).

64. Cf. Irenaeus fr. 13 (ANF, 1:570), and the testimony of the slave Christian *ministrae* in Pliny, *Epistle* 10.96 (although a pagan author admittedly unsympathetic to Christian discourse). The imperial cult eventually restricted the term *minister* to slaves, *magister* to freedmen (Bakker, p. 204), perhaps a useful distinction for contextualizing what Pliny understands when he writes

No monument of faith stood taller than the slave martyr Blandina.[65]

> All the wrath of the mob, the prefect, and the soldiers fell with overwhelming force on . . . Blandina, through whom Christ proved that the things people regard cheap, ugly, and contemptuous are deemed worthy of glory before God, by reason of her love for him which was not merely vaunted in appearance [μὴ ἐν εἴδει καυχωμένην] but demonstrated in achievement [ἐν δυνάμει δεικνυμένην]. All of us were in terror; and Blandina's fleshly mistress [τῆς σαρκίνης δεσποίνης], who was herself among the martyrs in the conflict [ἀγωνίστρια], was in agony lest because of her bodily weakness she [sc., Blandina] would not be able to make a bold confession of her faith.[66]

Blandina's female master agonized over not the pain of torture but the fear of her slave's lack of will to profess Christ. But, in sharp contrast to the pagan servile betrayers, Blandina supplies in the touchstone of torture unexpected proof of genuineness. In a physiognomic reversal, the *eidos* of Blandina's slave body — cheap, ugly, and contemptuous — turns out, in the end, to be the most beautiful and prized spectacle of divine power *(dynamis)*, the real "autopsy" and direct sighting of God.[67]

This irony extends to her very name (from the Latin: *blandus*, "cozening," "insidious," "insincere"). Torture proves Blandina to be the moral polarity of her name, which better labels the cozening betrayer slaves *not* being tortured. Her name is an etymological pun heightening the dramatic surprise. This use

---

that these slave women were Christian *ministrae* (we should not assume it to be an emic term actually used by Christian congregations in Bithynia).

65. Because of its adherence to flat reading, patristic scholarship on Blandina and other slave martyrs is a major disappointment. Garth Thomas, "La condition sociale de l'église de Lyon en 177," in *Les martyrs de Lyon (1977): Lyon 20-23 Septembre 1977*, ed. Jean Rougé and Robert Turcan, Colloques internationaux du Centre National de la Recherche Scientifique 575 (Paris: Centre National de la Recherche Scientifique, 1978), pp. 93-106, esp. pp. 99-101; William H. C. Frend, "Blandina and Perpetua: Two Early Christian Martyrs," in *Les martyrs de Lyon* (1977), pp. 167-77; Marie-Louise Guillaumin, "'Une Jeune Fille qui s'appelait Blandine': Aux origines d'une tradition hagiographique," in *Epektasis: Mélanges patristiques offerts au Cardinal Jean Daniélou*, ed. Jacques Fontaine and Charles Kannengiesser (Paris: Beauchesne, 1972), pp. 93-98.

66. *Letter of the Churches of Vienne and Lyon* 1.17-18 (Musurillo, pp. 66-67 = Eusebius, *HE* 5.1.17-18). The phrase ἐν δυνάμει δεικνυμένην might be an allusion to the *deiknymena* in Greco-Roman mystery religions; cf. Marvin W. Meyer, *The Ancient Mysteries: A Sourcebook of Sacred Texts* (1987; reprint, Philadelphia: University of Pennsylvania Press, 1999), p. 11; Lane Fox, pp. 143, 160.

67. Brent D. Shaw, "Body/Power/Identity: Passions of the Martyrs," *JECS* 4 (1996): 308-9; Perkins, *The Suffering Self*, pp. 113-14.

of names, to (mis)lead the reader to associate qualities of character in a certain episode only to develop the contrary as the story progresses, was a known literary technique of suspense and surprise in Greco-Roman novels. A cultural context for this literary phenomenon is ancient philosophic speculation on the origin and nature of language — whether etymology was meaning, and whether *name* and *essence* bear a necessary and internal relation to each other.[68] Blandina is not bland; Biblis is not a fragile strip of βιβλίς (Cyperus Papyrus); Pothinus has a pressing desire (ποθεινός) for martyrdom, as does Martyrus; Sanctus is blessed *(sanctus)*, for he says to his tormentors nothing but the declaration of his faith; or (in another martyrdom) Perpetua does not enjoy a long-lasting life; the slave Felicitas does not have good fortune, and so on. From this insight, the system of name giving in Christian martyrdoms suggests a fiction familiar from Greco-Roman novels.

The *Letter* continues:

> Yet Blandina was filled with such power that even those who were taking turns to torture [βασανίζοντας] her in every way from dawn to dusk were weary and exhausted. They themselves admitted that they were beaten, that there was nothing further they could do to her, and they were surprised [θαυμάζειν] that she was still breathing, for her entire body was broken and torn. They testified [μαρτυρεῖν] that even one kind [εἶδος] of torture was enough to release her soul, let alone the many they applied with such intensity. Instead this blessed woman like a noble [γενναῖος] athlete got renewed strength with her confession of faith: her admission, "I am a Christian; we do nothing to be ashamed of," brought her refreshment, rest, and insensibility to her present pain.[69]

The graphic blood and gore heighten the irony of a "faithful slave" by contrasting Blandina's reaction to torture with that of the pagan slaves to nontorture.

---

68. Blanche Brotherton, "The Introduction of Characters by Name in the *Metamorphoses* of Apuleius," *CP* 29 (1934): 36-52; Alexander Scobie, *Aspects of the Ancient Romance and Its Heritage: Essays on Apuleius, Petronius, and the Greek Romances,* Beiträge zur klassischen Philologie 30 (Meisenheim am Glan: Anton Hain, 1969), pp. 58-64; Gerald N. Sandy, "Serviles Voluptates in Apuleius' Metamorphoses," *Phoenix* 28 (1974): 243; R. De Smet, "The Erotic Adventure of Lucius and Photis in Apuleius' *Metamorphoses*," *Latomus* 46 (1987): 618-19; Arthur J. Droge, *Homer or Moses? Early Christian Interpretations of the History of Culture,* HUT 26 (Tübingen: Mohr Siebeck, 1989), pp. 104-8. Cf. Paul's ironic pun of *Onesimus* as the name of the slave (Philem. 11).

69. *Letter of the Churches of Vienne and Lyon* 1.18-19 (Musurillo, pp. 66-67 = Eusebius, *HE* 5.1.18-19).

The details make the scene dramatic, clear, and immediate, enabling the very experience of reading (or auditing) itself to be an act of autopsy.

The reader witnesses further, as Blandina is led out with others

> into the amphitheater to be exposed to the beasts and to give a public specta-
> cle [θέαμα] of the pagans' inhumanity, for a day of gladiatorial games was ex-
> pressly arranged for our sake. . . . Though their spirits endured much
> throughout the long contest, they were in the end sacrificed, after being
> made all the day long a spectacle to the world [θέαμα γενόμενοι τῷ κόσμῳ] to
> replace the varied entertainment of the gladiatorial combat. Blandina was
> hung on a post and exposed as bait for the wild animals that were let loose on
> her. She seemed to hang there in the form of a cross, and by her fervent
> prayer she aroused intense enthusiasm in those who were undergoing their
> ordeal, for in their torment with their physical eyes [διὰ τοῦ βλέπεσθαι] they
> saw in the person of their sister him who was crucified for them, that he
> might convince all who believe in him that all who suffer for Christ's glory
> [δόξης] will have eternal fellowship in the living God.[70]

The reader's autoptic gaze into the text sees what the onlookers in the narrative see. Hung on a cross, Blandina is a spectacle of the crucified Jesus Christ:

> But none of the animals had touched her, and so she was taken down from
> the post and brought back to the jail to be kept for another ordeal: and thus
> for her victory in further contests [ἀγῶνα] she would make irreversible the
> condemnation of the crooked serpent [Isa. 27:1], and tiny [μικρά], weak
> [ἀσθενής], and insignificant [εὐκαταφρόνητος] as she was, she would give
> inspiration to her brothers, for she had put on Christ [cf. Rom. 13:14; Gal.
> 3:27], that mighty [μέγαν] and invincible athlete, and had overcome the ad-
> versary in many contests, and through her conflict had won the crown of im-
> mortality [cf. 1 Pet. 5:4; James 1:12].[71]

Blandina's martyrdom transfigures her dishonored slave body into a religious monument of honor (τιμή) and nobility (εὐγένεια), which the freeborn
martyrs emulate, including her "fleshly" master. Such fidelity and endurance
in an unlikely figure resembles the moral exemplum of the "faithful slave" in
Greco-Roman literature, such as that of the freedwomen Epicharis, who

---

70. *Letter of the Churches of Vienne and Lyon* 1.37-42 (Musurillo, pp. 72-75 = Eusebius, *HE* 5.1.37-42).

71. *Letter of the Churches of Vienne and Lyon* 1.42 (Musurillo, pp. 74-75 = Eusebius, *HE* 5.1.42).

alone did not betray members of the Pisonian conspiracy (Tacitus, *Annals* 15.57).[72]

Conclusion

Recent scholarship has drawn important attention to martyrdom as a discourse that questioned ancient ideologies of the family. Martyrdom, writes Judith Perkins, "projects a subversion of the contemporary hierarchy through the power acquired by suffering."[73] Focusing on gender, scholars point to women martyrs who rejected their traditional place in the family. As significant as this recovery of Christianity's challenge to Greco-Roman hierarchies is, at its extreme this approach suggests that the "blood of the martyrs" overthrew the entire oppressive ideology of the ancient family and state.[74] The slave Blandina, for example, does display the reversal of normal domestic hierarchies in dramatic and forceful spectacle. Yet her loyalty to her mistress also reinforces ancient ideologies of slavery, in particular Roman *auctoritas* that requires the slave not simply to obey individual commands, but also to accept the master's point of view so fully as to be an extension of the master's will. The system of name giving suggests that Blandina is a fiction serving the author's faith and not a historical person. Even if historical, the effort by scholars to recover nonhegemonic voices, though laudable, has not sufficiently emphasized martyrology as the official, and so not the whole, story — the "public transcript" as opposed to the disguised "hidden transcript" of household subordinates that the practice of domination also created.[75]

Stories about slaves are admittedly not prevalent in martyrdoms but tend

---

72. Stuart G. Hall, "Women among the Early Martyrs," in *Martyrs and Martyrologies*, ed. Diana Wood (London: Blackwell, 1993), pp. 14-15; Jan Willem van Henten, "The Martyrs as Heroes of the Christian People: Some Remarks on the Continuity between Jewish and Christian Martyrology, with Pagan Analogies," in *Martyrium in Multidisciplinary Perspective: Memorial Louis Reekmans*, ed. M. Lambergts and P. van Deun (Leuven: Leuven University Press, 1995), p. 317, pointing to a parallel with the ignoble-becomes-noble theme of the Maccabean martyrs (2 Macc. 7:20-41). See also Carlin A. Barton, "Savage Miracles: The Redemption of Lost Honor in Roman Society and the Sacrament of the Gladiator and the Martyr," *Representations* 45 (1994): 54.

73. Perkins, *The Suffering Self*, p. 113. See also Cooper, p. 149.

74. Cées Mertens, "Les premiers martyrs et leurs rêves: Cohésion de l'histoire et des rêves dans quelques 'passions' latines de l'Afrique du nord," *RHE* 81 (1986): 15; rightly criticized by Judith B. Perkins, "The *Passion of Perpetua*: A Narrative of Empowerment," *Latomus* 53 (1994): 846 n. 29.

75. See Scott, pp. 1-16 and passim.

to favor the faithful slave topos. In contrast to what Tertullian and Justin say, the few martyr accounts involving slaves rarely show domestic betrayal, except by pagans whom Christians owned. Although it may not be surprising to discover early Christian apologies defending traditional Greco-Roman family values, to find these themes even in the few instances of slave martyrs is unexpected in light of the recent scholarly attention on the hierarchical reversal implied in martyrdom as subversive discourse. Early Christian martyrdom may indeed contest the prevailing ideology of the family in the case of gender as scholars like Perkins and others have shown, but not entirely in the case of slavery. Elements of that ideology do appear, especially the moral polarity of the slave as domestic enemy and faithful companion. In the case of slavery, therefore, early Christian discourse participated in the very ideology of the Greco-Roman family that it was trying to subvert.[76]

76. Earlier portions of this essay were read at the general meeting of the North American Patristics Society and a DePaul faculty colloquium. I wish to thank Virginia Burrus and David Brakke for their helpful criticisms and suggestions, but they are in no way responsible for whatever errors and shortcomings may remain. A 2000 summer research grant from DePaul University's College of Liberal Arts and Sciences made the completion of this article possible.

Female Slaves, *Porneia,*
and the Limits of Obedience

Carolyn Osiek

From a modern perspective, we would say the categories "women" and "slaves" are partially overlapping. Some women were slaves, but not all were; some slaves were women, but not all slaves were. But in fact, in ancient categories it is the expression "women slaves," which seems to us more inclusive, that is a conceptual contradiction. While women and slaves of the ancient Greco-Roman world shared much in common within the male perspective of the patriarchal household, they did not belong to overlapping categories. Both were in Aristotle's categories fit by nature to be ruled, not to rule. Both shared intimately in the life of the household, including its religion, economy, child production and nurturing, and burial. Wives and slaves entered the household from outside, with the possible exception of the *verna,* or house-born slave.

With the Roman marriage custom *sine manu* largely in place by the first century, the wife remained legally an outsider to her husband's family, yet shared in most of its benefits and liabilities. The slave brought into the family ceased to have any other identity outside the family of ownership, yet remained a marginal member. Both women and slaves in many ways remained in a state of perpetual liminality. Ancient literature regularly ascribes to one the vices of the other. But if females who were slaves had to be fitted either into the category of women or of slaves, the ancient thinker would have considered them slaves, not women. As females who were slaves, they were doubly fit by nature to be ruled and dominated.

It has become customary and helpful to distinguish between sex and gender, sex being biological differentiation between the male and female of a species, while gender is the cultural construction of that biological difference. Gender, what it is to be man or woman, masculine or feminine, as distinct from

---

Earlier versions of this paper were read at the Context Group, Portland, Oreg., in March 2000 and at the Societas Novi Testamenti Studiorum, Tel Aviv, August 2000. I am grateful to those who gave me helpful feedback at those sessions.

male or female, differs cross-culturally. In most slave systems, while slaves undeniably have a sex, they do not have gender.[1] Thus a male slave is not a man (ἀνήρ, *vir*), and therefore cannot have masculine traits ascribed to him nor socially constructed expectations of masculine behavior placed on him, nor can he claim any of the status inherent in the cultural construct of masculinity.[2] Consequently a female slave is not a woman (γυνή, *mulier*), and thus cannot have feminine traits ascribed to her nor the social expectations of a woman in her culture placed on her, nor can she claim any status privileges inherent in the cultural construct of womanhood. Therefore the safeguards built into the culture to protect women are not to be applied to female slaves, which is an added degree of alienation.

In Aristotle's *Politics* 1.1, gender, class, and even race are closely intertwined. Aristotle places free women and women who are slaves in entirely different categories. Female slaves are at the bottom of the dominated heap. They are not to be dominated as members of their sex, females who are by nature to be ruled by males with constitutional or royal rule as the intellect rules the appetites, but as slaves who are to be ruled despotically as the soul rules the body. All human beings who are as different as body from soul, as animal from person, these are by nature slaves (1254b11-13). But the female slave is doubly so and doubly images body that is to be conquered and dominated, both as female in sex and as slave in class.

In an honor/shame society such as that of the ancient Mediterranean, a woman's honor in the public male world consists in the sexual propriety or chastity appropriate to her state, even though many nuances must be made from culture to culture and from dominant male perspectives to insider female perspectives. But slaves by definition are totally lacking in honor, either ascribed or attributed, in their interactions with free persons. If born as slaves, they are born without honor; if enslaved later, they move into a classification in which honor no longer exists. Nothing they do, no matter how honorably they may conduct themselves, can acquire honor. They are simply outside the honor system. Thus slaves are not expected to behave honorably; hence the familiar topos of the lazy, dishonest, unreliable slave, and the equally well known topos

---

1. Elizabeth Spelman, *Inessential Woman: Problems of Exclusion in Feminist Thought* (Boston: Beacon Press, 1988), pp. 52-55; William G. Thalman, "Female Slaves in the *Odyssey*," in *Women and Slaves in Greco-Roman Culture: Differential Equations,* ed. Sandra R. Joshel and Sheila Murnaghan (London and New York: Routledge, 1998), p. 25.

2. Marilyn B. Skinner, introduction to *Roman Sexualities,* ed. Judith P. Hallett and Marilyn B. Skinner (Princeton: Princeton University Press, 1997), p. 14; quoted in Jennifer A. Glancy, "Three-Fifths of a Man: Slavery and Masculinity in Galatians" (paper, SBL Annual Meeting, 1999), p. 2.

of the exception that proves the rule, the slave who unexpectedly exhibits behavior that would be called honorable in a free person — to the amazement of the slaveholding class. Examples of the latter include Seneca's admission that a slave could rather be beaten with whips and killed than be struck by fist on the face and insulted verbally (*De constantia* 5.1), and Octavia's slave Pythias, who endured torture and insulted her torturer rather than slander her mistress (Dio Cassius 62.13.4).

To the female slave, therefore, honor, whether of character or of behavior, cannot be ascribed. The female slave can lay no claim to chastity or shame, which have no meaning. In the official view she cannot have sensitivity toward chastity. Her honor cannot be violated because it does not exist, though the property rights of her owner over her can be infringed upon for sexual violation, injury, or death by another who does not hold such property rights. No legal recognition is granted to the sexual privacy of the female slave. In recognition of the anomaly of this situation, the Hellenistic novels and Roman comedies are filled with unfortunate heroines unjustly enslaved, caught between slavery and prostitution, struggling to maintain their honor, vindicated in the end by having their citizen status restored.[3] The contrast between the true slave without honor and the freeborn heroine thrown into her lot was the stuff of romance.

A familiar story told to explain the origins of a festal day illustrates well the female slave's lack of honor and yet, ironically, her ability to act honorably. Plutarch (*Camillus* 33; *Romulus* 29) relates that after the Gauls sacked Rome in 390 B.C.E., some of Rome's Latin allies took advantage of the city's temporary weakness to demand its freeborn virgins and widows to be taken as wives. While the city fathers were in a quandary, a female slave, alternately called Tutula or Philottis, suggested dressing female slaves as freeborn women and sending them out to the Latins. This was done, and during the night from the Latin camp she gave the signal to the Romans, a burning torch from the top of a fig tree, when it was the opportune time to attack. As a consequence, relates Plutarch, July 7 is the *ancillae feriae,* the festival of female slaves, at which time they run out of the city in mock battle calling out Roman men's names, to picnic under a fig tree. The legend only works on the premise that female slaves dressed differently from freeborn women (not the case later on) but otherwise looked

---

3. T. Crisafulli, "Representations of the Feminine: The Prostitute in Roman Comedy," in *Ancient History in a Modern University,* ed. T. W. Hillard et al. (Sydney: Macquarie University, Ancient History Documentary Research Centre; Grand Rapids: Eerdmans, 1998), 1:225-26; Jennifer A. Glancy, "Obstacles to Slaves' Participation in the Corinthian Church," *JBL* 117 (1998): 481-501.

like them. Most importantly, underlying it is the assumption that female slaves have no sexual honor to be safeguarded, as did the freeborn women.

Orlando Patterson's *Slavery and Social Death* proposes a thesis: that slavery is symbolic execution, liminal social death, in some cultures indeed ritualized at the moment of official enslavement. It is human parasitism, in which a relation of domination causes one to grow stronger as the other suffers, yet paradoxically creates a relationship of dependence stronger in the dominator than in the dominated.[4] It is social death because by legal and official recognition the slave has no family history, identification, or country of origin except that assigned by his/her owner. ("Owner" is preferable to "master," since many women also owned slaves. The habitual use of "master" in both ancient and modern discussion is another way of marginalizing women, in this case, slaveholding women.) Slaves' names could be changed at the will of the owner. Even names which suggest geographical origin may not be accurate, but may have depended on an owner's preference or whim: a German slave with a Greek name, a Phrygian with a Canaanite name, etc., may denote place of *purchase* rather than of origin.[5] Even in situations, which must have been common in the Roman Empire, in which a slave knew well who his/her parents were, familial units could be broken and separated at any time, and blood relatives could be so distanced from each other that they would be unable to maintain contact. In a state of natal alienation, the slave has no past and no future, no ancestry and no possibility of creating a family lineage or bequeathing property to offspring. The slave cannot contract a legal marriage, even though slave marriages existed de facto (see Dale Martin's discussion of the inscriptional evidence elsewhere in this volume). The slave's children are not his/hers, but the owner's. The slave's total identity is that created by the owner and granted for the enhancement of the owner.

Like most studies of slavery and slave systems, Patterson's gives very little consideration to enslaved women except when examining aspects of family and reproduction. Even here, there is an additional factor to be taken into account with regard to female slaves. Besides natal alienation depriving slaves of a past, an additional reproductive alienation resulted because they usually had little choice in whether they would bear children or how much involvement they would have in nursing and raising them. In the slave sale records from Egypt, women in childbearing years commanded high prices and were frequently up

---

4. Orlando Patterson, *Slavery and Social Death: A Comparative Study* (Cambridge: Harvard University Press, 1982), pp. 293-94, 453 n. 1.

5. William L. Westermann, *The Slave Systems of Greek and Roman Antiquity* (Philadelphia: American Philosophical Society, 1955), p. 96.

for sale, whereas the sale records of women past childbearing years declined noticeably. In the surviving records, there are no sales of women over thirty-five, which may have provided some stability to their lives at that point. Some mothers were sold with small children, but no fathers with them nor couples together. The same records contain numerous instances of children, girls and boys, sold alone, sometimes several times before the age of puberty. Prices of girls seem to have surpassed those of boys in the surviving records of the first two centuries B.C.E. because of their reproductive potential.[6] There was a running legal discussion among the jurists about whether a purchaser could get a reimbursement for a female slave of childbearing age who failed to reproduce.

The Lives of Female Slaves

Attempted discussions of "slave breeding" in the literature on Roman slavery go nowhere. The expression conjures up whole populations of (female) slaves acquired and kept solely or primarily for the purpose of procreation. Nowhere is there any evidence of what would surely have been a very expensive, time-intensive, and not very lucrative practice. Rather, it seems that most slave populations in which males and females lived and worked together were encouraged to reproduce, and the raising of slave children, who in nearly all circumstances followed the servile status of their mother, was often left to others than their own parents. The *lex Papia Poppaea* of 9 C.E. gave freedom from *tutela* to freeborn women who produced three children, and freedwomen with four. Columella follows suit with his agricultural slaves, giving exemption from work to the slave mother of three and freedom to the one who produced more (*De re rustica* 1.8.19). Besides informing us that large families in any status must have been very unusual and general fertility low, he also tells us that large slave families were a rarity and extra incentive was needed for slaves to reproduce well. Columella would scarcely have offered rewards for what was an average number of children produced by a single female slave, nor was Augustus looking for excuses to waive *tutela.*

Wet nurses and child minders were often hired to nurse and raise children. Whether nurse or nursling was slave or free seems to have made little difference, except that the free nurse could contract for herself. Wet-nursing contracts extended from six months to three years, during which time the wet nurse was

6. Keith R. Bradley, *Slaves and Masters in the Roman Empire: A Study in Social Control* (New York: Oxford University Press, 1987), p. 53; Keith Hopkins, *Conquerors and Slaves* (Cambridge: Cambridge University Press, 1978), p. 159, quoted in Patterson, p. 167.

under contract not to become pregnant or have sexual intercourse. Though some seemed to think that nursing is a natural contraceptive, apparently most realized that it is not always effective. The further prohibition of sexual intercourse was intended to prevent alienation of affection from the child being nursed. If the wet nurse was a slave, she had no choice in the matter, but was subject to the contract arranged by her owner, thereby disrupting any normal familial relations she had.

Apparently it was regular procedure to have slave children nursed by a woman other than their mother, in order to free the mother for work and perhaps for further reproduction. Plautus's reference (*Miles gloriosus* 697) to "the nurse who suckles the *vernas*" implies a recognized figure for the nursing of slave children in some households.[7] But freeborn children were also often nursed by a slave or freedwoman, known as *mamma* or foster mother;[8] the first meaning of the word *mamma* is breast. Among the letters of the Pythagorean women philosophers, that of Myia to Phyllis with congratulations and advice to the new mother gives as first point of advice not that she should nurse her own baby, as Plutarch advises (*De liberis educandis* 5), but the necessity of finding a good nurse, one not given to drink or too much sleep, who should not be allowed intimacies with her husband, preferably a Greek rather than a foreigner.[9] Young female slaves were prized for their reproductive potential, yet had little or no control over their reproductive and child-nurturing activity. In subsequent discussion of this paper, Richard Saller noted that the evidence for wet-nursing contracts yields twice as many for female foundlings as for male, so it must have been considered worthwhile to invest in raising female slaves, even though they were not seen to be as labor-productive as males.

Female slaves as a group have been very little studied. All surviving evidence indicates a larger male slave population in Roman society than female,[10] for a number of reasons. Where child abandonment or other forms of infanticide are practiced in a society that favors males, more female children will be abandoned and die. A heavily agricultural slave society will depend more on males than females for labor, as also is the case for building, mining, shipping,

---

7. Westermann, p. 102 n. 4; Suzanne Dixon, *The Roman Mother* (London and New York: Routledge, 1988), pp. 17-18, 70-71.

8. Dixon, p. 146.

9. Mario Meunier, ed., *Femmes Pythagoriciennes: Fragments et Lettres de Théano, Périctioné, Phintys, Mélissa et Myia* (Paris: L'Artisan du Livre, 1932), pp. 8-9.

10. William V. Harris, "Towards a Study of the Roman Slave Trade," *MAAR* 36, ed. John H. D'Arms and E. C. Kopff (1980): 119-20; John Madden, "Slavery in the Roman Empire: Numbers and Origins," *Classics Ireland* 3 (1996). Online: http:/www.ucd.ie/%7Eclassics/96/Madden96.html, pp. 3-5.

and other forms of heavy labor. Even in household staffs, some studies indicate a larger male than female contingent, including the households of aristocratic women. Seventy-seven percent of Livia's household was male, as were 66 percent of the slaves and freedpersons of two other aristocratic households, along with 80 percent of the tomb inscriptions of deceased slave children of these households, and fifty-nine of sixty-one slaves in the urban *familia* of an early second-century Roman aristocrat in Alexandria.[11]

Such a large preponderance of males in the slave population raises serious questions about how this population was maintained. Either the surviving evidence for gender selection of slaves is skewed and there really were many more female slaves than we think, reproducing at a steady rate and not largely manumitted during childbearing years, or the slave population was woefully unable to reproduce itself and was dependent on large numbers entering its ranks through the known nonreproductive means: child abandonment, self-sale, prisoners of war, and importation from outside the empire.[12]

In every slave society, a larger number of female slaves are manumitted because of sexual relations with masters or other free males and for marriage, thus reducing further the available female slave population of childbearing age.[13] Many more female slaves were manumitted to marry their male owners than vice versa, though Dale Martin in his essay in this volume presents evidence of other apparent motivations for freeing female slaves, and the considerations cited above about the ability of the slave population to reproduce itself must be kept in mind. Marriages between freedmen and freeborn women were severely discouraged, and even penalized by the *Senatus consultum Claudianum.* Marriages between a male slave and his female former owner were also strongly discouraged, even when the woman was a freedwoman, yet they continued to occur regularly. Dedications to *patrona et coniux* are not that hard to find in *CIL.* Yet those to *patronus et coniux* are far more abundant. The early *lex Aelia Sentia* of 4 C.E. provided that a female slave could be manumitted earlier than the minimum age of thirty for the purpose of marriage. The overall status of women with regard to men is a factor here, combined with the dominative nature of the slave system: for women to "marry up" was considered favorably; to "marry down" was not, even for freedwomen. That is to say, there was less com-

---

11. Madden, p. 4; Susan Treggiari, "Family Life among the Staff of the Volusii," *TAPA* 105 (1975): 393-401; Treggiari, "Jobs in the Household of Livia," *PBSR* 43 (1975): 48-77.

12. This question is very much discussed currently. See, for example, Walter Scheidel, "Quantifying the Sources of Slaves in the Early Roman Empire," *JRS* 87 (1997): 156-69; William V. Harris, "Demography, Geography and the Sources of Roman Slaves," *JRS* 89 (1999): 62-75.

13. Patterson, p. 263; Madden, p. 4.

promise of honor involved for men to "marry down" than up. One of the accusations of the Christian theologian Hippolytus against his rival Callistus (a former slave) involved exactly that: Callistus sanctioned marriages of higher-status Christian women with lower-status males, presumably because of a dearth of high-status Christian men (*Refutatio* 9.12).

Female slaves were not spared the harsh treatment often encountered by their male counterparts. Slave whipping, beating, and torture were not confined to males, and references to such treatment, unless specifically applied to males, must be understood to apply to both sexes. Like a travesty of today's service industry, Roman society had professional torturers *(tortores)* who could be hired to punish slaves deemed to be in need of punishment (see Matt. 18:34) or to extract information in a nonjudicial setting. A chilling testimony is preserved in an inscription from Puteoli that specifies what materials the contractors are to provide for the private punishment of a slave, male or female, by *crux* or *furca,* and how and when the bodies are to be removed.[14] Juvenal refers in passing to sending the female attendants *(ancillae)* of a household to the *tortor* to get information about whether the actor-owner of the house who dresses like a woman is really a woman-chasing *vir* (*Satire* 6.029). Similarly, Pliny the Younger had two slave women *(ancillae),* who held the title of *ministrae* in their church, tortured to investigate Christian practices, though this was official judicial interrogation (*Epistle* 10.96.8). Ulpian specifies, in his legislation about the accountability of slaves under the same roof when their owner is murdered, that the female slave asleep in her mistress's chamber who does not at least cry out when her mistress is attacked is to be put to death (*Digest* 29.5.27). Nor were female slaves less to be feared in the case of rebellion. Diodorus Siculus, for instance, relates that in the Sicilian slave uprising of circa 135 B.C.E., one couple, Megallis and Damophilus of Enna, were known to have been especially abusive to their slaves, in contrast to their daughter, who tried constantly to undo the damage by kindness. When the slaves revolted, the daughter was given safe passage while Megallis was handed over to her female slaves, who tortured her and threw her off a cliff (34.10, 13, 39).

Sexual Availability

Inherent in the abusiveness of the slave-dominance relationship was the well-known vulnerability of the slave to sexual abuse. Aristotle's definition of a slave

---

14. Published by L. Bove in *Labeo* 13 (1967): 43-48; *AE* 1971, no. 88; translation in Jane F. Gardner and Thomas Wiedemann, *The Roman Household: A Sourcebook* (London and New York: Routledge, 1991), pp. 24-27.

is a human being who belongs by nature completely to another, a human being who is also an article of property (*Politics* 1.1254a7). Another way of defining the slave is as one who is answerable with his/her body, as to physical punishment, degrading forms of execution, and testimony under torture. Yet another manifestation of this bodily subjection was complete sexual availability to his/her owner and anyone to whom the owner granted rights,[15] all these forms of defenselessness resulting from the lack of honor or *dignitas* of the slave. Seneca remarked of the "passive" or dominated sexual partner: "Unchastity is a crime in the freeborn, a necessity for the slave, a duty for the freedman" [Impudicitia in ingenuo crimen est, in servo necessitas, in libero officium] (*Controversiae* 4.praef.10). This sexual vulnerability was no less for male than for female slaves, but it must have been particularly acute for females, and more complicated because of the possibility of pregnancy. The slave's lack of moral responsibility for sex initiated by a free man was implicit in Roman law, as was that of the initiator.[16] Under the *lex Aquilia, iniuria* could be claimed by a slave's owner against someone else who had, against the owner's will, committed "corruption" of a slave, but this is a form of violation of property rights. The crime of *stuprum* seems to have been understood as sexual intercourse in which one person was used to gratify another. *Stuprum* could be committed with a virgin, a widow, or a divorcée (*Digest* 48.5.6.1).[17] It could not be committed with a slave, presumably because the sole purpose of a slave was to be used.[18]

Examples of how this sexual availability was taken for granted abound in the literature. To cite only a few, Horace warns a recipient of his letter not to become enamored of someone else's girl or boy slave, lest the owner not give her/him to you (*Epistle* 1.18.72).[19] He also remarks, in a passage lamenting the difficulties of adultery with a matron, that he prefers the more readily available services of an *ancilla* or *verna puer* (*Satires* 2.115-19). Trimalchio feels no shame in having sexually serviced both his master and mistress for fourteen years, "for it is no shame to do what is commanded" (*Satyricon* 75).

This sexual availability of slaves seems to have been completely taken for

---

15. Moses I. Finley, *Ancient Slavery and Modern Ideology* (New York: Penguin Books, 1980), pp. 94-96.

16. Susan Treggiari, *Roman Marriage: Iusti Coniuges from the Time of Cicero to the Time of Ulpian* (Oxford: Clarendon, 1991), p. 301.

17. Treggiari, *Roman Marriage,* p. 263.

18. Diana C. Moses, "Livy's Lucretia and the Validity of Coerced Consent in Roman Law," in *Consent and Coercion to Sex and Marriage in Ancient and Medieval Societies,* ed. Angeliki E. Laiou (Washington, D.C.: Dumbarton Oaks, 1993), p. 46.

19. References given in Westermann, p. 74 nn. 112-14; other examples in Glancy, "Obstacles," pp. 483-90.

granted. There is an astonishing lack of specification about slaves even in the literature of marital advice. More ancient authors than might be supposed advocate the marital fidelity of husbands, including Aristotle (*Oeconomicus* 3) and Pythagoras (Iamblichus, *Life of Pythagoras* 47-48), but it is doubtful whether sex with one's own slaves is included. Plutarch, on the other hand, considers it normal for husbands to take their debauchery elsewhere, to go wide of the mark (ἐξαμαρτάνειν) with a ἑταίρα or slave. The wife should be grateful that he does so, reserving a more respectful approach for her (*Praecepta conjugalia* 140B). If Plutarch is consistent, then his advice about educating freeborn males not to be overbearing with slaves (δούλους μὴ περιυβρίζειν) does not prohibit rape of slaves, even though the word group ὑβρίζειν with its various prefixes can carry this meaning.[20]

Seemingly the sole dissenting voice, not surprisingly, is Musonius Rufus, who explicitly argues to the husband that if it is not shameful for a master to have sex with his own slave, especially if she is "unmarried" (an interesting reference to slave marriages), nevertheless let him think how he would feel if his wife had sex with a male slave (fragment 12). But the effects would be quite different in the two cases. The wife's action would be adultery, and the male slave could also be accused of adultery, for male slaves were legally capable of committing adultery with a married free woman. The husband's action would be legally neutral, and for the majority of men, morally neutral. Musonius's example is meant to be strictly moral, and exhibits the surprising, nearly egalitarian thinking about marriage for which he is known. His appeal can only be moral, since the legal implications in each case are considerably different: for the husband legal and (for most free males) moral indifference; for the wife strong social disapproval and a legal charge of adultery, which under Augustan law would require her husband to divorce her if he is aware of it.

Jewish and Christian Slave Owning

It is sometimes thought that Jews and Christians had different and more humane standards for the treatment of their slaves. Granted, there were special regulations governing the treatment of Hebrew slaves, and Torah contains many specifications about the treatment of slaves that severely restrict the power of owners over them. For example, neither male nor female slaves are to be made to work on the Sabbath (Exod. 20:10; 23:12; Deut. 5:14). Domestic slaves

---

20. Cf. LSJ, s.v.; Diodorus Siculus 34.12: what revolting slaves did to women; Athenagoras, *De resurrectione* 19.7.

are to be integrated as far as possible into family rituals (Exod. 12:44; Deut. 12:12, 18). A Hebrew debt-slave must be set free in the seventh year and sent away with gifts, unless he chooses to remain permanently (Deut. 15:12-17). Though verse 17 suggests the same for a female slave, freeing in the seventh year was not generally interpreted in that way for women (e.g., Exod. 21:7; *b. Qidd.* 18a). A Hebrew girl sold into slavery by her father must be married at marriageable age by master or his son, or released (Exod. 21:7-11).

Most of these protective regulations did not apply to non-Hebrew slaves, though a female prisoner of war might be taken as a wife, and freed if her captor no longer wants her, but not sold (Deut. 21:10-14). Philo justifies Hebrew ownership of non-Hebrew slaves, saying the law permits it because of the many situations requiring slaves (*Specialibus legibus* 2.123). Male and female slaves are free from work on the Sabbath, he reports, in anticipation of the full freedom they may attain if they serve well, because (in disagreement with Aristotle) no one is a slave by nature, but all are free (2.67-69). Owners should not be excessively cruel to their slaves, which would reveal their own cruel nature. If a slave dies from mistreatment, the owner is liable in court, yet if a whipped slave lives two to three days, the owner is not guilty of murder (3.137-43; cf. Exod. 21:20-21).

Ben Sirach says a slave is to be worked hard, comparably to a donkey, because an idle slave will look for freedom. The disobedient slave should be tortured, the lazy slave loaded with chains. An owner should not be ashamed to draw blood on the back (πλευρά, normally side or ribs) of a wicked οἰκέτης. Yet a single slave, the only one owned by a given person, should be treated as another self of the owner and not mistreated, lest he/she run away. And in the midst of these admonitions, quite incongruously, is one against being overbearing or unjust to anyone, probably an indication of the miscellaneous nature of the collected sayings (Sir. 33:25-30; 42:5).

Most interesting is a text that seems to have been altered from Hebrew to LXX in the direction of justifying sex with one's own slave. Exodus 20:17 already prohibited coveting the male or female slave of another. Sirach 41:22 NRSV (24 LXX; 27 Vg) reads: "Be ashamed of . . . gazing at another man's wife; of meddling with his servant girl (ἀπὸ περιεργίας παιδίσκης αὐτοῦ LXX) — and do not approach her bed," so that the meaning prohibits sex with another man's female slave as well as with his wife. Lucian and Origen read αὐτῆς for αὐτοῦ, so that the prohibition is of sex with the female slave of another man's wife. But the Hebrew had read *leka* (your), so that the text read "of meddling with *your* slave girl."[21] The Hebrew text therefore prohibited a male owner to have sex

---

21. *The Wisdom of Ben Sira,* translation and notes by Patrick W. Skehan, introduction and commentary by Alexander A. di Lella, AB 39 (New York: Doubleday, 1987), p. 479.

with his own female slave, but the LXX altered the reading to avoid that situation and prohibit instead sex with the female slave of another man, something that already carried a penalty in Roman and other legal systems. The Lucianic/ Origen reading made the prohibition even more specific, avoiding sex with the female slave of another man's wife, but further removed from the situation of sex with one's own slave.

There are frequent overtones in rabbinic literature of the problems of rabbis with their female slaves. Hillel was known to remark: "The more maidservants, the more lewdness" (*m. 'Abot* 2.7). Talmudic legislation protects the rights of owners and the honor of wives, but not of female slaves, in spite of the many stories of the chastity and loyalty of the female slave of Rabbi Judah the Patriarch. It was difficult for a freedwoman to marry anyone other than her former owner because of the assumption of her promiscuity (*t. Hor.* 2.11-12; *m. Yebam.* 61). Leviticus 19:20 forbids sexual relations with a female slave, but it is a case of someone else's slave. Leviticus 18:8, 15 intends to prohibit a father from having sex with his son's wife or vice versa (cf. 1 Cor. 5:1). In this context, see Amos 2:7, where in a list of wrongs committed by Israel, father and son have sex with the same female slave (*na'ărāh* MT; παιδίσκη LXX). But *Sifra Qedoshim* (9.13,92a col. 2 ed. Weiss on Lev. 20:12) excludes female slaves from the prohibition against father and son having sex with the same woman by explicitly referring only to the legitimate wife; thus concubines and female slaves are not included in the prohibition. Another story relates that a prince was thrown out of court for having sex with a slave girl, probably not because of moral impropriety but because he usurped his father's privilege.[22]

There is ample evidence of Christian ownership of slaves and of continued expectation of their obedience, though from the earliest years, nothing so severe as Sirach's comments are preserved. Much later there will be such severe comments and legislation. Under Constantine, for example, the death sentence was legislated for a free woman who had sex with her own slave,[23] and it was ruled that if a slave died as the result of whipping, the owner was not to be charged with murder, since the use of a whip was evidence of intent not to kill.[24] R. Saller

22. Genesis Rabbah 15.7, ed. Theodor-Albeck, p. 140; Tal Ilan, *Jewish Women in Greco-Roman Palestine: An Inquiry into Image and Status,* Texte und Studien zum Antike Judentum 44 (Peabody, Mass.: Hendrickson, 1996), pp. 205-10, with further examples.

23. *Codex Justinianus* 9.11.1 pr., in *Women's Life in Greece and Rome: A Sourcebook in Translation,* ed. Mary R. Lefkowitz and Maureen B. Fant (Baltimore: Johns Hopkins University Press, 1992), #144, p. 118.

24. *Codex Theodotianus* 9.12.1; Richard Saller, "The Hierarchical Household in Roman Society: A Study of Domestic Slavery," in *Serfdom and Slavery: Studies in Legal Bondage,* ed. M. L. Bush (London and New York: Longman, 1996), p. 119.

argues that later Christian thinking actually expanded the use of whipping to children, since all are created equal in the sight of God![25] Augustine opines that misbehaving slaves should be whipped for their own benefit, since it is no kindness to let someone fall into greater evil by not acting (*City of God* 19.16). He also reports as nothing extraordinary — in a story about his mother's virtue — that when the female slaves in his household of origin created tensions between Monica and her mother-in-law by slandering the daughter-in-law, Monica continued to be deferential to the older woman and thus regained her confidence. When the mother-in-law realized what was happening, she asked her son, Augustine's father, to have the slaves beaten. After that, there were no more problems (*Confessions* 9.9.20).

Several female slaves appear in early Christian texts, two not among believers: the slave girl in the high priest's household (Matt. 26:69, 71; Mark 14:66, 69; Luke 22:56;[26] John 18:16-17) and the female slave with the spirit of divination at Philippi (Acts 16:16-19), the latter left in a vulnerable position with loss of her ability to earn money for her owners. Among believers, there is Rhoda the doorkeeper in the house of Mary in Jerusalem (Acts 12:13). Mary's allusion to herself in Luke 1:38, 48 as the δούλη of God is of course metaphorical, but some of the connotations of female slavery are necessarily attached, especially her lack of honor, which only God can bestow on the honorless.

Beyond the New Testament, there are the two *ancillae,* called *ministrae* by their church, tortured by Pliny the Younger to obtain information about Christian meetings (*Epistle* 10.96): Blandina, the heroic figure of Lyon, and Felicitas of Carthage. Both Blandina and to a lesser extent Felicitas are portrayed as legendary examples of heroism with christological typology. Blandina, whose age is not told, is the rallying point for her fellow martyrs. Her suffering gives them courage to go on, and when she is hung on a stake and exposed to wild animals, her companions explicitly compare her to the crucified Christ. She is the last to die and most heroic in her endurance (*Acts of the Martyrs of Lyons and Vienne* [Eusebius, *Historia ecclesiastica* 5.1.41, 53-55]). Felicitas, of childbearing age, is pregnant at the time of her arrest. Nothing is ever said of the father of her child, no more than the mysterious silence about the husband of Perpetua and father of her newborn. Felicitas gives premature but successful birth in prison after being earnestly prayed over so that her pregnancy would not delay her execution beyond that of her companions. When she cries out in labor pains, a guard

25. Richard Saller, *Patriarchy, Property, and Death in the Roman Family* (New York: Cambridge University Press, 1994), pp. 152-53. See also Theodore S. de Bruyn, "Flogging a Son: The Emergence of the *Pater Flagellans* in Latin Christian Discourse," *JECS* 7, no. 2 (1999): 249-90.

26. In Luke, Peter addresses her as γύναι, an unusual form of address for a slave, but probably her slave status is not at issue here.

taunts her that she will have to suffer much more, whereupon she replies that then another will be suffering in her (*Acts of Perpetua and Felicitas* 15). She, like her companions, goes enthusiastically to death later in the arena.

Two possible freedwomen are Lydia the purple merchant of Acts 16 and Rhodê the former owner of Hermas in the *Shepherd Vision* 1.1. Of all the above, only the story of Felicitas yields any definite sexual or reproductive information, her pregnancy at the time of her arrest, with no mention of the identity of the father of her child. With Rhodê of the *Shepherd*, there is a possible allusion to a sexual encounter with her former slave, Hermas, in the ambiguous opening scene of her bathing in the Tiber under his admiring eye (*Vision* 1.1.2).

The apocryphal *Acts of Andrew* follows the usual pattern of apocryphal acts by featuring a female disciple of the apostle who is won over to chastity, to the dismay of a forlorn fiancé or husband. In this case the heroine Maximilla sends her female slave Eucleia, described as very beautiful but undisciplined, to bed with her husband Aegeates, who is apparently so drunk every night for eight months that he doesn't notice the difference. To keep her slave's loyalty, Maximilla bribes her with expensive gifts. But Eucleia finally begins boasting anyway to her fellow slaves, who see for themselves what is going on. When the plot is revealed, Aegeates punishes Eucleia (who is not his own slave) by cutting off her tongue, hands, and feet, leaving her to die of exposure. He crucifies his own three slaves who accepted bribes from Maximilla to keep quiet. The story is typical of the use of slaves, with no Christian difference whatever. Maximilla, in keeping with the theology of the text, is convinced that sexual intercourse even in marriage is sinful, yet does not hesitate to use her slave to fulfill that function to avoid confrontation with her husband. The description of Eucleia as naturally undisciplined repeats slave stereotypes. The cruel punishment of the slaves goes without comment, and the story moves on from there.[27]

Porneia

How was πορνεία understood in early Christianity? Lexical definitions are very general: fornication, illicit sex. To say that πορνεία means fornication is circular, and the concept of illicit sex only begs the question of what is considered illicit. Long ago Bruce Malina asked whether New Testament πορνεία included all unchastity, or whether the lexica and commentaries were influenced by a cultur-

---

27. The manuscript tradition of the various pieces of the Andrew legends is complex. The text probably originated in the late second century. For this story, see the translation by Wilhelm Schneemelcher, *NTA*, 2:139-41.

ally conditioned understanding of the New Testament. He noted that in the Hebrew Scriptures πορνεία carries connotations of idolatry or adultery, and that the πορνεία forbidden by Torah is not unnatural but unlawful sex. He concluded that, with the exception of the violation of a virgin, which is a different kind of offense, "pre-betrothal, pre-marital, non-commercial sexual intercourse between man and woman" is not a moral crime in Torah.[28] If that were the case in Israelite law, would sex with one's own slave, who is in Roman law entirely one's own property and a legal nonperson, be included?

Paul does not address the question we would like answered, whether sex between a slave and his/her owner constitutes πορνεία. Nor do we know whether the same-sex prohibitions of 1 Corinthians 6:9 would include it. The case presented in 1 Corinthians 5:1, specifically called πορνεία, is usually supposed to be incest and probably is, considering the wording of the sentence, which should best be rendered that the man has taken to himself his father's wife, that is, his stepmother. Presumably the father and the woman are no longer married or the situation would be called μοιχεία (adultery), not πορνεία. Paul's lack of interest in the woman is taken to mean that she is not a believer. Some, however, have raised the question whether a female slave is the object of the conflict, whether believer or not.[29] This seems unlikely, since the woman somehow belongs to the father (γυναῖκα τινα τοῦ πατρός) and a female slave is not likely to have been called simply his γυνή. She is more likely the father's legal wife or concubine.

1 Corinthians 6:15-20 is primarily about (Christian) male customers and prostitutes. The sacred temple metaphors recall cultic prostitution, whether or not it was still functioning in Roman Corinth. Here Paul teaches that sexual union with a prostitute (πόρνη, v. 15) violates the identity of the male Christian as a member of the body of Christ, and so violates the holiness of the community. Πορνεία is a sin against one's own body, which is a temple of the Holy Spirit, and must therefore be avoided (vv. 18-19). The context refers primarily if not only to prostitution, and that is not our concern here.

In 1 Corinthians 7:1-7 Paul begins his comments on sexuality and celibacy by saying, or partially repeating from the Corinthian correspondence to him: "It is well for an ἄνθρωπος not to touch a γυνή, but because of πορνεία, each man should have a wife, and each woman should have a husband." It would be appropriate to conclude from this statement that Paul argues against adultery, and also against prostitution, given the immediately preceding discussion in chapter 6. But it is overinterpretation to conclude from this statement that Paul

28. Bruce J. Malina, "Does Porneia Mean 'Fornication'?" *NovT* 14 (1972): 10-17.
29. Discussion in Glancy, "Obstacles," pp. 492-93.

limits "the legitimate range of sexual expression to marriage" and "implicitly suggests that slaves who oblige their masters sexually are engaged in *porneia*."[30] The use of the word γυνή in 7:1 personalizes and therefore suggests that the sexual use of female slaves is not envisioned here, just as the use of πόρνη in 6:15-16 depersonalizes the female involved and classifies the particular kind of sexual act that is discussed. Even the reference to lack of self-control (ἀκρασία) in 7:5 might therefore be understood to refer to adultery or prostitution. It is possible that the holiness language of 6:16-20 with its strong assertion of the unitive symbolism of sexual intercourse precludes the legitimacy of sexual exploitation of one's slave. But even if Paul does include sexual use of one's slave under ἀκρασία and πορνεία here, there still remains the question whether his audience would have understood it as such.

Similarly, the enigmatic 1 Thessalonians 4:3-5 exhorts abstention from πορνεία, adding that each Christian should keep one's own σκεῦος in holiness and honor. Whereas 1 Peter 3:7 uses the expression for "wife," its more familiar meaning in this kind of context is the human body or vulnerability (2 Cor. 4:7), or even the genitals (cf. LSJ and BAGD, s.v.; 1 Sam. 21:6 LXX). Again, there is no doubt that Christian moral teaching prohibits πορνεία. The question, still not clarified, is whether sex with one's own slave was included in what constituted πορνεία.

Obedient Slaves in Early Christianity

In the early years, Philemon, 1 Corinthians 7:21-23, Ephesians 6:5-8, Colossians 3:22-25, 1 Timothy 6:1-2, Titus 2:9-10, 1 Peter 2:18-25, and Ignatius, *Polycarp* 4.3, all speak to some degree of the submission and obedience expected of slaves. Philemon, of course, deals only with one specific male slave, Onesimus, and this case is not relevant here. None of the other texts distinguishes male from female slaves, so we must read both sexes into the passages unless there is compelling reason to do otherwise. 1 Corinthians 7:21-23 and Ignatius, *Polycarp* 4.3, both speak of expectations of manumission, and both discourage setting it as a priority. 1 Corinthians makes it a matter of indifference, and Ignatius speaks against an expectation that the church will be the agent of manumission, which must therefore have been a custom beginning to develop in some places. Ignatius's paternalistic advice continues to set the tone of the church's general attitude to slavery and slaves for years to come: let slaves not think to be manumitted at church expense, lest they become slaves of desire (ἐπιθυμία).

---

30. Glancy, "Obstacles," p. 496.

More to the point are the various household codes and advice to slaves. Ephesians 6:5-8 enjoins slaves to obey earthly owners with fear and trembling and simplicity of heart as they would Christ, not in appearance but as true slaves of Christ, as if serving the Lord, knowing that the reward from God will be the same for both slave and free. Likewise, Colossians 3:22-25 in very similar terms exhorts slaves to obey their owners in everything as if serving the Lord. Their inheritance is sure because they are really serving the Lord Christ. Colossians adds that the wrongdoer will also be repaid in kind. What does it mean to obey *in everything?* The stress of the authors of these two letters on the fact that obeying an earthly master is really obeying Christ would at first glance lead us to think that the authors did not intend to include sexual availability as one of the factors in obedience. Yet in the previous exhortation to wives, the reference to Christ as the husband of the church, as metaphoric loving but still dominant husband in marriage, certainly does include sexual union: "Wives, submit to your husbands as to the Lord . . . in everything" (Eph. 5:22, 24). Much of the rest of the passage about husbands and wives, Christ and the church, is clearly sexual in connotation (vv. 26-31). Given societal expectations, it cannot therefore be ruled out that the exhortation for slaves to obey in everything might include sexual service.

On the other side, it can be countered that some sayings in the same literature seem to exclude an atmosphere in which sexual exploitation of slaves could be countenanced. For instance, Ephesians 6:9 tells slave owners not to be overbearing or threatening (ἀνιέντες τὴν ἀπειλήν) because they too have an impartial heavenly Lord. Colossians 4:1 goes further with the same point to say that owners should relate to slaves with justice and fairness (τὸ δίκαιον καὶ τὴν ἰσότητα), but this refers mainly to showing partiality to one slave over another — a situation which could easily arise, however, in a concubinage relationship.[31]

Three different questions must be asked: First, what did a particular author intend to include under the category of obedience? Second, what did slave owners hear and do with these teachings? Third, how did slaves hear and understand what was given them as official teaching?

1 Timothy 6:1-2 is less explicit about theological underpinnings of servitude. Owners are to be regarded with full honor so that outsiders who will see disobedient slaves do not judge the teachings poorly. Slaves with believing owners are not to be less respectful for that reason, but to serve all the better. Titus

---

31. In discussion, Margaret MacDonald raised the interesting question whether the ideology of the household codes, if taken seriously, might prompt Christian slave owners to keep slave families together for the sake of the greater harmony of the household.

2:9-10 bids slaves to be submissive and pleasing in every way to their owners, not obstinate but completely faithful. The most difficult passage, 1 Peter 2:18-25, tells slaves to be submissive not only to kind and gentle owners but also to abusive ones, after the example of Christ, who suffered abuse.

Generations of women have been told to endure abusive husbands because it is God's will as set out in the Bible. What of slaves suffering not only physical but also sexual abuse from their owners? The text does not differentiate between good and bad believing owners, good and bad unbelieving owners, and there is no caveat or exception given to the total obedience that is expected, even to unjust and abusive owners. The incentive to full obedience continues further in the tradition. A later text, the Ethiopic *Apocalypse of Peter* 11, delights in describing special torments devised for special crimes. One group of men and women "who ceaselessly chew their tongues and are tormented with eternal fire . . . are the slaves who were not obedient to their masters. This then is their judgment forever."[32] The way the text specifies here, and in several other instances in the same context, "both men and women" suggests that the differences in men's and women's situations are taken fully into account and that the author explicitly wants to include both.

Even if the Christian authors of texts such as the above do not intend to include sexual use as part of slaves' obedience (and that is never clear), the question still remains how new Christians, used to the sexually abusive patterns of slavery as normal and morally neutral, would have heard these directives in the absence of anything more specific. It is intriguing that in the texts that have been preserved, no such exception to the demands of obedience is specified. We would like to know whether it was so specified in oral instruction, but there is no way to find out. It is also clear that not every instance of sexual exploitation in slavery would have been experienced by the victim as abusive. Many female slaves both Christian and not would have found a certain degree of status, security, and perhaps even power in the relationship, as long as they were not mistreated and not threatened by jealous wives. Some may have attained a great deal of power, like Marcia, the (probably) Christian concubine first of Quadratus, nephew of Marcus Aurelius, then of Commodus (Hippolytus, *Refutatio* 9.12; Dio Cassius 73.4.6-7; 22.4; 74.16.5), from which position she was able to do good to Christians she favored.[33] From a modern perspective and perhaps an ancient one as well, even if the victim feels fortunate, it is still abuse.

32. Translation by C. Detlef G. Müller, *NTA*, 2:632.

33. A cache of jewelry recently discovered at Pompeii contains a gold bracelet inscribed *dominus ancillae suae* (the master to his female slave), testimony that such relationships could be deeply affectionate (www.telegraph.co.uk, *Daily Telegraph*, December 9, 2000).

The *Apostolic Tradition* of Hippolytus gives a list of occupations and conditions of persons that might pose problems for admission to the church as catechumens. Among them, a male catechumen not living with a wife should be taught not to fornicate, but to take a lawful wife or remain as he is. Whether this precludes sexual exploitation of his own slave depends on whether the understanding of fornication included this form of exploitation at that point in Christian history. Again, a male living with a concubine should cease and take a lawful wife. While this situation may refer to a woman of free but inferior social status, it also covers the situation of a man using his female slave as common-law wife. Like most of the examples usually cited about sexual liaisons with slaves in the Greco-Roman texts, it implies a long-term relationship and says nothing about occasional sexual exploitation.[34] A slave concubine — and this is the only time in the *Apostolic Tradition* that "slave" is specified — who has reared her children and remained faithful to one man is not to be held blamable, but may be admitted (15-16). Here the situation of slave concubinage is recognized and opposed, but it is still not certain that occasional sexual abuse of one's own slave is included in the prohibition. A separate sexual standard is held for free men who are in control of their sexual activity and female slaves who are not.[35]

Thus what J. Glancy calls a "moral conundrum" is recognized. Either the Christian community had to exclude some slaves whose sexual behavior, through no fault of their own, could not follow the general moral standard, or the community tolerated some whose sexual behavior did not conform to those norms. This situation adds a new dimension to the implications of 1 Corinthians 7:21: Given the opportunity for manumission, should the sexually exploited female slave take it, even though otherwise slavery or freedom is held by Paul to be morally and soteriologically neutral?[36]

Glancy rightly poses the dilemma faced by early Christians: either it is not true, as was maintained even by Paul and ever since, that servile status was no impediment to membership in the church, or there were some forms of extramarital sex that were overlooked. By the fourth century, concepts of μοιχεία and πορνεία no longer follow the older Roman legal distinctions.[37] The old Ro-

34. Beryl Rawson, "Roman Concubinage and Other *De Facto* Marriages," *TAPA* 104 (1974): 279-305, makes the helpful clarification, against some earlier scholarship, that Roman concubinage carried no moral connotations but was only a factor of disparate or servile social status between the partners.

35. Glancy, "Obstacles," p. 482.

36. Glancy, "Obstacles," pp. 482-83.

37. Angeliki Laiou, "Sex, Consent, and Coercion in Byzantium," in *Consent and Coercion to Sex and Marriage in Ancient and Medieval Societies,* pp. 128-32.

man *stuprum* becomes the Byzantine φθορά. Slavery continued, but understanding of the problem developed. Basil of Cappadocia writes that a female slave who cohabits with a man against the will of her owner commits πορνεία, but that if the relationship continues after she is freed, it becomes γάμος, because contracts made by those under authority are invalid. This simply follows Roman law in part. But further in the same letter, he states that a woman raped by force is innocent, even a slave raped by her master (*Epistle* 199.40, 49). The passage is part of a series of opinions about the sexual guilt of women in various situations. The text still raises no suggestion of culpability on the part of the master. Basil acknowledges that the double standard is not right but is the custom (*Epistles* 188, 199). The *Apostolic Constitutions* (6.17.2) of the late fourth century forbid at least clerics from having a ἑταίρα or a household slave, an οἰκέτις, as concubine, perhaps considered legitimate by some when marriage for clerics was discouraged.

Other Christian writers by this time were speaking out against the sexual double standard, including the sexual availability of female slaves to their owners (e.g., Jerome, *Epistle* 77.3), but nearly always from the point of view of what is required of the virtuous Christian male, not the rights of the slave, and while they expressed their moral views, they also acknowledged that neither the government nor men themselves did much to change the custom.[38] Later in Byzantine law πορνεία explicitly includes intercourse with a female slave.[39] Though one's own slave is not specified, it can probably be presumed by this time. The crime is not *stuprum* but πορνεία, which has now become a legal offense.

Did earlier Christian writers not speak of sexual exploitation of one's slave because a prohibition was self-evident (unlikely), because it was not done by Christians (also unlikely given the prevailing acceptance in the culture), because it was too much of a problem to tackle (ignore it and maybe it will go away), or because they did not consider it a problem? I would argue that this was a part of the culture that they had not yet sorted out as something to reject explicitly, though there may have been some awareness of the problem. As is the case with so many innovations against cultural conveniences, it was to take several centuries before there was a firm awareness, and several more centuries before sufficient sanctions were in place to change the practice.

And yet has it been changed? The traffic in female slaves for both labor and sex is very active today even in the so-called Christian countries.

---

38. Discussion and more references in Antti Arjava, *Women and Law in Late Antiquity* (Oxford: Clarendon, 1998), pp. 202-20.

39. Laiou, p. 132.

V. Children

Death, Burial, and Commemoration
of Children in Roman Italy

Beryl Rawson

Deaths and funerals were frequent events in a society of high mortality, disease, recurrent epidemics, and hazardous everyday urban life, all of which applied to Roman Italy in the early centuries c.e.[1] Italian towns had laws to regulate disposal of the dead, the use of cemeteries and cremation points *(ustrinae)*, and the practice of undertakers.[2] Disposal of the dead within the town walls was forbidden, except for babies aged less than forty days. These babies were not sufficiently developed individuals to cause religious pollution, and could be buried under the walls of houses. For others, graves and monuments were clustered along the roads leading away from towns. Funeral processions along these roads were a frequent sight, although some of them took place at night. Children were inured to such sights from an early age. There was no escape from a constant consciousness of death. Monuments and inscriptions which commemorated the dead were numerous in a culture which set considerable store not only on proper disposal of the dead but also on leaving something of one's self for posterity.[3]

---

1. See A. Scobie, "Slums, Sanitation and Mortality in the Roman World," *Klio* 68 (1986): 399-433, for a detailed, if rather gloomy, discussion of these public health matters; Shaw on seasonal variations in mortality in Rome, Italy, and several western provinces (B. Shaw, "Seasons of Death: Aspects of Mortality in Imperial Rome," *JRS* 86 [1996]: 100-138); R. Duncan-Jones, "The Impact of the Antonine Plague," *JRA* 9 (1996): 108-36, on many aspects of epidemics, especially pp. 109-11 for frequency of serious epidemics.

2. See, for example, J. Bodel, "Graveyards and Groves: A Study of the *Lex Lucerina*," *AJAH* 11 (1986 [1994]): 1-133 and "Dealing with the Dead: Undertakers, Executioners and Potter's Fields in Ancient Rome," in *Death and Disease in the Ancient City*, ed. V. M. Hope and E. Marshall (London and New York: Routledge, 2000), pp. 128-51.

3. There has been debate about the affordability of tombs or epitaphs, but I am persuaded by the evidence of costs versus available resources and by the discernible Roman wish for some material and durable sign of one's existence. See discussion in R. Saller and B. Shaw, "Tombstones and Roman Family Relations in the Principate: Civilians, Soldiers and Slaves," *JRS* 74 (1984): 127-28.

The Roman effort to record something of a person's life on inscribed and sometimes sculpted stone has been called "the epigraphic habit," which has come to identify the spread of Roman culture, a spread most notable in the western parts of the empire but which can be seen in parts of the East also, where the cultivation of Roman practices proved desirable as the imperial period developed.[4] As cremation was the dominant form of disposal of the dead in the Roman world in the first two centuries c.e., epitaphs were usually placed on niches for cinerary urns, often in the communal buildings called columbaria. Epitaphs were thus often brief, but the kind of detail recorded is strikingly constant: it is detail about personal relationships, and overwhelmingly about close family relationships. Though succinct, these epitaphs have permitted illuminating reconstructions of family structure and sentiment.[5] Upper-class men might give prominence to magistracies and other features of public life; some artisans (male and female) recorded their trade; but many had little to record beyond their name and the names of those closest to them. The form of Roman nomenclature allows deductions about status and relationships.[6] The primary bonds evidenced for the subelite population are between husband and wife and between parents and children.[7] Shaw (1996) has now shown that this is the dominant pattern in those Christian epitaphs from fourth-century Rome which record personal relationships (although fewer such relationships are recorded than in pre-Christian epitaphs).[8] These relationships were not, of course, the only relationships of people in this society: some did not have family to commemorate them, and even those who did interacted in various ways with a wider range of people. But what they chose to record on (for many) their only "piece" of posterity was, overwhelmingly, close family relationships. Memorial rates need not be the only measure of sentiment and affection, but their importance cannot be underestimated.

It is sometimes alleged that in Roman memorials children are underrepresented, in the sense that the proportion of children in the total number of

---

4. Most of the Greek examples in R. Lattimore, *Themes in Greek and Latin Epitaphs* (Urbana: University of Illinois Press, 1962), are from the Roman period and from Asia Minor.

5. The fundamental work on this is Saller and Shaw, "Tombstones and Roman Family Relations in the Principate," and subsequent work by Saller and Shaw separately.

6. There is much recent scholarship based on nomenclature. The leading center of such work is in Helsinki, led by Heikki Solin. For some brief remarks on the implications of nomenclature, see B. Rawson, "The Roman Family," in *The Family in Ancient Rome: New Perspectives*, ed. B. Rawson (London and Sydney: Routledge; Ithaca, N.Y.: Cornell University Press, 1986), p. 13.

7. Saller and Shaw, p. 137.

8. Shaw, "Seasons of Death," pp. 100-38.

commemorations is lower than their probable mortality rate. But, age-group by age-group, children are the most heavily represented decadal group commemorated.[9] Children of all ages are commemorated, although there are comparatively few infants and there is an emphasis on children under ten years of age. That children should have been commemorated in such numbers, and sometimes in such elaborate style, is a remarkable feature of Roman culture. There is no parallel for it in earlier or later societies before the twentieth century.

In the absence of official death registers from antiquity, it is impossible to compare the rates of dedications for any age-group with actual death rates. Model life tables have been our best means of comparing the dedications with the probable mortality rates. Skeletal material from Roman Italy has been very sparse and not easily accessible. Two explanations for this are the practice of cremation and modern archaeologists' lack of interest until recently in the systematic collecting of bones. Even now, the excavation of cemeteries might uncover only part of the original burial ground, thus missing children or infants when these were buried in a separate area. Where children's burials have been uncovered, it is clear that the original burials were carefully done. The proportion of prenatal or perinatal deaths in these cemeteries is quite high.[10] Abandonment or infanticide need not be the only explanations for such deaths: this is one of the most dangerous periods in the existence of a fetus or infant, even in normal circumstances. The frequent epidemics which broke out struck all age-groups and status levels, but children were especially vulnerable to some illnesses, e.g., diarrhea and dysentery,[11] and had built up less resistance to other diseases than had older members of the population.

Special arrangements have always applied to young deaths in European

9. See, for examples, Shaw, "Latin Funerary Epigraphy and Family Life in the Later Roman Empire," *Historia* 33 (1984): 457-97, especially tables C-G, showing high representation of under-tens, especially in Rome and Roman Italy.

10. E.g., an African cemetery in an area settled by Roman veterans has yielded a large number of skeletons of young children, all carefully buried (P.-A. Février and R. Guery, "Les rites funéraires de la nécropole orientale de Sétif," *Antiquités Africaines* 15 [1980]: 91-124). Thirty-five percent of the burials were aged zero to five years; 14 percent were prenatal or perinatal births. Recently Soren and Soren have published a large work on their excavations at a site (Lugnano) in southern Umbria, about seventy kilometers north of Rome, which have revealed a fifth-century (C.E.) cemetery of forty-seven children, all carefully buried. All but one were infants or premature fetuses, all buried at about the same time. D. Soren and N. Soren, *A Roman Villa and a Late-Roman Infant Cemetery: Excavation at Poggio Gramignano, Lugnano in Teverina* (Rome: L'Erma di Bretschneider, 1999).

11. Celsus (*On Medicine* 2.8.30) specifies that children up to age ten were most affected by this condition (*deiectio*).

history. According to Ariès,[12] the bodies of such children were sewn into shrouds and disposed of in common graves from medieval times until at least the late seventeenth century. Even when church policy changed and young children were buried in a town cemetery, they were buried in a special section of their own. It is only in very recent times in Western societies that there has been any recognition of infant or perinatal deaths in public cemeteries. Even today, miscarriages, stillbirths, and the deceased newborn are usually dealt with by the hospital where they occur, and some hospitals have special areas set aside for the scattering of ashes or arrange for communal burials in a special part of a cemetery. Not so very long ago, such remains were disposed of as merely hospital waste. Nowadays it is not unknown (but probably not the general practice) for infants to have an identifiable, individual burial place in a public cemetery, sometimes with a tombstone and personal items associated with the infant. Even these burial places are likely to be in liminal areas, separate from the main part of the cemetery.[13]

Even if infants were often buried more carefully than was once thought, it is demonstrable that they were memorialized less frequently than were other children. Epitaphs for those under one year, or even under two years, are a small proportion of all extant epitaphs. Some reasons for this are clear. In most, perhaps all, societies, a child is not considered a "real" person until it has developed certain functions, e.g., ability to walk or speak. The very first few days after birth are especially a time of limbo, when chances of survival are at their lowest.[14] The Romans did not give an infant a name until the seventh day (for females) or eighth day (for males).[15] There is another danger period at four to six

12. P. Ariès, *The Hour of Our Death* (New York: Knopf, 1981; translated from the French original of 1977), pp. 297, 552.

13. I owe much to the excellent discussion of modern material by E. Scott, *The Archaeology of Infancy and Infant Death*, BAR International Series 819 (Oxford: Archaeopress, 1999), especially chap. 3. Further development away from anonymous burials of infants is reflected in a new Butterfly Garden in Perth (Australia), dedicated in January 2001. It was welcomed by families not only for its identifiable location for each infant's memorial (e.g., an inscribed pebble in a stream, or a specific plant with a small plaque), but also for its attractive and peaceful ambience, encouraging visits by parents and other children, thus integrating the deceased infant into the whole family. Although infant mortality is now low in Western societies, SIDS (sudden infant death syndrome, or "cot deaths") remains a danger and a particular source of angst and guilt for many parents. Older women spoke at the dedication of the way in which the experience of infant death had been suppressed in their youth.

14. Neonatal mortality rates are still comparatively high, especially in poorer countries. See T. Parkin, *Demography and Roman Society* (Baltimore and London: Johns Hopkins University Press, 1992), pp. 93-94, for figures and discussion.

15. Cf. problems in the early church about early baptism of an infant who is likely to die. In

months. The first birthday was a significant date for some official Roman purposes, e.g., for the child's Junian Latin parent to upgrade to full Roman citizen-
ship, and for calculating eligibility for the *ius trium liberorum* under Augustus's
legislation.

Children did not merit full-scale formal mourning until the age of ten, but
some form of mourning was considered appropriate from the age of one, and it
increased for each year of age. A fragment from the third-century jurist Ulpian
preserves these rules: "Parents are to be mourned for a year, as are children older
than ten years. Pomponius [a jurist of the mid–second century] says that in this
context a year is ten months — a plausible argument, since younger children are
mourned for as many months as they have lived down to the age of three; a child
younger than three years does not receive formal mourning but a marginal form
(non lugetur, sed sublugetur); a child less than a year old receives neither formal
mourning nor a marginal form *(neque lugetur neque sublugetur)*."[16] Such rules,
however, are intended to help people structure their public lives (e.g., what public activities they might attend, what clothing they should wear),[17] and are more
relevant to people with public responsibilities and a public image to uphold than
to people of lower strata. Similarly, the literature of the educated upper classes
contains ideals of comportment — self-restraint, dignity, philosophical consola-
tion. None of this tells us much about inner emotions or behavior, especially in
the mass of the population. But recent studies, drawing on the work of anthropologists, make a strong case for real grief and grieving for the death of the very
young even in societies of high infant mortality.[18]

It has recently been argued that the upper, educated classes were able to ex-
ternalize their grief in funerary ritual and philosophical, consolatory literature
— avenues less accessible to lower classes, who therefore expressed grief more
frankly and uninhibitedly.[19] But MacMullen pointed out twenty years ago that

---

the East the ritual interval between birth and baptism might be eight days or forty days. Parents
who allowed their children to die unbaptized were subject to severe penances; but if an infant of
seven days or younger died unbaptized, the parents' penance was considerably less severe (J.
Baun, "The Fate of Babies Dying before Baptism in Byzantium," in *The Church and Childhood*,
ed. D. Wood [Oxford: Blackwells, 1994], pp. 117-18).

16. *Fragmentum Vaticanum* 321, in *FIRA*, 2.536. A later legal text (the *Sententiae* attributed
to Paulus, probably late third century) prescribes a full year's mourning for children older than
six: *Sententiae* 1.21.13, in *FIRA*, 2.335.

17. E.g., Paulus (*Sententiae* 1.21.14) reports that a person in mourning must abstain from
banquets, ornamentation, and the wearing of purple and white ("qui luget abstinere debet a
conuiuiis ornamentis purpura et alba ueste").

18. E.g., M. Golden, "Did the Ancients Care When Their Children Died?" *GR* 35 (1988): 152-
63.

19. A. Gunnella, "Morte improvise e violente nelle iscrizioni latine," in *La mort au*

upper-class Romans did in fact indulge in "exaggerated and paraded grief" on some occasions.[20] Such grief was displayed for infant deaths by some notable Roman men, although we usually know of this only through the disapproval of one of their peers. Seneca wrote a long letter on the futility and ungratefulness of grieving at death (*Letters* 99). In it he takes his friend Marullus as an example of a mature man, who should know better, grieving extravagantly at the death of a young son *(filium paruulum)*: Seneca criticizes Marullus's emotional reaction (*molliter ferre:* 99.1). Seneca's arguments are that the boy had lived for so short a period that no hopes could have been invested in him; he might have turned out badly, as sons often did. Seneca grants that it is natural to show emotion at the time of death, but one should not overdo it so as to make a display (99.15-16). He grants also that one should not suppress memory of a lost one; it is less than human not to remember one's own dead, to bury memory with the body (99.23). It is good to speak often of the lost one, to remember his talk and jokes (even that of a very young one: *quamuis paruoli*). But those who mourn and miss those who died young *(in aetate prima raptum)* should put the death in perspective by realizing how short any life is in comparison with eternity (99.31). It is clear that Marullus was deeply moved by the death of the infant, and even Seneca, playing the rational philosopher, admits the human and individual qualities of the lost son.[21]

Within fairly general attitudes to infancy there can be significant cultural differences. MacMullen's classic work on "the epigraphic habit" showed that, within the western Mediterranean, young children received the highest percentage of epitaphs in large urban areas and amongst large slave populations. Northern Italy provides more evidence than southern Italy, and each provides more than Africa or Spain.[22] Within Rome itself, the Greek-speaking population contrasted strongly with the Latin-speaking in respect of the age-groups favored for mention on epitaphs. Epitaphs for children from birth to age nine account for over 30 percent of the ages specified in Latin epitaphs, but the

---

quotidien dans le monde romain: actes du colloque organisé par l'Université de Paris IV, ed. F. Hinard (Paris: de Boccard, 1995), pp. 9-22.

20. R. MacMullen, "Romans in Tears," *CP* 75 (1980): 254-55.

21. The poet Statius wrote a long (sympathetic) poem (*Siluae* 2.1) describing the grief exhibited by Atedius Melior at the death of his little foster child *(alumnus)* Glaucias. See Christian Laes in this volume. See also Juvenal 15.132-40 on compassion, or tenderness (*mollissima corda,* the same adjective Seneca used to describe Marullus's reaction to the death of his infant son); and Herodes Atticus, that pragmatic, often ruthless citizen of Athens and Rome in the mid–second century, powerful in political and cultural circles, could weep at the death of his newborn son (Fronto, *Letters* 1.6.7, Marcus Aurelius to Fronto; 1.8, in Greek, Fronto to Herodes).

22. See Shaw, "Latin Funerary Epigraphy and Family Life in the Later Roman Empire" and "Seasons of Death."

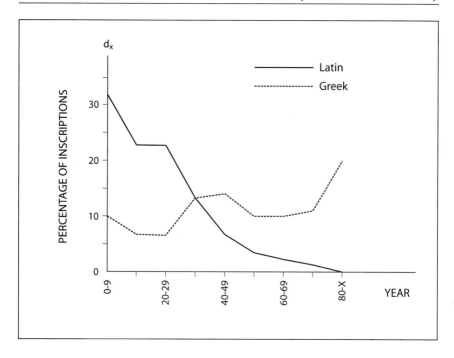

Figure 1. Age-group frequencies among 9,980 Greek and Latin
tomb inscriptions in Rome

Greek ones for these ages account for only 10 percent of Greek epitaphs specify-
ing ages. The graph in figure 1 illustrates this.[23] The other end of the age scale
shows an increase in Greek epitaphs after the age of thirty and again after the
age of seventy, whereas the proportion of Latin epitaphs decreases steadily with
age, especially after age thirty. These cultural differences are useful as a context
for assessing Christian funerary practices and attitudes to children. Some
Christians in Rome were Greek-speaking, and there were strong Christian
communities in Africa. Did the Christian epitaphs here conform to the non-
Christian? Shaw's work suggests that they did.[24] Thus the Christian epitaphs in

23. MacMullen ("The Epigraphic Habit in the Roman Empire," *AJP* 103 [1982]: 233-46), fig.
III, based on K. K. Ery, "Investigations on the Demographic Source Value of Tombstones Originating from the Roman Period," *Alba Regia* 10 (1969): 51-67. The work of M. Clauss, "Probleme
der Lebensalterstatistiken aufgrund römischen Grabinschriften," *Chiron* 3 (1973): 395-417, also
based on Ery, confirms the regional distinctions noted here and the Latin-Greek contrast.
24. See Shaw, "Latin Funerary Epigraphy and Family Life in the Later Roman Empire."

Africa, like the pagan ones, have much less emphasis on children than those in Rome and Italy. Carthage, an urban center, has a greater emphasis than do rural African areas, but still less than in Rome and Italy.[25]

It has sometimes been said that early Christian memorials gave great emphasis to children because of the special value Christianity attached to children. The allocation of space in the catacombs at Rome does not offer support for this. There are comparatively few slots for children, and the percentage of known Christian sarcophagi belonging to children is low.[26] Shaw reports the emphasis on bisomal slots (designed for two bodies) in the catacombs, predominantly for husband and wife with no provision for children.[27] Epitaphs, however, of Christians from Rome of the third to sixth centuries do have a more prominent place for children than did non-Christian epitaphs of the first two and a half centuries.[28] But was this a new element or an adoption and further development of earlier Roman practices?[29] In Christian populations in other cultures there was also accommodation to local culture, which resulted in a much lower profile for children if that was the context in which Christian groups settled or developed. What is needed is an analysis of Christian epitaphs region by region, to determine what elements (if any) are consistently Christian. Shaw's studies have taken us well along this path, and one hopes for more analysis of this kind based on his very extensive data set.

Shaw deduced from the inscriptions of Rome a valuation of children in the Christian community "over and above the level attributable to time and city living."[30] Thus the valuation of children in Rome, as evidenced in epitaphs, had increased as the city became larger and more prosperous and probably peaked in the late second or early third century. As the Christian community at Rome developed, it followed this pattern and (apparently) retained it even as Rome's size and prosperity declined in subsequent centuries (third to sixth). Shaw's calculations for various regions are shown in his table (4.3), "Percentage of Tomb-

25. Shaw ("The Cultural Meaning of Death: Age and Gender in the Roman Family," in *The Family in Italy from Antiquity to the Present*, ed. D. I. Kertzer and R. P. Saller [New Haven and London: Yale University Press, 1991], pp. 66-90, and "Seasons of Death") discusses the emphasis on children in Christian epitaphs of Rome, but does not distinguish between Greek and Latin epitaphs.

26. Based on the sarcophagi included in *RS* and J. Huskinson, *Roman Children's Sarcophagi: Their Decoration and Its Social Significance* (Oxford: Clarendon, 1996).

27. Shaw, "Seasons of Death."

28. Shaw, "The Cultural Meaning of Death."

29. The number of Christian epitaphs before the fourth century is small, and the number of pagan epitaphs dwindled during the third; so there is a discontinuity which makes this question difficult to answer.

30. Shaw, "Cultural Meaning of Death," p. 80.

stone Epitaphs Dedicated to Children under Ten Years of Age in the Earlier and Later Empire," reproduced below:

Region	1st-3rd centuries (ca. A.D. 1-250)	3rd-6th centuries (ca. A.D. 250-500)
Rome	27.7	34.4
Northern Italy	19.5	21.1
Spain	6.9	7.7
Africa: Carthage	16.9	22.5
Africa: Cirta	5.5	11.4
Africa: small centers	6.9	8.4

(Reproduced courtesy of Brent Shaw, University of Pennsylvania)

In the context of the Christian view that death was the birth of a new life, those who died young could be seen as deserving celebration for their early entry into paradise. Their epitaphs are not, however, very communicative on such matters, and the children are less often recorded in the context of (biological) family relationships.

Visual representations of children in Roman Italy are striking in number and style.[31] Most of these are funerary, so they provide another dimension for the study of children's death and commemoration. An iconographical comparison of Christian and other memorials for children from Rome is instructive. Because of the Christian view of death and an afterlife, their memorials show less interest in daily activities or details of past life: the focus is on heaven and the future. There is also less differentiation between children and adults.

Pre-Christian reliefs, friezes, altars, and *klinē* monuments provide a rich variety of representations of children and commemorations of their deaths. Sometimes these are retrospective, recording lives already lived, sometimes prospective, alluding to lives looked forward to. One striking combination of both types is on the altar of Q. Sulpicius Maximus,[32] where the inscriptions (Greek and Latin) record at considerable length the eleven-year-old boy's achievements already in composing and reciting a poem in Greek at a public competition (in 94 C.E.), and his parents' pride in him, while the sculpture represents the more adult, fully-fledged orator into which he had been expected to develop.

31. Cf. B. Rawson, "The Iconography of Roman Childhood," in *The Roman Family in Italy: Status, Sentiment, Space,* ed. B. Rawson and P. Weaver (Oxford: Clarendon, 1997), pp. 205-32.

32. D. Kleiner, *Roman Imperial Funerary Altars with Portraits* (Rome: Bretschneider, 1987), pls. XXVII. 3, XXVIII. 1-2; Rawson, "Iconography of Roman Childhood," fig. 9.9; *CIL* 6.33976.

There is particular pathos in the inscription and associated sculpture on an altar dedicated by Publicia Glypte for two infant boys, her son and her *uerna* (a slave born and raised in her own household) (fig. 2).[33] The inscription records each boy's details in separate columns, with Glypte's name running along the bottom of both columns:

D	M
NICONI FILIO	EVTYCHETI
DVLCISSIMO	VERNAE
QVI V MENS XI	QVI VIX AN I
DIEBVS VIII	MENS V DIEB X
PVBLICIA GLYPTE	FECIT

("To the departed spirits of
[col. 1] Nico, her sweet son, who lived for 11 months and 8 days; and
[col. 2] Eutyches, her home-born slave, who lived for 1 year, 5 months and 10 days; dedicated by Publicia Glypte")

Above the inscription are sculpted two figures of the little boys in togas, each holding a scroll, with a scroll box between them at their feet. The togas and the appurtenances of schooling are clearly prospective, foreshadowing the boys' futures (now cut off) as well-educated citizens. The representation of Eutyches is especially optimistic, as a slave would not normally look forward to a liberal education or wear a toga; but Glypte advertises what had been her intention — to give Eutyches his freedom and to raise him as a citizen and as a foster brother to Nico.[34] The sculpture on the pediment of the stone appears to be of Telephus, suckled by a hind, thus alluding to a fostering relationship. Glypte has raised the two boys almost as twins. Eutyches may already have been a surrogate son during Glypte's pregnancy, and she could have looked forward to having him as playmate and companion for her natural son, perhaps also to be suckled by the same nurse. A use of the Roman wolf, the *lupa Romana,* suckling Romulus and Remus would have made more explicit the close association of the two boys; but the Telephus myth is nevertheless relevant enough to suggest

33. Rome, Villa Albani. *CIL* 6.22972; Kleiner, pl. XL. 1; DAI EA 4553.

34. Publicia Glypte's cognomen suggests that she is more likely to be freed than freeborn. The status of Nico is uncertain. If he is a slave, it would be natural for the mother to hope to free him at the earliest opportunity — hence the representation of him in a toga. I prefer this interpretation, retaining the parallelism with Eutyches. But if he has the same nomen Publicius (suppressed) as his mother, he could be of freed status (freed either by her after her freedom or by their common owner) or (much less likely in this context) freeborn, born after her freedom.

Figure 2. Altar dedicated for two boys by Publicia Glypte,
early second century C.E.

that it was consciously chosen for this occasion.[35] Representations of the wolf were used for a variety of purposes in Roman art. In imperial art, especially from the late first century, it often had political and national purposes, symbolizing the origins of Rome and commemorating the foundation figures. The image encoded the eternity *(Aeternitas)* of Rome, and examples of this continued until the sixth century. In funerary art it can be found on altars, steles, and sarcophagi, but its use cannot be identified with any particular familial association. The *Aeternitas* implications did make it suitable for spouses, to symbolize their enduring relationship and their loyalty to each other. Its use by freedmen and freedwomen gave these new citizens the opportunity to proclaim their loyalty to Rome.

Although the wolf and the twins cannot be linked closely to specific familial relationships, there was an interest in the general image of a nurturing animal with an infant. The myths of the *lupa Romana,* of the hind and Telephus, and of the goat and Asclepius all preserved stories of the miraculous rescue of an infant and an animal's suckling of the infant at risk. It was the fostering and rearing aspect of the image, more than that of loyalty and eternity, which was to the fore when it was chosen for children; and sometimes it is not clear which myth, or which animal, is represented. A casual observer could well confuse one with another. Sometimes the *lupa Romana* is represented with only one child.[36] On an altar of the first century the hind image is on one side, the wolf on another.[37] These two images were for some purposes interchangeable.

Early Christianity eschewed these classical myths, and one might expect that the apparent idolatry of an animal would cause difficulties. Lactantius hints at this in his criticism of Roman religion *(Divine Institutes* 1.20.1-3). He begins his examples of specifically Roman cults with Lupa. "Lupa, as the nurse of Romulus, had divine honours conferred on her." But he tempers this criticism in order to make a more severe accusation: he could tolerate the wolf myth if its focus were only an animal, but *lupa* can refer to a prostitute, and it is that

35. Tombstones must often have been bought "off the shelf," and their appropriateness is sometimes not obvious. But (as pointed out by Monika Trümper, whom I thank) it would be very rare to find a ready-carved tombstone with a twinlike pair of boys on it. I also thank Carolyn Osiek for drawing attention to the unusualness of the toga for a *uerna.*

36. E.g., C. Dulière, *Lupa Romana. Recherches d'iconographie et essai d'interprétation* (Brussels and Rome: Institut historique Belge de Rome, 1979), fig. 257, cat. 62. The epitaph (*CIL* 6.8830) is dedicated to an imperial slave, Euporus, by his brother Achilles, an imperial freedman. Much of the detail here on the iconography of these myths is due to Dulière. See also *Lexicon Iconographicum Mythologiae Classicae,* ed. H. C. Ackerman and J.-R. Gisler, 8 vols. (Zürich: Artemis, 1981-97).

37. Dulière, fig. 263, cat. 55.

sort of woman (the wife of the peasant who took up the twins), he alleges, who is worshiped in this story. The image of the infant Romulus and Remus was not totally unlike the Christian nativity image, with similar association of animals and shepherds. And it is found connected with the crucifixion in a rare image of the late ninth century, on an ivory diptych showing Christ on the cross, with the cross standing on the back of the *lupa Romana* and her twins.[38] Dulière interprets this as old Rome serving as the foundation for the new religion and the new Christian Rome remaining *caput mondi*. But it is more probably a declaration of Christianity's defeat of the old pagan myths and religions.[39]

Sarcophagi were gradually coming into use at Rome from the early second century C.E. With their broader surfaces, they provided greater scope for ornamentation and for details of children's (and others') lives, and this must have been a stimulus to their increasing use. Common elements are the infant's first bath, the games and education of the growing child, and aspects of the child's funerary rites (laying out of the body, parents' mourning, and sometimes apotheosis of the child).[40] A well-known example is the sarcophagus of the young M. Cornelius Statius: a finely sculpted piece of the mid–second century, 1.49 meters long and 0.475 meters high, originally from Ostia but now in the Louvre in Paris. The four life stages portrayed are: the mother nursing the newborn baby, watched by the father; the father standing, dandling his infant son; the boy driving a goat cart (goats were a favorite pet for Roman boys; driving the cart a favorite game); the boy reading from a scroll to a seated man (probably a teacher, perhaps the father).[41] Sarcophagi were the natural container for inhumation, and thus for the remains of Christians who could afford them.[42] But Christians were less attracted to the details of everyday life or the mythological scenes so popular on non-Christian sarcophagi. On Christian sarcophagi, sculpted scenes came mostly from biblical stories, e.g. (in fig. 3) Jonah on the lid and, on the body of the sarcophagus, Mary and child and the procession

38. Dulière, fig. 233 and p. 203.

39. A declaration seen by J. Davies, *Death, Burial, and Rebirth in the Religions of Antiquity* (London and New York: Routledge, 1999), p. 194, in the placement of Christian burials and shrines "on top of older, defeated pagan religions and burial sites."

40. For examples, see Huskinson, *Roman Children's Sarcophagi*; R. Amedick, *Vita Privata (Die antike Sarkophagreliefs,* i.4) (Berlin: Schaubel, 1991); Rawson, "The Iconography of Roman Childhood."

41. Illustrations of the sarcophagus are in many publications, e.g., Huskinson, pl. II.1; Amedick, pls. 52.1-12, 53.4-5; B. Rawson, "Education: The Romans and Us," *Antichthon* 33 (1999): fig. 1.

42. Although comparatively expensive, sarcophagi were not used exclusively by the upper classes. Other members of Rome's population, e.g., ambitious freedmen, adopted this form of commemoration readily, as they had adopted other forms from the first century C.E. onward.

Figure 3. Sarcophagus of Aurelius, dedicated by parents (Christian)

of the Magi; Daniel and the lions; Adam and Eve; and the healing of a blind man. These stories could be used on adult or child sarcophagi; there was nothing particularly appropriate to children in the decoration of their sarcophagi. Examples of the life-cycle sequence, of the parents' mourning at the funeral couch of their child, or other age-specific scenes are not found on Christian children's memorials. The sarcophagus in figure 3, from early-fourth-century Rome, does have a half-figure portrait of the dead five-year-old Aurelius on the lid, with his epitaph.[43] The portrait is not particularly individualized: it is set against a curtain (a *parapetasma*) held by cupids. Huskinson points out that by the later third century compositions on sarcophagi were already becoming formulaic, and that figured elements had a subordinate role in decorative scenes.[44] So, as suggested above for inscriptions, Christian practice might have developed a preexisting trend rather than establishing some radically new symbolism or ideology.

The boy on the lid of figure 3 holds a scroll in his hand. This had been one of the attributes of scenes of education over a long, preceding period. Such attributes continued on Christian sarcophagi, as learning and teaching were important elements in the practice and promotion of Christianity. Zanker dis-

43. Huskinson, 10.9; *RS* 662.
44. Huskinson, p. 59.

Figure 4. Sarcophagus of girl, shown with scroll (Christian)

cussed this continuity of imagery under the heading "Christ as the Teacher of the True Philosophy."[45] From the late third century the dominant visual image of Christ in catacomb paintings and on sarcophagi was as the teacher of wisdom. Epitaphs, too, continued the praise of child prodigies for their precocious learning, e.g., a father Dalmatius commemorated his seven-year-old son (also Dalmatius) for his complete *ingeniositas* and *sapientia* (*ICUR* 1978 = *CIL* 6.33929). The further details of the boy's study of Greek and Latin literature are reminiscent of earlier non-Christian epitaphs. Only the date of death, and the reference to his being snatched away from human affairs *(ereptus est rebus humanis)*, indicate his Christian connection.

Girls are less often represented with these qualities. In Christian iconography the female *orans* (standing figure with hands outstretched or clasped high in prayer) is frequent, and such figures are sometimes accompanied by a scroll; but this represents religious piety rather than scholarly achievement. One small sarcophagus from a fourth-century catacomb in Rome, however, has on its front a bust portrait of a girl (not an *orans*) clasping a scroll (fig. 4).[46] Other figures on the sarcophagus include Cupid and Psyche and the Good Shepherd. Another, for a girl (Optata) of about three years of age, shows an *orans* figure

45. P. Zanker, *The Mask of Socrates: The Image of the Intellectual in Antiquity*, trans. A. Shapiro (Berkeley: University of California Press, 1995), pp. 289-97.

46. Huskinson, 10.8; *RS* 381.

with a box at her feet which might hold scrolls. Her epitaph praises her for sweetness of speech as well as of gesture.[47]

By rare chance Aurelius, of figure 3, has a brother attested on another sarcophagus; but the memorial to the brother Florentius does not have the Christian associations of Aurelius's. The inscription on Aurelius's sarcophagus identifies him as of equestrian status and is dedicated by his parents, Tullianus and Aristia. The equestrian Florentius Domitius Marianus, who died at age nine, has a dedication from the same parents, Tullianus and Aristia.[48] Whereas Aurelius is praised as "dulcissimo et incomparabili," is said to have left great grief to his parents, and is represented with a scroll, Florentius receives only one epithet, "dulcissimo"; there is no reference to his parents' grief; and he is represented as a full-length standing figure in military garb. None of the sculpted scenes on his sarcophagus has overtly Christian reference: they comprise cupids, the Seasons, Oceanus and Tellus, and urns of fruit. Further reconstruction of the family history is impossible without additional information, but one notes with interest the early deaths of two sons and their different representations. It is possible that the parents and their second son were converted to Christianity after the death of Florentius, who seems to have been destined for a normal equestrian career, including service as an officer in the Roman army. This sequence could explain the greater grief and affection attested for Aurelius when he died.[49] The iconography is vital here to alert us to the boys' different experience. The inscriptions alone probably would not have alerted us to this, unless the two dates — for death and then burial — for Aurelius suggested his Christian affiliation: "defunctus Non(is) Sep(tembribus)/depositus VII Idus Sep(tembres)." Shaw remarks on the importance to Christians of the date of death as the true birthday, when one was born again, into eternal life: "what was worth recording on one's burial marker was the temporal point of the transition into one's genuine life."[50] Here the inscription takes account of the eight-day period (nine days on Roman inclusive counting) between death and actual burial: it was only after that period that funerary rites were finalized and the deceased could begin the new life. This nine-day period shows continuity with pre-Christian funerary practice (reflected in the term *nouendialis* for certain

---

47. Huskinson, 10.13; *RS* 769. "hic Optata sita est, quam/tirtia rapuit aestas./lingua, manu numquam/dulcior ulla fuit./in pace."

48. Huskinson, 8.12; *RS* 663.

49. In spite of death's being celebrated as a welcome event by Christians, as noted below. If this reconstruction is correct, how does Florentius come to be buried in a Christian cemetery (that of Novatian)?

50. Shaw, "Seasons of Death," p. 103.

ceremonies),[51] at least for a family of this high status. Poorer, more humble corpses went to the grave much more quickly and simply.

Premature, untimely death (*funus acerbum*) stimulated pathos but also feelings of unease in ancient communities.[52] The spirits of those who died "before their time" (the *lemures*) were thought to wander restlessly at night and to need special attention from the living to appease them. Vergil describes them in the underworld as amongst the unhappy dead, caught in the mire across the Styx and far from the blessed fields of Elysium (*Aeneid* 6.427-29). They include infants, "snatched from the breast, on the threshold of life and robbed of the sweetnesses of life, carried off by a black day and drowned in the bitterness of death" [*infantumque animae flentes, in limine primo / quos dulcis uitae exsortis et ab ubere raptos / abstulit atra dies et funere mersit acerbo*]. The festival of the Lemuria in May recognized the presence of such wandering spirits amongst the living and propitiated them in order to hasten their return to the underworld.

This gloomy view of the afterlife was modified as the imperial period developed. There were still many statements of the "nothingness" or grimness beyond death, but there is evidence of the development of an alternative view, which placed the good and the innocent in the heavens rather than in some part of the underworld (however blessed). There had been a long tradition of associating the soul with the ether and the stars, e.g., in Neo-Pythagoreanism. Funerary monuments with astral symbolism are not common in Roman Italy, being more frequent in Roman Africa and in Gaul.[53] Such symbolism and its application to children were not, however, unknown at Rome. In 82 or 83 C.E., the emperor Domitian deified his deceased young son and represented him on coinage as an infant reaching up to seven stars above him. The mythological associations were of a son translated to the heavens as the star Arcturus to join his spiritual mother, the constellation the Great Bear, and summoned by his father Jupiter.[54]

One tombstone found in Rome which contains symbolism of this kind

---

51. Some sources define *nouendialis* as relating to ceremonies nine days after the funeral. But Servius (in *Aeneid* 5.64) is specific that after a seven-day lying-in-state at home, the corpse was cremated on the eighth day and buried on the ninth. Games for the dead were called *nouendiales*.

52. See my discussion of *funus acerbum* and a first-century (B.C.E.) inscription from Puteoli prescribing undertakers' duties: "The Express Route to Hades," in *Thinking Like a Lawyer*, ed. P. McKechnie (Leiden: Brill, 2002).

53. See J. Prieur, *La mort dans l'antiquité romaine* (Rennes: Ouest-France, 1986), pp. 132-38, for these associations. Prieur attributes the astral symbolism in Gaul, Spain, Britain, and the Danube provinces to Celtic influences.

54. Rawson, "Representations of Roman Children and Childhood," *Antichthon* 31 (1997): 78.

commemorates a ten-year-old girl, Iulia Victorina. Her epitaph, probably from the first century C.E., was dedicated to her as *filiae dulcissimae* by her parents, C. Iulius Saturninus and Lucilia Procula (*CIL* 6.20727). Her bust, on the front of the altar above the epitaph, is surmounted by a crescent moon. On the back of the stone is the bust of an adult woman whose head is backed by the rays of the sun. These two portraits may be taken to represent two phases of the deceased girl's passage to eternal life in the heavens: her initial abode in the moon and her later ascent to the sun.[55]

Another monument, probably late second or early third century C.E., discovered near Rome in 1935, is also dedicated to a child — the two-year-old Eutychos — and also has sculpture with apotheosis symbolism.[56] The marble comprises a relief of a boy on a horse above a bilingual inscription (Greek and Latin). A pendant (the *bulla*) round the boy's neck shows his freeborn status. A star sits above his head. His horse is being led upward to the skies by an eagle with outstretched wings, by means of a rope between its beak and the horse's mouth. The boy's right hand is raised, but unfortunately it is broken off and one cannot be sure whether it held an object (e.g., a torch) or was making a gesture (e.g., a wave of farewell). Four elegiac couplets in Greek make explicit the child's message of reassurance to his father that he is not beneath the earth in Hades but has been taken up by Jupiter's eagle to join the stars. Two initial couplets in Greek, which precede the child's message, report his age in the precise way familiar in Latin epitaphs: he lived for two years, two months, and almost five days; and the father's dedication at the end is in Latin: the imperial freedman Eutiches set it up for his sweet son ("[E]utiches Aug. lib. filio/[dul]cissimo fecit").

Seston points out that Eutychos's direct translation to the skies has saved him from the long period in limbo traditionally assigned to the prematurely dead. He sees a revulsion in the imperial period against the traditional view, because of parents' affection for their children. He sees this change in another epitaph from Rome, in which the little girl *(paruola)* Anullina proclaims her escape from the underworld and her translation to the stars, distinguishing between her earthly remains and her soul thus:

55. Prieur, p. 136; Kleiner, cat. 15, pl. X.3-4

56. Published in *AE* 1945, 119; discussed by W. Seston, "L'épitaphe d'Eutychos et l'héroisation par la pureté," in *Hommages à Joseph Bidez et à Franz Cumont* (Brussels: Latomus [Collection Latomus II], 1949), pp. 313-22; and P. Boyancé, *"Funus acerbum,"* REA 54 (1952): 275-89.

. . . SED MEA
DIVINA NON EST ITVRA SVB
VMBRAS   CAELESTIS
ANIMA. MVNDVS ME SVMP-
SIT ET ASTRA. CORPVS HABET
TELLVS ET SAXVM NOMEN
INANAE.[57]

Children's only claim to a heavenly destiny is their innocence, as they can claim no great achievements or virtues. Eutychos is characterized as having known neither the bad nor the good of life: οὐ κακὸν οὐδὲ ἀγαθὸν γνοὺς βίος ὅττι φέρει. Although there are no literary sources attesting this new view of the fate of children, and the funerary monuments illustrating it are few, we must recognize that the literary and monumental evidence for this period (late second and third centuries) is sparse compared with that for the previous two centuries. If the new view had become current in the general population, it could have provided an easy transition to the early Christian view of a blessed afterlife for those who died young.

The Christian view, however, was ambivalent about the fate of those who died young. As for all Christians, death for these children meant the beginning of a new life, a birth into their "real" life; thus the precise date of death is often recorded. But how could very young children, who had achieved nothing, have earned the reward of eternal life after death?[58] In particular, how could they achieve salvation if they were unbaptized? And in the early church baptism was normally available only to those who had reached an age of reason and free will. The anguish and despair of those experiencing the death of infants, and the high frequency of such deaths, forced reconsideration of access to baptism, and various compromises were settled on in different sections of the church; but the dilemma continued, especially in the strong Augustinian tradition of original sin. There was also a problem for Christians in any attempt to represent the dead as gods or heavenly beings. Tertullian gave strong expression to this at the

---

57. *CIL* 6.12087. "But my divine spirit will not go down below, beneath the Shades; it is destined for the skies. The heavens and the stars have taken me up. The earth contains my body, and my stone the name of a ghost."

58. Neither did they deserve punishment. They were virtually nonbeings. On the problems of purgatory, limbo, and nonexistence for deceased infants, and contrasts between the Eastern and Western Churches, see G. Gould, "Childhood in Eastern Patristic Thought: Some Problems of Theology and Theological Anthropology," in *The Church and Childhood*, ed. D. Woods (Oxford: Blackwells, 1994), pp. 39-52; and Baun, "The Fate of Babies Dying before Baptism in Byzantium."

end of the second century, in his criticism of pagans' attitudes to their own gods: "What honour do you pay to your gods which you do not equally offer to your dead? You erect temples to the gods — equally to the dead; you erect altars to the gods — equally to the dead; you inscribe the same letters in their inscriptions, you give the same form to their statues, according to each person's profession or business or age. An old man's representation is taken from Saturn, a youth's from Apollo, a girl's from Diana. . . ."[59] There are, therefore, no parallels in Christian art for the heroizing of mortals.

There is ample evidence, in various media, for a changing attitude to children and childhood — or at least a changing manifestation of feeling, and greater visibility of children in these media — in the imperial period in Roman Italy.[60] Detailed regional studies would be necessary to establish whether there is an adequate range of evidence beyond Roman Italy to discuss attitudes and representations; and, if there is, how these compare with one another and with those in Italy. We have seen above that there was significant cultural variation in the Roman Empire regionally and chronologically.[61] Even in one place, a large and heterogeneous city such as Rome, there was cultural diversity. It seems that Christianity accommodated to local culture in many ways wherever it took root, so it is unwise to generalize about "Christianity in the Roman world." Even "Christianity in Rome" will have varied according to class, immigrant or native-born status, language, and other factors. But in many respects Christians in the early centuries can be seen as a subset of the Roman population, not seeking to advertise themselves publicly as a sector apart. The nature of cultural change in Rome in the third century is difficult to map, because of the poorer evidence available, but trends which are identifiable in more general Roman culture can also be seen in early Christianity in Roman Italy, e.g., the emphasis on children in funerary inscriptions. Christian children, however, are less often memorialized as members of a biological family and less often represented iconographically in specifically child-related contexts. The change in iconographic fashion may have been a pre-Christian trend, but the development of Christianity must have hastened the reduction in the specificity of children's

---

59. Tertullian, *To the Nations* 1.10.25-36; cf. *Apology* 13.7.

60. See, e.g., Rawson, "The Iconography of Roman Childhood," on iconography, and "Representations of Roman Children and Childhood," on other art, inscriptions, papyri, law, and literature.

61. Martin's study of epitaphs from Roman Asia Minor illustrates differences between these and those from the Roman West (D. Martin, "The Construction of the Ancient Family: Methodological Considerations," *JRS* 86 [1996]: 40-60). On the dangers of generalizing from such a regional study, see B. Rawson, "'The Family' in the Ancient Mediterranean: Past, Present, Future," *ZPE* 117 (1997): 294-96.

activities and in the recording of parent-child relationships. Children were being perceived as part of a wider community, where all — adults and children — were brothers and sisters in faith and children of God. In a big crowded city like Rome, with high rates of mortality and where public and private merged, children always experienced a variety of relationships. The difference between Christian and non-Christian was in the lesser emphasis placed, in Christian funerary memorials, on close kin and the life lived as children.

Desperately Different? *Delicia* Children in the Roman Household

Christian Laes

Back in the eighties *L' histoire de la vie privée (A History of Private Life)* was conceived and elaborated by two leading French historians: Philippe Ariès and George Duby. Their aim was as ambitious as it was innovative: discovering and exploring the vast and largely unexploited domain of people's personal lives from the times of the Roman Empire till our twentieth century. The first volume (dealing with the Roman Empire, late antiquity, early Middle Ages in the West, and the Byzantine Empire) was entrusted to Paul Veyne.[1] With its critical and sometimes provocative remarks, its thoughtful and insightful comments, this volume proved an excellent introduction to the subject for a large public, as well as a continued source of inspiration for other scholars.

In the chapter on the family and its freedmen, one can read the following interesting lines:

> The Romans liked to have about the house a little boy or girl slave or foundling, whom they brought up *(alumnus, threptus)* because they were fond of the child *(deliciae, delicatus)* and found it cute. They kept the child with them at dinner, played with it, put up with its whims; sometimes they gave it a "liberal" education, in principle reserved for free men. This custom was useful because of its ambiguity: the pet child might be a plaything, but it might also be a sexual object. It might have been adopted in all innocence, or it might be the master's own child, enjoying his secret favor. I should also mention the

1. P. Veyne, ed., *A History of Private Life*, vol. 1, *From Pagan Rome to Byzantium*, trans. A. Goldhammer (Cambridge: Harvard University Press, Belknap Press, 1987).

I owe many thanks to Prof. E. Eyben and Prof. T. Van Houdt (Louvain) as well as Prof. D. Pikhaus (Gent) for their valuable suggestions and corrections in preparing this paper. During and after the conference, I benefited much from the comments of Suzanne Dixon, Dale Martin, Beryl Rawson, Hanne Sigismund Nielsen, and Richard Saller.

corps of adolescent valets that, had they been well born, we might be tempted to call pages; but they, too, were slaves.

Keeping a boy for sexual purposes was a minor sin for gentlemen of quality, and their inferiors smiled respectfully. . . .

Jealous wives refused to allow their husbands to kiss a beloved boy in their presence. Did husbands go further still when out of sight? By convention no one in good society asked such questions.[2]

Not only does this passage provide an excellent summary on the problem of Roman *delicia* children; it is also one of the few places where the issue occurs in a major survey on Roman cultural history. Research on *delicia* children has indeed, by reason of its subject matter, always been rather controversial, and that is perhaps a reason why not too much attention has been given to it. In fact, the most thorough treatment was done in 1892 by Th. Birt (not fortuitous in Latin!). Valuable contributions (with a large amount of evidence, unfortunately sometimes confused) were written by Aurigemma[3] and Mau.[4] After a silence of almost seventy years, attention was again drawn to the subject by Slater in a discussion on some passages of classical Roman poetry.[5] A fresh approach was taken by the Danish scholar Hanne Sigismund Nielsen.[6] Although she takes full account of the epigraphic evidence, her research is confined to Rome and *CIL* 6.

Valuable as these contributions are, they all suffer from one remarkable error of interpretation. Starting from a narrow definition of slave *delicia* children as found in literary sources, they discuss the use of the term in epigraphic evidence and conclude that the term could be used in a much wider sense. How far this wider sense also occurs in literary sources is insufficiently examined, and thus the authors have failed to notice the bearing this wider use can have on our understanding of the nature of the Roman family. It is therefore my purpose to elaborate upon Sigismund Nielsen's study by:

1. examining more closely the literary meaning of the terms *delicium/ delicatus;*

---

2. Veyne, p. 79.

3. S. Aurigemma, "Delicium," in E. de Ruggiero, *Dizionario epigrafico di antichità romane* (Rome: "L'erma" di Brettschneider, 1910), vol. 2.2, pp. 1596-1603.

4. A. Mau, "Deliciae," in *Pauly's Realenzyklopädie der klassischen Altertumswissenschaft* 4.2, ed. G. Wissowa, W. Kroll, and K. Mittelhaus (Munich: Drüchenmuller, 1901), vol. 4, 2, c. 2435-38.

5. W. J. Slater, "Pueri, turba minuta," *Institute of Classical Studies Bulletin* 21 (1974): 133-40.

6. H. Sigismund Nielsen, "Delicia in Roman Literature and in the Urban Inscriptions," *ARID* 19 (1990): 79-88.

2. examining the *delicia* as a key for our understanding of the Roman family;
3. expanding the epigraphic evidence to the other volumes of *CIL* and *AE*, and thus creating a complete corpus of Roman *delicia*; and
4. offering explanatory models from psychology, anthropology, and comparative sociology.

Literary Evidence

"*Delicius puer in delicio a domino* — a beloved boy cherished by his master," cites the *ThLL* (with a reference to Gloss. 5.496, 53: *dicius: dilicius*), pointing to a professional and technical use of the term: young slave children meant to entertain and amuse their masters. Some examples of this technical use exist. Manumission of slaves under thirty years of age was under special conditions regulated by law (*Digest* 40.2, 11-14), but *Digest* 40.2, 16 does not provide this exception for luxurious slaves ("in causis probandis . . . non ex luxuria . . . neque enim deliciis, sed iustis affectionibus"). Apparently these *delicia* could be regarded as a special category of slaves. In *Digest* 7.7.6, 3 it is said that masters are not entitled to compensation for loss of pleasure or affection of slaves ("Item voluptatis vel affectionis aestimatio non habebitur, veluti si dilexerit eum dominus aut in deliciis habuerit"). Manuals for agriculture point in the same direction: proprietors are recommended not to choose this type of slave for the function of overseer *(vilicus)* ("ex eo genere servorum qui corpore placuerunt"; Columella, *Re rustica* 1.8.1; cf. Palladius, *Agricultura* 1.16.18).

The technical meaning of the term seems to be reflected the most accurately by the Latin word *delicium:* all passages concerning persons quoted in the *ThLL* point to boys who could be slaves or servants. The other meaning of the word, pet animals, conveys some views on *delicia* children, which I will treat later. Other words can express the same meaning, though other meanings are often implied: the adjectives *delicatus, delicius,* and *deliciosus,* the substantives *delicia, -ae/deliciolae.*

Dispersed in writings of various ancient authors are passages concerning *delicia* children, enabling us to draw a sketch of how Romans viewed these children and what their functions were. Interpretation of the material contains the pitfalls which the ancient historian should always be aware of: the danger of generalizing from one attested case or including inappropriate material (passages where the term *delicia* is not used but presumed in the biased mind of the historian).

Pet children often appear in connection with Roman emperors, not rarely evoking a luxurious and frivolous, fickle atmosphere associated with those rul-

ers in our Hollywood "spectacle" movies depicting Roman luxury and deca-
dence. Cleopatra, with an Aphrodisian appearance, was accompanied by a cor-
tege of pretty Eros-like children when approaching Antony (Plutarch, *Vita
Antonius* 26.2: παῖδες δὲ τοῖς γραφικοῖς Ἔρωσιν εἰκασμένοι). Augustus had his
own favorite, Sarmentos. He is mentioned by Plutarch in order to underscore
the shocking disparity between the way Antony's friends were mistreated by
Cleopatra — served sour wine in Egypt — and how Octavian's slave Sarmentus
was served exquisite Falernian in Rome. Plutarch's description points in the direction of a technical use of the term *delicium* (*Vita Antonius* 59: Ὁ δὲ
Σάρμεντος ἦν τῶν Καίσαρος παιγνίων παιδάριον ἃ δηλίκια Ῥωμαῖοι καλοῦσι).
Augustus, who was also known for collecting charming slave children from all
over the empire as playmates (Suetonius, *Augustus* 83), and who, according to
more gossipy remarks, used to sleep with twelve boys and twelve girls (Aurelius
Victor, *Epitome* 1.22), married Livia, who had her own pet child, said to walk
around naked, an impudent boy, who attended her at banquets (Cassius Dio
48.44.3: παιδίον τι τῶν ψιθυρῶν οἷα αἱ γυναῖκες ὡς πλήθει ἀθύρουσαι
τρέφουσιν). Apparently the phenomenon was well known to the readers of
Cassius Dio and considered a typical habit for women. Ancient historians have
generally depicted Augustus in a positive way. References to his luxurious taste
for *delicia* children should therefore be considered a mild and lenient form of
mockery: even the emperor had his human weaknesses!

Yet another tradition exists, where *delicia* children are strongly linked to
the practice of pederasty, almost a standard feature in description of everyday
practice at the courts of wicked and depraved emperors.[7] Vitellius, a notorious
homosexual, had an affair with a very young *libertus* (Suetonius, *Vitellius* 12:
"adulescentulum mutua libidine constupratum . . . rursus in deliciis habuit"):
the boy ran away from him, was caught again and eventually sold. Vespasian's
wife, mother of Titus and Domitian, had previously been a *delicata* of a certain
Statilius Capella. This fact gives her a stigma of low birth (Suetonius, *Vespasian*
3). Titus's youth was notorious for sexual misbehavior: he mixed with all sorts
of effeminates, *exoleti*, *spadones*, and *delicati* (Suetonius, *Titus* 7.1-2). Hadrian is
said to have established his influence by cultivating Trajan's *delicati* (SHA,
Hadrian 4.5).[8] Domitian too had his own *delicium*, a castrated *Caesareus puer*,
extensively praised in Statius's *Silvae* (3, 4), as well as an "army" of *delicia*

7. C. A. Williams, *Roman Homosexuality: Ideologies of Masculinity in Classical Antiquity*
(Oxford: Oxford University Press, 1999), p. 34, for emperors and their sexual use of child slaves.
Although many stories exist about Tiberius and Nero, no explicit use of the term *delicia* occurs.

8. Also SHA, *Hadrian* 2.7: "fuitque in amore Traiani, nec tamen ei per paedagogos
puerorum quos Traianus impensius diligebat Gallo adfovente defuit." For Hadrian's pederasty:
also Cassius Dio 68.7.4 and 68.21.2.

(Cassius Dio 67.15.3: παιδίον τι τῶν γυμνῶν τῶν ψιθυρῶν — Dio resorts to the same words): one of them discovered, by chance, tablets containing names of persons to be executed. The tablets were put on the couch where the emperor rested and discovered by the naked *delicium*. The same story, though more elaborate, is told by Herodian about Commodus's favorite boy, Philocommodus. The author provides us with interesting information: "But he forgot about the little boy (παιδίον πάνυ νήπιον), who was one of those that fashionable Roman fops are pleased to keep in their households running around without any clothes on, decked out in gold and fine jewels. Commodus had such a favourite, whom he often used to sleep with. He used to call him Philocommodus, a name to show his fondness for the boy" (Herodianus 1.17 LCL).

It seems clear to me that most of these examples are meant to emphasize the immoral or at least luxurious way of life of the emperors concerned. Sex as a political invective is not an American invention, nor one of modern journalism![9] It is highly unreasonable to accept these testimonies as pictures of normal everyday life, presuming, e.g., that all *delicia* in Roman households normally walked around naked and gold-clad, as Mau and Aurigemma do. Still, it is perfectly possible that such crowds of children could be found at the imperial court.

Closely but not exclusively linked with the emperors is the habit of keeping deformed *delicia* children.[10] As these children were outside the social organism over which they presided, Roman rulers were able to indulge their monstrous craving to the full. Emperors considered such abnormal physiological condition analogous to their own uniqueness. The taste for collecting human monstrosities also pervaded the upper class of Rome; the belief that such persons were endowed with magical and supernatural powers may also have been of some importance. Lastly, an ennui on a massive scale combined with a perverse and inexhaustible taste for the exotic and the bizarre induced the emperor and wealthy Romans to pay exorbitant prices for human "monsters." Pliny informs us about Canopas, a dwarf of two feet five inches, the shortest man alive during Augustus's principate, *in deliciis Iuliae*, Augustus's granddaughter (*Naturalis historia* 7.38). Andromeda, the shortest woman alive, was a pet of the same Julia (7.75).

The existence of Alexandrian markets for tiny children, dwarfs, monsters, and other *curiosa* is well attested; Th. Birt has even suggested that the Hellenis-

9. W. Krenkel, "Sex und Politische Bibliographie," *Wissenschaftliches Zeitschrift Rostock* 20, no. 5 (1980): 65-76, and R. MacMullen, "Roman Attitudes to Greek Love," *Historia* 31 (1982): 484-502.

10. R. Garland, *The Eye of the Beholder: Deformity and Disability in the Graeco-Roman World* (Ithaca, N.Y.: Cornell University Press, 1995).

tic fancy in arts for depicting small Eros-like children has its origin in this everyday Alexandrian reality.[11] Evidence goes from literary fiction (*Anthologia Palatina* 5.178 is a beautiful poem on a merchant selling Cupids) to iconography (images of little Cupids sold in cages, as well as little fictile Amor figures) and allusion to harsh reality (dwarfs being kept small in little cages: Pseudo-Longinus, *Peri hypsous* 44.5). Ps-Quintilian is of particular use for our subject: "Habent hoc quoque delicia divitum. Gratus est ille debilitate, ille ipsa infelicitate distorti corporis placet" (*declamationes* 298). Pliny the Elder informs us on the decadent taste for hermaphrodites (*Naturalis historia* 7.34: "olim androgynos vocatos et in prodigiis habitos, nunc vero in deliciis"). Rome had its own market for *terata* (Plutarch, *De curiositate* 10), and we can safely assume that many markets existed outside Alexandria for those in search of such merchandise.[12]

For what purposes did the wealthy Romans of the principate keep these children? They could be used as playmates for younger children in a rich household: Seneca had his own *deliciolum* slave when he was young, and did not recognize him several years later, as aging had changed his appearance profoundly (Seneca, *Epistle* 12.3).[13] They were also known for their conversational skills, and it was therefore considered a habit of Sophists to enjoy them: Favorinus of Arles and Herodes Atticus kept a small Indian boy (ἄθυρμα): they found delight in his Indian accent and his presence at symposia (Philostratus, *Vitae sophistarum* 490). Archytas of Tarente is said to have found great delight in the children of his big household — especially when they attended symposia (Aelianus, *Varia Historia* 12.15/Athenaeus 12.519b). Besides, they could act as companions of wealthy Roman ladies: in one of his elegies (2.29A) the poet Propertius dreams about his reception by a crowd of tiny naked boys *(pueri minuti)* of his mistress Cynthia. No doubt this poetic fiction had some grounds in everyday reality.

We know of many Roman masters who kept such children as entertaining company. Trimalchio had his *delicium*, Croesus, a nasty and ugly kid, a creature with blear eyes and very bad teeth, beyond doubts a grotesque exaggeration deliberately made by Petronius to depict Trimalchio as a social parvenu

---

11. Th. Birt, "De amore in arte antiqua simulacris et de pueris minutis apud antiquos in deliciis habitis" (diss., Marburg, 1892).

12. J. P. Néraudau, *Être enfant à Rome* (Paris: Les Belles Lettres, 1984), pp. 353-55, 366-67, for many details on prices, merchandise, treatment, etc.

13. This use of child slaves is well attested (the term *delicia* not being used): e.g., Plautus, *Captives* 19-20, 982, 1012-13 (a father buys a four-year-old slave for his four-year-old son), or Juvenal 14.168-69. Septimius Severus also kept *pueruli collusores* for his little sons, who also attended meals together with their young masters (SHA, *Septimius Severus* 4.6).

(Petronius, *Satyricon* 28.64). Moreover, Trimalchio himself had been a *delicium* (76). Statius composed some touching elegies for deceased *pueri delicati*: of his friends Blaesus (*Silvae* 2.1) and Ursus (2.6) and for his own favorite (5.5).[14]

The case of Martial and his five-year-old *delicium* girl Erotion is well known (three emotional epigrams: 5.34; 5.37; 10.61), although the nature of their relationship is not very clear to us. About three hundred years later Ausonius celebrated his little slave girl Bissula, in a poem named after her (*Bissula* 4.1: "delicium, blanditiae, ludus, amor, voluptas"). Such children could be either house-born *vernae* or bought at slave markets. The epithet *Alexandrinus* suggests that they sometimes were of Egyptian origin, as attested by Statius when speaking about slave boys as merchandise of Pharian ships and put on a stand at the marketplace (*Silvae* 2.1.72-73/5.5.66-68).

There is, however, no need to overemphasize the exotic character of *delicia*: Varro mentions a special market in Capua for those fond of *pueri minuti* (Varro, in Nonius Marcellus, *De compendiosa doctrina* 141.18).

Other Meanings of *Delicium/Delicatus*

As I pointed out in the introduction, the terms *delicium/delicatus* appear to have been used in quite different contexts, where pretty jester-like slaves are clearly not meant. We may safely omit those meanings that do not have much bearing on our subject: *delicatus* as synonymous with "weak," "infirm," "suffering of bad health" (in Ps-Soranus 80, *infans delicatus* is opposite to *infans validus;* the Benedictine Rule 48 has a passage on infirmaries for "fratribus infirmis aut delicatis"). Other meanings are more relevant to us: spoiled children are called *pueri delicati* (Cicero, *De natura deorum* 1.102); "I have spoiled you too much" [nimiam te habui delicatam], says a husband to his wife (Plautus, *Menaechmi* 119); "we must not be too particular, when there is a sky above us all" [non debemus delicati esse], says Echion in the *Cena Trimalchionis* (Petronius 45); and also Christian writers know this use of the word: "I am a spoiled girl and cannot perform manual work" [puella sum delicata et quae meis manibus laborare non possum] (Jerome, *Epistle* 22.31.3).

Delicium and its synonyms could also be used to connote a depraved way of living and moral lasciviousness: the followers of Catilina are stigmatized as "pueri tam lepidi et delicati" (Cicero, *In Catilinam* 2.23), the gods should be

---

14. For detailed commentaries on Statius's poems, see H. Van Dam, *P. Papinius Statius, Silvae Book II: A Commentary* (Leyden: Brill, 1984), and F. Vollmer, *P. Papinii Statii, Silvarum Libri: herausgegeben und erklärt* (Leipzig: Teubner, 1898).

"seiunctum a delicatis et obscaenis voluptatibus" (Cicero, *De natura deorum* 1.113); to designate articles of luxury or simply luxury itself ("omnium deliciarum atque omnium artium puerulos"; Cicero, *Pro Sexto Roscio Amerino* 120); to characterize an anticonformist troupe of young men like Catullus.[15]

Finally, the use as a term of endearment is well known and abundantly attested (for which see ThLL, s.v. *delicia*, cols. 447-448): "mea voluptas, mea delicia" (Plautus, *Poenulus* 365); "Critias mea delicia" (Apuleius, *Apologia* 9); "meae deliciae, mei lepores" (Catullus 6, 1). This includes addresses to beloved family members: in his letters Cicero calls his daughter "Tulliola, deliciolae nostrae" (*Atticus* 1.8.3), and Macrobius quotes Augustus: "duas se habere filias delicatas, rem publicam et Iuliam" (*Saturnalia* 2.5.4). *Delicatus,* the most frequent of these synonyms, is often used in a negative sense, with connotations of effeminacy or weakness. The positive meaning ("beloved person") mostly occurs in sources from late antiquity and early Christianity (an exception is Plautus, *Rudens* 465). *Delicium,* considerably less attested, usually keeps its (semi)technical meaning of pet child or pet animal. The feminine noun *delicia* has the largest number of senses, ranging from "pleasure," "luxury," to "pet child/pet animal" or term of endearment. It is widely attested in all these meanings.[16]

The fact that *delicium* and synonyms could be used both to designate a group of pampered jester-like slave children and as a relational term denoting a family-like relationship with affection or closeness cannot be overemphasized and has, to my opinion, important consequences for our understanding of the Roman family. I shall return to this later. But first I will confront the literary facts with a large, though by its nature very different, body of evidence: the inscriptions.

Epigraphic Evidence

The present body of evidence is the result of a thorough search through the volumes of the *CIL* as well as the complete series of *AE*. Greek inscriptions have been considered to some extent (indices of *SEG*), but the search did not deliver significant results, nor did a search through the Duke D-base of Documentary Papyri.[17] Isolated inscriptions are silent witnesses: due to their fragmented and

15. Nielsen, "Delicia," p. 80.
16. *ThLL*, s.v. c. 450.
17. W. Peek, *Griechische Versinschrifte* (Chicago: Ares, 1988), no. 587,3 and 2030,10 (inscriptions for a child called ἄθυρμα). Another possible Greek equivalent, σπαταλάω (τὰ σπαταλῶντα

analytic character, they often leave us with more questions than answers. Only serial evidence can be of help, and the following tables can help to elucidate something about Roman *delicia*. The first diagram deals with the geographical spread of inscriptions for *delicia*.

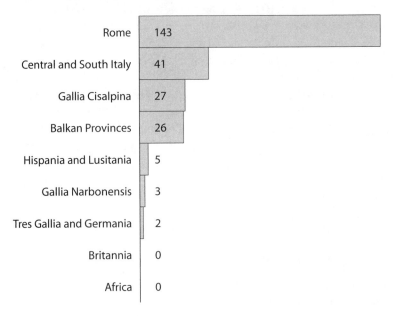

Rome	143
Central and South Italy	41
Gallia Cisalpina	27
Balkan Provinces	26
Hispania and Lusitania	5
Gallia Narbonensis	3
Tres Gallia and Germania	2
Britannia	0
Africa	0

The preponderance of Rome is significant: the nearer to Rome, the more *delicia* inscriptions there seem to be in a region; also, greater attention is paid to children in the epigraphic evidence of a big city.[18] Still, it remains remarkable that provinces with a rich epigraphic culture (like Africa) appear destitute of *delicia*; and the same can be said about provinces whose epigraphic corpora are equipped with excellent and detailed indices (Britannia and the African provinces).

What about the use of the different terms? I offer tables for those areas where the body of evidence is sufficient to draw some conclusions.

τῶν παιδίων, Theano in Pythagoras, *Epistle* 4.4), is not found in the inscriptions. I thank Prof. J. Strubbe (Leyden) and Prof. W. Clarysse (Louvain) for their help with searching in Greek inscriptions and papyri.

18. B. Shaw, "The Cultural Meaning of Death: Age and Gender in the Roman Family," in *The Family in Italy from Antiquity to the Present*, ed. D. I. Kertzer and R. P. Saller (New Haven, New York, and London: Yale University Press, 1991), pp. 66-90.

Rome

delicium	101		in deliciis	2
delicatus, -a	25		delicatissima	1
delicia	5		delicieis	1
delicius	4			
deli	4		(abbreviated or fragmented)	

Balkans

delicium	2	
delicatus, -a	20	
delicia	1	
delicius	0	
deli.	3	(abbreviated or fragmented)

Gallia Cisalpina

delicium	0	
delicatus, -a	23	
delicia	1	
delicius	0	
deli.	3	

Central and South Italy (*CIL* 4, 9, 10, 11, 14)

delicium	25	
delicatus, -a	10	
delicia	7	
deli.	2	(abbreviated or fragmented)

It seems thus as if certain proof for geographical differences in the use of the terms exists[19] (with Gallia Cisalpina and the Dacian provinces showing a deviating preference for the term *delicatus*), although I would ascribe this merely to local fashion. There seems to be absolutely no difference between the relationships designated by *delicium* or *delicatus;* and I would regard theories which see *delicati* as somewhat older (past childhood) slaves, or even primarily servants for homosexuals, as modern attempts to make clear distinctions which the ancients did not make themselves.[20]

19. Mau, c. 2437.

20. Van Dam, *Statius,* p. 73, takes *delicati* as older than *delicia* and sexual objects, and S. Lilja, *Homosexuality in Republican and Augustean Rome,* Societas scientiarum Fennica, Commentationes humanarum litterarum (Helsinki, 1983), p. 16, considers *delicati* as homosexual slaves. Already Aurigemma, p. 1578, demonstrated that such distinctions are flawed.

Counting distribution according to sex reveals the following results:

males   116 (45.5%)
females   118   (47%)
unknown   19   (7.5%)

The somewhat remarkable overrepresentation of females (56 percent) re-marked by Sigismund Nielsen[21] for the *delicia* in Rome is not corroborated by the evidence for the whole empire. More than that: my own counting for Rome does not support Nielsen's results (45 percent men, 47.5 percent women, and 7 percent *incerti*; it is striking that Nielsen does not have any *incerti* in her count-ing!). A male overrepresentation is normal in the inscriptions commemorating children and young people, and so it is the case with *delicia* inscriptions throughout the empire.

Concerning the relation between gender of the dedicator (eventually owner) and gender of the *delicium*, I found the following numbers:

Male(s)	male *delicia:*	45
female *delicia:*	34	
Female(s)	male *delicia:*	26
	female *delicia*	39
Male(s) + Female(s)	male *delicia*	13
	female *delicia*	19

Young people the *delicia* certainly were, as the table on ages proves:

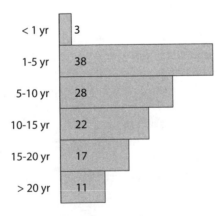

< 1 yr	3
1-5 yr	38
5-10 yr	28
10-15 yr	22
15-20 yr	17
> 20 yr	11

21. Nielsen, "Delicia," p. 83.

The majority were clearly under ten years of age when they died. The rarity of babies (less than one year) should not surprise us, since it is in accordance with the low degree of attention for such infants in epigraphic evidence.[22] The number over twenty may seem remarkable,[23] but is in accordance with the literary sources: the term was not restricted to its technical meaning of pretty child slaves, but could be used in a much broader context. Hence Romans did not limit the word too strictly to underage children, nor did they see it as a shameful thing to be commemorated thus even in older age (*AE* 1957, 217: a patronus and father [?] commemorating a fifty-year-old male *delicatus,* and *CIL* 10, 1875: a woman calling her forty-five-year-old husband a *verna delicatus Augustalis*).

The next table shows the social status of the commemorated *delicia,* based on onomastic evidence. Though difficulties and caveats in this kind of research are notorious, the findings reveal clear tendencies:

ing.:	11
ing. (?):	1
lib.:	25
lib. (?):	1
ing (?)/l(?):	44
servi	25
servi (?)	117
?	31

The majority were probably slaves, though approximately one-third of the *delicia* were free (in most cases manumitted, that is, also with a servile background). Manumission of slaves under thirty years was under special conditions regulated by law (*Digest* 40.2, 11-14), but the number of *liberti* is remarkable, since *Digest* 40.2, 16 does not provide an exception for manumission under thirty years for luxurious slaves ("in causis probandis . . . non ex luxuria . . . neque enim deliciis, sed iustis affectionibus"). I take this as a hint that not all *delicia* from inscriptions were actually considered exotic or luxurious slaves. Anyway, the numbers on social origin are in striking accordance with the findings for Rome.[24]

22. Under one year: *CIL* 14.899 (ten months, three days); *EE* VIII n. 190 (eleven months); and *AE* 1969/70, 241 = 1995, 716 (twenty-eight days; Lusitania).

23. Older than twenty: *CIL* 3.1903; 5.1137 + 3039 + 3474 (three women in their twenties); 6.7935 (thirty-five years old); 15482 (a husband calls his thirty-year-old wife *delicata*); 28253 (twenty-three years: *vixit delicatissima*); 33796; *AE* 1971, 44 (a *delicium populi*); 1957, 217 (a fifty-year-old male *delicatus*); *CIL* 10.1875 (a forty-five-year-old *verna delicatus Augustalis*).

24. Nielsen, "Delicia," p. 83.

The last table deals with epithets attributed to these *delicia* children. Though very easy to count and enumerate, the interpretation of the results is difficult, since they deal with the ambiguous sphere of human affectivity.

carissimus	11
bene merens	7
piisimus/pientissimus	6
dulcissimus	5
infelicissimus	3
caelitus	2
dulcis	2
puppa	2

wide range of epithets used only once[25]

Delicia received manifestly fewer epithet inscriptions than other relationship groups (only 44 times in 247 inscriptions, that is, 17 percent of the cases).[26] This undoubtedly interesting fact has given rise to assumptions which I would not hesitate to call incredibly naive and simplistic. It has been stated[27] that the lack of epithets points to a lack of affection, and that *delicia* were regarded as mere objects, even lust objects (here the moralistic approach of some commentators is clearly playing its part). First, it is very risky to make judgments about feelings derived from facts which can be ascribed to epigraphic habit. Second, the term *delicium* may very well have been understood by the ancients as affectionate (*delicatus* was used as an epithet for women and sons or daughters, as I will demonstrate below), so that no additional epithets were needed. Third, just as in literature, the possessive forms *suus* (used fifty-two times), *eius/eorum* (four times), *meus* (twice), *noster* (once) could have some emotional value to the dedicator.[28] Besides, focusing on the object role of *delicia* is in contradiction with explicit evidence from epigraphic poetry, which has by its nature more place for expression of feelings than conventional prose inscriptions do. One could think of *CIL* 10.4041 (= *CLE* 1075), where the father is said to wet the gravestone and to weary the ashes by his endless mourning (vv. 3-4: *ossa parens*

25. In alphabetic order: *amabilis, amans, amantissima, blandus, iocosa, issulus, parvulus, rarissimus, simplex, suavis.*

26. H. Sigismund Nielsen, "Interpreting Epithets in Roman Epitaphs," in *The Roman Family in Italy: Status, Sentiment, Space*, ed. B. Rawson and P. Weaver (Oxford and Canberra: Clarendon, 1997), pp. 169-204, is an excellent study on these matters.

27. E. Herrmann-Otto, *Ex ancilla natus. Untersuchungen zu den 'Hausgeborenen' Sklaven und Sklavinnen im Westen des römischen Kaiserreiches* (Stuttgart: Steiner, 1994), pp. 54-56.

28. Aurigemma, p. 1602, considers these words as epithets expressing affection.

maculat lacrumis cineremque fatigat/fletibus); the thirteen-year-old boy, apparently a good singer (v. 6: *formosum cantu*), is called *delicium domini* and *spes exspectata parentum* (v. 7). Also, the epitaph for the little twelve-year-old jeweler Pagus, again called *delicium domini, spes grata parentum* in verse 3 (*CIL* 6.9437 = *CLE* 403), has a sense for emotions.[29]

I summarize: in the question of emotional attachment to *delicia*, I would take an agnostic position. We simply cannot know about feelings and emotional bonds between dedicators and dedicatees. Yet I consider simplistic explanations emphasizing the exploitative mode in these relations flawed. No doubt *delicia* could be exploited, and certainly they sometimes were, but the spectrum of human experience and feelings is wider than that.

Delicia and Family Inscriptions

I have already pointed to the difficulties which arise in interpreting single inscriptions, and will illustrate this further with the following case. A funerary sculpture has the following text (*CIL* 11.6176):

> Sex. Titius Sex(ti) l(ibertus) Primus/VI vir/Lucianae benignae
> concubinae/Titiae Chreste l(ibertae)/Chloe delicium.

The image and the text together can provide us with the following story. Sextus Titius Primus was a freedman and had a concubine Luciana. We may speculate upon the origin of Titia Chreste: she may have been Luciana and Primus's daughter. When he was freed, he in turn bought her free and she became his *liberta*, or they may both have been freed by their master. But Luciana's single name may point to servile status: Did she remain a slave (most probably the couple stayed in the same household afterward), or did Sextus Titius Primus later make the acquaintance of (or perhaps buy) a slave with whom he lived together in concubinage? It is not necessary to presume that Luciana was in fact Chreste's biological mother. It is even not absolutely sure that Titius Primus was her bio-

---

29. But also prose inscriptions do sometimes show signs of affectivity: a *delicium* is called *issulus* (*CIL* 6.12156); little Grusoglosus (6.14786) is designated by the diminutive *parvulus* and the epithets *amabilis* and *infans flebilis;* a woman says farewell to her husband in moving verses (*CIL* 6.22102) speaking on behalf of herself, their son, and their *delicium* called *blanda dulcis pupa.* In *CIL* 6.25808 a *delicium* is said to leave his mother: *mammam gementem, plangentem, plorantem. CIL* 6.24888 *delicium* as *anima dulcissima;* 6.36525 (= *AE* 1901, 148) is a very emotional epitaph for a girl *in delicieis Vettiae* and beloved by her master; also *CIL* 10.5500, *delicium* as *pupa.* See also Aurigemma, pp. 1602-3.

logical father: she could have been entrusted to him as a quasi child by the master when they were still slaves. And what about the *delicium* Chloe? Only from the image is it clear that she was Chreste's pet child. She was almost certainly a slave. Did the *libertus* Titius Primus buy such a child to amuse his (quasi) daughter? Or, if we suppose that they stayed close to his former master's household, was she perhaps a slave child who was entrusted to Titia Chreste to be educated? The only thing we know absolutely for sure is that at a certain moment those four persons lived together and saw their union as something we would call a conjugal family: a couple, a (quasi) daughter, and a pretty little child.

It is no exaggeration to say that similar stories can be found for almost every one of the 247 *delicia* inscriptions, yet to assess them all would make this article not only rather a tedious read, but also a very speculative enterprise. It would be better to pay attention to some remarkable and well-established patterns, and to avoid speculation as much as possible.

Sometimes *delicium/delicatus* is used as an epithet with the words *filius/filia* to designate one's natural son or daughter.[30] To this may be added those inscriptions where parents mention their own natural children as somebody else's *delicium*.[31] CIL 5.2417 is worth mentioning here: a slave father says of his own *delicium* son that he would have been freed by their master soon: "qui si vixisset, domini iam nomina ferret." In these examples *delicium/delicatus* is clearly not synonymous with *filius/filia*. When biological children are meant, *delicium* can be added as a sort of epithet, or specification of a function (pet child of another person). It would therefore be hazardous to regard children only mentioned as *delicium* (for instance, by a couple) automatically as biological offspring.

Delicium/delicata could also serve as an epithet to denote one's spouse.[32]

Some inscriptions have what I would call a conjugal-family-like pattern:[33] a couple with a child, most probably not their own child, designated as *delicium*. In some cases this pet child is mentioned together with sons or daughters.[34]

---

30. *CIL* 2.7.445; *CIL* 6.8514, 28253; *CIL* 10.8316; *CIL* 13.3624; *CIL* 14.899, 3661; *AE* 1955, 25, and 1957, 217. Probably also *CIL* 6.25808 and 27827 for a *mamma* with the same *nomen gentilicium*.

31. *CIL* 5.2417; *CIL* 6.9437, 12096, 14786, 19616, 19673, 23257, 24158, 25046; *CIL* 10.4041; *EE* VIII n. 190; *AE* 1955, 25. All these examples deal with slave children.

32. *CIL* 5.7014; *CIL* 6.7935, 15482, 20874, 33796; *CIL* 10.1875, 5921; *CIL* 14.2737; *AE* 1967, 165. To these may be added: *CIL* 6.1842 and 7935 (men who have a woman and a female *delicium*).

33. R. Saller and B. Shaw, "Tombstones and Roman Family Relations in the Principate: Civilians, Soldiers and Slaves," *JRS* 74 (1984): 124-56.

34. *CIL* 3.1903, 1905, 2244; *CIL* 5.936, 1323 (?), 1410, 1460, 6064, 7014, and 8336; *CIL* 6.1892, 2336, 4776, 5180, 6612, 6638, 7135, 8824, 9375, 9567, 12156, 14321/32, 14443, 23072, 24786, 24888, 24829, 24962, 25529, 27075, 28342, 29055, 33594, 33696, 34393, 35793, 37699, and 39198; *CIL* 9.260,

Sometimes parents gave such a child to their children: we have an inscription for a twenty-three-year-old son and his eight-year-old *delicata* by his parents (*CIL* 6.7135) and a boy of fourteen who has his own *delicium* (*CIL* 9.4035).

Yet another interesting pattern exists. No small number of inscriptions show a (often freed) woman with a pet child sharing the same nomen.[35] These children may well have been slaves freed together with their mother, or she might have bought and freed them afterward. They could also be the offspring of an illegitimate alliance after the mother's liberation (the abbreviation *Sp. f.* — the child being *ingenuus* though illegitimate — is not used after the third century). It is interesting, however, that the term *filius/filia* is not used. I therefore believe that there is yet another possibility: they could have been slave children, put with a slave who was not the biological mother, to be brought up. Afterward they were freed together, and a sort of mother-child relation could evolve. This procedure of quasi adoption or transferring of children in the context of slave breeding (e.g., one slave nursing a number of children, so that the others could return to their work, or the separation of slave families by sale) is well attested for Roman times.[36]

A whole series of *delicia* inscriptions have their place outside the relationships of biological or nuclear family (spouses, sons and daughters): *delicia* are commemorated together with patrons, friends, brothers or sisters, parents, other slaves or freedmen.[37] Also, house-born *vernae* are sometimes called *delicia* (*CIL* 6.24158, 24947). Pet children could also be part of a larger household with many slaves: I found about fifteen slaves who had their own *delicium* slave, and one who seems to have had a free *delicium* (*CIL* 6.17401). In this context, mention should also be made of *delicia* performing service in the imperial household.[38]

1482 and 4811; *CIL* 10.5500, 5921, 5933, 5934, 6630; *CIL* 11.1477 and 3268; *CIL* 12.3582; *CIL* 13.3624; *CIL* 14.3661; *AE* 1896, 37, and 1935, 105.

35. Sometimes the woman is mentioned with a man/husband: *CIL* 3.2244, 2407, 2414; *CIL* 6.9375, 12355, 12357, 14559, 15071, 16055, 24888, 25529 (?), 27827, 37699; *CIL* 9.260; *AE* 1974, 296; 1984, 91; 1987, 253; and 1991, 24.

36. K. Bradley, "Wet-Nursing at Rome: A Study in Social Relations," in *The Family in Ancient Rome: New Perspectives,* ed. B. Rawson (London and Sydney: Croom, Helm; Ithaca, N.Y.: Cornell University Press, 1986), pp. 201-29, 211-12 (transferring of children in slave families), and K. Bradley, *Discovering the Roman Family* (Oxford and New York: Oxford University Press, 1991), pp. 3-13.

37. *CIL* 3.2503; *CIL* 5.141, 647, 1405, 1460 (?), 2180, 5148, 7023, 8346; *CIL* 6.1892, 9375, 14523, 24829, 24947, 26689, 27593, 28637, 32784, 34393; *CIL* 9.1713 and 4811; *CIL* 10.4370; *CIL* 11.900, 1228, 4472, 4811, 6829; *AE* 1974, 317.

38. Slaves of other slaves: *CIL* 3.2693, 8478; *CIL* 5.3039; *CIL* 6.4674, 5204, 5292, 6670, 10587, 12337, 16738, 17401, 17747, 25434, 25812, 38744; *CIL* 9.260; *CIL* 14.2369. In many cases there is some

Some scarce examples show two men having their own *delicium*: *CIL* 6.21689 has two men and one *delicium* (four years of age), whilst *CIL* 11.4472 has three men with two *delicia*, but unfortunately the last inscription is too fragmented to draw valid conclusions. *CIL* 5.3474 has two *liberti* and one *delicata* (twenty-six years of age), and *CIL* 6.25375 mentions two men and two *delicii*.

There seems to be a remarkable similarity between literary and epigraphic evidence. In both cases *delicium* points to children or young persons, in many cases of servile origin, meant to amuse and entertain their masters. In both cases we are warned against a too strict and technical interpretation of the term: *delicium/delicatus* can cover a wide spectrum of meanings (term of endearment for natural son, daughter, or wife).[39] Epigraphic evidence gave us a better image of the functioning of such children in the Roman household. It is now time to turn our attention to possible explanations for the phenomenon. At this point we may call in help from other disciplines: sociology, cultural history, and psychology or anthropology.

In Search of an Explanation: A Psychosociological Approach

No matter how one would judge the nature of *delicia* children and their masters' motivation, one can agree that they received some kind of special attention from their masters. The nomination "pampered pets" seems to fit them well. But what could compel Roman masters to give some children that very special kind of attention? A psychological explanation is offered by the ancient writers themselves: "It happens that some who stubbornly oppose marriage and procreation of children, have painful regrets afterwards, and find themselves mourning as cowards for their servants' child or their concubine's nursling being ill or dying" (Plutarch, *Moralia* 788E).

Beyond doubt this can be true, but modern demography has provided facts of which Plutarch could not have been conscious: the harsh demographic reality of child mortality with 50 percent of the children dying before reaching the age of five, and a life expectancy of thirty years. Besides, ancient people were confronted with squalid hygienic conditions and an overall presence of illness and disease that can be compared with the situation in less developed countries

uncertainty: the fact that only one name is mentioned does not always point to servile origin (affectivity or just saving of space can also be responsible for that). On slaves of other slaves: Herrmann-Otto, pp. 196-206. Imperial *delicia*: *CIL* 6.14959, 15570, 19616, 20237, 25046, 28637, 33156; *AE* 1955, 25.

39. It can also refer to popular artists: *CIL* 6.10151; *AE* 1903, 160; 1909, 75; 1968, 74; 1971, 44.

nowadays.[40] Many marriages were ended by death in childbirth. So we should not be surprised that some "survivor children" were spoiled exceedingly, even when they were mere slave children, or secret bastards (as is suggested also by Plutarch). For those who survived, childhood could be short and hard: child labor must have been a reality for many lower-class children, in the countryside or in the cities. Again it seems plausible to consider *delicia* children as one factor of compensation, an outlet of love for children.

Many of those children were of servile origin. Here one of the most striking contradictions of ancient society seems to emerge. On the one hand, various source material testifies to the warm emotional ties that could exist between masters and slaves. Slaves played a vital role in education of free children in the Roman household, and there can be no doubt that affectionate relationships arose between them that lasted when children became adults. In a sinister irony, this positive attitude coexisted with intensified violence toward slaves: extraordinary brutality in everyday life (one was free to do with his slaves whatever one wanted; torture of slaves was required in courts) and abuse of slaves as source of crude humor on stage.[41]

However contradictory these behaviors could seem, they can be explained as parts of the same complex of conflicting attitudes. In a society based on slavery and subordination, adolescents and adults could counteract and compensate their attitudes of affection and esteem toward some slaves by excessive brutality toward others. The mechanism also works the other way around: the violence to which many slaves were undoubtedly exposed could be compensated by love and affection for other slaves. I suggest that the keeping of *delicia* children could be one (though not the only) outlet for such affectionate feelings.[42] This social-psychological theory of compensation is also used by P. Veyne to explain what he calls "the self-evidence of

40. T. Parkin, *Demography and Roman Society* (Baltimore and London: Johns Hopkins University Press, 1992); R. P. Saller, *Patriarchy, Property, and Death in the Roman Family* (Cambridge: Cambridge University Press, 1994); R. S. Bagnall and B. W. Frier, *The Demography of Roman Egypt* (Cambridge: Cambridge University Press, 1994); W. Scheidel, *Death on the Nile: Disease and the Demography of Roman Egypt* (Leyden: Brill, 2001); A. Scobie, "Slums, Sanitation and Mortality in the Roman World," *Klio* 68, no. 2 (1986): 399-433; V. M. Hope and E. Marshall, eds., *Death and Disease in the Ancient City* (London and New York: Routledge, 2000).

41. M. Finley, *Ancient Slavery and Modern Ideology* (London: Chatto and Windus, 1980), and K. Bradley, *Slaves and Rulers in the Roman Empire* (Brussels: Latomus, 1984). Also R. P. Saller, "Corporal Punishment, Authority, Obedience in the Roman Household," in *Marriage, Divorce, and Children*, ed. B. Rawson (Oxford and Canberra: Clarendon, 1991), pp. 144-66.

42. For this part I am indebted to the insightful comments of M. Golden, *Children and Childhood in Classical Athens* (Baltimore and London: Johns Hopkins University Press, 1990), pp. 141-63.

slavery."[43] Slaves developed a kind of midway attitude between violent anger or resistance and submitting passivity: they loved their masters and felt themselves loved by them. Again the phenomenon of *delicia* children can be explained as an outlet of this survivors strategy.

It is well known that relations between Roman upper-class parents and children were characterized by physical and emotional distancing. This is far from claiming generic indifference among the upper class: the hopes invested in children were considerable. Nor is it to say that relations between Roman children and their parents could never be close and affectionate. What matters is that such affection was not required or self-evident.[44] Again I would return to the compensation theory and suggest that some parents gave the affective attention they did not or could not grant their own children (e.g., by dislocation of families, being entrusted to nurses) to some children called *delicia*.

Delicia as Jesters or Pet Animals: A Cultural-Historical Approach

The literary sources make clear that *delicia* were supposed to entertain their masters. A share of wit, babylike language, loquacity, or brutality was expected and appreciated by some keepers of those naughty pet children. When Augustus's wife Livia, who was formerly married to and pregnant of Nero, was attending a meal in the presence of her new and her former husband, one of her pet children brutally sneered upon her: "*What are you doing here? For your husband is reclining over there*" (Cassius Dio 48.44.3). Similarities with medieval court jesters immediately come to mind. The story in Cassius Dio and Herodian about the pet child reading the emperor's private wax tables is in fact paralleled by medieval stories about jesters reading their masters' letters.[45]

Comparative cultural history informs us that children and jesters were often put on the same footing: at the bottom of the social hierarchy or even outside it.[46] Children, like women and irrational animals, were also considered outsiders in Roman male social hierarchy, though it would be wrong to think

43. Veyne, pp. 55-56.

44. For this well-debated question, see, e.g., Bradley, *Discovering the Roman Family*, pp. 28-29, 56, 61; S. Dixon, *The Roman Mother* (London: Routledge, 1992); E. Eyben, "Fathers and Sons," in *Marriage, Divorce, and Children*, pp. 113-43; and Saller, "Corporal Punishment," pp. 144-66.

45. W. Mezger, *Hofnarren im Mittelalter. Vom tieferen Sinn eines seltsamen Amts* (Constance: Universitätsverlag, 1981), p. 67.

46. Mezger, pp. 53-60.

the Romans regarded them as lower beings: high hopes were invested in upper-class children.[47] I find it therefore quite plausible to compare the functioning of *delicia* children of rich or powerful masters with the medieval and modern habit of keeping jesters: they brought relief to their masters for the sorrows of every day, and dared to say truths nobody else would dare to tell them.

Veyne compared the keeping of pet children with the vogue of keeping pet animals in rich households.[48] There are certain grounds for this: both the Greek ἄθυρμα and the Latin *delicium/deliciae* can refer to pet animals too (cf. *ThLL* s.v.). Pet owners were from various economic, geographical, social, and intellectual backgrounds in both classical civilizations, pointing to a long-standing practice of roughly ten centuries of pet keeping in ancient Greece and Rome. Sometimes striking similarities with descriptions of human *delicia* occur: a lap-dog is said to lie in her master's or mistress's bosom (*CIL* 6.29896), to share her mistress's bed and to beam at her smile with gentle bites (13.488), to eat out of her master's hand and to drink from her cup (10.659); the same remarks are made about the *delicium* Glaucias in Statius, *Silvae* 2.1. Martial's *Epigrams* 1.109 is composed for the little puppy Issa, called *deliciae*. The humor and irony of this poem is based on the little animal being described as a human partner. The little girl Erotion is also compared with various and precious pet animals (*Epigrams* 5.37.1-14).[49] It has to be added, however, that no ancient writer actually equates these children with domestic animals. In fact, ancient authors explicitly criticized people for caring more for pet animals than children (Plutarch, *Pericles* 1.1, and *Moralia* 472c; Clement of Alexandria, *Paedagogos* 3.30; and Athenaeus 12.518f-519b).

Delicia and Pederasty: A Psychological and Anthropological Approach

It goes beyond saying that sometimes sex and sexual abuse are found in connection with the term *delicium*. Epigraphical evidence has shown that this does not always have to be the case (e.g., parents call their own children somebody

---

47. T. Wiedemann, *Adults and Children in the Roman Empire* (London: Routledge, 1989). Contra M. Golden, "Chasing Change in Roman Childhood," *AHB* 4 (1990): 90-94.

48. Veyne, p. 69; K. Bradley, "The Sentimental Education of the Roman Child: The Role of Pet-Keeping," *Latomus* 57, 3 (1998): 523-57; and L. Bodson, "Motivations for Pet-Keeping in Ancient Greece and Rome: A Preliminary Survey," in *Companion Animals and Us: Exploring the Relationship between People and Pets*, ed. A. L. Podberseck, E. S. Paul, and J. A. Serpell (Cambridge: Cambridge University Press, 2000), pp. 27-41.

49. See P. Watson, "Erotion: Puella Delicata?" *Classical Quarterly* 42 (1992): 253-65.

else's *delicia*).[50] Still, the fact remains that pet children could be used for erotic purposes.

Scholars have always been embarrassed by the issue, and moral condemnation has led them to strange pronouncements on the subject. In a most erudite work, Elisabeth Herrmann-Otto states that most *delicia* died young, in consequence of the severe sexual maltreatment by their masters.[51] Apart from the fact that one does not usually die from this cause, the question remains how this German scholar could assume a sexual relationship for all *delicia* mentioned in inscriptions, and besides, believe that this small number could be significant for life expectancy of pet children in the Roman Empire!

The amount of evidence for pederasty in Roman poetry is not easy to dismiss, and the reading of literature was primarily a public affair.[52] Recent research on iconographical evidence finds the evidence for pederasty considerable. The famous Warren Cup (the boy is a slave, as is clear from his lock) would be enough nowadays to put the artist in jail for indecent pornographic art with minors.[53] This article, however, is not primarily concerned with pederasty, and it would seem useful to search for evidence for sexual use of *delicia*, in a society where pedophilia apparently occurred. Such evidence exists unquestionably. The anecdotes on emperors and their favorites are intended as part of a literary tradition stressing the tyrant's lack of self-control in sexual matters. Denying erotic tones in Statius's poems would be absurd, as detailed commentaries have shown. Martial has some explicit testimonies: *Epigrams* 7.14 is about a woman who lost her *deliciae* (v. 2); the reason for her grief is explained in an obscene ending: "She has lost a boy numbering twice six years, whose cock was not yet eighteen inches long" (vv. 9-10). The boy Didymus is called *delicia* (12.75.6): Martial wrote three erotic epigrams for him.[54] Other evidence can be cited. Being buried together in one grave is an erotic commonplace (Ovid, *Metamorphoses* 4.157/Propertius 4.7.94), and it is attested in three inscriptions for *delicia* (*CIL* 6.5163, 21986, and 24345). Scholars also take the *pupulus* in Catullus 56 as a kind of *delicium*: the boy is engaged in sexual play with a girl, and the narrator hastens himself to join them. Seneca (*Epistles* 47.7; 95.24) deplores the abuse of young persons who serve their masters not only at table, but also in bed.

50. Cf. Nielsen, "Delicia," pp. 79-81.

51. Herrmann-Otto, pp. 309-10.

52. See, e.g., H. P. Obermayer, *Martial und der Diskurs über männliche "Homosexualität" in der Literatur der frühen Kaiserzeit* (Tübingen: Narr, 1998), and Williams, *Roman Homosexuality.*

53. J. R. Clarke, *Looking at Lovemaking: Constructions of Sexuality in Roman Art, 100 B.C.–A.D. 250* (Berkeley, Los Angeles, and London: University of California Press, 1998), pp. 85-86.

54. On which, see Obermayer, pp. 69-74.

How are we to cope with this evidence, which clashes severely with the moral values of our Western society? I propose four explanations for the complex enigma of Roman pederasty. Primarily, I believe the phenomenon is strongly linked and interwoven with the institution of ancient slavery.[55] Seneca has summarized the matter as follows: "Impudicitia in ingenuo crimen est, in servo necessitas, in liberto officium" (*Controversiae* 4.pref.10). Slaves were subject to "an unrestricted availability in sexual relations";[56] "Slaves of both sexes and of all ages were objects of carnal sexual pleasures,"[57] to quote two specialists on ancient slavery. These facts are paralleled by research in more recent slaveholder societies, in Jamaica.[58] Since Freud, psychiatrists distinguish between "true and sustained" pedophilia, and pedophile feelings that can arise suddenly and occasionally in many persons.[59] It seems plausible to assume that, instead of being repressed, such feelings could find an outlet in overall available young slaves.

The Dutch scholar L. Hermans discerns a change toward more intimate and companionate relations in Greek pederastic relations beginning in Hellenistic times, culminating in theoretical works such as Plutarch's *Amatorius* and pseudo-Lucian's *Amores*.[60] Beauty, exclusivity, free choice, and reciprocal sexual pleasure were elements of those new relationships, for which Hadrian and Antinoös could stand as examples. Since such alliances were disreputable and legally not allowed in Rome, at least for freeborn people of status and freeborn boys, a way out was again found in affectionate friendships with slaves, and that can partly explain the presence of *delicia* in the Roman household.

Roman housing could offer another explanation. Houses lacked any sense of what we would call privacy: there were generally no separate rooms for children. Servants, laborers, or slaves were omnipresent even in houses of poor families, and children slept together with slaves and nurses. Sexual intercourse could rarely be had without the danger of being watched, and children must have accidentally witnessed it.[61] Here again the Warren Cup is illuminating: it

55. On sex and slavery: Williams, pp. 30-38.

56. See Finley, p. 95, for many references.

57. Bradley, *Slaves and Rulers*, p. 118.

58. O. Patterson, *The Sociology of Slavery* (London: Tauris London, 1967), p. 42.

59. Many references in Watson, pp. 258-59.

60. L. Hermans, *Bewust van andere lusten. Homoseksualiteit in het Romeinse keizerrijk* (Amsterdam: Wereldbibliotheek, 1995). The results of this interesting research unfortunately only exist in Dutch!

61. D. Montserrat, *Sex and Society in Graeco-Roman Egypt* (London and New York: Kegan Paul, 1995); A. Wallace-Hadrill, *Houses and Society in Pompeii and Herculaneum* (Princeton: Princeton University Press, 1994), pp. 9, 44-45, 106-7, 113. Also S. Guijarro, "The Family in First-Century Galilee," in *Constructing Early Christian Families: Family as Social Reality and Meta-*

shows a boy watching a sexual act, while entering through a door, the act being perpetrated in what seems to have been an easily accessible room.[62] Besides, ancient people lacked some of the sense of prudery toward children in certain matters of body or sexuality: erotic art pervaded everyday life: wall paintings, utensils, ceramics, etc. Earlier confrontation with sex and thus earlier maturity in these matters are a logical consequence.

The last explanation seems more like a caveat. When speaking of sex, we are inclined to think of sexual intercourse. Yet erotic experience can be attained in very different ways. In the case of Erotion, for instance, it is almost impossible to imagine a relationship with intercourse — yet a relationship with affectionate body language seems very well possible. In such cases, various factors play a part. Sexual behavior is a culturally defined term.[63] How does a society understand the human body? What about personal integrity or privacy? Roman men used to kiss each other with a passionate tenderness (Catullus 9.9). Travelers nowadays experience how certain body gestures (men kissing each other) are approved of in certain countries and disliked in others. I imagine something like that, in the case of *CIL* 6.10674, where a master addresses his *alumnus* and says to kiss and lick him: "D(is) M(anibus/P(ublio) Aelio Dextriano/fecit M(arcus) Ulpius Pollo/alumno suo basio te/ling(o) te b(ene) me(renti) fecit."

This last point should be borne in mind, in order to avoid too strong moral, present-minded, and ahistorical condemnations in what is bound to be a matter of issue.

Delicia, the Roman Family, and Roman Concepts of Childhood

In this article, much attention has been paid to both the literary and the epigraphic use of *delicium* and related terms. It emerged that these words could be used in a wide range of situations and contexts. To put things sharply: Cicero could use the same word for addressing his beloved daughter Tullia (*Atticus* 1.8.3) as others used to designate the troupe of footboys of a decadent emperor, or as a master used for his beloved slave child, a substitute

---

phor, ed. H. Moxnes (London and New York: Routledge, 1997), pp. 42-66, is very useful for the whole of Roman antiquity.

62. Clarke, pp. 65-66; pl. 2.

63. In the Manchu tribe, a mother will routinely suck her small son's penis in public, but never kiss his cheeks. The latter deed is always considered sexual, so fellatio turns out to be the best way for expressing motherly affection (Clarke, pp. 15-16).

or a fostered child. What conclusion are we to draw from this? I think a very important one, which has not been fully recognized yet and which is related to the field of human affection and the concept of Roman family itself. Roman children were drawn into wide spheres of familial contacts and association. Large households with many servants and slaves, dislocating factors such as marital changes by sudden death or divorce, and frequent remarriages contributed to the fact that emotional ties were formed with people in close physical proximity. The concept of Roman family extended well beyond immediate blood connections or our modern core unit father-mother-children. What mattered was physical proximity: hence a Roman lady could have more intense affective "family-like" contacts with a servant's or a slave's child called *delicium* than with her own natural son from a previous marriage whom she left with her ex-husband.

In this context, other interesting questions arise, but the answers are due to remain somewhat speculative. How did Roman children cope with this great variety of very different persons who might play important roles in their social formation? How did Atedius's or Ursus's *delicia* (see Statius, *Silvae* 2.1 and 2.6) experience the fact of having their own parents and being loved by their masters? Can we imagine what it meant for the young Earinus to be Domitian's favorite? How did the young jeweler Pagus (see above) experience the apparently deep love of his father and his being *delicium* of the master? What was the psychic everyday reality of such a child? Since there are no autobiographies of children, we will never know. The closest we get is the story of Vitellius's young lover, who ran away from him, was caught again and eventually sold (Suetonius, *Vitellius* 12).

We do know something, however, about the impact of erotic *delicia* on Roman marriage. In epigrams women are frequently urged to accept the fact that their husbands have their pleasures with young slave boys (Martial, *Epigrams* 12.96). These boys are even present in Catullus's wedding hymn (61.144-46). That Roman women did not yield that easily emerges from passages like *Satyricon* 75, where Fortunata is angry with Trimalchio because he kissed a beautiful slave boy. Most illuminating is a story from the life of Marcus Aurelius (SHA 5.11) where he answers to his jealous wife that "she must let him have his pleasures with others: a wife is for honour, not for pleasure" [uxor enim dignitatis nomen est, non voluptatis].

I am also convinced that the phenomenon of *delicia* children is a key concept for our understanding of the Roman concept of childhood. Children were a constant source of anxiety to the Romans, and it is clear that pet children shared a special and privileged kind of care and attention (although that attention may sometimes seem strange to us). On the other hand, children were outsiders in the male social hierarchy, and *delicia* are also a perfect illustration of that. A separate category of child *delicia* did not exist. Deformed dwarfs, hunchback jesters, hermaphrodites, boys kept for sexual pleasure or cute pet children, they were all called *delicia*. Both types, the child as a social outsider and the child as a source of care and attention, are united in the flocks of prattling little children that inhabited the houses of rich Romans during the principate and were called *delicia*.

Delicia in the Christian Household: "Where Did All the *Delicia* Go?"

Early Christian families arose and developed in the context of the Roman household. Although this sounds rather like a commonplace, it is not without importance for our present research. Early Christians lived in a world where large households were a common phenomenon; beyond doubt they were familiar with the keeping of slave children and *delicia*.[64] Yet we would like to have more specific information: Do we know of Christian *delicia* children? Are we informed about early Christian opinions or behavior toward them?

Epigraphical evidence on Christian *delicia* children is extremely scarce. *CIL* 6.3221 (= 32784) is about a deceased man who recommends his *delicia*, called Miles, to his brother, and is considered by Diehl a probable Christian epitaph (see *ILCV* 1509). Yet this is far from sure. For research on this subject I had access to the not yet published database of the monumental *Inscriptiones Christianae Urbis Romae* series (vols. 2-6 and 9-10).[65] The results of a search on *delic-* were remarkably meager. In *ICUR* 6.15590 *deliciae* is probably used as a term of endearment by a father to his deceased son (but the inscription is very fragmented). *ICUR* 9.24124 (= *ILCV* 3211E) is the only clear example: "Respectus qui vixit/ann(os) V et menses/VIII dormit/in pace/delicium."

The silence of Christian epigraphy on *delicia* is very surprising; all the more so since all the material of *ICUR* comes from Rome, an area which has proved to be rich in pagan *delicia*, and since Shaw has shown that children are considerably more commemorated in Christian epitaphs.[66] This silence is not paralleled by diminished use of the term in Christian literary sources: in fact,

---

64. Moxnes, *Constructing Early Christian Families*. On Christian ideology and slavery, see the survey of Carolyn Osiek and David L. Balch, *Families in the New Testament World: Houses and House Churches* (Louisville: Westminster John Knox, 1997), pp. 174-93.

65. I owe thanks to Prof. Dorothy Pikhaus (Gent) and Prof. Carlo Carletti (Bari) for help in this research.

66. Shaw, "The Cultural Meaning of Death."

Christian writers use it as much as their pagan colleagues, often in moralistic passages (Mic. 1:16 Vg on the moral decline of Jerusalem: "decalvare et tondere super filios deliciarum tuarum"), but also in other contexts, as in reference to the Garden of Eden (*in paradiso deliciarum,* Jerome, *Epistle* 22.4.3; see also Augustine, *De genesi ad litteram* 8.3) or in reference to being loved by God (*ut dei delicata* in *Acts of Perpetua* 18).

How are we to explain this epigraphic silence? Firstly, we should not overstate matters. Comparison with pagan inscriptions is difficult, since they suddenly disappear in the fourth century, the period in which the majority of our Christian inscriptions emerge. Neither am I inclined to moralistic interpretations. Psychohistorians have pointed out that Christians (and especially monasteries) were the first to really respect children, to give them appropriate training and attention, and to protect them from damaging effects like pederasty.[67] The absence of *delicia* in the Christian epigraphical evidence would seem to be an argument in favor of this thesis. However, I find this hard to believe since the thesis would rest on a narrow interpretation of *delicia* as lust objects, which I have demonstrated to be flawed. Of course, Christian writers knew of this possible function of *delicia* (Arnobius, *Adversus nationes* 4.26: "Catamitus rapitur deliciarum futurus et poculorum custos," about Ganymedes), but would Ausonius write a cycle on his favorite Bissula when the keeping of such children was considered disreputable by Christians?

There is, however, a possibility of linking the phenomenon of the missing *delicia* with another theory. In some recent publications Sigismund Nielsen has argued for a gradual interest of early Christians in what we would call the conjugal family unit. On the basis of family tombs found in situ and an analysis of Roman family dining practice, she argues for a relative absence of the nuclear family in Roman times.[68] The ideal of the natural and biological unit of parents and children became established and cherished in early Christian literature. Far from being a definite proof, the absence of *delicia* children may point in the same direction. As I have shown, those children were for the most part not natural or legal offspring, but their existence was interwoven with slavery, quasi adoption, and dislocating factors. Christians considered these factors distorting

67. C. A. Mounteer, "Roman Childhood, 200 B.C. to A.D. 600," *Journal of Psycho-History* 14, no. 3 (1987): 233-54.

68. H. Sigismund Nielsen, "The Physical Context of Roman Epitaphs and the Structure of the 'Roman Family,'" *ARID* 23 (1996): 35-60; Nielsen, "Roman Children at Mealtimes," in *The Roman Family at Dinner: Aspects of the Communal Meal in the Hellenistic and Roman World,* ed. I. Nielsen and H. Sigismund Nielsen (Aarhus: Aarhus University Press, 1998), pp. 56-66; and G. Nathan, *The Family in Late Antiquity: The Rise of Christianity and the Endurance of Tradition* (New York: Routledge, 2000).

family relations, as is clear from Ambrose, *Abraham* 1.4, about the effects of masters having concubines and children of those wives: *solvit caritatem coniugii* (it ruins marital love), *superbas ancillas facit* (makes the slave women arrogant), *matronas iracundas* (the wives angry), *discordes coniuges* (the spouses quarreling), *concubinas procaces* (the concubines impudent), *inverecundos maritos* (the husbands untrustworthy). Did Christians refrain from keeping *delicia* for that reason?

Conclusion

In this article I have dealt with Roman *delicia* children. I have refrained from giving an exact, always matching definition for the term. *Delicia* can be natural children, substitute children, foster children, pampered pets, entertaining little jesters, objects for erotic pleasure. It is difficult to distinguish in each single case, since human behavior does not always allow classification in exact categories.

I began with a question: *Desperately different?* The phenomenon strikes modern readers as strange. We are not pleased with the idea of children being exchanged, being objects of entertainment or erotic pleasure. In that sense the ancients are indeed different from us. Still, I would not use these facts to propagate a naive, progressivist view of history, depicting ancient people as strange creatures, only gradually (psychogenetically) reaching the *culmen* of being human in our modern times. Instead I would stick to the presumption of fundamental comprehensibility, a basic similarity, which enables understanding and dialogue with people from the past. The Canadian scholar Mark Golden has valuable things to say on this subject: "Speculation about interpersonal relations must inevitably be sterile if we cannot assume some similarity or comprehensibility in the feelings of those long since beyond direct appeals for clarification."[69] Instead I plead for a careful consideration of demographical data, and the comparative use of cultural history, anthropology, and psychology.

It is my belief that by such careful and nuanced research, new elements on Roman childhood may continue to reveal themselves to us. There is thus no need for despair!

69. M. Golden, "Did the Ancients Care When Their Children Died?" *GR* 35 (1988): 152-63.

VI. Implications for Theological Education

Theological Education, the Bible, and History: Détente in the Culture Wars

Amy-Jill Levine

The significance of the Bible has become, no less than the construction of the family and the role of the church, a battlefield in theological education. Fueled by multicultural interests that prioritize the social location of the reader, postcolonial critiques that flag the ideologically driven and often pernicious composition of both canon and commentary, and a fascination with narrative possibilities which assign meaning-making to the interpreter rather than the text, the ship of biblical scholarship in some settings has cut loose its historical anchor. The hermeneutic privileging of what is in front of the text over the already-contested history behind it opens the canon to a myriad of new perspectives, and this is all to the good. However, the deposing whether overt, surreptitious, or even unintended of any understanding of the Scriptures of Judaism and Christianity in their cultural contexts threatens both to strip from theology and so theological education its historical moorings — the God of synagogue and church is a God manifested in history — and to facilitate particularly in Christian self-definition a proclamation marked by co-optation, if not triumphalism.

Although the doing of history remains an imprecise exercise, the continually tested results of its endeavors must remain, in my view, part of both theological education and ecclesial development. Bad history creates bad theology, and theology decoupled from history sells short the proclamation of the communities that trace their origins in part to Scripture. For example, historical attention helps the budding minister avoid the romantic albeit anti-Jewish sense that Jesus, or Paul, somehow liberated people from their horrible Jewish (or pagan) lives, even as it helps to preclude the anti-Catholic corollary: after this one brief shining moment fostered by Jesus and Paul, it's been downhill ever since via *frühkatholische* compromise.

At Vanderbilt Divinity School, one is just as likely to find a student who rejects the Bible as hopelessly antiquated, patriarchal, misogynistic, and elitist as one who accepts it as the divinely inspired, timeless, universal guide. The biblical studies classroom then becomes the locus for discussing nuances of and correctives to various cramped views, for appreciating the cultural embeddedness of the texts as well as their readers, and hence for developing methods by which the interpreter can facilitate the translation between ancient text and present context. Put otherwise: greater understanding of Jesus' earliest followers in their own settings and their own idiom helps prevent ministers from spewing either incomprehensible or injurious remarks from the pulpit. The more divinity students know about the cultural, social, and material settings of early Christianity, the better homileticians, counselors, theologians, ethicists, and ministers they will be. Similarly, the more biblical studies practitioners dialogue with classicists, the more precise our own contributions can be. Where two or three (from different disciplines but with common interests) are gathered, theological education can happen.

The papers presented at this conference as well as the discussions of them offer excellent resources for helping students to develop critical biblical awareness. Most immediately, the content of these papers, like that of Lyn Osiek and David Balch's *Families in the New Testament World*, forces students out of the fantasy of first-century Bible Land. Any move that disrupts the process of domestication — that is, of reading the ancient texts as if they were written yesterday — serves also to open up new understandings. Second, the papers and discussions provide a process model that would be profitably implemented in theological education more generally understood. Interdisciplinary conversation makes evident the dangers of parochialism: neither the modern church nor its ancient counterpart formed in a vacuum, and neither can be appreciated apart from a profusion of perspectives; understanding and appreciating Scripture are substantially enhanced when the words on the page are matched to the types of houses in which the people lived, the public monuments they saw, the foods they ate, the way they mourned their dead.

As wonderful as it is to have historians of early Christianity and formative Judaism talk with classicists, even rarer and, I suspect, even more wonderful would be finding in theological education biblicists talking with ethicists, theologians, pastoral care specialists, and other practitioners of practical theology. Although scholars of these latter fields often proceed with a consciousness of historical and cultural contingency, their grounding could be substantially improved. Many if not most Ph.D. programs in ethics, pastoral care, et al. do not require candidates to take courses in Bible or church history; what these candidates may have retained from an M.Div. or even undergraduate survey is often negligible. Such parochialism works in reverse as well: although understandings of the biblical text are necessarily shaped by Christianity's prevailing theological emphases, only infrequently do candidates for degrees in Bible do formal work in the chronologically later texts and issues.

The next step would be to have collaborative work among theologians and ethicists, classicists, and the experts in early Christianity as well as formative Judaism. Historically oriented studies of the early Christian family provide a necessary corrective to the stereotypes some ethicists and theologians (let alone biblical scholars) continue to promulgate, and highly encouraging is the attention today's most prominent pastoral theologians and ethicists are paying to the construction of families in antiquity. Epitomizing this concern are "Honor, Shame, and Equality in Early Christian Families," in Don Browning et al.'s *From Culture Wars to Common Ground*,[1] and Lisa Sowle Cahill's "Family Bonds and Christian Community: New Testament Sources," in her *Family: A Christian Social Perspective*.[2] Because these are such fine works, the following comments rely on their content to suggest how a more informed knowledge of the first century could lead to a less problematic, richer treatment of contemporary family configurations and possibilities.

When my students begin their work in Christian moral theology or ethics, they typically presuppose a self-congratulatory view: Jesus and the church, they believe, offered a more progressive message than anything else in their contexts. Not a few Christian students are wont to see the Jesus movement and the earliest Pauline churches as constituting a radical discipleship of equals with no gender bifurcation, class division, or sexual immorality. The view was forcefully presented during this conference in Timothy Sedgwick's citation of Cahill's view that the New Testament offers a "moral vision of a different order of 'mutuality, equality, and solidarity' among all people."[3]

Enhancing this stereotypically positive view is a stereotypically negative picture, the "different order," of surrounding cultures. Paganism becomes a hedonistic orgy of licentiousness and idolatry, while Judaism is a legalistic morass of purity regulations and patriarchal misogyny. The work of this conference illustrates, quite literally, the incorrectness of such views. By removing Jesus and the church from this cultural docetism and by complicating any simple reconstruction of their historical contexts, the conjoined work of classicists, scholars

---

1. Don S. Browning et al., *From Culture Wars to Common Ground: Religion and the American Family Debate*, Family, Religion, and Culture Series (Louisville: Westminster John Knox, 1997, 2000), pp. 129-54.

2. Lisa Sowle Cahill, *Family: A Christian Social Perspective* (Minneapolis: Fortress, 2000).

3. Timothy F. Sedgwick, "Theological Education and the Analogical Imagination," p. 339 in this volume. For a very helpful critique grounded not only in textual evidence but also in philosophic theory and linguistic exploration, see now John H. Elliott, "Jesus Was Not an Egalitarian: A Critique of an Anachronistic and Idealist Theory," *BTB* 32, 2 (2002): 79-91; as well as Kathleen Corley, *Women and the Historical Jesus: Feminist Myths of Christian Origins* (Santa Rosa, Calif.: Polebridge Press, 2002).

of Christian origins, and scholars of formative Judaism can better prepare the foundation upon which ethicists and theologians build.

Neither the literary evidence nor the material culture supports such constructions. To the contrary, these models overstate the extent of both social boundaries based on class and gender and the distinction between the church and other contemporaneous social groups. Epigraphic evidence demonstrates that Jewish and pagan women, as well as their Christian sisters, held positions of authority and influence in their religious organizations. Given women's public presence, property ownership, roles as patrons, and leadership in other religious movements, Christianity would be anomalous if women did not have prominent roles in its institutions as well.

The common claim that "most women in Hellenistic societies led lives confined mainly to the inner spaces of their living compound"[4] and that such women were then attracted to the liberating church has clearly been shattered by this conference's references to, *inter alia,* both the constraints upon and the public roles of female slaves, the fluidity of public and private spaces in the home, and women's participation in civic and religious festivals; biblicists might add women's frequent public appearances in the Gospels. The romantic view of the missionary struggling to meet with sympathetic women locked away in the homes of Antioch or Rome yields to the more mundane picture of the *insula,* where contact between men and women as well as between rich and poor was a quotidian occurrence. Christian slaves remained slaves; the rich and the poor remained in the states in which they were called; systemic changes in city or even domestic structures did not appear. Within the household, perhaps there was an additional familiarity practiced among Christian masters and slaves, men and women, but the texts provide little evidence of such; further, any such familiarity may have been encouraged less by claims to equality than by ongoing contact.

On the ground the Christian home looks no different than the neighboring homes of pagans, Jews, or Samaritans; in practice, the church in Antioch or Rome looked no different than synagogue gatherings, gatherings of Isis worshipers, or the meetings of numerous voluntary associations. Art, epigraphs, inscriptions, and house plans disrupt the stereotypical divide of male/female, public/private, even as they force nuance to the way Christian origins are read. To recognize, as David Balch points out, that fellowship meals may well have been held in rooms adorned by artistic depictions of the naked Iphigenia about to be sacrificed not only expands meanings attributed to Jesus' death, it also challenges more conservative views of aesthetics.[5]

4. Browning, p. 142.

5. Historians might investigate the means of determining whether the art represents more

One increasingly favorite theory utilized with the result of distinguishing the early followers of Jesus and Paul from their cultural milieux has been the appeal to purity legislation. For example, Timothy Sedgwick's reflections, following Cahill's *Family: A Christian Social Perspective*, see Jesus as "responding to and challenging . . . a religious ideology which organized economic and social status around purity laws." Engagement with historians and archaeologists tempers this view, which is itself demonstrated even by the New Testament writings as untenable. Jesus himself upholds rather than abrogates the purity legislation; had he not, Paul's encounter with Peter at Antioch (Gal. 2) and the Lucan depiction of the Jerusalem Council (Acts 15) would make no sense. The Gospels do not demonstrate people "outcast" (a common term in the discourse) because of purity issues; to the contrary, purity is rarely even educed by the text. Women appear in public, as do lepers; likely Jesus and those who traveled with him also would have been in impure states. If the Gospels do not find purity issues to be a problem, and the Gospels do not present a purity system fully mapped onto class and economic concerns — while kings and high priests can be in impure states, the slave may be pure — there is no reason the modern scholar should either. Next, and here the archaeologists are of great help, the presence of *miqva'ot* throughout Judea and the Galilee testifies to the ease by which certain forms of impurity, such as those created by menstruation or seminal emissions, may be treated. Finally, as the classicists demonstrate, purity is of concern also to Greek and Roman cultures (almost invariably overlooked by Christian thinkers with built-in stereotypes of Jewish culture).

The apologetic use of purity concerns is matched by appeal to the role of the child in early Christian households. Pastoral theologians and ethicists have long argued that the church, at least in the first two centuries, held a "deeper respect for children"[6] than did a culture such as "Jesus' social world" where children "are not generally regarded as having value in their own right."[7] Several of the conference papers detail the abundant love of some Greek and Roman parents for their children, even as we see as well in the Gospels the love of Jewish parents (in particular, Jairus, the synagogue ruler) for theirs. More, the papers demonstrate how complicated attitudes toward children were throughout the

---

than a dead metaphor. Martyred women may be displayed in banquet settings because they whet the appetite (they're sexy, and libido drives hunger) rather than for religious reasons. Classicists might also do more with the biblical potential of Greek art. To read Paul in the presence of *Laocoon* might also invite Adam: thwarting divine will, brought to death by a snake, having one son die and another be cursed, and looking spectacular (as one in the image of the divine must).

6. Browning, p. 131.

7. Cahill, p. 30.

empire — with contingencies concerning the child's age and relationship to the parent (biological or adopted child, slave, pet [*delicia* children]). Consequently re-creations of the early Christian view of children should be much more hesitant, especially concerning the first two centuries, for which there are precious little Christian epigraphic information and unclear and conflicted literary materials. The church is quite a marvelous and inspirational institution; there is no need to invent history to make it correspond to the values we hold near and dear today.

We might also be less sanguine in suggesting that Jesus' injunction that one become like a little child has direct value for children. To become like a child does not necessarily mean that one has "negligible status"; nor does it indicate acceptance of "social scorn."[8] It may refer in addition, or rather, to cases of dependency and familial constructs (here the family being the fictive kinship group), to celibacy, to lack of adult responsibilities, to the model of Adam and Eve. Second, scorn is not determined by age; the child of the emperor or of the wealthy is not scorned and in fact may be quite disobedient. Third, metaphoric associations need not and often do not translate into social change: to encourage Christians to become slaves to God likely failed to enhance the status of the household slave; to encourage the wealthy to divest their holdings and become poor need not help the poor (who have no choice in the matter). Perhaps the Gospel injunction should be read in light of issues of reciprocity (the inscriptions with *pientissimus*) or the treatment of the *deliciae* — in addition to/along with/over against those interpretations that stress asexuality, innocence, and dependence.

Speaking of sex, the papers and slides presented at this conference wreck any notion that attitudes toward sexuality or the human body remain consistent over time. Indeed, the material remains have the potential to shock even the more theoretically sophisticated student of early Christian literature. It is all well and good to read Foucault; it's something else to see a penis door knocker or fellatio illustrated on a candy dish. Once we realize the cultural construction of sexual mores, it becomes easier as well as more overtly necessary to reassess our own views of propriety and desirability. On the matter of sexuality, we might note, for example, that those earliest Christians weren't distressed by such displays of the human body engaging in very human activities. It should also be informative to note that masters — even those with churches in their homes — might have found it perfectly normal and righteous to have intercourse with their female slaves.

Concerning divorce, the standard view on the pastoral-theological front is

8. Cahill, p. 30.

that Jesus prohibited divorce because he objected "to the patriarchal patterns of unilateral divorce of Jewish wives by their husbands, a practice that filled the ranks of the poor primarily with rejected women."[9] Jesus is, rather, "an opponent of divorce and thereby a proponent of family stability."[10] Complicating these reductive views are both material remains and textual evidence. Ross Kraemer's observations on the Babatha Papyri, including widows' access to their husbands' estates, the strength of the *ketubah* (marriage contract — something that actually did protect women's rights), and the opportunity for polygamy begin to contest this view. Notices of Jewish women's ability to leave their husbands (legally, as in the case of the Herodian household; voluntarily, perhaps in the case of Johanna the wife of Herod's steward) further undermine it.

Jesus' program was not about preserving the biological family unit but rather about dismantling it in favor of fictive kinship groups: he forbids divorce, but he also encourages people to leave their families, as Mrs. Zebedee leaves her husband and Peter his mother-in-law. Luke understood the program: "There is no one who has left house or wife or brothers or parents or children, for the sake of the kingdom of God, who will not get back very much more in this age, and in the age to come eternal life" (Luke 18:29-30; cf. Matt. 19:27-30). The forbidding of divorce does not thereby lead to the conclusion that Jesus supported family stability: separation apart from divorce was not uncommon then (e.g., as the separation of slave families indicates), or now, for that matter. Given forced separations, by slavery, by war, by whatever, of parental couples, of parent and child, we see how this Gospel view might have caught on, for the

---

9. Browning, pp. 134-35. See also Cahill, p. 32: "If divorce was a mechanism for ensuring the primacy of male interests in patriarchal marriage, then Jesus upheld the right of women to protection. Prohibiting divorce had the practical effect of limiting arbitrary male control over women and of protecting women from the social consequences of the fact that they were valued primarily as sexual prizes, son producers, economic bargaining chips, and tokens of family political status." I suspect one could find a more balanced description of the way Jewish men in Jesus' time viewed their mothers, wives, and daughters, and how these women viewed themselves. Cahill's treatment of early Judaism is far better than most of this genre, yet she too elides chronological distinctions (first-century Judaism is not the same thing as the life reconstructed from Leviticus) and offers a monolithic model against which to place Christianity. For another example, p. 34: the "entire basis of Christian religious identity is faith and a personal commitment to act as a disciple; whereas in both Greco-Roman and Jewish culture of the first century, one belongs to a religious community by virtue of family identity and the traditions of one's kin group and its elders." To the contrary: were the master of a household to become a Christian, likely the other members would join as well; Jewish identity is also determined by practice, as the numerous examples of converts to Judaism in the first century (notably Helena of Adiabene) demonstrate; Judaism is determined not simply by familial affiliation, but also by practice and therefore by the "personal commitment" to follow *Halacha*.

10. Browning, p. 132.

church offered a new family structure. Jesus' injunctions against divorce are thus not indicative of a Jewish system out of control (the *ketubah* and *get* prevented this), but rather indicate precisely what the Gospels claim: a concern to create a new Eden (Matt. 19:3-9). Attracted to the movement were not wives tossed out on the street, but single women apparently in control of their own finances.[11] Sometimes we have social engineering, such as Augustus's family values programs; sometimes we have biblical idealism, such as what Jesus promoted.

While Paul did see "marriage as an individual decision," ethicists might want to rethink the common contrast, the claim that marriage was "a necessity for everyone, as was thought in ancient Judaism."[12] The evidence of this conference points to the vast array of familial configurations. There are also the unmarried, widowed, or otherwise single men at Qumran. If nothing else, these conference papers highlight the impossibility of stereotyping any group; of making sharp distinctions among Jews, Christians, and pagans; and especially, of thinking all relationships were of the "nuclear family of today"[13] variety. This can only be good news for those today outside the nuclear family.

Ancient Christian families, ancient families in general, were diverse in configuration, domicile, attitudes, and status — in this sense, they are much like today's families, Christian or no. But here the facile similarity stops. The world of the ancients is not our world — and we would be both intellectually sloppy and theologically naive were we to read the evidence of antiquity as if it were. Find models for modern views — yes, but do not do so by forcing a distinction, with Christianity always on the progressive end, between Christians and their non-Christian neighbors; by positing an ideal early tradition of radical egalitarianism now lost, which is bad history and inevitably leads to anti-Judaism and anti-Catholicism; or by suggesting a "natural" attitude toward sexuality rather than viewing sexual ethics as culturally constructed. In turn, ethicists and pastoral theologians, especially from Protestant traditions, might explore the very positive endorsement Jesus and Paul give to celibacy. Here, finally, is a shift from the prevailing ethos, but it is one too often overlooked today both because of America's family values system (manifest especially in churches, where the single person is often alienated) and perhaps because of residual cultural anti-Catholicism.

11. See the very helpful essays in Ross S. Kraemer and Mary Rose D'Angelo, eds., *Women and Christian Origins* (New York: Oxford University Press, 1999).

12. Browning, p. 139; no sources, primary or secondary, are cited in support of these or the other assertions concerning Judaism. The term "ancient Judaism" is less helpful than, e.g., "early Judaism"; the text does not use the equivalent "ancient Christianity."

13. Cahill, p. 19.

334

It is increasingly popular in theological education to speak of interfaith dialogue and globalization. So too it should be with the past: Why not learn from it rather than abstract the church or theological pronouncement out of it? Why not, indeed, celebrate the ancient churches even as we recognize the distinct cultural contexts of churches today? Perhaps such openness, and such recognition of alternative settings within which the gospel is not only preached but also adapted, will make those of us in theological education at the very least a bit more humble when we offer pronouncements on ethics, pastoral care, worship, and God.

There is no conclusion to the conjoining of the diverse disciplinary voices heard in the symposium and recorded in the pages of this volume. There is only ongoing explication to be undertaken with caution. In the first-century Mediterranean world, such a result would be celebrated by public encomium, or perhaps a commissioned statue. But we are not creatures of the past. Nevertheless, adaptation of the genre may be in order; the point is not to engage in frivolity, but, like the insistence on attention to material culture for understanding Christian origins, so too perhaps verse might cement the paths taken.

> To read social structures from ancient remains
> Or seek for the nuclear family
> Is a trek filled with guesswork and gaps and with pains;
> The *insula's* no sacred canopy.
>
> For the *domus* need not be a family's own space
> Even for Rome's upper classes;
> Commercial apartments comprise part of the place
> And the courtyard invites in the masses.
>
> Not *domus* nor *insula* but *vicus* we learn
> Comprises Rome's true social habit.
> It's the baths and the cookshops to which we must turn
> For antiquity's real urban fabric.
>
> Then to Delos we go, expecting a show
> Of the port's multicultural fixtures,
> But the domestic structures appear uniform
> With common liturgical pictures.
>
> Nor do Delian rooms evince architectural design
> Dividing public from private home places;
> To make the distinction, we've learned to refine
> Views of temporal models, not spaces.

The questions of gender, and function, and diet
In Israel apply more than a minimum;
But are we sure we are willing to regard the *Bayit*
As some sort of old condominium?

More new questions we bring up to Sepphoris sites:
Do *miqva'ot* exceed ritual function?
While there's not been a pig bone on acropolis' heights,
What of that peristyle junction?

There's more to be said, and more to be read
Of Babatha, Augustus, and Celsus.
This is only a start, a glimpse at the art
Of what material culture can tell us.

Theological Education and the Analogical Imagination

Timothy F. Sedgwick

As a theological educator in an Episcopal seminary, my primary responsibility is preparing persons for leadership in the church, mostly priests for parish ministry. More specifically, the focus of my teaching and writing as a moral theologian is to enable persons to articulate their understanding of Christian faith and life. In terms of Christian ethics this requires a constructive account of how God is present in our lives, what is needed to inform conscience in the making of moral decisions, and what are the disciplines and practices that shape persons in Christian faith and life.[1] Broadly speaking, my work is theological, ethical, and ascetical. In one sense I am at the end of the "food chain" in theological education, feeding critically or uncritically on the work of historians.

As my own work assumes, the end of theological education is expressed in the meaning of the word "tradition": to pass something on, in this case Christian faith as a living faith, however that might be expressed — as saving gospel, as holy piety, as liberation, as *theosis,* or whatever. What this involves is a hermeneutical arch that connects past to present. This arch is constructed by way of analogies since the past is neither absolute difference nor simple correspondence. As Paul Ricoeur describes this process in terms of what it means to be human, the past is appropriated in the configuration and refiguration of the self as given in practices told in narrative form.[2] As I want to develop in this response to the studies in this volume on households and the social world in late

---

1. This definition of the task of Christian ethics is framed in terms of enabling the articulation of leaders within the community of faith. Such an account has a double focus. It is directed to the formation of those within the community and to the world at large. On the nature of Christian ethics, see James M. Gustafson, "Christian Ethics," in *The Westminster Dictionary of Christian Ethics,* ed. James F. Childress and John MacQuarrie (Philadelphia: Westminster, 1986), pp. 87-90. On ethics and moral theology in the Anglican tradition, see Timothy F. Sedgwick, *The Christian Moral Life: Practices of Piety* (Grand Rapids: Eerdmans, 1999), pp. 25-51.

2. Paul Ricoeur, *Oneself as Another,* trans. Kathleen Blamey (Chicago: University of Chicago Press, 1992), pp. 152-68.

antiquity, moral theologians and all who serve communities of faith offer assessments of human life in terms of some narrative identity that configures human actions. If this telling of the Christian story is to refigure present practices adequately, the historical constructs used to interpret the past must be critically assessed.

Prior to the publications arising from the Family, Religion, and Culture Project — which includes the publication of Carolyn Osiek and David Balch's *Families in the New Testament World*[3] — the constructs of family and household were not critically assessed and developed. Rather, ethicists focused more narrowly on specific moral issues that arise within the boundaries or in breaking the boundaries of family — contraception, divorce and remarriage, premarital sexual relations, single sexual relations, extramarital sexual relationships, and homosexual relations — and then criticized or defended understandings of the family. The nature of the family and household was generally uncritically assumed and developed, first as a God-given order and then as an oppressive patriarchal order.[4] The collaborative work *From Culture Wars to Common Ground: Religion and the American Family Debate* and the work of Lisa Sowle Cahill, Roman Catholic moral theologian at Boston College, are among the first works in which a critical reassessment of the historical constructs of family and household has reframed issues of human sexuality and sexual relations.[5] Cahill's two books, *Sex, Gender, and Christian Ethics* and *Family: A Christian Social Perspective*, are in particular methodologically self-

---

3. Carolyn Osiek and David Balch, *Families in the New Testament World: Houses and House Churches* (Louisville: Westminster John Knox, 1997).

4. Two notable exceptions are Roger Mehl, *Society and Love: Ethical Problems of Family Life*, trans. James H. Farley (Philadelphia: Westminster, 1964); and James M. Gustafson, *Ethics from a Theocentric Perspective* 2 (Chicago: University of Chicago Press, 1984), pp. 153-84. Two classic contemporary texts evidence the failure to assess and develop this larger context. As representative of Protestant thought, see James Nelson, *Embodiment: An Approach to Sexuality and Christian Theology* (Minneapolis: Augsburg, 1978). As representative of Roman Catholic thought, see Anthony Kosnik, William Carroll, Agnes Cunningham, Ronald Modras, and James Schulte, *Human Sexuality: New Directions in American Catholic Thought* (New York: Paulist, 1977). For an account of liberal and conservative responses to the family since the 1960s, see Don Browning, Bonnie J. Miller-McLemore, Pamela D. Couture, K. Brynolf Lyon, and Robert M. Franklin, *From Culture Wars to Common Ground: Religion and the American Family Debate*, Family, Religion, and Culture Series (Louisville: Westminster John Knox, 1997; 2nd ed., 2000), pp. 157-246.

5. Browning et al., *From Culture Wars to Common Ground*, and Lisa Sowle Cahill, *Sex, Gender, and Christian Ethics* (Cambridge: Cambridge University Press, 1996) and *Family: A Christian Social Perspective* (Minneapolis: Fortress, 2000). These three books reflect the methodology of the Family, Religion and Culture Project. On the methodology of practical theology, see the appendix in Browning, pp. 337-39.

conscious about the integral relationship between the work of historical config-uration and normative judgments.

In developing a Christian ethic, Cahill understands that the narrative mean-ing of literary texts expresses moral visions and moral norms only as they recon-figure social practices and relationships. Therefore, "In interpreting the Bible for ethics, texts as literary units, the social settings assumed or projected by those texts, the layered revisions of biblical accounts in response to social factors, and the experience of the church today are all important pieces of the hermeneutical process." This enables us to understand "how specific New Testament moral atti-tudes and norms functioned against their own cultures, and thus to understand the sorts of moral relationships they might offer us as models today."[6]

Present concerns shape the process of conceptualizing past practices and relationships; at the same time, the concepts that construe these relations shape present understandings and judgments. If the present concern is with unjust social relationships between men and women, then those interests shape the description of gender relations. In turn, the historical description of gender re-lations will further focus present attention and concerns. This is most evident in groundbreaking studies such as Susan Brownmiller's *Against Our Will: Men, Women, and Rape* or Elisabeth Schüssler Fiorenza's study of women and leader-ship in the early Christian community.[7] Simply stated, moral visions and norms are a refiguration of our lives only in terms of those relations that are configured in the process of historical reconstruction.[8]

In developing her work on the family, Cahill identifies the constructs by which she construes the social setting of families and households of late antiq-uity in terms of economic, social, and gender relations. Economic exchange is determined by patron-client relationships; social roles are shaped by a culture of honor and shame; men and women relate to each other in terms of a patriar-chal hierarchy. Given these constructs, Cahill reads the literary texts of the New Testament as offering a moral vision of a different order of "mutuality, equality, and solidarity" among all people.[9] As she says:

6. Cahill, *Sex*, p. 293 n. 6.

7. Susan Brownmiller, *Against Our Will: Men, Women, and Rape* (New York: Simon and Schuster, 1975); Elisabeth Schüssler Fiorenza, *In Memory of Her: A Feminist Theological Recon-struction of Christian Origins* (New York: Crossroad, 1983).

8. Max Weber articulated this process of historical interpretation in terms of "ideal types." Grounded in the phenomenology of Edmund Husserl, Alfred Schutz has offered the most thor-ough analysis of Max Weber, ideal types, and historical interpretation. See Alfred Schutz, *The Phenomenology of the Social World*, ed. George Walsh and Frederick Lehnert (Evanston, Ill.: Northwestern University Press, 1967), esp. pp. 176-214.

9. Cahill, *Family*, p. 47.

Research into the social history of Palestine in Jesus' day, and of his followers in the next two generations, suggests that Jesus and the gospels are responding to and challenging highly stratified social relationships, especially those installed by a patron-client economy, a religious ideology which organized economic and social status around purity laws, and by a gender hierarchy within the patriarchal family. Early Christianity does not reject exchange relations, purity observance, or the family as such. But it does challenge and even reverse cultural criteria of inclusion and exclusion, and gauges all moral relations by their success in dislodging power elites and including "the poor."[10]

As if the construction of the social world and the construction of a moral vision and moral norms were not difficult enough, the historian of late antiquity and the Christian ethicist have a further task of historical reconstruction. Not only do the texts and practices of Christians suggest a moral life in tension with the prevailing social world of late antiquity, but the Christian moral life is grounded in religious meanings and practices. These meanings and practices must be construed in relationship to a moral vision and moral norms if Christian faith is to be understood as religious — and that is essential to Christian ethicists and, of course, to the leaders of religious communities that seek to pass on Christian faith as a living faith. The sources for this reconstruction include religious texts, visual images, and artifacts as they are interpreted in relationship to the social world about them. Peter Lampe's paper on early Christian meal practices and David Balch's paper on suffering — as construed by and as informing the meaning of death and resurrection — suggest the kind of historical work that is required to interpret how the religious world is variously shaped by and shapes the social world of late antiquity.[11] More broadly, as historians of late antiquity, biblical scholar Gerd Theissen and liturgical scholar Gordon Lathrop have sought to describe the symbolic world of early Christianity by a reconstruction of religious worlds of meaning and practice as they develop in response to the social and moral world of late antiquity.[12]

As historians develop new and often more detailed descriptions of the so-

---

10. Cahill, *Family*, p. 123.

11. See Peter Lampe's article and David Balch's article in this volume.

12. Gerd Theissen, *The Religion of the Earliest Churches: Creating a Symbolic World*, trans. John Bowden (Minneapolis: Fortress, 1999); and Gordon Lathrop, *Holy Things: A Liturgical Theology* (Minneapolis: Augsburg Fortress, 1993). Of course, drawing upon Weber's understanding of ideal types, the first methodologically self-conscious reconstruction of the religious world in relationship to the moral world is the work of Ernst Troeltsch, *The Social Teaching of the Christian Churches*, trans. Olive Wyon, 2 vols. (Louisville: Westminster John Knox, 1992; originally published in German in 1912 and English in 1931).

cial world of the past — for example, as papers in this collection describe the household in light of the archaeological evidence or the place of women, slaves, and children in light of burial inscriptions — the adequacy of historical constructs will be a matter of debate. Constructs such as the household, patron-client relations, honor-shame codes of behavior, or the patriarchal ordering of the social world may be contested or qualified because they are inadequate in interpreting historical data or, more broadly, fail to comprehend the complexity of the social world of the past. However, the work of the historian and the work of the ethicist require such constructs. Historical constructs may be qualified or rejected, but some such constructs are necessary to the work of both. They are the means and the only means by which historians can describe a social world and by which ethicists can describe a moral vision and moral norms as they arise in relationship to that social world. As a matter of theological education, the task of passing on the Christian faith as a way of life lived in relationship to God rests upon such historical reconstruction of the past.

As proposed in the focus of this collection of studies and in the work of ethicists drawing from such critical studies of the social world of late antiquity (such as Cahill and the authors of *From Culture Wars to Common Ground*), at the heart of the reconstruction of the moral world of late antiquity stands the household. The household is not to be understood narrowly as the private sphere opposed to the public. The household stands rather as the threshold where domestic relationships and practices connect members of a household to persons outside the immediate household. These relationships beyond the household are public in the sense that they form what persons understand it is to be a people. The household is not, therefore, to be considered the private sphere. There is no dichotomy between private and public. Instead, the house is best viewed as the domestic sphere — the sphere of those who live in the household — as that forms them in relationship to others as a people. Patron-client, honor-shame, and patriarchy are then the constructs by which economic, social, and gender relations are construed. The Christian moral vision and the norms for the Christian life are seen as calling for a different order, an order of "mutuality, equality, and solidarity" among all people. The power of this vision is given *via negativa,* in its contrast with the construal of the social world of late antiquity in terms of patron-client relationships, codes of honor and shame, and the power and privilege of males over females.

In turn, the religious meaning of Christian faith is interpreted in terms of this construction of the social world. The church begins in the household, centered in a shared, common meal where all are invited and welcomed as members of a household. By the fourth century, however, the Eucharist is a ritual meal of bread and wine celebrated by authorized priests in a church as a separate house. Such practices insured that the Eucharist would be regularly and uniformly celebrated as a celebration of a new people and not that of a particular family or people. On the other hand, the connection with table fellowship and hospitality could be lost from view. A ritual meal could spiritualize what was a real meal, the giving of thanks for the blessings of life and the sharing of the meal with all who come and all who are in need. This institutionalization of Christian faith could be for good or ill or both, depending upon one's perspective. But, whatever the perspective, the constructs of household and of the relations that constitute the household in forming a people offer a basis for developing the relationship between Christian faith and the moral life.

Still, there is no consensus about the constructs for understanding religious meanings and practices as these are given in the social world and as they shape and form the moral vision and norms of the Christian life. As indicated above, Gerd Theissen and Gordon Lathrop offer two distinct accounts. In light of these works, the basic constructs for understanding religious meanings and practices in relationship to the moral world might be developed in terms of worship and specifically the Eucharist as sacrifice, as table fellowship, and as hospitality. Each of these constructs has both a social meaning in late antiquity and, as given in texts and practices, a religious meaning for Christians. Like the constructs of household and of household relations, this holds the promise of understanding and developing religious meanings in light of their constitutive contexts.[13] As David Balch has explored in his paper in this volume, this would include the question of the nature and meaning of death and suffering as that connects and extends the human person to other persons and purposes.[14]

In terms of theological education, if leaders of the church are to pass on a living faith, they must themselves move back and forth between historical reconstruction (figuration) and moral and theological construction (refiguration). Unless they are able to do this, they will be captive to certain historical constructs in understanding the past and in presenting a constructive vision for the present. This may lead to crude and finally inadequate, reductionistic representations of Christian faith that reflect present interests. This is the case in both conservative and liberal renderings of Christian faith, for example, in the claim that, as revealed in the New Testament, it demands that wives be obedient to their husbands, or that it is narrowly a matter of political liberation understood as overthrowing the oppression of patriarchy. In both cases there is no assessment of the constructs that serve to figure and refigure, to construct and reconstruct, the nature of Christian faith in different social worlds. History describes

13. See Theissen, esp. pp. 136-60, and Lathrop, esp. pp. 139-58.
14. See Balch's article in this volume.

what is. Theology and ethics describe what ought to be. Never the twain shall meet. There is then no understanding how the constructs of the one determine the focus of the other. There is then no play of analogy, no play of imaginative variations, and no understanding of historical development.

In order to develop an analogical imagination that moves back and forth between historical construal of the past and theological-moral construal of Christian faith in the present, theological education must overcome the divide between the historical and the theological and ethical, as if one were objective description and the other normative truth, the one phenomenal and the other noumenal.[15] Those working in theology and ethics — in their own work and in the classroom — must engage the work of historical construction of the past in order to assess the focus, comprehension, and adequacy of the constructs that shape their constructive work. In turn, as theological educators, historians must assess their historical constructs in terms of their own interests and their adequacy in answering questions and furthering the purposes of theology and ethics. If they find lacking the constructs used by theologians and ethicists (as all constructs necessarily are), they need to suggest what constructs would be more adequate. This requires cross-disciplinary reading and, ideally, collaborative work, especially in the classroom.

The disciplinary interests of narrowly defined guilds of scholars, however, often narrow the focus of scholars on basic research within a field. These interests are often reinforced by standards for faculty reward and promotion. This must change if there is to be the needed collaborative work across disciplinary boundaries. This is more easily done in denominational seminaries. More difficult is developing such interdisciplinary work in university-based seminaries with doctoral programs (such as Boston, Chicago, Duke, Harvard, Notre Dame, Princeton, Union, Vanderbilt, and Yale). However, such collaborative, interdisciplinary work is especially needed in such programs because they provide the scholarship that most often defines or redefines the theological disciplines that shape theological education. These programs, moreover, train the majority of scholars and teachers for theological education, including those who will teach at denominational seminaries.

Perhaps what was most significant about the conference from which the papers in this volume originated was the collaborative work between historians of late antiquity and biblical scholars. What may be more difficult and more significant is developing the collaboration between historians and biblical scholars and scholars working in theology and ethics. And what may be most

15. See David Tracy, *The Analogical Imagination: Christian Theology and the Culture of Pluralism* (New York: Crossroad, 1981).

difficult and most significant is developing and sustaining such interdisciplinary work among faculty members in a way that is integral to the curriculum in schools whose purpose is theological education.

Why Family Matters for Early Christian Literature

Margaret M. Mitchell

Introduction: "Theological Education in My Context"

I have been asked to speak about the implications of the research presented in this conference "for theological education in my context." I shall start, therefore, by saying a few words about where I teach, in the Divinity School and in the Department of New Testament and Early Christian Literature in the Humanities Division at the University of Chicago. The traditional emphasis of this school, from its founding in 1891, has been on the historical contexts of biblical literature, both Greco-Roman and ancient Near Eastern, and the realia of the ancient world, including artifacts, architecture, manuscripts, and the social history of everyday life (our Oriental Institute's most famous fictional faculty member, you may recall, is Indiana Jones). I teach primarily graduate students, two-thirds of whom are master's and doctoral students preparing for careers as researchers and teachers of the New Testament and early Christian history, and roughly another third of whom are in the M.Div. program, training both for ordained ministry and for a whole range of nonordained positions in agencies, church-governing bodies, and various forms of educational and social service.

My area of teaching is primarily defined by texts — the New Testament and early Christian literature. This body of documents is of interest to these varied student populations for different reasons, at least on the face of things. My choice has been to seize upon this diversity of interpretive agendas as a pedagogical opportunity, so at least once a year I offer a course that overtly welcomes students who bring a range of questions, from "purely historical" to constructive theological and ethical, to history of religions, to ministerial, in order to create a context for conversation around a common text. In the spring of 1999 I taught Biblical Studies 436, "The Pastoral Epistles" (1 and 2 Timothy and Titus), in such a format, using books by three of the presenters at this conference: Carolyn Osiek and David Balch, *Families in the New Testament*

World,[1] and Margaret MacDonald's *Early Christian Women and Pagan Opinion: The Power of the Hysterical Woman.*

Our Chicago M.Div. students were perhaps less surprised at being expected to do serious historical and philological analysis of these biblical texts than were the Ph.D.s at actually having to talk about what these texts might mean beyond their ancient contexts. My not-so-covert purpose was to get these two groups (and the many positions mediating the two) well introduced to one another, given that particularly Ph.D. students in New Testament, early Christian literature, and the history of Christianity may well produce scholarship that would conceivably be of interest to contemporary believers and others for whom New Testament texts have some form of authoritative status, and *surely* they would teach such students after they graduate.

I began the course by questioning why these three peculiar little texts, 1 and 2 Timothy and Titus, were worthy of ten weeks of study. For example, if our interest was "Pauline theology," then undoubtedly we should read Romans instead; if Hellenistic ethics and paraenesis, then Aristotle's *Ethica Nicomachea* or Seneca's *Epistulae morales* would be more suitable; if ancient pseudepigraphical literature, then the Cynic and Socratic letters, or those attributed to Plato or Demosthenes, might more rightfully claim our attention. But in the face of these fine alternatives I offered my own reasons for focusing on the Pastoral Epistles: fascination with how the author, Paul, is constructed in these postmortem pseudepigraphical documents, and how the historical author of the letters creates simultaneously portraits of the recipients Timothy and Titus and the readership itself; with the development and permutations of Pauline theology in the next generations; with the relationship between the Pastorals and *The Acts of Paul and Thecla;* with the literary and historical relationships between the Pastorals and the emerging canonical collection of Paul's letters in the early second century; and with the legacy of these texts for Christian social existence, especially in regard to patriarchy and the suppression of women's leadership in churches. Having acknowledged my own motivations, I in turn asked the students about theirs. Fully seventeen of twenty-one in the room testified that from very early youth these texts, especially the prescriptions for male and female household and church roles, had been drummed into them as

---

1. In a most instructive contemporary illustration of the complexities of authorship, we had a marvelous debate in the class over whether it was David or Lyn who penned this sentence about the Pastorals on p. 123: "Second-generation, deutero-Pauline Christians acculturating to Roman imperial (tyrannical) society wrote a passive ethic into our canon." Almost simultaneously two students (each of whom was serendipitously a former student of one of our authors) vehemently claimed their own professor as the author! (Later detective work has ascertained that it was David Balch who penned the sentence.)

God's definitive word about Christian lifestyle. A large majority of the class said they were no longer fundamentalists or "in 'conservative' churches" (their words), but wanted to know if there were other interpretations or other information that might help them understand these texts — and live with them — better. I tell this story by way of preamble to illustrate a simple point: even scholarly researchers whose predominant perspective on the Christian family in antiquity is antiquarian, may — if one digs just a little below the surface — be influenced by a personal relationship with the subject matter as encountered somewhere on the terrain of their own lives.

Interpretive Propositions

With these opening observations about my own context in theological education as a backdrop, I would like to structure my response to the rich offerings of this conference in two ways. First I shall formulate four propositions about what this conference might or should mean for theological education in my context. Then I shall present one illustration of the significance of the findings presented here for the kind of textual interpretation in which I am usually engaged.

1. *It is simply a fact (whether allowed, welcomed, discouraged, or encouraged) that a major audience of this scholarship on families in antiquity, and early Christian families in particular, is Christian believers seeking to understand their present in relation to their (reconstructed) past, and their sacred texts which mirror, embody, and sometimes challenge the cultural norms and expectations of their day.*

Given this reality, scholars who produce carefully researched and composed arguments on these topics should not be surprised that there is a ready audience for them that extends more widely than classicists, historians, and anthropologists. I consider this to offer both a rare and a potentially dangerous opportunity. To lead with the good news: it is wonderful to see the level of intense curiosity and interest many Christian believers have for the ancient historical contexts which are the object of specialized research. Such a conversation can be to the advantage of both sides: rendering Christians less insensitive to the complex and different historical contexts of their ancient traditions, while also bringing ancient historians and the fruits of their illuminating research more into the limelight and general cultural conversation of today. It can be precisely at such points of common interest that the fields of historical and constructive studies can come together. But at the same time I have two concerns about this phenomenon. I have a serious distrust of the utilitarian impulse (on the side of either authors or readers) to make relevant what works or to make what works relevant. This especially worries me when it becomes a highly selective reading of ancient cultures and communities for parallels which may be facile comparisons to the now, the familiar, the debated (even as the "now" is often myopically perceived). In the face of this I instinctively wish to "save" classics and ancient historiography from those who wish to "raid the Loeb" for useful ancient data to throw on the fire of contemporary debates. But at the same time I have an anxiety about these historically questing Christians themselves, about their playing into a biblical hermeneutic of which I am quite cautious — i.e., the Bible (or early Christian experience as confirming or correcting it) deemed immediately and unquestionably *normative* for contemporary life. This is especially the case for social and sexual ethics (as with "the family") — which is often the sole subject of the vast array of biblical injunctions that are so treated — which seems to me an intolerable and disingenuous hermeneutical inconsistency. But I also fervently believe that one cannot be too well informed about one's sacred texts. So I would encourage inquisitive Christians to delve into this research, but not without serious and sustained conversation and debate at each turn about the complexities of its transferability and significance for specific modern concerns.

2. *A rich, varied, and textured historical-cultural sensibility of the ancient world is an inescapable prerequisite for the interpretation of the New Testament and early Christian literature.*

Given this assumption, the cultivation of such a sensibility is a central goal of my teaching, to which the conference topics, data, and analyses have contributed in many ways. In particular the conference has provided abundant material for the furnishing of one's imagination about lived realities in antiquity — which is the foundation of creative historical research.

3. *How and where people lived, with whom, in what kinds of social arrangements, being engaged in what sorts of pursuits, in the context of what social expectations are issues central to the task of cultivating the historical imagination anywhere.*

Consequently, I applaud New Testament studies moving out of its "Babylonian captivity" to the history of ideas into social history and rhetorical analysis of texts as performative utterances with persuasive, context-specific goals. (I still like the history of ideas, but find it much enriched in this way.) The move from "head hermeneutics" to "whole body hermeneutics" is just plain good historiography. Good method requires, however, that one not just map the general research on any topic in antiquity onto a particular group without justification. Thus my fourth and last proposition:

4. *Issues of family, household, domesticity, social relations are not a matter of simple "application" of the* Umwelt *to early Christian texts, nor can the New Testament texts just be randomly taken as another set of data to be mined, but, more sharply, these essential concerns of ancient life are at play — explicitly, implicitly, and in some fascinating and controversial ways — in these in-other-respects rather idiosyncratic and marginal pieces of first- to second-century Greek literature.*

It is on this basis that I would unhesitatingly argue for the historical legitimacy of bringing this scholarship into conversation with early Christian texts *and*, in turn, maintain that such writings can themselves be significant sources for the wider classical enterprise *because of* this explicit attention.[2]

Exegetical Illustration

Because of my just-stated fear of "parallelomania" (Samuel Sandmel, after all, wrote his famous article while on the faculty at the University of Chicago),[3] I do not wish now to go through, paper by paper, and indicate the many individual points of contact with New Testament writings I have been observing. But, as a text person, I find myself eager, after the rich and continual barrage of *portioned* documents we have experienced in the last three days, to cozy up to one text for a closer and more sustained look. As I have said, theological education where and how I practice it is a matter of textual interpretation. Hence I suggest we look together at one of the writings that was the object of study in the course with which I began my remarks, 1 Timothy (a relatively short piece of early Christian literature), in the light of the excellent papers we have heard. The thesis I would like to demonstrate is that there is hardly a topic discussed in this conference that is irrelevant to or absent from this text and its purpose. That fact perhaps says more than any individual point of contact: "family matters" in early Christian life and text.

In roughly the first quarter of the second century, an unknown Christian or Christians decided Paul had not written enough letters to satisfy their needs, likely because the letters then circulating which he *had* written were susceptible to interpretations they feared and vigorously rejected — especially, apparently, ascetic tendencies of renunciation of marriage, adoption of dietary restrictions, and adherence to νόμος (law) and μῦθοι ("myths," see 1:3-11), all due to the hypocritical "cauterized consciences" (4:2) of their opponents (fellow Christians

---

2. A point Suzanne Dixon also made in her presentation.
3. Samuel Sandmel, "Parallelomania," *JBL* 81 (1962): 1-13.

they deemed malformed by deceiving spirits). This led them to compose further letters bearing the apostle's name. Whether they did so in order deliberately to deceive is hard to say — the "Pastoral Epistles" they produced bear all the trappings of personalia, newsy news, names, greetings, and other paraphernalia characteristic of Greek pseudepigraphic letters, such as the Cynic or Socratic Epistles.[4] Of course, whether there was a defrauded original audience or not (does it take two to tango in literary deception?), the church soon received them as genuinely by Paul, and they have maintained that status, and have been read as such, through most of the succeeding centuries.

Fascinating for our conference is that this mysterious pseudepigraphical Paul wrote precisely in order to define, direct, and regulate the Christian οἶκος (household), and to connect as firmly as possible ecclesial self-identity with current Greco-Roman norms of household management and family relations (οἰκονομία). Reconceptualizing Paul's view of the church as the (metaphorical) οἰκοδομὴ τοῦ θεοῦ (building of God) into the οἶκος τοῦ θεοῦ ("household of God"; compare 1 Cor. 3:10 with 1 Tim. 3:15),[5] this author makes Pauline tradition into a παραθήκη to his "descendants" through Timothy (6:20), the spokesperson for an ἐκκλησία (assembly/church) governed by ἐπίσκοποι ("bishops"; literally "overseers") who can προστῆναι τοῦ ἰδίου οἴκου (3:4, 12), "preside over their own household," and therefore, by real analogy, over the οἶκος τοῦ θεοῦ ("household of god"; 3:15). Hence this author ironically begins where Andrew Wallace-Hadrill does — with defining the *domus* — and, like Wallace-Hadrill, the neo-Paul sees it as "a houseful rather than a household," because by his conveniently structured metaphorical double entendre it refers to the whole ἐκκλησία which met in an οἶκος, "house," and the individual οἶκοι (house[hold]s) which the

4. See Benjamin Fiore, *The Function of Personal Example in the Socratic and Pastoral Epistles,* AnBib 105 (Rome: Biblical Institute Press, 1986), and especially Lewis R. Donelson, *Pseudepigraphy and Ethical Argument in the Pastoral Epistles,* HUT 22 (Tübingen: Mohr/Siebeck, 1986).

5. Even with the considerable qualifications he makes late in the article (pp. 310-11), I find the thesis of David G. Horrell's recent article ("From ἀδελφοί to οἶκος τοῦ θεοῦ: Social Transformation in Pauline Christianity," *JBL* 120 [2001]: 293-311), that "the character of this significant degree of transformation [from the genuine Pauline letters to the Pastorals] may nevertheless be epitomized in the phrase 'from ἀδελφοί to οἶκος θεοῦ'" to be overstated, due to lexical rigidity (e.g., in arguing that the Pastorals use ἀδελφός [brother/sister] much less frequently than the genuine Paulines; he does not reckon with the fact that many of the uses of ἀδελφοί in the former are vocative addresses which naturally would be absent in these letters addressed to individuals whom Paul designates with other family terms) and a too-ready dismissal of counter-evidence for the broad claim that Paul "seldom, if ever, gives any direct instruction concerning the appropriate behavior required from other social groups within the household" (p. 305, with much too brief treatment of exceptions in n. 54).

members simultaneously inhabit. For this he brought Paul back from the dead to speak definitively.

Unfortunately, because the author and his (presumed) audience already know what these οἶκοι (the physical ones, that is) were like, the letter gives us little to add to the *domus/insulae* question, though it does give a definition of domestic tranquility that is hardly controversial: ἵνα ἤρεμον καὶ ἡσύχιον βίον διάγωμεν ἐν πάσῃ εὐσεβείᾳ καὶ σεμνότητι ["so that we might live a tranquil and quiet life in all piety and seemliness"] (2:2). This wish for a quiet life, however, is nicely understood within Wallace-Hadrill's emphasis on the *vicus,* neighborhood or street, as a social unit. Hence, for example, the stipulation about the ἐπίσκοπος in 3:7 — δεῖ δὲ καὶ μαρτυρίαν καλὴν ἔχειν ἀπὸ τῶν ἔξωθεν ["it is necessary that he has also a good testimony of repute *from the outsiders*"] — may be quite simply the local neighbors whose opinion still of course matters, even if they are οἱ ἔξωθεν (outsiders). One can only inquire here if this ἐπίσκοπος (bishop/overseer) who knew how to preside over *his own household* didn't jump from one tiny family (microcosm) to the whole ἐκκλησία (macrocosm) without perhaps the intermediate step of acting as *patronus* to a larger network of *insulae* such as some of the Delian units ("houses of all types combined in every conceivable combination") that Monika Trümper has shown to us. That new question helpfully complexifies a modern reader's move from oversight of 2.3 children to a whole diocese! Indeed, this raises the interesting possibility that neighborhood or street politics may have been a means of administrative apprenticeship on a larger scale for local early Christian leaders. The documented side-by-side presence of rich and poor in such urban settings may also shed light on a long-standing enigma of the Pastorals: the author's exhortation to οἱ πλούσιοι (the rich) to engage in benefactions (ἀγαθοεργεῖν, 6:18) when, just a few lines earlier, he had addressed οἱ βουλόμενοι πλουτεῖν ["those who wish to become rich"] (6:9). In a neighborhood or "block" setting, such mixed socioeconomic levels — and aspirations — are quite comprehensible.

Eric Meyers's discussion of Syro-Palestinian domestic architecture highlights a contrast with the urban Ephesian environment presupposed by 1 Timothy (1:3). But his treatment of the Villa of Dionysius at Sepphoris serves as a powerful reminder that Hellenism and Judaism are not binary pairs in this period, which greatly complicates the identification of the νομοδιδάσκαλοι ("teachers of the law") against whom this author inveighs (1:7), who are hardly like the scribes and Pharisees of the gospels, which at least attempt a Palestinian verisimilitude. But these νομοδιδάσκαλοι pay attention to myths and genealogies and forbid marriage, though they likewise abstain from certain foods (cf. the Halakic debates in Mark 7 and Synoptic parallels, etc.), yet on what basis we do not know precisely. Another of Meyers's points is even more probative, perhaps, for our example: the busyness and fluidity of use of domestic space, with women and men working together. Men's work, curiously enough, is only obliquely invoked in 1 Timothy, though the language of commerce is strongly at play in the polemics: the requirement that διάκονοι be pure of "shameful gain" (αἰσχροκερδεῖς, 3:8); the preaching of the gospel and exercise of church leadership depicted in economic terminology (4:10; 5:17-18, which with scriptural authority establishes a work-and-wages parity standard); and the concern for proper πορισμός ("profit"; 6:5-6), which this author redefines as εὐσέβεια ("piety"), just as the office of bishop is described as a καλὸν ἔργον ("good work"). "Women's work" is, however, directly enjoined upon them in 2:10, 5:10 (ἔργα καλά/ἀγαθά), and 5:13-14, where they are excoriated for being ἀργαί ("not busily employed," but περίεργοι, "being busybodies") and wished by the author to γαμεῖν, τεκνογονεῖν, οἰκοδεσποτεῖν ("marry, bear children, run households");[6] just as slaves engage in εὐεργεσία ("good work"; 6:2). But the actual physicality of trades, merchant occupations, or agricultural tasks is oddly distant here,[7] perhaps swept away by the metaphorical complex of ἔργα ἀγαθά ("good works"; 2:10; cf. 5:25; 6:18), διακονία ("service for the gospel"; 1:12; cf. 3:8, 12; 4:6), and prayer as occupation (2:1f.; 5:5). The author allows for simple needs — διατροφαὶ καὶ σκεπάσματα ("food and covering"; 6:8) — assumes they are in within reach, and counsels (with Stoic terminology) αὐτάρκεια ("self-sufficiency"; 6:6). But the actual work life of these families, so broadly assumed that the author can calque off its generic terminology to describe their religious well-being, remains tantalizingly obscured from the modern reader.

To move on to David Balch's wonderful topic, there are no explicit references to εἰκόνες (images/pictures) in 1 Timothy, but for this author Paul is himself the εἰκών (image) he is concerned to paint (see the "autobiographical portrait" of Paul as blasphemer turned apostle in 1:12-14). The focus here is on λόγος. Πιστὸς ὁ λόγος ("the word is to be trusted!"), he exclaims three times (1:15; 3:1; 4:9) — in keeping with his overall program of discursive rather than material παραθήκη (deposit). His metaphorical οἶκος τοῦ θεοῦ ("house[hold] of God") has no pictures on the wall, but the "window dressing" of linguistic doxology of the heavenly βασιλεύς (king) frames the letter (1:17; 6:15-16). There can be no pictures, for he describes a deity ὃν εἶδεν οὐδεὶς ἀνθρώπων οὐδὲ ἰδεῖν δύναται ["whom none among humans has seen or is even able to see"]. But that

6. See also the list of actions in 5:10. The same author will in 2 Tim. 3:6 express his terror at "home invasion" of γυναικάρια ("little womenfolk"), presumably when "home alone" and vulnerable, thus indicating a presumption of at least some gender-segregated use of the domestic space.

7. Less so in 2 Tim. 2:4-6, for example, but these may be laboring topoi no different from 1 Tim. 5:18, hence likewise at a remove from the actual social situation envisioned.

doesn't preclude verbal description of this God. Text replaces art, and theology happens in *ekphrasis.*[8]

Women are surely not invisible in 1 Timothy. The pseudepigraphic Paul harps on them constantly, prescribing their garments, hairstyles, jewelry, and most of all, social relations in the οἶκος. His calls for submission of women to male authority, even to the point of stigmatizing them by a most questionable reading of Genesis 2, clearly are, as Margaret MacDonald has shown in *Early Christian Women and Pagan Opinion* and in her paper here, a response to (for him) worrisomely inappropriate forms of female visibility that he fears are compromising the household structure of the ἐκκλησία and its stature in the eyes of outsiders. An analysis of this strategy can profitably draw upon an inverted form of Michael White's categorization of the domestic sphere: the author of 1 Timothy aims at creating *nonnegotiable space,* demarcating firm lines beyond which straying is not to be tolerated. He is engaged in what we might term "absolutist negotiation" (since surely White is right that all space is negotiated in some way) by the cessation and denial of negotiation itself. Women teaching? Nonnegotiable. Women domineering over a man? Nonnegotiable. Young widows who choose to remain so? Nonnegotiable. Women younger than sixty who seek support? Nonnegotiable. Women περιερχόμεναι τὰς οἰκίας (which we should now translate "making the rounds in the *vicus*") idly? Nonnegotiable.

But even in this invective — despite himself — this author might provide us with a surprising and overlooked glimpse at the object of Suzanne Dixon's quest: evidence of passionate marriages in antiquity. For one thing, as is often noted, this author castigates those who prohibit marriage (κωλύειν γαμεῖν in 4:3). But even more than that, in his rebuke and proscription of "younger widows" (νεώτεραι χῆραι), this author does not, as we might expect, excoriate them for πορνεία or μοιχεία ("sexual malfeasance" or "adultery"), but, rather, he reaches for a neologism to describe their wish for sexual satisfaction *in marriage:* ὅταν γὰρ καταστρηνιάσωσιν τοῦ Χριστοῦ, γαμεῖν θέλουσιν ["for when they 'wax wanton' against Christ, they wish to get married"] (5:11).

What Ross Kraemer's paper illustrates so effectively is the remarkable complexity and vicissitudes of ancient women's marital careers and experiences. Although the author of 1 Timothy wants his "enrolled widows" to be ἑνὸς ἀνδρὸς γυναῖκες ("wives of one husband" [5:9]), he also insists that they be over sixty years old. How likely would that be on sheer demographic grounds? Is the "one

8. A rhetorical form for "vivid description" meant to "turn the hearer into a spectator" (for full discussion and references, see Margaret M. Mitchell, *The Heavenly Trumpet: John Chrysostom and the Art of Pauline Interpretation,* HUT 40 [Tübingen: Mohr/Siebeck, 2000; Louisville: Westminster/John Knox, 2002], esp. pp. 101-4).

marriage" rule this author invokes a genuine reality for many women (as Berenice and Babatha, who occupy rather different ends of the social spectrum, should lead us to question)? The practical rarity of this is especially indicated by the preponderance of evidence that the initial marriage of a young woman or girl at puberty was often to a considerably older man.

The same question may be asked of the men who seek to be ἐπίσκοποι or διάκονοι ("bishops" or "deacons"), who are the recipients of the same injunction to absolute monogamy: μιᾶς γυναικὸς ἄνδρες ("husbands of one wife"; 3:2, 12). Would Christians, then, who followed such a rule, have stood out from their neighbors, and was it our author's deliberate intent that they do so?

It is at this point that 1 Timothy constitutes an astonishing example of Richard Saller's point, that male elite authors show no interest in portraying women's subjective experience in any realistic, empathetic, or accurate way. Could this fact be illustrated more precisely than by the author of 1 Timothy's audacious usurpation of access to women's internal life in his definition of the "true widow" in 5:5? He writes: "the true widow (ἡ ὄντως χήρα), left alone, has hope in God (μεμονωμένη ἤλπικεν ἐπὶ θεόν) and remains in supplication and prayers night and day; but the self-indulgent widow is (already) dead, though living" (ἡ δὲ σπαταλῶσα ζῶσα τέθνηκεν). By this brutal co-optation of women's subjectivity to his own limited and coercive norms and standards, the pseudo-Paul has made women's inner lives either a monotony of endless (harmless) prayer ("all-patriarchal prayer, all the time" news radio) or the silence of a living death — women's self-consciousness as the flatline EEG of a "vegetable" on life support. He simply allows for no alternative women's self-consciousness.

Women slaves are not separated out for particular treatment in 1 Timothy, or elsewhere in New Testament household codes, as Carolyn Osiek has shown. But no blueprint for the οἶκος τοῦ θεοῦ ("house[hold] of God") would be complete without mention of slaves. 1 Timothy 6:1-2 takes up two cases of slaves in early Christian ἐκκλησίαι ("assemblies/churches"): one concerning Christians enslaved to non-Christian masters, the other slaves with believing masters. The new Paul has commands for each. "Those who are slaves under the yoke, let them consider their own masters (οἱ ἴδιοι δεσπόται) worthy of all honor, lest the name of God and the teaching be blasphemed" (6:1). Christians who are slaves of "outsiders" must be sure not to contribute to the bad repute of the church in the eyes of the *vicus*.[9] Here Bert Harrill's identification of the *topos* of the slave as αὐτόπτης ("eyewitness") is inverted in line with the logic of the dual οἶκοι ("house[holds]"): the fear is not that the slave will betray the (earthly Christian master's) secrets to nonhouseholders, but will by insolent behavior

---

9. Βλασφημεῖν (to blaspheme) is a major concern that frames the letter (see 1:13, 20; 6:4).

implicitly cast false testimony against the divine δεσπότης (master), whose name (τὸ ὄνομα τοῦ θεοῦ) he or she bears.[10] The second prescription about slaves moves to another case: "Slaves who have believing masters (πιστοὶ δεσπόται), let them not think down on them because they are 'brothers and sisters,' but instead let them serve as slaves, *because* those who benefit from their good work (εὐεργεσία) are brothers/sisters and beloved." Carolyn Osiek's work makes us cast a dark eye on a passage such as this, wondering what its intended limits or nonlimits of compliance might be. The cloaking of the ideology of slave submission in the language of family (brothers, sisters, beloved) only intensifies the worry. The text also depends on another negative slave *topos* (mentioned by Harrill, as also by Saller as a reality on the ground): the nonworking, lazy slave who looks to turn any opportunity for shirking duty to her or his advantage.[11]

Dale Martin's "anecdotal" historical case studies in slave family relations urge us to fill in with our imaginations the wider circles involved in prescriptions such as are found in the Pastorals. There are important considerations that we too often neglect when reading such passages as 1 Timothy 6:1-2. Who else might be attached to these Christians slaves, wondering what *their* fate might be in the new household of God?[12]

What about children in 1 Timothy — are they visible or invisible? In the debate between Beryl Rawson and Hanna Sigismund Nielsen, we have witnessed a striking cultural paradox about parental love for children in an ancient world that experienced an intensely high rate of infant mortality (whether we accept Nielsen's 50 percent mortality rate or Saller's correction to 25 percent).[13] What that discussion crystallizes is the high social value and capital of τεκνογονία, "childbearing," and τεκνοτροφεῖν, "child rearing." These, too, are at the heart of the pseudepigraphical Paul's social and ecclesial program. Childbearing receives the highest possible (if heretical) compliment a Paulinist can give: usurping the place of πίστις Ἰησοῦ Χριστοῦ ("faith in Jesus Christ") in the

10. In addition to assuming the existence of female slaves, the author of 1 Timothy may well have in mind that women are slave owners, as expressed in his wish that the younger widows marry and, among other things, οἰκοδεσποτεῖν (5:14).

11. Interestingly, a version of this caricature — for nonslaves — is applied to the young widows as ἀργαί ("not busily employed") in 5:13.

12. The same holds for Ignatius, *Polycarp* 4.3, which is often imagined as a case of individual slaves seeking an amelioration of their own fate — singly (cf. 1 Cor. 7:17-24), a view which now requires adjustment (for the social historical context of the passage, see J. Albert Harrill, *The Manumission of Slaves in Early Christianity*, HUT 32 [Tübingen: Mohr/Siebeck, 1995], pp. 158-92).

13. In discussion, there was some agreement on the figures offered by Richard Saller: 25-30 percent mortality in first year, 50 percent by age ten.

genuine Paulines,[14] it is the very source of salvation — for *women,* that is (σωθήσεται διὰ τῆς τεκνογονίας ["she will be saved through childbearing"; 2:15]). Indeed, childbearing is the prescribed life-plan of the young widow, which has been interrupted by the first husband's death, but is meant for resumption in a second marriage (βούλομαι νεωτέρας γαμεῖν, τεκνοτροφεῖν ["I wish younger ones to marry, bear children"]), even as not just *bearing* but *raising* children is among the sure litmus tests of the "true widow" (5:10; cf. 3:4). For men, however, neither child begetting nor child rearing per se is stressed, just ἔχειν τέκνα ἐν ὑποταγῇ ("having children in a state of subservience"; 3:4). Obediently subordinate children serve as harbingers that the bishop will likewise "preside" over a "house[hold] of God" in such a way as to thwart all unruliness (cf. 3:12: τέκνων καλῶς προϊστάμενοι καὶ τῶν ἰδίων οἴκων ["presiding well over their children and over their own house(hold)s"]). But the passage contains not a word about an emotional bond; there are no explicit requirements that fathers (or mothers) *love* their children (or that a bishop love his ἐκκλησία). The point is proper paternal oversight, formed by the easy convergence of father and bishop as διδάσκαλος ("teacher"; compare διδακτικός, "with a capacity for teaching," in 3:2). This is, of course, not to deny that early Christian writers or readers loved their children, but 1 Timothy should be added to the volume of other evidence that likewise does not overtly express that value, which once again raises the difficult historiographical question we have often asked in this conference: whether something is "invisible" because it is assumed or because it is genuinely not present. Yet, although the emotional bond between the bishop and his children, or even the mother and the children for whom she is to provide τεκνογονία, is not stressed, there is one "familial" relationship in 1 Timothy that goes further. With that we turn to Christian Laes's paper.

Thankfully, I see no evidence of *deliciae* in 1 Timothy per se. However, although there is not a "pet child" in the text, there is a "darling" — an adopted son by *imitatio exempli* — Timothy (called γνήσιον τέκνον ["genuine child"] in 1:2).[15] The familial *topos* found in the genuine Paulines of Timothy's fidelity[16] is employed in this double pseudepigraphon to cast him as the son and heir to the Pauline deposit/legacy who, already himself moving off the stage into death and oblivion, must set these instructions he is receiving before a new generation of "brothers and sisters": ταῦτα ὑποτιθέμενος τοῖς ἀδελφοῖς ("setting them before the brothers and sisters"; 4:6). He is a fictional envoy on a fantastical visit

14. E.g., Gal. 2:16; 3:24; Rom. 4:5; 5:1.

15. The relationship is styled in even warmer fashion in 2 Tim. 1:2: ἀγαπητὸν τέκνον.

16. See especially Phil. 2:19-22: οὐδένα γὰρ ἔχω ἰσόψυχον, ὅστις γνησίως τὰ περὶ ὑμῶν μεριμνήσει . . . ὡς πατρὶ τέκνον σὺν ἐμοὶ ἐδούλευσεν εἰς τὸ εὐαγγέλιον (cf. 1 Cor. 4:17; 16:10; and yet also the brotherly language of 1 Thess. 3:2).

back from the dead Paul with a fresh social blueprint for subsequent genera-tions. Timothy is one literally "reared on the words" (ἐντρεφόμενος τοῖς λόγοις) of the faith and teaching he received from his father, Paul (4:6).

The abundance of grave inscriptions discussed in this conference leads us to appreciate well the cultural force of death in life in the Greco-Roman world. Given that the home was the primary venue for death, preparation of the corpse, and mourning, one might expect 1 Timothy's blueprint for the "house[hold] of God" to mention actual deaths and mourning habits of Chris-tians. But it does not. Death is leapfrogged by the peculiar religious logic of the Pauline gospel to which that author adheres; he never mentions death or "to die."[17] Life in the household of God, if lived with the εὐσέβεια (piety) appropri-ate to its host, gives a promise of future life extending beyond death: ἡ εὐσέβεια πρὸς πάντα ὠφελιμός ἐστιν ἐπαγγελίαν ἔχουσα ζωῆς τῆς νῦν καὶ τῆς μελλούσης ["but piety is beneficial in all respects, since it has a promise of life now and in the future"] (4:8). This is because the believers will come to share the life of their *pater:* "the one who dwells in unapproachable light is the sole guardian of immortality" (6:16). Hence the omission of treatment of what must greatly color the real existence of the addressees of the letter — the deaths of their chil-dren, their parents, their spouses — must be read as a kind of theological aver-sion of gaze from the visible to the invisible, a euphemistic glance away toward "the future life," the ultimate benefaction that only a household head can pro-vide — but only for those who live out the household ethic of the household of God in the now.

This existential point about death in life brings me to a concluding obser-vation. In our discussions on the *domus,* the οἶκος, we have had to try to catch something in midair, stop for a freeze-frame photo something which by its very definition is always moving, ever changing. Hence we are *always* at a hermeneutical disadvantage, trying to sketch a three-dimensional object on a two-dimensional sketch pad. The *domus,* in both its physical and human as-pects, was never a fixed or completed entity.

This reminds me of the ubiquitous specter one meets traveling throughout modern Syria and other places in the Middle East: the constant presence of cement side-beams to edifices in various stages of construction. The cement has been poured over steel cables, which now stick out of the top like the fuses of firecrackers awaiting a match or, as I often thought, a limb amputated from

17. The single exception in the Pastorals is the reference to hypostatized death in 2 Tim. 1:10: Χριστοῦ Ἰησοῦ καταργήσαντος μὲν τὸν θάνατον. This is another respect in which the Pas-torals differ from the genuine Pauline letters, such as 1 Thessalonians and 1 Corinthians, in which Paul confronts directly the theological meaning of the actual deaths of Christian believ-ers (see especially 1 Thess. 4:13-18 and 1 Cor. 15:1-58).

some rusty Frankenstein. To an American this common sight registers as a "blight on the landscape," for the unfinished rings as unsightly for a well-run society. That is why in our condo associations and suburban neighborhoods we have rules about the timely completion of building projects. But while there I was told that the reason one sees such "uncompleted" homes all over the Middle East is that each new beam constitutes a provision for posterity; suspicious of banks and other forms of invisible investment, many modern Arabs, when they get a sum of money, put it into literally concrete form by erecting yet another structural beam on a new house for their families. And they do this with full recognition that they themselves may never live in that house; they are investing for their family's future, for their children and beyond.

The incomplete beams of contemporary Syrian homes constitute a visual analogue for the family itself. "The family" is an entity that can only be appreciated across time — time that is not limited to any single life span (in this regard I was especially moved by Dale Martin's suggestion that some Greco-Roman gravestones contain memorials to children yet unborn, in the knowledge that they, too, will come to share the family grave anon). In the contemporary American context we are surrounded by illusions of permanence, illusions of completeness which may lead us to overlook the simplest and most important of realities: that what we have studied here — houses, households, families — were and always are "under construction."

Bibliography

Abrahamsen, Valerie. "Women at Philippi: The Pagan and Christian Evidence." *JFSR* 3 (1987): 17-30.

Aland, Kurt. "Bemerkungen zum Alter und zur Entstehung des Christogramms anhand von Beobachtungen bei p66 und p75." In *Studien zur Überlieferung des Neuen Testaments und Seines Textes*, pp. 173-79. ANTF 2. Berlin: De Gruyter, 1967.

Allen, J. "A Tabula Iliaca from Gandhara." *JHS* 66 (1946): 21-23.

Allison, P. A., ed. *The Archaeology of Household Activities.* London and New York: Routledge, 1999.

Alston, Richard. "Arms and the Man: Soldiers, Masculinity and Power in Republican and Imperial Rome." In *When Men Were Men: Masculinity, Power, and Identity in Classical Antiquity*, edited by Lin Foxhall and John Salmon, pp. 205-23. Leicester-Nottingham Studies in Ancient Society 8. London: Routledge, 1998.

Altink, Sietske. *Stolen Lives: Trading Women into Sex and Slavery.* New York: Haworth, 1995.

Amedick, R. *Vita Privata (Die antike Sarkophagreliefs i.4).* Berlin: Schaubel, 1991.

Anderson, J. G. C. "An Imperial Estate in Galatia." *JRS* 27 (1937): 18-21.

Anderson, William S. "Anger in Juvenal and Seneca." *University of California Publications in Classical Philology* 19, no. 3 (1964): 160-65.

Andreae, Bernard. *Laocoon und die Gründung Roms.* Kulturgeschichte der Antiken Welt 39. Mainz: Philipp von Zabern, 1988.

—————. *Laocoon und die Kunst von Pergamon: die Hybris der Giganten.* Frankfurt: Fischer Taschenbuch, 1991.

Arav, R. "Letter to the Editor." *BARev* 26, no. 5 (2000): 12, 14, 72, and 74.

Arbesmann, Rudolph, Emily Joseph Daly, and Edward A. Quain, trans. *Tertullian: Apologetical Works; and Minucius Felix: Octavius.* FC 10. Washington, D.C.: Catholic University of America Press, 1950.

Arce, J. "El inventario de Roma: Curiosum y Notitia." In *The Transformations of Urbs Roma in Late Antiquity.* Journal of Roman Archaeology Supplement Series 33. Edited by W. V. Harris. Portsmouth, R.I.: Journal of Roman Archaeology, 1999.

Ariès, Philippe. *The Hour of Our Death.* New York: Knopf, 1981. Translated from the French original, 1977.

Arjava, Antti. *Women and Law in Late Antiquity.* Oxford: Clarendon, 1998.

Aurigemma, S. "Delicium." In E. de Ruggiero, *Dizionario epigrafico di antichità romane,* vol. II, 2, pp. 1596-1603. Rome: "L'Erma" di Brettschneider, 1910.

Avigad, Nahman. *The Herodian Quarter in Jerusalem.* Wohl Archaeologial Museum. Jerusalem: Keter, 1989.

———. "Jerusalem." In *NEAEHL,* 2:729-53.

Avi-Yonah, Michael. *The Holy Land from the Persian to the Arab Conquest.* Grand Rapids: Baker Books, 1977.

Babcock, William S., ed. *Paul and the Legacies of Paul.* Dallas: Southern Methodist University Press, 1990.

Bagnall, Roger S., and Bruce W. Frier. *The Demography of Roman Egypt.* Cambridge: Cambridge University Press, 1994.

Baker, Cynthia. "Rebuilding the House of Israel: Gendered Bodies and Domestic Politics in Roman Jewish Galilee c. 135-300 C.E." Ph.D. diss., Duke University, 1997.

———. *Rebuilding the House of Israel: Architectures of Gender in Jewish Antiquity.* Stanford: Stanford University Press, 2002.

Bakker, Jan Theo. *Living and Working with the Gods: Studies of Evidence for Private Religion and Its Material Environment in the City of Ostia (100-500 AD).* Dutch Monographs on Ancient History and Archaeology 12. Amsterdam: J. C. Gieben, 1994.

Balch, David L. *Let Wives Be Submissive: The Domestic Code in 1 Peter.* Chico, Calif.: Scholars, 1981.

———. "The Suffering of Isis/Io and Paul's Portrait of Christ Crucified (Gal 3:1): Frescoes in Pompeian and Roman Houses and in the Temple of Isis in Pompeii." *Journal of Religion* 83, 1(January 2003): 24-55.

———. "Families and Households." In *Paul in the Greco-Roman World,* edited by J. Paul Sampley. Harrisburg, Pa.: Trinity Press International, 2003.

Barclay, John M. G. *Jews in the Mediterranean Diaspora: From Alexander to Trajan (323 BCE–117 CE).* Edinburgh: T. & T. Clark, 1996.

Barnard, Leslie W. "In Defence of Pseudo-Pionius' Account of Saint Polycarp's Martyrdom." In *Kyriakon: Festschrift Johannes Quasten,* 1:192-204. Münster: Aschendorff, 1970.

Barnes, Timothy D. "Legislation against the Christians." *JRS* 58 (1968): 32-50.

———. "Pre-Decian *Acta Martyrum.*" *JTS* 19 (1968): 509-31.

———. *Tertullian: A Historical and Literary Study.* 2nd ed. Oxford: Clarendon, 1985.

Barry, Kathleen. *Female Sexual Slavery.* New York and London: New York University, 1984.

Bartchy, S. Scott. "Slavery (Greco-Roman)." In *ABD,* 6:65-73.

Barton, Carlin A. *The Sorrows of the Ancient Romans: The Gladiator and the Monster.* Princeton: Princeton University Press, 1993.

———. "Savage Miracles: The Redemption of Lost Honor in Roman Society and the Sacrament of the Gladiator and the Martyr." *Representations* 45 (1994): 41-71.

Baun, J. "The Fate of Babies Dying before Baptism in Byzantium." In *The Church and Childhood,* edited by D. Wood, pp. 115-26. Oxford: Blackwells, 1994.

Beacham, Richard C. *The Roman Theatre and Its Audience.* Cambridge: Harvard University Press, 1992.

Beard, Mary, John North, and Simon Price. *Religions of Rome Vol. 1-2 A Sourcebook.* Cambridge: Cambridge University Press, 1998.

Benko, Stephen. *Pagan Rome and the Early Christians.* Bloomington: Indiana University Press, 1984.

Bergmann, Bettina. "The Roman House as Memory Theater: The House of the Tragic Poet in Pompeii." *Art Bulletin* 76, no. 2 (1994): 225-56.

Berry, Joanne, ed. *Unpeeling Pompeii: Studies in Region I of Pompeii.* Soprintendenza Archeologica di Pompei. Milan: Electa, 1998.

Betz, Hans Dieter. *Galatians.* Hermeneia. Philadelphia: Fortress, 1979.

Beyen, H. G. *Die Pompejanische Wanddekoration vom Zweiten bis zum Vierten Stil.* Vol. 2. The Hague: Martinus Nijhoff, 1960.

Birley, A. R. "Persecutors and Martyrs in Tertullian's Africa." In *The Later Roman Empire Today: Papers Given in Honour of Professor John Mann,* edited by D. F. Clark, M. M. Roxan, and J. J. Wilkes, pp. 37-68. London: Institute of Archaeology, 1993.

Birt, Th. "De amorum in arte antiqua simulacris et de pueris minutis apud antiquos in deliciis habitis." Diss., Marburg, 1892.

Black, Matthew. "The Chi-Rho Sign — Christogram and/or Staurogram?" In *Apostolic History and the Gospel: Biblical and Historical Essays Presented to F. F. Bruce on His Sixtieth Birthday,* edited by W. Ward Gasque and Ralph P. Martin, pp. 319-27. Grand Rapids: Eerdmans, 1970.

Bodel, Jean. "Graveyards and Groves: A Study of the *Lex Lucerina.*" *AJAH* 11 (1986 [1994]): 1-133.

———. "Dealing with the Dead: Undertakers, Executioners and Potter's Fields in Ancient Rome." In *Death and Disease in the Ancient City,* edited by V. M. Hope and E. Marshall, pp. 128-51. London and New York: Routledge, 2000.

Bodson, L. "Motivations for Pet-Keeping in Ancient Greece and Rome: A Preliminary Survey." In *Companion Animal and Us: Exploring the Relationship between People and Pets,* edited by A. L. Podberseck, E. S. Paul, and J. A. Serpell, pp. 27-41. Cambridge: Cambridge University Press, 2000.

Bömer, Franz. *Untersuchungen über die Religion der Sklaven in Griechenland und Rom.* 3 pts. Abhandlungen der Akademie der Wissenschaften in Mainz, Geistes- und sozialwissenschaftliche Klasse. Forschungen zur antiken Sklaverei 14 and 14.3. Revised by Peter Herz. Wiesbaden and Stuttgart: Franz Steiner, 1982, 1960, 1990.

Boserup, Ester. *Women's Role in Economic Development.* London: Allen and Unwin, 1970.

Bowersock, Glen. "The Babatha Papyri, Masada and Rome." *JRA* 4 (1991): 336-44.

Boyancé, P. "*Funus acerbum.*" *REA* 54 (1952): 275-89.

Boyarin, Daniel. *Dying for God: Martyrdom and the Making of Christianity and Judaism.* Figurae: Reading Medieval Culture. Stanford: Stanford University Press, 1999.

Bradley, Keith R. "The Age at Time of Sale of Female Slaves." *Arethusa* 11 (1978): 243-52.

———. "Slaves and the Conspiracy of Catiline." *CP* 73 (1978): 329-36.

———. *Slaves and Rulers in the Roman Empire.* Brussels: Latomus, 1984.

———. "Ideals of Marriage in Suetonius's *Caesares.*" *Rivista storica dell'antichità* 15 (1985): 77-95.

———. "Wet-Nursing at Rome: A Study in Social Relations." In *The Family in Ancient Rome: New Perspectives,* edited by B. Rawson, pp. 201-29. Ithaca, N.Y.: Cornell University Press, 1986.

―――. "On the Roman Slave Supply and Slavebreeding." In *Classical Slavery*, edited by M. I. Finley, pp. 42-64. London: Frank Cass & Co., 1987.

―――. *Slaves and Masters in the Roman Empire: A Study in Social Control*. New York: Oxford University Press, 1987.

―――. *Slavery and Rebellion in the Roman World, 140 B.C.–70 B.C.* Bloomington: Indiana University Press, 1989.

―――. *Discovering the Roman Family*. Oxford: Oxford University Press, 1991.

―――. *Slavery and Society at Rome*. Key Themes in Ancient History. Cambridge: Cambridge University Press, 1994.

―――. "The Sentimental Education of the Roman Child: The Role of Pet-Keeping." *Latomus* 34 (1998): 523-57.

Braund, David. "Bernice." In *ABD*, 1:677.

Brendel, Otto J. "Der Affen-Aeneas." *RM* 60-61 (1953-54): 153-59.

Brilliant, Richard. *Visual Narratives: Storytelling in Etruscan and Roman Art*. Ithaca, N.Y.: Cornell University Press, 1984.

Brooten, Bernadette J. *Women Leaders in the Ancient Synagogue*. BJS 36. Chico, Calif.: Scholars, 1982.

Brotherton, Blanche. "The Introduction of Characters by Name in the *Metamorphoses* of Apuleius." *CP* 29 (1934): 36-52.

Brown, Peter. "Aspects of the Christianization of the Roman Aristocracy." *JRS* 51 (1961): 1-11.

Browning, Don, et al. *From Culture Wars to Common Ground: Religion and the American Family Debate*. Family, Religion, and Culture Series. Louisville: Westminster/John Knox, 1997. Second Edition 2000.

Brownmiller, Susan. *Against Our Will: Men, Women, and Rape*. New York: Simon and Schuster, 1975.

Bruneau, Philippe, and Jean Ducat. *Guide de Délos*. Paris: Éditions E. de Boccard, 1983.

Bruneau, Philippe, Claude Vatin, et al. *L'îlot de la Maison des comédiens. Exploration archéologique de Délos XXVII*. Paris: Éditions E. de Boccard, 1970.

Brüning, A. "Über die bildlichen Vorlagen der Ilischen Tafeln." *Jahrbuch des Kaiserlichen Deutschen Archäologischen Instituts* 9 (1894): 136-65.

Brunt, Peter A. *Italian Manpower, 225 B.C.–A.D. 14*. Oxford: Oxford University Press, 1971.

―――. "Evidence Given under Torture in the Principate." *Zeitschrift der Savigny-Stiftung für Rechtsgeschichte (romanistische Abteilung)* 97 (1980): 256-65.

―――. "Aristotle and Slavery." In his *Studies in Greek History and Thought*, pp. 343-88. Oxford: Clarendon, 1993.

Buckler, John. "Plutarch and Autopsy." *ANRW* 2.33.6 (1992): 4788-4830.

Burrus, Virginia. "Torture and Travail: Producing the Christian Martyr." In *A Feminist Companion to Early Gnostic and Patristic Thought*, edited by Amy-Jill Levine. Sheffield: Sheffield Academic Press. Forthcoming.

Buschmann, Gerd. *Martyrium Polycarpi — Eine formkritische Studie: Ein Beitrag zur Frage nach der Entstehung der Gattung Märtyrerakte*. BZNW 70. Berlin: Walter de Gruyter, 1994.

―――. *Das Martyrium des Polycarp*. Kommentar zu den apostolischen Vätern. Göttingen: Vandenhoeck & Ruprecht, 1998.

Cahill, J. M. "Chalk Vessel Assemblages of the Persian/Hellenistic and Early Roman Periods." In *Excavations at the City of David, 1978-1985,* pp. 190-272. Qedem 33. Jerusalem: Hebrew University Institute of Archaeology, 1992.

Cahill, Lisa Sowle. *Family: A Christian Social Perspective.* Minneapolis: Fortress, 2000.

———. *Sex, Gender, and Christian Ethics.* Cambridge: Cambridge University Press, 1996.

Cameron, Alan. "The Date and Identity of Macrobius." *JRS* 56 (1966): 35-38.

Campenhausen, Hans von. "Bearbeitungen und Interpolationen des Polykarpmartyriums." In his *Aus der Frühzeit des Christentums: Studien zur Kirchengeschichte des ersten und zweiten Jahrhunderts,* pp. 253-301. Tübingen: Mohr Siebeck, 1963.

Canciani, F. "Aineias." In *LIMC,* edited by H. C. Ackerman and J.-R. Gisler, vol. 1.2, pp. 381-96. Zürich, 1981.

Carcopino, Jérôme. *Daily Life in Ancient Rome: The People and the City at the Height of the Empire.* New Haven: Yale University Press, 1968.

Carettoni, G., et al. *La pianta marmorea di Roma antica: forma urbis Romae.* Rome, 1960.

Castelli, Elizabeth A. "Visions and Voyeurism: Holy Women and the Politics of Sight in Early Christianity." *Protocol of the Colloquy of the Center for Hermeneutical Studies,* n.s., 2 (1995): 1-34.

———. "Gender, Theory, and the Rise of Christianity: A Response to Rodney Stark." *JECS* 6, no. 2 (1998): 227-57.

Chamonard, Joseph. *Le Quartier du théâtre. Étude sur l'habitation délienne à l'époque hellénistique.* Exploration archéologique de Délos VIII. Paris: Éditions E. de Boccard, 1922/24.

Chancey, M., and E. M. Meyers. "How Jewish Was Sepphoris in Jesus' Time?" *BARev* 26, no. 4 (2000): 18-33, 61.

Chini, P. "L'insula dell'Aracoeli." *Forma Urbis* IV, 6 (June 1999): 5-13.

Churchland, Patricia Smith. *Neurophilosophy: Toward a Unified Science of the Mind-Brain.* 3rd printing. Cambridge, Mass.: MIT, 1988.

Claridge, A. *Rome.* Oxford Archaeological Guides. Oxford: Oxford University Press, 1998.

Clark, Patricia. "Women, Slaves and the Hierarchies of Domestic Violence: The Family of St. Augustine." In *Women and Slaves in Greco-Roman Culture: Differential Equations,* edited by Sandra R. Joshel and Sheila Murnaghan. New York and London: Routledge, 1998.

Clarke, G. W. *The Octavius of Marcus Minucius Felix.* ACW 39. New York: Newman, 1974.

Clarke, John. "Hypersexual Black Men in Augustan Baths: Ideal Somatypes and Apotropaic Magic." In *Sexuality in Ancient Art,* edited by N. Kampen, pp. 184-98. Cambridge: Cambridge University Press, 1996.

———. *Looking at Lovemaking: Constructions of Sexuality in Roman Art, 100 B.C.–A.D. 250.* Berkeley, Los Angeles, and London: University of California Press, 1998.

Clauss, M. "Probleme der Lebensalterstatistiken aufgrund römischen Grabinschriften." *Chiron* 3 (1973): 395-417.

Coarelli, Filippo. *Da Pergamo a Roma: I Galati nella città degli Attalidi.* Rome: Quasar, 1995.

———. "La consistenza della città nel periodo imperiale: *pomerium, vici, insulae.*" In *La Rome impériale: démographie et logistique. Actes de la table ronde (Rome, 25 mars 1994).* Collection de L' École Française de Rome 230. Rome: École Française de Rome, 1997.

————. "The Odyssey Frescos of the Via Graziosa: A Proposed Context." *PBSR* 66 (1998): 21-37.

Cohen, David, and Richard P. Saller. "Foucault on Sexuality in Greco-Roman Antiquity." In *Foucault and the Writing of History,* edited by J. Goldstein, pp. 35-59. Oxford: Blackwell, 1994.

Cohen, Shaye J. D., ed. *The Jewish Family in Antiquity.* BJS 289. Atlanta: Scholars, 1993.

Coleman, K. M. "Fatal Charades: Roman Executions Staged as Mythological Enactments." *JRS* 80 (1990): 44-73.

Colin, Jean. *L'Empire des Antonins et les martyrs gaulois de 177.* Antiquitas, ser. 1; Abhandlungen zur alten Geschichte 10. Bonn: Rudolf Habelt, 1964.

Colini, Antonio Maria. "Storia e topografia del Celio nell'antichita." *Atti Pontifica Accademia romana di archeologia,* ser. III, 7 (1944): 164-70.

Conte, Gian Biagio. *The Rhetoric of Imitation: Genre and Poetic Memory in Virgil and Other Latin Poets.* Edited and translated with a foreword by Charles Segal. Ithaca: Cornell University Press, 1986.

Cooper, Kate. "Insinuations of Womanly Influence: An Aspect of the Christianization of the Roman Aristocracy." *JRS* 82 (1992): 150-64.

————. *The Virgin and the Bride: Idealized Womanhood in Late Antiquity.* Cambridge, Mass., and London: Harvard University Press, 1996.

————. "The Voice of the Victim: Gender, Representation and Early Christian Martyrdom." *BJRL* 80, no. 3 (1998): 147-57.

Corbier, M. "Child Exposure and Abandonment." In *Childhood, Class, and Kin in the Roman World,* edited by S. Dixon, pp. 52-73. London: Routledge, 2001.

Corley, Kathleen. *Women and the Historical Jesus: Feminist Myths of Christian Origins.* Santa Rosa, Calif.: Polebridge, 2002.

Cornell, T. J. "Aeneas and the Twins." *Proceedings of the Cambridge Philological Society* 21 (1975): 1-32.

Costin, Cathy Lynne. "Exploring the Relationship between Gender and Craft in Complex Societies: Methodological and Theoretical Issues of Gender Attribution." In *Gender and Archaeology,* edited by R. P. Wright, pp. 112-40. Philadelphia: University of Pennsylvania Press, 1996.

Crisafulli, T. "Representations of the Feminine: The Prostitute in Roman Comedy." In *Ancient History in a Modern University,* edited by T. W. Hillard et al., 1:222-29. Sydney: Macquarie University, Ancient History Documentary Research Centre; Grand Rapids: Eerdmans, 1998.

Crook, J. A. "Women in Roman Succession." In *The Family in Ancient Rome: New Perspectives,* edited by B. Rawson, pp. 58-82. Ithaca, N.Y.: Cornell University Press, 1986.

Curcio, G. *L'Angelo e la città. La città nel settecento.* Rome: Fratelli Palombi, 1987.

Dalby, Andrew. "On Female Slaves in Roman Egypt." *Arethusa* 12 (1979): 255-59.

D'Ambra, Eva. "The Calculus of Venus: Nude Portraits of Roman Matrons." In *Sexuality in Ancient Art,* edited by N. Kampen, pp. 219-32. Cambridge: Cambridge University Press, 1996.

D'Angelo, Mary Rose. "Women in Luke-Acts: A Redactional View." *JBL* 109, no. 3 (1990): 441-61.

————. "Women Partners in the New Testament." *JFSR* 6 (1990): 65-86.

D'Arms, John H. "Slaves at Roman Convivia." In *Dining in a Classical Context,* edited by William J. Slater, pp. 171-83. Ann Arbor: University of Michigan Press, 1991.

Davies, J. *Death, Burial and Rebirth in the Religions of Antiquity.* London and New York: Routledge, 1999.

Davies, Percival V. *Macrobius: "The Saturnalia."* New York: Columbia University Press, 1969.

Davis, Basil S. "The Meaning of προεγράφη in the Context of Galatians 3.1." *NTS* 45, no. 2 (1999): 194-212.

Dean-Jones, Lesley. "The Politics of Pleasure: Female Sexual Appetite in the Hippocratic Corpus." *Helios* 19, nos. 1-2 (1992): 72-91. Special issue, *Documenting Gender: Women and Men in Non-Literary Classical Texts,* edited by D. Konstan.

———. *Women's Bodies in Classical Greek Science.* Oxford: Clarendon, 1994.

De Caro, Stefano. "Ifigenia in Aulide su una Brocca Fittile da Pompei." *Bollettino d'Arte* 23 (1984): 39-50.

———, ed. *Le Collezioni del Museo Nazionale di Napoli: I Mosaici, Le Pitture, Gli Oggetti di Uso Quotidiano, Gli Argenti, Le Terrecotte Invetriate, I Vetri, I Cristalli, Gli Avori.* Milan: DiLuca Edizioni d'Arte, 1986.

De Caro, Stefano, and Luciano Pedicini. *The National Archaeological Museum of Naples.* Naples: Electa, 1996.

DeFilippo, Joseph G. "*Curiositas* and the Platonism of Apuleius' *Golden Ass.*" *AJP* 111 (1990): 471-92.

De Gieter, E. "Een sociaal profiel van vernae, alumni/-ae en deliciae." 2 vols. Diss., Gent, 1997.

Dehandschutter, Boudewijn. *Martyrium Polycarpi: Een literair-kritische studie.* BETL 52. Leuven: Leuven University Press, 1979.

———. "The Martyrium Polycarpi: A Century of Research." *ANRW* 2.27.1 (1993): 485-522.

Deines, R. *Jüdische Steingefässe und pharisäische Frömmigkeit: Ein archäeologisch-historisher Beitrag zum Verständnis von Joh 2,6 und der jüdischen Reinheitshalacha zur Zeit Jesu.* Tübingen: J. C. B. Mohr, 1993.

de Labriolle, Pierre Champagne. *La réaction païenne: étude sur la polémique antichrétienne du 1er au VIe. siècle.* 2nd ed. Paris: L'Artisan du livre, 1948.

Delehaye, Hippolyte. *Les passions des martyrs et les genres littéraires.* 2nd ed. Subsidia hagiographica 13b. Brussels: Sociéte des Bollandistes, 1966.

Delumeau, Jean. *La religion de ma mère: les femmes dans la transmission de la foi.* Paris: Cerf, 1992.

De Smet, R. "The Erotic Adventure of Lucius and Photis in Apuleius' *Metamorphoses.*" *Latomus* 46 (1987): 613-23.

Dickmann, Jens-Arne. "The Peristyle and the Transformation of Domestic Space in Hellenistic Pompeii." In *Domestic Space in the Roman World: Pompeii and Beyond,* edited by Ray Laurence and Andrew Wallace-Hadrill, pp. 131-36. Journal of Roman Archaeology Supplement Series 22. Portsmouth, R.I.: Journal of Roman Archaeology, 1997.

———. *Domus frequentata. Anspruchsvolles Wohnen im pompejanischen Stadthaus.* Studien zur antiken Stadt 4. Munich: Verlag Dr. Friedrich Pfeil, 1999.

Dixon, Suzanne. "The Marriage Alliance in the Roman Elite." *Journal of Family History* 10 (1985): 353-78.

————. *The Roman Mother.* London and New York: Croom Held, 1988.

————. *The Roman Family.* Baltimore: Johns Hopkins University Press, 1992.

————. "The Sentimental Ideal of the Roman Family." In *Marriage, Divorce, and Children in Ancient Rome,* edited by B. Rawson, pp. 99-113. Canberra and Oxford: Clarendon, 1991.

————, ed. *Childhood, Class, and Kin in the Roman World.* London: Routledge, 2001.

————. *Reading Roman Women.* London: Duckworth, 2001.

Downey, G. "Ekphrasis." *RAC* 4 (1959): 922-44.

Drexhage, H.-J. *Preise, Pieten/Pachten, Kosten und Loehne im Roemischen Aegypten bis zum Regierungsantritt Diokletians.* St. Katharinen: Scripta Mercaturae Verlag, 1991.

Droge, Arthur J. *Homer or Moses? Early Christian Interpretations of the History of Culture.* HUT 26. Tübingen: Mohr Siebeck, 1989.

duBois, Page. *Torture and Truth.* London: Routledge, 1991.

Ducrey, Pierre, Ingrid R. Metzger, and Karl Reber. *Le Quartier de la Maison aux mosaïques, Eretria. Fouilles et recherches VIII.* Lausanne: Éditions Payot, 1993.

Dulière, C. *Lupa Romana. Recherches d'iconographie et essai d'interprétation.* Brussels and Rome: Institut historique Belge de Rome, 1979.

Duncan-Jones, Richard. "The Impact of the Antonine Plague." *JRA* 9 (1996): 108-36.

Eck, Werner. "*Cum dignitate otium:* Senatorial *Domus* in Imperial Rome." *Scripta Israelitica Classica* 16 (1997): 162-90.

Eder, Walter. *Servitus Publica.* Forschungen zur antiken Sklaverei 13. Wiesbaden: Franz Steiner, 1980.

Elia, Olga. *Le Pitture della "Casa del Citarista." Fasc. 1. La Pittura Ellenistico-Romano: Pompei.* 2 vols. Rome: Istituto Poligrafico dello Stato, 1937.

Elliott, John H. "Jesus Was Not an Egalitarian: A Critique of an Anachronistic and Idealist Theory." *BTB* 32, 2 (2002): 79-91.

Elsner, Jas. *Art and the Roman Viewer.* Cambridge: Cambridge University Press, 1995.

Epstein, L. M. *Marriage Laws in the Bible and the Talmud.* Cambridge, 1942.

Erdkamp, Paul. "Agriculture, Underemployment, and the Cost of Rural Labor in the Roman World." *Classical Quarterly* 49 (1999): 556-72.

Ery, K. K. "Investigations on the Demographic Source Value of Tombstones Originating from the Roman Period." *Alba Regia* 10 (1969): 51-67.

Esler, Philip F., ed. *The Early Christian World.* Vol 2. London and New York: Routledge, 2000.

Euripides. *Iphigenia among the Taurians, Bacchae, Iphigenia at Aulis, Rhesus.* Translated by James Morwood. Oxford: Oxford University Press, 1999.

Evans, E. "Tertullian Ad Nationes." *VC* 9 (1955): 37-44.

Fairchilds, Cissie. *Domestic Enemies: Servants and Their Masters in Old Regime France.* Baltimore: Johns Hopkins University Press, 1984.

Fasola, U. M. *Peter and Paul in Rome: Traces on Stone.* Rome, 1980.

Feldherr, Andrew. *Spectacle and Society in Livy's History.* Berkeley and Los Angeles: University of California Press, 1998.

Feldman, Louis H. *Studies in Hellenistic Judaism.* AGJU 30. Leiden: Brill, 1996.

Février, P.-A., and R. Guery. "Les rites funéraires de la nécropole orientale de Sétif." *Antiquités Africaines* 15 (1980): 91-124.

Finley, Moses I. "Slavery." In *International Encyclopedia of the Social Sciences*, edited by David L. Shils, 14:307-13. New York: Macmillan and the Free Press, 1968.

―――. *The Ancient Economy*. Berkeley and Los Angeles: University of California Press, 1973.

―――. *Ancient Slavery and Modern Ideology*. Edited by Brent D. Shaw. 2nd Edition. Princeton: Markus Weiner, 1998.

Finney, Paul Corby. *The Invisible God: The Earliest Christians on Art*. Oxford: Oxford University Press, 1994.

Fittschen, Klaus. "Pathossteigerung und Pathosdämpfung. Bemerkungen zu griechischen und römischen Porträts des 2. und 1. Jahrhunderts v. Chr." *Archaeologischer Anzeiger* (1991): 253-70.

―――. "Wall Decorations in Herod's Kingdom: Their Relationship with Wall Decorations in Greece and Italy." In *Judea and the Greco-Roman World in the Time of Herod in the Light of Archaeological Evidence*, edited by K. Fittschen and G. F. Foerster. Göttingen: Vandenhoeck & Ruprecht, 1996.

Fitzgerald, William. *Slavery and the Roman Literary Imagination*. Roman Literature and Its Context. Cambridge: Cambridge University Press, 2000.

Flory, Marlene B. "Family in Familia: Kinship and Community in Slavery." *AJAH* 3 (1978): 78-95.

Fogel, Robert W. *Without Consent or Contract: The Rise and Fall of American Slavery*. New York: Norton, 1989.

Förster, Richard. "Laokoon-Denkmäler und Inschriften." *Jahrbuch des Kaiserlichen Deutschen Archäologischen Instituts* 6 (1891): 177-96.

Foucault, Michel. *The Use of Pleasure*, vol. 2 of *The History of Sexuality*. Translated by R. Hurley. New York: Vintage Books, 1990, from the 1984 original publication, *L'Usage des plaisirs* (Paris: Gallimard).

Fox, Robin Lane. *Pagans and Christians*. New York: Knopf, 1987.

Fraschetti, A. *Roma e il Principe*. Rome and Bari: Laterza, 1990.

Fraser, P. M., and E. Matthews. *A Lexicon of Greek Personal Names*. Oxford: Clarendon, 1997.

Frend, William H. C. *Martyrdom and Persecution in the Early Church: A Study of the Conflict from the Maccabees to Donatus*. Oxford: Basil Blackwell, 1965.

―――. "Blandina and Perpetua: Two Early Christian Martyrs." In *Les martyrs de Lyon (1977): Lyon 20-23 Septembre 1977*, edited by Jean Rouge and Robert Turcan, pp. 167-77. Colloques internationaux du Centre National de la Recherche Scientifique 575. Paris: Centre National de la Recherche Scientifique, 1978.

Friedman, Mordechai A. "Babatha's Ketubbah: Some Preliminary Observations." *IEJ* 46, nos. 1-2 (1996): 55-76.

Frier, Bruce W. "Roman Demography." In *Life, Death, and Entertainment in the Roman Empire*, edited by D. S. Potter and D. J. Mattingly, pp. 85-109. Ann Arbor: University of Michigan Press, 1999.

Frier, Bruce W., and Roger S. Bagnall. *The Demography of Roman Egypt*. Cambridge and New York: Cambridge University Press, 1994.

Fuks, A. "Marcus Julius Alexander." *Zion* 13-14 (1948-49): 15-17 (Hebrew).

Fullerton, M. D. "Pasiteles." In *The Dictionary of Art*, edited by Jane Turner, 24:227-28. New York: Grove Press, 1996.

Funaioli, Gino, ed. *Grammaticae romanae fragmenta collegit. Volumen prius.* Bibliotheca scriptorum Graecorum et Romanorum Teubneriana. Leipzig: Teubner, 1907.

Gagarin, Michael. "The Torture of Slaves in Athenian Law." *CP* 91 (1996): 1-18.

Gagé, Jean. Matronalia. Essai sur les dévotions et les organisations culturelles des Femmes dans l'ancienne Rome. Brussels: Latomus. 1963.

Gager, J. G., ed. *Curse Tablets and Binding Spells from the Ancient World.* Oxford: Oxford University Press, 1992.

Gallant, Thomas W. *Risk and Survival in Ancient Greece: Reconstructing the Rural Domestic Economy.* Stanford: Stanford University Press, 1991.

Galor, K. "The Roman-Byzantine Dwelling in the Galilee and the Golan: 'House' or 'Apartment'?" In *Miscellanea Mediterranea,* edited by R. R. Holloway, pp. 109-24. Providence: Brown University Press, 2000.

Gamrath, H. *Roma Sancta renovata: studi sull'urbanistica di Roma nella seconda metà del sec. XVI con particolare riferimento al pontificato di Sisto V (1585-1590).* Rome: L'Erma di Bretschneider, 1987.

Gardner, Jane F. *Women in Roman Law and Society.* Bloomington: Indiana University Press, 1986.

Garland, Andrew. "Cicero's *Familia Urbana.*" *GR* 39 (1992): 163-72.

Garnsey, Peter. *Social Status and Legal Privilege in the Roman Empire.* Oxford: Clarendon, 1970.

————. *Ideas of Slavery from Aristotle to Augustine.* The W. B. Stanford Memorial Lectures. Cambridge: Cambridge University Press, 1996.

George, Michele. "*Servus* and *Domus:* The Slave in the Roman House." In *Domestic Space in the Roman World: Pompeii and Beyond,* edited by Ray Laurence and Andrew Wallace-Hadrill, pp. 15-24. Journal of Roman Archaeology Supplement Series 22. Portsmouth, R.I.: Journal of Roman Archaeology, 1997.

Glancy, Jennifer A. "The Mistress-Slave Dialectic: Paradoxes of Slavery in Three LXX Narratives." *JSOT* 72 (1996): 71-87.

————. "Obstacles to Slaves' Participation in the Corinthian Church." *JBL* 117 (1998): 481-501.

————. "Three-Fifths of a Man: Slavery and Masculinity in Galatians." Paper, SBL Annual Meeting, 1999.

Glaserfeld, E. von. "Konstruktion von Wirklichkeit und der Begriff der Objektivität," in *Einführung in den Konstruktivsmus.* Munich: Oldenbourg, 1985.

Gold, Barbara K. "But Ariadne Was Never There in the First Place: Finding the Female in Roman Poetry." In *Feminist Theory and the Classics,* edited by N. S. Rabinowitz and A. Richlin, pp. 75-101. New York and London: Routledge, 1993.

Goldberg, M. Y. "Spatial and Behavioral Negotiation in Classical Athenian City Houses." In *The Archaeology of Household Activities,* edited by P. A. Allison, pp. 142-61. London and New York: Routledge, 1999.

Golden, Mark. "Did the Ancients Care When Their Children Died?" *GR* 35 (1988): 152-63.

————. *Children and Childhood in Classical Athens.* Baltimore, London: Johns Hopkins University Press, 1990.

Goldin, Claudia. *Understanding the Gender Gap: An Economic History of American Women.* New York: Oxford University Press, 1990.

Goldstein, J., ed. *Foucault and the Writing of History.* Oxford: Blackwell, 1994.

Goodman, Martin. "Babatha's Story." *JRS* 81 (1991): 169-75.

——. *Mission and Conversion: Proselytizing in the Religious History of the Roman Empire.* Oxford: Clarendon, 1994.

Goodspeed, Edgar J., ed. *Die ältesten Apologeten: Texte mit kurzen Einleitungen.* Göttingen: Vandenhoeck & Ruprecht, 1914.

Gould, G. "Childhood in Eastern Patristic Thought: Some Problems of Theology and Theological Anthropology." In *The Church and Childhood,* edited by D. Woods, pp. 39-52. Oxford: Blackwell, 1994.

Grant, Robert M. *After the New Testament.* Philadelphia: Fortress, 1967.

Greene, E. "Sappho, Foucault and Women's Erotics." *Arethusa* 29, no. 1 (1996): 1-14.

Greene, William Chase. *Moira: Fate, Good, and Evil in Greek Thought.* Cambridge: Harvard University Press, 1948.

Greenfield, Jonas. "'Because He/She Did Not Know Letters': Remarks on a First Millennium C.E. Legal Expression." *Journal of the Ancient Near Eastern Society* 22 (1993): 39-43.

Grubbs, Judith Evans. *Law and Family in Late Antiquity: The Emperor Constantine's Marriage Legislation.* Oxford: Clarendon, 1995.

Guidobaldi, F. "Le *domus* tardoantiche di Roma come 'sensori' delle trasformazioni culturali e sociali." In *The Transformations of Urbs Roma in Late Antiquity.* Journal of Roman Archaeology Supplement Series 33. Edited by W. V. Harris. Portsmouth, R.I.: Journal of Roman Archaeology, 1999.

Guidobaldi, Paola. *The Roman Forum.* Soprintendenza Archeologica di Roma. Milan: Electa, 1998.

Guijarro, Santiago. "The Family in First-Century Galilee." In *Constructing Early Christian Families: Family as Social Reality and Metaphor,* edited by H. Moxnes, pp. 42-66. London and New York: Routledge, 1997.

Guilhembet, J.-P. "La densité des *domus* et des *insulae* dans les XIV régions de Rome: selon les *Régionnaires* représentations cartographiques." *Mélanges d' archéologie et d' histoire de l' École française de Rome* 108 (1996): 7-26.

Guillaumin, Marie-Louise. "'Une Jeune Fille qui s'appelait Blandine': Aux origines d'une tradition hagiographique." In *Epektasis: Mélanges patristiques offerts au Cardinal Jean Daniélou,* edited by Jacques Fontaine and Charles Kannengiesser, pp. 93-98. Paris: Beauchesne, 1972.

Guillemin, A. M. *Pline et la vie littéraire de son temps.* Paris: Belles Lettres, 1929.

Gunnella, A. "Morte improvise e violente nelle iscrizioni latine." In *La mort au quotidien dans le monde romain: actes du colloque organisé par l'Université de Paris IV,* edited by F. Hinard, pp. 9-22. Paris: de Boccard, 1995.

Gustafson, James M. "Christian Ethics." In *The Westminster Dictionary of Christian Ethics,* edited by James F. Childress and John Macquarrie, pp. 87-90. Philadelphia: Westminster, 1986.

——. *Ethics from a Theocentric Perspective,* volume 2. Chicago: University of Chicago Press, 1984.

Guttentag, Marcia, and Paul E. Secord. *Too Many Women? The Sex Ratio Question.* Beverly Hills, Calif.: Sage, 1983.

Hall, Stuart G. "Women among the Early Martyrs." In *Martyrs and Martyrologies,* edited by Diana Wood, pp. 1-45. London: Blackwell, 1993.

Hallett, Judith. "The Role of Women in Roman Elegy: Counter-Cultural Feminism." *Arethusa* 6, no. 1 (1973): 103-24.

———. *Fathers and Daughters in Roman Society: Women and the Elite Family.* Princeton: Princeton University Press, 1984.

———. "Martial's Sulpicia and Propertios." *CW* 86.2 (1992): 199-24. Reprinted pp. 322-53 in *Woman's Power, Man's Game: Essays in Classical Antiquity in Honor of Joy K. King,* ed. Cynthia M. DeForest. Chicago: Bolchazy-Carducci, 1993.

Hallett, Judith, and M. B. Skinner, eds. *Roman Sexualities.* Princeton: Princeton University Press, 1997.

Halperin, David. "Historicizing the Subject of Desire: Sexual Preferences and Erotic Identities in the Pseudo-Lucianic Erōtes." In *Foucault and the Writing of History,* edited by J. Goldstein, pp. 19-34. Oxford: Blackwell, 1994.

Hanson, Anne. "The Roman Family." In *Life, Death, and Entertainment in the Empire,* edited by D. S. Potter and D. J. Mattingly, pp. 19-66. Ann Arbor: University of Michigan Press, 1999.

Harnack, Adolf von. *The Mission and Expansion of Christianity in the First Three Centuries.* Translated by James Moffat. Torchbook Edition, 1908. Reprint, with introduction by Jaroslav Pelikan, New York: Harper and Brothers, 1961.

Harrill, J. Albert. *The Manumission of Slaves in Early Christianity.* HUT 32. Tübingen: Mohr Siebeck, 1995.

———. "The Dramatic Function of the Running Slave Rhoda: A Piece of Greco-Roman Comedy (Acts 12.13-16)." *NTS* 48 (2000): 150-57.

———. "Paul and Slavery." In *Paul in the Greco-Roman World: A Handbook,* edited by J. Paul Sampley. Harrisburg, Pa.: Trinity Press International, forthcoming.

Harris, William V. "Towards a Study of the Roman Slave Trade." *MAAR* 36 (1980): 117-40. Edited by John H. D'Arms and E. C. Kopff.

———. "Demography, Geography and the Sources of Roman Slaves." *JRS* 89 (1999): 62-75.

Hawley, Richard, and Barbara Levick. *Women in Antiquity: New Assessments.* London: Routledge, 1995.

Heers, J. *Family Clans in the Middle Ages: A Study of Political and Social Structures in Urban Areas.* Amsterdam: North-Holland Publisher, 1977.

Heil, Christoph. "Die Rezeption von Micha 7,6 LXX in Q und Lukas." *ZNW* 88 (1997): 211-22.

Henten, Jan Willem van. *The Maccabean Martyrs as Saviours of the Jewish People: A Study of 2 and 4 Maccabees.* Supplements to the Journal for the Study of Judaism 57. Leiden: Brill, 1997.

———. "The Martyrs as Heroes of the Christian People: Some Remarks on the Continuity between Jewish and Christian Martyrology, with Pagan Analogies." In *Martyrium in Multidisciplinary Perspective: Memorial Louis Reekmans,* edited by M. Lambergts and P. van Deun, pp. 303-22. Leuven: Leuven University Press, 1995.

Hermansen, Gustav. "The Population of Imperial Rome." *Historia* 27 (1978): 129-68.

————. *Ostia: Aspects of Roman City Life.* Edmonton, Alberta: University of Alberta Press, 1982.

Herrmann-Otto, E. *Ex ancilla natus. Untersuchungen zu den 'Hausgeborenen' Sklaven und Sklavinnen im Westen des römischen Kaiserreiches.* Stuttgart: Steiner, 1994.

Hesse, Mary. "Is There an Independent Observation Language?" In *The Nature and Function of Scientific Theories,* edited by R. Colodny, pp. 36-77. Pittsburgh: University of Pittsburgh Press, 1970.

Hirschfeld, Y. *The Palestinian Dwelling in the Roman Byzantine Period.* Jerusalem: Franciscan Printing Press and Israel Exploration Society, 1995.

Hobson, Deborah. "The Role of Women in the Economic Life of Roman Egypt: A Case Study from First Century Tebtunis." *Echoes du Monde Classique/Classical Views* 28 (1984): 373-90.

Hoepfner, Wolfram, and Ernst-Ludwig Schwandner. *Haus und Stadt im klassischen Griechenland. Wohnen in der klassischen Polis I.* 2nd edition. Munich: Deutscher Kunstverlag, 1994.

Hoffmann, R. Joseph. *Celsus on the True Doctrine.* Oxford: Oxford University Press, 1987.

Hooper, R. W. "In Defence of Catullus' Dirty Sparrow." *GR* 32, no. 2 (1985): 162-78.

Horrell, David G., "From ἀδελφοί to οἶκος τοῦ θεοῦ: Social Transformation in Pauline Christianity." *JBL* 120 (2001): 293-311.

Hudson, Larry. *To Have and to Hold: Slave Work and Family Life in Antebellum South Carolina.* Athens: University of Georgia Press, 1997.

Huskinson, Janet. *Roman Children's Sarcophagi: Their Decoration and Its Social Significance.* Oxford: Clarendon, 1996.

Ilan, Tal. "Julia Crispina, Daughter of Berenicianus, a Herodian Princess in the Babatha Archive: A Case Study in Historical Identification." *JQR* 82, no. 3-4 (1992): 361-81.

————. *Jewish Women in Greco-Roman Palestine: An Inquiry into Image and Status.* Texte und Studien zum Antike Judentum 44. Tübingen: J. C. B. Mohr (Paul Siebeck), 1995. Reprint, Peabody, Mass.: Hendrickson, 1996.

————. "Josephus and Nicolaus on Women." In *Geschichte — Tradition — Reflexion. Festschrift für Martin Hengel zum 70 Geburtstag,* vol. 1, *Judentum,* edited by Hubert Cancik, Hermann Lichtenberger, and Peter Schäfer, pp. 221-62. Tübingen: J. C. B. Mohr (Paul Siebeck), 1996.

————. "Notes and Observations on a Newly Published Divorce Bill from the Judaean Desert." *HTR* 89, no. 2 (1996): 195-202.

————. *Mine and Yours Are Hers: Retrieving Women's History from Rabbinic Literature.* Leiden: Brill, 1997.

————. *Integrating Women into Second Temple History.* Texte und Studien zum Antike Judentum 76. Tübingen: Mohr Siebeck, 1999.

Insalaco, Antonio. "Vicus Caprarius: l'area archeologica," *Forma Urbis* VIII, 2 (Febbraico, 2003) 4-19.

Isaac, B. "The Babatha Archive: A Review Article." *IEJ* 42 (1992): 62-75.

Isager, Jacob. *Pliny on Art and Society: The Elder Pliny's Chapters on the History of Art.* 2nd ed. London: Routledge, 1998.

James, Sharon L. "Slave-Rape and Female Silence in Ovid's Love Poetry." *Helios* 24 (1977): 60-76.

Jameson, Michael. "Domestic Space in the Greek City-State." In *Domestic Architecture and the Use of Space*, edited by S. Kent, pp. 92-113. Cambridge: Cambridge University Press, 1990.

Jensen, Robin Margaret. *Understanding Early Christian Art*. New York: Routledge, 2000.

Johns, C. *Sex or Symbol? Erotic Images of Greece and Rome*. London: British Museum Press, 1982.

Johnson, A. C. *Roman Egypt: Economic Survey of Ancient Rome*. Vol. 2. Baltimore: Johns Hopkins University Press, 1936.

Jones, Lawrence P. "A Case Study in 'Gnosticism': Religious Responses to Slavery in the Second Century CE." Ph.D. diss., Columbia University, 1988.

Joshel, Sandra R. *Work, Identity, and Legal Status at Rome: A Study of the Occupational Inscriptions*. Norman: University of Oklahoma Press, 1992.

Joshel, Sandra R., and Sheila Murnaghan, eds. *Women and Slaves in Greco-Roman Culture: Differential Equations*. London: Routledge, 1998.

Kahil, Lilly, and Pascale Lilant De Bellefonds. "Iphigeneia." In *LIMC*, vol. 5.1, pp. 706-29. Zürich: Artemis, 1990.

Kampen, Natalie. *Image and Status: Roman Working Women in Ostia*. Berlin: Mann, 1981.

————, ed. *Sexuality in Ancient Art*. Cambridge: Cambridge University Press, 1996.

Käsemann, Ernst. *Pauline Perspectives*. Translated by Margaret Kohl. Philadelphia: Fortress, 1971.

Kellum, B. "The Phallus as Signifier: The Forum of Augustus and Rituals of Masculinity." In *Sexuality in Ancient Art*, edited by N. Kampen, pp. 170-98. Cambridge: Cambridge University Press, 1996.

Kennedy, George. *The Art of Persuasion in Greece*. Princeton: Princeton University Press, 1963.

Kent, S. *Domestic Architecture and the Use of Space: An Interdisciplinary Cross-Cultural Study*. Cambridge: Cambridge University Press, 1990.

Keuls, Eva C. *The Reign of the Phallus: Sexual Politics in Ancient Athens*. Berkeley: University of California Press, 1985.

Kilbourne, Brock, and James T. Richardson. "Paradigm Conflict, Types of Conversion, and Conversion Theories." *Sociological Analysis* 50 (1988): 1-21.

Kindstrand, Jan Fredrik. "The Greek Concept of Proverbs." *Eranos* 76 (1978): 71-85.

Klees, Hans. *Sklavenleben im klassischen Griechenland*. Stuttgart: Franz Steiner, 1998.

Kleiner, David. *Roman Imperial Funerary Altars with Portraits*. Rome: Bretschneider, 1987.

Knittlmayer, B., and W. P. Heilmeyer, eds. *Staatliche Museen zu Berlin: Die Antikensammlung. Altes Museum — Pergamon Museum*. Mainz: Philipp von Zabern, 1998.

Kokkinos, Nikos. *The Herodian Dynasty: Origins, Role in Society, and Eclipse*. Journal for the Study of Pseudepigrapha Supplement Series 30. Sheffield: Sheffield Academic Press, 1998.

Kolendo, Jerzy. "L'esclavage et la vie sexuelle des hommes libres à Rome." *Quaderni Camerti di Studi Romanistici = International Survey of Roman Law* 10 (1981): 288-97.

Koloski-Ostrow, A., and C. L. Lyons, eds. *Naked Truths: Women, Sexuality, and Gender in Classical Art and Archaeology*. London and New York: Routledge, 1997.

Kondoleon, C., and L. A. Roussin. "Mosaics." In *Oxford Encyclopedia of Archaeology in the Near East*, edited by Eric M. Meyers, 4:50-55. New York: Oxford University Press, 1997.

Konstan, David, ed. *Helios* 19, no. 1-2 (1992). Special issue, "Documenting Gender: Women and Men in Non-Literary Classical Texts."

Konstan, David, and Martha Nussbaum, eds. *Sexuality in Greek and Roman Society: Special Issue of Differences.* Providence: Brown University Press, 1990.

Kosnik, Anthony, et al. *Human Sexuality: New Directions in American Catholic Thought.* New York: Paulist, 1977.

Kraemer, Ross Shepard. "The Conversion of Women to Ascetic Forms of Christianity." *Signs* 6 (1980): 298-307.

————. *Her Share of the Blessings: Women's Religions among Pagans, Jews, and Christians in the Greco-Roman World.* Oxford and New York: Oxford University Press, 1992.

————. "Jewish Mothers and Daughters in the Greco-Roman World." In *The Jewish Family in Antiquity,* edited by Shaye J. D. Cohen, pp. 89-112. BJS 289. Atlanta: Scholars, 1993.

————. Review of *Jewish Women in Greco-Roman Palestine: An Inquiry into Image and Status,* by Tal Ilan. *JAOS* 118, no. 4 (1998): 570-73.

————. *When Aseneth Met Joseph: A Late Antique Tale of the Biblical Patriarch and His Egyptian Wife, Revisited.* New York and Oxford: Oxford University Press, 1998.

————. "Jewish Women and Women's Judaism(s) at the Beginning of Christianity." In *Women and Christian Origins,* edited by Ross Shepard Kraemer and Mary Rose D'Angelo, pp. 50-79. New York and Oxford: Oxford University Press, 1999.

————. "Berenice." In *Women in Scripture: A Dictionary of Named and Unnamed Women in the Hebrew Bible, Apocryphal/Deutero-Canonical Books, and the New Testament,* gen. ed., Carol Meyers, associate eds., Toni Craven and Ross S. Kraemer, pp. 59-61. Boston: Houghton-Mifflin, 2000. Reprint, Grand Rapids: Eerdmans, 2001.

————, ed. *Maenads, Martyrs, Matrons, and Monastics: A Sourcebook on Women's Religions in the Greco-Roman World.* Philadelphia: Fortress, 1988.

Kraemer, Ross Shepard, and Mary Rose D'Angelo, eds. *Women and Christian Origins.* Oxford and New York: Oxford University Press, 1999.

Krautheimer, R. *Corpus Basilicarum Christianarum Romae* 1.4, 267-303.

Kreeb, Martin. *Untersuchungen zur figürlichen Ausstattung delischer Privathäuser.* Chicago: Ares Publishers, 1988.

Kunze, Christian, "Zur Datierung des Laokoon und der Skyllagruppe aus Sperlonga." *Jahrbuch des Deutschen Archäologischen Instituts* 111 (1996): 139-223.

Laiou, Angeliki E. "Sex, Consent, and Coercion in Byzantium." In *Consent and Coercion to Sex and Marriage in Ancient and Medieval Societies,* edited by Angeliki E. Laiou, pp. 109-221. Washington, D.C.: Dumbarton Oaks, 1993.

Lampe, Peter. "Die Apokalyptiker — ihre Situation und ihr Handeln." In U. Luz, J. Kegler, P. Lampe, and P. Hoffman, *Eschatologie und Friedenshandeln.* 2nd ed. Stuttgart: Katholisches Bibelwerk, 1982.

————. *Die Stadtrömischen Christen in den ersten beiden Jahrhunderten.* 2nd ed. Tübingen: Mohr-Siebeck, 1989. ET: *From Paul to Valentinus: Christians at Rome in the First Two Centuries.* Minneapolis: Augsburg/Fortress, 2003.

————. *Die Wirklichkeit als Bild. Das Neue Testament als Grunddokument abendländischer Kultur im Lichte konstruktivistischer Epistemologie und Wissenssoziologie.* Neukirchen: Neukirchener, 2004.

————. "Wissenssoziologische Annäherung an das Neue Testament," *NTS* 43 (1997): 347-66.

Lampe, Peter, and Ulrich Luz. "Nachpaulinisches Christentum und pagane Gesellschaft." In J. Becker et al., *Die Anfänge des Christentums: Alte Welt und Neue Hoffnung*, pp. 185-216. Stuttgart: Kohlhammer, 1987.

Lander, Shira L. Review of *Jewish Women in Greco-Roman Palestine: An Inquiry into Image and Status*, by Tal Ilan, and of *Spinning Fantasies: Rabbis, Gender, and History*, by Miriam Peskowitz. *CCAR Journal: A Reform Jewish Quarterly* (summer 2000): 61-68.

Lang-Auinger, Claudia. *Hanghaus 1 in Ephesos. Der Baubefund. Forschungen in Ephesos VIII/3*. Vienna: Verlag der Österreichischen Akademie der Wissenschaften, 1996.

Lathrop, Gordon. *Holy Things: A Liturgical Theology*. Minneapolis: Augsburg Fortress. 1993.

Lattimore, R. *Themes in Greek and Latin Epitaphs*. Urbana: University of Illinois Press, 1962. Reprint of 1942 edition.

Laurence, Ray. "The Urban *Vicus*: The Spatial Organization of Power in the Roman City." In *Papers of the Fourth Conference of Italian Archaeology*, volume 1: *The Archaeology of Power*. Edited by E. Herring, R. Whitehouse, and J. Wilkins. London: Accordia Research Centre, 1991.

————. *Roman Pompeii: Space and Society*. London and New York: Routledge, 1994.

Laurence, Ray, and Andrew Wallace-Hadrill, eds. *Domestic Space in the Roman World: Pompeii and Beyond*. Journal of Roman Archaeology Supplement Series 22. Portsmouth, R.I.: Journal of Roman Archaeology, 1997.

Lavagne, Henri. "Römische Wandmalerei: Bilanz jüngerer Forschungen und neue Sichtweisen." In *Römische Glaskunst und Wandmalerei*, edited by Michael J. Klein, pp. 21-24. Mainz: Philipp von Zabern, 1999.

Lefkowitz, Mary R., and Maureen B. Fant, eds. *Women's Life in Greece and Rome: A Sourcebook in Translation*. Baltimore: Johns Hopkins University Press, 1992.

Lehmann-Hartleben, Karl. "The *Imagines* of the Elder Philostratus." *Art Bulletin* 23 (1941): 16-44.

Levenson, Jon D. "The Rewritten Aqedah of Jewish Tradition." In *The Death and Resurrection of the Beloved Son: The Transformation of Child Sacrifice in Judaism and Christianity*, pp. 173-99. New Haven: Yale University Press, 1993.

Levine, Lee I. *The Rabbinic Class of Roman Palestine in Late Antiquity*. Jerusalem: Yad Izhak Ben-Zvi, 1989.

————. "Beth-She'arim." In *Oxford Encyclopedia of Archaeology in the Near East*, edited by Eric M. Meyers, 1:309-11. New York: Oxford University Press, 1997.

————. *Judaism and Hellenism in Antiquity: Conflict or Confluence?* Peabody, Mass.: Hendrickson, 1998.

Lewis, Naphtali, ed. *The Documents from the Bar Kochba Period in the Cave of Letters: Greek Papyri*. JDS 2. Jerusalem: Israel Exploration Society, Hebrew University, Shrine of the Book, 1989.

Lexicon Iconographicum Mythologiae Classicae. Edited by H. C. Ackerman and J.-R. Gisler. 8 vols. Zürich: Artemis, 1981-97.

Lieu, Judith M. *Image and Reality: The Jews in the World of the Christians in the Second Century*. Edinburgh: T. & T. Clark, 1996.

————. "The 'Attraction of Women' in/to Early Judaism and Christianity: Gender and the Politics of Conversion." *JSNT* 72 (1998): 5-22.

Lindsay, Wallace M., ed. *Sexti Pompei Festi. De verborum significatu quae supersunt cum Pauli epitome.* Bibliotheca scriptorum Graecorum et Romanorum Teubneriana. 1913. Reprint, Hildesheim: Georg Olms, 1965.

Ling, Roger. "The Insula of the Menander at Pompeii: Interim Report." *Antiquaries Journal* 63 (1983): 34-57.

————. *The Insula of the Menander at Pompeii: The Structures.* Vol. I. Oxford: Clarendon, 1997.

Lloyd-Jones, Hugh. "Artemis and Iphigenia." *JHS* 103 (1983): 87-102.

Lo Cascio, E. "Le procedure di recensus della tarda repubblica al tardo-antico e il calcolo della popolazione di Roma." In *La Rome impériale: démographie et logistique: Actes de la table ronde (Rome, 25 mars 1994),* Collection de L' École Française de Rome 230. Rome: École Française de Rome, 1997.

————. "La popolazione." *Roma Imperiale. Una metropoli antica.* Rome: Carocci editore, 2000.

Löhr, Winrich A. "Der Brief der Gemeinden von Lyon und Vienne (Eusebius, h.e. V, 1-2 (4))." In *Oecumenica et Patristica: Festschrift für Wilhelm Schneemelcher zum 75. Geburtstag,* edited by Damaskinos Papandreou, Wolfgang A. Bienert, and Knut Schäferdiek, pp. 135-49. Stuttgart: W. Kohlhammer, 1989.

Löwy, Emanuel. "Der Schluss der Iphigenie in Aulis." *Jahreshefte des Österreichischen Archäologischen Institutes in Wien* 24 (1929): 1-41.

Luck, G., ed. *Arcana Mundi: Magic and the Occult in the Greek and Roman Worlds.* Baltimore: Johns Hopkins University Press, 1985.

Lugli, G. "Il valore topografico e giuridico dell'*insula* in Roma antica." *Rendiconti della Pontificia Accademia Romana di archeologia* 18 (1941-42): 191-208.

Lyne, R. O. M. *The Latin Love Poets from Catullus to Horace.* Oxford: Clarendon, 1980.

MacDonald, Margaret Y. *Early Christian Women and Pagan Opinion: The Power of the Hysterical Woman.* Cambridge: Cambridge University Press, 1996.

————. *Colossians and Ephesians.* Sacra Pagina Series. Edited by Daniel J. Harrington, S.J. Collegeville, Minn.: Liturgical Press, 2000.

Mack, Burton J. *The Lost Gospel: The Book of Q and Christian Origins.* San Francisco: Harper Collins, 1993.

MacMullen, Ramsay. "Romans in Tears." *CP* 75 (1980): 254-55.

————. "Women in Public in the Roman Empire." *Historia* 29 (1980): 208-18.

————. "The Epigraphic Habit in the Roman Empire." *AJP* 103 (1982): 233-46.

————. *Christianizing the Roman Empire (A.D. 100-400).* New Haven: Yale University Press, 1984.

————. *Changes in the Roman Empire: Essays in the Ordinary.* Princeton: Princeton University Press, 1990, especially "Judicial Savagery in the Roman Empire," pp. 204-17.

————. *Enemies of the Roman Order: Treason, Unrest, and Alienation in the Empire.* Cambridge: Harvard University Press, 1996.

Macurdy, Grace H. "Julia Berenice." *AJP* 56 (1935): 246-53.

————. "Royal Women in Judaea." In *Vassal Queens and Some Contemporary Women in the Roman Empire,* pp. 63-91. Johns Hopkins University Studies in Archaeology 22.

Baltimore: Johns Hopkins University Press; London: Oxford University Press, Humphrey Milford, 1937. Reprint, Chicago: Ares Press, 1993.

Madden, John. "Slavery in the Roman Empire: Numbers and Origins." *Classics Ireland* 3 (1996). Online: http:/www.ucd.ie/%7Eclassics/96/Madden96.html. 9 pages.

Magen, Y. "Jerusalem as the Center of Stone Vessel Industry during the Second Temple Period." In *Ancient Jerusalem Revealed*, pp. 244-56. Jerusalem: Israel Exploration Society, 1994.

Maiuri, Amedeo. *La Casa del Menandro e il suo Tesoro di Argenteria.* 2 vols. Rome: La Libreria dello Stato, 1933.

———. "La Parodia di Enea." *Bollettino d'Arte* 35 (1950): 108-12.

Majanlahti, A. "Mapping Rome: Urban Change in the Neighbourhood of Santa Caterina della Rota." *PBSR* 56 (2001): 393-95.

Malherbe, Abraham J. *Moral Exhortation: A Greco-Roman Sourcebook.* Library of Early Christianity. Philadelphia: Westminster, 1986.

Malina, Bruce J. "Does Porneia Mean 'Fornication'?" *NovT* 14 (1972): 10-17.

Malinowski, Francis X. "The Brave Women of Philippi." *BTB* 15 (1985): 60-64.

Marincola, John. *Authority and Tradition in Ancient Historiography.* Cambridge: Cambridge University Press, 1997.

Marinovic, L. P., E. S. Golubcova, I. S. Sifman, and A. I. Pavlovskaja. *Die Sklaverei in den östlichen Provinzen des römischen Reiches im 1.-3. Jahrhundert.* Stuttgart: Franz Steiner, 1992.

Martin, Dale B. *Slavery as Salvation: The Metaphor of Slavery in Pauline Christianity.* New Haven: Yale University Press, 1990.

———. "The Construction of the Ancient Family: Methodological Considerations." *JRS* 86 (1996): 40-60.

Martin, Victor, and Rodolphe Kasser, eds. *Papyrus Bodmer XIV: Evangile de Luc chap. 3–24. P75.* Cologny-Geneva: Bibliotheca Bodmeriana, 1961.

Martin, Victor, and J. W. B. Barns, eds. *Papyrus Bodmer II, Supplément: Evangile de Jean chap. 14-21. Nouvelle édition augmentée et corrigée avec reproduction photographique complète du manuscrit (chap. 1–21).* Cologny-Geneva: Bibliotheca Bodmeriana, 1962.

Masciardi, M. Manca, and O. Montevecchi. *I contratti di baliatico. Corpora Papyrorum Graecarum 1.* Milan: Azzate; Varese: Tipolitografia Tibiletti, 1984.

Maser, Peter. "Das sogenannte Spottkruzifix vom Palatin: Ein 'frühchristliches' Denkmal im Widerstreit der Meinungen." *Das Altertum* 18 (1972): 248-54.

Maslakov, G. "Valerius Maximus and Roman Historiography: A Study of the *Exempla* Tradition." *ANRW* 2.32.1 (1984), pp. 437-96.

Massaux, Édouard. *The Influence of the Gospel of Saint Matthew on Christian Literature before Saint Irenaeus,* vol. 2, *The Later Christian Writings.* New Gospel Studies 5.2. Macon, Ga.: Mercer University Press, 1992.

Mathews, Thomas F. *The Clash of Gods: A Reinterpretation of Early Christian Art.* Princeton: Princeton University Press, 1993.

Matson, David Lertis. *Household Conversion Narratives in Acts: Pattern and Interpretation.* JSNTSup 123. Sheffield: Sheffield Academic Press, 1996.

Mau, A. "Deliciae." In *Pauly's Realenzyklopädie der klassischen Altertumswissenschaft* 4.2, edited by G. Wissowa, W. Kroll, and K. Mittelhaus, c. 2435-38. Munich: Alfred Drückenmuller Verlag, 1901.

McCarthy, Kathleen. *Slaves, Masters, and the Art of Authority in Plautine Comedy.* Princeton: Princeton University Press, 2000.

McGinn, Thomas A. J. *Prostitution, Sexuality, and the Law in Ancient Rome.* Oxford: Oxford University Press, 1998.

McKee, B. R. "Household Archaeology and Cultural Formation Processes: Examples from the Cerén Site, El Salvador." In *The Archaeology of Household Activities,* edited by P. A. Allison, pp. 30-42. London and New York: Routledge, 1999.

Meeks, Wayne. *The First Urban Christians: The Social World of the Apostle Paul.* New Haven: Yale University Press, 1983.

Mehl, Roger. *Society and Love: Ethical Problems of Family Life.* Translated by James H. Farley. Philadelphia: Westminster, 1964.

Mertens, Cées. "Les premiers martyrs et leurs rêves: Cohésion de l'histoire et des rêves dans quelques 'passions' latines de l'Afrique du nord." *RHE* 81 (1986): 5-46.

Meunier, Mario, ed. *Femmes Pythagoriciennes: Fragments et Lettres de Théano, Périctioné, Phintys, Mélissa et Myia.* Paris: L'Artisan du Livre, 1932.

Meyer, Marvin W. *The Ancient Mysteries: A Sourcebook of Sacred Texts.* 1987. Reprint, Philadelphia: University of Pennsylvania Press, 1999.

Meyers, Carol. "Fumes, Flames or Fluids? Reframing the Cup-and-Bowl Question." In *Boundaries of the Ancient Near Eastern World: A Tribute to Cyrus Gordon,* edited by M. Lubetski, C. Gottlieb, and S. Keller, pp. 30-39. JSOTSup 273. Sheffield: JSOT, 1998.

Meyers, Eric M. "An Archaeological Response to a New Testament Scholar." *BASOR* 297 (1995): 17-26.

———. "The Ceramic Incense Shovels from Sepphoris: Another View." Festschrift for Ami Mazar. Forthcoming.

———. "The Pools of Sepphoris — Ritual Baths or Bathtubs?" *BARev* 26, no. 4 (2000): 46-49, 60.

———. "Roman-Period Houses from Galilee: Domestic Architecture and Gendered Spaces." *Albright/ASOR Centennial,* forthcoming.

———, ed. *Galilee through the Centuries: Confluence of Cultures.* Winona Lake, Ind.: Eisenbrauns, 1999.

Meyers, Eric M., and Carol L. Meyers. "Talmudic Village Life in the Galilean Highlands." *Bulletin of the Anglo-Israel Archaeological Society* (1982-83): 32-36.

Meyers, Eric M., E. Netzer, and C. L. Meyers. *Sepphoris.* Winona Lake, Ind.: Eisenbrauns, 1992.

Meyers, Eric M., J. F. Strange, and C. L. Meyers. *Excavations at Ancient Meiron.* Cambridge, Mass.: ASOR, 1981.

Mezger, W. *Hofnarren im Mittelalter. Vom tieferen Sinn eines seltsamen Amts.* Constance: Universitätsverlag, 1981.

Milik, J. T. "Le travail d'édition des manuscrits du Désert de Juda." *Volume du congrès Strasbourg* 1956 = VTSup 4. Leiden: Brill, 1956.

Mitchell, Margaret M. *The Heavenly Trumpet: John Chrysostom and the Art of Pauline Interpretation.* HUT 40. Tübingen: Mohr/Siebeck, 2000; Louisville: Westminster/John Knox, 2002.

Mohler, S. L. "Slave Education in the Roman Empire." *TAPA* 71 (1940): 262-80.

Moormann, Eric M. "'Vivere come un uomo': L'Uso dello Spazio nella Domus Aurea." In *Horti Romani: Atti del Convegno Internazionale, Roma, 4-6 maggio 1995*, edited by Maddalena Cima and Eugenio La Rocca. Rome: "L'Erma" di Bretschneider, 1998.

Morgan, Llewelyn. "The Autopsy of C. Asinius Pollio." *JRS* 90 (2000): 51-69.

Moses, Diana C. "Livy's Lucretia and the Validity of Coerced Consent in Roman Law." In *Consent and Coercion to Sex and Marriage in Ancient and Medieval Societies*, edited by Angeliki E. Laiou, pp. 39-81. Washington, D.C.: Dumbarton Oaks, 1993.

Moxnes, Halvor, ed. *Constructing Early Christian Families: Family as Social Reality and Metaphor*. New York and London: Routledge, 1997.

Muñoz, A. *Campidoglio*. Rome: Governaturo di Roma, 1930.

Murdock, George P., and Caterina Provost. "Factors in the Division of Labor by Sex: A Cross-Cultural Analysis." *Ethnology* 12 (1973): 203-25.

Murgatroyd, P. "Tibullus and the Puer Delicatus." *Acta Classica* 20 (1977): 105-19.

Nagy, R., E. M. Meyers, Z. Weiss, and C. L. Meyers, eds. *Sepphoris in Galilee: Crosscurrents of Culture*. Raleigh: North Carolina Museum of Art, 1996.

Nappo, Salvatore Ciro. "Alcuni esempi di tipologie di case popolari della fine III, inizio II secolo a.C. a Pompei." *Rivista di Studi Pompeiani* 6 (1993-94): 77-104.

———. "Urban Transformation at Pompeii in the Late Third and Early Second Century B.C." In *Domestic Space in the Roman World: Pompeii and Beyond*, edited by Ray Laurence and Andrew Wallace-Hadrill, pp. 92-120. Journal of Roman Archaeology Supplement Series 22. Portsmouth, R.I.: Journal of Roman Archaeology, 1997.

———. *Pompeii: Guide to the Lost City*. London: Weidenfeld and Nicolson, 1998.

Nardi, Enzo. *Procurato aborto nel mondo greco romano*. Milan: Giuffrè, 1971.

Nathan, G. *The Family in Late Antiquity: The Rise and Endurance of Tradition*. London, New York: Routledge, 2000.

Nautin, Pierre. *Lettres et Écrivains chrétiens des IIe et IIIe siècles*. Patristica 2. Paris: Cerf, 1961.

Nelson, James. *Embodiment: An Approach to Sexuality and Christian Theology*. Minneapolis: Augsburg, 1978.

Néraudau, Jean-Paul. *Être enfant à Rome*. Paris: Les Belles Lettres, 1984.

Neusner, Jacob, Ernest S. Frerichs, Peter Borgen, and Richard Horsley, eds. *The Social World of Formative Christianity and Judaism: Essays in Tribute to Howard Clark Kee*. Philadelphia: Fortress, 1988.

Nevett, Lisa. *House and Society in the Ancient Greek World*. Cambridge: Cambridge University Press, 1999.

Newsom, Carol A., and Sharon H. Ringe, eds. *The Women's Bible Commentary*. Louisville: Westminster John Knox, 1992.

Nielsen, Hanne S. "Delicia in Roman Literature and in the Urban Inscriptions." *ARID* 19 (1990): 79-88.

———. "The Value of Epithets in Pagan and Christian Epitaphs from Rome." In *Childhood, Class, and Kin in the Roman World*, edited by S. Dixon, pp. 165-77. London: Routledge, 2001.

———. "Roman Children at Mealtime." In *The Roman Family at Dinner: Aspects of the*

Communal Meal in the Hellenistic and Roman World, edited by I. Nielson and H. S. Nielson, pp. 56-66. Aarhus: Aarhus University Press, 1998.

———. "The Physical Context of Roman Epitaphs and the Structure of the 'Roman Family,'" *ARID* 23 (1996): 35-60.

Nordh, Arvast. *Libellus de regionibus urbis Romae.* Lund: C. W. K. Gleerup, 1949.

Obermayer, H. P. *Martial und der Diskurs über männliche "Homosexualität" in der Literatur der frühen Kaiserzeit.* Tübingen: Narr, 1998.

Oekland, Jorunn. "Women in Their Place: Paul and the Corinthian Discourse of Gender and Sanctuary Space." Ph.D. diss., University of Oslo, 2001.

Origen. *Contra Celsum.* Translated by Henry Chadwick. Cambridge: Cambridge University Press, 1953.

Origo, Iris. "The Domestic Enemy: The Eastern Slaves in Tuscany in the Fourteenth and Fifteenth Centuries." *Speculum* 30 (1955): 321-66.

Osborne, M. J., and S. G. Byrne, eds. *A Lexicon of Greek Personal Names.* Vol. 2. Oxford: Clarendon, 1994.

Osiek, Carolyn, and David L. Balch. *Families in the New Testament World: Households and House Churches.* Louisville: Westminster John Knox, 1997.

Packer, John. "La Casa di via Giulio Romano." *Bulletino della Commissione archeologica Communale in Roma* 81 (1968-69): 127.

Paris, Rita. "Le Testimonianze Pittoriche a Roma." In *Romana Pictura: La pittura romana dalle origini all'età bizantina,* edited by Angela Donati, pp. 73-84. Milan: Electa, 1998.

Parish, David. "The Architectural Design and Interior Décor of Apartment I in Insula 2 at Ephesus." In *Fifth International Colloquium on Ancient Mosaics, Bath 1987,* edited by Roger Ling, pp. 143-58. Journal of Roman Archaeology Supplement Series 9. Portsmouth, R.I.: Journal of Roman Archaeology, 1995.

Parker, Holt. "Loyal Slaves and Loyal Wives: The Crisis of the Outsider-within and Roman *Exemplum* Literature." In *Women and Slaves in Greco-Roman Culture: Differential Equations,* edited by Sandra R. Joshel and Sheila Murnaghan, pp. 152-73. London: Routledge, 1998.

Parkin, Timothy. *Demography and Roman Society.* Baltimore and London: Johns Hopkins University Press, 1992.

Patterson, Jeremy R. "Living and Dying in the City of Rome: Houses and Tombs." In *Ancient Rome: The Archaeology of the Eternal City,* edited by J. Coulson and H. Dodge. Oxford: Oxford University School of Archaeology, 2000.

Patterson, Orlando. *Slavery and Social Death: A Comparative Study.* Cambridge: Harvard University Press, 1982.

Pearce, T. E. V. "The Role of the Wife as Custos in Ancient Rome." *Eranos* 72 (1974): 16-33.

Pedroni, L. "Per una lettura verticale della Forma Urbis Marmorea." *Ostraka* 1 (1992): 223-30.

Penwill, J. L. "Slavish Pleasures and Profitless Curiosity: Fall and Redemption in Apuleius' *Metamorphoses.*" *Ramus* 4 (1975): 49-82.

Perkins, Judith B. "The *Passion of Perpetua:* A Narrative of Empowerment." *Latomus* 53 (1994): 837-47.

———. *The Suffering Self: Pain and Narrative in the Early Christian Era.* London: Routledge, 1995.

Peskowitz, Miriam. "Family/ies in Antiquity: Evidence from Tannaitic Literature and Roman Galilean Architecture." In *The Jewish Family in Antiquity*, edited by Shaye J. D. Cohen, pp. 9-38. Atlanta: Scholars, 1993.

————. *Spinning Fantasies: Rabbis, Gender, and History.* Berkeley and Los Angeles: University of California Press, 1997.

Peterson, J. M. "House Churches in Rome." *VC* 23 (1969): 264-72.

Phillips, C. R. "Seek and Go Hide: Literary Source Problems and Greco-Roman Magic." *Helios* 21, no. 2 (1994): 107-14.

Pirson, Felix. *Mietwohnungen in Pompeji und Herkulaneum. Untersuchungen zur Architektur, zum Wohnen und zur Sozial- und Wirtschaftsgeschichte der Vesuvstädte.* Studien zur antiken Stadt 5. Munich: Verlag Dr. Friedrich Pfeil, 1999.

Polito, Eugenio. *I Galati Vinti: Il Trionfo sui Barbari da Pergamo a Roma.* Soprintendenza Archeologica di Roma. Milan: Electa, 1999.

Pomeroy, Arthur J. "Trimalchio as Deliciae." *Phoenix* 46 (1992): 45-53.

Pomeroy, Sarah B. *Goddesses, Whores, Wives, and Slaves: Women in Classical Antiquity.* New York: Schocken Books, 1976.

————. "Women in Roman Egypt: A Preliminary Study Based on Papyri." In *ANRW* II.10.1 (1988): 708-12.

————. *Xenophon, "Oeconomicus": A Social and Historical Commentary.* Oxford: Oxford University Press, 1994.

Pompei: Pitture e Mosaici. Enciclopedia Italiana. 9 vols. Rome: Arti Grafiche Pizzi, S.P.A., 1990-99.

Potter, David. "Martyrdom as Spectacle." In *Theater and Society in the Classical World*, edited by Ruth Scodel, pp. 53-88. Ann Arbor: University of Michigan Press, 1993.

Prieur, J. *La mort dans l'antiquité romaine.* Rennes: Ouest-France, 1986.

Quilici, L. "Il Campo Marzio occidentale." *Città e Architettura nella Roma Imperiale, ARID* 10 (1983): 59-85.

————. "Roma. Via di S. Paolo alla Regola. Scavo e recupero di edifici antichi e medioevali." *Notizie degli Scavi ser. VIII* 40-41 (1986-87): 175ff.

Rabinowitz, Nancy S., and Amy Richlin, eds. *Feminist Theory and the Classics.* New York and London: Routledge, 1993.

Radt, Wolfgang. "Pergamon. Vorbericht über die Kampagne 1992." *Archäologischer Anzeiger* (1993): 366-69.

Raepsaet-Charlier, Marie-Thérèse. "Tertullien et la législation des mariages inégaux." *RIDA* 29 (1982): 253-63.

Rajak, Tessa. "Dying for the Law: The Martyr's Portrait in Jewish-Greek Literature." In *Portraits: Biographical Representation in the Greek and Latin Literature of the Roman Empire*, edited by M. J. Edwards and Simon Swain, pp. 39-67. Oxford: Clarendon, 1997.

Rathbone, Dominic. *Economic Rationalism and Rural Society in Third-Century A.D. Egypt: The Heroninus Archive and the Appianus Estate.* Cambridge: Cambridge University Press, 1991.

Rawski, Conrad H. *Petrarch's Remedies for Fortune Fair and Foul.* 5 vols. Bloomington: Indiana University Press, 1991.

Rawson, Beryl. "Family Life among the Lower Classes at Rome in the First Two Centuries of the Empire." *CP* 61 (1966): 71-83.

―――. "The Roman Family." In *The Family in Ancient Rome: New Perspectives*, edited by B. Rawson, pp. 1-57. London: Routledge; Ithaca, N.Y.: Cornell University Press, 1986.

―――. "'The Family' in the Ancient Mediterranean: Past, Present, Future." *ZPE* 117 (1997): 294-96.

―――. "The Iconography of Roman Childhood." In *The Roman Family in Italy: Status, Sentiment, Space*, edited by B. Rawson and P. Weaver, pp. 205-32. Oxford: Clarendon, 1997.

―――. "Representations of Roman Children and Childhood." *Antichthon* 31 (1997): 74-95.

―――. "Education: The Romans and Us." *Antichthon* 33 (1999): 81-98.

―――. "The Express Route to Hades." In *Thinking Like a Lawyer*, edited by P. McKechnie. Leiden: Brill, 2002.

―――, ed. *Marriage, Divorce, and Children in Ancient Rome*. Oxford: Clarendon, 1991.

Reitz, Christiane, and Ulrike Egelhaaf. "Ekphrasis." *Der Neue Pauly*, edited by H. Cancik et al., 3 (1997): 942-50.

Remus, Harold. *Pagan-Christian Conflict over Miracle in the Second Century*. Cambridge, Mass.: Philadelphia Patristics Foundation, 1983.

Rice, Ellen E. "Prosopographica Rhodiaka, Part II: The Rhodian Sculptors of the Sperlonga and Laocoon Statuary Groups." *Annual of British School at Athens* 81 (1986): 233-50.

Richlin, Amy. *The Garden of Priapus: Sexuality and Aggression in Roman Humor*. New Haven: Yale University Press, 1983; reprinted 1992 with special introduction.

―――. "Zeus and Metis: Foucault, Feminism, Classics." *Helios* 18, no. 2 (1991): 1-21.

―――. *Pornography and Representation in Greece and Rome*. New York: Oxford University Press, 1992.

Ricoeur, Paul. *Oneself as Another*. Translated by Kathleen Blamey. Chicago: University of Chicago Press, 1992.

Riemann, H. "Paedagogium Palatini." In *Paulys Real-Encyclopädie* 18/1, edited by G. Wissowa and W. Kroll, pp. 2205-24. Stuttgart: J. B. Metzler, 1939.

Rigsby, Kent J. *ZPE* 102 (1994): 192-93.

Rinaldoni, M. C., and A. S. Scarponi. "Edifici antichi nei sotterranei di Palazzo Spada." *Forma Urbis* IV, 3 (March 1999): 4-13.

Robinson, Olivia. "Slaves and the Criminal Law." *Zeitschrift der Savigny-Stiftung für Rechtsgeschichte (romanistische Abteilung)* 98 (1981): 213-54.

Rodriguez-Almeida, E. "Forma Urbis marmorea, nuove integrazioni." *Bulletino della Commissione archeologica Communale in Roma* 82 (1970-71): 105ff.

―――. *Forma Urbis Marmorea: aggiornamento generale 1980*. Rome: Quasar, 1981.

Rostovtzeff, M. I. *Social and Economic History of the Roman Empire*. Oxford: Oxford University Press, 1957.

Rougé, Jean, and Robert Turcan, eds. *Les martyrs de Lyon (177): Lyon 20-23 Septembre 1977*. Colloques internationaux du Centre National de la Recherche Scientifique 575. Paris: Centre National de la Recherche Scientifique, 1978.

Roussel, Pierre. *Délos, colonie athénienne*. Paris: Éditions E. de Boccard, 1916; 2nd ed., 1987.

Rousselle, A. *Porneia: On Desire and the Body in Antiquity*. Oxford: Blackwell, 1988. French original, Paris: Presses universitaires, 1983.

Rowlandson, Jane. *Women and Society in Greek and Roman Egypt: A Sourcebook.* Cambridge: Cambridge University Press, 1998.

Rozenberg, Silvia. "The Absence of Figurative Motifs in Herodian Wall Painting." In *I Temi Figurativi nella Pittura Parietale Antica (IV sec. a.C.–IV sec. d.C.),* edited by D. S. Corlàita. Bologna: University Press, 1997.

Rubenstein, Richard L. "Atonement and Sacrifice in Contemporary Jewish Liturgy." In *After Auschwitz: Radical Theology and Contemporary Judaism.* Indianapolis: Bobbs-Merrill, 1966.

Rutgers, L. V. "Incense Shovels at Sepphoris?" In *Galilee through the Centuries: Confluence of Cultures,* edited by E. M. Meyers. Winona Lake, Ind.: Eisenbrauns, 1999.

Saavedra, Christine Tina. "Women on the Verge of the Roman Empire: The Socioeconomic Activities of Iberian Women." Ph.D. diss., University of Chicago, 2000.

Sadvrska, Anna. *Les Tables Iliaques. Centre d'Archéologie Méditerranéenne de l'Académie Polonaise des Sciences.* Warsaw: Panstwowe Wydawnictwo Naukowe, 1964.

Salerno, Luigi, Luigi Spezzaferro, and Manfredo Tafuri. *Via Giulia: una utopia urbanistica del 500.* Rome: Aristide Stadeerini, 1973.

Saller, Richard P. "Familia, Domus, and the Roman Concept of the Family." *Phoenix* 38 (1984): 336-55.

———. "Slavery and the Roman Family." In *Classical Slavery,* edited by M. I. Finley, pp. 65-87. "Slavery and Abolition" special issue 8. London: Frank Cass, 1987.

———. *Patriarchy, Property, and Death in the Roman Family.* New York: Cambridge University Press, 1994.

———. "The Hierarchical Household in Roman Society: A Study of Domestic Slavery." In *Serfdom and Slavery: Studies in Legal Bondage,* edited by M. L. Bush, pp. 112-29. London and New York: Longman, 1996.

———. "Symbols of Gender and Status Hierarchies in the Roman Household." In *Women and Slaves in Greco-Roman Culture: Differential Equations,* edited by S. Murnaghan and S. Joshel, pp. 85-91. London: Routledge, 1998.

———. "Pater Familias, Mater Familias, and the Gendered Semantics of the Roman Household." *CP* 94 (1999): 182-97.

Saller, Richard P., and Brent D. Shaw. "Tombstones and Roman Family Relations in the Principate: Civilians, Soldiers and Slaves." *JRS* 74 (1984): 124-56.

Salzman, Michele Renée. "Aristocratic Women: Conductors of Christianity in the Fourth Century." *Helios* 16 (1989): 207-20.

———. "How the West Was Won: The Christianization of the Roman Aristocracy in the West in the Years after Constantine." In Carl Deroux, ed., *Studies in Latin Literature and Roman History, Collection Latomus* 217 (1992): 451-79.

Sandy, Gerald N. "Serviles Voluptates in Apuleius' Metamorphoses." *Phoenix* 28 (1974): 234-44.

Satlow, Michael. *Jewish Marriage in Antiquity.* Princeton: Princeton University Press, 2001.

Schalles, Hans-Joachim. "Pergamon: Sculpture." In *Dictionary of Art,* edited by Jane Turner, 24:413-16. New York: Grove Press, 1996.

Scheer, Tanja. "Forschungen uber die Frau in der Antike. Ziele, Methoden, Perspektiven." *Gymnasium* 107 (2000): 143-72.

Schefold, Karl. "Die Troiasage in Pompeji." *Nederlands Kunsthistorisch Jaarboek* 5 (1954): 211-24.

————. *Der religiöse Gehalt der antiken Kunst und die Offenbarung.* Kulturgeschichte der Antiken Welt 78. Mainz: Philipp von Zabern, 1998.

Scheidel, Walter. "The Most Silent Women of Greece and Rome: Rural Labor and Women's Life in the Ancient World (I)." *GR* 47 (1995): 202-17.

————. "The Most Silent Women of Greece and Rome: Rural Labor and Women's Life in the Ancient World (II)." *GR* 48 (1996): 1-10.

————. "Reflections on the Differential Valuation of Slaves in Diocletian's Price Edict and in the United States." *Münstersche Beiträge zur antiken Handelsgeschichte* 15 (1996): 67-79.

————. "Quantifying the Sources of Slaves in the Early Roman Empire." *JRS* 87 (1997): 159-69.

Scherrer, Peter, ed. *Ephesos. Der Neue Führer.* Vienna: Österreichisches Archäologisches Institut, 1995.

Schneider, André. "Notes critiques sur Tertullian, Ad Nationes I." *Museum Helveticum* 19 (1962): 180-89.

Schürer, Emil. *The History of the Jews in the Age of Jesus Christ.* A new English version revised and edited by G. Vermes, F. Millar, and M. Goodman. 3 vols. Edinburgh: T. & T. Clark, 1973-87.

Schüssler Fiorenza, Elisabeth. *In Memory of Her: A Feminist Theological Reconstruction of Christian Origins.* London: SCM Press, 1983.

————, ed. *Searching the Scriptures: Volume 2, A Feminist Commentary.* New York: Crossroad, 1994.

Schutz, Alfred. *The Phenomenology of the Social World.* Edited by George Walsh and Frederick Lehnert. Evanston, Ill.: Northwestern University Press, 1967.

Scobie, Alexander. *Aspects of the Ancient Romance and Its Heritage: Essays on Apuleius, Petronius, and the Greek Romances.* Beiträge zur klassischen Philologie 30. Meisenheim am Glan: Anton Hain, 1969.

————. "Slums, Sanitation and Mortality in the Roman World." *Klio* 68 (1986): 399-433.

Scott, E. *The Archaeology of Infancy and Infant Death.* BAR International Series 819. Oxford: Archaeopress, 1999.

Scott, James C. *Domination and the Arts of Resistance: Hidden Transcripts.* New Haven: Yale University Press, 1990.

Sedgwick, Timothy F. *The Christian Moral Life: Practices of Piety.* Grand Rapids: Eerdmans, 1999.

Seston, W. "L'épitaphe d'Eutychos et l'héroisation par la pureté." In *Hommages à Joseph Bidez et à Franz Cumont,* pp. 313-22. Brussels: Latomus (Collection Latomus II), 1949.

Settis, Salvatore. *Laocoonte: Fama e stile.* Rome: Donzelli, 1999.

Shaw, Brent D. "Latin Funerary Epigraphy and Family Life in the Later Roman Empire." *Historia* 33 (1984): 457-97.

————. "The Cultural Meaning of Death: Age and Gender in the Roman Family." In *The Family in Italy from Antiquity to the Present,* edited by D. I. Kertzer and R. P. Saller, pp. 66-90. New Haven and London: Yale University Press, 1991.

————. "Body/Power/Identity: Passions of the Martyrs." *JECS* 4 (1996): 296-312.

————. "Seasons of Death: Aspects of Mortality in Imperial Rome." *JRS* 86 (1996): 100-138.

Simon, Erika. "Laokoon und die Geschichte der Antiken Kunst." *Archäologischer Anzeiger* (1984): 643-72.

————. "Laokoon." In *LIMC*, vol. 6.1, pp. 196-201. Zürich: Artemis, 1992.

Skinner, Marilyn B. "Zeus and Leda: The Sexuality Wars in Contemporary Classical Scholarship." *Thamyris* 3, no. 1 (1996): 103-23.

Skoie, M. "Sublime Poetry or Feminine Fiddling: Gender and Reception: Sulpicia through the Eyes of Two Nineteenth Century Scholars." In *Aspects of Women in Antiquity*, edited by Lena Larsson Lovén and Anita Strömberg, pp. 169-82. Jonsered, Sweden: Paul Åstrom, 1998.

Slater, W. J. "Pueri, turba minuta." *Institute of Classical Studies Bulletin* 21 (1974): 133-40.

Smallwood, Mary G. *The Jews under Roman Rule, from Pompey to Diocletian: A Study in Political Relations*. SJLA 20. Leiden: Brill, 1976. Reprint, 1981.

Smith, R. R. R. "The Imperial Reliefs from the Sebasteion at Aphrodisias." *JRS* 77 (1987): 88-138.

————. "Simulacra Gentium: The Ethne from the Sebasteion at Aphrodisias." *JRS* 77 (1988): 50-77.

————. Review of *Plinius und der Laocoon*, by B. Andreae. *JRS* 79 (1989): 213-17.

————. Review of *Laokoon und die Gründung Roms*, by B. Andreae. *Gnomon* 63 (1991): 351-58.

Snyder, Graydon F. *Ante Pacem: Archaeological Evidence of Church Life before Constantine*. Macon, Ga.: Mercer University Press, 1985.

Solin, Heikki, and Marja Itkonen-Kaila. *Graffiti del Palatino*. Acta Instituti Romani Finlandiae 3. Helsinki: Helsingfors, 1966.

Soren, D., and N. Soren. *A Roman Villa and a Late-Roman Infant Cemetery: Excavation at Poggio Gramignano, Lugnano in Teverina*. Rome: L'Erma di Bretschneider, 1999.

Spelman, Elizabeth V. *Inessential Woman: Problems of Exclusion in Feminist Thought*. Boston: Beacon Press, 1988.

Spinazzola, Vittorio. *Pompei alla Luce degli Scavi Nuovi di Via dell'Abbondanze (Anni 1910-1923)*. Vol. 2. Edited by S. Aurigemma. Rome: La Libreria dello Stato, 1953.

Stark, Rodney. *The Rise of Christianity: A Sociologist Reconsiders History*. Princeton: Princeton University Press, 1996.

Stark, Rodney, and W. S. Bainbridge. "Networks of Faith: Interpersonal Bonds and Recruitment in Cults and Sects." *American Journal of Sociology* 85 (1980): 1376-95.

Ste. Croix, G. E. M. de. *The Class Struggle in the Ancient Greek World*. London: Duckworth, 1981.

Stehle, E. "Venus, Cybele and the Sabine Women: The Roman Construction of Female Sexuality." *Helios* 16, no. 2 (1989): 143-64.

Stenger, H., and H. Geisslinger. "Die Transformation sozialer Realität: Ein Beitrag zur empirischen Wissenssoziologie." *Kölner Zeitschrift für Soziologie und Sozialpsychologie* 43 (1991): 247-70.

Stern, Menahem. *Greek and Latin Authors on Jews and Judaism*. 3 vols. Jerusalem: Israel Academy of Sciences and Humanities, 1974-80.

Strecker, Georg. *Theology of the New Testament.* Translated by M. Eugene Boring. Louisville: Westminster John Knox, 2000.

Teugels, Lieve. Review of *Integrating Women into Second Temple History,* by Tal Ilan. *Journal for the Study of Judaism* 31, no. 3 (2000): 322-25.

Thalman, William G. "Female Slaves in the *Odyssey.*" In *Women and Slaves in Greco-Roman Culture: Differential Equations,* edited by Sandra R. Joshel and Sheila Murnaghan, pp. 22-34. London and New York: Routledge, 1998.

Theissen, Gerd. *The Gospels in Context: Social and Political History in the Synoptic Tradition.* Translated by Linda M. Maloney. Minneapolis: Fortress, 1991.

————. *The Religion of the Earliest Churches: Creating a Symbolic World.* Translated by John Bowden. Minneapolis: Fortress, 1999.

Thomas, Garth. "La condition sociale de l'église de Lyon en 177." In *Les martyrs de Lyon (1977): Lyon 20-23 Septembre 1977,* edited by Jean Rougé and Robert Turcan, pp. 93-106. Colloques internationaux du Centre National de la Recherche Scientifique 575. Paris: Centre National de la Recherche Scientifique, 1978.

Thurston, Bonnie Bowman. *The Widows: A Women's Ministry in the Early Church.* Minneapolis: Fortress, 1989.

Tomei, Maria Antonietta. *Museo Palatino.* English Edition. Ministero per I Beni Culturali e Ambientali. Roma: Electa, 1997.

Tracy, David. *The Analogical Imagination: Christian Theology and the Culture of Pluralism.* New York: Crossroad, 1981.

Treggiari, Susan. "Domestic Staff at Rome in the Julio-Claudian Period, 27 b.c. to a.d. 68." *Histoire Sociale* 6 (1973): 241-55.

————. "Family Life among the Staff of the Volusii." *TAPA* 105 (1975): 393-401.

————. "Jobs in the Household of Livia." *PBSR* 43 (1975): 48-77.

————. "Jobs for Women." *AJAH* 1 (1976): 76-104.

————. "Lower Class Women in the Roman Economy." *Florilegium* 1 (1979): 65-86.

————. *Roman Marriage: Iusti Coniuges from the Time of Cicero to the Time of Ulpian.* Oxford: Clarendon, 1991.

Trevett, Christine. *Montanism: Gender, Authority, and the New Prophecy.* Cambridge: Cambridge University Press, 1996.

Troeltsch, Ernst. *The Social Teaching of the Christian Churches.* 2 volumes. Translated by Olive Wyon. Louisville: Westminster/John Knox, 1992.

Trümper, Monika. *Wohnen in Delos. Eine baugeschichtliche Untersuchung zum Wandel der Wohnkultur in hellenistischer Zeit.* Internationale Archäologie 46. Rahden in Westfalia: Verlag Marie Leidorf GmbH, 1998.

Van Andringa, W. "Autels de Carrejour, organisation vicinale et Rapports de voisinage à Pompéi." *Rivista di Studi Pompeiani* XI (2001): 47-86.

Van Dam, H. J. *P. Papinius Statius, Silvae Book II: A Commentary.* Leyden: Brill, 1984.

Van Minnen, Peter. "Did Ancient Women Learn a Trade outside the Home? A Note on SB XVIII 13305." *ZPR* 123 (1998): 201-3.

Vasaly, Ann. *Representations: Images of the World in Ciceronian Oratory.* Berkeley: University of California Press, 1993.

Vergil. *Eclogues, Georgics, Aeneid.* Translated by William Heinemann. LCL. Cambridge: Harvard University Press, 1974.

Vial, Claude. "Délos indépendante." *Bulletin de Correspondance Hellénique,* suppl. X (1984).

Vogt, Joseph. "The Faithful Slave." In *Ancient Slavery and the Ideal of Man,* pp. 129-45. Cambridge: Harvard University Press, 1974.

Vollmer, F. P. *Papinius Statii, Silvarum Libri: herausgegeben und erklärt.* Leipzig: Teubner, 1898.

Von Salis, Arnold. *Antike und Renaissance.* Zürich: Eugen Rentsch, 1947.

Walker, Susan. "Women and Housing in Classical Greece." In *Images of Women in Antiquity,* edited by Averil Cameron and Amelie Kuhrt. London: Routledge and Kegan Paul, 1983.

Wallace-Hadrill, Andrew. "The Social Structure of the Roman House." *PBSR* 56 (1988): 43-97.

————. "Rome's Cultural Revolution." Review of *The Power of Images in the Age of Augustus,* by Paul Zanker. *JRS* 79 (1989): 157-64.

————. "Houses and Households: Sampling Pompeii and Herculaneum." In *Marriage, Divorce, and Children in Ancient Rome,* edited by Beryl Rawson. Canberra: Oxford University Press and Humanities Research Centre, 1991.

————. *Houses and Society in Pompeii and Herculaneum.* Princeton: Princeton University Press, 1994.

————. "Rethinking the Roman Atrium House." In *Domestic Space in the Roman World: Pompeii and Beyond,* edited by Ray Laurence and Andrew Wallace-Hadrill, pp. 219-40. Journal of Roman Archaeology Supplement Series 22. Portsmouth, R.I.: Journal of Roman Archaeology, 1997.

————. "Case e abitanti a Roma." In *Roma Imperiale: Una metropoli antica,* edited by Elio Lo Cascio. Rome: Carocci, 2000.

————. "Emperors and Houses in Rome." In *Childhood, Class, and Kin in the Roman World,* edited by S. Dixon. London and New York: Routledge, 2001.

————. "Rome Finds Its Pevsner: Delights and Challenges of Mapping the Ancient City." *Times Literary Supplement,* 11 May 2001 (a review of LTUR vols. 1-6), pp. 3-4.

Walsh, P. G. "The Rights and Wrongs of Curiosity (Plutarch to Augustine)." *GR* 35 (1988): 73-85.

Walzer, Richard. *Galen on Jews and Christians.* London: Oxford University Press, 1949.

Watson, Alan. "Roman Slave Law and Romanist Ideology." *Phoenix* 37 (1983): 53-65.

Watson, P. "Erotion: Puella Delicata?" *Classical Quarterly* 42 (1992): 253-68.

Weaver, Paul R. C. "Children and Freedmen (and Freedwomen)." In *Marriage, Divorce, and Children in Ancient Rome,* edited by Beryl Rawson. Oxford: Clarendon, 1991.

Wegner, J. R. *Chattel or Person? The Status of Women in the Mishnah.* Oxford: Oxford University Press, 1988.

Weidmann, Frederick W. "The Martyrs of Lyons." In *Religions of Late Antiquity in Practice,* edited by Richard Valantasis, pp. 398-412. Princeton Readings in Religions. Princeton: Princeton University Press, 2000.

Westermann, William L. *The Slave Systems of Greek and Roman Antiquity.* Philadelphia: American Philosophical Society, 1955.

Whelan, Caroline F. "Amica Pauli: The Role of Phoebe in the Early Church." *JSNT* 49 (1993): 67-85.

White, Deborah Gray. *Ar'n't I a Woman?* New York: Norton, 1985.

White, L. Michael. *The Social Origins of Christian Architecture.* HTS 42. Baltimore: Johns Hopkins University Press, 1990, vol. 1; Cambridge: President and Fellows of Harvard College, 1997, vol. 2.

———. *Texts and Monuments for the Christian Domus Ecclesiae in Its Environment.* Vol. 2. HTS 42. Valley Forge, Pa.: Trinity Press International, 1997.

White, L. Michael, and O. Larry Yarbrough, eds. *The Social World of the First Christians: Essays in Honor of Wayne A. Meeks.* Philadelphia: Fortress, 1995.

Wiedemann, Thomas. *Greek and Roman Slavery.* 1981. Reprint, London: Routledge, 1988.

———. *Adults and Children in the Roman Empire.* London: Routledge, 1989.

Wilken, Robert L. *The Christians as the Romans Saw Them.* New Haven and London: Yale University Press, 1984.

Williams, Craig. *Roman Homosexuality: Ideologies of Masculinity in Classical Antiquity.* Oxford: Oxford University Press, 1999.

Williams, Gordon. "Some Aspects of Roman Marriage Ceremonies and Ideals." *JRS* 48 (1958): 16-29.

Williams, Sam K. *Jesus' Death as Saving Event: The Background and Origin of a Concept.* HTRHDR 2. Missoula: Scholars, 1975.

Wilson, Stephen G., and Michel Desjardins, eds. *Text and Artifact in the Religions of Mediterranean Antiquity: Essays in Honour of Peter Richardson.* Waterloo, Ontario: Wilfrid Laurier Press, 2000.

Wilson, Walter T. *Love without Pretense: Romans 12.9-21 and Hellenistic-Jewish Wisdom Literature.* WUNT 46, 2nd ser. Tübingen: Mohr Siebeck, 1991.

Winkler, John J. *The Constraints of Desire: The Anthropology of Sex and Gender in Ancient Greece.* New York: Routledge, 1990.

Wiplinger, Gilbert. "Die Wohneinheiten 1 und 2 im Hanghaus 2 von Ephesos." *Jahreshefte des Österreichischen Archäologischen Instituts in Wien* 66 (1997): 75-86.

Wissowa, Georg. *Religion und Kultus der Römer.* Munich: Beck, 1912, rep. 1971.

Wright, Benjamin G., ed. *A Multiform Heritage: Studies on Early Judaism and Christianity in Honor of Robert A. Kraft.* Atlanta: Scholars, 1999.

Wulf, Ulrike. *Die hellenistischen und römischen Wohnhäuser von Pergamon.* Die Stadtgrabung Teil 3. Altertümer von Pergamon XV,3. Berlin and New York: Walter de Gruyter, 1999.

Yadin, Yigal. *Finds from the Bar Kochba Period in the Cave of Letters.* Jerusalem: Israel Exploration Society, 1963.

———. *"Bar Kokhba": The Rediscovery of the Legendary Hero of the Second Jewish Revolt against Rome.* New York: Random House, 1971.

Yadin, Yigal, Jonas C. Greenfield, and Ada Yardeni. "Babatha's Ketubbah." *IEJ* 44, nos. 1-2 (1994): 75-101.

Yardeni, Ada. *Nahal Se'elim Documents.* Jerusalem: Israel Exploration Society and Ben Gurion University in the Negev Press, 1995.

Zanker, Paul. "Augustan Political Symbolism in the Private Sphere." In *Image and Mystery in the Roman World: Papers Given in Memory of Jocelyn Toynbee.* Gloucester, 1988.

———. *The Powers of Images in the Age of Augustus.* Translated by Alan Shapiro. Ann Arbor: University of Michigan Press, 1988.

————. *The Mask of Socrates: The Image of the Intellectual in Antiquity.* Translated by A. Shapiro. Berkeley: University of California Press, 1995.

————. *Pompeji. Stadtbild und Wohngeschmack.* Mainz: Verlag Philipp von Zabern, 1995, translated as *Pompeii: Public and Private Life.* Cambridge, Mass.: Harvard University Press, 1998.

————. "Immagini come Vincolo: Il Simbolismo Politico Augusteo nella Sfera Privata." In *Roma: Romolo, Remo e la fondazione della città. Roma, Museo Nazionale Romano,* pp. 84-91. Milan: Electa, 2000.

Zeitlin, Froma I., John J. Winkler, and David M. Halperin, eds. *Before Sexuality: The Construction of Erotic Experience in the Ancient Greek World.* Princeton: Princeton University Press, 1990.

Zintzen, Clemens. "Die Laocoonepisode bei Vergil." *Akademie der Wissenschaften und der Literataur (Mainz), Abhandlungen der Geistes- und Sozialwissenschaftlichen Klasse* 10 (1979): 67-72.

Acknowledgments

Color Plates

Plate 1: Drawing by M. Trümper after Monika Trümper, *Wohnen in Delos. Eine baugeschichtliche Untersuchung zum Wandel der Wohnkultur in hellenistischer Zeit.* Internationale Archäologie 46 (Rahden/Westf.: Verlag Marie Leidorf, 1998), fig. 7.

Plate 2: Drawing by M. Trümper after Monika Trümper, *Wohnen in Delos. Eine baugeschichtliche Untersuchung zum Wandel der Wohnkultur in hellenistischer Zeit.* Internationale Archäologie 46 (Rahden/Westf.: Verlag Marie Leidorf, 1998), fig. 37.

Plate 3: Drawing by M. Trümper after Philippe Bruneau and Claude Vatin et al., *L'îlot de la Maison des comédiens,* Exploration archéologique de Délos XXVII (Paris: Éditions E. de Boccard, 1970), plate A.

Plate 4: Drawing by M. Trümper after Philippe Bruneau and Jean Ducat, *Guide de Délos* (Paris: Éditions E. de Boccard, 1983), plan VI.

Plate 5: National Archaeological Museum, Naples, inventory 9112. Published by permission of Soprintendenza per i Beni Archeologici delle province di Napoli e Caserta.

Plate 6: Published by permission of Soprintendenza per i Beni Archeologici delle province di Napoli e Caserta.

Plate 7: National Archaeological Museum, Naples, inventory 9089. Published by permission of Soprintendenza per i Beni Archeologici delle province di Napoli e Caserta.

Plate 8: Published by permission of Soprintendenza Archeologica di Pompei.

Plate 9: Published by permission of Soprintendenza Archeologica di Pompei.

Plate 10: Published by permission of Soprintendenza Archeologica di Pompei.

Plate 11: Published by permission of Soprintendenza Archeologica di Pompei.

Figures in Monika Trümper, "Material and Social Environment of Greco-Roman Households in the East: The Case of Hellenistic Delos"

Figure 1: after Philippe Bruneau and Claude Vatin et al., *L'îlot de la Maison des comédiens*, Exploration archéologique de Délos XXVII (Paris: Éditions E. de Boccard, 1970), p. 18, fig. 12.

Figure 2: after Philippe Bruneau and Claude Vatin et al., *L'îlot de la Maison des comédiens*, Exploration archéologique de Délos XXVII (Paris: Éditions E. de Boccard, 1970), p. 34, fig. 29.

Figure 3: after Wolfram Hoepfner and Ernst-Ludwig Schwandner, *Haus und Stadt im klassischen Griechenland. Wohnen in der klassischen Polis I,* 2nd ed. (München: Deutscher Kunstverlag, 1994), p. 214, fig. 208.

Figure 4: after Ulrike Wulf, *Die hellenistischen und römischen Wohnhäuser von Pergamon*. Die Stadtgrabung Teil 3. Altertümer von Pergamon XV,3 (Berlin/New York: Walter de Gruyter, 1999), p. 204, fig. 81.

Figure 5: after Pierre Ducrey, Ingrid R. Metzger, and Karl Reber, *Le Quartier de la Maison aux mosaïques, Eretria*. Fouilles et recherches VIII (Lausanne: Éditions Payot, 1993), p. 32, fig. 25.

Figure 6: after Salvatore Ciro Nappo, "Alcuni esempi di tipologie di case popolari della fine III, inizio II secolo a.C. a Pompei," *Rivista di Studi Pompeiani* VI (1993-94): figs. 5, 6, 19, 22, 25.

Figure 7: after Felix Pirson, *Mietwohnungen in Pompeji und Herkulaneum. Untersuchungen zur Architektur, zum Wohnen und zur Sozial- und Wirtschaftsgeschichte der Vesuvstädte*. Studien zur antiken Stadt 5 (München: Verlag Dr. Friedrich Pfeil, 1999), p. 24, fig. 6.

Figures in Beryl Rawson, "Death, Burial, and Commemoration of Children in Roman Italy"

Figure 1: Courtesy of Ramsay MacMullen, Yale University

Figure 2: DAI, Rome, Neg. EA 4553

Figure 3: Photo Pontificia Commissione di Archeologia Sacra 662

Figure 4: DAI, Rome, Neg. 581387; photographer Sansaini

Index of Modern Authors

Index of Scripture and Other Ancient Literature